Johannes Chan

Financial Restructuring and Reform
in Post-WTO China

International Banking and Finance Law Series

VOLUME 4

The titles published in this series are listed at the end of this volume

Asian Institute of International Financial Law
www.AIIFL.com
University of Hong Kong

Financial Restructuring and Reform in Post-WTO China

Editors

James R. Barth
Milken Institute and Auburn University

Zhongfei Zhou
Shanghai University of Finance and Economics

Douglas W. Arner
University of Hong Kong

Berry F.C. Hsu
University of Hong Kong

Wei Wang
Fudan University

KLUWER LAW
INTERNATIONAL

Published by:
Kluwer Law International
P.O. Box 316
2400 AH Alphen aan den Rijn
The Netherlands
E-mail: sales@kluwerlaw.com
Website: http://www.kluwerlaw.com

Sold and distributed in North, Central and South America by:
Aspen Publishers, Inc.
7201 Mc Kinney Circle
Frederick, MD 21704
USA

Sold and distributed in all other countries by:
Turpin Distribution Services Ltd.
Stratton Business Park
Pegasus Drive, Biggleswade
Bedfordshire SG18 8TQ
United Kingdom

ISBN 90-411-2573-6

Table of Contents

Chapter 2
Banking Regulatory Law Reforms in China: A Long Way
to Go Towards International Standards   **45**

Chapter 8
Financial Conglomerates in the People's Republic of China   **273**

Chapter 9
Financial Institution Insolvency in the PRC   **325**

Editors and Contributors

Editors:

James R. Barth
Senior Finance Fellow, Milken Institute; and Lowder Eminent Scholar in Finance, Auburn University.

Zhongfei Zhou
Professor of Law and Vice President, Shanghai University of Finance and Economics; and Deputy Director, China Society of International Economic Law, China Law Society.

Douglas W. Arner
Associate Professor; Director, Asian Institute of International Financial Law; and Director, LL.M. (Corporate & Financial Law) Programme, Faculty of Law, University of Hong Kong.

Berry F.C. Hsu
Associate Professor of Law, Faculty of Architecture, and Deputy Director, Asian Institute of International Financial Law, Faculty of Law, University of Hong Kong.

Wei Wang
Associate Professor, Law School, Fudan University; and Research Fellow, Asian Institute of International Financial Law, Faculty of Law, University of Hong Kong.

Contributors (in alphabetical order):

Douglas W. Arner
As above.

James R. Barth
As above.

Michael E. Burke
Associate and Member, International Practice Group, Williams Mullen PC, Washington, DC; and Visiting Fellow, Asian Institute of International Financial Law, Faculty of Law, University of Hong Kong.

Berry F.C. Hsu
As above.

Andreas Kellerhals
Professor of Law and Director, Europa Institut and LL.M. Programme in International Business Law, Zurich University; and Research Fellow, East Asian International Economic and Policy Programme, Faculty of Law, University of Hong Kong.

Jingwei Li
Associate Professorship Research Fellow, Research Institute of International Trade, University of International Business and Economics, Beijing.

Changyuan Lin
Assistant Professor, Institute of Law, Chinese Academy of Social Sciences.

George A. Walker
Professor in International Financial Law, Centre for Commercial Law Studies, Queen Mary, University of London.

Qun Wan
Legal Counsel, Fortis, Shanghai; and Research Fellow, Asian Institute of International Financial Law, University of Hong Kong.

Wei Wang
As above.

Yong Yang
Deputy Director, Supervisory Rules and Regulations Department, China Banking Regulatory Commission.

Lusong Zhang
Manager, Business Development, Hong Kong Exchanges and Clearing, Beijing; and Research Fellow, Asian Institute of International Financial Law, Faculty of Law, University of Hong Kong.

Zhongfei Zhou
As above.

Foreword

This book addresses, from a legal perspective, the ongoing process of financial restructuring and reform in post-WTO China. The structure of this book is as follows. Chapter 1, 'The WTO and Financial Restructuring in China', provides an overview of the impact of the WTO on China's financial markets and financial law systems. Chapter 2, 'Banking Regulatory Law Reforms in China: A Long Way to Go towards International Standards', discusses reform of banking law and regulation in post-WTO China. Chapter 3, 'Independence and Accountability of the People's Bank of China: A Legal Perspective', addresses the role of the central bank in China's financial system, focusing on issues of independence and accountability of the People's Bank of China (PBOC), China's central bank. Chapter 4, 'Implementation of China's WTO Commitments: The Compliance Issue in Banking', analyzes China's compliance with WTO obligations in the area of banking. Chapter 5, 'Financial Restructuring and China's Asset Management Companies', discusses the role of asset management companies (AMCs) in China's ongoing banking restructuring and liberalization. Chapter 6, 'Liberalization and Reform of China's Securities Markets after WTO Accession', analyzes the development of securities markets in China, the challenges being faced and the impact of the WTO. Chapter 7, 'Insurance in China: Liberalization and Restructuring Post-WTO', describes insurance and its development in China, focusing on the role of the WTO in liberalization. Building upon the discussions in the previous chapters, a new topic in China, financial conglomerates, is discussed in Chapter 8, 'Financial Conglomerates in the People's Republic of China'. Chapter 9, 'Financial Institution Insolvency in the PRC', in turn, studies the issue of financial institution insolvency and restructuring – key issues in China, as noted in previous chapters. Finally, Chapter 10, 'China's Banking Law and Free Trade Agreements: The Case of CEPA', discusses the double impact of the WTO and one of China's regional trade agreements, CEPA, on China's banking law.

In producing a book of this nature, we have been supported by many others. In particular, we would like to thank the following:

- The Asian Institute of International Financial Law (<www.aiifl.com>) of the University of Hong Kong (HKU), especially Charles Booth and Flora Leung: This work was partially supported by a grant from the HKU's University Research Committee (URC) to AIIFL to the support the URC Strategic Research Theme of China business and law studies;
- The Research Grants Committee (RGC) of the University Grants Committee (UGC): This work was partially supported by a grant from the RGC of the HKSAR, China (Project No. HKU 7401/05H).

In addition, this project benefited greatly from our participation from November 2002 through September 2004 in a technical assistance project funded by the Asian Development Bank, Technical Assistance to the People's Republic of China for Banking Laws and Regulations. The final report of the project, which represented the efforts of a twenty-plus member team, *Banking Laws and Regulations: Asian Development Bank Funded Technical Assistance: PRC 3890 – Final Report* (Washington DC: International Law Institute Dec. 2003), is available at <www.adb.org/Documents/Reports/TA3890/>. In this respect, we would especially like to thank Marshall M. Mays and the International Law Institute for their support.

Without their support and those of our partners and families, the production of this volume would not have been possible.

James R. Barth, Zhongfei Zhou, Douglas W. Arner, Berry F.C. Hsu and Wei Wang
September 2006

Preface

Since 1979, China has been in the midst of a process of liberalization of financial services, which has been accelerated under its WTO obligations. Such liberalization increases the vulnerability of China to financial crises, with domestic and international implications. To reduce its vulnerability, China is seeking to develop a robust financial system by restructuring its financial regulatory and institutional structure in accordance with international standards. This process requires structural choices to be made in respect of financial services liberalization commitments and international financial standards. These choices will have a significant impact upon the development of China's financial system.

The ongoing reform of China's financial system raises many challenges. At the international level, there is at present no explicit linkage between the required legal infrastructure that must be in place for the development of a robust financial system and financial liberalization under the WTO. At the domestic level, weaknesses remain, which are likely to be brought to the surface by financial liberalization resulting from WTO accession and implementation. China's challenge is to strike an appropriate balance between a robust financial system and WTO compliance. Measures taken in this connection will also be indicative of potential disputes that may arise with other WTO members, including Hong Kong and Taiwan.

In December 2006, China's two protective measures of geographical limitation and client limitation will be eliminated. The result will be fewer market-access limitations for foreign investors in banking, with the exception of capital requirements. In this context, it is interesting to know how Chinese financial regulators will deal with the liberalization issue arising from the WTO. This question is precisely the focus of this book. This study of China's financial reform under the WTO is meaningful for other developing and developed countries, as well as for China.

Most of the authors of this book have participated in Chinese financial reform projects supported by the World Bank, the Asian Development Bank, and other international financial institutions. This book can be seen as the fruit of their labours and of their transnational cooperation. Such cooperation has been facilitated by the Asian Institute of International Financial Law, at the University of Hong Kong, which played the pivotal role in assembling the authors and giving this book its high degree of coherence.

Professor Joseph J. Norton
James L. Walsh
Distinguished Faculty Fellow in
Financial Institutions Law and
Professor of Law
Dedman School of Law
Southern Methodist University
September 2006

Professor Ross P. Buckley
Professor of Law
Tim Fischer Centre for
Global Trade and Finance
Faculty of Law
Bond University

Chapter 1

The WTO and Financial Restructuring in China

James R. Barth, Zhongfei Zhou, Douglas W. Arner, Berry F.C. Hsu, and Wei Wang

The People's Republic of China (PRC) entered the World Trade Organization (WTO) on 11 December 2001. As part of its accession to the WTO and the implementation of the General Agreement on Trade in Services (GATS) and its annexes in regard to financial services, China made numerous commitments in respect to financial-services liberalization. These commitments address banking, securities and insurance activities and institutions, as well as motor vehicle finance.

I. CHINA'S GATS/WTO COMMITMENTS IN FINANCIAL SERVICES

China's WTO accession documents related to financial service trade include the Protocol on Accession of the People's Republic of China ('China Accession Protocol'), Schedule of Specific Commitments on Services ('Schedule'), and the Working Party Report. The three legal documents are interrelated and interconnected. The China Accession Protocol is the leading document, annexed by the Schedule and some parts of the Working Party Report. All

Barth et al., *Financial Restructuring and Reform in Post-WTO China*, pp. 1–43.
© 2007 Kluwer Law International BV, The Netherlands.

of the official documents respecting China's accession are not in the Chinese language, for example, the Schedule is 'authentic only in the English language'.[1]

I.A.   HORIZONTAL COMMITMENTS

China's commitments respecting financial services can be divided into two main categories: horizontal and specific. The horizontal commitments apply to financial services, as well as all service sectors included in the Schedule. China made the following horizontal commitments:

First, it is permitted to establish foreign capital enterprises (wholly-foreign-owned enterprises), joint-venture enterprises, branches, and representative offices in China.

Second, all land in the PRC is State-owned. Use of land by enterprises and individuals is subject to maximum term limitations, such as 50 years or 70 years.

Finally, managers, executives and specialists as senior employees of a representative office, branch or subsidiary in China shall be permitted entry for a period of time.

I.B.   SPECIFIC COMMITMENTS IN FINANCIAL SERVICES

The following sections outline China's specific commitments related to banking, insurance and securities.

I.B.1.   Banking

China's commitments with respect to banking services mainly address geographic coverage, clients, licensing and national treatment.

                           Geographic coverage
For foreign-currency business, no geographic restrictions will be placed upon accession. For local-currency business, the geographic restriction will be phased out within five years after accession to the WTO (end-2006). All geographic restrictions will be removed.

                           Clients
For foreign currency business, foreign financial institutions are permitted to provide services in China without restriction as to clients upon accession. For local-currency business, within five years after accession (end-2006), foreign financial institutions will be permitted to provide services to all Chinese clients.

---

1. See *China Accession Protocol*, Annex 9. See also *China Accession Protocol*, final para.

Foreign financial institutions licensed for local-currency business in one region of China can service clients in any other region that has been opened for such business.

Licensing

The criteria for authorization to deal in China's financial services sector are to be solely prudential; in other words, the criteria must contain no economic-needs test or quantitative limits on licenses. Within five years after accession (end-2006), any existing non-prudential measures restricting ownership, operation or juridical form of foreign financial institutions, including on internal branching and licenses, shall be eliminated. Financial institutions must meet the following asset requirements in relation to forms of business establishment:

– Subsidiary: Total assets of more than USD 10 billion at the end of the year prior to filing the application.
– Branch: Total assets of more than USD 20 billion at the end of the year prior to filing the application.
– Chinese-foreign joint bank or finance company: Total assets of more than USD 10 billion at the end of the year prior to filing the application.

Qualifications for foreign financial institutions to engage in local-currency business are three years' business operation in China and profitability for two consecutive years prior to the application; otherwise, none.

I.B.2.   Insurance

China's commitments with respect to insurance services address form of establishment, geographic coverage, business scope, licenses and national treatment.

Form of establishment

Foreign non-life insurers are permitted to establish as a branch or as a joint venture with 51 per cent foreign ownership. Since the end of 2003, foreign non-life insurers have been permitted to establish as a wholly-owned subsidiary; in other words, with no form of establishment restrictions. Upon accession, foreign life insurers are permitted 50 per cent foreign ownership in a joint venture with the partner of their choice. The joint venture partners can freely agree to the terms of their engagement, provided the partners remain within the limits of the commitments contained in the schedule.

For brokerage of insurance of large-scale commercial risks and brokerage of reinsurance and brokerage of international marine, aviation, and transport insurance and reinsurance, the limitations on foreign equity shares have been gradually relaxed. From December 2006, wholly foreign-owned subsidiaries will be permitted.

Geographic coverage

Geographic restrictions on foreign life and non-life insurers, as well as insurance brokers were eliminated at the end of 2004.

Business scope

Upon accession, foreign non-life insurers will be permitted to provide 'master policy' insurance/insurance of large-scale commercial risks, with no geographic restrictions. In accordance with national treatment, foreign insurance brokers will be permitted to provide 'master policy' coverage no later than Chinese brokers, under conditions no-less favourable. Foreign non-life insurers are permitted to provide insurance of enterprises abroad as well as property insurance, related liability insurance and credit insurance of foreign-invested enterprises in China upon accession. Since the end of 2003, foreign non-life insurers have been permitted to provide the full range of non-life insurance services to both foreign and domestic clients.

Foreign insurers are permitted to provide individual (not group) insurance to foreigners and Chinese citizens upon accession. Since the end of 2004, foreign insurers have been permitted to provide health insurance, group insurance and pension/annuities insurance to foreigners and Chinese citizens. Upon accession, foreign insurers are permitted to provide reinsurance services for life and non-life insurance as branches, joint ventures, or wholly foreign-owned subsidiaries, without geographic or quantitative restrictions on the number of licenses issued.

Licenses

Upon accession, licenses are issued with no economic needs test or quantitative limits on licenses. Qualifications for establishing a foreign insurance institution are as follows:

- be a foreign insurance company with more than 30 years of establishment experience in a WTO member;
- have a representative office for two consecutive years in China; and
- have total assets of more than USD 5 billion at the end of the year prior to application, except for insurance brokers.

Upon accession, insurance brokers must have total assets in excess if USD 500 million this threshold amount being reduced on each anniversary of accession by USD 100 million. In December 2005, the threshold was reduced to USD 200 million.

I.B.3.   Securities

China made comparatively fewer commitments in its securities sector [2] than it did in the banking and insurance sectors respectively, and the securities

---

2. The PRC Securities Law defines a 'securities company' as a limited liability company or limited company given approval to engagein securities business and divides securities compa-

sector will open at a slower pace than either the banking or insurance sectors. This slower pace is due in part to the Chinese government's desire not to have transnational capital flows potentially disrupt China's securities markets. These commitments include forms of establishment, business scope, licensing, and national treatment.

Forms of establishment

Upon WTO accession, China committed to:

– allow foreign securities firms to engage directly in B-share business without a Chinese intermediary;
– permit the representative offices of foreign securities firms to become Special Members of all Chinese stock exchanges; and
– allow foreign investors to establish joint venture fund management companies (FI-FMCs) provided that foreign interest in an FI-FMC not exceed 33 per cent of the venture's registered capital.

By the third anniversary of WTO accession (end-2004), China committed to:

– increase the foreign investment limit in a FI-FMC to 49 per cent of the venture's registered capital; and
– allow foreign investors to form joint venture securities companies (JVSCs), provided that the maximum foreign interest in such entity is limited to 33 per cent of the JVSC's registered capital. [3]

Business scope

China's Schedule of Specific Commitments does not define the permitted business scope for foreign invested securities ventures as comprehensively as for foreign invested banking or insurance ventures. Upon accession, China committed to permit foreign securities institutions to engage directly – without a

---

nies into two categories: comprehensive securities companies and brokerage-type securities companies (art. 118 and 120). Under art. 129, comprehensive securities companies' scope of business may include securities brokerage business; securities proprietary business; securities underwriting business; and other securities businesses, as approved by the CSRC. Pursuant to art. 130, brokerage type securities companies can only operate a brokerage business.
3. In its Services Sector Horizontal Commitments, the Chinese government notes that foreign investment in an equity joint venture shall be no less than 25 per cent of the venture's registered capital. This situation is consistent with the terms of China's Equity Joint Venture Law. However, on 30 December 2002, MOFTEC, SAT, SAIC, and SAFE jointly issued Issues Relevant to Strengthening the Administration of the Examination, Approval, Registration, Foreign Exchange Issues and Taxation of Foreign-invested Enterprises Circular ('FIE Circular'), effective 1 January 2003. The new circular generally requires all FIEs to comply with the Equity Joint Venture Law's examination, approval and registration requirements, and reiterates the 25 per cent foreign-equity interest requirement. The FIE Circular appears to create a 'Special FIE', with less than 25 per cent foreign-equity interest. The Special FIE will not be eligible for any preferential tax policy. It is unclear whether Special FIEs will be permitted in China's securities sector.

Chinese intermediary – in B-share business (brokering B-shares); to permit representative offices of foreign securities firms to become Special Members of all Chinese stock exchanges; and to permit FI-FMCs to engage in domestic securities investment fund management. By the third anniversary of WTO accession (end-2004), China committed to allow JVSCs to underwrite A-shares directly, to underwrite and broker B-shares, H-shares, and government and corporate bonds, and to establish investment funds.

Licensing
As in other financial services sectors, the criteria for licensing in China's securities sector are prudential and contain no economic needs test or quantitative limit on licenses.

National treatment
China placed no limitations on national treatment, apart from those national treatment restrictions related to the presence of natural persons, as provided in the Horizontal Commitments (as described previously).

II.   CHINA'S FINANCIAL REGULATORY SYSTEM

The PRC has a legal and institutional framework based on civil law and supporting the development of a socialist-market economy. This section first presents an overview of the PRC legal system, and then examines its overall financial regulatory structure.

II.A.   OVERVIEW OF CHINA'S LEGAL STRUCTURE

Legislative power in China does not rest exclusively in the hands of the National People's Congress (NPC) and its Standing Committee. Instead, legislative power depends on the level of legislation involved. According to the PRC Legislation Law of 2000, in the broadest sense, seven types of laws exist:

- laws;
- administrative regulations;
- local regulations;
- autonomous regulations;
- separate regulations;
- rules of departments under the State Council; and
- rules of local governments[4]

---

4. Legislation Law, art. 2.

II.A.1.   Laws

In the strictest sense, laws refer only to those rules enacted by the NPC and its Standing Committee. The NPC enacts and amends basic laws governing criminal offences, civil affairs, State institutions and other basic laws, while the Standing Committee of the NPC enacts and amends laws other than those within the power of the NPC.[5] Because the NPC only holds one national conference each year, the NPC Standing Committee enacts most laws.

II.A.2.   Administrative Regulations

The State Council formulates administrative regulations in accordance with the Constitution and laws enacted by the NPC and its Standing Committee. The main purpose of administrative regulations is to implement the laws and deal with the administrative matters within the powers of the State Council; these laws, therefore, are binding for all of the PRC, with the exceptions of the HKSAR and Macau SAR.

II.A.3.   Local Regulations

China's local regions include three forms: provinces, autonomous regions and municipalities directly under the Central Government, each of which has its own local People's Congress and corresponding Standing Committee. These local People's Congresses and Standing Committees can formulate local regulations, provided the regulations do not conflict with the Constitution, national laws and/or administrative regulations.[6] In contrast to the nationally binding scope of laws and administrative regulations, local regulations are effective only within the relevant local area. The local congresses at the level of comparatively larger cities in provinces and autonomous regions can also formulate local regulations subject to approval by provincial-level congresses.

II.A.4.   Autonomous Regulations and Separate Regulations

With respect to the political, economic and cultural characteristics of the local nationalities, local People's Congresses in autonomous areas, including autonomous regions at provincial level and autonomous prefectures or counties at lower level, may formulate autonomous regulations and separate regulations.[7] All autonomous regulations and separate regulations must be approved by a higher People's Congress.

---

5.   Ibid., art. 7.
6.   Ibid., art. 63.
7.   Ibid., art. 66.

II.A.5.   Rules of Departments

Article 71 of the Legislation Law states:

> 'The ministries and commissions of the State Council, the People's Bank of China, the State Audit Administration as well as the other organs endowed with administrative functions directly under the State Council may, in accordance with the laws as well as the administrative regulations, decisions and orders of the State Council and within the limits of their power, formulate rules.
>
> Matters governed by the rules of departments shall be those for the enforcement of the laws or the administrative regulations, decisions and orders of the State Council'.

The binding scope of the rules of departments is similar to that of administrative regulations, that is, the whole territory of China. The two terms 'administrative regulations' and 'rules of departments' are easily confused. In fact, administrative regulations – *Xingzheng Fagui* or *Xingzheng Tiaoli* – refer only to regulations issued by the State Council, while rules of departments – *Xingzheng Guizhang* or *Xingzheng Banfa* – refer only to rules issued by departments or ministries under the State Council. Therefore, all measures issued by the main financial regulatory agencies – PBOC, CBRC, CIRC and CSRC, all of which are discussed later in this chapter – should be termed 'rules' rather than 'regulations'.[8]

II.A.6.   Rules of Local Governments

The local governments of the provinces, autonomous regions, municipalities directly under the Central Government and the comparatively larger cities can formulate local rules.[9]

II.B.   FINANCIAL LAW AND REGULATION IN CHINA

The forms of law described in the previous section are not all relevant to finance. Given the uniform nature of China's financial market, China's financial laws take mainly three forms: financial laws, financial administrative regulations and financial rules. Following China's entry to the WTO, many laws, regulations, rules and other measures were abolished or amended, and this abolition and amendment process is still ongoing.

---

8. The US Trade Representative (USTR) misused the term of 'regulations' in its report. See *USTR 2003 National Trade Estimate Report on Foreign Trade Barriers*, p. 64. <www. ustr.gov/reports/nte/2003/>, 18 April 2003.
9. Legislation Law, art. 63.

To better understand financial markets and related law and regulation in China, it is useful to have an overall understanding of China's regulatory structure. In essence, China has adopted a financial structure, and related legal and institutional framework, based on a sectoral model similar to that of the US prior to the enactment of the Gramm-Leach-Bliley Financial Services Modernization Act of 1999. Under this sectoral structure, financial markets, institutions and laws are separated into individual financial sectors, namely banking, securities and insurance. As a result, the main financial regulatory agencies in China and their scope of authorities and competencies are as follows:

- People's Bank of China (PBOC): Central banking, financial stability and monetary policy
- China Banking Regulatory Commission (CBRC): Banks and banking business
- China Securities Regulatory Commission (CSRC): Securities business
- China Insurance Regulatory Commission (CIRC): Insurance business

In addition, a number of other agencies are also often involved in various ways, including:

- National Development and Reform Commission (NDRC): Financial and development policy and planning
- Ministry of Finance (MOF): Allocation of budgetary resources, as well as some exercise of state-ownership rights
- State-Owned Assets Supervision and Administration Commission (SASAC): Exercise of state-ownership rights

These agencies, plus a range of others, together comprise the State Council, which in many ways is the primary decision-making body in respect to overall financial and economic policy and related legal and institutional issues. Based on this background, the following three sections discuss banking, securities and insurance markets and the related legal and institutional framework in China.

III.   BANKING

China's banking sector is evolving from a simple and closed system in which the government controls almost all credit allocation to an increasingly sophisticated and open system in which multiple institutions perform diverse financial functions. Meanwhile, banking laws and regulations have paced, and often led, development of the banking system and banking practices. Undoubtedly, both globalization and China's transition from a planned economy to a market economy have made an overwhelming contribution to such evolution.

III.A.   DEVELOPMENT OF CHINA'S BANKING INSTITUTIONS

The banking sector plays a dominant role in China's financial market, making up more than 90 per cent of the total assets of all financial institutions.[10] Following continuous efforts directed towards transformation into a modern banking system over the last two decades, China, has developed a system in which the PBOC acts as the central bank, the state-owned commercial banks perform the dominant financial role under the primary supervision of the CBRC, and a variety of financial organizations coexist.

At the same time, China has implemented a three-tier system in its banking market. The first tier banking institutions consist of the four largest state commercial banks, also known as the big four SOCBs, which are: the Agricultural Bank of China (ABC), the Bank of China (BOC), the China Construction Bank (CCB), and the Industrial and Commercial Bank of China (ICBC). These four SOCBs still perform the most important role in the domestic financial market, accounting for more than half of deposits taken and loans granted in the entire banking system.[11] The combined assets of these banks would place them among the fifty largest banking institutions in the world,[12] though there are significant problems with asset quality.

The second-tier banking institutions are the policy banks. It is usually quite common for a transition economy to implement state policies through bank loans. To construct a separate commercial banking system, three policy banks were restructured in 1994, with the intention of alleviating the burden of the dual roles; in other words, policy and commercial roles, of state-specialized banks.[13] The three policy banks are the Agricultural Development Bank, China Development Bank, and Export-Import Bank of China.[14] These state-development banks must assume their own financial risks, protect their asset values and must not compete with commercially based financial institutions.[15] Funding for these banks is mainly raised through bond issuance – large retail issues, though not bonds in the sense of liquid or tradable instruments.[16] Each of these banks has

---

10. X. H. Tong et al., *Financial Services in China: The Past, Present and Future of a Changing Industry* (Singapore: China Knowledge Press Private Limited, 2005).
11. 'Balance Sheet of Assets and Liabilities of State-Owned Commercial Banks', *Annual Report of People's Bank of China 2003* (Beijing: Research Institute of People's Bank of China), available at <www.ripbc.com.cn/yjxxw/jinrongnianbao/2003.htm>.
12. 'Top 1,000 World Banks', [2004] *The Banker* (London: Financial Times Business Information), p.168.
13. Decision of the State Council on Financial System Reform', art. 2, National Distribution (*guo-fa*) 1993, no. 91 (Beijing: State Council, 25 December 1993).
14. Notice of the State Council in Restructuring the Agricultural Development Bank of China, National Distribution (*guo-fa*) 1994', no. 25 (Beijing: State Council, 19 April 1994); Notice of State Council in Restructuring the State Development Bank of China, National Distribution (*guo-fa*) 1994, no. 22 (Beijing: State Council, 17 March 1994).
15. Decision of the State Council on Financial System Reform 1993, art. 2.
16. Ibid.

been assigned specific mandates in carrying out state policies.[17] In effect, these banks are state credit-granting agencies.

The third-tier banking institutions incorporate national, regional and local commercial banks. As of 2004, there were eleven national and regional commercial banks – all of which are joint-stock.[18] One of these banks, the Minsheng Bank, was incorporated in 1996 as the first private bank since the foundation of the PRC.[19] So far, four of these banks have been publicly listed on the Shanghai Stock Exchange and one on the Shenzhen Stock Exchange.[20] These joint-stock banks are permitted to engage in extensive banking business, and their creation was intended to increase competition in China's domestic market.[21] Although a large bulk of their shares are still under the control of the State, the banks are relatively less-subject to political interference, and therefore, their operation appears more dynamic, and performance is superior to their state-owned competitors.

In addition, city and rural commercial banks, which have evolved from city and rural cooperatives respectively, are vested with specific functions relating to local development, for example for small and medium enterprises in city areas and agricultural development in the countryside.[22] In 1995, the PBOC reorganized city credit cooperatives into city cooperative banks in thirty-five pilot cities under the auspices of the respective municipal governments.[23] By the end of October 2005, 150 city commercial banks[24] and nine rural commercial banks existed.[25] Market shares of these types of banks are extremely small, because their business scope is limited to the city in which the banks are founded, and their asset quality is rather poor due to a large amount of policy lending required by the local governments. City commercial banks, however, have become merger and acquisition targets of foreign institutions with the phased-in opening of China's financial market following the country's entry into the WTO.

---

17. Ibid.
18. *Total Assets and Total Liabilities in 2004* (Beijing: China Banking Regulatory Commission, January 2005), available at <www.cbrc.gov.cn/english/index.htm>.
19. *Annual Report of People's Bank of China 2002* (Beijing: People's Bank of China, 2002), p. 68.
20. *2003 Fact Book* (Shanghai: Shanghai Stock Exchange, 2003), available at <www.sse.com.cn/en_us/cs/about/factbook/factbook_us2003.pdf>; *SSE Share Information* (Shenzhen: Shenzhen Stock Exchange, September 2003), available at <www.szse. com.cn/sse/en/mktinfo/3-3.asp>.
21. Decision of the State Council on Financial System Reform 1993.
22. Ibid., art. 3(3).
23. Ibid.
24. 'Latest Developments in China's Banking Reform, Opening-up and Supervision', Press Conference of the State Council of the PRC, December 5, 2005, <www.cbrc. gov.cn/english/con_main/main1.jsp#> 5 December 2005.
25. News of the CBRC, July 18, 2005, available at <www.cbrc.gov.cn/Chinese/con_main/main1.jsp#>. Note that rural credit cooperative banks – *nongcun hezuo yinhang* – are not commercial banks. For this reason, in this dissertation, Chinese-funded banks do not include rural credit cooperative banks.

Since the first foreign banking institution was permitted to operate in Shenzhen in 1981, foreign banks have developed rapidly. By the end of October 2005, foreign-funded banks had established 238 operational entities in 23 cities in China, including 181 foreign bank branches, 14 foreign-funded banks with legal personality,[26] and 238 representative offices of foreign banks.[27] In addition, 138 foreign-funded banks had been approved to operate RMB business, including 73 banks approved to operate RMB business for non-foreign-funded enterprises, 15 foreign-funded banks to provide online banking services in China, 41 foreign-funded banks to carry out derivative transactions in China, and five foreign bank branches to offer custodian services for securities investment by qualified foreign institutional investors (QFII) in China. With the phase-out of geographical and business restrictions for foreign banks and full liberalization in the banking sector by 2006 under China's WTO commitments, foreign players will likely have an increasing impact on China's financial system in terms of their management expertise and diversified financial products, as well as international business networks.

Although the state banks still account for the dominant part of China's financial market, private capital including foreign investment is playing an increasingly active role. Aside from traditional approaches, such as establishing wholly foreign-owned banks and joint-venture banks with domestic financial institutions, the increasingly prevalent method for foreign players is to expand market shares in China through purchasing and holding equity stakes of domestic banks, particularly joint-stock banks and city commercial banks.[28] Certainly, the limitations on equity holdings of overseas financial institutions in Chinese financial institutions constrain the pace of foreign business expansion in China.[29]

The central bank and the banking supervisory body have also evolved as China moves towards the creation of a market economy. During the long period from its establishment in 1948 until the late 1970s, the PBOC was the only de facto banking institution in China; assuming the dual roles of both the central and commercial bank.[30] In 1983, it was determined that the PBOC should function only as a central bank and all of its commercial business was transferred to the four commercial banks: ABC, BOC, CCB and ICBC.[31]

---

26. Foreign-funded banks with legal personality consist of wholly-foreign-funded banks and Sino-foreign Equity Joint Venture Banks.
27. 'Latest Developments in China's Banking Reform, Opening-up and Supervision', Press Conference of the State Council of the PRC, 5 December 2005, available at <www.cbrc.gov.cn/english/con_main/main1.jsp#>.
28. X.H. Tong et al., supra note 10, p. 114.
29. Measures Governing the Equity Investment in Chinese Financial Institutions by Overseas Financial Institutions, art. 8 and 9, no. 6 (Beijing: CBRC, 8 December 2003).
30. X.L. Dai (ed.), *A Fifty Years' History of the People's Bank of China: The Development of the Central Banking System* (Beijing: Chinese Financial Press, November 1998), p. 22.
31. Decision of the State Council on the Specialization of Central Bank Functions by the People's Bank of China, para. 2 (Beijing: State Council, 17 September 1983).

The organizational reform of the PBOC in 1998 was a major step forward towards freeing the PBOC from the various types of local interference common under the provincial network system.[32] In the past, the PBOC was organized into economic regions, and its provincial branches were under dual supervision of both their head office and provincial governments.[33] In strengthening the independence of the PBOC, the State Council has reorganized it and replaced the provincial network with nine trans-provincial branches.[34]

Previously, each regional office of the PBOC had supervisory power over the banking institutions within its jurisdiction, independent of the regional governments.[35] As a result, the PBOC inevitably had conflicting roles as a regulator and central banker. A balance was needed between maintaining rapid economic growth and prudential supervision of banking institutions. The risk, therefore, was that the PBOC might have been compelled to soften its regulatory control over risky banking institutions in accordance with State economic development policies. This uncertainty contributed to an increasing number of non-performing loans (NPLs) in the banking system. To resolve this dilemma, the CBRC was established in April 2003 to assume the regulatory functions of the PBOC;[36] namely supervising banking and non-banking financial institutions – with the exception of insurance and securities firms- to ensure the stability of their operations,[37] and to help these firms strengthen defences against financial risks.[38] The PBOC continues its role as a central bank with its focus on formulating and implementing monetary policy and safeguarding financial stability.[39] The PBOC concentrates on regulations in regard to monetary conditions and financial system liquidity with the aim of promoting economic growth and monetary stability; while the CBRC focuses on the strength of financial institutions with a focus on controlling financial risks. The functions of the PBOC and the CBRC, however, seem to overlap in some areas, because both have the responsibility to prevent and minimize financial risks.

A task of highest priority for China's government has been to transform SOCBs into independent, transparent and commercialized banking institutions. During the period in which the PBOC fulfilled both central and

32. *Country Finance – China* (London: Economist Intelligence Unit, August 2004), p. 10.
33. Decision of the State Council on the Specialization of Central Bank Functions by the People's Bank of China.
34. Notice of State Council Approval of People's Bank of China Provisional Branch Restructuring, National Distribution (*guo-fa*) 1998, no. 33 (Beijing: State Council, 17 October 1998).
35. Ibid., para. 2.
36. Decision of the Standing Committee of National People's Congress on the Exercise of Regulatory and Supervisory Functions by the China Banking Regulatory Commission in Place of the People's Bank of China (Beijing: 26 April 2003).
37. Banking Supervision Law, 2003, art. 1.
38. Ibid., art. 3.
39. Notice of the Central Committee Office on the Adjustment of Major Functions, Internal Organizations and Staff of the PBOC, available at <www.pbc.gov.cn/detail.asp?col=100&ID=1012&keyword=>.

commercial roles, the ABC and CCB of the time, which originated through restructuring the corresponding banking institutions, merely performed specialized functions of the PBOC.[40] Through a gradual process, the ABC and CCB were made independent of the PBOC and the Ministry of Finance, and took over the commercial role of the PBOC.[41] In 1984, the State Council formalized the specialized functions of the big four SOCBs.[42] Prior to the Decision of the State Council on Financial System Reform in 1993, the concept of state commercial banks was murky. Although the Council accepted deposits and channelled money into lending activities, the SOCBs functioned essentially as specialized banks under the PBOC and acted primarily as state agencies, implementing governmental policies in granting credit to SOEs with little regard for profitability.[43] In 1993, the State Council formally adopted the socialist market economy, and the big four specialized state banks were restructured as commercial banks.[44] Despite this restructuring, and the establishment of the policy banks to assume policy loans in 1994,[45] the SOCBs continue to suffer from a tremendous volume of NPLs, due to a large extent to inefficient corporate governance and excessive lending to loss-making SOEs at the strong intervention of both central and local governments.

As described previously, widespread asset-quality problems in China's state banking sector can be attributed largely to the underperforming SOEs, poor banking and directed lending. Prior to 1983, SOE funding came directly from government financial grants, which have since been gradually substituted with bank loans,[46] and by 1985, loans granted by the SOCBs became the only funding source for the SOEs.[47] The SOEs relied on bank loans as an implicit financial subsidy, including low-interest-rate loans and defaulted principal and interest.[48] As a result, the big four SOCBs themselves acted as quasi-state agencies in

---

40. X.T. Yang, et al. (eds.), *The General History of China's Finance* (Beijing: Chinese Finance Publishing House, 2000), pp. 223–226.
41. Decision of the State Council on the Specialization of Central Bank Functions by the People's Bank of China, para. 3.
42. Notice of the State Council on the Approving the People's Bank of China Report on the Division of Lending Functions among the Specialized Banks, para. 2 (Beijing: State Council, 30 May 1984).
43. The Provisional Rules of Banking Management, arts 3 & 14, National Distribution (*guo-fa*) 1986, no. 1 (Beijing: State Council, 7 January 1986).
44. Decision of the State Council on Financial System Reform 1993, Preface.
45. Ibid.
46. Transfer to the People's Bank of China Regarding Uniform Management of Operating Funds of State Own Enterprise, National Distribution (*guo-fa*) 1983, no. 100 (Beijing: State Council, 25 June 1983).
47. *National Budget: Infrastructure Finance will be provided by Loans than State Funds*, Budget Brief (*ji-zi*) 1984, no. 2580 (Beijing: National Accounting Commission, Ministry of Finance, and Chinese Construction Bank, 14 December 1984).
48. J. Lin, F. Cai and Z. Li, *The China Miracle: Development Strategy and Economic Reform* (Hong Kong: The Chinese University Press, 2003), p. 221. See also *The Chinese Economy: Fighting Inflation, Deepening Reforms* (Washington, D.C., World Bank, 1996), p. 17.

maintaining SOE operations and further securing social stability.[49] The central government controlled all credit allocation through strict plans implemented by the PBOC in pursuit of government economic policies, and therefore, prudential regulation was seemingly impossible for the SOCBs.[50] Despite the asset problems created among the SOCBS, this approach nonetheless supported rapid economic growth in China over the past two decades.[51]

The outbreak of Asian financial crises triggered a new round of reforms in China's financial sector – commonly viewed as having similar potential risks, in spite of not being adversely affected by the crisis. Those reforms included strengthening prudential practices in the banking system, such as the introduction of the asset-liability management system in place of credit planning in 1998, and the establishment of vertical management, both in the central bank and commercial banks, to reduce administrative intervention. In addition, two large bank bailouts were carried out to strengthen the reforms: in 1998, RMB 270 billion (USD 33.33 billion) of capital was injected into the four SOCBs through special government bond issuance to boost their capital bases,[52] and in 1999, RMB 1.4 trillion (USD 172.84 billion) of NPLs were transferred from the big four SOCBs to the four newly established asset management companies (AMCs).[53] Because no parallel institutional reform measures were put in place to secure the return of the capital infusion, the financial bailouts have not turned the large SOCBs into healthy institutions. Because China has committed to liberalize widely its banking sector by 2006, it has become necessary to intensify the transformation of the SOCBs in order for them to face the increasing competition and maintain national economic development.[54]

Accordingly, in 2003, an all-round reform initiative, featuring a three-step strategy, was launched to enhance the shareholding system in the SOCBs. The first step, financial restructuring, is illustrated by the following cases: in January 2004, BOC and CCB received USD 45 billion in capital injections in the form of foreign reserves,[55] and in April 2005, ICBC received USD 15 billion of

---

49. J. Lin, F. Cai and Z. Li, Ibid, pp. 221–222.
50. N. R. Lardy, *China's Unfinished Economic Revolution* (New York, Brookings Institution Press, 1998), p. 83.
51. Ibid., p. 220.
52. Resolution by Standing Committee of National People's Congress on Approving the State Council's Advice that Supplementing the Capital Reserves of the Solely State-Owned Commercial Banks through Issuing Special Government Bonds, 1998 (Beijing: NPC Standing Committee, 28 February 1998).
53. Notice of the People's Bank of China, etc. on Establishing China's Cinda Asset Management Company (*guoban-fa*) 1999, no.33 (Beijing: Office of the State Council, 4 April 1999); Notice of the People's Bank of China, etc. on Establishing China's Huarong, Great Wall and Orient Asset Management Company (*guoban-fa*) 1999, no. 66 (Bejing: Office of the State Council, 21 July 1999).
54. PBOC News Release, 'State Council Decides to Introduce Shareholding System in Bank of China and China Construction Bank' (Beijing: PBOC, 6 January 2004). See <www.pbc.gov.cn/english//detail.asp?col=6400&ID=352&keyword=sharehold-ing>.
55. Ibid.

fresh capital in the same form.[56] Here, the financial restructuring is intended to create favourable conditions for further shareholding restructuring and listing (likely to take place in at least Hong Kong), which are regarded as the second and third steps, respectively.[57] Both CCB and BOC have completed their structural adjustment from solely state-owned institutions to limited corporations following the capital injections.[58] For the sake of thorough and fundamental transformation, China's policymakers have imposed a stiffer regime of corporate governance and a set of strict assessment indicators on the SOCBs that benefit from these pilot recapitalizations.[59] These measures, however, have not yet removed the fundamental problems of the SOCBs, and concerns about corporate governance and substantial transformation in the entities mean further steps are expected to propel full commercialization.

III.B.   DEVELOPMENT OF BANKING LAWS AND REGULATIONS

China's legal framework for banking mainly takes three forms: banking laws, banking administrative regulations and banking rules. The main banking laws, which are the Law on the People's Bank of China ('PBOC Law' – the central bank law) and the Law on Commercial Banks ('Commercial Banking Law'), were enacted by the NPC and its Standing Committee, respectively, in 1995, and both were amended in 2003.

Prior to the enactment of the PBOC Law and the Commercial Banking Law in 1995, no substantial banking law existed in China, and the legal system that regulated the banking market in China was comprised mainly of administrative regulations stipulated by the State Council and a variety of rules or measures by the PBOC and other government departments. The Provisional Regulations on Banking Management, issued by the State Council in 1986, was the first comprehensive legislation in China to regulate the banking sector.[60] However, the legislation was relatively rough and simple due to the immature markets

---

56. PBOC News Release, 'State Council Decided to Carry out Shareholding Reform in the Industrial and Commercial Bank of China' (Beijing: PBOC, 21 April 2005). See <www.pbc.gov.cn/english/detail.asp?col=6400&id=517>.
57. Ibid.
58. PBOC News Release, 'Bank of China Co. Ltd Inaugurated', available at <www.pbc.gov.cn/english//detail.asp?col=6400&ID=419&keyword=Huijin>; PBOC News Release, 'Speech by Mr. Xie Ping, General Manager of Central Huijin Investment Company, at the Inauguration Ceremony of China Construction Bank Co. Ltd'. See <www.pbc.gov.cn/detail.asp?col=4200&ID=128>.
59. PBOC News Release, 'State Council Decides to Introduce Shareholding System in Bank of China and China Construction Bank' (Beijing: PBOC, 6 January 2004). See www.pbc.gov.cn/english//detail.asp?col=6400&ID=352&keyword=shareholding; also, CBRC, *Guidelines on Corporate Governance Reforms and Supervision of Bank of China and Construction Bank of China* (Beijing: CBRC, 11 March 2004). See <www.cbrc.gov.cn/english/index.html>.
60. Regulations on Banking Management (Beijing: State Council, 7 January 1986).

of the time. The promulgation of the two banking laws alongside the Law on Security (*Danbaofa*) and the Law on Negotiable Instruments (*Piaojufa*) was a milestone for China's banking legislation, marking the formation of a modern banking legal system in China.

The 1995 PBOC Law was enacted to provide supervision and administration of banking operations, making and implementation of currency policy.[61] The PBOC of the time had very wide supervisory powers, including authorization, auditing deposits and loans, settlement of accounts, addressing bad debts and business affairs of banking institutions, and taking appropriate supervisory actions including suspension, termination and take-overs of banking institutions as necessary.[62] Notwithstanding this, the detail of day-to-day supervision of banking institutions was implemented through administrative guidelines issued by the PBOC.[63] These guidelines have the force of law, as the PBOC has legal capacity to make administrative rules or measures.[64] To formulate monetary policy, a monetary policy committee was set up within the PBOC in 1997. Additionally, the PBOC is granted a series of market-oriented instruments to realize monetary policy and adjust financial markets, i.e. deposit reserve system, basic interest rates, rediscounting business, re-lending, and open market operations.[65] Corresponding to the creation of the CBRC, the amendment to the PBOC Law was enacted in December 2003 to refocus and refine the independent role of the PBOC as a central bank in making and implementing monetary policy and in safeguarding overall financial stability.[66] As a part of those amendments, anti-money-laundering was added on the list of responsibilities of the PBOC.[67] The amended PBOC Law has also expanded the powers of the PBOC in imposing monetary as well as other administrative penalties on wrongdoers.

The operation of the CBRC is legally based on the Law on Banking Regulation and Supervision ('Banking Supervision Law'), promulgated in 2003. The CBRC has assumed many functions and authorities previously exercised by the PBOC. The Banking Supervision Law provides the CBRC with unambiguous powers to approve or revoke banking licenses, to supervise the operations and to take over administration of banks in distress, and to dismiss or restrict the authority of directors and senior managers. A remarkable provision in this law is the clear establishment of prudential operation as the core principle for banking business.[68]Reducing NPLs, restructuring state banks and

---

61. PBOC Law 1995, art. 2.
62. Ibid., arts 31, 32 and 64.
63. Ibid., art. 31.
64. Legislation Law, arts 71 and 82.
65. Ibid., art. 23.
66. PBOC Law 2003, art. 2.
67. Ibid., art. 4(10).
68. Banking Supervision Law 2003, art. 21.

implementing prudential practices in accordance with international standards are set as top tasks for the CBRC.[69]

The Commercial Banking Law was passed in 1995 and amended in December 2003, providing a legal foundation for the construction of China's commercial banking system. The Commercial Banking Law formulates a series of provisions governing the establishment and organizational structure of commercial banks, banking business rules as well as relevant legal liabilities in view of developing a market-oriented commercial banking system. In the 1995 version the independence of SOCBs in granting loans was highlighted.[70] However, the Commercial Banking Law required commercial banks to develop their lending business under the guidance of state industry policies supporting the national economy and social development,[71] which left ample opportunities to local governments to meddle with the affairs of the commercial banks under the guise of providing direction on industrial policies. A major change in the 2003 amendment is that the power of the State Council to direct commercial banks to grant specific loans is abolished,[72] which is one step forward toward autonomy of banking institutions. Also, the 2003 amendment has strengthened corporate governance by imposing stiffer penalties on corporate wrongdoers of banking institutions.[73] The amendment puts safety as the top priority for banking operations whereas efficiency was stationed as the first principle in the 1995 version.[74] The most extensive revisions are seen in relation to legal responsibilities. Essentially, the revisions lay out in detail the monetary penalties for negligence or malfeasance by banks.

The revised PBOC Law and Commercial Banking Law do not change the overall sectoral structure of China's financial system and related legal framework.[75]

An effective banking legal framework should protect banking institutions from problematic borrowers. However, China's banking sector is still facing legal barriers in protecting creditor rights. Firstly, the banking law does not in substance prohibit political interference in the banking system. Although both the PBOC Law and Commercial Banking Law prohibit political interference in the loan granting process,[76] they leave ample opportunity for such

---

69. *The CBRC identified supervisory priorities for the coming years for the wholly state-owned commercial banks and joint shareholding commercial banks* (Beijing, CBRC, 4 September 2003), available at <www.cbrc.gov.cn/english/module/viewinfo.jsp?infoID=472>.
70. Commercial Banking Law 1995, art. 4 and 41.
71. Ibid., art. 34.
72. Commercial Banking Law (Amendment) Decision, art. 11 (Beijing: NPC Standing Committee, 27 December 2003) deleting Commercial Banking Law 1995, art. 41(2).
73. Commercial Banking Law (Amendment) Decision, arts 27 & 34, amending Commercial Banking Law, arts 76 & 78 & adding art. 89.
74. Commercial Banking Law (Amendment) Decision, art. 2 (Beijing: NPC Standing Committee, 27 December 2003).
75. Commercial Banking Law 1995, art. 43.
76. PBOC Law 1995, art. 7; Commercial Banking Law 1995, art. 41.

interference as no provision imposes any penalty for breach of this prohibition. Moreover, the policy-directed supervision and arrangement of branches based on administrative regions enable local governments to exert profound influence over business decisions of the commercial banks. Secondly, the law of bankruptcy and mortgage in China does not provide adequate protection for creditors. Severe political meddling in SOE bankruptcies leaves little protection for the interests of banking institutions since local authorities put stability in their jurisdictions as the top priority and clearly one which may be affected by the failure of regional SOEs in maintaining employment. The costly procedure to realize mortgaged assets is also a barrier to protecting the interests of banking institutions as creditors. To protect local interests, local governments always try to prevent the foreclosure of mortgaged property by interfering with the valuators, auctioneers, courts, and other administrative agencies involving in the valuation and sale of mortgaged property.[77] Thirdly, the banking institutions have limited powers to supervise the operation of problematic debtors. Under the current legal framework banking institutions cannot invest in non-banking financial industries and other enterprises. Further legislative authority is required to improve this situation.

China's banking supervisory system is undergoing fundamental transformation from a simple credit control model to a sophisticated risk-based model. Credit planning had previously been the most important approach for the PBOC to implement monetary policies through controlling the loan limits of the banking institutions. As a significant instrument to realize national economic policies, it was not completely abolished until 1998 when a management system based on the asset-liability ratio was formally put in practice.[78] The asset-liability ratio management system, to a large extent, was a major step in liberalizing the operations of the banking sector and implementing a sound supervisory mechanism. Credit and asset quality were usually ignored under the previous system supervision when the ratio of credit to deposits within a banking institution did not exceed 75 per cent.[79] The newly launched risk-based supervisory approach puts more emphasis on banking risk through strengthening capital requirements and tightening credit risk management rather than just controlling the growth of credit lending.

Non-transparent operational systems are more vulnerable to risks of underestimating and hiding banking problems, and therefore transparency is a major issue for China's banking sector to address. China's banking sector has been rife with transparency problems resulting from an inaccurate loan

---

77. F. Zhou (editor), *The Debt Work-Out for SOEs in China* (Beijing: Peking University Press, 2003), pp. 239–40.
78. *Almanac of China's Finance and Banking* (Beijing: Editorial Board of Almanac of China's Finance and Banking, 1999), p. 7.
79. Commercial Banking Law 2003, art. 39(2).

classification system, incomplete financial reporting requirements, unauthentic auditing reports, and unreasonable taxation standards. To control the expansion of financial risks, in 2002, the PBOC enacted Interim Measures for the Information Disclosure of Commercial Banks, which set the minimum requirements for commercial banks in terms of information disclosure and also the principles of authenticity, accuracy, integrity, and comparability when disclosing information.[80] Financial reports, various kinds of risk management, corporate governance and major events must be disclosed to meet the minimal requirements of this Measure.[81] Also, penalties can be imposed on relevant responsible persons who provide false financial statements or false auditing reports.[82] This is emphasized further under the Banking Supervision Law.[83] As the pilots of financial reform, the BOC and CCB are charged with stricter responsibility in keeping transparent operations.[84]

Following the creation of the CBRC, a series of supportive administrative regulations, which cover risk management, internal controls, capital adequacy, asset quality, loan loss provisioning, risk concentrations, connected transactions, and liquidity management, were formulated in line with international standards to ensure the implementation of the prudential rules.[85]

The Regulation Governing Capital Adequacy of Commercial Banks was claimed to incorporate a number of recommendations of the proposed Basel II Capital Accord,[86] Under the Regulation all commercial banks are required to meet the international standard of 8 per cent capital adequacy ratio and 4 per cent for core capital adequacy ratio by 2007,[87] including supervisory review and information disclosure.[88] and the risk weight is stipulated as 100 per cent for all types of business enterprises and individuals, including SOEs.[89] The CBRC is provided extensive powers to take corrective actions in relation to inadequately

---

80. Interim Measures for the Information Disclosure of Commercial Banks, arts 3 & 5 (Beijing: PBOC, 21 May 2002).
81. Ibid., art. 8.
82. Ibid., arts 27 & 28.
83. Banking Supervision Law 2003, arts 33, 35, 36, 45 & 46
84. CBRC, *Guidelines on Corporate Governance Reforms and Supervision of Bank of China and Construction Bank of China* (Beijing: CBRC, 11 March 2004), <www.cbrc.gov.cn/english/index.htm>.
85. Banking Supervision Law 2003, art. 21.
86. Regulation Governing Capital Adequacy of Commercial Banks, no.2 2004 (Beijing: CBRC, 23 February 2004); *The New Basel Capital Accord* (Basel: Bank for International Settlements, 11 October 2003), available at <www.bis.org/publ/bcbsca.htm#pgtop>.
87. *The responses to the press by the senior official of the China Banking Regulatory Commission on issues relating to the New Capital Accord* (Beijing: CBRC, 14 September 2003), available at <www.cbrc.gov.cn/english/module/viewinfo.jsp?infoID=468>.
88. Regulation Governing Capital Adequacy of Commercial Banks, arts 7 & 53.
89. Ibid., art. 23.

capitalized institutions [90] and to exert penalties on senior management members if the capital reserve is significantly below the threshold.[91]

To ensure that commercial banks will develop their risk-taking activities on the basis of risk management capacity and capital strength, credit risk management plays an important part in the new supervisory system. Larger banking institutions have already begun implementing the two-dimensional rating system as recommended by Basel II.[92] In 2004, the Guidelines on Market Risk Management of Commercial Banks was issued by the CBRC, which require commercial banks to enhance market risk management by identifying, measuring, monitoring, and controlling the market risks arising from all their activities.[93] To ensure the capture of risks and adjustment to the changing environment, another important measure, the Provisional Rules on Assessment of Internal Controls of Commercial Banks, was issued to encourage commercial banks to establish systematic, transparent, and documented internal control systems.[94] Connected transactions between commercial banks and their insiders or shareholders are also strictly regulated.[95] In addition, on an experimental basis, the old four-category loan system based on payment experience has been replaced with a five-category system in accord with international standards,[96] and banking institutions are required to draw adequate loss reserve funds according to the Guidelines on Banking Loan Loss Provisioning[97] before computing reliable profit-reporting and capital.[98]

Constructing sound corporate governance structures within China's banking institutions is set as a crucial point to ensure the success of China's banking reform. In 2002, the Guidelines on Corporate Governance in Joint-Stock Commercial Banks, as well as the Guidelines on Independent Directors and Outside Supervisors of Joint-Stock Commercial Banks, were released to provide a legalbasis for the establishment of effective governance mechanisms within

---

90. Ibid., art. 40(3).
91. Ibid., art. 41(1).
92. *The responses to the press by the senior official of the China Banking Regulatory Commission on issues relating to the New Capital Accord* (Beijing: CBRC, 14 September 2003), available at <www.cbrc.gov.cn/english/module/viewinfo.jsp?infoID=468>.
93. Guidelines on Market Risk Management of Commercial Banks, art. 1, no. 10 2004 (Beijing: CBRC, 16 December 2004).
94. Provisional Rules on Assessment of Internal Controls of Commercial Banks, arts 4 & 7, no. 9 2004 (Beijing: CBRC, 20 August 2004).
95. The Administrative Measures for the connected transactions between commercial banks and their insiders or shareholders (Beijing: CBRC, 2 April 2004).
96. Notices of People's Bank of China on the Full Implementation of the Five-grade Loan Classification System, Bank Distribution (*yin-fa*) no. 263 1999 & no. 416 2001 (Beijing: PBOC, 15 September 1999 & 31 December 2001).
97. PBOC, Guidelines on Banking Loan Loss Provisioning (*yin-fa*) no. 98 2002 (Beijing: PBOC, 2 April 2002).
98. Provisional Measures for Monitoring and Assessing the Distressed Assets of Commercial Banks, art. 4 (Beijing: CBRC, 25 March 2004).

joint-stock commercial banks.[99] Establishing modern corporate governance has always been a top goal in reforming China's state banking sector. However, state ownership itself makes this task rather difficult. After receiving capital infusions, three pilot banks, namely BOC, CCB, and ICBC, were requested to implement a shareholding system with strict corporate governance at its centre.[100]

Foreign banks in China have benefited considerably from the improving legal environment. China's entry to the WTO accelerates the openness of legal system for foreign participants. As a result, the major legislation regulating the operations of foreign financial institutions in China, i.e. the Regulations on the Administration of Foreign-Funded Financial Institutions as well as its detailed implementation rules, were much revised, so as to be more compliant with GATS/WTO rules and more favourable to foreign participants.[101] The Rules Governing the Equity Investment in Chinese Financial Institutions by Overseas Financial Institutions issued by the CBRC,[102] which raised the maximum foreign equity holding in Chinese financial institutions, encourages foreign counterparts to participate in the reforms of domestic banks through helping them improve service quality and competitiveness. However, a series of prudential requirements and limits on foreign equity participation in Chinese banks are set to prevent possible risks and market monopoly associated with foreign investment.[103] The promulgation of these regulations and rules has significantly improved the transparency and efficiency of the legal framework, making China's policy more encouraging and attractive for foreign involvement with domestic financial institutions.

Also, the participation of foreign investors in the restructuring of China's SOEs and SOCBs has received strong legal support from the government. In 2003, the Interim Provision on Restructuring State-owned Enterprises with

---

99. PBOC, Guidelines on Corporate Governance of Joint-Stock Commercial Banks, no. 15 2002 (Beijing: PBOC, 4 June 2002); PBOC, Guidelines on Independent Directors and Outside Supervisors of Joint-Stock Commercial Banks, no. 15 2002 (Beijing: PBOC, 4 June 2002).

100. PBOC News Release, 'State Council Decides to Introduce Shareholding System in Bank of China and China Construction Bank' (Beijing: PBOC, 6 January 2004). See: <www.pbc.gov.cn/english//detail.asp?col=6400&ID=352&keyword=shareholding>; PBOC News Release, 'State Council Decided to Carry out Shareholding Reform in the Industrial and Commercial Bank of China' (Beijing: PBOC, 21 April 2005). See <www.pbc.gov.cn/english/detail.asp?col=6400&id=517>; Also: CBRC, *Guidelines on Corporate Governance Reforms and Supervision of Bank of China and Construction Bank of China* (Beijing: CBRC, 11 March 2004). See <www.cbrc.gov.cn/english/index.htm>.

101. State Council, Regulation on the Administration of Foreign-Funded Financial Institutions, no. 340 2001 (Beijing: State Council, 20 November 2001); CBRC, Detailed Rules on the Implementation of the Regulation on the Administration of Foreign-Funded Financial Institutions, no. 4 2004 (Beijing: CBRC, 26 July 2004).

102. CBRC, Measures Governing the Equity Investment in Chinese Financial Institutions by Overseas Financial Institutions, no. 6 2003 (Beijing: CBRC, 8 December 2003).

103. Measures Governing the Equity Investment in Chinese Financial Institutions by Overseas Financial Institutions, art. 8 and 9.

Foreign Investment was issued by the SETC providing a basic framework for foreign capital to enter into the strategic restructuring of SOEs.[104] The legal framework addressing NPL problems through absorbing foreign capital began to take shape in 2001 when the Provisional Rules on Drawing Foreign Capital into the Asset Restructuring and Disposal by Financial Asset Management Companies was enacted as an administrative rule.[105] It expressly states that all AMCs may receive foreign capital in the restructuring and disposing of NPLs. However, it only offers limited guidance to foreign investors in disposing of NPLs, and the relating legal and regulatory problems have yet to be resolved. [106] In addition, settlement for redundant employees of SOEs is still a delicate and problematic issue for foreign investors as the government still puts top priority on such issues as resettling employees, guaranteeing their lawful rights and interests, and maintaining social stability.[107]

The system dealing with banking exit is inadequate in China. So far, there is no specific legal regime governing the exit of financial institutions, though the legal basis for closure of financial institutions can be found in the Bankruptcy Law for general enterprises, the PBOC Law, Banking Supervision Law, Commercial Banking Law, and Company Law as well as some administrative regulations. Nonetheless, Regulations on the Cancellation of Financial Institutions, enacted by the State Council and taking effect in 2001, is currently the most comprehensive legal document providing the administrative resolution for financial institutions in distress in China.[108] In practice, one regional joint-stock bank, several trust and investment companies, and some deposit-taking credit cooperatives were closed during 1997–2001.[109] Apparently, China's banking supervision has been more focused on market entrance. A robust exit policy, however, should be clearly defined in legal measures, under which a failed bank must be removed from the market. A set of rules in detail should also be established to classify the standards and procedures regarding the exit of financial institutions.

In conclusion, the creation of the CBRC, together with the revised commercial banking and central bank laws marked a big and firm step forward not only for the effective bank regulation in China, but also for the reform of the whole system. Hopefully, the introduction of such prudential measures

---

104. Provisional Rules on Reorganization of SOEs by Using Foreign Fund, 42 2002 (Beijing: State Economic & Trade Commission, 8 November 2002).
105. The Provisional Rules of Attracting Foreign Capital into Asset Restructuring and Disposition of Asset Management Companies, no. 6 2001 (Beijing: Ministry of Foreign Trade & Economic Cooperation, 26 October 2001).
106. D. Liu, 'Foreign Investment in NPL Assets: Is China's Legal Environment Up to the Task?', *China Law & Practice* (May 2003), pp. 27–8.
107. Provisional Rules on Reorganization of SOEs by Using Foreign Fund, art. 4(3)
108. Regulations on the Cancellation of Financial Institutions, State Council Decree No. 324 (Beijing: State Council, 23 November 2001).
109. *Almanac of China's Finance and Banking* (Beijing: Editorial Board of Almanac of China's Finance & Banking, 2002), p. 9.

will assist China's banking institutions to operate in line with international practices, improve asset quality, and address NPLs. As all Chinese banks will gradually adopt the corporate system and offer shares to the public, including foreign strategic investors, the regulatory authority will have to take more robust measures to maintain greater transparency in banks' operations and ensure their ultimate accountability for the interests of investors as well as the State.

IV.   SECURITIES

China's securities market and related legal framework have evolved gradually, though not always smoothly, alongside the country's liberalization and economic reform. Nonetheless, both the market and its regulation have now achieved certain level of maturity.

IV.A.   DEVELOPMENT OF SECURITIES MARKETS

China's securities markets have been developing since the 1980s, in tandem with the market reforms and the liberalization of the country's economy. In July 1981, issuance of treasury bonds began in China. Six years later, a secondary market for the trading of treasury bonds was established, though not entirely successfully. By the mid-1980s, state enterprises had begun to issue both shares and corporate bonds.[110]

China's securities markets formally took shape with the establishment of the two domestic stock exchanges: the Shanghai Stock Exchange and Shenzhen Stock Exchange in December 1990 and June 1991 respectively. The two stock exchanges were initially only regional markets. At that time, only 14 joint stock companies were listed in China with a total equity capital of RMB 600 million (USD 74 million), and a total market value of around RMB 11 billion (USD 1.36 billion).[111] The small-scale market had little effect on the country's economic life. Most enterprises preferred bank loans to share issuance in the securities market despite the low availability of bank loans. China's securities market was at its experimental stage, and was regarded as a capitalist phenomenon and thus contradicting the country's socialist ideology.

In the process of China's liberalization and economic reform, the Communist Party of China gradually changed its ideology of socialism to one in support of the development of a socialist market economy, which greatly benefited the development of the country's securities markets. In 1992, the first

---

110. CSRC, 'China's Securities and Futures Markets' April 2004, available at <www.csrc. gov.cn>.
111. See Z. Huoqi, 'How about the Publicly-held Corporations: A Comment on the Development of the Publicly-held Corporations,' *People's Daily*, 6 February 1999, p. 5.

governmental regulatory agency for the securities market, namely the Securities Commission of the State Council, was established. In April 1993, the State Council promulgated the first influential legislation concerning market regulation: the Provisional Regulations for the Administration of the Issuance and Trading of Stock (ITS).[112] In December 1993, the Company Law was enacted, which was of great significance for the development of China's securities markets. At the same time, many normative documents related to the regulation of these markets were promulgated. The development in legislation inspired market growth. As a result, the securities market experienced rapid expansion in 1993 and 1994. By the end of 1994, the number of listed companies on the Shanghai and Shenzhen Stock Exchanges rose to 181 and 291 respectively, with respective equity capitalization of RMB 35.8 billion (USD 4.42 billion) and RMB 63.8 billion (USD 7.88 billion). The total market value of China's securities market amounted to RMB 354.2 billion (USD 43.73 billion).[113] Enterprises gradually realized the advantages of raising capital through stock issuance.[114]

In the market development, however, various new problems arose. The rapid expansion of the market generated a sizeable gap between the demand for, and supply of, capital. Consequently, the secondary market experienced adjustment. Taking into consideration the market volume and scale, the Chinese government became more careful in approving applications for stock issuance since 1994. By the end of 1995, the number of listed companies increased only by 32 on the two domestic stock exchanges. As compared to the previous year, the market value dropped by RMB 2 billion (USD 246.9 million).[115]

The second period of marked growth of the Chinese securities market occurred during 1996 and 1998. By the end of 1998, the number of listed companies in the Chinese market had risen to 745, and the market capitalization had increased to RMB 2 trillion (USD 246.9 billion). The Shanghai and Shenzhen Stock Exchanges had by then grown into national markets.[116]

In December 1998, the most important statute for China's securities markets, the Securities Law, was promulgated, which greatly promoted the development and the regulation of the markets. Since that time, the China Securities Regulatory Commission (CSRC) has established its status as the competent authority for the Chinese securities markets. The accumulation of the government's experience in market regulation and the development of the related legal system guarantee market growth. From that time, these markets have entered a period of standardization and steady development.

---

112. This statute is still valid even after the Securities Law of China came into force in July 1999 – though the major part of the ITS has been replaced by the Securities Law.
113. See Z. Huoqi, *supra note 111.*
114. The most apparent advantage is that enterprises are free from the pressure of returning principal, although this does not include paying interest, as will take place with bank loans. This makes equity financing less risky than debt financing.
115. See Z. Huoqi, *supra note* 111, p. 6.
116. Ibid., p. 3.

During their development, China's securities markets are becoming more open to the outside world. Since its accession to the WTO in December 2001, China has been actively fulfilling its commitments by allowing the establishment of foreign-invested securities companies and fund management companies. In addition, China is making efforts to attract foreign investment to its securities markets by launching the Qualified Foreign Institutional Investor (QFII) scheme, which opens up China's domestic 'A' share market to overseas investors. As a result of this policy, the development pace of the Chinese securities markets has accelerated.

Currently, China's securities market offers seven types of financial instruments, which include: 'A' shares,[117] 'B' shares,[118] treasury bonds, treasury bond repurchase agreements, corporate bonds, convertible bonds and securities investment funds (close-end and open-end). The offering and trading of shares and close-end investment fund units have been dematerialized, with trading and settlement procedures standardized across the market for all participants. Insurance companies are permitted to invest in the securities market indirectly by means of purchasing securities investment funds. The Social Security Fund can entrust approved asset management institutions to invest in the securities market on its behalf.

By September 2005, a total of 1,381 companies were listed on the Shanghai and Shenzhen Stock Exchanges, with a total market capitalization and float value of RMB 3.34 trillion (USD 429.63 billion) and RMB 1.07 trillion (USD 135.8 billion), respectively. The number of investor accounts totalled 73.13 million.[119] As China developed domestic securities markets, it also encouraged domestic companies to enter international capital markets. By the end of 2003, 93 domestic companies listed overseas.[120]

By the end of April 2004, 34 fund management companies were running more than 100 funds – including both close-end and open-end funds – in China. The scale of investment funds totalled 256.3 billion shares, with net assets of RMB 267.9 billion (USD 33.1 billion). The market value of shares held by funds amounted to 11 per cent of the float market value of 'A' shares.[121] By the end of 2003, China had issued RMB 628 billion (USD 77.5 billion) of treasury bonds and RMB 35.8 billion (USD 4.42 billion) of corporate bonds. The turnover for treasury bonds trading in thespot market and bond repurchases were RMB

---

117. Common shares denominated in RMB.
118. Domestically listed common shares denominated in RMB and quoted in US dollars (on the Shanghai Stock Exchange) or HK dollars (on the Shenzhen Stock Exchange).
119. Statistics available at <www.csrc.gov.cn>.
120. CSRC, 'China's Securities and Futures Markets' April 2004, available at <www.csrc. gov.cn>.
121. 'Current Situation of the Chinese Securities Market (*Muqian Zhongguo Zhengquan Shichang Xianzhuang*)', 7 June 2004, available at <news1.jrj.com.cn/new>.

575.6 billion (USD 71.1 billion) and RMB 5.3 trillion (USD 654.32 billion), respectively.[122]

Conventional debt issuance by central and state governments and financial institutions began in the early-1980s in China, but has suffered hiatuses caused by economic, institutional or irregular shocks. The contemporary form of debt issuance has evolved only since 1994. While issuance by the central government and state organizations has become substantial, a true market for notes and bonds has always been modest, with only peripheral trading liquidity available to investors of all types. Corporate bonds have an irregular history: state organizations were permitted to issue bonds in a semi-regulated fashion in the mid-1980s and the results became chaotic.[123] Similarly, in the early-1990s, markets in exchange-traded and OTC interest rate and bond futures and options were wholly speculative in use, became discredited and were prohibited by 1995. Issuance by SOEs is now modest, non-state enterprise issuance trivial and secondary trading virtually non-existent. New interest rate and exchange rate derivatives will be permitted with the eventual implementation of reform guidelines announced in 2004.

The growing breadth of financial intermediation in China means that professional and investor interest in issuance and trading is profound, and a limited number of approved investment firms now engage in trading state sector debt issues with the considerable sophistication known in major markets, despite the general illiquidity.[124] Their success on an observable scale requires the loosening of symbiotic links between state banks and government typical of Asia's domestic money markets, in which banks and their regulators form a circle that restricts the use of debt instruments by other parties.[125]

Since 2002, China's central authorities[126] have accumulated a strong understanding of the practicalities of building robust market and issuance infrastructures for debt instruments of all kinds, not least due to amassing attention of foreign and multinational organizations and transaction-seeking private sector banks. There is, however, a profound need for commensurate legal and

---

122. CSRC, 'China's Securities and Futures Markets', April 2004, available at <www.csrc. gov.cn>.
123. Scott and Ho identify four separate phases of issuance of non-government, non-financial bonds since 1980, encouraged by two competing sets of laws and at least three waves of regulation. D. Scott and I. Ho, *China's Corporate Bond Market* (Washington: World Bank, 2004).
124. An early and influential example is described in L. Huaizhong, 'Challenges to, and opportunities for, investing in China bond markets' (November 2003), mimeo presentation to the Asian Bond Market Forum, University of Hong Kong, available at <www.aiifl.com>.
125. A problem addressed by M. Mohanty, 'Improving liquidity in government bond markets: What can be done?', Basel: BIS Papers 11 (2002).
126. Especially CSRC, PBOC, Ministry of Finance and NDRC, which until 1995 was the lead bond regulator, before losing status after market failures. Early in 2004, the State Council endorsed the principle of modern markets for government and corporate debt, and in the regulated use of commodity, interest rate and equity derivatives. All initiatives required new legislation.

regulatory reform, both enabling in nature and specific to markets or instruments. The speed at which implementation can occur is limited by competing political interests, the outcomes of past quasi-market developments, the need for policy sequencing and by the timetable for China's service sector WTO obligations, which set more demanding and hasty agendas for banking and insurance reform than for changes in the securities industry. CSRC and PBOC policy heads are also aware that time pressure may be subsumed to the tactics required to secure new legislation.

The solution adopted by agencies such as CSRC and PBOC is twofold. First, to use a problem-solving approach, the agencies seek legislative support in the NPC for pilot projects or single transactions, both to demonstrate their value and to make clear the need for overarching reform in accordance with prior declarations of intent by the State Council. Second, to prevent reform leading to shocks and uncertainty, these agencies combine the creation of modern debt markets with the pressing need for a market structure to recycle impaired assets from the balance sheets of state banks.

The outstanding debt securities market capitalization was USD 483.3 billion as of the end of 2004, of which 63.3 per cent and 33.6 per cent were central government and financial issues, respectively. Net issuance in 2004 was USD 42.9 billion (2003 USD 63.2 billion), ignoring non-negotiable retail targeted bonds – approximately one-third of the gross amount in issue. Annual gross Treasury bond issuance since 2001 exceeds USD 70.0 billion. Central government issues fixed and floating rate treasury bills (2–5 years) and bonds (since 2002 of up to 30 years' tenor) and sanctions financial institution bonds. Most of this debt is bought by commercial banks for liquidity requirements or under a system of mandatory allocation. A growing non-bank financial institutional sector has a lesser investment and trading role.

To sum up, China's securities markets have been developing rapidly since 1992 with remarkable progress in market size, infrastructure development, legal framework and market maturity. It is now the third largest in Asia after Tokyo and Hong Kong.[127] As a result, the securities markets have become the key components of China's socialist market economy and play an important role in the reform of SOEs, improving resource allocation, facilitating structural adjustment and propelling economic growth. The Chinese government is continuing its efforts to develop a modern financial system and build an effective and efficient securities markets.

IV.B.   STRUCTURE OF THE PRC SECURITIES LEGAL SYSTEM

Markets are always influenced and guided by legislation. At the same time, legislation is made to meet the needs of reality and evolves with the development

---

127. *Doing Business with China*, in association with the China Association of International Trade, Ministry of Foreign Trade & Economic Cooperation, (China Link, London; Sterling VA: Kogan Page, 2003), p. 282.

of markets. The cultivation of an effective regulatory framework has been a key cornerstone for the development of China's securities markets. Its aim is to ensure that the market is orderly and fair.

IV.B.1.   Share Classification System in The Chinese Securities Market

Before introducing the legal framework for the China's securities market, it is necessary to explain a crucial background to this framework: the share classification system in China's securities market and related ownership structure in listed companies. As the whole legal system is divided into pieces in the light of the classification of shares, it is reasonable to say that this structure stems from the share classification system in China's stock market, which is mainly based on the legal status of shareholders.

Interests traded on China's securities market are divided into several share categories. Two of the principal share categories are 'A' Shares and 'B' Shares. Generally speaking, 'A' shares are initially designed for domestic investors and 'B' shares are for overseas investors. Based on the identity of investors, 'A' shares are further classified as state shares, legal person shares and individual shares.

According to statistics, among all the domestic listed companies, 65 per cent have the state as their largest shareholder, and 31 per cent have a legal person as their largest shareholder.[128] As state shares and legal person shares are under the division of 'A' share market, obviously the scale of the 'B' share market is much smaller than that of the 'A' share market. According to the CSRC statistics in September 2005, among the 1381 companies listed in the domestic stock market, 1326 issued 'A' shares, while only 109 issued 'B' shares.[129] In general, the state accounts for an average of two-thirds of the ownership of listed companies, in the form of either state shares (directly) or legal person shares (indirectly).[130]

The implication of this classification system is that different classes of shares are governed by different issuing and trading rules, and markets for various categories of shares are isolated from each other. In China's stock markets, different categories of shares are not convertible among each other. First, 'A' shares and 'B' shares cannot convert between each other. Second, classes of shares under the 'A' share category are also not convertible to each other. Finally, transfers within the same class of share may also be limited. Usually, the only category of 'A' shares that can be publicly transferred are individual shares,[131] while state shares and legal person shares that consist of the major

---

128. L. Maosheng and Y. Dejun (eds.), 'Report on the Problems of the Chinese Securities Market' (*Zhongguo Zhengquan Shichang Wenti Baogao*) (Social Science Publishing House, 2003), p. 79.

129. The data are available at <www.csrc.gov.cn>.

130. See Z. Xin, 'Regulating Chinese M&A', 29 August 2002, available at <www. financeasia. com>.

131. F. Liufang, 'China's Corporatization Experiment', 5 *Duke J. Comp. & Int'l L.*149 (1995), p. 212.

part of ownership in most Chinese listed companies are not allowed to convert and trade freely on the stock market.[132] In a word, the scheme of issuing categories of shares by one company, with state shares and legal person shares essentially non-publicly tradable, results in the artificial segregation of the securities market and its low liquidity.

Fortunately, the negative effects of the classification of ordinary shares and the segregation of the securities market have been commonly recognized in the PRC and the country is working to eliminate the classification of shares based on the nationality and identity of shareholders during the process of China's extension of its interconnection with the outside world. China has unveiled legislation that tends to dismantle the dichotomy between shares reserved for citizens and those reserved for foreigners. Foreign investors have been able to participate in China's 'A' share market, as well as its 'B' share market, and can improve their position in relation to the majority.[133] At the same time, the CSRC announced in February 2001 that domestic individual investors in the PRC could open trading accounts for 'B' shares, which since their debut were reserved only for overseas investors.[134]

As a larger step, the Chinese government is prudently carrying out experimental reform by selling down part of shares held by the state and legal persons and gradually permitting these shares to be traded freely in the secondary market[135] for the purpose of appropriate settlement of the long-existing problem in the securities market, which is regarded as the key obstacle for the development of this market. Because the reform is at a very early stage, results remain to be seen.

IV.B.2.   Overview of China's Securities Legal System

Along with the development of its securities markets, China's regulatory mechanism concerning the markets has also been gradually improved. Initially,

---

132. T. Tao, 'The Burgeoning Securities Investment Fund Industry in China: Its Development and Regulation', 13 *Colum. J. Asian L.* 203 (1999), p. 229.
133. This statement refers to the implementation of rules such as the Administration of Securities Investments in China by Qualified Foreign Institutional Investors Tentative Procedures (2002) and the Notice on Relevant Issues Concerning the Transfer to Foreign Investors of Listed Company State-owned Shares and Legal Person Shares (2002).
134. See ''B' Share Opens to Domestic Investors', *China Daily*, 20 February 2001, available at <www.china.org.cn>.
135. The experiment was launched in April 2005, symbolized by the CSRC Notice on the Issues Concerning the Reform of the Split Share Structure among Listed Companies, promulgated on and effective as of 29 April 2005. On 4 September 2005, the CSRC promulgated the Administrative Measures on the Split Share Structure Reform of Listed Companies. The term 'split-share structure', refers to the phenomenon that state shares and legal person shares are not permitted to be traded freely in China's secondary stock market, and are therefore segregated from publicly tradable shares, such as individual shares and foreign capital shares.

the regulatory authority was dispersed among a number of central governmental departments and local governments. A dual regulatory system later evolved, with the Securities Commission of the State Council being responsible for macro control and the CSRC exercising specific regulatory functions. The promulgation of the Securities Law (1998) then firmly and clearly established China's securities regulatory regime with centralized and unified regulation and supervision of the securities markets by the CSRC at the core, supported by self-disciplinary regulation by the stock exchanges and the Securities Industry Association.

Meanwhile, under the principle of 'rule of law, regulation and supervision, self-discipline and standardization', a legal system regulating the securities markets has gradually taken shape.[136] Since 1992, the PRC has promulgated numerous normative documents in relation to the regulation of its securities markets. Legislation in this field includes securities issuance rules, securities listing and trading rules, information disclosure rules, rules regulating securities organizations and specialized organizations, legal responsibility system governing securities activities and so on.

Within this framework, three general categories of normative documents exist in light of their various formulating bodies and binding forces: national laws by the National People's Congress (NPC) or its Standing Committee, administrative regulations by the State Council and departmental rules, mainly by the CSRC, as well as operational rules by the stock exchanges. The Company Law, the Securities Law and the Securities Investment Fund Law are the three basic national laws that govern the PRC's securities markets. The administrative regulations by the State Council either fill in the legislative blanks in related areas or provide specific details on related legal regimes. The departmental rules issued by the CSRC in accordance with relevant laws and administrative regulations are intended to provide necessary particulars and supplements for relevant laws and regulations, thereby constituting the important elements and major part of the PRC's legal system governing the securities markets.

IV.B.2.a.   *Securities laws*

As described previously, three laws are highly relevant to the regulation of the securities markets in China.

On 29 December 1993, the Standing Committee of the NPC adopted the Company Law, which came into effect on 1 July 1994 and was amended on 25 December 1999 and 27 October 2005.[137]

The Company Law promotes a fundamental change in the organizational structure of enterprises in China. This law seeks to provide a nationwide standard of establishing and operating limited liability companies and companies

---

136. See *Doing Business with China*, p. 283.
137. The new amendment took effect on 1 January 2006.

limited by shares in the country. In this way, the Company Law aims to provide a part of the entire legal framework that will be essential to transforming
China's SOEs – which almost solely comprised China's economy prior to its
reform, starting in 1978 – into independent entities, and thus fostering overall
domestic economic growth.[138] This Law stipulates the establishment and the
organization of limited liability companies and companies limited by shares, as
well as the responsibilities of corporate management. Part V of the Law provides the issuance and assignment of shares by companies limited by shares.
This law also includes provisions on the issuance of company bonds (Part VII).
Each of these factors makes the Law vital to the regulation of the securities
market.

The amendment made in 2005 aims to encourage investment and promote
the establishment of companies and the development of domestic capital markets through granting greater autonomy to companies.

On 29 December 1998, the Standing Committee of the NPC promulgated
the Securities Law. The law took effect 1 July 1999. The law is the first national
securities law in China and is the fundamental law that comprehensively regulates activities in the securities market.

The Securities Law applies to the issuance and trading in the PRC of shares,
corporate bonds and other securities designated by the State Council.[139] The
Law contains provisions governing various aspects of the securities market,
such as:

- the issuance of securities;
- securities trading
- takeovers by listed companies;
- administration of stock exchanges;
- securities companies;
- securities registration and settlement organizations;
- securities trading services organizations;
- securities industry associations;
- securities regulatory bodies.

The Securities Law is vital to the development of China's securities markets,
because the law endeavours to:

'standardize the issuance and trading of securities, protect the lawful
rights and interests of investors, safeguard the economic order and public
interests of society and promote the development of the socialist market
economy'.[140]

138. S. Huo, 'Comment: the Company Law of the People's Republic of China', 13 (1995) *UCLA
      Pacific Basin Law Journal* 373, p. 376.
139. Securities Law, art. 2.
140. Ibid., art. 1.

For this purpose, the law establishes the principles of securities-related activities as 'openness, fairness and equitability'.[141] In addition, the law serves to enhance the objectivity and transparency in China's securities regulatory process.

On 27 October 2005, China revised the Securities Law with the purposes of promoting the healthy growth of the securities markets, strengthening the regulation of the markets and improving the protection for investors. The amendment took force as of 1 January 2006.

On 28 October 2003, the Standing Committee of the NPC enacted the Securities Investment Fund Law, effective as of 1 February 2004. This law is formulated to regulate securities investment funds, to safeguard the lawful rights and interests of investors and other parties involved, and to promote the healthy development of securities investment funds and the securities market.[142]

This law is applicable to investment fund activities within the PRC carried out through the public sale of shares of funds to raise securities investment funds administered by fund managers and held in custodians, and that engage in securities investment, using a portfolio of assets for the profits of fund shareholders.[143] Fund operating methods can be close-end, open-end or otherwise.[144]

The law stipulates provisions, for example, in regard to:

- fund managers;
- custodians;
- placement and trading of funds;
- subscription and redemption of funds;
- operations and information disclosure;
- modification and termination of contracts;
- liquidation of funds;
- rights and interests of fund holders and their exercising, supervision and administration of funds,
- legal liabilities.

IV.B.2.b.   *Securities regulations*

In this category, the following four normative documents are predominately under the enforcement by the CSRC for the regulation of China's securities markets.

On 22 April 1993, the State Council promulgated the Provisional Regulations for the Administration of the Issuance and Trading of Stock (ITS), which

---

141.   Ibid., art. 3.
142.   Securities Investment Fund Law, art. 1.
143.   Ibid., art. 2.
144.   Ibid., art. 5.

came into force on the same day, with a purpose to further China's goal of majority state ownership and minority private equity participation in the stock market.[145] Issued just after the formal establishment of China's securities market, this Regulation is the first comprehensive statute for the regulation of this market. The ITS deals with the application and approval procedures for public offerings of, and trading in, stock, takeovers of listed companies, deposit, settlement and transfer of listed stock, disclosure of information with respect to a listed company, enforcement of law, and penalties and dispute settlement.

Due to limited knowledge of securities markets and the government's persistent vigilance towards capitalism, this statute takes a conservative attitude towards these new markets. The ITS was predominantly superseded by the Securities Law, when the new Law came into force in 1999.

On 4 July 1994, the State Council promulgated the Overseas Offering and Listing Regulations to meet the requirements of raising fund overseas by joint stock companies. These regulations deal mainly with the issuance, subscription, trading and declaration of dividends and other distributions of foreign capital stock listed abroad, as well as information disclosure, and articles of association of companies limited by shares having foreign capital stock listed abroad.

On 25 December 1995, the State Council promulgated the Domestic Listed Foreign Shares Regulations. These Regulations apply to the issuance, subscription and trading of domestic listed foreign capital shares, and declaration of dividends and other distributions of such shares, and disclosure of information by companies limited by shares.

On 2 June 1999, the State Council promulgated the Trading of Futures Regulations, which came into force on 1 September 1999. These regulations aim to regulate futures transactions, strengthen the supervision and regulation of the futures market, guarantee normal market order, control market risk and protect the lawful rights and interests of participants and public interests.

IV.B.2.c.   *Securities rules*

As discussed previously in this section, departmental rules are the major components of the PRC's securities legal system, and the total numbers of these rules run in the hundreds. For this reason, a complete list and introduction for all of these rules is impossible here. For the purpose of clarification, the following table lists several relatively important rules issued by the CSRC as examples.

---

145.   B. Chun, 'A Brief Comparison of the Chinese and United States Securities Regulations Governing Corporate Takeovers', 12 (1998) *Colum. J. Asian L.*, 105.

Table: China's Securities Rules

Securities Rule Title (English)	Issuing Date	Effective Date
Provisional Measures on the Administration of Securities and Futures Investment Consultation	25 December 1997	1 April 1998
Interim Rules on the Administration of Qualification of Senior Officials in Securities Operation Institutions	11 November 1998	11 November 1998
Rules on the Administration of Representative Offices of Foreign Securities Institutions in China	21 April 1999	21 April 1999
Implementing Measures for Convertible Bonds of Listed Companies	26 April 2001	26 April 2001
Guidelines for Establishing the System of Independent Director among Listed Companies	16 August 2001	
Standards for the Content and Format of Information Disclosure by Listed Companies (No.1 to 22).	15 March 2001 – 8 October 2003	15 March 2001 – 8 October 2003
Opinions on Several Issues Concerning Foreign Investment in Listed Companies	5 November 2001	
Administration of Stock Exchanges Procedures	12 December 2001	12 December 2001
Rules for the Administration of Securities Companies	28 December 2001	1 March 2002
Code of Corporate Governance for Listed Companies in China	7 January 2002	7 January 2002
Administration of Futures Broker Companies Procedures	17 May 2002	1 July 2002

Table: Contd.

Securities Rule Title (English)	Issuing Date	Effective Date
Administration of Futures Exchanges Procedures	17 May 2002	1 July 2002
Rules for Establishing Foreign-Invested Fund Management Companies	1 June 2002	1 July 2002
Administration of the Takeover of Listed Companies Procedures	28 September 2002.	1 December 2002
Notice on Relevant Issues Concerning the Transfer to Foreign Investors of Listed Company State-owned Shares and Legal Person Shares	1 November 2002	1 January 2003
Administration Measures on the Qualifications of Personnel Engaged in the Securities Industry	16 December 2002	1 February 2003
Interim Measures on the Sponsor System for Securities Public Offerings	9 October 2003	1 February 2004
Interim Measures on the Public Offering Review Committee of the CSRC	5 December 2003	5 December 2003
Administration of Securities Investment Funds Operations Procedures	29 June 2004	1 July 2004
Administration of the Sale of Securities Investment Funds Procedures	25 June 2004	1 July 2004
Rules of Administration of Securities Investment Fund Management Companies	16 September 2004	1 October 2004
Several Regulations Concerning Strengthening the Protection for the Lawful Rights and Interests of Public Shareholders	7 December 2004	7 December 2004

Table: Contd.

Securities Rule Title (English)	Issuing Date	Effective Date
Administrative Measures on the Split Share Structure Reform of Listed Companies	4 September 2005	4 September 2005
Rules of Administration of Securities Investment in China by Qualified Foreign Institutional Investors	24 August 2006	1 September 2006

Following China's accession to the WTO, the CSRC has rectified and amended all the rules and administrative approval procedures to comply with relevant securities commitments. The CSRC has also promulgated several new rules for this purpose. At the same time, both the Shanghai and Shenzhen Stock Exchanges have revised their rules of management on memberships and on 'B' share trading seats, in compliance with China's WTO commitments.

V. INSURANCE

Development of insurance markets and the related legal and institutional framework has been more straightforward than that of banking or securities, largely as a result of the lack of any such market and related framework in the context of a centrally planned economy. Markets and their framework thus have developed in parallel with the move towards a socialist market economy in China.

V.A. INSURANCE LAW

In 1995, the Standing Committee of the NPC enacted China's first Insurance Law. At that time, insurance regulation rested with the PBOC.[146] In 1998, the CIRC was established and the insurance regulatory function was transferred from the PBOC to the CIRC.[147]

Article 148 of the Insurance Law 1995 is similar to Article 92 of the Law on Commercial Banks 2003, and stipulates that the establishment of foreign-fund-participated insurance companies or branches of foreign

---

146. For example, the PBOC issued the Interim Rules of Administration of Insurance in 1996, which stated that the PBOC was in charge of insurance regulation. See 'Interim Rules of Administration of Insurance', art. 65. This interim rule was abolished after the CIRC issued the Rules of Administration of Insurance Companies in 2000.
147. See Notification on the Establishment of the CIRC (*Guowuyuan Guanyu Chengli Zhongguo Baoxian Jiandu Guanli Weiyuanhui de Tongzhi*), *Guofa* [1998], no. 37.

insurance companies shall be subject to this insurance law, but the laws and regulations specifically related to foreign related insurance companies, if any, shall prevail. In October 2002, the Standing Committee of the NPC amended the Insurance Law 1995,[148] at least partially to make the law consistent with China's WTO commitments.[149] Article 154 of the Insurance Law 2002, for example, replaced Article 148 of the Insurance Law 1995, adding wholly-foreign-funded insurance companies as one of the forms of foreign-invested insurance companies.[150]

V.B.   INSURANCE RULES

In accordance with Article 2 of the Rules on Administration of Insurance Companies,[151] the CIRC is entitled to supervise insurance companies by the authorization of the State Council.[152] The first duty of the CIRC granted by the State Council is 'to formulate policies and rules concerning commercial insurance'.[153] For the purpose of formulating insurance rules, the CIRC formulated a special rule on how to formulate insurance administrative rules, that is, the Rules on the Formulation Procedures of Insurance Administration Rules,[154] by which such rules generally take the name of 'rules' or 'detailed rules of implementation'.[155] The following table lists the most-relevant CIRC insurance rules:

Table: CIRC Insurance Rules

Insurance rule title (English)	Issue date	Effective date	Document number
Interim Rules on Administration of Investment in Securities Investment Fund by Insurance Companies	29 October 1999	29 October 1999	*Baojianfa* [1999] No. 206. This rule was slightly amended in 2000, *Baojianfa* [2000] No. 96

---

148. The amended Insurance Law came into force as of 1 January 2003.
149. See the statement of CIRC's chairman, Wu Dingfu, available at <www.circ.gov.cn/news/wudingfu.htm>.
150. According to China's insurance commitments, within two years of China's accession, foreign non-life insurers will be permitted to establish as wholly-owned subsidiaries.
151. CIRC published this rule in January 2000.
152. See Organic Law of the State Council 1982, art. 10.
153. See Notification on the Establishment of CIRC.
154. Baojianfa [1999] no.111, repealed by the Rules on the Formulation Procedures of the CIRC, effective as of 1 May 2006.
155. The term 'Guiding' is suitable for insurance regulation or insurance activities in part, while the term 'Banfa' is suitable for detailed rules on insurance regulation or insurance activities; 'Detailed Implementation Rule' is suitable for a complete and detailed rules for the enforcement or operation of one particular law or regulation. See art. 3 of the Rules on the Formulation Procedures of Insurance Administration Rules.

Table: Contd.

Insurance rule title (English)	Issue date	Effective date	Document number
Interim Rules on Investment in Insurance Companies	1 April 2000	1 April 2000	*Baojianfa* [2000] No. 49. This rule amended *Baojianfa* [1999] No. 270.
Rules on Administration of Insurance Assessors	16 November 2001	1 January 2002	CIRC Decree [2001] No. 3 Some articles of this rule was amended in 2002 to be inconsistent with the WTO.
Rules on Establishment of Reinsurance Companies	17 September 2002	17 September 2002	CIRC Decree [2002] No. 4
Provisions on the Administration of Marketing Departments of Insurance Companies	1 February 2002	1 March 2002	Joint Decree by CIRC and State Administration for Industry and Commerce
Provisions on the Administration of the Amount of Solvency and Relevant Regulatory Index of Insurance Companies	24 March 2003	24 March 2003	CIRC Decree [2003] No. 1
Rules on Administration of Representative Offices of Foreign Insurance Companies	15 January 2004	1 March 2004	CIRC Decree and [2004] No. 1
Rules on Administration of Insurance Companies	15 March 2004	15 June 2004	CIRC Decree and [2004] No. 3
Detailed Rules for Implementation of Regulations of the PRC on Administration of Foreign-funded Insurance Companies	13 March 2004	15 June 2004	CIRC Decree [2004] No. 4
Rules on Administration of Insurance Agencies	11 November 2004	1 January 2005	CIRC Decree [2004] No. 14

Table: Contd.

Insurance rule title (English)	Issue date	Effective date	Document number
Rules on Administration of Insurance Brokers	11 November 2004	1 January 2005	CIRC Decree [2004] No. 15
Rules on Administration of Reinsurance	14 October 2005	1 December 2005	CIRC Decree [2005] No. 2
Rules on Administration of Representative offices of Foreign Insurance Companies in China	12 July 2006	1 September 2006	CIRC Decree [2006] No. 5

China's insurance law is under the impact of the GATS/WTO. For example, according to China's insurance commitments, upon accession, a 20 per cent cession of all lines of the primary risks for non-life, personal accident and health insurance business with an appointed Chinese reinsurance company shall be required; one year after accession, 15 per cent shall be required; two years after accession, ten per cent shall be required; three years after accession, five per cent shall be required; and four years after accession, no compulsory cession shall be required. To be in line with the commitments, China amended its Insurance Law in 2002, to state that insurance companies shall engage in reinsurance business according to relevant rules issued by the CIRC, eliminating the former provision with a 20 per cent legal reinsurance requirement for non-life insurance business.[156]

VI.   CONCLUSION

As China advances towards a socialist market economy, the country's financial sector has been transformed, opening many opportunities and challenges. The preference of the Chinese government for strictly controlling financial resources, in spite of its necessity at this stage of transition, is one of the major obstacles for financial institutions and markets to function independently and efficiently. However, reforming China's financial architecture in line with international standards does not necessarily enhance the functioning of its financial system, because China is experiencing a radical transformation from a planned economy to a socialist market economy. Nevertheless, restructuring China's financial sector into an independent, transparent and commercialized system is essential both for a sound financial market and sustainable economic development.

---

156.   See Art. 102 of Insurance Law 2002, c.f. Art. 101 of the Insurance Law 1995.

China's developing legal system has been facilitating the transformation of its financial sector, and the rapid economic growth in China is correlated with the progression in its legal development.[157] As a transition country, however, China's efforts to reform its financial system under a rule-based framework is far from perfect. For this reason, the measures adopted to resolve problems must proceed through trial and error; this goal can hardly be achieved in strict compliance with a formal legislative process. The need for flexibility and expediency must be balanced against the costs of 'legislative forbearance'; in other words, relaxing the strict rule of law. Reform of China's corporate and financial law is highly challenging because it must maintain a balance between global competition and maintain social stability in post-WTO China. However, a well-functioning legal framework with efficient judicial system, credible supervisory authorities with sufficient enforcement capacity, and an efficient administrative structure with less corruption, are crucial for constructing and maintaining a healthy financial system. Although the special environments of the transition process, including social, political, and economic aspects, constrain the legal regime, good legal mechanisms should, and can, be adopted to provide with adequate restrictions on the power of the government and sufficient incentives for market participants.

Effective legal infrastructure that serves to establish and enforce property rights and contracts, as well as creditor and shareholder rights, underpins a sound and stable financial system.[158] Disparity between extensive legislation and insufficient compliance, however, is a problematic issue for China, in common with other transition economies.[159] As a result, cultivating a credit culture through improved legal enforceability is crucial.

In compliance with the WTO Agreement, China's legal system must be transparent and consistent across the entire country.[160] A process is ongoing to abolish or amend many financial laws, regulations and rules not in accordance with the WTO commitments. However, uniformity in the implementation of laws and the WTO Agreement cannot be realized, insofar as China's legal system is still taking an ad hoc piecemeal approach in the context of transition. Regulations, rules, decisions and orders make up the largest part of China's legal system, with their advantage of adapting rapidly to the developing economy; but these regulations and so on often lack clarity, certainty, universality, and stability. In addition, legislative competition among government agencies seeking rents through issuance of regulations, orders, and complex procedures further complicates market participation.

---

157. R. Peerenboom, *China's Long March toward Rule of Law* (Cambridge: Cambridge University Press, 2002), pp. 463–464.
158. European Bank for Reconstruction and Development (EBRD), *Transition Report 1998* (London: EBRD, 1998), p. 116.
159. Ibid., pp. 108–109.
160. D. Blumental, 'Reform or Opening? Reform of China's State-owned Enterprises and WTO Accession: The Dilemma of Applying GATT to Marketizing Economies', 16 *UCLA Pacific Basin Law Journal* 198, p. 234.

Besides the previously mentioned problem caused by the basic systematic flaws of China's securities market, there are some other pitfalls in the legal system that are worthy of attention.

First, an overly administrative approach is adopted in financial market regulation. Government intervention is still much wider and deeper than necessary. Market participants have not enjoyed sufficient freedom and power to take decisions. This problem originated in the centrally planned economic system adopted by China before the country's reform towards a socialist market economy, and the problem commonly exists in the regulation of economic activities, including financial activities. Though China has acted to change this situation, much work remains to be done.

Second, many statutes are imprecise and lack detail. Though the legal system seems to be comprehensive, insufficient detail is available for practice in some normative documents. The major components of the legal system contain numerous basic principles, which in practice are far too general to apply. Not all of the normative documents contain applicable procedures or arrangements. Specific implementing rules must be improved gradually.

Third, the protections for public investors and minority shareholders are relatively weak. Due to the dominance of the State and legal persons as the major shareholders among Chinese listed companies, minority shareholders – in most cases, public investors – require better protection from the abuse of majority ownership. However, many legal mechanisms necessary for this protection have not been established or recognized in the Chinese legal system. Investors sometimes cannot find proper weapons to safeguard their lawful rights and interests.

Fourth, many issues that have arisen, or are arising, in China's financial markets during their development and liberalization remain unaddressed. Securitization, management buyouts, stock options and other activities and objects common in well-developed markets and mature legal systems worldwide must be addressed by regulation in China. The need for this type of development is vital for the further development of the Chinese market.

In short, the Chinese legal system is far from perfect. In summary of the various defects in this system, the most critical defects are the lack of legal foundation for the functioning of market and the artificial separation between the regulations for investors with different statuses.

As a result of its reform program, China has produced an economy with one of the most rapid growth rates in the world and is regarded as a miracle. In this process, the financial markets must contribute more to the national economy and performing functions such as raising capital, optimizing resource allocation, and improving corporate governance. These goals can best be achieved through the improvement of the legal system, as well as ensuring that all the normative rules are strictly observed and implemented.

In conclusion, this chapter has focused on the financial markets and related legal and institutional frameworks in China, in the context of China's liberalization commitments under the WTO. The current trend of financial regulation in China is that increasingly, financial rules apply equally to both domestic and foreign financial institutions. The recent rule issued by the CBRC, Guideline for Administration of Credit-granting Risks for Group Customers, applies to commercial banks, which include Chinese-funded banks, joint-equity banks, wholly-foreign-funded banks and foreign bank branches.[161] Important to note, however, is that according to this rule, policy banks, city cooperatives, rural cooperatives and trust investment companies all must follow this guideline;[162] which means not only equality among domestic and foreign banks, but also equality among domestic banks. This trend is especially obvious in the insurance sector, which reflects the fact that the WTO national treatment obligation is clearer in China's insurance laws than in banking laws.

Since entering the WTO at the end of 2001, China has made outstanding progress in opening up financial services trade and gradually eliminated restrictions on financial market access and national treatment. Foreign-funded banks are permitted to engage in RMB business in an increasing number of cities. The fundamental laws and rules that reflect WTO commitments relating to financial sectors have been formulated, among which are three important regulations and rules: the Regulation on Administration of Foreign-Funded Financial Institutions (banking), the Regulation on Administration of Foreign-funded Insurance Companies (insurance) and the Rules for Establishing Foreign-invested Securities Companies (securities). Although China will likely formulate additional financial regulations and rules, as well as revise relevant financial rules and measures, the new foreign-funded financial law framework has been established.

From these newly published financial laws, regulations and rules, two significant tendencies can be discerned. The first is that China's financial regulation system is moving forward along a path of prudential regulation in the process of performing its WTO commitments and obligations. The second is that increasing numbers of laws, regulations and rules in China apply to both foreign and domestic financial institutions, with equal treatment. The experience of the past five years shows that China is seriously and positively implementing its WTO financial commitments. While some issues, such as high capital requirements, still exist, and it is possible that some issues will remain for quite some time, one of the advantages of the WTO is that it provides a multilateral mechanism to resolve those problems, through consultations, the TRM (or final TPRM for China) and the Dispute Settlement Mechanism. In fact, China's accession to the WTO has not caused a 'flood' of litigation, as predicted by some commentators.

The real challenge for China's financial services sector, however, will occur after the end of the five-year transitional period, which happens in December 2006. For this reason, China's financial laws, regulations and rules must be well-prepared and adjusted for real WTO challenges in the near future.

---

161. See Art. 2 of CBRC Order [2003] no. 5.
162. See Art. 30 of CBRC Order [2003] no. 5.

Chapter 2

Banking Regulatory Law Reforms in China: A Long Way to Go Towards International Standards

Zhongfei Zhou

Over the past three years, China's banking system has undergone a critical change. In March 2003, the banking regulatory system in China was significantly restructured, with the result that the banking regulatory function was split from the central bank (People's Bank of China, or PBOC), and a new regulatory agency, the China Banking Regulatory Commission (CBRC), was created. In December 2003, in response to this restructuring, the National People's Congress (NPC) amended the Commercial Banking Law, as well as the Central Banking Law, both of which took effect in 1995, and adopted a new law, the Banking Supervision Law (BSL). Since taking over the banking regulatory power from the PBOC, the CBRC has paid increased attention to the introduction of international standards and practices in its regulatory and supervisory process, with numerous regulatory and supervisory rules being amended and issued.

I.   BANKING REGULATORY SYSTEM

The importance of regulatory structure in the efficiency and effectiveness of banking regulation is increasingly acknowledged by countries around the

Barth et al., *Financial Restructuring and Reform in Post-WTO China*, pp. 45–76.
© 2007 Kluwer Law International BV, The Netherlands.

world, with emphasis given to the question of whether, and to what extent, the achievement of regulatory objectives is influenced by the particular institutional structure within which regulators operate. A number of countries split banking regulatory function from central banking function, while others have established a single mega regulator. However, which institutional structure is more efficient and effective is still an issue that is widely debated. In China, it seemed that little debate had taken place on whether the banking regulatory function should be separated from the PBOC, and the government made a rather straightforward decision on establishment of the CBRC, which obtained approval of the NPC at the first session of the 10th NPC on 5 March 2003. According to the explanation given by the State Council to the NPC, the change was intended to make the PBOC focus more on monetary policy formulation and implementation and other macro policies in the financial sector, leaving bank regulation to the CBRC as a specialist regulatory agency.[1]

I.A.   PBOC's Role in Banking Regulation

Following this institutional restructuring, the NPC grants the CBRC the banking regulatory power through the BSL. Under the BSL, the CBRC is delegated to regulate and supervise banking financial institutions, financial asset management companies, trust and investment companies, finance companies, financial leasing companies and other financial institutions.[2] However, it would be wrong to assume that the PBOC would no longer perform banking regulatory functions. Under the PBOC Law, the PBOC continues to hold banking regulatory powers in some specific areas and under specific circumstances. First, the PBOC is authorized to examine the activities conducted by financial institutions, entities and individuals in relation to deposit reserves, special loans,[3] Renminbi, inter-bank loans, foreign exchanges, bullions, exchequer, settlement and anti-money laundering.[4] All institutions, whether financial or non-financial, and individuals that engage in activities in these areas are subject to regulation and supervision of the PBOC.

Second, the PBOC has the power to conduct an overall examination of a banking financial institution if the banking financial institution runs into payment difficulty which would thereby cause financial risks.[5] Approval from the State Council, however, is the precondition for this type of examination.

---

1. W. Zhongyu, 'Explanations on the Restructuring Scheme of the State Council', 5 March 2003.
2. BSL, art. 2.
3. Under article 32 of the PBOC Law, special loans are defined to mean loans issued by the PBOC to financial institutions, approved by the State Council, for special purposes. It can be concluded that lender-of-last-resort lending is included in specific loans.
4. PBOC Law, art. 32.
5. Ibid., art. 34.

Finally, the PBOC can recommend the CBRC to conduct examination of banking financial institutions, based on the needs of implementation of monetary policy and maintenance of financial stability.[6] The CBRC shall respond within 30 days of receiving the recommendation.[7]

I.B.   CBRC'S ROLE IN BANKING REGULATION

Although the CBRC has the power to regulate all financial institutions except securities companies and insurance institutions, which are regulated by the China Securities Regulatory Commission and China Insurance Regulatory Commission, respectively, this does not mean that the provisions of the BSL can be applied equally to these non-banking financial institutions (and policy banks). It might, therefore, be inappropriate that the BSL stipulates that regulation of non-banking financial institutions and policy banks be governed by those provisions for banking financial institutions.[8] In my opinion, the basic reason for imposing more regulation on commercial banks than on any other commercial entities is that commercial banks take deposits from the public and the failure of this type of bank would damage the interests of the public and give rise to systemic risk. The nature of the business of non-banking financial institutions is different from banking financial institutions. Having the CBRC regulate financial institutions, as it does with banking financial institutions, would be both unnecessary and costly.

I.B.1.   Regulatory Objectives

Under the BSL, the regulatory objectives of the CBRC are first to facilitate lawful and sound operations of the banking industry and second to maintain the public's confidence in the banking industry.[9] The CBRC itself announced on its website that its regulatory targets are as follows:

- to protect the interests of depositors and customers through prudential and effective regulation;
- to enhance market confidence through prudential and effective regulation;
  to promote the public's awareness of modern finance though education;
- to attempt to reduce financial crimes.[10]

---

6. Ibid., art. 30.
7. Ibid.
8. BSL, art. 2.
9. Ibid., art. 3(cf). The Core Principles for Effective Banking Supervision explicitly provide that an effective system of banking supervision will have clear responsibilities and objectives for each agency involved in the supervision of banking organizations. Basle Committee on Banking Supervision, *The Core Principles for Effective Banking Supervision,* Principle 1.
10. Available at the CBRC's website: www.cbrc.gov.cn (English version available).

The meanings of the two terms 'objective' and 'target' are difficult to distinguish in Chinese. This author's understanding is that the regulatory targets are the embodiment of the statutory objectives. In regard to the statutory objectives, the BSL requires the CBRC to protect fair competition in and promote the competitive force of the banking industry.[11] This requirement can be considered as the standard with which the CBRC must comply in conducting its operations. This judgment is partly justified by the CBRC's declaration of its regulatory standards, which include

- to promote financial stability and facilitate financial innovation simultaneously;
- to enhance the competitive force of the country's financial industry in the international financial services;
- to set appropriate regulatory limitations and reduce unnecessary restraints;
- to encourage fair and orderly competition;
- to establish accountability of the regulators and regulates;
- to use its regulatory resources in an efficient and economic way.[12]

It is acknowledged that a well-defined statutory objective against which the agency's performance can be measured is traditionally viewed as a key requirement for holding independent agencies accountable.[13] However, unlike a central bank, whose objectives can be measured in the form of an explicit inflation target, the regulatory objectives of a banking regulatory agency are multiple and non-operational, and therefore hard to measure.[14] Despite the difficulty in measuring whether, or the extent to which, a banking regulator achieves its objectives, this author argues that the clearly articulated statutory objectives themselves can provide a basis for holding a banking regulator accountable. The lack of measurability in the statutory objectives does not make entirely impossible assessing a regulator's performance according to the objectives. The statutory objectives stipulated by the BSL, and the regulatory targets, as well as the regulatory standards, established by the CBRC indeed expose its performance to the checks and balances by its accountees. In addition, the accountability of the CBRC would be heightened by the legal requirements under which the

---

11. BSL, art. 3.
12. Available at the CBRC's website: www.cbrc.gov.cn (English version available). These standards are apparently quite similar to those stipulated in the UK's Financial Services and Markets Act 2000. See the Financial Services and Markets Act, Part 1, Section 2(3).
13. E. Hüpkes, M. Quintyn and M.W. Taylor, *The Accountability of Financial Sector Supervisors: Principles and Practice,* IMF Working Paper (WP/05/51, March 2005), p. 10.
14. In regard to the discussions on the difficulty in measuring the objectives of a banking regulator, see ibid, pp. 10–15. See also C. Goodhart, *Financial Regulations: Why, How, and Where Now?* (1998), pp. 61–72, in the discussion of the difficulty in quantifying the benefits and costs of banking regulation and supervision.

CBRC should make its regulatory and supervisory processes public[15] and be subject to auditing and surveillance by competent authorities.[16]

I.B.2.   CBRC's Independence and Accountability

An accountable banking regulator must also be independent. An independent banking regulator must be free from political interference, as well as from regulatory capture by interest groups. The BSL explicitly prohibits local governments, governmental departments of all levels, social organizations and individuals from interfering with the CBRC's discharge of functions.[17] In addition, the fit and proper requirements for the regulators of the CBRC can, to some degree, promote the CBRC's independence.[18] However, as part of the State Council, the CBRC can never be entirely cut off from its close relationship with the government. The inseverability between the CBRC and the State Council would, no doubt, undermine the protection of its independence provided by these legal arrangements.

In the discharge of its functions, the CBRC is constrained by deference to several principles. The statutory principles include lawfulness, openness, fairness and efficiency.[19] The principle of lawfulness requires the CBRC to regulate and supervise banks in accordance with laws and regulations. Openness or transparency is regarded as the basis for the emerging international consensus on the basic requirements for financial stability. This principle requires not only that banking laws, regulations and rules be made public, but also that the CBRC regulate and supervise banks on a consistent and transparent basis. The principle of fairness is intended to level the playing field and create competitive equality between banks, with national laws and rules to be applied as uniformly as possible. The efficiency principle relates to the way in which the CBRC shall allocate and use its regulatory resources. In conducting its supervisory activities, the CBRC should use the cost-effective analysis to ensure that the benefits of regulation can be proportionate to the burden which is imposed on banks or on the conducting of an activity.

---

15.   BSL, art. 12.
16.   Ibid., art. 14.
17.   Ibid., art. 5.
18.   Under the BSL, the regulators of the CBRC shall have the professional skills and working experiences as required for performing their functions; shall perform their duties with integrity and in accordance with laws and regulations; shall not take advantage of their positions to seek inappropriate gains, or concurrently hold a position in enterprises, including financial institutions; and shall keep the state secrets and bank secrets for the banks supervised and other parties concerned. See BSL, art. 9–11.
19.   Ibid., art. 4.

I.B.3.   CBRC's Rule-Making Power

The BSL vests upon the CBRC the power to make rules, in addition to a general banking regulatory power.[20] Under the BSL, the CBRC is authorized to formulate and issue rules in relation to regulation and supervision of banks and their businesses.[21] The CBRC also has the power to formulate prudential rules on bank operations by which banks must abide.[22] The rules made by the CBRC must be in line with laws and regulations. In practice, however, determining whether rule-making by the CBRC is consistent with laws and regulations is often difficult. According to the Implementing Rules for the Regulations on the Administration of Foreign Financial Institutions amended in July 2004 (known as 'the Implementing Rules for Foreign Banks' in the remainder of this chapter), for example, the CBRC can take special supervisory measures against a foreign bank that does not satisfy the requirements for unallocated profits, exposures on large customers and fund flows.[23] The special supervisory measures include:

- a verbal warning;
- submission of a written report;
- restriction on businesses or fund outflows;
- provision of a guarantee letter;
- special requirements for risk management;
- supplementation of capital or operating fund;
- accreditation of special supervisors for a violating bank;
- senior management change within a specified period;
- other prudential supervisory measures.[24]

---

20. The BSL clearly authorizes the CBRC to examine and approve a bank's establishment, modification, termination, and business scope. See ibid, art. 16.
21. Ibid., art. 15.
22. Ibid., art. 21.
23. Implementing Rules for Foreign Banks, art. 95. Article 95 of the Implementing Rules for Foreign Banks provides for the circumstances under which the CBRC may take special regulatory measures against a violating foreign bank:

    - for a foreign bank branch, the sum of its unallocated profits and net losses and profits of the current year becomes negative, and the sum of the absolute value of the negative and the deficiencies in loan loss provisioning exceeds 30 per cent of its operating fund;
    - the balance of credit-granting by a foreign bank to all large customers – which are defined as customers whose balance of credit granting from a foreign bank exceeds 10 per cent of the bank's capital or operating fund – exceeds eight times the bank's capital or operating fund;
    - for a foreign bank, the cumulative amount of the funds flowing out of China exceeds the fund flowing into China in a month;
    - other imprudent operations.
24. Ibid., art. 96.

Although the Regulations on the Administration of Foreign Financial Institutions promulgated by the State Council in December 2001 (referred to as Foreign Bank Regulations for the remainder of this chapter) authorize the CBRC to punish or take measures against a foreign bank's violations, the Foreign Bank Regulations also emphasize that the punitive measures should be taken in accordance with laws and regulations.[25] In the author's opinion, however, the measures, which require a violating foreign bank to supplement capital or operating capital and accredit a special supervisor to a violating foreign bank to provide surveillance and guide for the foreign bank's daily operations, may lack legitimacy. Under the current Chinese laws and regulations, both of which are superior to the rules made by the CBRC in legal validity, none require a foreign bank, if it satisfies the capital requirements, to supplement its capital, even if it falls within the situations stipulated in article 95 of the Implementing Rules for Foreign Banks. Nor do the laws and regulations permit the CBRC to send its supervisors to provide surveillance and guidance – which, in many cases, is indistinguishable from undue interference – for a violating bank's daily operations, in which a foreign bank obtains autonomy delegated by the Company Laws and Banking Laws.[26]

I.B.4.   CBRC's Enforcement Powers

Under the BSL and Commercial Banking Law (referred to as the CBL of 2003 for the remainder of this chapter), the CBRC possesses a wide range of enforcement powers to enable itself to carry out its functions and achieve its statutory objectives. These enforcement powers include business suspension for rectification, withdrawal of business license, imposition of fine and administrative penalty, prohibition on employment in banks, confiscation of illegal gains and others. During the period of restructuring a credit-crisis-hit bank, or liquidating a closed bank, the CBRC can request the border control authority to prevent the directors and senior management in direct charge from leaving China, and apply to the judicial authority to prohibit the directors and managers from diverting or transferring their properties, or creating other rights on their properties.[27] In addition, the CBRC also has the power to inspect the bank accounts of the banks and persons suspected of violation of laws and regulations, and can apply to the judicial authority to freeze the bank accounts of the banks and persons suspected of diverting or concealing illegal funds.[28]

---

25. Foreign Bank Regulations, art. 35.
26. In the author's opinion, the measure – that is, restricting a violating foreign bank's businesses and fund outflows – is not incompliant with the laws and regulations. The reason for this belief is that the measure can be considered to be one of the early interventions stipulated by article 37 of the BSL.
27. BSL, art. 40.
28. Ibid., art. 41

II.   REGULATION OF BANK ENTRY

In virtually all banking systems, regulation begins at the market access stage.
While bank entry regulation cannot guarantee that a bank will be well run
after it is permitted to open, it can provide the possibility to reduce the number of unstable institutions that enter the banking system, keep dishonest or
inexperienced people from operating banking and prevent 'over-banking'. In
addition, restricted entry can help create the charter – or franchise – value of a
bank, which produces an incentive for bank owners to avoid risks that would
jeopardize its charter.[29] However, entry requirements adopted for the purpose
of promoting safe and sound banking may adversely affect banking competition and increase barriers to trade in banking services. Similarly, easier market
access may also diminish access barriers, but reduce the charter value of banks
and increase the pressures on banks to engage in riskier activities, which might
lead some banks to fail. For these reasons, a banking law must strike the balance with respect to the safety and soundness, competition and the lowering of
regulatory barriers.

II.A.   ENTRY REQUIREMENTS

The Basel Committee's Core Principles for Effective Banking Supervision
requires the licensing authority to set the minimum standards for bank establishments. These standards include an assessment of the bank's ownership
structure, directors and senior management, its operating plan and internal controls, and its projected financial condition.[30] The entry requirements
stipulated in the CBL of 2003 also include these types of mandatory and discretionary aspects. Under the CBL of 2003, applicants who want to set up a
commercial bank must meet the following requirements:[31]

    – a set of articles of association in accordance with the CBL of 2003 and
      the Company Law;
    – the minimum amount of the registered capital;
    – qualified directors and senior bank management of the proposed bank;
    – a sound internal organization and management system;
    – a business site, safety measures and other facilities relevant to the bank's
      operations.

First, the fit and proper test is extended to all directors of the board of directors
and senior management, rather than simply to the chairman of the board,

---

29. G. Gorton, 'Bank Regulation: When "Banks" and "Banking" Are Not the Same', *Oxford
     Review of Economic Policy*, Vol. 10, p. 107 (Winter 1994).
30. Basle Committee on Banking Supervision, *Core Principles for Effective Banking Supervi-
     sion*, Principle 3.
31. CBL of 2003, art. 12.

the president and other senior management. Accordingly, the BSL grants the CBRC the right to make qualification checks of a bank's directors and senior management, and to formulate relevant rules.[32] In addition, under the CBL of 2003, anyone who meets any of the following conditions is disqualified from holding the position of director or senior management at a bank:[33]

- has received criminal penalties for committing economic crimes or is deprived of political rights for committing a crime;
- holds the position of a director or manager of a bankrupt company or enterprise and is personally liable for the bankruptcy;
- is the legal representative of a company or enterprise whose business permit has been revoked due to illegal acts, and is personally liable for the revocation;
- fails to repay a large amount of personal debts at maturity.

Second, in approving an application for bank establishment, under the CBL of 1995, the licensing authority would consider the need for economic development and competition in the banking industry.[34] Some countries, such as the US, Japan and Australia, set out economic needs in their laws.[35] However, the economic needs standard loses the dimension of leveling the playing field for prospective applicants, in particular for foreign applicants, and instead constitutes a bank-entry barrier. The standard had come under criticism because it was often invoked to withhold new bank authorizations, even if applicants fulfilled the establishment standards. In view of this, for example, as early as the 1970s, the EC attempted to phase out the economic needs standards as a precondition for granting a license, given that the applicant's head office was located in an EC Member State.[36] As in the EC, the Chinese legislature removed the economic needs standard and added an open clause in the amended CBL of 2003, which requires an applicant to satisfy other prudential requirements,[37] although what precisely these other prudential requirements are is left to the discretion of the CBRC.

---

32. BSL, art. 20. In March 2003, the PBOC, the former banking regulator, issued the Measures on the Administration of Qualifications of Senior Management of Financial Institutions, which is still in force.
33. CBL of 2003, art. 27.
34. CBL of 1995, art. 12.
35. For example, in acting on any application to establish a Federal branch or agency proposed by a foreign bank, the Comptroller shall take into account the effects of the proposal on competition in the domestic and foreign commerce of the US. See 12 U.S.C. section 3102 (c).
36. See First Council Directive 77/780 of 12 December 1977 on the Coordination of Laws, Regulations and Administrative Provisions Relating to the Taking up and Pursuit of the Business of Credit Institutions, art. 3(2)(a), 1977 O.J. (L322) 30.
37. CBL of 2003, art. 12.

Third, the CBL of 2003 revises the provisions on the initial capital requirements of a bank. The minimum capital subscription is RMB 1 billion for a nationwide bank[38] rather than for a general commercial bank in the CBL of 1995. In parallel to the removal of the economic needs standard, the CBRC is delegated to adjust the initial capital requirement above the statutory minimum amount for prudential reasons rather than for economic needs.[39]

II.B.   APPLICATION PROCEDURES

Under the CBL of 2003, the application process involves two steps. First, a bank applicant must submit to the CBRC the following documents:

- an application letter which states the name of the prospective commercial bank, location, registered capital, business scope and other information;
- a feasibility study report;
- other documents required by the CBRC.[40]

Second, if the CBRC considers the documents submitted by the applicant at the first stage to be satisfactory, the CBRC will require the applicant to complete a formal application form and submit the following documents:[41]

- draft articles of association;
- qualification credentials of the prospective directors and senior management;
- certification on verification of capital subscriptions issued by a lawful institution engaging in capital verification;
- a list of shareholders, their subscriptions and shares;
- a certificate of creditworthiness of the shareholders who hold more than five per cent of the registered capital and other relevant information;
- operating policies and plans;
- business site, safety measures, and other information regarding facilities of the business;
- other documents required by the CBRC.

The application procedure is, in fact, a process through which the CBRC conducts a critical examination of whether an applicant meets the mandatory and discretionary establishment standards. The statutory application procedures reflect the introduction of international standards, for example, the Basle Committee's Core Principles for Effective Banking Supervision, by the Chinese banking legislature.

---

38. Ibid., art. 13.
39. Ibid.
40. Ibid., art. 14.
41. Ibid., art. 15.

First, the legislature focuses strongly on an assessment of the bank ownership structure and the shareholder qualification. According to the BSL, in approving an establishment application, the CBRC shall review the sources of the capital subscription, financial strength, ability to supplement capital, and the integrity of a shareholder.[42] The qualification checks are extended not only from proposed senior management to directors and senior management, as discussed previously, but also from a shareholder who holds 10 per cent or more of the registered capital under the CBL of 1995[43] to a shareholder who holds five per cent or less of the registered capital. In addition to licensing a new bank, the CBRC is also granted the authority to review and approve a proposal for a change in significant ownership in an existing bank to make the criteria for a new entrant comparable to those for approving a bank. The term 'significant', here, is defined as five per cent of the total capital in the CBL of 2003, as opposed to 10 per cent under the CBL of 1995.[44]

Second, acceptable operating plans are always an element used by the licensing authority to review the application.[45] In virtually all banking systems, the licensing authority will, in considering an application, assess the type of business, planned future business, proposed expansion, profitability, and future prospects by reviewing the information furnished by the applicant. Under the Chinese practice, the feasibility study report and the operating plan describe and analyze the market area from which the proposed bank expects to draw the majority of its business and to establish a strategy for the proposed bank's ongoing operations. These documents encompass plans for the future of business development, potential profitability and other factors that affect prospective operations.

Third, in most countries, banking law or licensing authorities require a minimum initial capital requirement. A bank's capital can provide a base to support its proposed strategic plan, further growth, and start-up costs, and can also serve as a cushion against unexpected losses. In comparison to other countries' legislation and practice, Chinese banks face a higher minimum capital requirement. Although this type of higher requirement also increases the difficulty for bank entry, it indeed provides a starting point to ensure that a bank is managed in a safe and sound manner.

Following the example of foreign banking legislation, the BSL clearly requires the CBRC to decide whether to approve or disapprove a banking establishment application within six month of receiving the application. In case of disapproval, the CBRC must state the grounds of the refusal.[46] However, both the CBL of 2003 and BSL do not provide whether the CBRC can revoke a

---

42. BSL, art. 17.
43. See CBL of 1995, art. 15, and CBL of 2003, art. 15.
44. See ibid., art. 24, CBL of 1995, art. 24.
45. See Basle Committee on Banking Supervision, *Core Principles for Effective Banking Supervision*, p. 17.
46. BSL, art. 22.

bank's license in the event that the approved bank does not appear to have fulfilled, or does no longer fulfill, one or more of the entry criteria.[47]

II.C.   PERMISSIBLE ACTIVITIES

The banking business, particularly the activity of taking deposits from the public, should be reserved for an institution licensed as a bank, and therefore the use of the word 'bank' in names should be controlled as far as possible.[48] In line with the requirement, institutions and individuals are strictly prohibited from conducting banking activities, and from using the word 'bank' in their company names without the expressed approval of the CBRC.[49]

Under the CBL of 2003, a commercial bank is permitted to perform part or all of the following businesses:[50]

- Take deposits from the public.
- Issue short, medium and long-term loans.
- Provide domestic and foreign settlement services.
- Accept and discount negotiable instruments.[51]
- Issue financial bonds.
- Act as an agent to issue or cash government bonds, and underwrite government bonds.
- Trade in government bonds and financial bonds.[52]
- Engage in inter-bank lending and borrowing.[53]
- Trade in, or trade in as an agent, foreign exchanges.

---

47. The Basle Committee on Banking Supervision argues that it is important that the criteria for issuing licenses be consistent with those applied in ongoing supervision, so that they can provide one of the bases for withdrawing authorization when an established institution no longer meets the criteria. Basel Committee on Banking Supervision, *Core Principles for Effective Banking Supervision*, p. 15.
48. Ibid., p. 15.
49. BSL, art. 19; CBL of 2003, art. 11.
50. CBL of 2003, art. 3.
51. The CBL of 2003 extended the scope of business for a bank to include acceptance of negotiable instruments. Banks, however, had been traditionally permitted to accept negotiable instruments.
52. Trading in financial bonds was newly added into the scope of business of a bank by the CBL of 2003, although banks had been permitted to conduct this type of activity. The PBOC, however, shall be responsible for supervising financial bonds issuing and trading in inter-bank bond markets. See the Law of PBOC, arts. 4(4) and 32(4); CBL of 2003, art. 76(2).
53. According to Article 46 of the CBL of 2003, in engaging in inter-bank lending and borrowing, a bank must comply with the relevant rules of the PBOC regarding inter-bank lending and borrowing. See also the Law of PBOC, arts. 4(4) and 32(4), and the CBL of 2003, art. 76(2). The supervisory allocation in this regard is that the PBOC is responsible for examining whether a bank meets the requirements for entry into inter-bank markets, while the CBRC is responsible for examining whether a bank that has entered inter-bank markets is qualified to perform inter-bank businesses.

- Conduct bank card business.[54]
- Provide letter of credit services and guarantee.
- Act as an agent to collect and pay money, and act as an insurance agent.
- Provide safety box services.
- Perform other activities approved by the CBRC.

In addition to these permissible activities, a commercial bank is permitted to conduct settlement and sale of foreign exchanges subject to the approval of the PBOC.[55] Under the CBL of 1995, a bank was required to issue loans to specific State Council-approved projects,[56] which were often criticized as a non-market-based practice. For this reason, the CBL of 2003 removes this provision, and loans of this type are left to policy banks. With respect to inter-bank lending and borrowing, the maximum time limit was set at four months in the CBL of 1995, while the CBL of 2003 leaves the time limit to the prerogative of the PBOC.[57] Given that disposing of real estate and equity would be time consuming, the CBL of 2003 extends the limit of one year to two years within which a bank must dispose of the real estate and equity acquired from execution of mortgage and pledge.[58] Under both the CBL of 1995 and the CBL of 2003, banks are prohibited from investing in trust, stock, real estate, non-bank financial institutions, and enterprises. However, in response to strong calls to relax the grip on cross-industry activities of banks, the CBL of 2003 adds an exception to this general prohibition; that is, unless otherwise provided for by the state. Despite ambiguity of the term 'state', this exception apparently leaves room for banks to expand their activities into other industries.

Based on the statutory business scope, a bank should determine its own business activities in the articles of incorporation and submit these activities to the CBRC for approval.[59] For the business products that fall within the approved business scope, the CBRC shall adopt an approval and recording approach. In other words, the CBRC shall determine which products shall undergo approval procedures or be reported for the record.[60]

---

54. Although bank card business did not fall within the business scope of a bank under the CBL of 1995, banks had already been permitted to conduct these types of activities for several years.
55. CBL of 2003, art. 3. This implies that, in doing this business, a bank must be subject to the supervision of both the CBRC and PBOC. Under article 76 of the CBL of 2003, the PBOC can impose administrative penalties on a bank that conducts settlement and sale of foreign exchanges without the prior approval of the PBOC.
56. CBL of 1995, art. 41.
57. CBL of 1995, art. 46; CBL of 2003, art. 46.
58. CBL of 2003, art. 42.
59. Ibid., art. 3.
60. BSL, art. 18. Before the promulgation of the BSL, the CBRC issued the Decision on Adjusting Bank Entry and Procedures on 29 May 2003. Subject to the Decision, a domestic commercial bank that wishes to conduct the following businesses was no longer required to obtain the prior approval from the CBRC:

    – factoring services to domestic traders;
    – clearing services for securities transactions as an agent;

III.   ONGOING REGULATION

A strict licensing process does not imply that a bank will be operated in a safe and sound manner. The safe and sound operations of a bank depend, to a large extent, on prudential regulation and supervision. Prudential regulation and supervision covers legal, administrative and non-legally binding rules or standards established by legislature, competent authorities and international organizations. In particular, prudential regulation include capital adequacy requirements, large exposure and connected lending controls, liquidity adequacy, and provisioning while prudential supervision is defined to cover on-site examination conducted by supervisors or external auditors and off-site examination.

III.A.   CAPITAL ADEQUACY

Capital adequacy has become a code word for, or synonymous with, enhanced and broadened bank regulation at both the international and domestic levels.[61] The low level of capital adequacy has excruciated the Chinese banking regulator and banks themselves. Due to the chronic problems inherent in banks, and the lack of effective supplementary rules, the eight per cent capital adequacy requirement stipulated in the CBL of 1995 had not given rise to a significant increase in the capital adequacy level of Chinese banks. However, the increasing importance of capital adequacy to bank safety and soundness had been gradually recognized by the Chinese banking regulator and banks.

The CBL of 2003 reconfirms the eight per cent capital adequacy requirement for a bank to issue a loan.[62] Apparently, the amended law does not correct

---

    – insurance businesses as an agent;
    – custody of investment accounts assigned to securities firms by institutional investors;
    – custody of trust assets;
    – custody of annuity accounts of an enterprise.

A domestic commercial bank that sought to conduct the following businesses was no longer required to file with the CBRC for the record:

    – discount of negotiable instruments with interest paid by the purchaser or by the party designated under the contract;
    – overdraft services to legal entities;
    – collection of proceeds from sales of trust products.

A foreign-funded bank who wanted to conduct the following businesses was no longer required to file with the CBRC for the record:

    – factoring services to domestic traders;
    – discount of negotiable instruments with interest paid by the purchaser or by the party designated under the contract;
    – overdraft services to legal entities.

61.   J.J. Norton, *Devising International Bank Supervisory Standards* (1996), p. 247.
62.   CBL of 2003, art. 39(1).

the weakness in the CBL of 1995, that is, the capital adequacy requirement for other on and off-balance sheet activities falls outside regulation. To remedy this defect, the CBRC, based on the prudential rules making power granted by the BSL,[63] issued the Measures on Administration of Capital Adequacy of Commercial Banks (referred to as Capital Adequacy Measures for the remainder of this chapter) in February 2004. Although China announced that it would not abide fully by the Basel II in the near future, the Capital Adequacy Measures adopt the basic framework and main contents of the Basel II and the Amendments to the Capital Accord to Incorporate Market Risks issued by the Basle Committee on Banking Supervision in January 1996.

The Capital Adequacy Measures require banks to provide a capital charge for credit and market risks arising from on and off balance sheet activities. The classification and definition of capital, and the approach to calculating risk weights and risk-weighted assets are essentially similar to those in the Basel capital documents.[64] The calculation of capital adequacy is expressed as follows:[65]

> Capital adequacy ratio
>> = (total capital − deductions[66]) / (credit risk − weighted assets
>> + 12.5 × capital charge for market risk) 8%

> Core capital adequacy ratio
>> = (core capital − deductions[67]) / (credit risk − weighted assets
>> + 12.5 × capital charge for market risk) 4%

Under the Capital Adequacy Measures, banks are required to disclose information in relation to capital adequacy, including objectives and policies of risk management, scope of consolidated accounts, capital, capital adequacy, credit risks and market risks. Appendix 5 of the Capital Adequacy Measures set out the items that must be disclosed in each of these five categories. The board of directors is responsible for information disclosure, and the contents disclosed must be approved in advance by the board.

Consistent with Basel II, the Capital Adequacy Measures enhance the banking regulator's supervisory review of capital adequacy of a bank. Under

---

63. BLS, art. 21.
64. With respect to calculating market risk-based assets, the Capital Adequacy Measures simply translate the relevant sections of the Basel's Amendments to the Capital Accord to Incorporate Market Risks of January 1996.
65. Capital Adequacy Measures, art. 11.
66. In calculating capital adequacy ratio, goodwill, equity investment by a bank in unconsolidated financial institutions, and equity investment by a bank in the real estates and enterprises not for its own use shall be deducted. Ibid, art. 14.
67. In calculating the core capital adequacy ratio, goodwill, 50 per cent of equity investment by a bank in unconsolidated financial institutions and 50 per cent of equity investment by a bank in the real estates and enterprises not for its own use shall be deducted. Ibid, art. 15.

the Capital Adequacy Measures, the board of directors must bear the ultimate responsibility for capital adequacy management, while senior management is responsible for implementation of capital adequacy policies.[68] A bank is required to report to the CBRC its consolidated capital adequacy ratio semi-yearly, and unconsolidated capital adequacy ratio on a quarterly basis.[69]

More importantly, the Capital Adequacy Measures introduce the 'prompt corrective action' system into the Chinese banking regulatory and supervisory process. Under the Capital Adequacy Measures, the system classifies banks into three categories, according to their capital adequacy level: adequately capitalized, under-capitalized, and significantly undercapitalized:[70]

	Total capital adequacy	*Core capital adequacy*
Adequately-capitalized	$\geq 8\%$	and $\geq 4\%$
Undercapitalized	$\leq 8\%$	or $\leq 4\%$
Significantly undercapitalized	$\geq 4\%$	or $\leq 2\%$

As a bank's capital declines below the required levels, increasingly stringent restrictions and requirements apply to the bank. To prevent the capital of an adequately capitalized bank from falling below the minimum level, the CBRC shall take the following intervening measures:[71]

– require the bank to improve its rules and systems of risk management;
– require the bank to enhance its ability to control risks;
– require the bank to strengthen analysis and forecast of capital adequacy;
– require the bank to make a feasible and practicable capital maintenance plan;
– restrict the bank from engaging in particular high-risk activities.

In the event that a bank becomes undercapitalized, the CBRC shall take the following corrective measures:[72]

– issue a supervisory letter, which specifies:
  – the description of capital adequacy situation of the bank;
  – corrective measures to be taken;
  – the detailed plan for carrying out the corrective measures;
– require the bank to make a feasible and practical capital restoration plan within two months of receiving the CBRC's supervisory letter;

---

68. Ibid., art. 33 and 34.
69. Ibid., art. 35.
70. Ibid., art. 38.
71. Ibid., art. 39.
72. Ibid., art. 40.

- require the bank to restrict its asset growth;
- require the bank to reduce the size of risky assets;
- require the bank to restrict purchase of fixed assets;
- require the bank to limit the payment of dividends and other incomes;
- impose more-stringent requirements or limitations on a bank's expansion of institutions and activities.

In addition to these measures, the CBRC has the power to require the bank to suspend all but low-risk activities, and refuse the bank's application to establish additional institutions and conduct new lines of business based on the bank's risk levels and implementation of the bank's capital restoration plan.[73]

A significantly undercapitalized bank faces a longer list of corrective measures. In addition to the corrective measures taken against an undercapitalized bank, the CBRC can impose two additional measures on a significantly undercapitalized bank. The CBRC can first require the bank to reshuffle its senior management, and second, the CBRC can appoint a conservator for the bank, facilitate the bank's reorganization or even close the bank.[74]

In the author's opinion, some corrective measures set out in the Capital Adequacy Measures may lack a legal basis. First, under the Capital Adequacy Measures, an adequately capitalized bank can be restricted from conducting high-risk activities for the purpose of preventing the bank's capital adequacy from falling below the minimum level. However, according to the BSL, the CBRC can suspend part of a bank's business activities only if the bank violates prudential operation rules and fails to make corrections within a specified period, or if the bank's act seriously endangers its safe and sound operations, and causes damage to the lawful interests of depositors and other customers. For an adequately capitalized bank that satisfies the minimum total and core capital adequacy requirements, the CBRC has the power to conduct any approved activities, even if these approved activities fall into the category of high risk. For this reason, the CBRC lacks the legitimacy to restrict an adequately capitalized bank from engaging in particular high-risk activities.

Second, according to the Capital Adequacy Measures, the CBRC can appoint a conservator for a significantly undercapitalized bank. By contrast, the CBL of 2003 and BSL provide that the precondition for appointing a conservator is that the bank concerned is, or is likely to be, in a credit crisis and seriously threatens the interests of depositors and other customers.[75] In China, however, neither laws nor regulations have so far provided that a significantly undercapitalized bank is a bank in a credit crisis or would threaten the interests of depositors. The CBRC also lacks legitimacy to appoint a conservator

---

73.   Ibid.
74.   Ibid., art. 41.
75.   CBL, art. 64; BSL, art. 38.

for a significantly undercapitalized bank, unless a law enacted by the NPC, or a regulation made by the State Council, so announces.

III.B.   RISK CONCENTRATIONS

In any banking system, depositor protection and the stability of the banking system are closely linked to the quality of assets. Excessive concentration of risks is a well-documented cause of bank failure. For this reason, supervisors often rely on a set of parameters, which can be expressed in the form of formal limits, guidelines and reporting thresholds to assess a bank's risk diversification. The CBL of 2003 sets a stringent limit on risk concentrations, under which the ratio of the balance of loans to a single borrower and the bank's capital shall not exceed 10 per cent.[76]

Several weaknesses are inherent in risk-concentrations control in China's banking law. First, the risk-concentration control is limited only to loans, exclusive of other on and off balance sheet activities. Second, the law fails to define 'single borrower', and leaves unclear whether, as in EU or USA laws, two or more borrowers that constitute a single risk can be regarded as a single borrower.[77] Third, the law pays inadequate attention to country and sectoral exposures within the general framework of risk concentrations. Finally, the law entirely ignores the mechanism for reporting large exposures.

In April 2004, the CBRC issued the Measures on the Administration of Insider and Shareholder Connected Transactions of Commercial Banks (which is referred to as Connected Transaction Measures for the remainder of this chapter) which make several amendments to the CBL of 2003 with respect to risk-concentration control. The Connected Transaction Measures define a connected transaction to include all on and off balance sheet activities conducted between a bank and its connected parties.[78] The Connected Transaction

---

76. CBL, art. 39(4).
77. In October 2003, the CBRC issued the Guidelines on the Administration of Credit-granting to a Group Customer by a Commercial Bank. Pursuant to the Guidelines, a group customer is defined to include the following enterprises receiving a bank's credits:

    – controlling directly or indirectly other enterprises in the form of shares or management, or being controlled by other enterprises;
    – being jointly controlled by the third-party enterprise;
    – being jointly controlled, directly or indirectly, by a major investor, key management or a family member to whom the customer is closely related;
    – having other connected relations so that the bank can transfer assets and profits inconsistent with a fair price. See the Guidelines on the Administration of Credit-granting to a Group Customer by a Commercial Bank, art. 3. According to a general understanding, a group customer can be regarded as constituting a single risk. Under the Guidelines, credit-granting by a bank to a group customer can exceed 15 per cent of the bank's capital. See Ibid., art. 12. In other words, in China's banking regulation two or more borrowers constituting a single risk have not been taken as a single borrower.
78. See Connected Transaction Measures, art. 18.

Measures broadly define a connected party, and includes a connected natural person, connected legal person, and other connected organizations.[79] The term 'connected natural person' refers to:

- a bank's insider person;[80]
- key natural person shareholder,[81]
- close relatives of an insider person and key natural person shareholder,
- controlling natural person shareholder;
- director
- key management of a connected legal person and other organizations of a bank;[82] other natural persons having material influence on a bank.[83]

A connected legal person is defined to include:

- a bank's major non-natural person shareholder
- a legal person or other organizations controlled directly or indirectly by an enterprise[84] that also controls the bank
- a legal person or other organizations controlled directly, indirectly or jointly materially influenced by a bank's insider person,
- key natural shareholder and their close relatives,
- other legal persons or organizations directly, indirectly or jointly controlling or having material influence on a bank.[85]

Pursuant to the Connected Transaction Measures, credit granting by a bank to a connected party shall not exceed 10 per cent of the bank's capital, while credit granting to a group customer to which a connected legal person or organization belongs shall not exceed 15 per cent of the bank's capital.[86] The Connected Transaction Measures, therefore, maintain the same limit as stipulated by the CBL of 2003 for risk concentrations. Because the Connected Transaction Measures permit credit granting to a group customer to exceed 10 per cent limit,

---

79. The CBL of 2003 prohibits a bank from extending an unsecured loan to its related party. The term 'related party' is defined to include:

    - the director, supervisor, management or staff in charge of granting credit, and these individuals' close relatives;
    - a company, enterprise or other organization in which these individuals have investments or hold a position of senior management. CBL of 2003, art. 40.
80. An insider person is deemed to be a bank's director, senior management of head office and branches, other staff who possess the power to choose or participate in granting credit and transferring assets. Connected Transaction Measures, art. 7.
81. A key natural person shareholder is defined as a shareholder who holds or controls five per cent or more of a bank's shares or voting rights. Ibid.
82. Under the Connected Transaction Measures, the terms 'legal person' and 'other organizations' do not include a commercial bank. See Ibid, art. 8.
83. Ibid., art. 7.
84. The term 'enterprise' does not include a state-owned asset management company. Ibid.
85. Ibid.
86. Ibid., art. 32. A bank's credit granting to all group customers shall not exceed a total of 50 per cent of its bank. Ibid.

these Measures indicate that a group customer could not, even if the group customer could – in many cases – constitute a single risk in many cases, be regarded as a single borrower, and is not, therefore, subject to the 10 per cent risk concentration limit.

III.C.   PROVISIONING

The main purpose of loan-loss provisioning is to recognize potential future calls on banks' capital resources and to make due allowance for these future calls. Regulations or rules on loan classification and provisioning vary across countries. In some countries, the rules are developed by private sector accounting standard-setting bodies, while in others the rules are issued by Parliament, the Ministry of Finance or the banking regulator. In China, the CBL of 2003 sets forth a general rule on provisioning, under which a commercial bank shall set aside bad debt provisions and write off bad debts.[87]

In December 2001, the PBOC – China's former banking regulator – issued the Guiding Principles for Loan Risk Classifications, which remain in force after the CBRC took over the banking regulatory authority. Under these Guiding Principles, loans are classified, based on their risk levels, into five categories: standard, mentioned, sub-standard, doubtful and loss, with the latter three categories being non-performing loans.[88]

A standard loan implies that a borrower can perform the loan contract and no sufficient reason exists to doubt that the principal and interest will not be repaid in full and on time.

A mentioned loan implies that, although a borrower is able to repay the principal and interest, negative factors currently exist that influence the borrower's repayment.

A substandard loan is a loan in which a borrower has obvious repayment difficulties, under which the principal and interest cannot be fully repaid depending solely on the borrower's normal incomes, and the chance of loss is probable, even if collateral is executed.

A doubtful loan is a loan whose principal and interest are not fully repaid by a borrower and that will incur a relatively large loss, even if collateral is executed.

A loss loan is a loan whose principle and interest are uncollectible, even after all necessary measures or legal procedures are adopted.

In addition to these factors, arrears are important factors in classifying loans. In cases in which the number of days in arrears, including the extended due days, exceed a fixed time period, and the loan's accrued interest is not calculated in the current income and loss, the loan shall be classified at least

---

87. CBL, art. 57.
88. Guiding Principles for Loan Risk Classifications, art. 4.

in the sub-standard loan category.[89] Loans extended in violation of laws and regulations shall be classified at least in the specified loan category.[90]

In April 2002, the PBOC issued the Guidelines on Provisioning for Bank Loan Losses, which the CBRC still applies. According to these Guidelines, loan loss provisions are classified into general provisions, specific provisions and special provisions.[91]

General provisions are created against the possible, but unidentified losses; the amount of which is set aside based on a fixed percentage of the balance of the total loans.[92] The Guidelines set a benchmark of one per cent of the year-end balance of loans against which the adequacy of a bank's general provisions is assessed.[93] A bank must, on a quarterly basis, establish its general provisions that qualify for inclusion in the supplementary capital, according to the CBRC's Capital Adequacy Measures.[94]

Specific provisions are established to cover the identified losses of a specific loan, the amount of which is set aside based on the loss level of each loan after the loan is risk-classified according to the Guiding Principles for Loan Risk Classifications.[95] A bank can set side its specific provisions on a quarterly basis according to the following criteria:[96] provisions for mentioned loans are created at two per cent; sub-standard loans are created at 25 per cent, with a floating range of 20 per cent; doubtful loans are created at 50 per cent, with a floating range of 20 per cent; and loss loans are created at 100 per cent.

Special provisions are in place against particular countries, regions, sectors, or risks of particular types of loans.[97] The quarterly percentage for special provisions is left to the discretion of a bank according to special risks, loss possibility and historical loss experience of various types of loans, for example, various countries, sectors and so on.[98]

Important to note is that the competent authority takes a different approach to loan loss provisions for city commercial banks. In November 2002, the PBOC issued its Opinions for Implementing Five-category Classification of Loan Quality at City Commercial Banks. Under the Opinions, specific provisions for mentioned loans, sub-standard loans, doubt loans, and loss loans are set aside at not less than two per cent, 20 per cent, 40 per cent, and 100 per cent of the uncollateralized amount of the loan concerned, respectively. The uncollateralized amount is defined as the difference between the principal and interest of the loan and the value of collateral.

---

89. Ibid., art. 9.
90. Ibid., art. 10.
91. Guidelines on Provisioning for Bank Loan Losses, art. 2.
92. Ibid.
93. Ibid., art. 4.
94. Ibid., Capital Adequacy Measures, art. 12.
95. Guidelines on Provisioning for Bank Loan Losses, art. 2.
96. Ibid., art. 5.
97. Ibid., art. 2.
98. Ibid., art. 6.

In practice, banks must comply with the rules of the Ministry of Finance in term of loan loss provisions. The Ministry of Finance issued the Accounting System of Financial Enterprises in 1993 and 2001, respectively. Strangely, different banks are permitted to apply the two different versions of the accounting system.[99] The main difference between the 1993 and 2001 version is that, under the 1993 version, a bank does not need to set aside sufficient loan loss provisions, even if the amount of non-performing loans is carried on the balance sheet, while the 2001 version requires a bank to set aside sufficient loan loss provisions and to write off its profit or capital in the event of a deficiency in provisions.

To make China's accounting system consistent with international accounting standards, on 1 September 2005, the Ministry of Finance issued the Temporary Rules on Recognition and Measurement of Financial Instruments[100] (which are referred to as Financial Instruments Rules for the remainder of this chapter), which are essentially a Chinese version of IAS 39 Financial Instruments: Recognition and Measurement made by the International Accounting Standards Board. Under the Financial Instruments Rules, a bank is required to assess, at each balance sheet date, whether any objective evidence of impairment exists.[101] If any such evidence exists after the initial recognition of a financial asset, the bank is required to establish provisions for impairment on the financial asset.[102] Objective evidence of impairment includes, among other things:

- significant financial difficulty of the issuer;
- an actual breach of contract, such as a default or delinquency in interest or principal payments;
- a high probability of bankruptcy,
- a financially restructuring,
- the disappearance of an active market in an asset due to significant financial difficulties.[103]

For financial assets carried at amortized cost, the amount of the impairment loss of a financial asset is measured as the difference between the asset's carrying amount and the present value of estimated future cash flows, discounted at the financial asset's original effective interest rate.[104]

---

99. The four biggest state-owned banks, for example, used the 1993 version of the accounting system before 2003. In 2004, the financially restructured Bank of China and Bank of Communications began to use the 2001 version. Some joint-stock banks continue to use the 1993 version.
100. Available at <www.mof.gov.cn/news/20051215_2202_11142.htm>.
101. Financial Instruments Rules, art. 33.
102. Ibid.
103. Ibid., art. 34.
104. Ibid., art. 35.

So far, the attitudes of the CBRC towards the Financial Instruments Rules have been unknown. According to China's traditional practice, banks shall be subject to the regulation of the Ministry of Finance on financial asset-loss provisions. Apparently, the Ministry of Finance's rules are geared towards the losses of specific financial assets, and therefore deal with specific provisions. In the author's opinion, this approach has two implications for banks. First, specific provisions based on the five-category classification of loan quality will be superseded by the new approach introduced in the Financial Instruments Rules. Second, general provisions and special provisions under the Guidelines on Provisioning for Bank Loan Losses also remain in effect.

III.D.   ON AND OFF-SITE EXAMINATIONS

The supervisory process requires the collection and analysis of information to assess banks' current condition and make judgments about their future prospects. This can be achieved through on-site or off-site examinations.

The CBL of 2003 and BSL both authorize the CBRC to conduct on-site examinations of banks.[105] Under the BSL, the CBRC shall conduct on-site examination of business activities and risk profiles of a commercial bank,[106] while under the CBL of 2003, the CBRC has the power to conduct examinations at any time against a bank's deposits, loans, settlement and non-performing loans.[107]

In conducting on-site examinations, the BSL authorizes the CBRC to take the following supervisory measures:[108]

- to enter the location of a bank to conduct an examination;
- to enquire with bank staff, and require the staff to provide explanations on examined matters;
- to have full access to, and make copies of, a bank's documents and materials related to on-site examination, and to seal documents and materials that are likely to be removed, concealed or destroyed; and
- to examine a bank's information technology infrastructure for business operations and management.

To ensure the legitimacy and fairness of on-site examination, the BSL requires that without the approval from the responsible person in the CBRC, examiners are not permitted to conduct on-site examinations. In conducting examinations,

---

105. The CBL also authorizes the PBOC to conduct examinations of banks according to articles 32 and 34 of the PBOC Law. CBL of 2003, art. 62.
106. BSL, art. 24.
107. CBL of 2003, art. 62.
108. BSL, art. 34.

no fewer than two examiners are required, who must present legal identification and the examination notice upon examination.[109]

A common practice is for the banking supervisor to depend on external auditors to conduct on-site examinations in several countries. The reports of external auditors are an important complement to the supervisory devices available to the banking supervisor to assess the situations of a bank. Neither the CBL of 2003, nor the BSL explicitly provides for the role of an external auditor in on-site examination. However, from article 33 of the BSL and article 56 of the CBL of 2003, it can be concluded that a bank is required by the CBRC to submit its auditing report.[110] In addition, Chinese laws do not address the issue of the auditor's reporting duty to the CBRC. An implied term of the auditor's contract is that auditors are under a duty of confidentiality to their clients. For this reason, if no law applies to break legitimately such a duty of confidentiality, the auditor cannot report directly to the CBRC information in regard to an audited bank's secrecy. All information flows between the CBRC and external auditors must be channeled through the audited bank. This approach, however, can impair the role of external auditing in the supervisory process. It is, therefore, suggested that a law made by the NPC should lay down the auditor's reporting duty to the CBRC.

Off-site examinations rely on the data that banks submit in their supervisory report and on the information required by supervisors. By reviewing and analyzing these reports, supervisors can check a bank's adherence to prudential requirements. The BSL authorizes the CBRC to conduct off-site examination of a bank's business activities and risk profiles, establish an information system for supervision of a bank and analyze and assess a bank's risk levels.[111] The CBRC has the power to require a bank to submit a balance sheet, income statements and other financial reports.[112]

Under the BSL, the CBRC shall establish the bank rating system and risk warning system, and, based on the rating assigned and the risk level of a bank, determine the frequency and scope of on-site examinations, and measures to be taken.[113] To enforce the provision, the CBRC issued the Risk Rating System for Joint-Stock Commercial Banks in February 2004, under which the elements of capital, asset, earning and liquidity (CAMELS) are introduced. The elements of CAMELS consist of quantitative and qualitative factors, while management and sensitivity to market risk are only subject to a qualitative factors assessment. All elements and factors, with the exception of sensitivity to market risk, are assigned various score points, as described in the following table.

---

109. Ibid.
110. Article 33 of the BSL provides that the CBRC has power to require a bank to submit its audit report prepared by certified accountants. Article 56 of the CBL of 2003 requires a bank to publish its audit report.
111. Ibid., art. 23.
112. BSL, art. 33; CBL of 2003, art. 55 and 61.
113. BSL, art. 27.

Table 1: unit: point

	Quantitative Factors	*Qualitative Factors*
Capital	– capital adequacy (30) – core capital adequacy (30)	– components and quality of capital (6) – impact of the overall financial situations of a bank on its capital (8) – impact of the assets of a bank on its capital (8) – accessibility of a bank to capital markets or to other sources to increase its capital (8) – management of capital (10)
Asset Management	– non performing loans (15) – expected loan losses (10) – credit granting to a largest single customer or group customer (10) – coverage of provisions (20) – non-credit assets loan losses (5)	– changes in non-performing loans and other non-performing assets and their impact on a bank's overall asset safety (5) – sectoral exposures and their impact on a bank's asset safety (5) – credit risk management procedures and their effectiveness (10) – soundness and effectiveness of loan risk classification system (10) – guaranteed loans and mortgaged (pledged) loans and their management (5) – risk management of non-credit assets (5)
Management		– corporate governance of a bank (50) – internal control system (50)
Earning	– ROA (15)	– cost, income, profitability and their tendency (15)

Table 1: Contd.

	Quantitative Factors	Qualitative Factors
	– ROC (15) – interest recovery ratio (15) – asset expense ratio (15)	– quality of profitability and its impact on business development and loss provisions (15) – financial budget and settlement system and soundness and effectiveness of financial management (10)
Liquidity	– liquidity ratio (20) – RMB excessive reserve ratio (10) – foreign currency reserve ratio (5) – ratio between loans and deposits (10) – ratio between foreign currency loans and deposits (5) – inter-bank borrowing and lending net (10)	– composite, change, and stability of the fund sources (5) – asset and liability management policy and fund distribution (5) – liquidity management (20) – ability of a bank to meet the demand for liquidity in the form of active liabilities (5) – ability of management to effectively identify, monitor, and control a bank's positions (5)
Sensitivity		– sensitivity of profitability and asset value to a reverse change in interest rates, foreign exchange rates, commodity prices or property prices – ability of the board of directors and senior management to identify, measure, monitor, and control market risk exposures – nature and complexity of interest rate risk exposures originating from non-trading book positions – nature and complexity of market risk exposures originating from trading book activities and abroad activities

In addition to the score points, the individual elements – with the exception of sensitivity to market risk – are assigned various weights: capital adequacy is assigned 20 per cent, asset safety 20 per cent, management 25 per cent, earning 20 per cent, and liquidity 15 per cent. The composite score of a bank is gained by calculating the sum of each element's weighted scores. Based on the ratings, the CBRC shall take various supervisory measures against a bank. For example, if an individual element is rated below three – a composite score is between 60 and 75 points – the CBRC shall enhance supervision of the element and conduct on-site examination of the specific element, if required. For a bank with a composite rating below four – a composite score is between 50 and 60 points – the CBRC shall increase the frequency of on-site examinations, keep a close watch on the bank's operations and limit the bank's market entry in terms of additional institution establishment and new business.

IV. DEALING WITH PROBLEM BANKS

The existence of problem banks can undermine the entire financial system. For this reason, problem banks must either be put on a path that will restore their financial strength or be closed in a timely fashion. The CBL of 2003 and BSL set forth a number of mechanisms to deal with problem banks, which include:

- handling unexpected events;
- early interventions;
- conservatorship;
- reorganization;
- suspension for internal rectification;
- bank closure;
- bankruptcy.

Among these mechanisms, handling unexpected events, early interventions, and reorganization are newly introduced by the two banking laws, while the rest of the problem bank resolutions are revised to a varying extent.

IV.A. HANDLING UNEXPECTED EVENTS

According to the BSL, the CBRC shall establish a system for detecting and reporting a bank's unexpected events.[114] The BSL defines an unexpected event to refer to an event which is likely to cause a bank systemic risk and seriously threaten social stability.[115] As soon as the CBRC detects this type of event, the individual in charge at the CBRC shall be reported immediately. In cases in which the person in charge considers it necessary to report to the State Council,

---

114. BSL, art. 28.
115. Ibid.

this person must submit this report immediately, and at the same time inform this fact to the PBOC, the Ministry of Finance and other relevant departments.[116] To handle an unexpected event in a timely and effective manner, the CBRC is required to coordinate with the PBOC, the Ministry of Finance and other relevant departments to set up a system for handling unexpected events, lay down a preventive scheme, determine the body and staff responsible for handling the event, and clarify their responsibilities, measures and procedures.[117]

IV.B.   EARLY INTERVENTIONS

Most bank failures do not occur instantaneously, but rather result from losses over time. The early intervention mechanism is intended to prevent a problem bank from deteriorating and to correct problems before they grow too large and, in any event, before these problems lead to losses to depositors. For the first time, the BSL introduces the early intervention system. In cases in which a bank violates prudential rules, the CBRC shall order the bank to make corrections within a specified period; if the bank fails to do so, or if the bank's actions seriously threaten the sound operations of the bank and causes damage to the lawful interests of depositors and other customers, the CBRC may, upon approval from the person in charge, take the following measures:

- order the bank to suspend some of its business activities, and refuse the bank's application for new lines of business;
- restrict payments of dividends and other income;
- restrict asset transfers;
- order the bank's controlling shareholders to transfer their shares or restrict the rights of relevant shareholders;
- order the bank to shuffle directors and senior management, or restrict these individuals' rights;
- refuse the bank's application to establish additional institutions.[118]

Obviously, many of the interventions are geared toward the rights or powers granted by the company law to a bank. The CBRC cannot deprive or restrict any of these interventions without a law being adopted by the NPC. The BSL, as the NPC-adopted law, legitimately authorizes the CBRC to intervene in a bank's exercise of these types of rights and powers.

    The bank that is subject to early interventions shall submit its rectification report to the CBRC after taking corrective measures. The CBRC shall terminate the measures taken against the bank within three days after the bank proves compliant with relevant prudential rules.[119] However, the law does not

---

116.   Ibid.
117.   Ibid., art. 29.
118.   Ibid., art. 37.
119.   Ibid.

stipulate the period during which a bank can rectify its problems. Nor does the law provide how the CBRC shall deal with a bank that does not satisfy the prudential rules after taking corrective measures.

IV.C.   Conservatorship and Reorganization

Under the CBL of 2003, in the event that a bank is – or is likely to be – in a credit crisis, and therefore seriously threatens the interests of depositors, the CBRC can appoint a conservator for the bank.[120] The BSL introduces the same provision for conservatorship, but with one minor difference. Under the BSL, the right to threaten the interests of other customers is added.[121] In other words, in cases in which a credit-crisis-hit bank seriously threatens the interests of depositors, the bank concerned can be under conservatorship according to the CBL of 2003, whereas under the BSL, this type of bank could receive conservatorship only if the interests of both depositors and other customers were seriously threatened. Although the distinction between the interests of depositors and of other customers is blurred, the two NPC-adopted laws still both stipulate various conditions for applying conservatorship. Which condition is applied in appointing a conservator for a problem bank, however, remains unknown.

As a new resolution for a problem bank, the BSL provides for bank reorganization. The conditions for applying a reorganization resolution are exactly the same as those for appointing a conservator according to the BSL.[122] Apparently, the resolution, conservatorship or reorganization that would be used depends solely on the CBRC's decision. In addition, the law does not clarify the types of bank reorganization, simply requiring bank reorganization to be conducted according to laws or the State Council's regulations. However, so far, none of the laws or regulations in regard to bank reorganization has been made public.

IV.D.   Suspension for Internal Rectification

Suspension for internal rectification can be defined to specify that a problem bank is ordered by the CBRC to suspend its business and to rectify its problems. This resolution is regarded as one of the penalties imposed on, or the legal responsibilities assumed by, a problem bank. In the author's opinion, this resolution can also be taken as one of the problem bank resolutions.

Articles 44 and 45 of the BSL provide that if a bank commits one of the acts defined by the BSL with particularly serious circumstances, or fails to make corrections within a specified period, the CBRC has the authorization

---

120.   CBL of 2003, art. 64.
121.   BSL, art. 38.
122.   Ibid.

to suspend the bank's business for internal rectification.[123] The CBL of 2003 also sets out a long list of cases under which a bank can be under suspension for internal rectification. Some of the cases are the same as those in the BSL. Again, important to note is that the application of suspension for internal rectification must satisfy the requirement of 'particularly serious circumstances or failing to make corrections'.[124]

---

123.   The acts set out in article 44 of the BSL involve:

  – establishing a branch without approval;
  – modifying or terminating a bank without approval;
  – conducting an activity without approval or being filed for record in violation of the provisions;
  – raising or lowering interest rates of deposits and loans in violation of the provisions.

  The acts in Article 45 of the BSL involve:

  – appointing directors and senior management without qualification checks;
  – refusing or hindering on or off-site examinations;
  – providing false or important-facts-concealed statements, reports and other documents and materials;
  – failing to disclose information as required;
  – seriously violating prudential rules;
  – refusing to implement the early intervention measures as provided for in article 37 of the BSL.

124.   Articles 74–77 of the CBL of 2003 list the cases for applying suspension for internal rectification:
  Article 74:

  – establishing a branch without approval;
  – splitting or merging a bank without approval, or failing to apply for approval concerning bank modifications in violation of the provisions;
  – raising or lowering interest rates in violation of the provisions, or absorbing deposits or issuing loans by any other illegal means;
  – leasing or renting its business permit;
  – buying and selling foreign exchanges by itself or as an agent without approval;
  – buying and selling government bonds or issuing or trading in financial bonds without approval;
  – engaging in trust and investment or securities business, investing in real estate property not for its own use or in non-bank financial institutions and enterprises in violation of the provisions;
  – issuing unsecured loans or secured loans to its connected parties on conditions favorable to those in issuing similar loans to other borrowers.

  Article 75:

  – refusing or hindering examinations conducted by the CBRC;
  – providing false or important-facts-concealed statements, reports and other documents and materials;
  – failing to abide by the provisions on capital adequacy, deposit-loan ratio, liquidity ratio, risk concentration ratio, and other provisions on asset-liability management of the CBRC.

  Article 76:

  – settling or selling foreign exchanges without approval;

Some ambiguities exist in the CBL of 2003 and the BSL in terms of suspension for internal rectification. Under article 75(3) of the CBL of 2003, in the event that a bank fails to comply with prudential rules and to make corrections within a specified period, the CBRC can order the bank to suspend its business for internal rectification. By contrast, under article 45(5) of the BSL, the bank is subject to suspension for internal rectification only if the bank seriously violates prudential rules and fails to make corrections. While differentiating the line between 'seriously violate' and 'fails to comply with' is difficult, the various laws use the degree of violation as a condition for applying suspension for internal rectification. In addition, the condition for suspension for internal rectification – that is, that a bank violates prudential rules and fails to make corrections within a specified period – is exactly the same as one of the conditions for applying early interventions.[125] As a result, the CBRC can choose between the two resolutions to deal with the bank falling within the case.

IV.E. BANK CLOSURE

Bank closure is one type of involuntary termination of banks. Article 70 of the CBL of 2003 provides that the reason for closing a bank is to revoke the bank's business permit. Both the CBL of 2003 and BSL set out the cases for revoking a bank's business permit. These cases are exactly the same as those for suspension for internal rectification.[126] In this regard, however, conflicts still exist between the CBL of 2003 and BSL. Article 45(5) of the BSL provides that the CBRC is authorized to revoke a bank's business permit if the bank seriously violates prudential rules and fails to make corrections within a specified period. Under article 75 (3) of the CBL of 2003, by contrast, revocation of a business permit does not require the degree of violation as stipulated in article 45(5) of the BSL. By the same token, a bank that falls within the case can be subject to early interventions under the BSL or be revoked its business permit under the CBL of 2003. Apparently, a bank that engages in the same violation can receive a completely different treatment under the different laws.

An important note is that the BSL also provides for the conditions leading to bank closure. Under article 39 of the BSL, in which a bank conducts business in violation of laws, has poor management pr engages in other misconduct, and

---

 – issuing, or trading in financial bonds on the inter-bank bonds markets or borrowing funds from abroad without approval;
 – engaging in inter-bank borrowing or lending in violation of the provisions.
Article 77:
 – refusing or hindering examinations conducted by the PBOC;
 – providing false or important-facts-concealed statements, reports and other documents and materials;
 – failing to pay deposit reserves according to the ratios as prescribed by the PBOC.
125. BSL, art.37.
126. BSL, art. 44 and 45; CBL of 2003, art. 74–77.

the bank's continued existence would seriously threaten financial orders and cause damage to the public interests, the CBRC has the power to close the bank. In the author's opinion, however, closing a bank is a severe punishment and all conditions for bank closure should be clearly listed and defined in the law. The term 'other misconduct' in Article 39 of the BSL would leave too much room for the CBRC's discretion.

V.   CONCLUDING REMARKS

The past three years have seen the establishment of the basic legal framework for Chinese banking regulation at the NPC, State Council and CBRC level, covering capital adequacy, risk concentration, risk management, and corporate governance. These law or rule-making bodies pay a great deal of attention to the introduction of international standards and practices. The Capital Adequacy Measures, for example, adopt the basic contents of the Basle Committee's documents on capital adequacy and prompt corrective action prevailing in many countries. In addition to laying down mandatory rules, the CBRC tends to issue guidelines and standards to increase the flexibility of its supervisory process. Bear in mind, however, that in the process of establishing the Chinese banking law framework over the past years, the legislature and regulator have attempted to make international supervisory standards and practices fit into China's political and economic situations. As discussed previously, success and failure coexist in the process, and most likely China's banking regulation will become increasingly closer to international standards.

Chapter 3

Independence and Accountability of the People's Bank of China: A Legal Perspective

Zhongfei Zhou and Jingwei Li

I.   INTRODUCTION

Central bank independence has received a great deal of attention in literature and in practice. A widespread fear is that the government is focusing on short-term economic growth and has strong incentives for monetary expansions. It would, therefore, be beneficial to the public, and reduce inflationary bias, if monetary authority were to be delegated to an independent central bank that is not subject to elections and shows a longer temporal dimension.[1] Although this type of general consensus in regard to the necessity of central bank independence has been reached, scholars are still divided over many issues of central bank independence, ranging from the concept and types of independence, to the measurement of central bank independence.

Some authors define central bank independence as the absence of political interference[2], while others incorporate freedom from "industry capture' into

---

1. See P. de Sousa, "ndependent and Accountable Central Banks and the European Central Bank", *European Integration Online Papers*, Vol. 2, 2001, no. 9, p. 3, available at <eiop.or.at/eiop/texte/2001-009a.htm>.
2. See R. Lastra, *Central Banking and Banking Regulation* (1996), p. 10. Dr. Lastra posits that (central bank) independence indicates the absence of political interference and implies the

the concept, in addition to independence from political interference.[3] Based on different legal criteria, *de jure* central bank independence is classified into different types.[4] In general, however, these different types consist of similar legal components. A well-documented weakness of central bank independence measurement is different weights being assigned to the same components by authors, as coding legal independence is a subjective process.

In a democratic society, accountability, as a mechanism of checks and balances, is an essential and constituent element of a modern political order. By placing decision and implementation of monetary policy into the hand of independent central bank, individuals must be available to whom central bank must be accountable. Some have argued that delegation of powers to unelected officials can only be acceptable in a democratic society if central banks are – one way or anther – accountable to democratically elected institutions.[5]

China's central bank, the People's Bank of China (PBOC), previously was burdened with central banking and commercial banking functions. With the adoption of the 1995 People's Bank of China Law (the 1995 PBOC Law),[6] the PBOC was granted the pure status of central bank responsible for monetary policies and financial regulation. In 2003, the National People's Congress of China (NPC) split banking regulation function from the PBOC and set up a specific banking regulatory agency, the China Banking Regulatory Commission, while the PBOC is specifically in charge of monetary policy matters. Accordingly, the 1995 PBOC Law and 1995 Commercial Banking Law were amended and a new banking law, the Banking Supervision Law, was adopted in December 2003.[7]

Academic and practical concerns in regard to central bank independence in China are much less drastic than in other countries. In regard to central bank accountability, the issue does not seem to have attracted the attention of scholars and practitioners. For the purpose of this chapter, we will analyze

---

widest possible room for manoeuvre in the conduct of the policies delegated to the central bank.

3. See T. Lybek and J. Morris, *Central Bank Governance: A Survey of Boards and Management*, IMF Working Paper WP/04/226 (December 2004), p. 4, which posits that central bank autonomy implies that the central bank is able to resist undue influences from government, industry, and other interests.

4. For example, Lybek and Morris divide central bank independence into four types: goal autonomy, target autonomy, instrument autonomy, and limited autonomy. See Lybek and Morris, supra note 3, p. 9. Sousa identifies three types, including personal independence, financial or economic independence and political independence. See Sousa, supra note 1, p. 2. Maliszewski simply classifies central bank independence into political and economic independence. See W.S. Maliszewski, *Central Bank Independence in Transition Economies*, CASE Working Paper, LSE (September 2,000), p. 6.

5. J. de Haan et al, *Accountability of Central Banks: Aspects and Quantification* (manuscript, May 1998), p. 3.

6. The Law of the People's Bank of China of 1995 (1995 PBOC Law) (*Zhong Guo Ren Min Yin Hang Fa*), available at <www.pbc.gov.cn/detail.asp?col=310&ID=537>.

7. The Banking Supervision Law of 2003 (*Yin Hang Ye Jian Du Guan Li Fa*), available at <www.cbrc.gov.cn/mod_cn00/jsp/cn004002.jsp?infoID=297&type=1>.

independence and accountability of the PBOC, in light of China's central bank law, based on a comparative study of central bank laws in other countries. The second part of this chapter discusses the independence of the PBOC from the perspective of functional, personal and financial independence. The third part creates a basic legal framework of the accountability of the PBOC by means of a general theory of democratic accountability. Finally, this chapter concludes with a general assessment of independence and accountability of the PBOC.

II.   INDEPENDENCE OF THE PBOC

As discussed in the previous section, central bank independence can be assessed within the various categories covering similar legal components. In this chapter, we will classify central bank independence into functional, personal, and financial independence to assess the *de jure* independence of the PBOC.[8]

II.A.   FUNCTIONAL INDEPENDENCE

Central bank independence is not an end in and of itself, but is a means for a central bank to carry out its mandates designated by laws, independently of any other authority. In the opinion of the authors, functional independence of central bank can be assessed with respect to the autonomy of central bank to determine and achieve the monetary policy objective, and to carry out the bank's other legal functions.

---

8. In some countries, central bank law contains a formal declaration of central bank independence, while very few countries declare central bank independence in their Constitution. In the former case, the degree of central bank independence declared differs somewhat. Article 12 of the German central bank law, for example, provides that the Deutsche Bundesbank shall be independent and not subject to instructions from the Federal government; to the greatest degree possible without prejudice to the bank's tasks, the Bundesbank supports the general economic policy of the Federal government. Article 7 of the 2003 PBOC Law declares that the PBOC, under the leadership of the State Council, independently implements monetary policies, performs its functions and carries out its operations without interference from any local governments, governmental agencies of all levels, social organizations, and individuals. The Philippines and Chile both constitutionize central bank independence. Under the Philippine Constitution, the Congress establishes an independent central monetary authority. See 1987 Constitution of the Philippines, art. 12, sect. 20. The same section also stipulates the qualifications for members of the governing body of the central bank. Chapter 12 of 1980 Chilean Constitution is entitled 'Central Bank', under which some dimensions of central bank independence are stipulated, including a provision that an autonomous body of a technical nature with patrimonial assets of its own, known as the Central Bank, is established. See 1980 Chilean Constitution, art. 97 and 98.

II.A.1.   Monetary Policy

The autonomy to determine and implement the monetary policy objectives most notably reflects a central bank's functional dependence. Lybek and Morris classify the degree of autonomy into four types: goal autonomy, target autonomy, instrument autonomy and limited autonomy.[9]

According to Lybek and Morris, goal autonomy gives the central bank the authority to determine its primary objective from among several objectives stipulated in the central bank law; goal autonomy, therefore, is the broadest degree of autonomy.

With target autonomy, the central bank has one clearly defined primary objective included in the central bank law.

Instrument autonomy implies that the government or the legislature – rather than the central bank – decides on target of the monetary policy, but the central bank can use any instrument necessary to implement the monetary policy target subject to the central bank law.

Limited autonomy indicates that the government determines the monetary policies – objectives and targets – and also influences the implementation of the policy. The central bank, therefore, is regarded essentially as a government agency.

A widely recognized fact is that the Federal Reserve System (or simply the "Fed") in the US typically enjoys goal autonomy. Under the Federal Reserve Act, the Board of Governors of the Fed and the Federal Open Market Committee shall maintain long-run growth of the monetary and credit aggregates commensurate with the economy's long-run potential to increase production, so as to promote effectively the goals of maximum employment, stable prices and moderate long term interest rates.[10] Although, literally speaking, the law does not entrust the Fed with the responsibility for determining the primary objective among these various competing objectives, it is apparent that the law gives the Fed the discretion to deal with the time inconsistency problem which the government may frequently face, to prioritize the objectives and to determine the instruments to achieve the objectives.

The Statute of the European System of Central Banks (ESCB) and of the European Central Bank (ECB) provides, with clarity and legal certainty, that the ESCB has only one primary objective, maintaining price stability.[11] The ESCB, therefore, falls within the scope of target autonomy. With the primary objective of maintaining price stability, the ESCB has the autonomy to define and implement the monetary policy of the Community.[12]

A good example of instrument autonomy is the Reserve Bank of New Zealand. Under the Reserve Bank Act of New Zealand, the central bank's

---

9. Lybek and Morris, supra note 3, pp. 10–13.
10. Federal Reserve Act, art. 225a.
11. See Statute of the ESCB and of the ECB, art. 2.
12. Ibid., art. 3.1.

primary function is to formulate and implement monetary policy directed to the economic objective of achieving and maintaining stability in the general level of prices.[13] The Minister of Finance, in agreement with the Governor,[14] fixes policy targets for the central bank's implementation of its primary functions during the term of the Governor.[15]

Under the 2003 PBOC Law, the PBOC is delegated to formulate and implement monetary policy,[16] the objective of which is to maintain monetary value stability, and in this way facilitate economic growth.[17] However, these types of provisions do not imply that the law entrusts the PBOC with goal autonomy or target autonomy. As a general precondition for the PBOC's operations, the law requires the PBOC to formulate and implement its monetary policy under the leadership of the State Council.[18] More importantly, with respect to the yearly amount of money supply, interest rates, exchange rates and other important matters determined by the State Council, the PBOC can implement its decision only after obtaining the prior approval of the State Council.[19] In practice, 'approval of the State Council' is subject to various interpretations. No matter what the interpretation, however, the requirement for approval indicates that the PBOC has not been entrusted with true independence to determine important monetary policy matters.

In the area of monetary policy implementation, although Article 23 of the 2003 PBOC Law provides that the PBOC can use the monetary policy instruments to implement monetary policy, this does not mean that the PBOC enjoys complete authority to use whatever instruments it sees fit to implement monetary policy. As described in the previous paragraph, a precondition is that formulation and implementation of monetary policy by the PBOC shall be under the leadership of the State Council.[20] In addition, Article 7 of the 2003 PBOC Law stipulates that the PBOC independently implements monetary policy according to law under the leadership of the State Council. The term 'leadership of the State Council' can be interpreted as holding the PBOC accountable to the State Council, but the law does not clarify this point, and leaves the room for direct government involvement in the implementation of monetary policy. In addition, according to the 2003 PBOC Law, the PBOC

---

13. Reserve Bank Act of New Zealand, art. 8.
14. In regard to the sample of the agreement between the Minister of Finance and the Governor, see Lastra, supra note 2, pp. 65–68. The agreement consists of a price stability target, measurement of price stability, deviations from the targets, renegotiation of the targets and implementation.
15. Supra note 13, art. 9(1).
16. 2003 PBOC Law, art. 4(1).
17. Ibid., art. 3.
18. See Ibid., art. 2.
19. Ibid., art. 5. For example, in the PBOC's announcement of an initial 2.1 per cent revaluation and shift to a managed float against a basket of currencies on 20 July 2005, the PBOC indicated that this type of currency reform move was approved by the State Council. See Y. Li, 'Renminbi has been 'floated'', *China Securities Daily* (22 July 2005), p. 1.
20. Ibid., art. 2.

may use the monetary policy instrument determined by the State Council.[21] It might be concluded that the State Council may impose upon the PBOC the monetary policy instrument which it considers fit. As a result, the authority of the PBOC in implementing monetary policy would probably be affected adversely.

In many central banks, there is a monetary policy board or committee. The central bank law usually delegates the determination of money policy to the Policy Board. In the case of goal autonomy, the Policy Board determines the prioritized objective while in the case of target autonomy, it determines the targets.[22] Under both the 1995 PBOC Law and the 2003 PBOC Law, the PBOC is required to set up a monetary policy committee, the functions, structure and working procedures of which are set by the State Council.[23] It should be noted, however, that the monetary policy committee is only an advisory institution with respect to formulation of monetary policy by the PBOC.[24] Its functions are to discuss and provide suggestions on monetary policy matters based on a comprehensive analysis of macro-economic situations and according to the controlling targets for the state's macro-economy.[25] It is apparent that the monetary policy committee within the PBOC does not have any decisive role in monetary policy matters. The 2003 PBOC Law may recognize the disadvantage in the 1995 PBOC Law and amended the latter by adding a sub-article under which the monetary policy committee of the PBOC shall play an important role in the state's macro-economic control, and formulation and adjustment of monetary policy.[26] Without a legitimate status in independently determining monetary policy, however, it remains on paper that the monetary policy committee plays an important role.

Within goal autonomy and target autonomy, in theory, direct government involvement in monetary policy should be eliminated.[27] Consider the EU, for example: in exercising the powers and carrying out the tasks and duties, the ECB, national central banks and even members of their decision-making bodies are prohibited from seeking or taking instructions from Community

---

21. Ibid., art. 23(6).
22. Lybek and Morris argue that a central bank with instrument autonomy would not have a policy board as the policy is set by the government. See Lybek and Morris, supra note 3, p. 21, footnote 20. This argument is valid only if a policy board is defined as independent.
23. 1995 PBOC Law, art. 11; 2003 PBOC Law, art. 12.
24. Regulations on Monetary Policy Committee of the PBOC (*Zhong Guo Ren Min Yin Hang Huo Bi Zheng Ce Wei Yuan Hui Tiao Li*], art. 2. The State Council issued the Regulations on 25 April 1997, available at <www.pbc.gov.cn/huobizhengce/ huobizhengceweiyuan-hui/huobizhengceweiyuanhuitiaoli.asp>.
25. Ibid., art. 3.
26. 2003 PBOC Law, art. 12.
27. It is, however, still reasonable and acceptable that the central bank law requires the central bank to support the general economic policies of the government without prejudice to the primary monetary policy objective, as many central bank laws with goal autonomy and target autonomy, for example, the US Federal Reserve Act, the Act concerning the Deutsche Bundesbank and the Statute of the ESCB and of the ECB, do.

institutions or bodies, from any government of a Member State or from any other body.[28] In addition, the Community institutions and bodies, as well as the governments of the individual Member States, are prohibited from seeking to influence the members of the decision-making bodies of the ECB or of the national central banks.[29] However, several central bank laws permit the participation of the government in central bank meetings. A government is represented at a central bank meeting with right to vote in some cases,[30] and without right to vote in others.[31] In the latter case, some central bank laws grant the government representative the right to postpone a vote.[32]

As discussed previously, the PBOC is not free from government pressure in the area of formulating, and even implementing, monetary policy. That the authority of the monetary policy committee of the PBOC is reduced in formulating monetary policy is not surprising. The monetary policy committee is not only an advisory institution, but also has a strong representation of government officials. Under the Regulations on Monetary Policy Committee of the PBOC, the monetary policy committee consists of the Governor, two Deputy Governors, one deputy Minister of Finance, one deputy director of the National Planning Commission, one deputy director of the National Economic and Trade Commission and other financial regulators.[33] Each member

---

28. Statute of the ESCB and of the ECB, art. 7.
29. Ibid.
30. In the survey conducted by Lybek and Morris, 24 per cent of the 50 central bank laws permit government officials to have right to vote on the policy board. See Lybek and Morris, supra note 3, at 29 (Table 6). Cf: When the Fed was set up in 1913, the government had a direct role. The Secretary of the Treasury and the Comptroller of the Currency represented on the Board of Governors. In 1935, the Congress removed these two officials from the Board of Governors in an effort to strengthen the independence of the Fed from political pressures within the government. S. Cecchetti, 'Central Bank Accountability in Formulating Monetary Policy', Remarks at the Seminar on Current Legal Issues Affecting Central Banks (14 May 1998), pp. 3–4.
31. For example, the Deputy Minister of Finance in Canada is a member of the Board of Directors of the Bank of Canada, but does not have right of vote. See Bank of Canada Act, art. 5(1) (2).
32. For example, under the Bank of Japan Act, the Minister of Finance, while attending the Policy Board meetings for monetary control matters, may request that the Policy Board postpone a vote on monetary control matters until the next Board meeting. The Policy Board shall determine whether or not to accommodate the request. See Bank of Japan of Bank Act, art. 19(2) (3).
33. Regulations on Monetary Policy Committee of the PBOC, art. 5. Due to government agency restructuring, the composition of the current monetary policy committee is quite different from that stipulated in the Regulations. The current monetary policy committee consists of:
    – the Governor;
    – two Deputy Governors;
    – one Deputy General Secretary of the State Council;
    – one deputy Minister of Finance;
    – one Deputy Director of the National Development and Reform Commission;
    – Director of the National Bureau of Statistics;

of the monetary policy committee has right to vote.[34] Therefore, if the PBOC accepts the advice of the monetary policy committee in formulating its monetary policy, the Committee's decision would, no doubt, be affected – whether positively or negatively – by the views of the government officials serving on the monetary policy committee.

Obviously, the PBOC does not have *de jure* goal autonomy and target autonomy in formulating and implementing monetary policy. As a result, it becomes impossible that the PBOC could be given *de facto* goal autonomy and target autonomy. Whether or not the PBOC is entrusted with instrument autonomy is at issue, because legal ambiguity exists in light of the leadership role the State Council plays in implementation of the PBOC of monetary policy. It might be safe to conclude that the PBOC falls between instrument autonomy and limited autonomy.

II.A.2.   Other Functions of the PBOC

With the exception of monetary policy, the PBOC is authorized to fulfil other functions as an issuing banker, government's banker and bankers' banker.[35] Despite its limited authority in formulating monetary policy, the PBOC has a relatively high degree of operating autonomy. Under article 5 of the 2003 PBOC Law, the PBOC has the autonomy to decide and implement any monetary policy matters other than the yearly amounts of money supply, interest rates, exchange rates and other important matters which are determined by the State Council. The central bank law also precludes intervention by local governments, governmental departments of any level, social organizations or

---

     – Director of the State Administration of Foreign Exchange;
     – three Chairpersons of the banking, securities and insurance regulatory commissions;
     – the President of the Bank of China;
     – a professor of finance.

34.   Ibid., art. 15(3).
35.   The PBOC performs the following functions:

     – issues orders and rules related to performance of its functions;
     – formulates and implements monetary policy, according to law;
     – issues and regulates the circulation of Renminbi;
     – regulates and supervises inter-bank borrowing and lending markets, and inter-bank bond markets;
     – administers foreign exchange and supervising inter-bank foreign exchange markets;
     – regulates and supervises gold markets;
     – possesses, administers, and operates foreign exchange reserves and gold reserves;
     – manages the exchequer;
     – maintains orderly operations of payment and settlement system;
     – guides and plans anti-money laundering in financial sectors, and be responsible for monitoring laundered money;
     – handle statistics, surveys, analyses and forecast in terms of financial sectors;
     – participate in international financial activities as the central bank of the state;
     – performs other functions prescribed by the State Council. 2003 PBOC Law, art. 4.

individuals into the PBOC's operations.[36] This point is the result of a lesson learned from traditional weaknesses arising from close relations between the PBOC branches and local governments.[37]

Whether the law can prevent a central bank from providing monetary financing for the government is one of the benchmarks of central bank independence, because separation of monetary and fiscal policy is integral to the central bank's achieving price stability, and without limits for direct financing of government budget deficits, the central bank would face difficulties in achieving price stability. Lending to the government may take two forms: direct credit to the government and purchase of government securities. Ideally, direct credit to the government and purchase of government securities directly from the issuers should be prohibited. However, in some countries, central bank laws permit the central bank to lend directly to the government subject to amount and time limitations.[38] As in many other countries, the 2003 PBOC Law prohibits the PBOC from directly lending to the governments of all levels and buying government bonds and securities.[39] As a monetary policy instrument, the central bank law permits the purchase of government bonds and securities in the open market.[40]

Under the 2003 PBOC Law, the objectives of the PBOC are to maintain financial stability and orderly operations of the payment systems.[41] Both of these objectives are crucial to ensuring price stability. Apparently, the central bank law entrusts the PBOC with a high degree of autonomy to deal with the payment and settlement matters, because the central bank law does not require the PBOC to conduct this job under the leadership of the State Council.[42] With

---

36. 2003 PBOC Law, art. 7.
37. Before 1998, the PBOC was structured in line with the country's administrative areas. Each province, prefecture and county, accordingly, has a central bank branch, sub-branch and agency. Each of these branches of the PBOC is inflicted with heavy interventions from local governments due to the close relations of each branch with local governments in personnel appointment and logistic support. In 1998, the PBOC was restructured into nine regional branches and two local operating branches, with all branches under the vertical leadership of the PBOC headquarters. For information on the history of the PBOC, see the PBOC website at <www.pbc.gov.cn/renhangjianjie/lishiyange.asp> (31 December 2005).
38. For example, the Bank of Canada can make loans or advances for periods not exceeding six months to the government of Canada or the government of any province on the pledge or hypothecation of readily marketable securities or guaranteed by Canada or any province. Bank of Canada Act, art. 18(i). By contrast, the financing of government deficits through direct overdrafts and purchase of debt instruments by European Central Bank or national central banks is prohibited in EU. See Statute of the ESCB and of the ECB, art. 21.1.
39. 2003 PBOC Law, arts. 29 and 30.
40. Ibid., art. 23(5).
41. Ibid., art. 2 and 4(9).
42. Article 27 of the 2003 PBOC Law reads:

'The PBOC shall organize or assist in organizing the payment and settlement system between financial institutions, ordinate the payment and settlement matters between financial institutions, and provide the payment and settlement services, the detailed rules of which shall be laid down by the PBOC'.

respect to the function of maintaining financial stability, China's central bank law does not clearly stipulate that the PBOC must play the lender-of-last-resort role. Whether silence on this issue is the result of the Chinese legislature, following the 'constructive ambiguity' approach, or if the legislature is completely ignoring the issue is unclear.[43] Some clauses in the 2003 PBOC Law, however, relate to the PBOC's lender of last resort and maintenance of financial stability functions. The PBOC can extend to financial institutions specific-purpose loans, which are determined by the State Council.[44] The PBOC can also provide loans to specific non-banking financial institutions subject to the decision of the State Council.[45] It can be concluded that the loans extended by the PBOC in both cases can include emergency liquidity assistance for the purpose of maintaining financial stability.[46] According to the law, these two types of loans can only be issued under the decree of the State Council. In other words, the PBOC has no authority – or limited authority – to determine provision of emergency liquidity loans to banks and other financial institutions.

Article 4 includes an open clause on the functions of the PBOC in the 2003 PBOC Law, to the effect that the PBOC may perform other functions determined by the State Council.[47] While it may be well intended to increase the PBOC's flexibility in performing its central banking functions to adapt itself to the changing situations, governments might use this type of clause to impose on the PBOC non-central banking functions that are more in the nature of myopic government behaviour. This leaves room for the government to intervene in the PBOC, which indeed the government does under the aegis of the law. The weakness can be rectified to some degree by adding that the functions determined by the State Council should be consistent with the central bank law.

---

43. On the PBOC's lender-of-last-resort role, see Z. Zhou, "A Study on Lender of Last Resort on a Comparative Law Basis", *Jurists Review* (*Fa Xue Jia*, Renmin University Law School), Vol. 3, 2005, p. 154.
44. 2003 PBOC Law, art. 22.
45. Ibid., art. 30.
46. Whether a central bank may bail out non-banking financial institution is open to dispute. During the stock market crash of October 1987, Alan Greenspan announced that the Fed was prepared to provide liquidity to securities markets. In June, 2005, the PBOC injected money – the amount of which was not disclosed – into China Galaxy Securities Co. Ltd, a wholly state owned securities company, for the purpose of restructuring the securities firm through Central Huijin Investment Co. Ltd, an investment arm of the PBOC. See *First Finance Daily* (Chinese), 16 June 2005. A PBOC official was reported to have said that the PBOC allocated RMB 10 billion as a start-up fund for financing the proposed Securities Investor Protection Fund. The PBOC official's speech was a response to the rumour that the PBOC would directly provide loans to trouble-incurred securities firms. See *Finance Daily* (Chinese), 19 June 2005.
47. *See* 2003 PBOC Law. art. 4(13).

II.B.   PERSONAL INDEPENDENCE

It has been argued that central bank independence can be further strengthened by personal independence of a central bank. Personal independence is assessed by tenure, nomination, dismissal, remuneration, qualification of the governor and other senior members of a central bank.[48] Many authors propose that the more reasonably the law arranges the personnel affairs of a central bank, the more a central bank can resist undue influences from the government.

II.B.1.   Qualification Requirements

Usually, the governor and other senior members of a central bank are subject to a range of qualification requirements stipulated by the central bank law. The qualification requirements consist roughly of professional, fit and proper, and personal requirements. Professional requirements mean professional skills in the financial or economic sectors. Fit and proper requirements refer to a candidate's integrity. Personal requirements pay attention to age limits and citizenship. The former two requirements are intended to provide guarantees for independence of central bankers to perform their functions as a central banker with professional skills and good moral standing would have greater ability to resist undue influences, while the latter requirements are essentially based on the currency sovereignty concern.

Countries such as Canada introduce two of the three qualification requirements. Under the Bank of Canada Act, the Governor and Deputy Governor must have financial experience, be a Canadian citizen and be under 75 years of age.[49] In a majority of countries, professional qualification requirements are compulsorily required for senior members of a central bank, although the contents of these requirements can vary. Unfortunately, however, both the 1995 and 2003 PBOC Laws are completely silent on the qualification requirements.[50] By contrast, the Regulations on Monetary Policy Committee of the PBOC explicitly stipulate the qualification requirements for the members of the monetary policy committee, including professional, fit and proper, and personal requirements. Under the Regulations, the members of the monetary policy committee must satisfy the following requirements: less than 65 years old, in principle, and a Chinese citizen; fair and honest, and devoted to duties, with no record of violations; and professional skills and experiences in the areas

---

48. In many countries, a central bank has two or three governing bodies, including policy board (monetary policy committee), implementation board, advisory board, supervisory board, and management board. Members of these various boards can have various qualifications, tenure and appointment and dismissal procedures.
49. Bank of Canada Act, art. 6.
50. Article 13 of the 1995 PBOC Law and Article 14 of the 2003 PBOC Law require that the central bank staff abide strictly by their duties and be prohibited from abusing their powers and engaging in malpractices out of their own interests. This provision is not about the requirement for a candidate's qualification.

of macro-economy, finances and banking.[51] Considering that the Governor and two of the Deputy Governors are *ex officio* members of the monetary policy committee, the qualification requirements for the members of the monetary policy committee can be regarded, to some extent, as those for the Governor and Deputy Governor of the PBOC.

II.B.2.   Appointment

To ensure the appointment of a qualified person and depoliticized appointment, a double-veto approach is followed in many central bank laws to appoint the governor and other senior members of a central bank. A double-veto approach means that one body nominates and another body appoints, or one body appoints and another body approves. In many cases, to balance the interests of the various groups, members of a central bank are nominated and appointed by various bodies. In Germany, members of the governing board are appointed by the German chancellor, among whom the president, vice president and two other members are nominated by the Federal government and the other four members are nominated by the Bundesrat in agreement with the Federal government.[52] In Korea, members of the monetary board are recommended individually by several bodies, such as the Minister of Finance and Economy, the Governor of the central bank, the Chairman of the Financial Supervisory Commission and the Chairman of the Korean Chamber of Commission, while the Governor and other members are appointed by the President and the Governor, respectively.[53] The Chairman and Vice Chairman of the US Fed Board are designated by the president, by and with the advice and consent of the Senate, among the members of the Fed Board, who are appointed by the President, by and with the advice and consent of the Senate.[54]

Chinese legislature also applies the double-veto approach to the appointment process. Under the 2003 PBOC Law, the Governor is nominated by the Premier of the State Council, approved by the NPC, and appointed and dismissed by the President of the PRC, while Deputy Governors are appointed and dismissed by the Premier of the State Council.[55] The law, however, is silent on the nomination of the Deputy Governor. In regard to members of the monetary policy committee of the PBOC, the Governor, the Director of the State Administration of Foreign Exchange and the Chairman of the China Securities Regulatory Commission are the *ex officio* members of the monetary policy committee, and other members are nominated by the PBOC or after

---

51.   Regulations on Monetary Policy Committee of the PBOC, art. 8.
52.   Act concerning the Deutsche Bundesbank, art. 7(3).
53.   Bank of Korean Act, art. 13.
54.   Federal Reserve Act, sect. 241 and 242.
55.   2003 PBOC Law, art. 10. The standing committee of the NPC shall decide the governor during recess. See ibid.

consultation with other relevant governmental departments and appointed by the State Council.[56]

It would be an eisegesis if one understands the double-veto arrangement of the 2003 PBOC Law from the perspective of depoliticizing the appointment process.[57] In fact, the candidate for the Governor of the PBOC is decided by the Central Committee of the Chinese Communist Party in advance. So it is impossible for the Governor candidate nominated by the Premier to be vetoed by the NPC which is dominated by the members of the Central Committee of the Chinese Communist Party. Also, the possibility is next to nothing that the NPC would dismiss the Governor during his term of office for reasons of disqualification. This is because if the Governor proved disqualified, the Central Committee of the Chinese Communist Party would discuss and decide the candidate for the Governor before the members of the NPC made a recall motion.

II.B.3.   Dismissal

In many countries, senior members of a central bank cannot be dismissed during their term of office without legal grounds. Protection against arbitrary dismissal of a central banker serve to alleviate the fear of a central banker of being removed by political authorities due to the failure to following the latter's instructions. Grounds for dismissal are clearly stipulated by law and include crimes, serious misconduct, gross negligence, permanent mental or physical incapability, adjudicated bankruptcy and even absence of meetings.[58]

Both the 1995 and 2003 PBOC Laws do not explicitly stipulate the grounds for dismissal of a central banker. However, three articles relate to dismissal grounds. According to the 2003 PBOC Law, a central banker would incur administrative or criminal penalty if they commit any of the following activities:

- provide loans to local governments, governmental departments of all levels, non-banking financial institutions and entities and individuals;
- provide guarantees to entities and individuals;
- use the issuance funds presumptuously;
- divulge state secrets or commercial secrets;
- embezzle property;

---

56. Regulations on Monetary Policy Committee of the PBOC, art. 6.
57. However, it would also be naïve to conclude that the double-veto arrangement in the US could depoliticize the appointment process. According to Chang's study, both the US president and Senate influcnced the Fed's monetary policy through appointment of members of the Fed. See K. Chang, 'The President Versus the Senate: Appointments in the American System of Separated Powers and the Federal Reserve', *Journal of Law, Economics and Organization*, Vol. 17 (October 2001), p. 343.
58. The Bank of England may, with the consent of the Chancellor, remove a person from office as Governor or Deputy Governor or director of the Bank if they are absent from meetings of the court for more than three months without the consent of the court. See Bank of England Act, sch. 1, para. 8.

- take bribes;
- Abuse power;
- Neglect duty.[59]

According to a general understanding, when a central banker is convicted of crime, the banker must be dismissed from office; however, banker cannot be removed from office if administrative penalty is imposed upon them. However, in China's political practices, it is unusual for officials subjected to administrative penalty to remain in their position.

II.B.4.   Term of office

In most central bank laws, the term of office of governors are fixed and is usually longer than the term of the body which nominates or appoints them. It has been argued that the legal guarantee for a longer term of office for governors can reduce the risk of political appointment and prevent reappointment that result from electoral cycles. The term of office for governors and other senior members of a central bank vary, ranging from three years to 14 years or more, with the governor typically serving for five years.[60] For example, the European national central bank statutes must contain a minimum term of office of five years for a governor.[61] Very few central bank laws do not specify the term of office. Silence on the term can indicate an unlimited term. In Denmark, the terms of office of the members of the Board of Governors are indefinite, but are required to retire at 70 years of age.[62]

China is among the few countries which do not stipulate the term of office for governors.[63] No provision on the term, however, does not imply an indefinite term. The deliberate omission can reflect the dilemma of the legislature in balancing between the term of governors and the government. In the opinion of the authors, it might be inappropriate to apply to Chinese practices the basic theory in regard to the security of longer tenure office of governors. Even if the term of office of the Governor of the PBOC is longer than that of the government that nominates the Governor, the Governor still does not dare to refuse the instructions from the government. The reason is because Governors would worry about their political treatment after they stepped down, as their refusal of the government's instructions, which are in many cases decisions of the Communist Party, are often regarded as deviations from the Party's policy.

---

59. 2003 PBOC Law, art. 48, 50 and 51.
60. See Lybek and Morris, supra note 3, p. 36.
61. Statute of the ESCB and of the ECB, art. 14.2.
62. See Lybek and Morris, supra note 3, p. 37.
63. However, under the Regulations on Monetary Policy Committee of the PBOC, the term of office of the members of the monetary policy committee who are the president of a state-owned commercial bank or the expert in finance is two years. Regulations on Monetary Policy Committee of the PBOC, art. 10.

II.B.5.   Conflict of Interest

If central bankers hold simultaneous jobs in other sectors during their term of office in the central bank, a conflict of interest would not be avoided and personal independence would be jeopardized. For this reason, many central bank laws provide for a number of measures to compel central bankers to be fully devoted to their central bank responsibilities. Some central bank laws require central bankers to perform their functions on a full-time basis.[64] Others prohibit a central banker from being an officer or director, or from holding stock in financial institutions, and even in any private and public entity.[65] Some countries go so far as to forbid a central banker from being a member of the parliament and of a political party.[66]

The conflict of interest restriction is extended even further to the activities conducted by central bankers after their term expires. The basic intent of the restriction is to restrain a central banker, after they leave office, from entering into employment with a public or private entity, which could exert influence on the central banker while in office, to avoid being captured, typically in the later term of office. In the US, for example, members of the Fed Board shall be ineligible for two years subsequent to the expiration of their term from holding any office, position or employment in any member bank, if the members fail to complete their entire fourteen-year term.[67]

By the same token, the Chinese central bank law adopts similar measures to avoid conflicts of interest. Under the 2003 PBOC Law, the Governor, Deputy Governors and other staff of the PBOC shall not hold posts concurrently in any other financial institutions, enterprises or funds. The law, however, does not seem to prohibit a central bank staff from holding jobs concurrently in entities

---

64. For example, members of the US Fed Board shall devote all of their time to the business of the Fed Board. See Federal Reserve Act, sec. 241. The Governor or deputy Governor of the Bank of England shall work exclusively for the Bank. See the Bank of England Act, sch. 1. para. 1 and 2. The Governor and deputy Governor shall devote the whole of their time to their duties. See Bank of Canada Act, art. 6(2).

65. For example, members of the US Fed Board shall not be an officer or director or hold stock in banks, trust companies or the Federal Reserve Bank. See Federal Reserve Act, sec. 244. The Governor, Vice Governors, Assistant Vice Governors and staff of the Bank of Korea shall not be engaged in any business on a commercial basis other than their duties, and shall not hold other duties concurrently unless approved by the relevant appointer. See the Bank of Korea Act, art. 41.

66. For example, no Senator or Representative in the US Congress shall be a member of the Fed Board or an officer or director of a Federal Reserve Bank. See the Federal Reserve Act, sec. 303. The appointment of the member of the monetary policy council of National Bank of Poland shall be recalled in the event that the member concerned is a member of a political party or trade union. See the Act on the National Bank of Poland, art. 13. Members of the Monetary Board of the Bank of Korea shall not join a political party and shall not involve in political movements. See the Bank of Korea Act, art. 19.

67. See the Federal Reserve Bank Act, sect. 242.

other than those described previously. In addition, the law does not stipulate any punishment for a staff member who violates the prohibition. It is unclear whether a violating staff member would be dismissed, remain or suffer from some other punishment.

II.C.   FINANCIAL INDEPENDENCE

It is generally argued that, even if a central bank obtains functional and personal independence, the overall independence of the central bank would not be safeguarded if it does not have the autonomy to determine financial resources to fulfil its mandate. Financial independence can be assessed mainly from the perspective of capital subscription and determination of budget.

A central bank must have an initial capital to cover its risks. Determining the appropriate level of a central bank's initial equity capital is highly difficult. The capital can reach up to EUR 2.5 billion, as in Germany, and also can be zero, as in Korea.[68] The capital of the PBOC is subscribed by the state, but the law does not specify the amount of the capital.[69] Understanding that the Ministry of Finance requires that the capital of the PBOC must not be increased or decreased without prior approval of the Ministry of Finance, therefore, is difficult.[70]

The capital of a central bank can be subscribed to by the government solely, the government and non-government investors jointly or non-government investors solely. The capital of the Deutsche Bundesbank is owned by the Federal Republic of Germany.[71] The capital stock of the Bank of Canada is issued to the Minister of Finance to be held by the Minister on behalf of the Queen in right of Canada.[72] The Bank of Japan is owned jointly by the government and non-governmental persons with the government subscription not less than 55 per cent.[73] The share capital of the National Bank of Belgium is subscribed by the Belgian State and any other bearers in the ratio of 50:50.[74] The Swiss central bank is an example of a non-governmental subscriber. Under Swiss National Bank Law, Swiss citizens, Swiss public law corporations as well as general and

---

68. Under the Act in regard to the Deutsche Bundesbank, the central bank's capital amounts to EUR 2.5 billion. See the Act in regard to the Deutsche Bundesbank, art. 2. Under the Bank of Korea Act, the Bank of Korea is a special legal person without capital. See the Bank of Korea Act, art. 2.
69. 2003 PBOC Law, art. 8.
70. Ministry of Finance, Financial System for the PBOC (January 2,000) (*Zhong Guo Ren Min Yin Hang Cai Wu Zhi Du*), art. 10, available at <www.pbc.gov.cn/detail.asp?col=832&ID=59>.
71. See Act in regard to the Deutsche Bundesbank, art. 2.
72. Bank of Canada Act, art. 17(2).
73. Bank of Japan Act, art. 8.
74. Statute of the National Bank of Belgium, art. 3.

limited partnerships and legal entities whose main office is in Switzerland are eligible to be entered in the share register or to subscribe for new shares.[75]

It can be difficult to determine which of the subscription approaches, government subscription and non-government subscription, is best equipped to reduce the risk of undue influences from the subscribers. In theory, both of the approaches could not exempt a central bank from being captured, if possible, by the subscribers as the owner of the central bank, whether it is government capture or industry or private capture. In the opinion of the authors, however, the key to withstanding capture depends on how the law limits the powers of the shareholders. If the law deprives the shareholders, whether government shareholders or non-government shareholders, of voting rights and any other decision-making powers,[76] the door for government, industry and private capture would be closed. In China, although the central bank law says nothing of the voting rights of the Ministry of Finance as the representative of the state shareholder, the Ministry of Finance would not influence the activities of the PBOC in the capacity of the shareholder, because the central bank law clearly prohibits any governmental department from interfering with the central bank's activities.[77]

The government can intervene in a central bank's operations by means of its appropriation channels. Therefore, if a central bank must be funded by the government for its operating expenses, the bank's independence would be impaired. This is also true if a central bank is funded by industry. Fortunately, most central banks are permitted to avail themselves of their own profits to supply funds for their operating expenses. In China, the central bank, without government appropriations, offsets expenditure with its income, according to its budget.[78] In addition, a central bank's independence would be strengthened if the central bank has the power to determine its own budget. The US Fed's independence benefits partly from the autonomy to determine its budget. The Fed has the power to assess member banks to contribute funds for its operating

---

75. National Bank Law of Switzerland, art. 7. Cf, Sousa awards the greatest weight (one point) to the Swiss central bank, because the Swiss government does not own any central bank's capital. See Sousa, supra note 1, at Appendix Table 4.

76. The twelve Reserve Banks of the US are largely owned by the private member banks in their respective Federal Reserve districts. Each member bank subscribes to an amount of stock equal to six per cent of its own paid-up capital stock and surplus in the Reserve Bank in its district. See the Federal Reserve Act, sect. 282. In addition, the Reserve Banks are authorized to offer non-voting stock to the public and to the United States. Ibid., sect. 283 and 285. Clearly, this scheme is not the typical shareholder arrangement in the private sector. Ownership of the Reserve Bank stock does not denote the usual attributes of control and financial interest. See the Board of Governors of the Federal Reserve Systems, *The Federal Reserve System: Purposes and Functions* (7th ed., 1984), p. 10.

77. 2003 PBOC Law, art. 7.

78. See Y. Liang, 'Finance and Accounting of the PBOC', in *Series Lectures on the PBOC Law* (1995), p. 113. Mr. Liang was, at that time, the deputy director of the accounting department of the PBOC.

expenses,[79] and to determine freely the compensation of its employees without being restricted by government service pay scales.[80] By contrast, the PBOC has its own independent budget, separate from the government budget.[81] The PBOC's budget, however, must be subject to the review and approval of the Ministry of Finance.[82] This might force the PBOC to succumb to the Ministry of Finance to obtain the financial means necessary to carry out its tasks.

III.   ACCOUNTABILITY OF THE PBOC

The term 'accountable', as defined in the *Oxford Dictionary of English*, refers not only being held responsible for one's action, but also to be required to justify and explain one's actions and decisions.[83] Central bank accountability, therefore, implies that the central bank must explain, justify and assume responsibility for its performance to the body that delegates authority to the central bank.

Some have argued that central bank accountability and independence are contradictory, and that a completely independent central bank is lack of accountability, and vice versa. This argument seems to mischaracterize the relationship between central bank independence and accountability. We agree with the view proposed by Quintyn and Taylor that independence and accountability is complementary:[84] central bank independence and accountability are not of a trade-off nature.[85] A fully independent central bank may still have a high degree of accountability, while a less-independent central bank may be unaccountable. Important to note, here, is that 'accountable to whom' must not be interpreted as 'control by whom', or even 'intervention by whom'. Accountability is a mechanism of checks and balances exerted by the accountee to accountor, which depends, to a great extent, on the legal arrangements. Properly designed legal arrangements must include mechanisms for granting a central bank sufficient independence, while holding the central bank accountable for

---

79. Federal Reserve Act, sect. 243.

80. Ibid., sect. 244. The Fed's operations are not included in the budget, nor does the President review the budget. Executive Office of the President of the US, *Budget of the United States Government, Fiscal Year 1999* app. 1165 (1998), cited from S.A. Ramirez, 'Depoliticizing Financial Regulation', *William and Mary Law Review* (February 2,000), Vol. 41, no. 109.

81. 2003 PBOC Law, art. 38.

82. Ibid. See also Ministry of Finance, Financial Administration System for the PBOC, art. 3 and 41. Cf: The US Fed has occasionally been subject to government budgetary oversight and audit; however, the general rule is that the Fed need not submit its budget annually to Congress for approval. See Ramirez, supra note 80, p. 525.

83. See *Oxford Dictionary of English* (2nd ed., Revised, Oxford University Press, 2005), p. 11.

84. M. Quintyn and M.W. Taylor, *Regulatory and Supervisory Independence and Financial Stability*, IMF Working Paper (WP/02/46, March 2002), no. 39, p. 29.

85. Haan et al argue that the relationship between central bank independence and democratic accountability is characterized not primarily by a trade-off between the two principles. Although some aspects of accountability can interfere with central bank independence, the concepts are definitely not at odds with each other. Haan et al, supra note 5, p. 20.

its delegated tasks. For these reasons, we disagree with the argument by other authors that a central bank with goal autonomy is unaccountable.[86] Where properly designed legal arrangements are available, any central bank, whether with goal autonomy, target autonomy, instrument autonomy, or with limited autonomy, can have a high degree of accountability.

The basic contents of accountability include accountable for what, to whom and how to be accountable. Accordingly, central bank accountability consists of performance accountability, institutional accountability and instrument accountability.

III.A.   PERFORMANCE ACCOUNTABILITY

Performance accountability refers to the extent to which the objectives of a central bank, in terms of monetary policy and other delegated functions, are achieved. In a democracy, only elected politicians have the power to determine the monetary policy objectives and other functions of a central bank. Typically, these objectives and functions are explicitly defined in the form of law. Legitimacy of the objectives and functions is both a precondition of central bank accountability and a yardstick to evaluate central bank accountability. For this reason, we argue that the monetary policy objectives and functions of a central bank must be determined by the legislature, in the form of law, rather than by the government. The 2003 PBOC law includes an open clause, in which the PBOC must perform other functions determined by the State Council. As discussed previously,[87] this provision not only increases the possibility of government interventions, but also reduces the legitimacy of the PBOC accountability.

Multiple objectives are criticized, first as having a lack of accountability for ambiguous ranking, and second as being difficult to evaluate central bank performance. In our opinion, however, the two justifications are problematic. Legal certainty with respect to central bank objectives is the utmost guarantee for central bank accountability. Whether in the case of multiple objectives – and whether or not the objectives are prioritized – or a single objective, the law-based objectives, in themselves, provide a sound basis for holding a central bank accountable for its pursuing objectives. With multiple objectives, the law grants the central bank the right to determine the objective among several unranked objectives. The US Fed, for example, does not have

---

86. Eijffinger and Hoeberichts conclude that the argument that central bank independence and accountability are contradicting is only correct as far as decisions in regard to the ultimate goal of, and final responsibility for, monetary policy. For this reason, they argue that a central bank must not have goal independence. S. Eijffinger and M. Hoeberichts, *Central Bank Accountability and Transparency: Theory and Some Evidence*, Discussion Paper 6/00 Economic Research Centre of the Deutsche Bundesbank (November 2,000), p. 1. Cf. Briault found an inverse relationship between central bank accountability and central bank goal independence in evaluating 14 central banks. Cited from Sousa, supra note 1, p. 7.
87. See supra note 47 and accompanying text.

explicit hierarchical objectives: stability and growth of the economy, maximum employment, stable prices and the soundness of the financial and payments systems.[88] These broadly defined and unranked objectives do not imply a lack of accountability; instead, it seems to us to be just the contrary: that the US Fed is not only held accountable for its choice of objective, but also held more accountable in the case of choosing two or more objectives than in the case of a single objective. The ECB, for example, is labelled a democratic deficit for the ECB's power to decide under what circumstances the objective of supporting the general economic policies can prevail over the objective of price stability.[89] Misunderstanding can arise in regard to the ECB's power to determine the objective. As a matter of fact, there is a hierarchy of objectives stipulated by the Statute of the ESCB and of the ECB, under which the primary objective of the ESCB is to maintain price stability and without prejudice to the primary objective, it is to support the general economic policies in the Community.[90] This clear hierarchy implies that other objectives can be pursued by the ESCB only when they do not conflict with the primary objective, and in most cases the ECB is bound to the primary objective. This is why Lybek and Morris posit that the ECB has only target autonomy with which a central bank has one clearly defined primary objective stipulated in the law,[91] and the ECB is less accountable in what concerns to the 'final responsibility for monetary policy' aspect, and more accountable in the case of the 'ultimate objectives'.[92] As with the Statute of the ESCB and of the ECB, the 2003 PBOC Law stipulates the objective of the PBOC is to maintain monetary value stability so as to facilitate economic growth.[93] In this sense, the PBOC is held accountable for its ranked statutory objectives.

With respect to central bank performance evaluation, it is understandable that a single objective with a quantified target particularly enables the accountor to evaluate central bank performance more effectively. The typical example is the Policy Target Agreement of the Reserve Bank of New Zealand under which the Governor agrees with the government a tight target range for inflation. No doubt, easiness and effectiveness to evaluate central bank helps enhance central bank accountability. However, lack of such a yardstick to evaluate the

---

88. See Federal Reserve Act, sec. 225a.
89. See Haan et al., supra note 5, p. 4, which argues that the ECB has some room for manoeuvre with respect to the goals of monetary policy. The ECB has too much goal independence.
90. See the Statute of the ESCB and of the ECB, art. 2. The former part of article 2 of the Statute of the ESCB and of the ECB reads:

'In accordance with Article 105(1) of this Treaty [establishing the European Community], the primary objective of the ESCB shall be to maintain price stability. Without prejudice to the objective of price stability, it shall support the general economic polices in the Community with a view to contributing to the achievement of the objectives of the Community as laid down in Article 2 of this Treaty [establishing the European Community]'.

91. *See* Lybek and Morris, supra note 3, p. 11.
92. Sousa, supra note 1, p. 8.
93. 2003 PBOC Law, art. 3.

performance of central bank does not in itself mean lack of accountability. Furthermore, instead of facilitating performance control, a wrongly determined evaluation yardstick would undermine central bank accountability.

In our opinion, heavier government interventions in central bank activities would make it hard to hold a central bank accountable for its performance as the central bank performance and the government behaviour are blurred. In China, the government plays a crucial role in determining monetary policies and other important central bank activities as discussed above. For example, the PBOC has provided billions of loans to trouble financial institutions, most of which were extended under the order of the government and became non-performing loans. Obviously, it is unfair to hold the PBOC responsible for these loans. We tend to conclude that a less independent central bank may not always have more accountability, rather may have less accountability.

III.B.   INSTITUTIONAL ACCOUNTABILITY

When a central bank is delegated authority, it must be subject to checks and balances by any of the parties involved. In a democracy, these involved parties are three branches of government: legislature (parliament), executive and judiciary.

Given that price stability is a public good, a central bank is, in the broadest sense, to the public at large. However, the public would not directly check the performance of a central bank, and instead elect a parliament to represent their interests. For this reason, central bank accountability relates first and foremost to parliament. Parliament holds the central bank accountable through its lawmaking powers, described as *ex ante* accountability and *ex post* accountability.[94] By *ex ante* accountability, this implies that the parliament has the power to grant the legitimacy of the central bank's existence, determine the objectives and mandate of central bank, and set the rules with which central bank must comply. *Ex post* accountability refers to a mechanism whereby parliament has the power to change the legal basis of the central bank, and reformulate the objectives, mandate and rules of central bank.[95] To enhance *ex ante* and *ex post* accountability, parliament requires the central bank to establish institutionalized contacts with itself, most often in the form of law, so that parliament has the opportunity to review and assess the performance of the central bank on a regular basis.

Institutionalized contacts take various forms. Central bank law generally requires a central bank to submit, on a regular – at least annual – basis, its report

94. See Haan et al, supra note 5, p. 6.
95. Some have argued that the mere threat of a change to the law will ensure that even independent central banks will, in general, be in accordance with the wishes of elected politicians. See ibid., p. 13.

directly to parliament[96] or to the Minister of Finance,[97] or to appear before the parliament.[98] Under the 2003 PBOC Law, the PBOC shall submit to the Standing Committee of the NPC its reports in regard to monetary policies and operations of financial sectors.[99] In addition, because few politicians of the NPC possess expertise in finance and economy and have difficulty understanding these reports, the PBOC, as a matter of practice, reports implementation of monetary policies to the special committee on finance and economy of the NPC on a quarterly basis. Although no law requires that the PBOC must attend the inquiries of the NPC, a common practice is for the Governor to answer the *ad hoc* inquiries made by the representatives or special committee of the NPC.

Traditionally, central banks have been accountable to the government, in particular where a central bank has a performance contract with the government. It has been argued that an overriding mechanism of the government would enhance central bank accountability. The overriding mechanism includes three types: the right to issue instructions, the right to approve, suspend, annul or defer decisions, and the right to censor decisions on legal grounds.[100] The UK Treasury, after consultation with the Governor, may by order give the Bank of England directions on monetary policy, if satisfied that the directions are required in the public interest and by extreme economic circumstances.[101] It seems to us that this type of overriding mechanism is indistinguishable from government interventions. In China, the government can, according to the central bank law, be heavily involved in the determination and implementation of monetary policies and other important central bank activities. As discussed

---

96. The US Fed Board, for example, shall transmit to the Congress independent written reports. Federal Reserve Act, sect. 225a. The US Fed Board shall annually make a full report of its operations to the Speaker of the House of Representatives. Federal Reserve Act, sect. 247.
97. The Bank of Japan, for example, shall, approximately every six months, prepare and submit to the Diet through the Minister of Finance, a report on the Policy Board's decisions in regard to monetary control matters. Bank of Japan Act, art. 54. The Bank of England Act provides that the Chancellor shall lay copies of every report before Parliament after receiving the annual report submitted by the Bank of England. Bank of England Act, sect. 4(1) (6).
98. The Governor of the Bank of Korea, for example, shall attend and reply where the National Assembly or any of the Assembly's committee requests the Governor to attend, in connection with the report submitted. Bank of Korea Act, art. 96.
99. 2003 PBOC Law, art. 6.
100. See Haan et al., supra note 5, p. 6.
101. Bank of England Act, sect. 19 (1). Similar examples include the Bank of Canada Act and the Bank of Korea Act. Under the Bank of Canada Act, if the Bank of Canada and the Minister of Finance have different opinions on monetary policy, the Minister can, after consultation with the Governor, and with approval of the Governor in Council, give to the governor of the bank a written directive on monetary policy, and the bank shall comply with that directive. Bank of Canada Act, art. 14(2). According to the Bank of Korea Act, where any decision taken by the Monetary Board is judged to contradict the government economic policy, the Ministry of Finance and Economy may request the Monetary Board to reconsider decision. Bank of Korea Act, art. 92.

previously, we argue that the governmental involvement in the PBOC activities reflects the low degree of the PBOC's independence; and at the same time does not indicate the PBOC accountability to the government.[102] However, the government can, of course, use the overriding mechanism as a stick to achieve accountability. In the sense of enhancing accountability, in our opinion, the law must clearly provide not only for the detailed contents of an overriding mechanism, but also for the conditions and procedures for applying them. Legal certainty on the overriding mechanism can provide guarantees for the mechanism not to be used as a tool for political intervention by the government, but rather as a tool for holding the central bank to greater accountability. By contrast, because the government's instruction and approval of the PBOC's important activities are never taken as the overriding mechanism for enhancing accountability of the PBOC, it is not unusual that the central bank law does not stipulate any conditions and procedures for the government's instruction and approval.

An agency functions through its decisions and activities. Those who are affected by the agency's decisions and activities, therefore, should have the right of legal redress in court. Judiciary accountability serves to ensure that a central bank takes action consistent with its governing statutes and observes the due process requirements. However, particular areas of a central bank action are essentially non-reviewable. In the US, for example, the Fed's power over monetary policy probably is not reviewable, because these decisions are committed to the agency's discretion and it is unlikely that any particular person could establish any statutory 'core of interests' intended for protection.[103]

In China, under the Law of Administrative Procedure, the court only accepts the lawsuit against specific administrative acts (*juti xingzheng xingwei*) of an administrative agency, while abstract administrative acts (*chouxiang xingzheng xingwei*) fall outside the jurisdiction of a court. It is generally accepted that an abstract administrative act is one made by an agency with a general binding force against unspecific persons and matters, and a specific administrative act is one with a specific binding force against specific persons and matters. Obviously, the PBOC's decisions and activities on monetary policy are one of the abstract administrative acts and are free of judicial review. In addition to monetary policy, the PBOC is authorized to perform some specific administrative acts, for example, issuing permits to trade in bond and

---

102. C.f. Haan et al. argue that the simple fact that government can override the central bank does not necessarily add to the democratic accountability of monetary policy. See Haan et al., supra note 5, p. 7.

103. Ramirez, supra note 80, p. 528. In *Association of Data Processing Serv. Org. v. Camp* (1970), the judge set forth the 'legal interest' test that plaintiffs must satisfy to sue an agency. Ibid., no. 129. In *Committee for Monetary Reform v. Board of Governors of the Fed. Reserve Bd.* (1985), it was held that members of a group of private interest harmed by monetary policy lacked the standing to challenge Fed action or structure. Ibid., no. 130. In *Reuss v. Balles* (1978), it was held that a Congressperson lacked the standing to challenge the composition of the Federal Open Market Committee of the Fed. Ibid., no. 130.

foreign exchange markets. In the event that a person challenges the PBOC's action in this regard, this person can sue the PBOC.

III.C.   INSTRUMENT ACCOUNTABILITY

Instrument accountability refers to transparency of central bank performance. Transparency is a guarantee mechanism for democratic accountability of a central bank. Without transparency, the effectiveness of other arrangements concerning central bank accountability is discounted. Because transparency must not be left to the discretion of the central bank, the central bank law must prescribe particular procedures with respect to the transparency of the central bank performance.[104] To enhance transparency, generally speaking, the central bank must prescribe the requirements for the publication of the report on central bank performance and of the minutes of central bank meetings.

Whether, and to what extent, the central bank explains its performance in the report to be disclosed publicly varies among the central bank laws. The Bank of England Act clearly prescribes the details of the published annual report, which contains a review of the Bank's performance in relation to its objectives and strategy, and a statement of the Bank's objectives and strategy,[105] and the published quarterly report[106], which contains a review of the monetary policy decisions, an assessment of the developments in inflation and an indication of the expected approach to meeting the Bank's objectives.[107] The Statute of the ESCB and of the ECB obliges the ECB to publish reports on the activities of the ESCB at least quarterly.[108] Whether, and to what extent, the ECB will include details on the past performance and the future development of monetary policy is left to the ECB's discretion. Under the 2003 PBOC Law, the PBOC shall prepare and publish its annual report.[109] In practice, the PBOC publishes the report on implementation of monetary policy on a quarterly basis. According to the PBOC, the report focuses on how the PBOC implements monetary policy to achieve the monetary policy objective, which is determined by the State Council. The report contains five parts:

   – a summary of monetary credits;
   – implementation of monetary policy;
   – an analysis of financial markets;
   – an analysis of macro-economy; and
   – projections and prospects.

---

104. See Eijffinger and Hoeberichts, supra note 86, p. 3.
105. Bank of England Act, sect. 4(3), (4)(b) and (5).
106. The period may not be quarterly and be determined jointly by the Treasury and the Monetary Policy Committee. Ibid., sect. 18(3)(b).
107. Ibid., sect. 18(2).
108. Statute of the ESCB and of the ECB, art. 15.1.
109. 2003 PBOC Law, art. 41.

Some have argued that transparency will be improved if the minutes of the central bank meetings are made public.[110] The reasoning is that publication of minutes would enable the public to follow the course of debate among the central bank members and understand why decisions are made,[111] to more easily hold central bank members accountable for their behaviour. In many countries, to provide real-time information to the public, the central bank first releases to the public a brief statement in regard to the monetary-policy decisions taken, and several weeks later publishes the minutes to describe the reasons behind the decisions. Under the Bank of England Act, for example, the Bank of England shall publish a statement as to the actions decided at the meeting as soon as practicable after each meeting of the monetary policy committee, except if immediate publication of the decision at the meeting would likely impede or frustrate the achievement of the intervention's purpose,[112] and before the end of the period of six weeks, beginning with the day of the meeting publish minutes of the meeting.[113] The 2003 PBOC Law does not require the PBOC to publish the minutes of its meetings. However, as a matter of practice, the PBOC has published the summary of its meetings some time after its meetings. For example, the PBOC published a brief of the quarterly meetings of the monetary policy committee soon after the meetings. This type of brief usually lists the achievements made, a summary of current economic situations and actions to be taken in the implementation of future monetary policy. Although only those who have expertise in economy and finance could catch different, perhaps important, information between the lines of the briefs, these briefs indeed provide a comparative means for the public to assess the PBOC's performance.

Whether voting records must be revealed is still open to discussion. Some authors argue that the publication of votes could prevent poor central bankers from adopting inappropriate policies and ensure high-quality independent judgments, because they want to maximize respect for their own professional judgment and integrity.[114] Other leading central banks, including the US Fed

---

110. Some substitutions apply for publishing the meeting minutes. The Reserve Bank of New Zealand does not publish any minutes. The reason is because the Governor, rather than a collegial body, makes monetary policy decisions. Under Article 10.4 of the Statute of the ESCB and of the ECB, the proceedings of the meetings of the Governing Council shall be confidential, and the Governing Council can decide to make the outcome of its deliberations public. In practice, the European Parliament calls for a summary of the minutes of the Governing Council meetings to be published, and the Governing Council holds a press conference immediately after the Governing Council meetings, in which the latest decisions are explained.

111. J. von Hagen, *The ECB: Transparency and Accountability* (manuscript, December 1998), p. 7.

112. Bank of England Act, sect. 14(1) and (2).

113. Ibid., sect. 15(1).

114. See Hagen, supra note 111, p. 8; C. Randzio-Plath and T. Padoa-Schioppa, *The European Central Bank: Independence and Accountability* (Center for European Integration Studies, Policy Paper B16, 2,000), p. 17.

and the Bank of Japan, have now also taken this view.[115] The Bank of England is required to include the voting preference of members in the published minutes.[116] By contrast, other authors fear that making voting records public could undermine the credibility of a decision taken by only a slight majority and induce central bankers to bow to short-sighted political pressure.[117] The Statute of the ESCB and of the ECB takes the view of not requiring publication of voting records. In our opinion, disclosing how individual central bankers vote could expose them to the public's surveillance and, therefore, make the central bankers more accountable to the public.

IV.   CONCLUDING REMARKS

Fears that the central bank would be captured by the government and interest groups, and would not be subject to the usual political checks and balances if the central bank were to become highly independent have lead to the need to ensure central bank independence and accountability. A widespread perception is that independence and accountability are of a trade-off nature and ultimately incompatible: more independence means less accountability, and vice versa. As discussed previously, central bank independence and accountability is complementary and mutually reinforcing. Both are law-based. Legal arrangements are a starting point of central bank independence and accountability. However, *de jure* independence and accountability do not reflect *de facto* independence and accountability. Nor do legal independence and accountability guarantee that a central bank will be free from government or interest group interventions and be accountable to the accountees.

Only when legal arrangements for central bank independence and accountability fit into the political culture and system of a country, can they yield policy effectiveness. Some arrangements which take effect in other countries may be useless in facilitating independence and accountability in China. The proposal that security of longer-tenures of office for the central bank Governor, for example, would avoid political appointment of the Governor and enhance central bank independence might be invalid in China. As a member of the Communist Party, a Governor of the PBOC who refuses the instructions of the State Council would be eventually subject to the discipline by the Communist Party. The longer term of the Governor, therefore, would be unable to alleviate the Governor's concerns about being disciplined when the Governor does not comply with the government's instructions. The effectiveness of legal arrangements for central bank accountability depends, to a large extent, on

115. See Randzio-Plath and Padoa-Schioppa, ibid., p. 17.
116. Bank of England Act, sect. 15(4).
117. See J.-E. Sturm, *Accountability, Democracy and Central Bank Independence: The Case of Euro Area*, Paper for the Seminar on International Monetary Integration (24 March 2005), p. 13.

the supporting mechanisms, such as the transparency of political process, the traditional separation between the government, central bank and industries and the monitoring role of the media. The PBOC which lacks independence, therefore, may face increased interventions from the government rather than enjoy more accountability in light of the absence of the supporting mechanisms in China, in addition to incomplete legal arrangements for PBOC accountability.

According to the *de jure* standards discussed in this chapter, in the area of formulating and implementing monetary polices, the PBOC falls between instrument independence and limited independence, and is granted a relatively high degree of autonomy to perform other central banking functions. Even if the PBOC has a low degree of independence, it is still less accountable to the State Council, NPC and the public. To improve the PBOC independence and accountability, the first step we suggest is to reform the central bank law based on the prevailing standards, in combination of China's particular political and economic regimes.

Chapter 4

Implementation of China's WTO Commitments: The Compliance Issue in Banking

Wei Wang

I.　　　INTRODUCTION

The development of China's banking law post-WTO is generally discussed in the part of introduction of this book. This chapter focuses more closely on the issue of the compliance of China's banking law post-WTO with the WTO agreements and China's WTO commitments. The chapter examines whether China has seriously and carefully implemented its WTO commitments related to banking services, as claimed by the CBRC.[1]

II.　　　IMPLEMENTATION OF THE WTO AGREEMENTS IN CHINA

The PRC Constitution is silent on how to implement international treaties in China. It is unclear from Chinese existing laws whether China has adopted a

---

1.　Speech of L. Mingkang, Chairman of the CBRC, at the Press Conference on 5 December 2005, <www.cbrc.gov.cn/mod_cn00/jsp/cn004002.jsp?infoID=1767&type=1>; see also *Trade Policy Review*, Report by the People's Republic of China, WT/TPR/G/161, para. 51 (17 March 2006) (China stated that all market access commitments in the field of trade in services have been implemented through the revision and adoption of sector-specific laws, administrative regulations and department rules).

Barth et al., *Financial Restructuring and Reform in Post-WTO China*, pp. 105–122.
© 2007 Kluwer Law International BV, The Netherlands.

monism (direct application of treaties) or dualism (transformation of treaties into municipal law)[2] or something in between[3] when applying international law.

Article 142 of the General Principles of the Civil Law of the People's Republic of China (*Zhonghua Renmin Gongheguo Minfa Tongze*) stipulates that an international treaty shall prevail if a conflict arises between the international treaty concluded by or acceded to China and a China's civil law.[4] In addition, other civil laws apply that contain similar sentences that give the prevailing status of international treaties over domestic law when in conflict, for example, the PRC Maritime Law (*Haishangfa*),[5] the PRC Negotiable Instrument Law (*Piaojufa*),[6] and the PRC Civil Procedure Law (*Minshi Susongfa*).[7] However, these rules do not apply to non-civil law matters, for example, administrative litigations. These rules also do not necessarily require direct application of international treaties in the PRC, because the rules only touch upon the conflicting situations between international treaties and the PRC civil law. The main body of the PRC law in regard to the WTO refers to administrative law, from which one cannot find a similar sentence such as Article 142 of the PRC General Principles of the Civil Law. Despite the lack of a statute regulating the application of the WTO agreements in China, in practice, the WTO agreements do not seem to have a direct effect in China. Generally speaking, a Chinese court (People's Court) cannot invoke a WTO agreement or a provision in the China Accession Protocol as the legal basis of making a judgment.

After China entered the WTO, the Supreme People's Court attempted, given the sluggishness of the legislature, to resolve the issue of implementation of WTO agreements through judicial interpretations. In August 2002, the Supreme People's Court promulgated the first judicial interpretation on administrative cases related to the WTO – *Rules on Relevant Issues*

---

2. For the general introduction of the differences of monism and dualism, see Ian Brownlie, *Principles of Public International Law* (6th ed., Oxford University Press, 2003) pp. 31–33. For the terms 'direct application' and 'transformation', see John H. Jackson, *Status of Treaties in Domestic Legal Systems: a Policy Analysis*, in *The Jurisprudence of GATT and the WTO: Insights on Treaty Law and Economic Relations* (Cambridge University Press 2000), pp. 328–329, note 1 and 3, discussions of 'direct application' refers to a 'direct', statute-like role in the domestic legal system of the international treaty, while 'transformation' means to place a general treaty norm into the domestic jurisprudence.
3. See J.H. Jackson and A.O. Sykes, *Questions and Comparisons*, in *Implementing the Uruguay Round* (Clarendon Press, Oxford 1997), pp 457 and 461, which argues that the domestic legal effect of the international obligation is uncertain in many countries with an in-between attitude.
4. General Principles of the Civil Law of the People's Republic of China was promulgated on 12 April 1986 and took effect as of 1 January 1987.
5. See the PRC Maritime Law, art. 268. The PRC Maritime Law was enacted by the 28th meeting of the Standing Committee of the 7th NPC on 7 November 1992 and took effect on 1 July 1993.
6. See the PRC Negotiable Instrument Law, art. 96. The PRC Negotiable Instrument Law was enacted by the 13th Meeting of the Standing Committee of the 8th NPC on 10 May 1995 and took effect on 1 January 1996.
7. See the PRC Civil Procedure Law, art. 238. The PRC Civil Procedure Law was enacted by the 4th session of the 7th NPC on 9 April 1991 and took effect on the same day.

in Adjudicating Administrative Litigations Relating to International Trade.[8] Article 7 of the *Rules on Relevant Issues in Adjudicating Administrative Litigations relating to International Trade* actually excludes the WTO agreements from the legal basis of making a judgment by listing an exhaustive legal sources to be invoked by the Chinese courts, which include only 'laws, administrative regulations and relevant local regulations'. The other two judicial interpretations that immediately followed the *Rules on Relevant Issues in Adjudicating Administrative Litigations Relating to International Trade* reiterate the exhaustive legal sources to be invoked by the Chinese courts, without specifying any WTO agreement.[9] The Chief Justice of China – who is also the Chairman of the Supreme People's Court – Xiao Yang, expressly stated that WTO rules must not be directly implemented in the Chinese judicial system.[10]

The China's legislature also indirectly accepts the mode of transformation application of the WTO agreements. China's then MOFCOM Minister, Lü Fuyuan, when explaining the reasons for revising China's Foreign Trade Law to the Standing Committee of the National People's Congress, stated that 'China, after entry to the WTO, fulfils its WTO commitments by way of transforming those commitments and WTO rules into China's domestic laws'.[11] This explanation did not meet any objection from the National People's Congress.

From an academic perspective, the prevailing view is that the WTO agreements must be implemented by way of transforming into China's domestic laws.[12] This view is also supported by the statement of a representative of China in paragraph 67 of the Working Party Report: 'The WTO Agreements would

8. *Fashi* [2002] no. 27, effective as of 1 October 2002.
9. See Article 6 of *the Rules of Relevant Issues of Application of Laws in Adjudicating Administrative Cases concerning Countervailing* (promulgated by the Supreme People's Court on 21 November 2002, and came into force on 1 January 2003, *Fashi* [2002] no. 36; See also Article 6 of *the Rules of Relevant Issues of Application of Laws in Adjudicating Administrative Cases concerning Anti-dumping* (promulgated by the Supreme People's Court on 21 November 2002 and came into force on 1 January 2003, *Fashi* [2002], no. 35.
10. X. Yang, *A Speech at a Trial Work Seminar for the People's Courts (Renqing Xinxingshi, Yingjie Xintiaozhan, Wei Rushihou de Jingji Fazhan he Shehui Jinbu Tigong Sifa Baozhang – zai Renmin Fayuan Rushihou Shenpan Gongzuo Zhuotanhui shang de Jianghua)*, 20 November 2001, in *World Trade Organization and the People's Court* (*Rushi Yu Renmin Fayuan*) 5, edited by the Political Department of the Supreme People's Court (The People's Court Press, 2002).
11. L. Fuyuan, 'Explanation on the Revised Draft Foreign Trade Law of the People's Republic of China', address at the 6th meeting of the Standing Committee of the 10th National People's Congress, 22 December 2003, *Gazette of the Standing Committee of the National People's Congress of the People's Republic of China* (2004), no. 4, p. 254.
12. See M. Yaping and X. Yifan, *The Issue of Implementing WTO agreements in China* (*WTO Xieding zai Woguo Guonei Shiyong de Wenti*), in the *Study of Contemporary International Law: China and International Law in the 21st Century* (Shanghai People's Publishing House, 2002), pp. 215–216, which strongly objects the direct application of the WTO agreements based on the theory of national sovereignty; and to Z. Xin, *Domestic Effect of the WTO Agreement in China: Trend and Implications* (2002) 3 J.W.I. 913, 934; and H. Liyu, 'The Implementation of WTO rules and China's Domestic Legislations' (*WTO Guize de Shiyong yu Zhongguo Guonei Lifa*) [2004] *Chinese Journal of International Economic Law* 4 (*Guoji Jingjifa Luncong*), pp. 218 and 228. See also D.C. Clarke, 'China's Legal System and the

be implemented by China in an effective and uniform manner through revising its existing domestic laws and enacting new ones fully in compliance with the WTO Agreement'.[13] In fact, paragraph 67 of the Working Party Report was the main reason for the exclusion of WTO agreements as applicable laws in administrative litigations by Supreme People's Court.[14] Although the transformation method will increase transaction costs, as compared with the method of direct application,[15] the method could give China more room to manoeuvre when fulfilling its WTO commitments.

III.   CHINA'S BANKING LAW FRAMEWORK

China's banking law framework is composed of four tiers, banking laws, in the narrow sense, made by the NPC and its Standing Committee; banking administrative regulations by the State Council; banking rules by the CBRC; and other banking normative documents by the CBRC and the PBC.[16]

III.A.   BANKING LAWS

On 27 December 2003, the Standing Committee of the NPC passed China's first separate banking supervision law, the Law on Banking Regulation and

---

WTO: Prospects for Compliance', *Wash. U. Global Stud. L. Rev.* 2, pp. 97 and 99, arguing that China's WTO obligations will not become Chinese domestic law until Chinese domestic law incorporates those obligations.

13. See para. 67 of the *Report of the Working Party on the Accession of China*. However, the issue of implementation of WTO agreements by China has not been completely resolved. First, the PRC Constitution is silent with respect of the implementation of international treaty in China. Second, paragraph 67 of the *Report of the Working Party on the Accession of China* has no binding force because it is not contained in paragraph 342 as commitments incorporated in China's Accession Protocol. Third, paragraph 68 of the *Report of the Working Party on the Accession of China* , which is contained in paragraph 342 as binding commitments, specifies that, if administrative regulations, departmental rules or other measures were not in place within expected time frames, authorities would still honour China's obligations under the WTO Agreement and Protocol. Does that mean China's courts would directly invoke WTO agreements or articles if there were no corresponding domestic regulations or rules? There is no clear answer.

14. L. Guoguang, Speech at a News Conference, in the *People's Court Daily* (*Renmin Fayuan-bao*), 30 August 2002. Li Guoguang was one of the vice chairmen of the Supreme People's Court of P.R.C. at that time.

15. See J.H. Jackson and A.O. Sykes, *Questions and Comparisons*, in Implementing the Uruguay Round 457 (Clarendon Press, Oxford 1997), pp. 461–463.

16. Interesting to note is that the CBRC and the PBC occasionally jointly issue banking rules with some ministries or commissions under the State Council. For example, the PBC, CBRC and China Securities Regulatory Commission (CSRC) jointly issued the Measures for Administration of Pilots of Fund Management Companies Established by Commercial Banks (*Shangye Yinhang Sheli Jijin Guanli Gongsi Shidian Guanli Banfa*) on 20 February 2005, 'PBC, CBRC and CSRC Decree' [2005] *Gazette of the PBC,* no. 3, pp. 3–5.

Supervision (Banking Supervision Law 2003),[17] together with the 2003 amendments to the PBC Law 1995 (PBC Law 2003)[18] and the 2003 amendments to the Commercial Banking Law 1995 (Commercial Banking Law 2003)[19] all of which took effect as of 1 February 2004. The three banking laws are at the highest level in China's banking law framework.

III.B.　　　　BANKING ADMINISTRATIVE REGULATIONS

In addition to the three banking laws are banking administrative regulations made by the State Council. Currently, at least five banking administrative regulations exist, which include:

- the Regulation on Administration of Savings;[20]
- the Measures on Punishment of Illegal Financial Activities;[21]
- the Provisions on the True Name System of Personal Deposit Accounts;[22]
- the Regulation on Dissolution of Financial Institutions;[23]
- the FFFI Regulation 2001.[24]

The banking administrative regulations are at the second level of China's banking law framework.

17.　Banking Supervision Law 2003 (*Yinhangye Jiandu Guanlifa*), adopted at the Sixth Meeting of the Standing Committee of the Tenth NPC on 27 December 2003, effective 1 February 2004, *Gazette of the NPC* (2004), no. 1; also available in *Falü Huibian* (People's Publishing House, 2004), pp. 131–142.
18.　Decision on the Amendment of the Law on the PBC, adopted at the Sixth Meeting of the Standing Committee of the Tenth NPC on 27 December 2003, *Gazette of the NPC* (2004), no. 1, pp. 23–25. For the entire text of the PBC Law 2003, see *Gazette of the NPC* (2004), no. 1, pp. 26–30; also available in *Falü Huibian* (2003), supra note 869, pp. 150–160.
19.　Decision on the Amendment of the Law on Commercial Banks, adopted at the Sixth Meeting of the Standing Committee of the Tenth NPC on 27 December 2003, *Gazette of the NPC* (2004), no. 1, pp. 32–35. For the Commercial Banking Law 2003, see *Gazette of the NPC* (2004), no. 1, pp. 36–44.
20.　Regulation on Administration of Savings (*Chuxu Guanli Tiaoli*), State Council Decree no. 107, promulgated on 11 December 1992, effective 1 March 1993, *Gazette of the State Council* (1992), no. 31, pp. 1,339–1,344.
21.　Measures on Punishment of Illegal Financial Activities (*Jinrong Weifa Xingwei Chufa Banfa*), State Council Decree no. 260, promulgated on 22 February 1999, effective as of the same day, *Gazette of the State Council* (1999), no. 8, pp. 244–251.
22.　Provisions on the True Name System of Personal Deposit Accounts (*Geren Cunkuan Zhanghu Shimingzhi Guiding*), State Council Decree no. 285, promulgated on 20 March 2000, effective as of 1 April 2000, Gazette of the State Council (2000), no. 15, pp. 10–11.
23.　Regulation on Dissolution of Financial Institutions (*Jinrong Jigou Chexiao Tiaoli*), Decree no. 324 of the State Council, promulgated on 23 November 2001, effective as of 15 December 2001, *Gazette of the State Council* (2002), no. 1, pp. 13–16.
24.　Regulation on Administration of Foreign-Funded Financial Institutions, State Council Decree no. 340 (20 December 2001).

III.C.   BANKING RULES

The third level of China's banking law framework refers to relevant banking regulatory rules issued by the CBRC and the PBC. The forms of banking rules include 'provisions' (*guiding*), 'measures' (*banfa*), 'Detailed Rules for Implementation' (*shishi xize*) and so on.[25] There is a subtle difference between 'provisions' and 'measures'. Generally speaking, the title of 'provisions' is suitable for financial activities in part or in whole. The title of 'measures' is suitable for detailed rules on financial activities.[26]

Now, the CBRC takes the main responsibility for making China's banking regulatory rules. The Banking Supervision Law 2003 states that, in accordance with the law and the administrative regulations, the banking regulatory institution of the State Council, in other words, the CBRC, shall formulate and issue rules governing the supervision over banking institutions and their operations.[27] This article clearly empowers the CBRC to formulate banking rules.

The current banking rules in China are a mixture of rules issued by both the PBC and the CBRC. This situation increases the difficulty of finding proper banking regulatory rules, considering the huge amount of rules issued by the PBC prior to the establishment of the CBRC. The PBC and the CBRC have recognised the problem and, since 2003, have been working to better define the banking rules of the PBC. On 17 December 2004, the PBC and the CBRC jointly issued an announcement, declaring the initial result of the defining 110 rules originally made by the PBC,[28] among which eleven PBC banking rules remain valid under the common monitoring and enforcement by the PBC and the CBRC,[29] 61 PBC banking rules are succeeded by the CBRC,[30] 38 PBC banking rules were repealed from date of the announcement.[31]

III.D.   OTHER BANKING NORMATIVE DOCUMENTS

One of China's legal characteristics is the existence of a great number of 'other normative documents' (*qita guifanxing wenjian*), such as circulars or notices (*tongzhi*); letters or replies (*han* or *pifu*); announcements (*gonggao*); or other

---

25. Interim Rules on the Formulation Procedures of Basic Financial Rules (*Jinrong Yewu Jiben Guizhang Zhiding Chexu Guiding Shixing*), art. 8, issued by the PBC on 30 March 1991, effective as of 1 July 1991, *Yinfa* [1991], no. 166, available at <www.law-lib.com/lawhtm/1991/7506.htm>.
26. Ibid.,
27. Banking Supervision Law 2003, supra note 17, art. 15.
28. Announcement of the PBC and the CBRC [2004], no. 20, 17 December 2004, *Gazette of the PBC* (2004), no. 18–19, pp. 3–8 (referred to for the remainder of this document as the announcement of the PBC and the CBRC).
29. Ibid., sect. 1, Annex 1.
30. Ibid., sect. 2, Annex 2.
31. Ibid., sect. 3, Annex 3.

measures (*cuoshi*), issued by ministries, commissions of the State Council or by other institutions endowed with administrative functions directly under the State Council. These institutions should not be ignored, because these institutions often revise or supplement higher-level administrative regulations and rules. Because the normative documents are outside the scope of the Legislation Law, these documents do not have a formal status in the Chinese legal system. However, these documents can be invoked in administrative judgments at the discretion of People's Courts.[32] In fact, those administrative measures have binding force.[33]

According to Article XXVIII(a) of the GATS, 'measure' refers to any measure by a WTO Member, whether in the form of a law, regulation, rule, procedure, decision, administrative action, or any other form. Any other form is an all-inclusive expression. In addition, Part I:2(2) of the China Accession Protocol states:

> 'China shall apply and administer in a uniform, impartial and reasonable manner all its *laws, regulations and other measures* of the central government as well as *local regulations, rules and other measures* issued or applied at the sub-national level (collectively referred to as '*laws, regulations and other measures*') pertaining to or affecting trade in goods, services, trade-related aspects of intellectual property rights ('TRIPS') or the control of foreign exchange. (Emphasis added)

The expression in the China Accession Protocol implies that measure includes any measure, such as a law, a regulation, a rule, a procedure, a decision, an administrative action and so on, which echoes the definition in the GATS. From the expression in the China Accession Protocol, *laws* and *regulations* are parallel to *other measures*, so *other measures* include any measures 'pertaining to or affecting trade in goods, services, TRIPS or the control of foreign exchange', except for laws and regulations.

In number, other banking normative documents are the majority of China's banking law. However, no clear, reasonable, substantive distinction exists between 'banking rules' and 'other banking normative documents'. The obvious difference between them is in form only; that is, 'banking rules' usually take the form of 'decree' (*ling*), while 'other banking normative documents' take the form of inferior 'document' (*wen*). Another difference in form is that 'banking rules' come only from the head office of the CBRC, but 'other banking normative documents' may come from local offices of the CBRC.

---

32. Para. 2 of Article 62 of the Interpretations of the Supreme People's Court on Relevant Issues of the Administrative Procedural Law of the PRC (*Zuigao Renmin Fayuan guanyu Zhixing Zhonghua Renmin Gongheguo Xingzheng Susongfa Ruogan Wenti de Jieshi*), adopted at the 1,088th Meeting of the Adjudication Committee of the Supreme People's Court on 24 November 1999, available at <www.court.gov.cn/lawdata/explain/executivecation/200303200097.htm>.
33. Administrative Law (*Hu Jianmiao, Xingzhengfa Xue*) (2nd ed., China, Law Press, 2003) pp. 245–246.

IV.   COMPLIANCE WITH WTO OBLIGATIONS
                 IN BANKING

IV.A.   COMPLIANCE WITH MARKET ACCESS AND NATIONAL TREATMENT:
                 NEW DEVELOPMENT OF CHINA'S BANKING LAW UNDER THE WTO

In December 2003, the Standing Committee of the National People's Congress
of the PRC amended China's Commercial Banking Law, as well as the PBC
Law. This amendment is the first amendment on the Commercial Banking Law
after the Law was promulgated in 1995. However, the main purpose of the
amendment is not for the compliance with the WTO, but for the compliance
with the creation of the CBRC; in other words, for the transfer of most banking supervision power from the PBC to the CBRC.[34] As a matter of fact, the
new Banking Supervision Law 2003, the amended PBC Law, and the amended
Commercial Banking Law have nothing to do with the implementation of the
WTO Agreements. In China, with respect to banking, WTO obligations, particularly market access and national treatment obligations are implemented by
revising or formulating inferior banking regulations, banking rules, and other
banking normative documents.

IV.A.1.   Five Announcements since 2001

From China's entry to the WTO to the end of 2005, China made five announcements to implement its WTO commitments in banking services.

First, the PBC issued an announcement in December 2001, including eliminating restrictions on clients of foreign exchange business, opening Shanghai and Shenzhen for foreign-funded financial institutions to engage in RMB
business, Tianjin and Shanghai to apply for RMB business, permitting these
businesses to set up foreign-funded auto financing companies, foreign-funded
financial leasing companies and so on.[35]

Second, one year later, the PBC issued another announcement to further
implement China's WTO commitments, opening Guangzhou, Zhuhai, Qing-
dao, Nanjing and Wuhan for RMB business.[36]

Third, after succeeding to most banking regulatory power, the CBRC
became the main banking regulator to implement China's WTO commitments
in banking. In October 2003, the CBRC issued an announcement to further
open Jinan, Fuzhou, Chengdu and Chongqing for foreign-funded banks to
deal with RMB business.[37]

---

34. L. Mingkang, Chairman of the CBRC, *Explanation on the Amendment Bill to the Commer-
    cial Banking Law of the PRC*, address to the fourth meeting of the Standing Committee of
    the Tenth NPC on 22 August 2003.
35. PBC Announcement [2001] no. 1.
36. PBC Announcement [2002] no. 26, 6 November 2002.
37. Announcement of the CBRC on Further Opening RMB Business to Foreign-Funded
    Financial Institutions, CBRC Announcement [2003] no. 2, 24 October 2003.

Fourth, according to China's WTO Schedule, the CBRC issued another announcement to further open China's banking in 2004,[38] expanding RMB business to Kunming, Beijing, Xiamen, Xi'an and Shenyang. In addition, in this announcement, China relaxed restrictions on the qualifications of foreign-funded financial institutions to engage in RMB business in Western and North-eastern areas to encourage foreign investment in those areas.

Fifth, at the end of 2005, the CBRC announced to open Shantou and Ningbo for RMB business, and open Ha'erbin, Changchun, Lanzhou, Yinchuan and Nanjing of its own accord in advance to increase RMB city number from 18 to 25.[39] In this announcement, China further provided more favourable treatment to foreign-funded banks which desire to invest in Western and Northeastern areas of China.

From the five consecutive announcements made by China's banking regulators, it can be concluded that China has properly implemented its WTO commitments in regard to the elimination of geographical restrictions on RMB business. The five announcements have facilitated market access of foreign-funded banks in China. Through end-2005, 72 foreign banks from 21 countries and regions established 254 operational institutions in China, and 177 foreign banks from 40 countries and regions established 240 representative offices.[40]

IV.A.2. Revision of the FFFI Regulation in 2001

One week after China entered the WTO, the State Council of the PRC issued a new version of the Regulation on Administration of Foreign-Funded Financial Institutions (FFFI Regulation 2001), which replaced the Regulation on Administration of Foreign-Funded Financial Institutions of the 1996 (FFFI Regulation 1994). This type of revision resulted from China's entry to the WTO. China's specific commitments on banking services, particularly those limitations on market access, are incorporated into the FFFI Regulation 2001. However, important to note is that the FFFI Regulation 2001 is not simply a repeat of China's banking commitments under the WTO. In fact, the Regulation includes many new conditions and restraints on foreign financial institutions, some of which are highly debated, as discussed later, to be inconsistent with WTO obligations and commitments.

IV.A.3. Revision of DRI in 2004

In 2002, the PBC issued the Detailed Rules for Implementation of the Regulation on Administration of Foreign-Funded Financial Institutions (DRI 2002).

---

38. Announcement of the CBRC on Relevant Issues of Further Opening Banking, CBRC Announcement [2004], 24 November 2004.
39. Announcement of the CBRC on Relevant Issues of Further Opening Banking, CBRC Announcement [2005], 3 December 2005.
40. *Trade Policy Review*, Report by the People's Republic of China, WT/TPR/G/161, para. 52.

The DRI 2002 also resulted from the implementation of China's WTO obligations and commitments. Two years later, the DRI 2002 was replaced by the DRI 2004 issued by the CBRC. In addition to reflecting the change of banking regulatory function from the PBC to the CBRC, the DRI 2004 also reflected the requirements of further opening China's banking based on the WTO obligations and China's WTO commitments.[41]

Interesting to note is that one of the principles in revising the DRI 2002 is the equal application of the DRI to both Chinese-funded banks and foreign-funded banks,[42] which is also the requirement of WTO national treatment obligations. In addition, WTO national treatment obligations are reflected in Article 92 of the Commercial Banking Law 2003, which states:

> 'Foreign-funded commercial banks, Sino-foreign joint equity commercial banks and branches of foreign commercial banks shall be governed by the provisions of this Law; where other laws and administrative regulations provide otherwise, the provisions of those laws and regulations shall prevail'.[43]
>
> Therefore, the Commercial Banking Law 2003 generally applies to both foreign-funded banks and domestic-funded banks unless otherwise provided.

IV.B.   COMPLIANCE WITH WTO TRANSPARENCY OBLIGATIONS

During the negotiations relating to China's entry to the WTO, some WTO Members expressed concerns about the lack of transparency regarding the laws, regulations and other measures that applied to matters covered in the WTO Agreement. In particular, some Members noted the difficulty in finding and obtaining copies of regulations and other measures undertaken by various ministries.[44] China promised that none of the information required by the WTO Agreement or the China Accession Protocol to be disclosed would be withheld as confidential information except for very special reasons.[45] China further promised only those laws, regulations and other measures 'that are published

---

41. Reply of the CBRC Officials at the Press Conference of the CBRC on Revising the DRI, 3 August 2004, available at <www.cbrc.gov.cn/mod_cn00/jsp/cn004002.jsp?infoID=817&type=1>.
42. Ibid.,
43. The Commercial Banking Law 1995 (Article 88) included a similar provision. In addition, Article 49 of the Banking Supervision Law states:

     'Where it is otherwise provided for the regulation and administration of foreign-funded banking financial institutions, Sino-foreign joint equity banking financial institutions and the branches of foreign banking financial institutions established within the People's Republic of China in other laws and administrative regulations, the relevant laws and administrative regulations shall prevail.'
44. Report of the Working Party on the Accession of China, para. 324.
45. Ibid., para. 333.

and readily available to other WTO Members, individuals and enterprises' can be enforced.[46] Therefore, it is China's obligation to publish all normative measures affecting trade in financial services.[47]

Theoretically, the simplest way to find all laws, regulations, administrative rules and other measures related to China's WTO obligations is to look to the lists provided by China's government to the WTO. In accordance with paragraph V(a) of Annex 1A to the China Accession Protocol (Information to be Provided by China in the Context of the Transitional Review Mechanism), China should regularly provide updated lists of all laws, regulations, administrative guidelines and other measures affecting the trade in services to the WTO, including the date of publication and the date of entry into force. China did provide such a list to the WTO.[48] The list, however, did not satisfy the WTO requirement because it included only a portion of the laws, regulations, or other measures affecting trade in services, especially in financial sectors.

The list made by China's government is too simple and omits a few important laws, regulations and a number of rules, especially notices with actual binding force. One of the characteristics of the list notified by China is that it mainly covers market access of foreign financial service suppliers, ignoring provisions on business operation, or on market exit. The transparency obligation runs through every aspect of trade in financial services, thus relevant laws, regulations, rules or other measures to be made public should not be those concerned market access alone. Even with respect to laws that address market access, numerous binding laws, regulations, rules or other measures have not been notified by China to the WTO. This issue was raised by some WTO Members during the transitional review in the WTO. For example, the EC paid much attention to China's transparency, especially in the insurance sector.[49] In the banking sector, Japan was of the view that 'Chinese authorities issue licenses to foreign banks by non-transparent rules and procedures. . . . '[50]

Another issue related to transparency is the issue of translations. China has committed to make available to WTO Members translations in one or more of the official languages of the WTO 'all laws, regulations and other measures' affecting, inter alia, trade in services, in no case later than 90 days after implementation or enforcement.[51] However, so far, China has provided only a small number of these translations and always lags behind the time limit.[52] In February 2003, the State Council issued a notice on translations

---

46. China Accession Protocol, Part I: 2(C).1.
47. Ibid.,
48. See Communication from the People's Republic of China, 'Notification under Section 18 of China's Protocol of Accession to the Council for Trade in Services', S/C/W/218, 22 October 2002.
49. See Communication from the European Communities and their Member States, S/FIN/W/18, 23 September 2002, para. 1.
50. See Communication from Japan, S/FIN/W/21, 1 October 2002, para. 9.
51. See China's Working Party Report, para. 334.
52. For those related to financial services, see Notification Pursuant to Article III:3 of the GATS, S/C/N/215, 24 December 2002; S/C/N/221, 24 December 2002; S/C/N/222,

of administrative regulations.[53] According to this notice, the administrative
department that drafted the administrative regulation, or a leading administrative department in case of more than two departments involved in drafting,
is responsible for translation of such regulation. The Legal Office of the State
Council (*Guowuyuan Fazhiban*) is liable for reviewing and approving official
English translations, with general responsibility for translation quality.[54] The
work of translation, review and approval must be completed within 90 days
of the date of promulgation of a regulation.[55] Important to note is that this
notice merely covers administrative regulations. Neither laws that are subject
to the purview of the NPC, nor rules formulated by administrative departments – for example, regulatory commissions – are addressed in the document.
Therefore, the translation and notification of laws and rules, which provide
for the majority of binding legal documents in China, is still a prominent
problem.

IV.C.   ECONOMIC NEEDS TEST

Paragraph 2 of Article 12 of the Commercial Banking Law 1995 provided that
the PBC must consider economic development needs and banking competition
status when examining an application for establishment of a commercial bank.
In China's Service Schedule, China undertakes not to impose any measure that
requires taking an economic needs test in the process of approving licensing
applications for foreign-funded banks.[56] Therefore, the economic needs test in
the Commercial Banking Law 1995 was repealed by the Commercial Banking
Law 2003.[57]

However, the economic needs tests still exist in some financial rules. For
example, according to the Rules on Administration of Establishment of Operation Networks in the Same City by Commercial Banks,[58] one of the principles
in approving operation networks is that such establishment of networks must

---

24 December 2002; S/C/N/223, 24 December 2002. S/C/N/224, 24 December 2002;
S/C/N/225, 24 December 2002.
53. Notice on the Work of Reviewing and Approving Official English Translations of Administrative Regulations (*Guowuyuan Bangongting Guanyu Zuohao Xingzheng Fagui Yingwen
Zhengshi Yiben Fanyi Shending Gongzuo de Tongzhi*), issued by the General Office of the
State Council on 24 February 2003, *Guobanfa* [2003] no. 10.
54. See ibid., para. 1.
55. See ibid., para. 3.
56. One of China's WTO commitments is that, 'criteria for authorization to deal in China's
financial services sector are solely prudential (i.e., contain no economic needs test or quantitative limits on licenses . . . Upon accession, licenses will be issued with no economic needs
test or quantitative limits on licenses'. See China Schedule.
57. Para. 2 of art. 12 of the Commercial Banking Law 2003 states: 'other prudential conditions
shall also be met for the establishment of a commercial bank'.
58. See PBC Decree [2002] no. 3, art. 4.

be appropriate to the development level and operational situation of the local banking business, and satisfy the banking service demands of local communities. This type of test is a typical economic needs test, which is in violation of China's WTO commitments. This requirement applies not only to domestic banks, but also to foreign-funded banks.[59]

As another example, according to the Interim Rules on Intermediary Business of Commercial Banks, to engage in an intermediary business commercial banks must satisfy 'the objective demands of financial market development'.[60]

Compared with banking laws, insurance laws are more consistent with the WTO commitment regarding economic needs tests. Article 15(1) of the Rules on Administration of Insurance Companies stipulated that one of the conditions to apply for the establishment of a branch of an insurance company was to be beneficial to the development of the local insurance market. This typical economic needs test rule is inconsistent with China's WTO commitments, and therefore was repealed in 2002.[61] The Insurance Law amended in October 2002, however, reserved a similar article, reflecting the difficulty and sluggishness of amending the law in the NPC.[62] The effect of changing the rule is seriously diminished while the relevant law remains unchanged.

V. WTO TRANSITIONAL REVIEW OF CHINA'S BANKING LAW

To monitor China to comply with WTO obligations, the WTO designed the Transitional Review Mechanism (TRM) for China.[63] The TRM is unique. Nothing similar could be found in any other WTO agreements or in WTO history.[64] With this mechanism, the General Council and the subsidiary bodies of the WTO shall review the implementation by China of the WTO agreements and the provisions of the China Accession Protocol.[65] Compared with the Trade

---

59. See ibid., [2002] no. 3, art. 2.
60. See PBC Decree [2001] no. 5, art. 5.
61. See Decision on Amendment of the Rules on Administration of Insurance Companies (*Guanyu Xiugai Baoxian Gongsi Guanli Guiding de Jueding*) by CIRC on 15 March 2002, CIRC Order [2002] no. 3.
62. Para. 2, art. 72 of the Insurance Law reads: 'The insurance regulatory agency, when examining establishment of insurance companies, should consider the needs of development and fair competition of insurance industry'.
63. Ibid., part I:18.
64. See the Chinese representative's speech at the meeting of Committee on Trade in Financial Services of the WTO on 22 July 2002, S/FIN/M/36, (26 September 2002), para. 56.
65. A total of sixteen WTO subsidiary bodies are involved in TRM, including:

– Council for Trade in Goods;
– Council for Trade-Related Aspects of Intellectual Property Rights;
– Council for Trade in Services;

Policy Review Mechanism (TPRM)[66] applicable to other WTO Members, the
TRM is relatively strict.[67] Through the TRM, other WTO Members can monitor and urge China to make its laws, regulations, rules and relevant measures
consistent with the WTO agreements. For China, the TRM is both a burden and
an opportunity. In each year's review process, China must face the challenges
from other WTO Members, answer various difficult questions on its domestic
laws, regulations, rules or policies, and defend itself with every possible reason.
In view of the importance of the TRM, the General Office of the State Council
of the PRC (*Zhonghua Renmin Gongheguo Guowuyuan Bangongting*)[68] issued
to local governments at provincial level, departments and commissions of the
central government a special circular on how to deal with this matter.[69] In this
circular, the General Office pointed out the main reason for the significance of
the TRM affairs; that is, the TRM, as well as notification and enquiry matters,
has a direct impact on China's reputation in the WTO.[70]

- Committee on Balance-of-Payments Restrictions;
- Committee on Market Access (covering also ITA);
- Committee on Agriculture;
- Committee on Sanitary and Phytosanitary Measures;
- Committee on Technical Barriers to Trade;
- Committee on Subsidies and Countervailing Measures;
- Committee on Anti-Dumping Measures;
- Committee on Customs Valuation;
- Committee on Rules of Origin;
- Committee on Import Licensing;
- Committee on Trade-Related Investment Measures;
- Committee on Safeguards;
- Committee on Trade in Financial Services.

66. TPRM, in The Legal Texts: The Result of the Uruguay Round of Multinational Trade (Cambridge University Press 1999), pp. 380–382.
67. Under the TPRM, the ordinary frequency of reviews are once every two years, four years, six years (which is the most common frequency) or even longer for least-developed-country Members, based on the impact of individual Members on the functioning of the multilateral trading system. See TPRM, ibid., §C(ii).
68. The State Council (*Guowuyuan*) is China's highest administrative agency and is responsible for the National People's Congress (NPC) and its Standing Committee. See Article 85 and 92 of the PRC Constitution (*Xianfa*), adopted at the Fifth Session of the Fifth NPC on 4 December 1982, effective 4 December 1982, amended in 1988, 1993, 1999 and 2004, in *Falü Huibian* [2004] (People's Publishing House, 2005), pp. 1–83. The General Office of the State Council is the internal organ led by the Secretary General of the State Council, which deals with routine business of the State Council. See Article 7 of the Organic Law of the State Council (*Guowuyuan Zuzhi Fa*), adopted at the Fifth Session of the Fifth NPC on 10 December 1982, effective 10 December 1982, *Gazette of the State Council* (1982), no. 20, pp. 948–949.
69. Circular of the General Office of the State Council on Accomplishing the Work of Notification, Enquiry and Review of Trade Policies after China's Accession to the WTO (*Guowuyuan Bangongting Guanyu Zuohao Woguo Jiaru Shijie Maoyi Zuzhi Youguan Maoyi Zhengce Tongbao Zixun he Shenyi Gongzuo de Tongzhi*), *Guobanfa* [2002], no. 50, 29 September 2002, *Gazette of the State Council* 16 (2002), no. 31.
70. Ibid, §1.

V.A.   ISSUES RAISED IN THE TRM MEETINGS

From 2002 to 2005, the WTO made four rounds of transitional reviews on China, during which many compliance issues were raised. For example, many countries, particularly the EC members and Canada, stated that China's minimum working capital requirements for branches of foreign banks were high. Some WTO members claimed that approval of local Currency business for foreign bank branches in China was on a branch-by-branch basis. In 2002 and 2003, EC and Canada raised the issue of one year interval between approval of a branch and submission of another branch.

According to Article 30 of the FFFI Regulation 2001, a foreign bank can only fund up to 70 per cent of its foreign currency loans with funds deposited in China, and at least 30 per cent of its loan funding must be from abroad, which limits the ability of foreign banks to lend foreign currency without bringing in foreign currency from abroad. This issue was raised by Canada in 2004.

Some WTO members showed an interest in China's treatment to foreign-funded banks, including the United States, EC,[71] Canada, Australia, Japan and Chinese Taipei.[72] For example, in 2002, the EC asked whether the high minimum capital requirements for foreign bank branches were consistent with national treatment. In 2003, the EC further asked why 30 per cent of the working capital of foreign bank branches must be deposited at a Chinese local bank rather than at a foreign bank.

From the issues raised in TRM meetings, one can see that WTO members have attached great importance to the WTO compliance issue, which is closely related to China's banking laws, regulations and rules, particularly the special foreign banking regulations and rules.

V.B.   CHINA'S RESPONSES: PRUDENTIAL CARVE-OUT

China did not provide written responses to the above questions raised by various WTO Members, and all China's replies were from China's oral statements at TRM meetings.[73] In those meetings, China stated that it was making every possible effort to fulfil its WTO commitments with regard to financial services since accession to the WTO.[74]

---

71. In the WTO, the European Union (EU) is referred to as the European Communities (EC). The EC's 25 Member States are also WTO members in their own rights. See the European Communities and the WTO, available at <www.wto.org/english/thewto_e/countries_e/european_communities_e.htm>.

72. The official name of Chinese Taipei in the WTO is the Separate Customs Territory of Taiwan, Penghu, Kinmen and Matsu, which became a WTO Member on 1 January 2002. See Protocol of Accession of the Separate Customs Territory of Taiwan, Penghu, Kinmen and Matsu, WT/L/433 (23 November 2001).

73. In China's opinion, China has no legal obligation to provide written answers for TRM purpose under section 18 of the China Accession Protocol. See para. 46 of S/FIN/M/37.

74. S/FIN/M/37, para. 16.

First, with respect to banking services, China argued that the capital requirements were consistent with Chinese financial development level, and for the purpose of protecting the interests of domestic depositors and the safety and soundness of China's financial system.[75] In regard to banking branching restrictions and approval procedures, China stated that the requirements are prudential. In regard to the intervals between applications, China also argued that these intervals were also for prudential purposes.[76] As to the issue of 30 per cent working capital deposit at a local bank, China argued that the rule was based on prudential regulation and to avoid financial risks. On the issue of the 70 per cent limit on foreign bank holding of foreign currency deposits, China's reply was also based on prudential considerations.

From China's replies in the TRM meetings, one can discern that a key defence employed by China is of prudential carve-out.[77] The Annex on Financial Services fails to set standards for determining whether a measure taken by a WTO member is prudential or non-prudential. In addition, the Annex does not mention any of the so-called international standards or the role of international organizations. For this reason, no clear definition of prudential carve-out is available under the WTO. As a result, determining whether China's defences based on prudential considerations are legally prudential or not is extremely difficult under the current framework of the WTO. Obviously, China's banking regulators identified, and began to exploit, a loophole of the WTO regime, which should not be criticised per se.

VI.   CONCLUSION

China's banking regulators have paid a great deal of attention to the implementation of WTO obligations and the compliance issue since China's entry into the WTO. Observing China's financial legislation, one can find the speed of financial legislation becomes faster and faster. For example, from 2003 to 2005, the newly established CBRC made more than 200 financial rules and other normative documents.[78] It would be an exaggeration to claim that each of the 200 financial rules and documents is to implement China's WTO obligations and

---

75. Ibid., para. 21.2(a).
76. Ibid., para. 60.
77. The first sentence of paragraph 2(a) of the Annex on Financial Services is the so-called prudential carve-out, which empowers a WTO member to take prudential regulatory measures on financial service trade. The second sentence of the Annex on Financial Services is a trade-off of the first sentence, providing that such measures permitted by the first sentence shall not be used as a means of avoiding the Member's commitments or obligations under the GATS.
78. Speech of Liu Mingkang, the Chairman of the CBRC, at the Press Conference on 5 December 2005, <www.cbrc.gov.cn/mod_cn00/jsp/cn004002.jsp?infoID=1767&type=1>.

commitments, but it is safe to say that most of these rules and documents are influenced, directly or indirectly, by the WTO. For example, the minimum capital requirements for establishment of foreign bank branches have been gradually decreased from the range of RMB 100 million to 600 million in 2002,[79] to the range of RMB 100 million to 500 million in 2004[80] and then to the range of RMB 100 million to 400 million in 2006.[81] The minimum capital requirements for wholly-foreign-funded banks and Sino-foreign equity joint venture banks to establish branches to engage in RMB business is reduced from RMB 300 million to RMB 200 million.[82] In regard to the 70 per cent limit on foreign bank holding of foreign currency deposits, China has committed to reduce the limit in 2006,[83] which means that China will revise the relevant article of the FFFI Regulation 2001.

Indeed, the impact of the WTO on China's banking law is embodied not only in one or two banking laws, regulations or rules, but in a change to the entire body of China's banking law structure; and the impact is not interim, but permanent. The compliance issue between WTO obligations and China's banking law will not disappear with the end of the transitional period for China's banking services in December 2006. On the contrary, the issue will continue to coexist with the WTO, and develop with the development of the WTO and new financial commitments in the future.

On the whole, most WTO Members have given China positive feedback for its performance of WTO commitments, particularly developing countries, such as India, Pakistan and Cuba.[84] Even the US government admits that a number of positive developments have occurred, such as that China has reduced capital requirements in certain financial services sectors, and opened up the auto financing sector.[85]

Finally, the compliance issue is further complicated by the ambiguous concept of prudential carve-out of the Annex on Financial Services under the WTO framework. Prudential reason has become China's main defence against the complaints from some WTO members, particularly the complaints on the high capital requirements for establishment of foreign bank branches. Paragraph 2(a) of the Annex on Financial Services does not define the concept of prudential carve-out, or clearly identify the distance between the carve-out and GATS obligations, and therefore China, as well as other WTO members, have significant room for manoeuvre. From the gradual decrease of minimum capital requirements for foreign bank branches, although China has used the

---

79.   See DRI 2002, arts. 31–36, issued by the PBC, effective 1 February 2002.
80.   See DRI 2004, arts. 31–36, issued by the CBRC, effective 1 September 2004.
81.   Speech of Liu Mingkang, supra note 78.
82.   Ibid.
83.   Ibid.
84.   S/FIN/M/37, paras. 30, 35 and 64.
85.   USTR, 2003 Report to Congress on China's WTO Compliance, 11 December 2003, p. 4.

prudential carve-out, China has not abused it. In fact, in Articles 5 and 9 of the DRI 2004, the CBRC has listed various prudential conditions for establishment of foreign-funded financial institutions, including reasonable corporate governance structure, sound risk management system, good internal control system, effective management information system, qualified management, good business records, good assets, effective anti-money laundering measures and no significantly illegal records.

Chapter 5

Financial Restructuring and China's Asset Management Companies*

Berry F.C. Hsu, Douglas Arner, and Qun Wan

I.   INTRODUCTION

On 11 December 2001, the People's Republic of China (China) completed its process of joining the institutional framework of the international economic system through its accession to the World Trade Organization (WTO). Since accession, China's volume of foreign trade has increased twofold, from USD 500 billion to USD 1 trillion.[1] The process to complete its integration into the global economic system, as well as to reduce trade conflicts and to further support domestic restructuring and development, however, requires China's currency, the renminbi (RMB), to be fully convertible.[2] The key factor that limits continued capital account liberalization and free convertibility of the RMB is the level of confidence in China's banking system – both domestic and foreign. As one aspect of WTO accession, China has committed to fully

---

*   The authors wish to acknowledge the valuable comments of Dr. Wei Wang, Research Fellow, Asian Institute of International Financial Law, Faculty of Law, University of Hong Kong.
1.   'Dancing with "Wolves"', 48:1 *Beijing Review* (January 2005), p. 2.
2.   W. Stance, 'Banking and Finance', in L. Brahm (ed.), *China after WTO* (Beijing, China Intercontinental Press, 2002), p. 318.

opening its banking sector to foreign participation by the end of 2006.[3] To meet the challenges of foreign competition and to secure the benefits of financial liberalization and economic growth in the context financial and political stability, China has embarked on major banking restructuring, focusing on the performance and financial condition of its state-owned and controlled banks, including balance sheet restructuring through recapitalization and disposal of non-performing loans (NPLs). In respect to financial condition, China is implementing the 1988 Basel Capital Accord and has committed to the implement the Basel II framework at some point in the future,[4] which requires its banking institutions to maintain a certain minimum capital adequacy level. Crucial to the development of a competitive environment for banking services since its WTO accession are China's specific commitments stipulating regulation of China's banking sector,[5] including specific commitments that the regulatory framework for banking contain no economic needs tests or quantitative limits on licenses.[6] In addition, since 2002, any existing non-prudential measures restricting ownership, operation and juridicial form of foreign financial institutions, including internal branching, and licenses are required to be eliminated.[7] These commitments to prudential regulation of banking means that China's state-owned enterprises (SOEs) can no longer rely on direct or indirect state support through loans from government owned or controlled commercial banks, but rather must compete for financing in a commercial, market-based context.

The law and policy approach applied to banking restructuring in China, particularly to balance sheet issues and asset problems such as NPLs, reflect China's developing legal system and can be used as a basis against which to measure the development of the rule of law in China. This article focuses on one mechanism of bank restructuring: asset management companies (AMCs), their institutional characteristics and roles in China's banking system, and the legal issues surrounding banks' operations. This article is intended to address the law and policy issues related to disposal of NPLs in China's banking system.

While China's effort to build an effective legal system to support its socialist market economy include many imperfections, as well as many challenges confronting its future development, at the same time, China's corporate and financial law reforms must strike a balance between economic competitiveness and the maintenance of social stability in post-WTO China. Despite this

---

3. See D. Arner, Z. Zhou, M. Bushehri, B. Hsu, J. Lou and W. Wang, *Financial Regulation and the WTO: Liberalization and Restructuring in China Two Years Post-Accession*', EAIEL Policy Paper 1 (East Asian International Economic Law and Policy Programme, May 2004).
4. T. Liu, Deputy Governor, People's Bank of China to Basel Committee on Banking Supervision, 'Letter dated 30 May 2001'.
5. I. Horizontal Commitments, 'Part II – Schedule of Specific Commitments on Services, List of Article II MFN Exemptions', *Report of the Working Party on the Accession of China*.
6. Ibid.
7. Ibid.

conflict, China's efforts to build an effective legal system cannot be discredited.[8] One cannot ignore the reality that the high growth rates that underlie China's economic development – and, therefore, social stability – are correlated to progression in the country's legal development.[9] Numerous studies support the assumption that the rule of law is positively correlated with economic development.[10] Still, the issue of whether successful economic development depends on the rule of law is debatable.[11] Nevertheless, the Asian financial crisis in the late 1990s was a result of inadequate economic planning, weak regulatory mechanisms, lack of enforcement of prudential rules and poor transparency.[12] For these reasons, the legal framework, as well as the economic, historical and political context in which that system operates, must be addressed in China's banking reform.[13]

This chapter first discusses the background of China's banking reform and the role of the AMCs. Through an historical understanding of the causes and implications of NPLs in China, this article then analyzes the measures adopted to address NPLs. No panacea exists to solve China's NPL problems. While experience from other jurisdictions is helpful, China has its own unique economic, historical and political environment. Accordingly, the measures adopted to resolve China's NPL problems in its process of transition from central planning to a social market economy must proceed through a process of trial and error. This fact is particularly relevant because China's developing legal system lacks significant expertise and experience in market-related law and economics. However, the pressure to expedite banking reform increases as full liberalization of the banking sector at the end of 2006 becomes closer. Given the magnitude of NPLs and the risks of social instability, the measures taken must be immediate and decisive as new problems are revealed. These goals can hardly be achieved in strict compliance with the rule of law, for example, through the formal legislative process. As a result, 'legislative forbearance', in other words, relaxing the strict rule of law, has been, and continues to be, the pragmatic approach adopted. However, such relaxation must not be utilized to 'rule by law'. Rather, the strict observance of legislative formality over policy must be relaxed only where necessary and essential to cure the legislative defects in the

---

8. S. Lubman, 'Bird in a Cage: Chinese Law Reform After Twenty Years', 20 *NW. J. Int'l L. and Bus.* 383 (2000), p. 384.

9. R. Peerenboom, *China's Long March toward Rule of Law*, (Cambridge: Cambridge University Press, 2002), pp. 463–464.

10. *Legal and Judicial Reform: Strategic Directions* (Washington, D.C.: Legal Vice-Presidency, World Bank, 2004), p. 16.

11. Peerenboom, *China's Long March toward Rule of Law*, supra note 9, p. 450.

12. B. Hsu, 'Is the Financial Crisis over in the Hong Kong Special Administrative Region? An Evaluation of the HKSAR's Banking Framework', 16:2 *Banking and Finance Law Review* (2001) pp. 275–301.

13. See D. Arner, *Law, Financial Stability and Economic Development* (New York: Cambridge University Press 2006 forthcoming).

banking reform. The real issue is whether or not sufficient evidence is available of a genuine undertaking to develop a legal system that fits post-WTO China.

Second, this chapter examines the legal issues that affect the successful operation of the AMCs. The topics that are discussed include AMC corporate governance, state policy, property rights and foreign participation, as well as SOE restructuring. The theme of this article is 'policy functions as law'. The disposal of NPLs through the AMCs illustrates how this feature of the Chinese legal system operates from a practical, rather than a jurisprudential, perspective.

II.   BACKGROUND: AMCs IN CHINA

In addressing NPLs as part of the process of banking restructuring, the Central People's Government (CPG) of China adopted a series of measures, including recapitalization, debt-equity swaps, mergers, NPL disposals and closing insolvent banking institutions. This section first discusses banking reform in China that lead to the establishment of AMCs. Next, this section analyses the AMC concept and finishes with an examination of legal aspects of the reform.

II.A.   BANKING REFORM IN CHINA

In December 1993, in its measures to reform the banking sector to enhance the role of financial services in the national economy, China's State Council issued a decision that addressed the financial system.[14] These measures were intended to separate state policy banks from state commercial banks as a preliminary objective, as the boundary between these two types of banks began to blur under the planned economy system.[15] This decision provided directives to transform the state specialized banks into state commercial banks.[16] Accordingly, China has implemented a three-tier system for its state-owned banks. The first tier banking institutions are the nation's four largest state-owned commercial banks (SOCBs), which are:

- the Agricultural Bank of China (ABC);
- the Bank of China (BOC);
- the China Construction Bank (CCB);
- and the Industrial and Commercial Bank of China (ICBC).[17]

---

14. *Decision of the State Council on Financial System Reform*, National Distribution (*guo-fa*) 1993, no. 91 (Beijing, State Council, 25 December 1993), Preface.
15. Ibid.
16. Ibid., sect. 3.
17. Ibid., sect. 3(1).

As of the end of 2003, these SOCBs accounted for, respectively, some fifty-nine per cent of deposits and fifty-five per cent of all loans granted in the entire banking system.[18] These four SOCBs, therefore, dominate China's banking system. The second tier banking institutions are the policy banks created to alleviate the burden of the policy and commercial roles of specialized banks.[19] In 1994, the three policy banks were restructured to assume their own financial risks in carrying out specific state policies.[20] The third tier banking institutions consist of national, regional, and local commercial banks.[21] In addition, a number of other banking institutions vested with specific functions for local development.[22]

In China, the fundamental legal structure that underlies the banking system is the Constitution of the People's Republic of China (PRC Constitution), which stipulates the leadership of the Chinese Communist Party (CCP) and the socialist path.[23] From 1953 to the late 1970s, the People's Bank of China (PBOC) was the only *de facto* banking institution in China and assumed both central and commercial banking roles.[24] The existing SOCBs at that time, restructured from banking institutions that existed prior to the establishment of the PRC, were merely performing their specialized functions.[25] Although the SOCBs accepted deposits and channelled money into lending activities, these banks were primarily public bodies that acted as state agencies, implementing governmental policies in granting credits to SOEs. Through a gradual process, the SOCBs became independent of the PBOC and the Ministry of Finance (MOF) and took over the commercial banking role of the PBOC.[26] In 1984, the State Council formalized the specialized functions of the SOCBs.[27] Before 1983, the funding of SOEs came directly from the state. In 1983, the State

18. 'Balance Sheet of Assets and Liabilities of State-Owned Commercial Banks', *Annual Report of People's Bank of China 2003* (Beijing, People's Bank of China, 2003), available at <www.ripbc.com.cn/yjxxw/jinrongnianbao/2003.htm> (Beijing, Research Institute of People's Bank of China) (31 January 2005).

19. 'Decision of the State Council on Financial System Reform' [1993] *National Distribution* (*guo-fa*), no. 91 (Beijing, State Council, 25 December 1993), sect. 2.

20. Ibid.

21. *Annual Report of People's Bank of China 2002* (Beijing, People's Bank of China, 2002), p. 68.

22. Decision of the State Council on Financial System Reform, supra note 19, sect. 3(3).

23. Constitution of the People's Republic of China, 1982 (revised in 1988, 1993, 1999 and 2004) (referred to in this chapter as the 'PRC Constitution'), Preface.

24. X. Dai (ed.), *A Fifty Years History of the People's Bank of China: The Development of Central Banking System* (Beijing, Chinese Financial Press, November 1998), pp. 22–23.

25. Ibid., pp. 20–22.

26. *Decision of the State Council on the Specialization of Central Bank Functions by the People's Bank of China* (Beijing, State Council, 17 September 1983), para. 3.

27. *Notice of the State Council on Approving the People's Bank of China Report on the Division of Lending Functions among the Specialized Banks* (Beijing, State Council, 30 May 1984), para. 2.

Council decided to substitute bank loans in place of state grants.[28] From 1985, loans granted by the SOCBs were the only source of funding for the SOEs,[29] which relied on bank loans as indirect subsidies, for example, through low interest rates and frequent default on principal and interest.[30] In other words, the SOCBs assumed the state's role in indirectly providing employment and maintaining social stability.[31] It was impossible for the SOCBs to be regulated under a prudential system, because most SOEs made investment decisions in accordance with state policies.[32] Consequently, NPLs accumulated rapidly in the SOCBs,[33] because China's economy has grown similarly rapidly during the past two decades.[34]

As China continues its transformation from a planned economy to a social-ist market economy, the SOCBs now must perform the role of 'real' banking institutions.[35] The SOCBs must transform themselves from state agencies to banking institutions, performing commercial roles under a prudential regu-latory system. In reality, some of the less-efficient SOEs still operate for the sole purpose of maintaining employment to maintain social security for their workers and former workers, for example, housing, medical benefits, unem-ployment benefits and pensions.[36] The poor performance of these banks is also partly due to the constraints imposed by state policies, such as price controls which curb earnings.[37] It is unlikely that any state agency would allow any of these less-efficient SOEs to go bankrupt, because the state has a statutory duty to arrange for the re-employment of any laid-off workers and to guarantee their basic necessities.[38] Any deviation from this practice may create social discontent and possibly lead to social instability – the paramount concern of the CCP.

28. 'Transfer to the People's Bank of China Regarding Uniform Management of Operating Funds of State Own Enterprise', [1983] *National Distribution (guo-fa)*, no. 100 (Beijing, State Council, 25 June 1983).
29. 'National Budget: Infrastructure Finance will be provided by Loans than State Funds', [1984] *Budget Brief (ji-zi)*, no. 2580 (Beijing, National Accounting Commission, Ministry of Finance and China Construction Bank, 14 December 1984).
30. J. Lin, F. Cai and Z. Li, *The China Miracle: Development Strategy and Economic Reform*, (Hong Kong, Chinese University Press, 2003), p. 221. See also *The Chinese Economy: Fighting Inflation, Deepening Reforms* (Washington, D.C., World Bank, 1996), p. 17.
31. Lin, Cai and Li, supra note 30.
32. *Notice of the State Council on the Approving the People's Bank of China Report on the Division of Lending Functions among the Specialized Banks* (Beijing, State Council, 30 May 1984), para. 2.
33. Lin, Cai and Li, supra note 30, pp. 221–222.
34. N. Lardy, *China's Unfinished Economic Revolution* (New York, Brookings Institution Press, 1998), p. 220.
35. 'Decision of the State Council on Financial System Reform', [1993] *National Distribution (guo-fa)*, no. 91 (Beijing, State Council, 25 December 1993), Preface.
36. Lin, Cai and Li, supra note 30, pp. 218–220; *The Chinese Economy: Fighting Inflation, Deepening Reforms* (Washington, D.C., World Bank, 1996), p. 17.
37. Ibid.
38. Law of People's Republic of China on Enterprise Bankruptcy (For Trial Implementation) (1986), art. 4.

Therefore, reforming the SOCBs in China goes beyond simply injecting money into the banking system and implementing prudential banking regulations. The social safety net system can no longer depend on state-supported bank loans. In response, China has been reducing subsidies through its fiscal and banking systems, promoting competition and enhancing corporate governance.[39]

In the past, the extent of NPLs in the SOCBs was not readily apparent. A 2002 study found that the then-existing system understated NPLs by an average of fifteen per cent.[40] In the same year, some analysts suggested that the total NPLs could be over 40 per cent of all loans, as opposed to 25 per cent under the then-existing system as reported by the PBOC.[41] The monopoly status of the SOCBs and their close links with the national economy mean that bankruptcy is not a possible solution to China's banking problems due to the tremendous social and economic costs bankruptcy demands. Given the concentration of banks, the closure of any SOCB would, in all likelihood, generate serious bank runs and, potentially, the collapse of the entire banking system and perhaps China's financial and economic system. Considering the poor profitability of the SOCBs and their weak risk-control systems,[42] seeking to address NPL problems solely through growth underpinned by deregulation ('growing out of the problem') is also not an appropriate means,[43] although clearly this does have a role. Transition issues, such as social and political stability, as well as sustainable economic growth suggest that a mild approach is more suitable in China's peculiar circumstances. With reference to international experience in the management and disposition of NPLs, the AMC concept must be both a feasible and expeditious way to improve the financial condition of China's SOCBs.[44]

II.B.   THE AMC CONCEPT

China has adapted the AMC concept on the basis of experiences of other jurisdictions, for example, inter alia, Finland, Japan, Sweden and the United States. The ultimate objective of an AMC is to resolve its NPL portfolio and achieve maximum value. In achieving this objective, a number of techniques are available to address NPLs through the AMC framework. This objective and

---

39. The Chinese Economy, supra note 36, p. 17.
40. *China Banking System Outlook: China's Banks Walk a Tight Rope* (Hong Kong, Moody's Investors Service, October 2002), p. 11.
41. Ibid.
42. 'Development and Supervision of Wholly State-Owned Commercial Banks', *Almanac of China's Finance and Banking* [2003] (Beijing, Editorial Board of Almanac of China's Finance and Banking, 2003), pp. 66–67.
43. F. Montes-Negret and L. Papi, *The Polish Experience in Bank and Enterprise Restructuring*, World Bank Working Paper 1705 (Washington D.C., 1996), p. 2.
44. The Second Plenary Session of the Ninth National People's Congress: *Working Report by the Central Government*, March 1999.

the related techniques inevitably involve complicated legal issues. The success in achieving this objective depends highly on the relevant law, legal institutions and supporting institutional framework. For example, unless the issues in respect to property rights related to these assets are addressed, enabling the banking system to work on commercial principles would not be an easy task. In the first auction of an NPL portfolio by Huarong AMC to foreign and domestic purchasers, a consortium led by Morgan Stanley paid RMB 10.8 billion for four out of five pools of assets.[45] However, this consortium paid only eight-to-nine cents on the dollar, because of the legal risks that arose from uncertain property rights.[46]

According to economists, two problems are associated with NPLs:

- the stock problem: old loans that are non-performing;
- the flow problem: new loans that may also be non-performing.

Accordingly, two approaches have been employed to solve NPL problems.[47] In cases in which the entire banking system – and perhaps the real economy – are suffering systemic problems, the stock solution can be adopted to dispose large volumes of bad debts and restructure distressed banking institutions.[48] This approach includes liquidating distressed banking institutions, disposing of impaired assets and restoring viable but illiquid banking institutions.[49] In restructuring problematic banking institutions, timely disposal of NPLs is crucial to a successful and expedited bank restructuring.[50] In non-systemic crisis contexts, the flow approach enables problematic banking institutions to recapitalize over time by elevating operational profits through relaxation of regulatory requirements.[51] This approach to resolution is known as 'financial

---

45. 'Morgan Stanley Consortium completes China's largest NPL portfolio sale', Press Release by Morgan Stanley, (Beijing, 13 March 2003), available at www.morganstanley.com/cgi-bin/morganstanley.com/pressroom.cgi?action=load&uid=157 (30 January 2005).
46. N. Chan, 'Huarong loan auction draws strong response', *South China Morning Post* (Hong Kong, 21 October 2003), p. B3.
47. A. Sheng (ed.), *Bank Restructuring: Lessons from the 1980s* (Washington D.C., World Bank, 1996), p. 40; C. Dziobek and C. Pazabasioglu, *Lessons from Systemic Bank Restructuring: A Survey of 24 Countries*, IMF Working Paper WP/97/161 (Washington D.C., 1997), pp. 7–8; D. Klingebiel, *The Use of Asset Management Companies in the Resolution of Banking Crises: Cross-Country Experience,* World Bank Policy Research Working Paper 2284 (Washington D.C., 2000), p. 3.
48. Ibid.
49. Ibid.
50. Ibid.
51. Regulatory forbearance is applied to deal with banking problems by lowering capital adequacy requirements, making tax treatments more liberal, relaxing loan loss reserves and provisioning requirements and implementing lenient accounting standards. The prerequisites to employ this approach are that the crisis is temporary and the banks are fundamentally sound. An important assumption is that the banks must gradually recapitalize themselves by improving their profits. See Box 2, 'Forbearance: Never? If Ever, When? And How?' in S. Claessens, 'Experiences of Resolution of Banking Crises', in *Strengthening the*

forbearance'.[52] A number of countries have applied stock and flow models to dispose of and manage NPLs, as well as to perform corporate restructurings.[53] According to international experience, two structural models are generally adopted in managing and recovering impaired assets: decentralized and centralized.[54] The decentralized solution leaves the NPLs on the books of banking institutions and establishes an internal asset management unit, in other words, a 'bad bank', to dispose of the bad assets.[55] Usually these units are subsidiaries of the distressed banking institutions, and their major task is to manage the transferred problem assets and to recover as much from these assets as possible.[56] The centralized approach requires the transfer of problem assets to a single organization with the sanction of the state because of their quality and scale.[57]

The AMC concept is a workable solution in dealing with NPLs and restructuring impaired banking institutions. According to a recent study, of 26 banking crises worldwide, in nine cases an AMC strategy was adopted.[58] This approach has been employed in helping to resolve problems brought to the surface by the Asian financial crises (1997–1998) in a number of Asian countries, including Indonesia, Korea and Malaysia.[59] Economists have examined the advantages and disadvantages of these two approaches,[60] types of assets, magnitude of the problem, depth of markets and characteristics of debtors contributing to the structural arrangement of AMCs.[61] Regardless of the corporate governance structure of the AMC, a sound legal framework is essential in managing and disposing assets effectively from their transfer to debt recovery.[62] The AMCs should be vested with legal privileges in ensuring clear title to transferred assets and lowering transaction costs, for example, simplifying notification obligations of creditors in transferring assets.[63] The legal framework should include effective bankruptcy, corporate and securities law along with

    Banking System in China: Issues and Experience, Bank of International Settlement Policy Papers 7 (Basel, 1999), p. 283.
52. Klingebiel, supra note 47, p. 3.
53. Sheng, supra note 47, p. 40; Dziobek and Pazabasioglu, supra note 47, pp. 7–8; Klingebiel, supra note 47, pp. 3–4.
54. Klingebiel, supra note 47, p. 4.
55. Klingebiel, Ibid., p. 4; C. Lindgren, *Financial Sector Crisis and Restructuring: Lessons from Asia, Occasional Paper* 188 (Washington D.C., International Monetary Fund, 1999), p. 3.
56. Ibid.
57. Ibid.
58. Klingebiel, supra note 47, p. 2.
59. In handling huge NPLs after the Asian financial crises, Korea, Malaysia, Thailand and Philippines set up AMCs to accelerate the disposition of mounting bad assets and to help the revival of unviable banks.
60. S. Ingves, S. A. Seelig and D. He, *Issues in the Establishment of Asset Management Companies,* International Monetary Fund Policy Discussion Paper, PDP/04/3 (Washington D.C., 2004), pp. 9–10; D. Klingebiel, supra note 47, pp. 4–6.
61. Ingves, Seelig and He, supra note 60, p. 8.
62. Ibid., pp. 11–12.
63. Ibid.

well-trained lawyers and an effective judiciary.[64] To avoid conflict of interests arising from China's thin secondary debt market and complex relationship among banking institutions, corporate borrowers and AMCs, a legal environment drawing foreign investment into the domestic NPL market can expedite the disposition of NPLs and the restructuring of troubled enterprises.[65] However, China's legal infrastructure has yet to be fully developed.

The causes of NPLs are dependent upon historic, economic, political and legal factors. Accordingly, vehicles adopted for resolving NPLs should be flexible. AMCs are no exception.[66] In Korea and the United States, AMCs were employed to dispose of NPLs is as short a time frame as possible.[67] In Sweden and Finland, AMCs were employed to restructure disabled corporate borrowers and troubled banking institutions.[68] Studies have shown that AMCs with clearly defined and consistent objectives are more likely to be successful than those with mixed and conflicting goals.[69] AMCs with the narrow objective of disposing NPLs at a rapid pace tend to be more effective than those with wider objectives, such as supporting corporate restructuring.[70] A sound corporate governance structure is crucial for AMCs to achieve satisfactory performance.[71] Legal mechanisms should be implemented to ensure the independence, transparency and accountability of AMCs.[72] In addition, AMCs must be free from political pressure, with their own budgets, balance sheets and independent legal status.[73] Independent auditing and regular publication of relevant information are required to maintain transparency.[74] From an economic perspective, AMCs must be profit-oriented and should provide incentives to motivate employees and management to achieve their objectives.[75] The legal framework of China's AMCs should address these issues.

II.C.   THE DEVELOPMENT OF AMCS IN CHINA

As noted above, in 1993, the State Council issued the *Decision on Financial System Reform* separating policy loans from the state-owned specialized banks with

---

64. Ibid.
65. G. Ma and B. Fung, *China's Asset Management Corporations*, Bank of International Settlement Working Paper 115 (Basle, 2002), p. 15.
66. For details of financial crises and resolution mechanism, as well as major features of AMCs, including types, governance structure, objectives, funding, management, the process of the asset transfer and disposition and the legal environment in which AMC operates, see Klingebiel, supra note 47, Annex Table 1–10.
67. Ibid., pp. 13–15.
68. Ibid., pp. 18–19.
69. Ingves, Seelig and He, supra note 60, pp. 5–6.
70. Klingebiel, supra note 47, pp. 2–3.
71. Ingves, Seelig and He, supra note 60, p. 13.
72. Ibid., pp. 13–18.
73. Ibid., pp. 13–14.
74. Ibid., pp. 14–15.
75. Ibid., p. 18.

the ultimate aim of transforming them into state-owned commercial banks.[76] Two years later, two pieces of banking legislation, the Law of the People's Bank of China ('PBOC Law') and the Commercial Banking Law, were enacted to reinforce the commercialization of the banking sector. However, it was not until the recapitalization scheme in 1998,[77] and the closure of a number of distressed financial institutions in 1999,[78] that the CPG made serious attempts to improve the profitability and competitiveness of the SOCBs. Despite the implementation of the basic legal and regulatory framework to enhance the competitiveness of China's banking institutions, the most imminent issue to address was the NPL problem. In 1999, the State Council created four AMCs as provisional institutions to address these issues.[79] While there no legal provision stipulated that the corporate life of the AMCs, the life of AMCs is generally considered to be ten years, because their issued bonds have a ten year maturity period.[80] The AMCs are designated to take over the NPL assets of the SOCBs on a debt-equity swap basis. Each SOCB is assigned an AMC, in other words, Great Wall for ABC, Orient for BOC, Cinda for CCB and Huarong for ICBC,[81] with nearly RMB 1.4 trillion NPLs in total initially transferred.[82]

The AMCs were created halfway through China's three-year SOE rescue program – a program launched in 1997 to rescue inefficient large and medium-sized SOEs through restructuring their management to transform them into modern corporate entities.[83] The AMCs are expected to play an active role in this process. Legally, the AMCs were created as part of the banking reforms in commercializing the SOCBs. The reforms include divesting most NPLs from

---

76. Sect. 3, *Decision of the State Council on Financial System Reform*, National Distribution (*guo-fa*) 1993, no. 91 [1993] (Beijing, State Council, 25 December 1993).
77. Resolution by Standing Committee of National People's Congress on Approving the State Council's Advice Supplementing the Capital Reserves of the Solely State-Owned Commercial Banks through Issuing Special Government Bonds, Standing Committee of National People's Congress (Beijing, 28 February 1998).
78. J. Zhu, 'Closure of Financial Institutions in China', in *Strengthening the Banking System in China: Issues and Experience,* Bank of International Settlement Policy Papers 7 (Basel, 1999), p. 309.
79. Notice of the People's Bank of China, Etc. on Establishing China's Cinda Asset Management Company (*guoban-fa*) no. 33 [1999] (Beijing, General Office of the State Council, 4 April 1999; Notice of the People's Bank of China, etc. on Establishing China's Huarong, Great Wall and Orient Asset Management Company (*guoban-fa*) no. 66 [1999] (Beijing, General Office of the State Council, 21 July 1999).
80. Ma and Fung, supra note 65, p. 1.
81. Notice of the People's Bank of China, Etc. on Establishing China's Cinda Asset Management Company (*guoban-fa*) no. 33 [1999] (Beijing, General Office of the State Council, 4 April 1999); Notice of the People's Bank of China, etc. on Establishing China's Huarong, Great Wall and Orient Asset Management Company (*guoban-fa*) no. 66 [1999] (Beijing, General Office of the State Council, 21 July 1999).
82. 'Financial Asset Management Companies', [2002] *Almanac of China's Finance and Banking* (Beijing, Editorial Board of Almanac of China's Finance and Banking, 2002), p. 52.
83. H. Sheng, 'Report on Reform and Turnaround of China's State-Owned Enterprises', *Gazette of the Standing Committee of National People's Congress* (Beijing, National People's Congress, 15 January 2001).

the SOCBs, maximizing the recovery value of the transferred NPLs, relieving the heavy debt burden of SOEs and improving the governance structure of SOEs through the debt-equity swap scheme.[84] The debt-equity swap scheme, which converts selected debt claims to AMC-held equity stakes in selected SOEs, is an important strategy in restructuring SOEs by releasing their debt burden and enhancing state supervision over their management.[85] Therefore, the arrangements pertaining to their ownership structure and their operation focus on policy objectives rather than profit-orientation. Experience from other jurisdictions has shown that most AMCs have multiple objectives, because they are often set up in response to systemic banking crises, which are often closely related to corporate performance.[86] Therefore, expediting corporate restructuring and promptly disposing of bad assets are often designated as two parallel objectives of AMCs. These AMC objectives are also valid in the case of China. Because SOEs still dominate China's economic landscape, it was inevitable that the nation's AMCs would engage in corporate restructuring, because most NPL assets they acquired arose from loans obtained by the SOEs.

In 2000, the State Council promulgated rules regulating AMCs (the 'AMC Regulations').[87] However, the AMCs were under the respective jurisdiction of the PBOC, the MOF, as well as the China Securities Regulatory Commission (CSRC).[88] The China Banking Regulatory Commission (CBRC) was established in April 2003 and assumed the regulatory functions of the PBOC, including regulation of banks, AMCs and trust and investment companies,[89] with the main task of maintaining a sound and safe financial system.[90] The PBOC continues its role as China's central bank, including with a new mandate to support financial stability in addition to monetary policy.[91] However, both are arms of the State Council and, therefore, their regulatory functions are certainly affected by political considerations.

---

84. Sect. 1, 2 and 19, AMC Regulations, State Council Decree 2000, no. 297 (Beijing, State Council, 10 November 2000).
85. Sect. 19, AMC Regulations, State Council Decree 2000, no. 297 (Beijing, State Council, 10 November 2000).
86. Klingebiel, supra note 47, p. 7.
87. AMC Regulations, State Council Decree 2000, no. 297 (Beijing, State Council, 10 November 2000) (referred to in this chapter simply as 'AMC Regulations').
88. Ibid., sect. 4.
89. Decision of the Standing Committee of the National People's Congress on the Exercise of Regulatory and Supervisory Functions by the China Banking Regulatory Commission in Place of the People's Bank of China (Beijing, Standing Committee of National People's Congress, 26 April 2003).
90. Art. 1 and 3, Law of the People's Republic of China on Banking Regulation and Supervision, 2003.
91. Notice of the Central Committee Office on the Adjustment of Major Functions, Internal Organizations and Staff of the PBOC, available at <www.pbc.gov.cn/detail.asp?col=100&ID=1012&keyword=> (30 January 2005).

III.   THE LEGAL FRAMEWORK OF CHINA'S AMCS

The absence of legislative provisions to clarify the real status of the AMCs, as well as their uncertain corporate life, affects the AMCs' operation.[92] This section discusses the jurisdiction of the AMCs and their regulatory framework. However, much of the regulatory framework related to the AMCs relies on state policy rather than legislation. This legislative forbearance may be justified on the basis of flexibility and expediency in disposing NPLs, but the legislation also risks violating the principles of the rule of law.

III.A.   THE MANDATES OF THE AMCS

The AMCs are state-owned non-banking financial institutions with their own independent legal identities.[93] Under the AMC Regulations, in managing and disposing NPLs, APCs can engage in:

- debt collection;
- leasing, transferring or restructuring acquired assets;
- debt-equity swaps and holding equity stakes in enterprises for a period of time;
- issuing bonds and borrowing from financial institutions;
- listing recommendation and security underwriting; and
- financial and legal consultation, project evaluation, as well as other business activities approved by the PBOC and the CSRC.[94]

AMCs have a mandate to maintain their assets and minimize losses.[95] They can purchase NPL assets from the SOCBs subject to criteria established by the State Council,[96] and manage and dispose these assets.[97] Naturally, their corporate governance inherits the traditional problems of all SOEs in China in dealing with complex financial issues with limited experience and expertise and in the absence of clear, non-political rules.

The AMCs have the mandate to purchase NPL assets according to their book value.[98] Because their rates of recovery are more likely to occur at a lower level than book value, AMCs have often been criticized as a failure.[99] When

---

92. J. Zheng, 'Investigation on Asset Disposal of Beijing Office of the Four AMCs', *Almanac of China's Finance and Banking 2002* (Beijing, Editorial Board of Almanac of China's Finance and Banking, 2002), p. 745.

93. Sect. 2, AMC Regulations, State Council Decree 2000, no. 297 (Beijing, State Council, 10 November 2000).

94. Ibid., sect. 10.

95. Ibid., sect. 3.

96. Ibid., sect. 11.

97. Ibid., sect. 2.

98. Ibid., sect. 12.

99. S. Gao, 'Difficulties in evaluating the AMCs', [2005] *21st Century Business Herald* (Guangzhou, 17 January 2005).

foreign investors are involved, the pressure of 'losing state assets' restricts NPL disposition.[100] Therefore, it would be unrealistic to evaluate the performance of AMCs solely on recovery value. However, loans scheduled to be written off are excluded from this mandate.[101] Still, the loans are restricted to those created prior to 1996.[102] The rationale is that, prior to 1996, most loans created by the SOCBs were policy loans.[103] Since 1996, the SOCBs have had to bear the credit risks of their lending.[104] The MOF injected RMB 10 billion into each AMC as registered capital.[105] The purchase of NPL assets is financed by loans granted by the PBOC originally designated to the SOCBs and bonds issued to the SOCBs.[106] Although no law or policy stipulates that the State guarantees these types of bonds, these bonds are nevertheless implicitly backed by the state.[107] The State Council fixes the annual interest of these loans at 2.25 per cent.[108] Accordingly, the state is indirectly subsidizing SOCBs in writing off their NPLs through the AMC vehicles.

III.B.   LEGISLATIVE FORBEARANCE

To maximize the recovery value of transferred NPLs, AMCs are empowered to take drastic measures in management and disposal.[109] As in other jurisdictions, special laws and regulations have been implemented to grant the AMCs wider powers in disposing NPLs.[110] The subordinate legislation, which stipulates

---

100. Z. Li, 'Whether the AMCs Sell State Assets Cheaply', [2005] *21st Century Economic Report* (Beijing, 10 January 2005).
101. Para. 4, Notice of the People's Bank of China, etc. on Establishing China's Huarong, Great Wall and Orient Asset Management Company (*guoban-fa*) [1999] no. 66 (Beijing, Office of the State Council, 21 July 1999).
102. Ibid.
103. G. Xiao, *Property Rights and China's Economic Reform* (Beijing, China's Social Science Publishing House, 1997), p. 395; Lardy, supra note 34, pp. 91–92; *The World Bank China 2020, Series: Development Challenges in the New Century* (Washington, D.C., World Bank, September 1997), p. 31.
104. Ibid.
105. Sect. 5, AMC Regulations, State Council Decree 2000, no. 297 (Beijing, State Council, 10 November 2000).
106. Ibid., sect. 14.
107. Ma and Fung, supra note 65, pp. 6–7. This fact was also confirmed indirectly by officials of the People's Bank of China in a reception for journalists. See 'Answers by the Men in Charge from the People's Bank of China to the Journalists on Problems Concerning the Implementation of 'Financial Asset Management Company Regulations', *Almanac of China's Finance and Banking 2001* (Beijing, Editorial Board of Almanac of China's Finance and Banking, 2001), p. 247.
108. Sect. 14, AMC Regulations, State Council Decree 2000, no. 297 (Beijing, State Council, 10 November 2000).
109. Sect. 10, AMC Regulations, State Council Decree 2000, no. 297 (Beijing, State Council, 10 November 2000).
110. Ingves, Seelig and He, supra note 60, pp. 11–12.

the status, powers and liabilities of the AMCs, is the AMC Regulations, an administrative regulation enacted by the State Council in 2000 under the PRC Constitution.[111] The enabling act of the Regulation is a provision of the PRC Banking Supervision Law which provides that 'where the laws [i.e. *legislation*] and administrative regulations provide otherwise the regulation and supervision of policy banks and asset management companies, these provisions shall prevail.'[112]

However, according to the PRC Legislation Law, laws are paramount over all subservient administrative regulations codifying state policies.[113] *A fortiori*, the PRC Banking Supervision Law, enacted by the Standing Committee of the National People's Congress (NPC), cannot prevail over the PRC Legislation Law, which is a 'fundamental law' enacted by the full NPC.[114]

In practice, policies issued by the various state agencies, as well as judicial interpretations issued by the Supreme People's Court, constitute the core regulatory framework of the AMCs. In facilitating the transfer of NPLs from the SOCBs to the AMCs and the recovery process, extensive powers are granted to the AMCs.

Still, there is little legal support in China for legislative forbearance. However, 'policy functions as law' is an important feature of the Chinese legal system in its transformation from a planned economy to a socialist market economy.[115] The very fact that China is now progressing towards a socialist market economy, as a state policy, is a clear violation of the PRC Constitution, which stipulates that 'the state shall practice economic planning on the basis of socialist public ownership'.[116] In constructing the institutional framework, policies often prevail over formal arrangements, such as laws and regulations.[117] This also applies to China's AMCs. In March 1999, the Working Report of the CPG recommended 'gradually setting up the AMCs to dispose current NPLs and implementing strict responsibility for the quality of new loans'.[118] Subsequently to the Report, Cinda AMC was established and a series of policy documents were

---

111. Article 89(1), PRC Constitution, 1982 (revised in 1988, 1993, 1999 and 2004).
112. Article 48, *Law of the People's Republic of China on Banking Regulation and Supervision*, 2003 (referred to in this chapter simply as the 'PRC Banking Supervision Law').
113. Article 79, Law of People's Republic of China on Legislation, 2000 (referred to in this chapter simply as 'PRC Legislation Law').
114. Article 7, PRC Legislation Law, 2000.
115. J. Chen, 'Policy as Law and Law as Policy: The Role of Law in China's Development Strategy', in C. Antons (ed.), *Law and Development in East and Southeast Asia* (London and New York, Routledge Curzon, 2003), pp. 255–256.
116. Article 15, PRC Constitution, 1982 (revised in 1988, 1993, 1999 and 2004).
117. J. Zhang, *Legal Change Pattern and Political Stability: China's Experience and Its Implications in Economics of Law*, available at <article.chinalawinfo.com/article/user/article_display.asp?ArticleID=22893> (11 March 2005).
118. 'Working Report by the Central Government', The Second Plenary Session of the Ninth National People's Congress (Beijing, March 1999).

promulgated to define the status and jurisdiction of the AMCs.[119] The Decisions of Reform and Development of SOEs,[120] approved by the Central Committee of the CCP in September 1999, confirmed the establishment of the first AMC. One month later, an additional three AMCs were approved.[121] Although the NPC had proposed that the NPL problem should be resolved through the AMC concept, its activation was nevertheless signalled by the CCP. In practice, policy steers China's economic and political reform. Policy is the foundation of law, and law is the institutionalization of policy.[122] In other words, laws merely implement the policies of the CCP.[123] Because the CCP's policies have evolved during this transitional period, China's legal system has had to take an ad hoc and piecemeal approach.[124] Therefore, the legal framework regulating AMCs in this evolving system consists of regulations, rules, decisions and orders made under various ad hoc policies. Accordingly, statues, administrative regulations, orders and so on lack clarity, certainty, universality and stability.[125]

China's legislative hierarchy includes laws (as legislation is also known), administrative regulations, local regulations, autonomous regulations and special rules.[126] The NPC and its Standing Committee are empowered to enact laws.[127] The State Council can make administrative regulations under the PRC Constitution or empowering laws.[128] The NPC and its Standing Committee can invest the State Council with power to make administrative regulations within the scope of their legislative power.[129] The State Council can then recommend the NPC and its Standing Committee to enact these regulations into laws whenever practicable.[130] China's legislative system, therefore, has incorporated an experiential feature designed to meet the needs of a rapidly changing and developing economy. However, the differing interests among various government departments and local governments have resulted in inconsistency of

---

119. 'Notice of the People's Bank of China, Etc. on Establishing China's Cinda Asset Management Company' *(guoban-fa)* [1999] no. 33 (Beijing, General Office of the State Council, 4 April 1999).
120. 'Decisions on Some Important Issues of Reform and Development of State-Owned Enterprises', Fourth Plenary Session of the 15th Central Committee of China Communist Party (Beijing, Central Committee of China Communist Party, 27 September 1999) .
121. 'Notice of the People's Bank of China, Etc. on Establishing China's Huarong, Great Wall and Orient Asset Management Company' *(guoban-fa)* [1999] no. 66 (Beijing, Office of the State Council, 21 July 1999).
122. P. Keller, 'Legislation in the People's Republic of China', 23:3 *U.B.C. Law Rev.*, p. 643.
123. J.F. Chen, 'Policy as Law and Law as Policy: the Role of Law in China's Development Strategy', in C. Antons (ed.): *Law and Development in East and Southeast Asia* (London and New York: Routledge Curzon, 2003), p. 256.
124. Ibid.
125. Ibid.
126. Article 2, PRC Legislation Law, 2000.
127. Ibid., art. 7.
128. Ibid., art. 56; Article 89, PRC Constitution, 1982 (revised in 1988, 1993, 1999 and 2004).
129. Art. 56, PRC Legislation Law, 2000.
130. Ibid.

these administrative regulations.[131] Legislative competition among government agencies to seek rents by issuing regulations, orders and complex procedures further complicates the matter.[132]

The legal framework regulating AMCs in China is a relatively complex and evolving system, composed of administrative regulations made by the State Council and two judicial interpretations of the Supreme People's Court, as well as a number of administrative orders, decisions and opinions made by various departments and commissions of the State Council.[133] These administrative regulations, orders and so on are specifically tailored for the AMCs. In addition, a number of non-AMC-specific regulations are applicable to the AMCs. For example, the Provisional Rules on SOE Reorganization[134] provides a basic framework for the entry of foreign capital to restructure SOEs. Although the legal framework that regulates the AMCs relies heavily on administrative regulations, orders and so on, no law exists to harmonize and rationalize these regulations and orders. Because these regulations, orders and so on are made by different government departments with different mandates, conflicts inevitably arise; a situation that is inconducive to attracting foreign capital to China's NPL market.[135]

The enforceability of the special laws and policies under which the AMCs operate has yet to be improved. The policy-dominated regulatory framework implies that the AMCs cannot enjoy the certainty of legal support and are vulnerable to outside interference. Conversely, policies have the advantage of flexibility and expediency. For example, the Decisions of Reform and Development of SOEs, made by the Central Committee of CCP as a practical guideline, permits non-listed SOEs to transfer their land use rights allocated by the state upon approval.[136] The granting fees, paid by the assignee of the land use rights

---

131. J.W. Zhang, *Legal Change Pattern and Political Stability: China's Experience and its Implications in Economics of Law*, available at <article.chinalawinfo.com/article/user/article_display.asp?ArticleID=22893> (11 March 2005).

132. Ibid.

133. For example:

   – Provisional Rules on Drawing Foreign Capital into the Asset Restructuring and Disposal by Financial Asset Management Companies;
   – Circular of the General Office of the State Council on Transmitting the Opinions on Exerting Further Efforts in the Work of Debt-Equity Swap of State-owned Enterprises of the State Economic and Trade Commission, the Ministry of Finance and the People's Bank of China;
   – Measures on the Asset Disposition of Financial Asset Management Company.

134. 'Provisional Rules on Reorganization of SOEs by Using Foreign Fund 2002', no. 42 (Beijing, State Administration for Industry and Commerce, 26 October 2001).

135. Y. Du, 'Trying to Solve the Problems in Approving the Sale of NPLs to Foreign Investors', [2004] *21st Business Herald* (Guangzhou, 8 January 2004).

136. 'Decisions on Some Important Issues of Reform and Development of State-Owned Enterprises', The Fourth Plenary Session of the 15th Central Committee of China Communist Party (Beijing, Central Committee of China Communist Party, 27 September 1999), Para.7(4).

to the assignor enterprise, may then be used to increase its capital, reduce debts or undertake structural adjustment.[137] This policy is beneficial to the AMCs because some of the use rights on land owned by them, which originate from NPLs, are allocated without paying fees to the state. The local land department must approve the mortgage of allocated land-use rights[138]. Some local governments, however, would only permit the transfer of land-use rights when these types of rights are granted rather than allocated and all the granting fees are paid under the PRC Urban Real Estate Management Law.[139]

The Law of the People's Courts stipulates that 'the Supreme People's Court gives interpretation on questions in regard to specific application of laws and decrees in adjudicating cases'.[140] This, in effect, empowers the Supreme People's Court to make judicial interpretations. This power is also provided in the Resolution on Strengthening the Work of Law Interpretation, approved by the Standing Committee of the NPC in 1981, that the Supreme People's Court can interpret laws in adjudicating cases.[141] However, the power to enact laws is the exclusive jurisdiction of the NPC and its Standing Committee,[142] and the role of the court, which has no legislative power, is to interpret laws.[143] In addition, 'legislative interpretation', which occurs when a provision in a law or decree require further definition as to its limits or supplementary stipulations, is entrusted to the Standing Committee of the NPC.[144] Legislative interpretation has the same binding force as legislation.[145] Under the PRC Constitution, the Standing Committee has the final interpretation power subject to the veto of the full NPC.[146] The court cannot make new law under the guise of judicial interpretation. As in common law countries, the line is often blurred. In China, the court most often

---

137. Ibid.
138. 'Provisional Rules of the Assignment and Transfer of the Right to the Use of State-Owned Land in Urban Areas', State Council Decree 1990, no. 55 (Beijing, State Council, 1990), sect. 44.
139. Article 15, Law of the People's Republic of China on Urban Real Estate Management, 1994.
140. Article 33, Law of the People's Republic of China on Organization of the People's Courts, 1979 (revised in 1983 and 1986).
141. Sect. 2, Resolution on Strengthening the Work of Law Interpretation, 1981 (Beijing, Standing Committee of National People's Congress, 10 June 1981).
142. Article 58, PRC Constitution, 1982 (revised in 1988, 1993, 1999 and 2004). Article 7, PRC Legislation Law, 2000.
143. Article 123, PRC Constitution, 1982 (revised in 1988, 1993, 1999 and 2004). Article 33, Law of the People's Republic of China on Organization of the People's Courts, 1979 (revised in 1983, 1986).
144. Sect. 1, Resolution on Strengthening the Work of Law Interpretation, 1981 (Beijing, Standing Committee of National People's Congress, 10 June 1981); Article 67(4), PRC Constitution, 1982 (revised in 1988, 1993, 1999 and 2004); Article 42, PRC Legislation Law, 2000.
145. Article 47, PRC Legislation Law, 2000.
146. Articles 67(11), 64, 67(1) and (4), PRC Constitution, 1982. (revised in 1988, 1993, 1999 and 2004)

exercises its power actively in interpreting laws.[147] Although the court can only exercise judicial power under the PRC Constitution in adjudicating cases before it,[148] the court often declares new rules or regulations in adjudicating cases.[149] It can be argued that the court exceeds its jurisdiction and such practice is not conducive to the rule of law.[150] Two judicial interpretations given by the Supreme People's Court in 2000 and 2001, however, have cleared most of the AMCs' legal barriers. This would circumvent the intention of the laws in cases such as notice of obligation to creditors, change of registration of mortgaged rights and maximum amount of mortgages. These will be discussed later in this article.

The problem of the AMCs is aggravated by the policy-based transfer of NPLs. First, since most transferred NPLs arose from policy loans, the restructuring of these assets by AMCs would face intervention from parties with vested interests. Second, the SOEs, which are the root of the NPLs, were established under the planned economy system and politically they have to provide the social security net to employees and retired employees. This is a burden the AMCs must resolve in avoiding social instability. The titles of transferred assets are encumbered by socio-economic issues, such as housing, medical benefits, pensions and other social security measures to the workers and retired workers. Therefore, this affects asset prices.[151] The successful operation of such a program very much depends on how it is implemented by the relevant policies and law. However, China's legal infrastructure is still developing.

III.C.   THE REGULATORY FRAMEWORK OF THE AMCS

Regulatory authority over China's AMC is divided among a number of agencies, i.e. CBRC, CSRC, MOF and PBOC, each of which is established under its own law and with its own respective mandates and powers.[152] All of these

147. N. Liu, *Judicial Interpretation in China* (Hong Kong and Singapore, Sweet & Maxwell Asia, 1997), p. 78.
148. Under the PRC Constitution, the Supreme People's Court is the highest judicial organ, but the court's interpretive role is not mentioned. Article 127, PRC Constitution, 1982 (revised in 1988, 1993, 1999 and 2004). See: N. Liu, supra note 35, p. 78; Article 33, Law of the People's Republic of China on Organization of the People's Courts, 1979 (revised in 1983 and 1986). Resolution on Strengthening the Work of Law Interpretation, 1981 (Beijing, Standing Committee of National People's Congress, 10 June 1981), sect. 2.
149. Liu, supra note, pp. 78 and 90. It has been pointed out that since 1978 the Standing Committee has rarely exercised its power to interpret legislation.
150. Liu, supra note, pp. 89–91.
151. In the first auction of NPL portfolio by Huarong AMC to foreign and domestic investors, it was reported that the consortium led by Morgan Stanley paid only eight to nine cents on the dollar. See N. Chan, 'Huarong loan auction draws strong response', *South China Morning Post* (Hong Kong, 21 October 2003), p. B3.
152. PRC Banking Supervision Law, 2003; Law of the People's Republic of China on Securities, 1998 (revised in 2004), Chapter 10; Major Mandates of the Ministry of Finance, available at <www.mof.gov.cn/wwwroot/C120020517181417291/index/index.jsp> (Beijing, Ministry

agencies are represented on the AMCs' supervisory boards.[153] Since their interests in the AMCs are different, their regulatory policies toward the AMCs often conflict. As the only shareholder of the four AMCs, the MOF takes charge of the development of the AMCs and ultimately would have to bear their losses under the reasonable assumption that they eventually incur substantial financial losses.[154] The PBOC is more interested in their loan recovery. The CBRC enforces the relevant laws and regulations respecting the AMCs, and it has a duty to control financial risks and maintain stability in the banking system.[155] The CSRC, as the major regulator supervising the securities business in China, oversees the securities activities of the AMCs. Because members of senior management of the AMCs are appointed by the state,[156] whether the various state agencies could deal with AMCs impartially without preferential treatment is doubtful.

If these regulatory agencies are combined into a single superagency, the overlapping supervisory costs, as well as effort, can be avoided. One solution is to establish a central body to supervise the CBRC, CSRC, MOF and PBOC in coordinating the regulatory framework of the financial sector. This may, however, not be politically acceptable. One regulatory objective is to maintain and promote the fairness, efficiency, competitiveness, transparency and orderliness of the financial sector. In avoiding differing interpretation of policies and laws by different state agencies, regulations from various state agencies, such as CBRC, CSRC, MOF and PBOC, should be harmonized and rationalized. Like any piece of law, substance, such as the enforcement mechanism, rather than the form is what counts. The root of the problems in regulating the financial sector rests with the conflicting roles in enforcing the regulations rather than the banking law and policies.

IV.   CORPORATE GOVERNANCE OF AMCs

China's AMCs are state-owned, non-banking financial institutions with power to manage enterprises.[157] The AMCs are headquartered in Beijing with local

---

of Finance, 1 February 2005); Law of the People's Republic of China on People's Bank of China, 1995 (revised in 2003), Chapter 1.

153. See websites of the four AMCs: Supervisory Board: <www.cindamc.com.cn/introduce/about_supervise.html> (1 February 2005); Corporate Structure: <www.chamc.com.cn/jianjie/jie4.htm> (1 February 2005); Organizational Structure <www.coamc.com.cn/dongfang/include/center/zzjg.asp> (1 February 2005); and Corporate Bylaws <www.gwamcc.com/aboutus/index1.asp> (1 February 2005).

154. Sect. 32, AMC Regulations, State Council Decree 2000, no. 297 (Beijing, State Council, 10 November 2000).

155. Art. 1, PRC Banking Supervision Law, 2003.

156. AMC Regulations, State Council Decree 297 (Beijing, State Council, 10 November 2000), sect. 8.

157. 'Development and Supervision of Financial Asset Management Companies', *Almanac of China's Finance and Banking 2003* (Beijing, Editorial Board of Almanac of China's Finance and Banking, 2003), p. 74.

branch offices established in areas most adversely affected by NPLs, such as Wuhan, Shenyang and so on.[158] Although each AMC corresponds to a SOCB, no equity link exists between the two. Therefore, each AMC is independent from its corresponding SOCB. In strengthening the state supervision over the business operations of the AMCs, a supervisory board has been established in each AMC under the AMC Regulations and the Provisional Ordinance of the Supervisory Board in Key State-owned Financial Institutions.[159] No modern corporate governance structure is in place in these AMCs. Each AMC has a supervisory board and its management structure includes a chief executive and several deputy chief executives.[160] An independent board of directors has yet to be appointed for each AMC. The chief executive, appointed directly by the State Council, is responsible for the management and business operation of the AMC.[161] Members of the supervisory board are responsible to the State Council, which appoints these board members.[162] The supervisory board looks after the finances of the AMCs and supervises the chief executive and principal managers, with the ultimate purpose of protecting state property and interests.[163] The head office takes charge of the entire business of each AMC, and the local branches have no independent legal status and run their business without the authorization of the headquarters. However, effective governance mechanisms are essential in ensuring their profit-orientation free from political interference, since AMCs are state-owned enterprises funded by the MOF. The AMCs' independence, transparency and accountability have yet to be improved.

Because the AMCs were established as state agencies intended to handle the legacy of the SOCBs and SOEs, AMCs are vulnerable to political pressure. The parallel objectives of expediting corporate restructuring and disposing NPL assets promptly that the AMCs must achieve are often conflicting and leave room for state interference. For example, in the debt-equity swap scheme, the State Economic and Trade Commission (SETC) is empowered to select the enterprises capable of taking part in the scheme, and the AMCs can

---

158. *Organizational Structure of Cinda AMC*: <www.cindamc.com.cn/cindaen/Organizational Structure.html> (1 February 2005); *Corporate Structure of Huarong AMC*: <www. chamc.com.cn/English/our%20company/corp.htm> (1 February 2005); *Organization of Orient AMC*: <www.coamc.com.cn/dongfang/include/english/zzjg.asp> (1 February 2005); and *Organization Structure of Great Wall AMC*: <www.gwamcc.com/en/aboutus/index4.asp> (1 February 2005).

159. AMC Regulations, State Council Decree 2000, no. 297 (Beijing, State Council, 10 November 2000) sect. 9. The Provisional Ordinance of the Supervision Committee of State-Owned Key Financial Institutions, State Council Decree 2000, No. 282 (Beijing, State Council, 15 March 2000).

160. Sect. 8, AMC Regulations, (Beijing, State Council Decree No. 297, 10 November 2000).

161. Sect. 8, AMC Regulations, State Council Decree No. 297 (Beijing, State Council, 10 November 2000).

162. 'The Provisional Ordinance of the Supervision Committee of State-Owned Key Financial Institutions' State Council Decree 2000, no. 282 (Beijing, State Council, 15 March 2000).

163. Excerpt from the Huarong AMC Corporate Bylaws, available at <www.chamc.com.cn/jianjie/jie3.htm> (1 February 2005).

only review the qualifications of enterprises and make conversion agreements with SOEs.[164] Inevitably, the SETC must consider state policy in the selection process. Transparency in regard to their operation and performance is important to enhance accountability and to protect them from outside intervention. International experience suggests that the financial report of an AMC should be audited by an independent auditor regularly to ensure the accuracy of its financial statements and to ensure exposure of financial risks to stakeholders in a timely way.[165] The periodic reports of AMCs should be published to ensure transparency.[166] However, the requirements to disclose financial information on AMCs still remain inadequate. No comprehensive regulation is in place to regulate the disclosure of business information by the AMCs.[167]

The AMCs, in addition, are financial institutions without the requisite human resources. The incentive mechanisms for staff are not well-developed. Prior to issuing the Measure of Assessing the Disposition of NPLs of the AMCs[168] by the MOF, the AMCs adopted the salary scale of the SOCBs.[169] The AMCs could not offer bonuses, welfare or other allowances, and the incentive mechanism of the AMCs must conform to the salary limits approved by the state.[170] In reality, the AMCs do not have sufficient experienced and skilled employees to manage and dispose of NPLs. Therefore, establishing a sound incentive system is important to attract and motivate employees and mangers to pursue the AMCs' objectives. Since the NPL assets were transferred at their book value,[171] no effective mechanism is available to evaluate the performance of the AMCs and their employees.

V.   STATE POLICY TOWARDS DISPOSING NPLs

As of the end of August 2000, the value of NPL assets transferred from the SOCBs and China Development Bank (CDB) to the AMCs was RMB

---

164. AMC Regulations, State Council Decree 2000, no. 297 (Beijing, State Council, 10 November 2000), sect. 18.
165. Ingves, Seelig and He, supra note 60, pp. 14–15.
166. Ibid.
167. AMC Regulations, State Council Decree 2000, no. 297 (Beijing, State Council, 10 November 2000), sect. 29 and 30; Financial Asset Management Company Financial Regulations (Trial) (*cai-jin*) 2000, no. 17 (Beijing, Ministry of Finance, 30 June 2001), sect. 11.
168. Measures for Financial Asset Management Companies Regarding Handling and Assessing Distressed Assets (Trial Implementation) (*cai-jin*), no. 251 (Beijing, Ministry of Finance, 12 November 2001).
169. Notice on Financial Issues of Asset Management Company, (*cai-zhai*), no. 265 (Beijing, Ministry of Finance, 23 December 1999), sect. 3.
170. Ibid.
171. AMC Regulations, State Council Decree, no. 297 (Beijing, State Council, 10 November 2000), sect. 12.

1.39 trillion;[172] specifically, twenty per cent of SOCBs' loans or eighteen per cent of China's gross domestic product in 1998 terms.[173] Under the AMC Regulations, the AMCs can acquire assets, including NPL assets.[174] The types of NPL assets transferred were restricted to the overdue, dead and loss loans under the former loan classification system that were issued by the SOCBs and CDB before the end of 1995, and the loans scheduled to be written off are excluded.[175] Overdue loans are defined as loans outstanding when the contract expires (including the extension period),[176] and dead loans refer to outstanding loans which are overdue after the prescribed period (including the extension period), or any loan and/or overdue loans that are less than the prescribed years, but for which the borrower has ceased production or the project construction has stopped.[177] Loans are classified as loss loans in accordance with the instructions of the MOF.[178] An official interpretation clarifies the transferable NPL assets as:[179]

- overdue and dead loans lent by the SOCBs before 1995 and formed in 1998;
- unrecoverable loans as to the end of September 1999;
- part of CDB's NPLs;
- if issued after 1995, loans approved by the State Council to be converted into equity;
- interests chargeable to the profit and loss account of all of these types of loans.

The three major types of assets acquired by the AMCs are debt, equity and real property, of which debt comprises the largest share of assets: approximately 72 per cent.[180] Most of these NPLs, however, are unsecured.[181] Seven per cent

---

172. 'Financial Asset Management Companies', *Almanac of China's Finance and Banking 2001* (Beijing, Editorial Board of Almanac of China's Finance and Banking, 2001), p. 49.
173. Ma and Fung, supra note 65, p. 2.
174. Sect. 11 and 12, AMC Regulations, State Council Decree No. 297 (Beijing, State Council, 10 November 2000). Any interest not chargeable to profit and loss account is transferred without compensation.
175. Notice of the People's Bank of China, etc. on Establishing China's Cinda Asset Management Company (*guoban-fa*) [1999], no. 33 (Beijing, General Office of the State Council, 4 April 1999), para. 4. Notice of the People's Bank of China, etc. on Establishing China's Huarong, Great Wall and Orient Asset Management Company (*guoban-fa*) [1999], no. 66 (Beijing, General Office of the State Council, 21 July 1999).
176. General Lending Principles 1996 (Beijing, People's Bank of China, 28 June 1996), sect. 34.
177. Ibid.
178. Ibid.
179. 'Answers by the Men in Charge from the People's Bank of China to the Journalists on Problems Concerning the Implementation of Financial Asset Management Company Regulations, *Almanac of China's Finance and Banking 2001* (Beijing: Editorial Board of Almanac of China's Finance and Banking, 2001), p. 246.
180. Gao, supra note 90.
181. P. Xie and D. Li, 'Difficulties, Effects and Future in the Operation of China's AMCs', in J. Wu (ed.), *Comparative Studies* (Beijing: CITIC Publishing House, 2003), vol. 9, p. 164.

of the assets managed by the AMCs are real property and 47 per cent are manu-facturing.[182] The former asset type is easier to recover. In the case of Great Wall AMC, it was estimated that 56 per cent of NPL carve-outs are credit lending, and only 44 per cent are secured loans, of which 25 per cent are void guaranties and mortgages. In 47 per cent of the cases, the debtors either went bankrupt or disappeared.[183] The SOE equity holdings of the AMCs mainly arose from the debt-equity swap scheme, as well as from the assets transferred from the SOCBs. Each AMC must deal with a wide range of debtors across the entire country. For example, assets purchased by Cinda AMC involve 58,900 debtors, covering 31 provinces.[184] Industrial sector debts mainly come from traditional business, including real estate, coal, chemical, building materials, textile and so on.[185] Huarong AMC took over 72,000 debtors,[186] and Orient AMC took over more than 20,000 enterprises, including over 70,000 loans.[187] Approximately 1.95 million debtors are involved in the acquired assets by Great Wall AMC.[188] Realistically, the diversity of the AMCs' asset portfolios and the number of debtors make it difficult for the AMCs to manage and dispose of NPLs.

As discussed previously, the scope of NPL assets acquired by the AMCs are largely restricted to loans issued before 1995.[189] This policy-based criterion implies that the state would only assume responsibility for NPLs arising from loans granted before 1995.[190] However, this implication is misleading, because nearly one-third of all loans granted by SOCBs before 1995 were policy loans, which comprised the majority of NPLs.[191] Under the Commercial Banking Law enacted in 1995, the SOCBs finally became independent commercial enti-ties.[192] For historical reasons, the commercialization of the SOCBs overrides the moral-hazard problem that AMCs can rely on the state in the future. The advantage of transferring the NPL assets to the AMCs at their book values[193]

---

182. Ma and Fung, supra note 65, p. 12.
183. Xie and Li, supra note 181, p. 164.
184. *Business Operation*, see <www.cindamc.com.cn/cindaen/BusinessOperation.html> (Beijing, Cinda AMC) (1 February 2005).
185. Ibid.
186. *Company Profile*, see <www.chamc.com.cn/English/our%20company/gongsijianjie.htm>. (Beijing, Huarong AMC) (1 February 2005).
187. *Corporate Introduction*, see <www.coamc.com.cn/dongfang/include/english/e_about.asp> (Beijing, Orient AMC) (1 February 2005).
188. 'Financial Asset Management Companies', *Almanac of China's Finance and Banking 2002* (Beijing, Editorial Board of Almanac of China's Finance and Banking, 2002), p. 53.
189. Notice of the People's Bank of China, etc. on Establishing China's Cinda Asset Manage-ment Company (*guoban-fa*), no. 33 [1999] (Beijing, General Office of the State Council, 4 April 1999) para. 4. Notice of the People's Bank of China, etc. on Establishing China's Huarong, Great Wall and Orient Asset Management Company (*guoban-fa*) no. 66 [1999] (Beijing, General Office of the State Council, 21 July 1999).
190. Ma and Fung, supra note 65, pp. 2–3.
191. Xiao, supra note 103, p. 395; Lardy, supra note 34, pp. 91, 92; *China 2020*, supra note 103, p. 31.
192. Law of People's Republic of China on Commercial Banks, 1995 (revised in 2003), art. 4.
193. AMC Regulations, State Council Decree, no. 297 (Beijing, State Council, 10 November 2000), sect. 12.

can outweigh the transaction costs, because the magnitude and complexity of these assets make valuation infeasible.[194] For this reason, the AMCs will inevitably undertake huge losses in disposing of NPLs. In the absence of law or authoritative guidelines, making decisions to dispose of AMC assets would be difficult, because the burden of causing loss in state assets is high.[195]

Under the AMC Regulations, the registered capital of each AMC is RMB 10 billion.[196] With the exception of China Orient AMC, which has 40 per cent of its registered capital in US dollars because parts of its NPL assets are foreign currency loans, the registered capital of each AMC is in RMB.[197] The funding of the AMCs mainly comes from the MOF, loans from the PBOC and bonds issued to the SOCBs.[198] Under an order of the MOF, the priority of AMCs' repayment is the interest of the bonds that the AMCs issued to the SOCBs, followed by the interest of the loans borrowed from the PBOC, and finally bond principal and loan principal.[199] At the end of December 2004, the total disposition of NPLs by the four AMCs amounted to RMB 675 billion, and the cash recovery reached 20.3 per cent.[200] Because most transferred assets come from those traditional industry sectors with lower quality collateral, a high recovery rate was not expected. However, the pressure of paying bond and loan interest requires additional funding to the AMCs.[201]

In alleviating the financial burdens and expediting the disposal process, the AMCs enjoy certain privileges relating to finance and taxation. Under an order of the State Planning Commission – now the National Development and Reform Commission, or NDRC – all regional authorities and departments must take appropriate measures in alleviating the unreasonable burdens of the AMCs, and intermediary agencies of the community should offer preferential treatment to the AMCs in charging their fees, including assessment fees, notary fees and auditing and legal services fees.[202] The Supreme People's Court

194. M. Zhu and J. Huang, 'Discussion on China's AMC', no. 12 [1999] *Journal of Economic Research*, p. 6.
195. J. Zheng, 'Investigation on Asset Disposal of Beijing Office of the Four AMCs', *Almanac of China's Finance and Banking 2002* (Beijing, Editorial Board of Almanac of China's Finance and Banking, 2002), p. 743.
196. AMC Regulations, State Council Decree 297 (Beijing, State Council, 10 November 2000), sect. 5.
197. Notice of the People's Bank of China, etc. on Establishing China's Huarong, Great Wall and Orient Asset Management Company (*guoban-fa*), no. 66 [1999] (Beijing, General Office of the State Council, 21 July 1999), sect. 2.
198. Sect. 14, AMC Regulations, State Council Decree 2000, no. 297 (Beijing, State Council, 10 November 2000).
199. Notification by the Ministry of Finance Concerning Issues of Financial Asset Management Companies' Bonds and Re-Borrowing Interests Payment (*cai-jin*) no. 261 (Beijing, Ministry of Finance, 6 December 2001), sect. 2.
200. China Banking Regulatory Commission, 'The CBRC released the statistics regarding non-performing assets disposal by AMCs in 2004', *Press Release* (Beijing, 13 January 2005) <www.cbrc.gov.cn/english/index.htm> (30 January 2005).
201. Ma and Fung, supra note 65, pp. 11–12.
202. Notification by the State Planning Commission Concerning the Regulations of the Service Charge for the Intermediary Service Confronted by Financial Asset Management

permitted the AMCs to pay specific service fees at half price.[203] In 2001, an order issued jointly by the MOF and State Administration of Taxation provided a series of preferential treatments for AMCs in paying taxes.[204]

VI.   PROPERTY RIGHTS OF TRANSFERRED
                       AMC ASSETS

The transfer of RMB 1.39 billion of NPL assets from the SOCBs to the AMCs in 1999 was the largest disposal of financial assets in China's history. This was also the first time the CPG addressed the NPL issue seriously.[205] Naturally, this type of mandatory transfer package also granted the AMCs more legal power in the management and disposition of NPLs. Nevertheless, the legal issues pertaining to the transfer warrant further discussion. The most important issue is the validity of loans sold by the SOCBs. The second issue is the transfer of creditor rights, as well as ancillary rights attached to these rights. The third issue is the relevant provisions in Chinese company law. The experience of the Resolution Trust Company (RTC) in the United States and the debt restructuring practice of SOEs in Poland show that privileges and quasi-judicial powers granted to AMCs are effective in protecting their rights in seeking remedies.[206] As an example, in the United States, the RTC was authorized to invalidate burdensome contracts and to override certain laws of the states.[207] Naturally, it can be argued that this violates the rule of law. However, this authorization is also necessary and essential in China's circumstances, considering the country's poor credit culture and magnitude of NPLs.

The situation in China is quite different from other transitional economies. Economic reform in China is progressing at a faster speed than its legal development, because legislative innovation requires time to adapt. The rule of law is an ideal objective for China's legal development to achieve. A balance must be struck between this idealistic theory and the urgent need to meet the global challenge and to enhance the quality of life of the population in post-WTO China. Strict adherence to the rule of law must be carried out by humans,

---

Companies During Their Acquisition and Disposal of Distressed Assets (*ji-jiage*) no. 391 [2001].

203. Notification by the Supreme People's Court Concerning Litigation Fare of Legal Cases With Respect to Financial Asset Management Companies' Assets Formed by Acquisition, Management and Disposal of State-Owned Banks' Non-Performing Loans (Beijing, Supreme People's Court, 25 October 2001).
204. Notice of Ministry of Finance, etc. on Taxation Policies for China Cinda, etc. Financial Asset Management Companies (*cai-shui*) [2001], no. 10.
205. AMC Regulations (Beijing, State Council Decree 2000 No. 297, 10 November 2000).
206. Klingebiel, supra note 47, Annex Table 3; F. Montes-Negret and L. Papi, *The Polish Experience in Bank and Enterprise Restructuring*, World Bank Working Paper 1705 (Washington D.C., 1996), p. 7.
207. Klingebiel, supra note 47, Annex Table 3.

which cannot be perfect. However, any deviation from the rule of law should be exercised with utmost caution and should be restricted; for example, deviation from rule of law would not be applicable in criminal justice, where the rights of the citizens are in jeopardy. In banking reform, legislative forbearance, insofar as necessary and essential in ascertaining the legitimate property rights of the creditors must be permitted in addressing fraud and procedural defects which cannot be promptly addressed by the legislative process. In China, banking reform, which supports its economic development, should have priority over legal and political development, as maintaining social stability is a perquisite to the successful implementation of rule of law and democracy. The following sections illustrate how the legal inflexibility is circumvented by administrative policies in enabling the AMCs to achieve their objectives in disposing NPLs.

VI.A.   THE TRANSFER OF NPL ASSETS

In accordance with Chinese contract law, the transfer of NPL assets from the SOCBs to the AMCs is contractual in nature.[208] A creditor can transfer its contractual right to a third party, depending on the nature of the contract, the agreement itself and the provisions of laws.[209] Under the Commercial Banking Law, banking business does not cover disposing loan assets.[210] Because banking is a highly regulated business, the legality of these types of disposals is questionable. To avoid doubt, the State Council approved the transfer of RMB 1.39 billion in NPL assets,[211] and its legitimacy was further strengthened by an administrative regulation issued by the State Council in 2000.[212] However, the validity of subsequent transfers of NPL assets by the AMCs to third-party investors remains uncertain. The AMC Regulations only affirms the validity of the assets transferred from the SOCBs to the AMCs, but falls short of addressing subsequent disposals by the AMCs to other investors. In any event, under the PRC Legislation Law, the Regulations cannot conflict with the laws enacted by the NPC or its Standing Committee.[213] Among the assets transferred, a substantial portion is real property. The AMCs exercise their mortgagee rights to acquire some of these assets. The sale of real estate must

---

208. Article 79, Law of the People's Republic of China on Contract, 1999.
209. Ibid.
210. Article 3, Law of the People's Republic of China on Commercial Banks, 1995, as revised in 2003.
211. Notice of the People's Bank of China, etc. on Establishing China's Cinda Asset Management Company (*guoban-fa*), no. 33 [1999] (Beijing, General Office of the State Council, 4 April 1999); Notice of the People's Bank of China, etc. on Establishing China's Huarong, Great Wall and Orient Asset Management Company (*guoban-fa*), no. 66 [1999] (Beijing, General Office of the State Council, 21 July 1999).
212. AMC Regulations, State Council Decree 2000, no. 297 (Beijing, State Council, 10 November 2000).
213. Art. 79, PRC Legislation Law, 2000.

comply with Chinese land law and other regulations in regard to the transfer of land use rights.[214] Foreign investors would take account of the creditor rights in making investment decisions.

VI.B.   NOTICE OF CREDITOR

Under Chinese contract law, the creditor has an obligation to serve notice on the debtor in regard to the transfer of contractual rights.[215] Otherwise, the debtor is not bound by the transfer.[216] The total number of debtors involved in the RMB 1.39 billion asset transfer exceeds two million nationwide.[217] Therefore, it seems impossible to notify all debtors to fulfil the legal obligation. The AMC Regulations, however, states that where AMCs acquire original creditor rights, debtors, guarantors and other related contracting parties must perform their obligations in accordance with original contracts.[218] However, whether or not such a decree of the State Council can circumvent the requirement of a legislative provision of the NPC is doubtful. In avoidance of doubt, the Supreme People's Court issued two judicial interpretations in 2001 and 2002 simplifying transfer procedures and securing the rights of AMCs. Under these interpretations, a transferor SOCB is deemed to have served its notice by publishing it in leading national or provincial newspapers.[219] In addition, the notice can be served by notifying the debtor in court during legal proceedings.[220] These special interpretations and rules on serving notice ascertain the rights of the AMCs in the assets transferred. However, because these rules only apply specifically to AMCs and not to other creditors, the rules fail to provide equality under the law.

---

214. Law of the People's Republic of China on Land Administration, 1986 (revised in 1988, 1994, 1998 and 2004); Law of the People's Republic of China on Urban Real Estates Administration, 1994.
215. Law of the People's Republic of China on Contract, 1999, art. 80.
216. Ibid.
217. *Business Operation*, see: <www.cindamc.com.cn/cindaen/BusinessOperation.html> (Beijing, Cinda AMC) (1 February 2005). Company Profile, see: <www.chamc.com.cn/English/our%20company/gongsijianjie.htm> (Beijing, Huarong AMC) (1 February 2005). Corporate Introduction, see: <www.coamc.com.cn/dongfang/include/english/e_about.asp> (Beijing, Orient AMC) (visited on 1 February 2005); 'Financial Asset Management Companies', *Almanac of China's Finance and Banking 2002* [2002] (Beijing, Editorial Board of Almanac of China's Finance and Banking, 2002), p. 53.
218. AMC Regulations, State Council Decree 2000, no. 297 (Beijing, State Council, 10 November 2000), sect. 13.
219. Regulations Concerning Laws Involving the Rulings of the Supreme People's Court on Legal Cases With Respect to Financial Asset Management Companies' Assets Formed by the Acquisition, Management and Disposal of State-Owned Banks' Non-Performing Loans (*fa-shi*) 2001, no. 12 (Beijing, Supreme People's Court, 11 April 2001), sect. 6.
220. Ibid.

VI.C.   TRANSFER OF SECURED INTERESTS

The NPL assets can have some value if their loans are secured by way of mort-gage. Chinese contract law allows the transfer of mortgage.[221] Some mortgaged properties, including land-use rights, real estate, forest, transportation vehicles and equipment, as well as other movables and pledged rights, must be regis-tered as third parties.[222] The Security Law, and its judicial interpretations by the Supreme People's Court in 2000, does not mention re-registration requirements that arise from either the amendment of a security contract or the assignment of both principal and the ancillary security contracts.[223] However, a number of relevant ministerial regulations apply. For example, the Administration of Urban Real Property Mortgage Procedures of the Ministry of Construction requires amended registration after any variation of the security contract.[224] The AMCs should comply with the same legal requirement in protecting their interests against third parties. In practice, however, the change of mortgagee requires the assistance of the mortgagor, who often prefers not to cooperate to avoid its contracting obligations. Transaction costs are attached to com-pliance with this legal requirement. In protecting the interests of the AMCs, the Supreme People's Court issued an interpretation in 2001 that provided the AMCs with immediate mortgagee rights. The interpretation stated that the registration of mortgaged rights attached to the assets acquired by the AMCs from the SOCBs remains valid upon the assignment of the principal creditor rights.[225] As a result, the original registration remains in force, and the burden of the AMCs to re-register the transferred mortgages is waived.

The AMC Regulations merely provide a basic business framework for the AMCs. In practice, conflicts exist between the AMC Regulations and the rel-evant law and regulations. Under Chinese contract law, for example, various provisions apply on notice of transfer of asset (creditor rights), the mortgage ceiling and so on. The Supreme People's Court made two judicial interpre-tations in 2001 and 2002, which respectively provided specific and practical guidelines in regard to the notice obligations of creditors, the change of reg-istration of mortgaged rights and the mortgage ceiling. These interpretations confer privileges to the AMCs in securing their rights as creditors. However, the legitimacy of the interpretations remains to be examined. One may doubt

---

221. Law of the People's Republic of China on Contract, 1999, art. 81.
222. Law of the People's Republic of China on Security, 1995, art. 42, 41, 78 and 79.
223. Law of the People's Republic of China on Security, 1995 and Judicial Interpretations by the Supreme People's Court on Applying Security Law (*fa-shi*), no. 4 [2000] (Beijing, Supreme People's Court, 8 December 2000).
224. Administration of Urban Real Property Mortgage Procedures 1995, no. 56 (Beijing, Ministry of Construction, 9 May 1997 and revised on 15 August 2001), sect. 35.
225. Regulations Concerning Laws Involving the Rulings of the Supreme People's Court on Legal Cases With Respect to Financial Asset Management Companies' Assets Formed by the Acquisition, Management and Disposal of State-Owned Banks' Non-Performing Loans (fa-shi), no. 12 [2001] (Beijing, Supreme People's Court, 11 April 2001), sect. 8.

the binding force of these judicial interpretations. The question is whether judicial interpretation can circumvent a provision of the laws enacted by the NPC. Because only AMCs enjoy the privileges, other creditors would incur higher transaction costs to secure similar rights. This violates equality under the law and fair market competition. More importantly, because the judicial interpretation made in 2001 merely secures AMC-acquired assets, subsequent transactions between the AMCs and other investors are still uncertain. This situation would discourage overseas investors.

VI.D.   CREDITOR RIGHTS OF AMCS

Like other creditors, the legal framework should provide sufficient avenues to enforce debts. Otherwise, the NPL assets have very little value. The laws on collateral and litigation in this respect, however, are archaic. As creditors, the AMCs must rely on their privileges in securing their rights. When the debtors are in default, the realization of creditor rights depends strongly on the recovery of related collateral. A sound litigation procedure is crucial as the last resort for creditors in securing their interests.

VI.D.1.   Collection of Collateral

Under Chinese security law, any mortgage term that operates to transfer the mortgaged property to the creditor in default of payment is void.[226] In case of default, the mortgagor and mortgagee must reach an agreement to pay the mortgagee after valuating the mortgaged property, or by auctioning or selling off the property so that the mortgagor can receive their equitable interest from the proceeds of sale, if any.[227] If no agreement is reached, the mortgagee must obtain relief from the court.[228] If relief is granted, the mortgagee can apply to the court to enforce his rights over the mortgaged property.[229] The court can then order the valuation of the mortgaged property for auctioning.[230] This provision is intended to protect the mortgagor from unconscionable mortgage terms.[231] However, these provisions have transaction costs attached and create uncertainty for the mortgagee. First, the *ex post* agreement must be made between the creditor and debtor if the creditor intends to recover his debt directly through auctioning or selling collateral; however, in most cases, the debtor is unlikely to cooperate. The judicial channel is costly and time-consuming, but it is the best

---

226.   Article 40, Law of the People's Republic of China on Security, 1995.
227.   Ibid., art. 53.
228.   Ibid.
229.   C. Huang (ed.), *New Explanation on Security Law and Relevant Regulations* (Beijing, People's Court Press, 2000), pp. 774–775.
230.   Ibid.
231.   Ibid., p. 773.

remedy available for creditors. Due to the close relationship among the courts, local governments and debtor SOEs, judicial independence remains doubtful.[232] Second, intervention from local governments makes recovering proceeds from the any collateral more difficult for the AMCs. A typical example is the mortgage of land-use rights. In China, land-use rights are usually the most valuable assets of SOEs, and creditors rely on these rights to secure their lending. However, to protect local interests, local governments always attempt to prevent the foreclosure of mortgaged property by interfering with the appraisers, auctioneers, courts and other administrative agencies involved in the valuation and sale of mortgaged property.[233]

In addition, outdated regulations do not encourage creditors to seek remedy in court. Under the Regulations on State-owned Industrial Enterprises Transformation of Operating System, the SOE's superior department must approve any mortgage of all its equipment.[234] In practice, this approval is rarely granted. Courts have ruled that these types of mortgages are non-binding.[235] In circumventing these archaic rules, the Supreme People's Court in 2002 directed the inferior courts not to render mortgages on machines and workshops of SOEs ineffective.[236] The registration system in China, however, is incomplete. As discussed earlier, except a few ministerial rules requiring the re-registration of mortgages after any variation to security contracts or terms,[237] there is no re-registration requirement arising from either amendment of security contracts or assignment of both principal and ancillary security contracts.[238] There is no uniform registration system nation-wide regarding requirements, procedures, fee charge standards and other particulars.[239] This incomplete registration system makes it more difficult for creditors to ascertain the property holdings of debtors.

232. F. Zhou (ed.), The Debt Work-Out for SOEs in China (Beijing, Peking University Press, 2003), pp. 162(164 and 243.
233. Ibid., pp. 239–240.
234. Article 15, *Regulations on State Owned Industrial Enterprises Transformation of Operating System, State Council Decree No. 123*, Beijing, State Council, 23 July 1992).
235. Xie and Li, supra note 181, p. 165.
236. Reply by the Supreme People's Court on the Binding Force of Mortgage Contracts Involving the Machinery Equipments of State-Owned Enterprise as Mortgaged Property (*fa-shi*), no. 14 [2002] (Beijing, Supreme People's Court, 18 June 2002).
237. Administration of Urban Real Property Mortgage Procedures, no. 56 [1997] (Beijing, Ministry of Construction, 9 May 1997, and revised in 15 August 2001), sect. 35.
238. Law of the People's Republic of China on Security, 1995 and Judicial Interpretations by the Supreme People's Court on Applying Security Law (*fa-shi*), no. 4 [2000] (Beijing, Supreme People's Court, 8 December 2000).
239. D. Wang, 'Developments and Prospects in China's Security Law', *China Law and Practice* (April 2003), p. 21.

VI.D.2.   Litigation

The law on limitation of action – in other words, the statute of limitations – in China further erodes the creditor rights of the AMCs. Under the General Principles of Civil Law, the limitation of action in civil cases is two years, unless otherwise stated by law.[240] This would pose a problem for the AMCs. The limitation period for AMCs to enforce their rights over NPL assets may have lapsed and AMCs often have difficulty locating the debtors and guarantors who are liable.[241] Some may even refuse to acknowledge receiving the statement of claims issued by the AMCs to avoid their liabilities.[242] In protecting the interests of the AMCs, the Supreme People's Court made two interpretations in 2001 and 2002, respectively, stating that a notice or announcement issued by the AMCs in regard to the transfer of creditor rights in leading national or provincial newspapers with the statement of claims bars the limitation period from running.[243] In addition, these interpretations operate retroactively to the date when the AMCs acquire the NPL assets from the SOCBs.[244]

VI.E.   THE PROVISIONS OF CHINESE COMPANY LAW

The top priority of AMCs is the disposal of their NPL assets. In addition to meeting the interest payments of their bonds, the assets the AMCs hold are depreciating. However, Chinese company law has yet to be enhanced in addressing these problems. The NPL assets acquired by the AMCs can be classified as creditor rights, equity rights and real property.[245] Equity shareholdings account for 21 per cent of the NPLs.[246] The validity of transferring creditor rights by the AMCs to other investors is uncertain. The shareholder rights of the AMCs

---

240. Article 135, General Principles of Civil Law, 1986 (Beijing, National People's Congress, 12 April 1986).
241. J. Zheng, 'Investigation on Asset Disposal of Beijing Office of the Four AMCs', *Almanac of China's Finance and Banking 2002* [2002] (Beijing, Editorial Board of Almanac of China's Finance and Banking, 2002), p. 743.
242. Ibid.
243. Regulations Concerning Laws Involving the Rulings of the Supreme People's Court on Legal Cases With Respect to Financial Asset Management Companies' Assets Formed by the Acquisition, Management and Disposal of State-Owned Banks' Non-Performing Loans (*fa-shi*) no. 12 [2001] (Beijing, Supreme People's Court, 11 April 2001), sect. 10; Reply of the Supreme People's Court Concerning Correspondence Concerning Questions Related to the Implementation of the '12 Articles' Judicial Interpretation by the Supreme People's Court (*fa-han*) no. 3 [2003] (Beijing, Supreme People's Court, 7 January 2002).
244. Ibid.
245. The Provisional Rules of Attracting Foreign Capital into Asset Restructuring and Disposition of Asset Management Companies, 2001 No. 6 [2001] (Beijing, Ministry of Foreign Trade and Economic Cooperation (26 October 2001), sect. 5.
246. Gao, supra note 90.

in SOCBs arose from the debt-equity swap scheme.[247] This scheme enables the AMCs to recover their debts by helping to revive failed enterprises through alleviating their debt burden. Under the debt-equity swap scheme, debts owed by the SOEs to the SOCBs were converted into shareholdings held by the AMCs. Accordingly, the SOEs save paying interest on those debts and have their debt ratio reduced. Under the legal framework, the AMCs can dispose of their interests in the SOEs by selling their shareholdings to the SOEs through share buy-backs, to third parties or publicly listing the shares through the stock exchanges.[248]

Under Chinese company law, shareholders of a joint-stock enterprise – in other words, a limited liability company – may not redeem their share capital after the enterprise is registered.[249] Similarly, sponsors and subscribers of an enterprise limited by shares cannot redeem their share capital after paying their subscriptions or contributing their capital in lieu, save under limited circumstances.[250] In addition, an cannot purchase its own shares except to reduce its capital or to merge with another enterprise that holds the enterprise's shares.[251] After buying back its shares, the enterprise must cancel these shares within ten days, register the capital change in accordance with the law, and make a public announcement subsequently.[252] Share buy-backs will reduce the capital of the enterprise, which in turn would affect the interests of creditors. Therefore, implementing measures to protect creditor rights is essential. According to Chinese company law, the reduction of the registered capital of an enterprise must be approved by the shareholder meeting.[253] In addition, an enterprise must present a balance sheet and detailed inventory of assets for consideration.[254] The enterprise must inform its creditors of the planned reduction within ten days following the date on which the resolution to reduce its capital is adopted and make at least three announcements in newspapers within 30 days.[255] Creditors have the right to claim full repayment of their debts, or corresponding guarantees from the enterprise, within 30 days of the date of receipt of the notice, or within 90 days of the date of the first public announcement of for those who received the notice.[256]

247. AMC Regulations, State Council Decree 2000, No. 297 (Beijing, State Council, 10 November 2000), sect. 16.
248. Ibid., sect. 21.
249. Article 34, Law of the People's Republic of China on Company, 1993 (revised in 1999).
250. Ibid., art. 93.
251. Ibid., art. 149.
252. Ibid., art. 149.
253. Ibid., art. 104(8).
254. Ibid., art. 186.
255. Ibid.
256. Ibid.

   To avoid the adverse effects of these provisions on AMCs, the AMC Regulations permits SOEs to buy-back their shareholdings from the AMCs. [257] Because the AMCs must pay interest on their bonds, they may have to realize their shareholdings in the SOEs to meet this obligation. Share buy-back by the enterprise was at one time employed as the most significant channel, due to the large number of legal barriers, both for private investors to purchase state-owned shares, and for most SOEs to go public. However, the provisions of Chinese company law make buy-back of shares by SOEs difficult. As an enterprise's capital is reduced after buying back its shares, the shareholders' general meeting must approve this type of transaction.[258] It is especially complicated for a joint-stock enterprise, which must have at least two, and not more than 50, shareholders.[259] If the shareholders of the enterprise fall outside this legal requirement, the validity of these types of transaction is in doubt. In reality, a number of SOEs have complained that share buy-back reduces its capital base, and therefore also increases its debt ratio.[260] In protecting the interest of the AMCs in debt recovery, share-buy back is a requisite term in close to 90 per cent of the debt-equity swap contracts.[261] As share buy-back could not be enforced in most debt-equity swap cases, and therefore was abolished by an administrative order of the State Council in 2003.[262] The risk also exists that the shareholdings of such SOE are not be diversified. However, an AMC can always transfer its shareholdings in a SOE to other investors.[263]

   The transfer of shares held by the AMCs faces several legal limitations. First, in the scheme of debt-equity conversion, an AMC becomes the sponsor shareholder of the newly established joint-stock enterprise. According to Chinese company law, the shares held by the sponsor of a joint-stock enterprise cannot be transferred within three years from the date of incorporation.[264] Second, because the shares held by the AMCs in SOEs are state-owned shares,[265]

257. AMC Regulations, State Council Decree 2000, No. 297 (Beijing, State Council, 10 November 2000), sect. 21.
258. Law of the People's Republic of China on Company, 1993 (revised in 1999), article 103.
259. Ibid., art. 20.
260. Industrial Policy Department, State Economic and Trade Commission, Working Progress in Debt-Equity Swap Scheme, 30 May 2001, available at: <www.setc.gov.cn/was40/detail?record=33&channelid=37134&presearchword=%D5%AE%D7%AA%B9%C9> (Beijing, State Economic and Trade Commission) (29 January 2005).
261. Zhou, supra note 233, p. 131.
262. Circular of the General Office of the State Council on Transmitting the Opinions on Exerting Further Efforts in the Work of Debt-Equity Swap of State-owned Enterprises of the State Economic and Trade Commission, the Ministry of Finance and the People's Bank of China (*guoban-fa*) [2003] no. 8 (Beijing, General Office of the State Council, 23 February 2003), sect. 3(15).
263. AMC Regulations, State Council Decree 2000, No. 297 (Beijing, State Council, 10 November 2000), sect. 21.
264. Law of the People's Republic of China on Company, 1993 (revised in 1999), art. 147.
265. Provisional Measures for Management of State Share of Stock Limited Companies 1994 (Beijing, Management Bureau of State-owned Assets and State Commission of Institutional Reform, 3 November 1994), sect. 2.

the shares' liquidity is subject to policy restrictions. Although the state-owned shareholders can transfer their shares to other enterprises and natural persons in and outside China,[266] how and at what price these shares are sold must follow prescribed procedures. State-owned shares can only be sold by agreement, which must be approved by relevant state agencies.[267] In addition, the selling price of state-owned shares cannot be lower than the par value of each share.[268] The lengthy and complicated approval procedures create uncertainty and increase transaction costs in disposing these shares. Selling prices based on impractical assessment rather than market discipline would limit the freedom of bargaining.

A thin secondary debt market with limited players makes it more difficult for the AMCs to dispose of their NPL assets at a reasonable price. Although the revised Commercial Banking Law opens the door for commercial banks to invest in enterprises within China, the law is still an exception.[269] The extent of this law requires further enactment. Commercial banks are not usually permitted to make investment in enterprises in China.[270] Securities and insurance companies cannot purchase the equity holdings of the AMCs, because the scope of their business is restricted by law.[271] Other private investors face great difficulties in entering the NPL market, due to insufficient funds and policy discrimination.[272] Foreign participation also encounters serious legal restrictions, as will be discussed in detail in a subsequent section.

Listing SOEs through the stock exchanges enables the AMCs to dispose of their shareholdings and promotes share diversification in the SOEs. In addition to the requirements of share capital and the diversification of shareholders, an enterprise that applies to list its shares must have been in operation for three or more years and must have made profits for the past three consecutive years.[273] Obviously, the SOEs in which the AMCs hold shares usually do not meet these requirements. Accordingly, the AMCs will take a longer time to dispose of their NPL assets through the stock exchanges. In addition, even if

---

266. Opinions on Behaviour Model Concerning State Shareholders of Stock Limited Companies in Exerting Shares (*guozi-qi*) [1997] no. 32 (Beijing, Management Bureau of State-owned Assets and State Commission of Institutional Reform, 24 March 1997), sect. 15.
267. Notification by the Ministry of Finance on Management of State Shares of Stock Limited Companies (*cai-guan*) [2000] no. 200 (Beijing, Ministry of Finance, 19 May 2000).
268. Supra note 266, sect. 17.
269. Decision of the Standing Committee of the National People's Congress on Revising the Law of People's Republic of China on Commercial Banks, 2003 (Beijing, Standing Committee of the National People's Congress, 27 December 2003), sect. 13.
270. Law of People's Republic of China on Commercial Banks, 1995 (revised in 20003), art. 43.
271. Law of the People's Republic of China on Securities, 1998 (revised in 2004), art. 129 and 130.
272. 'Critical Challenge on AMCs' Selling NPLs to Foreign Capital', available at: <finance.sina.com.cn/g/20041124/11411177640.shtml> (visited on 07 March 2005).
273. Law of the People's Republic of China on Company, 1993 (revised in 1999), art. 153.

the restructured SOE could be listed, state-owned shares and state corporate shares are not tradable in China's stock markets and their transfer can only be made by agreement. Accordingly, the SOE shares held by the AMCs are not highly liquid. In addition, state approval is required to list or transfer shares of large SOEs related to national development.[274]

VII.   FOREIGN PARTICIPATION

In the late 1970s, China began its open door policy. Since that time, the legal framework for foreign investment has continued to improve. In 2003, the Interim Provisions on Restructuring State-owned Enterprises with Foreign Investment was issued by the SETC and provides a basic framework for foreign capital to enter into the strategic restructuring of SOEs.[275] The profound relationship among the interested parties in China, for example, AMCs, SOCBs and SOEs, calls for participation of independent outside investors to dispose of NPL assets. Foreign partners are more likely to deal at arms length with these parties. In addition, these partners would bring in new financial resources, management skill and experience in assisting the AMCs to dispose of the NPL assets and in developing a secondary debt market. The legal framework for addressing the NPLs problems through absorbing foreign capital began to take shape in 2001 when the Provisional Rules on Drawing Foreign Capital into the Asset Restructuring and Disposal by Financial Asset Management Companies was enacted as an administrative regulation.[276] The legislation expressly states that all AMCs can receive foreign capital in restructuring and disposing of NPL assets. However, it only offers limited guidance to foreign investors in disposing of NPL assets and the related legal and regulatory problems have yet to be resolved.[277] In addition, foreign participation is regulated by the Catalogue of Industries for Guiding Foreign Investment.[278] Although China's WTO accession liberalizes the investment of overseas funds, some selected industries, for example, banking, finance companies and trust and investment companies,

274. Circular of the General Office of the State Council on Transmitting the Opinions on Exerting Further Efforts in the Work of Debt-Equity Swap of State-Owned Enterprises of the State Economic and Trade Commission, the Ministry of Finance and the People's Bank of China (*guoban-fa*) 2003 No. 8 [2003] (Beijing, General Office of the State Council, 23 February 2003), sect. 3(20).
275. Provisional Rules on Reorganization of SOEs by Using Foreign Fund [2002] no. 42 (Beijing, State Economic and Trade Commission, 8 November 2002).
276. Provisional Rules of Attracting Foreign Capital into Asset Restructuring and Disposition of Asset Management Companies [2001] no. 6 (Beijing, Ministry of Foreign Trade and Economic Cooperation, 26 October 2001).
277. D. Liu, 'Foreign Investment in NPL Assets: Is China's Legal Environment Up to the Task?', *China Law and Practice* (May 2003), pp. 27–28.
278. Catalogue of Industries for Guiding Foreign Investment [2004] no. 24 (Beijing, State Development and Reform Commission and Ministry of Commerce, 30 November 2004).

are still considered restricted industries, which makes foreign participation in these industries difficult.[279]

Under the Provisional Rules of Attracting Foreign Capital,[280] issued by the Ministry of Foreign Trade and Economic Cooperation (MOFTEC – now the Ministry of Commerce) in 2001, the AMCs are empowered to sell or transfer their creditor rights to foreign investors.[281] Debts purchased by foreign purchasers become foreign debts.[282] In China, the borrowing, use and repayment of foreign debt and contingent foreign debts are under strict state supervision.[283] All foreign debts, external guarantees, utilization of foreign debt and repayment must comply with the provisions of relevant laws and administrative regulations and measures.[284] However, in the absence of comprehensive laws and regulations on the transfer of debts from domestic creditors to foreign investors, the integration of debts sold by the AMCs to foreign investors into a uniform management system of foreign debt is a challenging issue. In 2004, the State Administration of Foreign Exchange (SAFE) issued a notification concerning the management of foreign debts arising from NPL assets.[285] This notification provides specific rules regulating the registration, approval and guarantee of foreign debts, as well as remittance of proceeds and so on.[286]

Under the Provisional Rules of Attracting Foreign Capital, the AMCs can dispose of their shares in non-listed SOEs.[287] However, the legislation is silent as to whether or not the AMCs can sell their shares in SOEs. In China, various rules apply on transfer of shares between listed and non-listed enterprises. In addition to restrictions on the transfer of shares held by the sponsors of an enterprise who cannot transfer their shares within three years after the date of incorporation,[288] an industrial restriction applies on foreign investment. Although market access for foreign investors was expanded after China's WTO accession, some industries remain off-limits to foreign capital. The two major

---

279. Catalogue for Restricted Foreign Investment Industries, Catalogue of Industries for Guiding Foreign Investment [2004] no. 24 (Beijing, State Development and Reform Commission, 30 November 2004), s. 7(1).
280. The Provisional Rules of Attracting Foreign Capital into Asset Restructuring and Disposition of Asset Management Companies [2001] no. 6 (Beijing, Ministry of Foreign Trade and Economic Cooperation, 26 October 2001).
281. Ibid., sect. 5(3).
282. Provisional Measures for Management of Foreign Debts (2003) no. 28 (Beijing, State Development and Planning Commission, 8 January 2003), sect. 2.
283. Provisional Measures for Management of Foreign Debts, 2003 No. 28 (Beijing, State Development and Planning Commission, 8 January 2003), sect. 8.
284. Ibid.
285. Notification on Foreign Exchange Administration Involving Using Foreign Capital to Dispose of NPLs by AMCs (hui-fa) (2004) no. 119 (Beijing, State Administration of Foreign Exchange, 17 December 2004).
286. Ibid.
287. The Provisional Rules of Attracting Foreign Capital into Asset Restructuring and Disposition of Asset Management Companies 2001 No. 6 (Beijing, Ministry of Foreign Trade and Economic Cooperation, et al., 26 October 2001), sect. 6.
288. Law of the People's Republic of China on Company, 1993 (revised in 1999), art. 147.

documents of the state on access of foreign capital classified these investors as encouraged, restricted and prohibited industries.[289] As noted previously, banking, finance companies, trust and investment companies are still considered to be restricted industries, which makes foreign participation more difficult for these companies.[290]

In the new round of SOE reform that commenced at the beginning of this century, the strategy of increasing foreign participation in the restructuring of SOEs has received wide support. Under the Provisional Rules on SOE Reorganization, a basic framework for the entry of foreign capital into the strategic restructuring of SOEs began to operate on 1 January 2003.[291] Foreign funds can be used to restructure SOEs and enterprise with state-owned shares into foreign-funded enterprises with the exception of financial companies and listed enterprises.[292] According to the provisional rules, an AMC can transfer its creditor rights in a SOE to a selected foreign investor, and the transferred SOE can then be restructured into a foreign-funded enterprise, or an AMC can sell all or part of the state-owned shares the AMC holds to selected foreign investors. Selected foreign investors must meet the following conditions:

– the management qualifications and technical skills required by the restructured enterprise;
– good business credit standing and management skills; and
– good financial standing and economic strengths.[293]

However, the scope of foreign investment is still restricted by the national industrial policies.[294] The transfer of creditor rights must be approved by holders of state-owned property rights of the restructured enterprise; and the transfer of state-owned share rights of an enterprise must be approved at the shareholders' general meeting.[295] The arrangement for redundant employees of the transferred SOE is still problematic for foreign investors. The priority of China's current policy is to maintain social stability. This puts additional burdens on foreign funds and consequently influences the selling price of the assets that

---

289. Catalogue of Industries for Guiding Foreign Investment 2004 No. 24 (Beijing, State Development and Reform Commission and Ministry of Commerce, 30 November 2004); Regulations on Guiding Foreign Investment Direction, State Council Decree [2002], no. 346 (Beijing, State Council, 11 February 2002).
290. 'Catalogue for Restricted Foreign Investment Industries', Catalogue of Industries for Guiding Foreign Investment 2004 No. 24 (Beijing, State Development and Reform Commission, 30 November 2004), sect. 7(1).
291. Provisional Rules on Reorganization of SOEs by Using Foreign Fund [2002] no. 42 (Beijing, State Administration for Industry and Commerce, 26 October 2001).
292. Provisional Rules on Reorganization of SOEs by Using Foreign Fund [2002], no. 42, op. cit, sect. 2.
293. Ibid., sect. 5.
294. Ibid., sect. 6.
295. Provisional Rules on Reorganization of SOEs by Using Foreign Fund 2002 No. 42, op. cit, sect. 7.

the AMCs hope to sell.[296] The restructuring parties, including the holders of state-owned property rights, the creditors of the state-owned enterprises that assign their credits, the enterprises that sell their assets, and the restructured enterprise must come up with a proper settlement plan before employees may be restructured, and the plan must be approved by the employee representative assembly.[297] The restructured enterprise must use its existing resources to meet the expenses, such as delayed salaries of the employees, un-rebated funds and overdue social security premiums.[298] The enterprise and the employees are entitled to a bilateral choice, in other words, the enterprise as employer and the workers as employees have their respective rights to choose whether to continue the employment contract.[299] The employment contract of employees retained must be renewed or altered.[300] Those employees whose contracts are terminated are entitled to compensation.[301] Employees who are transferred to social security organizations shall have their social security premiums paid in a lump sum, as prescribed by law.[302] The money for these payments is deducted from the net assets of the enterprise before its restructuring or as a priority payment from the proceeds of the disposed state-owned assets.[303] The procedure of applying for the approval of the restructuring is rather complicated and time-consuming.[304]

In utilizing foreign capital, techniques and management and improving the corporate governance of listed companies, a 2002 joint notice of the CSRC, MOF and SETC provides that shares in a joint-stock enterprise, whether state-owned or not, can be assigned to foreign investors.[305] However, the transfer is restricted to those listed in the Catalogue of Foreign Investment Industries.[306] The requirements for controlling shareholding or relatively controlling shareholding to be a Chinese party remain unchanged after the transfer.[307] The transfer must be open to public bidding following prescribed procedures.[308] After the transfer, the listed enterprises shall carry on the original policies and will not enjoy the treatments available to foreign invested enterprises.[309]

---

296. N. Chan, 'Huarong loan auction draws strong response', [2003] *South China Morning Post* (Hong Kong, 21 October 2003), p. B3.
297. Provisional Rules on Reorganization of SOEs by Using Foreign Fund [2002], no. 42 (Beijing, State Administration for Industry and Commerce, et al., 8 November 2002), sect. 8.
298. Ibid.
299. Ibid.
300. Ibid.
301. Ibid.
302. Ibid., sect. 8.
303. Ibid.
304. Ibid., sect. 9.
305. Notice of the Related Issues on Transfer of the State-owned Shares and the Legal Person Owned Shares in the Listed Companies to Foreign Investors (*zhengjian-fa*) [2002] no. 83 (Beijing, China's Securities Regulatory Committee, 1 November 2002).
306. Ibid., sect. 2.
307. Ibid.
308. Ibid., sect. 3 and 4.
309. Ibid., sect. 9.

As to the disposition of real property, China's WTO accession has liberalized investment opportunities for foreign investors. In the newly amended *Catalogue for Industries for Guiding Foreign Investment*, the development and construction of residential buildings is listed as an encouraged industry.[310] However, massive land development, as well as luxury hotels, villas, top office buildings and development and operation of large theme parks are still restricted to domestic investors.[311]

The AMCs are empowered to establish foreign invested enterprises with foreign capital by injecting share rights and real properties they hold.[312] Since 2002, when Huarong AMC established two separate joint-venture AMCs with Morgan Stanley Consortium and Goldman Sachs to dispose of NPLs,[313] several joint-venture AMCs received approval in the second international bidding.[314] Creditor rights, however, are not considered to be an eligible investment under Chinese company law.[315] Accordingly, foreign investors are reluctant to purchase creditor rights from the AMCs in establishing joint-venture AMCs. This situation creates difficulty because the majority of NPL assets held by the AMCs are creditor rights. The major function of joint-venture AMCs is to manage, restructure and dispose NPL assets, and the parties share the liabilities and proceeds according to the contracts. Joint investment fund enterprises may also be set up by the AMCs and foreign partners to diversify the disposal of NPL assets.[316] The joint-venture AMCs can make subcontracts or set up trusteeship of their asset portfolios with overseas institutions to expedite disposition.[317] The regulatory hurdles related to the transfer of state-owned assets to foreign companies, including the time-consuming procedures for government approval, increase transaction costs for foreign investors to enter into China's bad-debt

---

310. 'Catalogue for Encouraging Foreign Investment Industries', *Catalogue of Industries for Guiding Foreign Investment 2004*, no. 24 (Beijing, State Development and Reform Commission, 30 November 2004), sect. 8(1).
311. 'Catalogue for Restricted Foreign Investment Industries', *Catalogue of Industries for Guiding Foreign Investment 2004*, no. 24 (Beijing, State Development and Reform Commission, 30 November 2004).
312. Provisional Rules of Attracting Foreign Capital into Asset Restructuring and Disposition of Asset Management Companies [2001] no. 6 (Beijing, Ministry of Foreign Trade and Economic Cooperation, 26 October 2001), sect. 6.
313. 'No. 1 United AMC with Morgan Stanley and Rongshen AMC with Goldman Sachs', Press release, website of Huarong AMC: *Joint AMCs Get Approved in International Bidding of Huarong*, at <www.chamc.com.cn/xinxi/searchnews.asp> (31 January 2005).
314. W. Li, 'Huarong: Joint Projects in Disposing Assets Get Approved', [2004] *International Financial Newspaper* (Beijing, 13 December 2004).
315. Law of the People's Republic of China on Company, 1993 (revised in 1999), art. 24.
316. Provisional Rules of Attracting Foreign Capital into Asset Restructuring and Disposition of Asset Management Companies 2001 No. 6 (Beijing, Ministry of Foreign Trade and Economic Cooperation, 26 October 2001), sect. 6.
317. 'Huarong Getting Approval on the Establishment of Joint AMC' <www.chamc.com.cn/xinxi/searchnews.asp> (25 February 2005).

market,[318] which would impair their role in disposing of NPLs.[319] In addition, the valuation and pricing of NPLs are problematic, because the original transfer is at book value.[320] This can be remedied by permitting more investors into the market and implementing transparent and fair procedures to determine the asset value. The absence of legislative forbearance in alleviating the legal barriers of foreign participation indicates that China is still cautious about foreign investors.

VIII.	RESTRUCTURING STATE-OWNED ENTERPRISES

The debt-equity swap scheme is an important strategy in relieving the SOEs' debt burden and enhancing state supervision over their management. Under a policy of strict separation of financial business in China's financial markets, banking institutions cannot hold shares in enterprises.[321] Therefore, these institutions can hardly exert any influence as creditors on the operation of the SOEs. The debt-equity swap scheme initiated a new restructuring scheme for the SOEs. The high NPL level in the SOCBs is correlated to the high-debt level of the SOEs.[322] The state policy of replacing financial appropriation with bank loans from the early 1980s resulted in huge debt burden on SOEs developing during the last two decades.[323] The introduction of the AMC concept is intended to enhance the recovery of NPLs, to resolve financial risks, to balance the books of large and medium-sized SOEs, and to restructure the SOEs into modern corporations.[324] The dismantling of insider influence in the SOEs and diversifying their shareholdings are important tasks of the AMCs.

---

318. Ibid. The Morgan Consortium won the bid in November 2001, and the joint-venture AMC received approved until November 2002. The final transfer of assets was made in February 2003. See R. Hu, 'Internal and External Discovery', [2004] *Oriental Outlook* (Beijing, 30 May 2004).

319. K. Richardson, 'Chinese Banks' Bad Loans Draw More Scrutiny; Failed December Auction to International Investors Undercuts Beijing Cleanup', [2004] *Wall Street Journal (Eastern Edition)* (New York, 15 January 2004), p. A12. It was reported that 'A second international auction by Huarong, held last month, fell far short of expectations. Out of 22 pools of debt at the auction, only three received bids that met the minimum reserve prices set by Huarong'.

320. C. Wu, 'Grey Area in Disposing of Trillions of China's NPLs', [2005] *Southern Weekend* (Guangzhou, 27 January 2005).

321. Law of People's Republic of China on Commercial Banks, 1995 (revised in 20003), art. 43.

322. Lin, Cai and Li, supra note 30, pp. 221–222; F. Zhou, supra note 233, pp. 10–11.

323. F. Zhou, supra note 233, pp. 8–11.

324. Notification by State Economic and Trade Commission Concerning the Regulation, Operation and Management Consolidation of Debt-to-Equity Swapped Enterprises [2000] no. 921 (Beijing, State Economic and Trade Commission, 6 November 2000). Circular of the General Office of the State Council on Transmitting the Opinions on Exerting Further Efforts in the Work of Debt-Equity Swap of State-Owned Enterprises of the State Economic and Trade Commission, the Ministry of Finance and the People's Bank of China (*guoban-fa*) [2003], no. 8 (Beijing, General Office of the State Council, 23 February 2003).

Although the debt-equity swap scheme enables the AMCs to restructure non-performing SOEs, it is the SETC which selects the participating SOEs.[325] The AMCs can only review the qualifications of SOEs and make conversion agreements with them.[326] The ultimate decision must be approved by the State Council after consulting the SETC, MOF and PBOC.[327] The SETC inevitably has to consider state policy demands rather than the commercial interests of the AMCs in its selection process. The two criteria set up to select SOEs are whether or not:

- the loans arose before 1995 and the high debt level was mainly caused by the lack of capital, the float of foreign exchange rates, or enterprise expansion during the planned economy; and
- the SOE has quality products with market competitiveness, better management capability, an effective scheme for laid-off workers and so on.[328] All participating SOEs must establish a modern corporate system under relevant laws and regulations[329] and must be restructured into joint-stock enterprises.[330] The converted equity holdings are the capital contributions of the AMCs and the restructured assets form the share capital of the SOEs. The aggregated amount of equity each AMC owns in an SOE is not restricted by their net asset value.[331] The AMCs assumes the market risks of their shareholdings.

After negotiations with the SOEs, local governments, relevant government departments, the SETC selected 601 SOEs, of which 508 SOEs joined the debt-equity swap scheme with debt conversion amounting to RMB 405 billion.[332]

325. AMC Regulations, State Council Decree 2000, No. 297 (Beijing, State Council, 10 November 2000), sect. 18.
326. Ibid.
327. Ibid.
328. Understanding Debt-Equity Swap Scheme in Ten Aspects [25 October 1999], available at: <www.setc.gov.cn/was40/detail?record=128&channelid=37134&presearchword%D5%AE%D7%AA%B9%C9> (Beijing, State Economic and Trade Commission) (29 January 2005). See also: 'Financial Asset Management Companies', *Almanac of China's Finance and Banking 2001* (Beijing, Editorial Board of Almanac of China's Finance and Banking, 2001), p. 49.
329. Notification by State Economic and Trade Commission Concerning the Regulation, Operation and Management Consolidation of Debt-to-Equity Swapped Enterprises [2000], no. 921 (Beijing, State Economic and Trade Commission, 06 November 2000), para. 4. Circular of the General Office of the State Council on Transmitting the Opinions on Exerting Further Efforts in the Work of Debt-Equity Swap of State-Owned Enterprises of the State Economic and Trade Commission, the Ministry of Finance and the People's Bank of China (*guoban-fa*) [2003] no. 8 (Beijing, General Office of the State Council, 23 February 2003), para. 1.
330. Ibid.
331. AMC Regulations, State Council Decree 2000, No. 297 (Beijing, State Council, 10 November 2000), sect. 16.
332. 'Financial Asset Management Companies', *Almanac of China's Finance and Banking 2001* (Beijing, Editorial Board of Almanac of China's Finance and Banking, 2001), p. 49.

This covers 29 per cent of all NPL assets acquired by the AMCs. On 1 April 2000, the NPLs of these SOEs which participated in the scheme became share capital.[333] These selected SOEs have no obligation to pay interest on these NPLs. According to a State Statistic Bureau survey, this type of interest amounted to RMB 3.7 billion and accordingly the debt-equity ratio of these SOEs fell to below 46 per cent,[334] from approximately 70 per cent in the early 1990s.[335] However, it was estimated that nearly 90 per cent of debt-equity swap contracts impose a duty on the SOE to buy-back their shares within a fixed time.[336] This, however, would result in increasing their debt level, and would not be conducive to diversifying their shareholders.

Most of the non-profit making assets of the SOEs arise from their social policy burden, including nurseries, schools and health and social services for the employees and their dependents.[337] Severing the non-performing or non-profitable assets of the SOEs and then injecting the assets into new companies is an option in restructuring SOEs.[338] Although it is addressed both in official documents and conversion contracts that local governments must support the relief of social burdens from the SOEs,[339] financial difficulties of local governments have postponed most of their commitments.[340] After the debt-equity swap, the SOEs are obliged to implement efficient corporate governance structures, at the

---

333. Circular of the General Office of the State Council on Transmitting the Opinions on Exerting Further Efforts in the Work of Debt-Equity Swap of State-Owned Enterprises of the State Economic and Trade Commission, the Ministry of Finance and the People's Bank of China (*guoban-fa*) [2003] no. 8 (Beijing, General Office of the State Council, 23 February 2003), para. 1(6).

334. 'Financial Asset Management Companies', *Almanac of China's Finance and Banking 2001* (Beijing, Editorial Board of Almanac of China's Finance and Banking, 2001), p. 49.

335. F. Zhou, supra note 233, pp. 8–9.

336. Industrial Policy Department of the State Economic and Trade Commission, *Working Progress in Debt-Equity Swap Scheme* [30 May 2001], available at <www.setc.gov.cn/was40/detail?record=33&channelid=37134&presearchword=%D5%AE%D7%AA%B9%C9> (Beijing, State Economic and Trade Commission) (29 January 2005).

337. Y. Lin and C. Li, *Reforms of China's State-Owned Enterprises and Financial Structure*, Working Paper No. C2003027 (Beijing, China Centre for Economic Research, 6 October 2003).

338. Notification by State Economic and Trade Commission Concerning the Regulation, Operation and Management Consolidation of Debt-to-Equity Swapped Enterprises [2000] no. 921, (Beijing, State Economic and Trade Commission, 6 November 2000), para. 3(2).

339. Notification by State Economic and Trade Commission Concerning the Regulation, Operation and Management Consolidation of Debt-to-Equity Swapped Enterprises [2000], no. 921 (Beijing, State Economic and Trade Commission, 6 November 2000), para. 6(1).

340. Industrial Policy Department of the State Economic and Trade Commission, *Working Progress in Debt-Equity Swap Scheme* [30 May 2001], available at: <www.setc.gov.cn/was40/detail?record=33&channelid=37134&presearchword=%D5%AE%D7%AA%B9%C9> (Beijing, State Economic and Trade Commission) (29 January 2005).

same time that the AMCs exert their shareholder rights.[341] Under the guidelines of SETC, this would include the division of rights and duties among the
shareholders' general meeting, the board of directors, the board of supervisors and the management.[342] The AMCs exert their influence over the SOEs
by their seats on boards of directors and boards of supervisors.[343] Accordingly,
the SOEs can supervise major decisions of SOEs, but cannot interfere with
their daily business. Although the AMCs have the power to employ or dismiss
senior management staff and to supervise the management through the two
governing boards, under Chinese company law, the role of the AMCs is limited, because the principle of 'cadres should be subject to party control' is still
a significant requirement in selecting managers.[344] Therefore, in some cases, the
AMCs could not choose the management, even in cases in which they controlled 100 per cent of the shares.[345] In addition, the AMCs do not have the
resources to sit on every governing board of every SOE. Because the AMCs
are more interested in recovering their stakes in the SOEs as soon as possible,
they are not concerned with the long-term interest of the SOEs.

The settlement for laid-off workers has been a delicate issue for local governments and enterprises, as well as all parties involved in the restructuring
of SOEs.[346] Several documents require that, when the property rights of an
SOE are transferred to an outside investor, the employee representative assembly of the enterprise concerned must be consulted if the legitimate rights and
interests of the staff are affected.[347] The relocation of employees and other

---

341. AMC Regulations, State Council Decree 2000, no. 297 (Beijing, State Council,
     10 November 2000); *Circular of the General Office of the State Council on Transmitting
     the Opinions on Exerting Further Efforts in the Work of Debt-Equity Swap of State-Owned
     Enterprises of the State Economic and Trade Commission, the Ministry of Finance and
     the People's Bank of China (guoban-fa)* [2003] no. 8 (Beijing, General Office of the State
     Council, 23 February 2003), para. 1.
342. Ibid.
343. AMC Regulations, State Council Decree [2000] no. 297 (Beijing, State Council, 10 Novem-
     ber 2000), sect. 20.
344. Circular of the General Office of the State Council on Transmitting the Opinions on
     Exerting Further Efforts in the Work of Debt-Equity Swap of State-Owned Enterprises
     of the State Economic and Trade Commission, the Ministry of Finance and the People's
     Bank of China (*guoban-fa*) [2003] no. 8 (Beijing, General Office of the State Council,
     23 February 2003), para. 1(7).
345. Zhou, supra note 233, p. 130; Xie and Li, supra note 181, p. 167; T. Zhou, 'Procedural
     Principles and Running Risks of Debt-Equity Swap Scheme', 1 (2000) *Journal of Economic
     Research*, p. 27.
346. *Interim Measures for the Management of the Transfer of the State-owned Property Right of
     Enterprises 2003* (Beijing, State-owned Assets Supervisory and Regulatory Commission
     and MOF, 31 December 2003). The same regulations can be found in *Measures for Enter-
     prise Merger and Acquisition 1989 (tigai-jing)* no. 38 (Beijing, State Institutional Reform
     Committee, et al. 19 February 1989); *Provisional Measures for the Sale of Property Right
     of State-Owned Small Enterprises* 1989 (Beijing, State Institutional Reform Committee, et
     al. 19 February 1989); and *Provisional Rules on Reorganization of SOEs by Using Foreign
     Fund 2002*, no. 42 (Beijing, State Economic and Trade Commission, 8 November 2002).
347. *Interim Measures for the Management of the Transfer*, Ibid., art. 11.

matters are subject to the approval of the employee representative assembly.[348]
The employee relocation program relating to the transfer enterprise concerned
must also be examined by the Ministry of Labour and Social Security.[349] However, these conditions put a greater burden on investors, and worker unrest often
prevents the normal running of an enterprise and can even force the government to invalidate the property right transfer agreement.[350] Since the staff and
workers of SOEs are called 'masters' whose rights are legally protected,[351] their
unrest against the restructuring of SOEs have legitimacy to some extent when
their welfare and interests are adversely affected. The local governments often
settle such unrest by sacrificing the interests of outside investors in maintaining stability.[352] This obviously violates the rule of law and discourages outside
investors to rescue the SOEs.

The debt-equity swap scheme was evaluated in 2004, four years after
its introduction.[353] The Opinions on Promoting and Regulating State-Owned
Enterprises' Debt-Equity Swap was issued intending to correct irregularities
and strengthen supervision.[354] In addressing the irregularities of the scheme,[355]
it requires accelerating follow-up work in respect to the registration of new companies established from the debt-to-equity swap, and sets the deadline for registering new companies.[356] These types of new companies are required to adopt
modern corporate governance.[357] With the exception of the industries prohibited or restricted by the State, the shareholdings of the AMCs are encouraged to
be publicly sold to domestic and foreign investors on a commercial basis.[358] The
issues of resettling employees, guaranteeing their lawful rights and interests,

348. Ibid.
349. Article 28 and 29, *Interim Measures for the Management of the Transfer of the State-
    owned Property Right of Enterprises* 2003 (Beijing, State-owned Assets Supervisory and
    Regulatory Commission and MOF, 31 December 2003).
350. J. Wang, 'The Privatization of State-Owned Enterprises in China: The Laws and Reality',
    Cross-Strait Law Review, no. 5 (Beijing: Tsinghua University Press, 2004), pp. 61–62.
351. Article 9, *Law of People's Republic of China on Industrial Enterprises Owned by the Whole
    People*, 1988.
352. Wang, supra note 350, p. 70.
353. *Notice on Clearing and Inspecting the Enterprises in the Debt-Equity Swap Scheme 2004*
    (Beijing, State-owned Assets Supervisory and Regulatory Commission, 29 October 2004).
354. *Notice of the General Office of the State Council on Transmitting the Opinions of the
    Ministry of Finance and Other Departments on Promoting and Regulating State-owned
    Enterprises' Debt-to-equity Swap (guoban-fa)* [2004] no. 94 (Beijing, General Office of
    State Council, 30 December 2004).
355. Z. Ke and S. Wang, 'SASAC Inspection to Look into Debt-Equity Swap', *21ˢᵗ Business
    Herald* (Guangzhou, 29 November 2004).
356. *Notice of the General Office of the State Council on Transmitting the Opinions of the
    Ministry of Finance and Other Departments on Promoting and Regulating State-owned
    Enterprises' Debt-to-equity Swap (guoban-fa)* [2004] no. 94 (Beijing, General Office of
    State Council, 30 December 2004), sect. 1.
357. Ibid., sect. 3.
358. Ibid., sect. 4(1).

and maintaining social stability are still a priority.[359] Therefore, the roles of the AMCs in restructuring SOE under the debt-equity swap scheme are still challenging.

IX.   CONCLUSION

The privilege given to the SOCBs to dispose of their NPLs creates unfair market competition for those viable banking institutions with good management. If banking reform is to be successful, it is inevitable that the AMCs should be given privileges, challenging fair market principles. However, because China is still a developing economy and the country's efforts to reform its banking system under a rule-based framework could hardly be perfect, its law and policy, as well as its judicial process, have yet to become internationally acceptable. Nevertheless, these discussions have demonstrated China's sincere efforts to implement fully its banking reform commitments. According to the public choice theory, China's ruling elite could use banking reform to accelerate domestic reforms, as people acting in their self-interest have no motivation to support the reforms. China could exploit banking reform to enhance its legal infrastructure and eliminate protection of vested interest groups. In this process, administrative polices are employed to address legislative defects and omissions. These discussions have shown the merits of such legislative forbearance. However, a balance must be struck in undertaking urgent banking reform through legislative forbearance and strict adherence to the rule of law.

     The social environment is not favourable to disposal of NPL assets, including debt evasion and default by enterprises.[360] Every legal framework has its limit. The transaction costs in addressing these issues often outweigh the benefits of strict legal enforcement. China's banking reform nevertheless would result in eliminating many vested interests, as SOEs would no longer rely to such an extent on the SOCBs for funding, and foreign and domestic investors would be forced to play by the identical rules. In using banking reform to restructure SOEs, the upshot would limit state intervention in the markets and enhance transparency in governance. It would, however, be overly optimistic to expect the AMCs to play an active role in transforming SOEs into modern companies, because their operational and financial risks, such as the management of SOEs, their human resource constraints and their financing capability, as well as the emphasis on speed of their cash recovery policy, have yet to be addressed. All these require an experienced and skilled work force which China is developing. However, regardless of the benefits in banking reform derived from legislative forbearance, the ultimate objective is to enact all the policies

---

359. Ibid., sect. 4(3).
360. China Banking Regulatory Commission, 'The CBRC held a supervisory working conference to strengthen NPL disposal,' *Press Release* (Beijing, 29 December 2004), available at <www.cbrc.gov.cn/english/module/viewinfo.jsp?infoID=1100> (15 March 2005).

into laws. Without the rule of law, China's economic development can only be short-lived. Legislative forbearance should only be de facto tolerated in this crucial period of China's transitional economy.

Market discipline is being introduced to China's AMCs. In addition to the RMB 1.4 trillion NPL purchase, the four AMCs have taken over other NPL assets from the SOCBs. More importantly, the transfer is based on market competition rather than state direction. In 2004, Cinda AMC won the bid by defeating the other three AMCs in selling NPLs.[361] Following the recapitalization of USD 45 billion into the BOC and the CCB at the end of 2003, Cinda AMC and Orient AMC were entrusted to take over and dispose of RMB 197 billion of NPL assets written off from the balance sheets of CCB and BOC.[362] This deal is significant in that the transfer was not made at the book value of the assets but rather at the price determined by the MOF.[363] This indicates that the AMCs will continue to play a significant role in the resolution of China's NPLs.

After four years of operation, the time has come to assess whether or not legislative forbearance in regulating AMCs is adverse to China's banking reform. In January 2005, the CRBC released statistics reporting that the NPL ratio of the major commercial banks including the four SOCBs and the twelve joint-stock banks for the past year has been reduced by 4.6 per cent, in other words, by RMB 394.6 billion, to 13.2 per cent, which comes to RMB 1,717.7 billion.[364] This year is the third consecutive year of reported declines in NPL ratio.[365]

The development of the AMCs, however, is still facing many challenges. According to a report of China's National Audit Office (NAO), substantial irregularities exist at the four AMCs, the NPL disposal process was opaque with insider dealing, asset valuation has often been gratuitous, and incidents involving artificial biddings and auctions have occurred.[366] This followed a CBRC news release reporting that the AMCs have been constantly violating laws and regulations. The NAO confirmed that a total of RMB 6.7 billion was involved in these cases.[367] Stricter regulations have been put into operation in the past year to strengthen the supervision of the transfer, disposition and management of NPLs. Accordingly, more stringent responsibilities are imposed on the AMCs

---

361. *Cinda Pondering Massive NPL Sale*, available at <news.xinhuanet.com/english/2005–02/01/content_2533107.htm> (25 February 2005).
362. *AMCs Entrusted with Massive NPL Disposal*, available at <news.xinhuanet.com/english/2004–05/17/content_1473160.htm> (25 February 2005).
363. 'The PBC and the CSRC demonstrate their resolution in transferring RMB 197 billion NPLs' [1970], *21st Century Business Herald* (Guangzhou, 22 May 2004).
364. China Banking Regulatory Commission, 'The CBRC released the NPL statistics for 2004', Press Release (13 January 2005) <www.cbrc.gov.cn/english/index.htm> (31 January 2005).
365. Ibid.
366. B. Hu, 'Bank Chief Seen Heading Huarong; Likely Posting Comes amid Increasing Criticism of State-Owned Asset Managers,' *South China Morning Post* (Hong Kong: January 3, 2005), p. 3.
367. 'Audit finds four AMCs violating regulations,' *People's Daily* (Beijing, 21 January 2005).

and their management.[368] Although detailed procedures and responsibilities have been implemented to reduce the risk of selling NPLs below value,[369] their initial transfer at book value makes proper valuation and asset pricing rather difficult. The wider ramifications that arise in the disposal of NPLs, such as the arrangement of employees and social welfare of retired and laid-off workers, have made timely development of the bad debt market more difficult. In December 2004, the Ministry of Labour and Social Security announced that laid-off workers from SOEs will be covered by unemployment insurance.[370] This move should enhance the quality of the NPL assets.

As discussed, the legal framework regulating China's AMCs is a developing system. In addressing the irregularities at the AMCs, the legal, policy and market environment must be enhanced. On a positive side, the CBRC has taken measures on strengthening corporate governance, enhancing supervision, as well as improving the market infrastructure for disposing NPLs.[371]

---

368. *Notification on Identifying Responsibility in Transferring NPLs from State-Owned Commercial Banks (cai-jin)* 2004 No. 77 (Beijing, the Ministry of Finance, 22 October 2004). *Measures on the Asset Disposition of Financial Asset Management Company (cai-jin)* 2004 No. 41 (Beijing, the Ministry of Finance, 30 April 2004).
369. *Measures on the Asset Disposition of Financial Asset Management Company (cai-jin)* 2004 No. 41 (Beijing, the Ministry of Finance, 30 April 2004).
370. 'SOE reforms expected to end within three years', *People's Daily* (Beijing, 21 December 2004).
371. H. Zhou, 'CBRC Strengthening Supervision over AMCs, and Some Regulations Are Going to Come out', *Securities Daily* (Beijing, 30 December 2004).

Chapter 6

Liberalization and Reform of China's Securities Markets after WTO Accession

Michael E. Burke and Lusong Zhang

I.   INTRODUCTION

China's securities markets have slowly been developing since the early 1980s, when several informal – and unofficial – stock markets began trading in Shanghai, Shenzhen, Chengdu and other cities. In 1985, Shanghai Yanzhong Industrial made the first public offering of standardized equity in Chinese history.[1] The Shanghai and Shenzhen stock exchanges began operations in December 1990 and June 1991, respectively. In 1998, the Standing Committee of the National People's Congress (NPC) promulgated the *Securities Law*, the first national, comprehensive securities regulation.[2] The development pace has accelerated in recent years, and the securities sector commitments China made in acceding to the World Trade Organization (WTO) are quickening an already

---

1. S. Green, *China's Stock Market: A Guide to its Progress, Players, and Prospects 9* (Profile Books, Ltd, 2003) (referred to simply as 'Green' in this chapter).
2. Securities Law of the People's Republic of China, adopted at the 6th Meeting of the Standing Committee of the Ninth National People's Congress on 29 December 1998, effective as of 1 July 1999, and amended on 27 October 2005 with the new amendments effective as of 1 January 2006) §121, available at LEXIS PRCLEG1084 (referred to simply as 'Securities Law' in this chapter).

Barth et al., *Financial Restructuring and Reform in Post-WTO China*, pp. 171–243.
© 2007 Kluwer Law International BV, The Netherlands.

fast pace of development. The liberalizations contained in China's securities sector WTO commitments, and the securities sector liberalization the Chinese government has undertaken outside of the WTO context, do not come without risk. In a 34-nation survey of jurisdictions that liberalized some part of their financial services sector, including their securities sector, between the 1970s and 1997, almost all experienced some form of financial crisis within five years of liberalization.[3] Many of the economies worst hit by the Asian Financial Crisis (AFC) had liberalized their financial systems, including their securities markets, just prior to the AFC's outbreak and, over the past ten years, liberalization without appropriate reform to develop a robust financial system has been a significant – if not the dominant – factor in financial crises worldwide.

Liberalization and reform are central themes in the Chinese government's effort to develop a modern financial system and to build an effective and efficient securities market. Liberalization without reform creates an atmosphere conducive to excessive risk-taking. In early 2004, the State Council released the Opinions on Promoting Reform and Development of Capital Markets (Capital Market Opinions), a long-term strategy for further liberalization and reform of China's securities market.[4] Through the Capital Market Opinions, the State Council directed relevant governmental departments to:

- implement more effectively the existing verification and approval system for stock issuance;
- enable securities companies to issue shares and corporate bonds;
- address issues related to non-tradable shares of listed companies;
- establish better corporate governance structures among listed companies;
- improve exit mechanisms for listed companies; and
- regulate more efficiently intermediaries such as accounting firms and law firms.

The Capital Market Opinions also call for the development of corporate bond markets, and the continued opening of China's securities sector to foreign investors. At the same time, the Chinese government has indicated that it plans to make the renminbi capital account convertible in the medium term.

Despite the Capital Market Opinions, China's securities markets remain at a unique junction. Market indices have been sliding for the past six years and many listed companies are of poor quality.[5] Investor confidence in market

3. Albert Berry and Clemente Ruiz, *Firm Size and the Impacts of Financial Liberalization and Integration, in* Critical Issues in International Economic Reform, Albert Berry and Gustavo Indart, eds. (Transaction Publishers, 2003) 189.
4. *Promoting the Reform, Opening Up and Stable Development of the Capital Markets Several Opinions (Guo Fa)* [2004] no. 3 (State Council, 31 January 2004 and reprinted at China Law & Practice 3700/04.01.31) (referred to as Capital Markets Opinions in this chapter).
5. See, for example, 'Shares Dip to 68-month low; 40-odd Stocks Dive', [2005] *China Daily,* WLNR 1451774 (2 February 2005); 'Shares Drop to Six-Year Low,' [2005] *China Daily,* WLNR 5051551 (31 March 2005).

integrity is low.[6] The securities market is too heavily focused on equity listings and the market is not adequately regulated. These facts suggest that China's securities market may be vulnerable to liberalization risk. Therefore, China's financial system may be exposed to some of the same pressures that affected AFC-affected nations prior to 1997, and reforming China's securities market can mitigate the impact of such risks.

Section II of this chapter reviews China's securities sector WTO commitments, including analyzing the securities sector commitments in context with its other financial services commitments. Section III discusses the regulations implementing China's securities sector commitments, as such existed on 31 December 2005, and Section IV reviews particular problems and issues that have arisen with this type of implementation. Section V analyzes the securities sector liberalizations China made between 11 December 2001 and 31 December 2005 outside the context of WTO, including the Qualified Foreign Institutional Investor (QFII) system. Section VI reviews the economic literature on the sequencing of liberalization and reform, analyzes the risks facing China's securities sector, and suggests certain risk-mitigating reforms. Section VII discusses the importance of institutional investors to securities market development and stability, and Section VIII attempts to predict, in economic terms, how liberalization will affect China's securities markets and overall economy. Section IX concludes with recommendations for the Chinese government in regard to reforming its securities sector.

II. CHINA'S SECURITIES SECTOR COMMITMENTS

Liberalization and reform are the dominant themes of Chinese economic development, including securities sector development. Given the limited access foreign investors enjoyed prior to WTO accession, the market access commitments significantly liberalize China's securities sector.[7] This section of the chapter reviews China's securities sector WTO commitments, and places these commitments in context temporally – how China's securities sector commitments evolved over time – and in context with China's other financial services commitments.

Prior to WTO accession foreign investment banks could not underwrite securities, manage investment funds, offer or perform any other

---

6. See 'Survey Shows Stock Market Top Concern', [2005] China Daily, WLNR 3117688 (1 March 2005); 'Investors' Confidence Hurt', [2002] China Daily, WLNR 7420802 (18 April 2002).

7. As some have opined, certain services commitments are radical and the attendant efficiency gains will benefit the Chinese economy as a whole. See, for example, *China's Growth and Integration into the World Economy: Prospects and Challenges*, International Monetary Fund Occasional Paper 232 (Eswar Prasad ed., 2004); J. Wang, 'Dancing with Wolves: Regulation and Deregulation of Foreign Investment in China's Stock Market', 5 *Asian-Pac. L. & Pol'y J.* (2004), pp. 1–61.

securities-related service or become a member of any Chinese stock exchange.[8] The services schedule Chinese negotiators submitted in connection with a failed 1994 accession bid did not contain any securities sector commitments.[9] Before its WTO accession, the Chinese government stated that its services commitments would not include any securities sector liberalization.[10] As late as April 1999, when the then-premier Zhu Rongji visited the White House in an unsuccessful attempt to win final American approval of China's WTO accession bid, Chinese negotiators had not scheduled any securities sector commitments.[11]

Many concepts seemed to underlie a restrictive approach.[12] For example, because most publicly-traded Chinese companies were state-owned enterprises (SOEs), the government was reluctant to allow any level of foreign ownership of state assets. The Chinese leadership was also concerned about the potential destabilizing effects of large-scale cross-border capital flows.[13] The Chinese government wanted to protect domestic securities companies until they had sufficient experience and competence to compete against foreign securities companies.

The shift from not making any securities sector commitments has been attributed to pressure applied by U.S. negotiators. Table 1, below, describes each of China's securities sector commitments.

China made market access liberalization commitments in 14 of the 18 financial services sectors, including five of five in the insurance sector, six of seven in the banking sector and four of six in the securities sector, including the one sector overlapping banking and securities.[14] Despite the significance of these

---

8. R. Janda and M. Jing, 'China's Great Leap of Faith: Telecommunications and Financial Services Commitments', in S. Ostry et al. (eds.), *China and the Long March to Global Trade: the Accession of China to the World Trade Organization* 78 (Routledge, 2002); see also N. Lardy, *Integrating China into the World Economy* (Brookings Institution Press, 2002), p. 67.
9. See A. Mattoo, 'The Services Dimension of China's Accession to the WTO', in D. Bhattasali et al. (eds.), *China and the WTO: Accession, Policy Reform, and Poverty Reduction Strategies* (Oxford University Press, 2004), p. 121.
10. Janda and Jing, supra note 8, p. 66.
11. Ibid., p. 87.
12. Ibid.
13. See Green, supra note 1.
14. People's Republic of China Schedule of Specific Commitments, GATS/SC/135 (14 February 2002) (referred to in this chapter as 'PRC Services Schedule'); see also Annex on Financial Services, General Agreement on Trade in Services, 15 April 1994, Marrakech Agreement Establishing the World Trade Organization, Annex 1B (referred to in this chapter as 'Financial Services Annex'). As provided in the Financial Services Annex, insurance and insurance-related services include:
    – Direct insurance (including co-insurance):
      – life;
      – non-life;
    – Reinsurance and retrocession;
    – Insurance intermediation, such as brokerage and agency;
    – Services auxiliary to insurance, such as consultancy, actuarial, risk assessment and claim settlement services.

Table 1: China's Securities Sector Commitments

Commitment	Target Implementation Date	Implementing Regulation	Date of Implementing Regulation
Foreign securities firms can engage directly in B-share business without a Chinese intermediary.	11 December 2001	Administrative Rules of the Shenzhen Stock Exchange Regarding Foreign Institutions' B-Share Seats and the Interim Measures of the Shanghai Stock Exchange Regarding Foreign Securities Institutions' Applications for B-Share Seats.	19 June 2002, and effective as of the same date
Representative offices of foreign securities firms can become members of Chinese stock exchanges.	11 December 2001	Provisions of the Shenzhen Stock Exchange on the Administration of Special Foreign Members and the Interim Provisions of the Shanghai Stock Exchange Regarding the Administration of Special Foreign Members.	25 July 2002, and effective as of the same date
Foreign investors can form a joint venture investment fund management company, with foreign interest limited to 33 per cent of the entity's registered capital.	11 December 2001	China Securities Regulatory Commission, Establishment of Fund Management Companies with Foreign Equity Participation Rules.	Issued 1 June 2002, and effective 1 July 2002.

Table 1: Contd.

Commitment	Target Implementation Date	Implementing Regulation	Date of Implementing Regulation
Foreign investors can increase their interest in a joint venture investment fund management company to 49 per cent of the entity's registered capital.	11 December 2004	Not issued as of 31 December 2004	
Permit foreign investors to form a joint venture securities company, with foreign interest limited to 33 per cent of the entity's registered capital.	11 December 2004	China Securities Regulatory Commission, Establishment of Securities Companies with Foreign Equity Participation Rules.	Issued 1 June 2002, and effective 1 July 2002

commitments, China's financial services market access commitments contain some significant limitations. In the insurance sector, China tempered its market

---

The banking sector, as illustrated in the Annex on Financial Services, includes:
- Acceptance of deposits and other repayable funds from the public;
- Lending of all types, including consumer credit, mortgage credit, factoring and financing of commercial transaction;
- Financial leasing;
- All payment and money transmission services, including:
  - credit, charge and debit cards;
  - travellers checks;
  - bankers drafts;
- Guarantees and commitments;
- Trading for own account or for account of customers, whether on an exchange, in an over-the-counter market or otherwise, the following:
  - money market instruments (including checks, bills and certificates of deposits);
  - foreign exchange;
  - derivative products including, but not limited to, futures and options;
  - exchange rate and interest rate instruments, including products such as swaps, forward rate agreements;
  - transferable securities;
  - other negotiable instruments and financial assets, including bullion; and
- Money broking.
The securities sector, as illustrated by the Financial Services Annex includes the 'Trading for own account or for account of customers' item in the banking sector illustrative list, as well as:
- Participation in issues of all types of securities, including underwriting and placement as agent (whether publicly or privately) and provision of services related to such issues;
- Asset management, such as cash or portfolio management, all forms of collective investment management, pension fund management, custodial, depository and trust services;
- Settlement and clearing services for financial assets, including securities, derivative products and other negotiable instruments;
- Provision and transfer of financial information, and financial data processing and related software by suppliers of other financial services;
- Advisory, intermediation and other auxiliary financial services on all the activities, including credit reference and analysis, investment and portfolio research and advice. Financial Services Annex at §5(a). Comparatively, division 71 of the United Nations Central Product Classification (CPC) version 1.1 provides a broader and more granular scope to securities-related services than the informational scope contained in the Financial Services Annex:
- subclass 71200, investment banking services, covers securities underwriting services; services of guaranteeing the sale of an issue of securities at a stated price from the issuing corporation or government and reselling it to investors; and engaging to sell as much of an issue of securities as possible without making a guarantee to purchase the entire offering from the issuer;
- subclass 71511, mergers and acquisition services, covers services of counsellors and negotiators in arranging mergers and acquisitions;
- subclass 71512, corporate finance and venture capital services, covers services of arranging corporate financing including debt, equity and venture capital financing and venture capital financing services;

access commitments with form of establishment, geographic, business scope, capital and experience requirements.[15] China's banking sector commitments

– subclass 71519, other services related to investment banking, covers other services related to investment banking NEC, but does not include portfolio management, trust and custody services, cf. 7153; stock price quotation services made available through an information server, cf. 84300; or supply of financial news to the news media, cf. 844);
– subclass 71521, securities brokerage services, covers brokerage services – that is, bringing together purchasers and sellers of the same instrument) for securities; services of acting as a selling agent of units, shares or other interests in a mutual (investment) fund; sales, delivery and redemption services of government bonds; and brokerage options);
– subclass 71522, commodity brokerage services, covers brokerage services for commodities and commodity futures including financial futures; brokerage financial derivatives, other than options; but does not include brokerage of options cf. 71521);
– subclass 71523, processing and clearing services of securities transactions, covers computer-based clearing and settlement for interchange of debits, credits and transfer of ownership of securities;
– subclass 71531, portfolio management services, covers managing portfolio assets of others, on a fee or commission basis; but does not include advisory services on personal financial planning not involving decision-making on behalf of clients, cf. 71551 or the buying and selling of securities on a transaction fee basis, cf. 71521;
– subclass 71532, trust services, covers estate and trust management and administration services; services of acting as a trustee of investment funds or pension funds; and services of acting as trustee for securities (administrative services related to the issue and registration of securities, and payment of interest and dividends;
– subclass 71533, custody services, under instructions, provides the services of the safekeeping of and accounting for valuable and usually income-bearing personal property, including securities; safekeeping services safe deposit services; security custody services; and audit confirmation services with respect to customers' securities held for safekeeping; and
– subclass 71551, financial consultancy services, covers financial advisory services; market analysis and intelligence; but does not include:
  – insurance and pension consultancy services, cf. 71690;
  – mergers and acquisitions services, cf. 71511;
  – corporate finance and venture capital services, cf. 71512;
  – portfolio management, trust and custody services, cf. 7153;
  – advisory services on taxation matters, cf. 823;
  – financial management consulting services (except business tax), cf. 8311).

United Nations Statistics Division, Central Product Classification Version 1.1, ST/ESA/STAT/SER.M/77/Ver.1.1, E.03.XVII.3 (March 2002), available at <unstats. un.org/unsd/cr/registry/regcst.asp?Cl=16&Lg=1> (1 March 2005). Ultimately, countries that make financial services commitments retain the right to define, for themselves, the scale and scope of securities-related services and commitments. Ibid., at §5(a). Most nations reference their commitments to the illustrative list in the Annex on Financial Services, although some will reference a CPC code to further define the scope of a commitment. One suggested area of work for the GATS Financial Services Committee is reconciliation between the Annex illustrations of financial services and the more comprehensive CPC codes. See, for example, Committee on Trade in Financial Services, *Report of the Meeting Held on 13 July 2000*, S/FIN/M/27 (23 August 2000), p. 21; Council for Trade in Services Special Session, *Communication from Switzerland*, S/CSS/W/71 (4 May 2001), p. 11; Council for Trade in Services Special Session, *Communication from Colombia*, S/CSS/W/96 (July 19, 2001), p. 10; Committee on Trade in Financial Services, *Report of the Meeting Held on 18 March 2002*, S/FIN/M/34 (26 April 2002), p. 11.
15. PRC Services Schedule, supra note 14, at §II.7.A.

similarly are limited.[16] The insurance and banking sector commitments are defined with reference to the GATS Annex on Financial Services illustrative framework, while the securities sector commitments are defined by its limits on market access.[17]

China's securities sector commitments contain restrictions on the required form of entity, capital requirements and scope of business for foreign service providers.[18] Capital requirements, experience prerequisites and limits on scope of business have been set out in relevant implementation regulations and limit the liberalizing effect of China's securities sector commitments.[19] China's securities sector commitments do not schedule greater foreign participation over the financial services implementation period ending in 2007.[20] In addition, China's Schedule of Specific Commitments does not define the permitted business scope for foreign-invested securities ventures as comprehensively as it does for foreign-invested banking or insurance ventures, allowing the Chinese government potential leeway in limiting foreign access to China's securities industry. Thus, China made comparatively fewer securities market access commitments than in banking and insurance sectors.

III.   IMPLEMENTATION OF ITS SECURITIES SECTOR COMMITMENTS

China's WTO implementation efforts are a focus of significant scrutiny, as evidenced by the annual transitional reviews conducted by the WTO pursuant to 18 of China's Accession Protocol, annual reports compiled by the Office of the United States Trade Representative, and analyses by various industry groups. Increasing international attention is being focused on China's implementation of its securities sector commitments. With the exception of increasing the limit on foreign investment in a FI-FMC to 49 per cent by 11 December 2004, China largely has implemented its securities sector commitments. The Chinese government, in fact, implemented its JVSC commitments two and one-half

---

16. Ibid., at §II.7.B.
17. Ibid.
18. Ibid., A communication from the Republic of Korea proposed that all WTO members should gradually abolish all limits on equity sharing. Council for Trade in Services Special Session, *Communication from the Republic of Korea*, S/CSS/W/86 (11 May 2001) 10.
19. See, for example, China Securities Regulatory Commission, *Establishment of Securities Companies with Foreign Equity Participation Rules*; (issued by the China Securities Regulatory Commission on 1 June 2002 and effective as of 1 July 2002) [hereinafter JVSC Rules]; China Securities Regulatory Commission, *Establishment of Fund Management Companies with Foreign Equity Participation Rules* (issued by the China Securities Regulatory Commission on 1 June 2002 and effective as of 1 July 2002) [hereinafter FI-FMC Rules].
20. Further, China's securities sector commitments do not contain the same form of phase-out as contained in the insurance and banking sectors wherein foreign services providers may form, within a stated period of time, wholly foreign-owned entities. *PRC Services Schedule*, supra note 14, at §II.7.B.

years ahead of schedule.[21] This section of the chapter will review the relevant legislative and regulatory actions the Chinese government has made in an effort to implement its WTO securities sector commitments.

III.A.   B-SHARE BUSINESS

The Shenzhen Stock Exchange (SZSE) and the Shanghai Stock Exchange (SHSE) implemented regulations on 19 June 2002 enabling foreign securities companies to obtain a B-Share trading seat (the B-Share Seat Rules).[22] The B-Share Seat Rules require that an application package include a long list of specified documents, the specified application fee (HKD 600,000 for the SZSE, USD 75,000 for the SHSE), and the first year's management fee (HKD 30,000 for the SZSE, USD2,415 for the SHSE).[23] Exchanges are to make a decision on a completed application within fifteen days of receipt.[24] A foreign securities company may purchase a B-Share seat from an existing B-Share seat holder rather than applying for a seat from the relevant exchange; however, the B-Share

---

21. *Janda and Jing*, supra note 8, at 78; see also Lardy, supra note 8, at 67.
22. Shenzhen Stock Exchange, *Administrative Rule of the Shenzhen Stock Exchange Regarding Foreign Institutions' B-Share Seats,* issued by the Shenzhen Stock Exchange on 19 June 2002 and effective as of the same date; Shanghai Stock Exchange, *Interim Measures of the Shanghai Stock Exchange Regarding Foreign Securities Institutions' Applications for B-Share Seats*, issued by the Shanghai Stock Exchange on 19 June 2002 and effective as of the same date. These rules are collectively referred to as the B-Share Seat Rules. For a discussion of the various designations of shares in a Chinese public company, see Green, supra note 1, p. 16.
23. These documents include:

   – an application form signed by the an authorized representative of the foreign securities institution;
   – a copy of its Certificate of Qualification for Operation of Foreign Stocks issued by the CSRC;
   – a copy of the foreign securities institution's business license issued by its home jurisdiction;
   – a copy of its securities business license issued by the relevant authorities of its home jurisdiction;
   – its articles of association;
   – its financial statements for the last year audited by an accounting firm;
   – the resumes of the major directors, senior executives and professionals of the foreign institution; and
   – a brief introduction of the foreign securities institution.

   B-Share Seat Rules, supra note 22, at §§1–5. Interestingly, the B-Share Seat Rules adopted by the Shenzhen Stock Exchange lowered the B-Share initial fee from HKD 1,000,000 to HKD 600,000 in an attempt to lure more players to the mainland stock market. S. Yeung and C. Chan, 'Shenzhen Bourse Cuts Seat Prices to Attract Foreigners', [2002] *South China Morning Post*, 25 June 2002, p. 3.
24. B-Share Seat Rules, supra note 22, at §6.

Seat Rules do not specify the applicable procedures for this type of transfer.[25] B-Share seat holders can only use the seat to engage in B-Share trading.[26] A foreign B-Share seat holder is subject to the relevant exchange's disciplinary standards and punishment.[27] Disputes between the exchange and foreign B-Share seat holders are to be governed by Chinese law and are to be settled through negotiation or arbitration if negotiation fails.[28]

As of 31 December 2005, foreign brokers held 39 of the 99 total B-Share seats on the SHSE.[29] As of end-December 2004, the SZSE included a total of 52 B-Share Seats, although the SZSE did not break down this data by domestic

---

25. A B-Share seat cannot be withdrawn or returned to the exchange, but can be transferred between securities companies with the consent of the relevant exchange. Ibid.
26. Foreign B-Share seat holders are required to appoint two persons to be primary contacts between the relevant exchange and the foreign securities company. A foreign B-Share seat holder is to submit the previous year's audit report to the relevant exchange within four months after the end of each fiscal year. Foreign B-Share seat holders are to keep relevant records for 20 years. B-Share seat holders are to notify the relevant exchange within five days of specified material events, such as an amendment to the foreign securities institution's formation documents. Ibid., at §§7–12.
27. The relevant exchange may punish violations of relevant exchange rules by foreign B-Share seat holders through:

    – a fine;
    – public criticism;
    – a warning;
    – limitation of trading;
    – suspension of B-Share seat – the seat cannot be transferred during the suspension; and
    – termination of the seat.

    Any party that objects to any punishment levied on it can, within fifteen days of receipt of the notification of decision on punishment, apply to the exchange for reconsideration of such punishment; however, the punishment is not stayed during the period of reconsideration. Ibid., at §17.
28. Ibid., at §18.
29. Shanghai Stock Exchange, *List of Overseas B Share Brokers*, available at <www.sse.com.cn/sseportal/en_us/ps/bshare/bsbl02.html> (5 February 2006). The Overseas B-Share Brokers on the SHSE are Jardine Fleming Securities Co., Ltd.; CLSA Ltd.; East Asia Securities Co., Ltd.; PBI Securities (Hong Kong) Co. Ltd.; ABN AMRO Asia Ltd.; ING Baring Securities (HK) Co., Ltd.; Chinalines Securities Investment Co., Ltd.; Nava SC China Securities Co., Ltd.; SG Securities (HK) Ltd.; Daiwa Securities SB Capital Markets (HK) Ltd.; Nomura International (HK) Ltd.; Yamaichi Intl. (HK) Co., Ltd.; Masterlink Securities (HK) Co., Ltd.; SBC Warburg Securities Co., Ltd.; Merrill Lynch International Inc.; Goldman Sachs (Asia) Securities Ltd.; Worldsec International Limited; Bear Stearns & Co. Inc.; Morgan Stanley Dean Witter Asia Ltd.; Pacific Capital (Asia) Ltd.; Indosuez W.I. CAR Securities Ltd.; NSC Securities (Asia) Ltd.; Credit Suisse First Boston (HK) Ltd.; Paribas Capital Market Ltd.; ICEA Securities Ltd.; Wanguo Securities Ltd.; Deutsche Securities Asia Ltd.; DBS Securities Hong Kong Ltd.; Vickers Ballas Hong Kong Ltd.; Sassoon Overseas Services Ltd.; Core Pacific Securities Intl. Ltd.; CSC Securities (HK) Ltd.; OCBC Securities Private Ltd.; LG Investment Securities Ltd.; KGI Asia Ltd.; Platinum Securities Co., Ltd.; and HSBC Securities (Asia) Ltd. Ibid.

and foreign seat holders.[30] China's B-Share markets are not an attractive market for foreign securities companies, because the B-Share markets are small and illiquid and overpopulated with existing traders. By the end of October 2005, 109 issuers had issued B-Shares, a much smaller figure than the 1,358 issuers on the A-Share market as of the same date.[31] In addition, as of the end of October 2005, only 86 issuers had issued both A and B-Shares.[32] Each exchange also sets the maximum per-transaction commission rate a B-Share trader can charge a customer at the greater of USD 1 or 0.3 per cent of the trading value.[33]

The Chinese government has attempted to foster growth of the B-Share market by enabling certain foreign-invested enterprises to convert their foreign investment shares into B-Shares and list such shares.[34] In addition, prior to WTO accession in February 2001, the China Securities Regulatory Commission (CSRC) implemented regulations allowing domestic individual investors to open B-Share trading accounts and trade B-Shares in foreign currency. Nonetheless, the B-Share market is somewhat of a failure and the B-Share trading seat liberalization will have a minimal effect on China's securities market. In fact, the B-Share trading seat commitment may be without consequence in the near future, as the Chinese government continues to study unification of the B-Share and A-Share markets.[35]

III.B.   SPECIAL MEMBERSHIP ON CHINESE STOCK EXCHANGES

On 24 July 2002, the SZSE issued the Provisions of the Shenzhen Stock Exchange on the Administration of Special Foreign Members and the SHSE issued the Interim Provisions of the Shanghai Stock Exchange Regarding the Administration of Special Foreign Members, known collectively as the

---

30. Shenzhen Stock Exchange, 2004 Fact Book (Shenzhen Stock Exchange, 2004) at 30–31, available at <www.szse.cn/upfiles/attach/1389/2005/03/11/1038050000.pdf> (5 February 2006) (referred to in this chapter as the 'SZSE 2004 Fact Book').
31. China Securities Regulatory Commission, *Statistical Report System Information, Listed Companies Monthly Report Table 3–1, Summary by Share Categories*, available at <www.csrc.gov.cn/en/statinfo/index1_en.jsp?path=ROOT%3EEN%3EStatistical%20Information%3EListed> (22 November 2005).
32. Ibid.
33. Shanghai Stock Exchange, *Introduction to the B-Share Trading System*, available at <www.sse.com.cn/sseportal/en_us/ps/bshare/tsi.shtml> (17 March 2005).
34. Ministry of Foreign Trade and Economic Cooperation, *Questions Relevant to the Conversion of Non-listed Foreign Investment Shares of Foreign-invested Companies Limited by Shares into B Shares for Circulation Supplementary Circular* (issued by the Ministry of Foreign Trade and Economic Cooperation on 16 August 2002 and effective as of the same date), which enables certain FIEs to convert their foreign investment shares into B-Shares).
35. Approximately 160 brokerages hold B-share seats at the Shenzhen exchange chasing turnover of between HKD 2 million and HKD 3 million a day, compared to HKD 6 billion for a weak day in Hong Kong. S. Yeung and C. Chan, 'Shenzhen Bourse Cuts Seat Prices to Attract Foreigners', [20020] *South China Morning Post* (25 June 2002), p. 3.

Special Member Regulations. Both took effect the day of issuance, and enable a foreign securities company's representative office, after one year of operations, to become a special foreign member of the SHSE or SZSE.[36] The Special Member Regulations require that the applicant representative office's parent have international securities business experience, good reputation and achieved good operating results, although none of these terms is defined in the relevant regulations. A Special Member does not have the same rights as a regular Member. Special Members can make proposals and accept the services supplied by the exchanges, but do not have voting rights at the general meeting of exchange members. For this reason, Special Members do not have the right to vote on management and supervision issues related to the exchange.[37]

The Special Member Regulations have received scant attention from the press and groups reviewing China's WTO implementation record. As of the end of 2004, the SHSE included 269 Members, while the SZSE had 189 Members. Neither exchange provides data on the number of foreign Special Members.[38] A quick review of each exchange's Member roster did not indicate that many foreign securities companies had become Special Members. Allowing foreign securities companies to become Special Members of a Chinese exchange will have a limited effect on China's securities markets. Few foreign securities companies would want to become a Special Member in and of itself, but may want to become a Special Member if necessitated by the scope of the company's operations through a Joint Venture Securities Company, Foreign Invested Fund Management Company or QFII, as the case may be. As a positive externality to their membership, foreign Special Members may improve governance of exchanges, but, as stated above, will not have significant impact on China's securities markets.

---

36. Shenzhen Stock Exchange, *Provisions of the Shenzhen Stock Exchange on Administration of Special Foreign Members* (issued by the Shenzhen Stock Exchange on 24 July 2002 and effective as of the same date); Shanghai Stock Exchange, *Interim Provisions of the Shanghai Stock Exchange Regarding the Administration of Special Foreign Members* (issued by the Shanghai Stock Exchange on 24 July 2002 and effective as of the same date), which are collectively referred to as the Special Member Provisions in this chapter. A resident representative office is an agency established to engage in non-business operations within Chinese territory, as reviewed and approved by the CSRC. Applicants must:

 – comply with the relevant Chinese laws and regulations, the exchanges' articles of association, rules and other relevant regulations;
 – implement the exchanges' decisions;
 – accept the exchanges' annual and interim examination;
 – submit annual operation reports and report material changes;
 – coordinate and communicate with their parents on the operation and affairs concerning the exchanges;
 – pay membership fees and relevant charges according to the exchanges' regulations.

 Special Member Provisions §11.
37. Ibid., at §10.
38. *SZSE 2004 Fact Book,* supra note 30, pp. 30–31.

III.C.   JOINT VENTURE SECURITIES COMPANIES

On 1 June 2002, the CSRC promulgated the Establishment of Securities Companies with Foreign Equity Participation Rules (Securities JV Rules), effective as of 1 July 2002, and implementing China's WTO commitment in this area two and a half years ahead of schedule. Chinese and foreign investors may form and operate a Joint Venture Securities Company (JVSC), provided that the foreign equity interest (collectively or individually) in the JVSC does not exceed 33 per cent of the JVSC's registered capital.[39] To form a JVSC, promoters can invest in an existing Chinese securities company, or form a new entity by joint promotion of Chinese and foreign parties.[40] A JVSC must be structured as a limited liability company and must have minimum registered capital of RMB 500 million.[41]

The foreign party to a JVSC must, *inter alia*, be a licensed securities firm from a jurisdiction whose securities regulator has signed a memorandum of understanding on regulatory cooperation with the CSRC and maintained an effective regulatory cooperative relationship with the CSRC. In addition, the foreign party must have 10 years' operational experience in its home country.[42] At least one of the Chinese parties to the JVSC must be a domestically funded securities company.[43] The JVSC's chairman of the board, general manager and

---

39. JVSC Rules, supra note 19, at §10.
40. Rather than form a JVSC through application, to create a JVSC, a foreign investor can acquire a stake in an existing Chinese securities company. The lines of business permitted for a domestic Chinese comprehensive securities company, but not permitted for a JVSC, must be spun off before a domestic Chinese comprehensive securities company can be converted into a JVSC. The requirements on a JVSC's equity ratio, scope of business, qualification requirements in respect to the shareholders and the requirement of at least one domestic shareholder holding no less than one-third of the equity interest will apply in the formation through acquisition process. See, generally, ibid; see also B, Shouyun, 'New Rules on JV Securities Companies: A Limited Opening of China's Securities Industry', *China Law & Practice*, 16(8) (October 2002). The foreign investors must find Chinese partners that have sufficient cash or non-cash assets to make their capital contribution. Ibid.
41. JVSC Rules, supra note 19, §6; Securities Law, supra note 2, at §121.
42. In addition, an applicant must:

     – have not been subject to any material disciplinary actions or sanctions by a securities regulator or judicial authority in the three years prior to its JVSC formation application;
     – have appropriate risk control that have satisfied the legal requirements of its home-jurisdiction securities regulator;
     – have effective internal control processes;
     – possess a good reputation and good business achievements; and
     – comply with any other CSRC required conditions.

     However, the regulation does not clarify whether the business history of the foreign shareholders' predecessors counts towards the ten-year requirement. JVSC Rules, supra note 19, §6.
43. Ibid., at §8. If more than one Chinese party participates in a JVSC, at least one – but not necessarily all – must be a domestically funded securities company. In such a case, the Chinese party that is not a securities company must satisfy the qualifications to be a

deputy general managers must be Chinese nationals, however, the foreign party can appoint a foreign national to serve as the chairman, general manager or deputy general manager, upon CSRC consent.[44] As discussed in Section III, the JVSC formation process is somewhat involved.[45]

The Securities JV Rules and JVSC structure will have a moderate impact on China's securities markets. As of the end of 2005, 133 securities companies, including four JVSCs, did business in China; an increase of 23 companies since the end of 2001.[46] Although domestic securities companies have been seeking strategic alliances, and many foreign investment banks desire a local partner, the pool of Chinese securities companies able to partner in a JVSC is small, as is the number of qualified professionals required to fill executive positions in a JVSC.[47] The market for the services a JVSC could offer is small in absolute terms, and such services could be provided in Hong Kong or other financial centres. As with B-share trading seats, the commissions a JVSC can charge for

---

shareholder in a securities company. Each potential five per cent holder in a JVSC must be approved by the CSRC. A Chinese shareholder cannot be a five per cent holder in a JVSC if the shareholder:

- has been subject to any sanction due to operating in any material violation of laws or regulations during the three years prior to the application;
- has had aggregate losses in excess of 50 per cent of its registered capital;
- is insolvent or unable to pay debts that come due;
- has a total amount of debts in excess of 50 per cent of its net assets;

Other circumstances also apply, as prescribed by the China Securities Regulatory Commission (CSRC), Administration of Securities Houses Procedures, issued by the China Securities Regulatory Commission on 28 December 2001 and effective as of 1 March 2002, reprinted at China Law & Prac. 3700/01.12.28.

44. JVSC Rules, supra note 19, at §11; see also China Securities Regulatory Commission, *Tentative Measures on the Administration of the Employment Qualifications of Senior Management Personnel of Securities Operating Entities* (issued by the China Securities Regulatory Commission on 9 October 2004 and effective as of 15 November 2004), reprinted at *China Law & Prac.* 3700/04.10.09, at §5; FI-FMC Rules, supra note 19, at §9, which specifies the requirements for the chairman, general manager or deputy manager in a joint venture fund management company.

45. First, the JVSC's representative must submit application documents to the CSRC. If approved, the JVSC may enter into a preparatory phase. The JVSC must file a second application with the CSRC for a Permit for the Operation of Securities Business. A JVSC cannot engage in any securities-related business without first obtaining this type of permit. Promoters must then apply to the Ministry of Commerce for approval as a foreign invested enterprise and, upon approval, register with State Administration for Industry and Commerce. JVSC Rules, supra note 19, at §§12-7.

46. Committee on Trade in Financial Services, *Report of the Meeting Held 23 November 2004*, S/FIN/M/47 (26 November 2004), p. 25 (referred to in this chapter as the 23 November 2004 Report); China Securities Regulatory Commission, *List of JV Securities Companies* (as of December 2005), available at www.csrc.gov.cn/en/jsp/detail.jsp?infoid=1136943742100& type=CMS.STD (6 February 2006).

47. Asia Society, *Conference Report on China's Capital Markets: Where Will WTO-Sparked Reforms Lead?* (9 May 2002), available at <www.asiasociety.org/publications/capitalmarkets02.html> (5 February 2006) (referred to in this chapter simply as the Asia Society Conference Report).

services are set administratively, and pressures already-thin profit margins.[48] Most importantly, as discussed in Section IV, the QFII structure provides a more attractive vehicle to offer most of the same services a JVSC could offer. The QFII structure will lessen the impact of the JVSC structure on China's securities markets.

III.D.   FUND MANAGEMENT WITH FOREIGN EQUITY

The CSRC issued the Establishment of Fund Management Companies with Foreign Equity Participation Rules (FI-FMC Establishment Rules) on 1 June 2002, which took effect 1 July 2002.[49] On 12 July 2002, the CSRC clarified that the Relevant Issues in the Examination and Approval Procedures for the Establishment of Fund Management Companies Circular issued on 7 January 2002 and the Several Issues Concerning Major Changes of Fund Management Companies Circular issued on 21 March 2002 apply to foreign-invested fund management companies.[50] The FI-FMC Establishment Rules and related clarifications are the first legal basis for foreign investment into China's funds industry, and enable foreign investors to form a Foreign Invested Fund Management Company (FI-FMC) to engage in the same services as a domestic fund management company.

An FI-FMC must be structured as a limited liability company and established by:

– application made by the FI-FMC's promoters; or
– acquisition by a foreign investor – through transfer or subscription – of shares in an existing fund management company.[51]

---

48. Chinese economist Wu Xiaoqiu has predicted that, in the next five years, the number of companies dealing in securities in China will be reduced by nearly 100 firms; an indicator of an oversupply of Chinese securities companies, Green, supra note 1, p. 201. Huaou (China-Europe) International Securities Co., Ltd. was the first JVSC to be formed, co-funded by Chinas Xiangcai Securities and the Credit Lyonnais Securities (Asia) Ltd. (CLSA) of France. The JVSC was registered in Shanghai with a registered capital of RMB 500 million. Xiangcai Securities has a 67 per cent stake in the joint venture, and the remaining 33 per cent will be taken by CLSA. See 'Foreign early birds move into securities', [2005] *China Daily,* available at <www.chinadaily.com.cn/english/doc/2004–04/05/content_320663.htm> (6 February 2005).
49. On 20 December 2001, the CSRC published for public comment a set of draft rules related to the establishment of FI-FMCs. In the accompanying notice, the CSRC indicated that the comment period would be 11 days and would conclude on 31 December 2001. The CSRC did not promulgate the finalized FI-FMC Rules until 1 June 2002.
50. Statement by a CSRC spokesperson on issues relevant to the establishment of fund management companies (including fund management companies with foreign equity participation), *China Law & Prac.,* 16(8) (October 2002), pp. 119–131.
51. FI-FMC Rules, supra note 19, at §12. Upon a first approval, the FI-FMC applicants can only prepare for the opening of business by the joint venture. Foreign investors who buy into an existing domestic fund with the intention of converting the fund into an FI-FMC start

The CSRC must approve the FI-FMC's initial formation and commencement of business operations, and:

- each fund an FI-FMC promotes;
- the top-level managers in an FI-FMC;
- transfers of any FI-FMC shares;
- the law firms and accounting firms that assist in preparing a FI-FMC's application materials and the prospectus for a fund; and
- each company in which a fund invests.

The CSRC has empowered itself, in the FI-FMC Establishment Rules, to impose whatever additional prudential requirements it deems appropriate.

Of the four WTO-related liberalizations, the FI-FMC structure will have the most significant impact on China's securities markets due to the relatively underdeveloped state of China's fund management sector, China's large amount of household savings, and the prospect of future pension reform.[52] As of the end of December 2005, foreign investors had formed 20 FI-FMCs.[53] Note that certain challenges remain for FI-FMCs, including:

- the requirement that 65 per cent of a fund's non-cash assets be invested in the sector identified in the fund's name;
- the limitation that directors of a fund management company cannot directly or indirectly trade stocks in China or elsewhere or work at any other for-profit enterprise; and
- the amount of allowable control a foreign investor may exercise over the FI-FMC. In addition, China's first integrated, national investment funds law became effective on 1 June 2004, which means that implementing regulations and other interpretations could alter the regulatory landscape.

IV.   IMPLEMENTATION CHALLENGES

Despite the significant efforts made by the Chinese government, its WTO compliance record in the securities sector is not perfect. Although the Securities JV Rules were issued two and a half years early, the B-Share Seat Rules, Special

---

at this step in the examination and approval process. The FI-FMC must make a second application to the CSRC for an operating license after the preparation is complete and before the actual commencement of operation by the joint venture. The CSRC must act upon the application within thirty days of formal receipt. Ibid., at §14.

52. Allianz AG and Guotai Junan Securities Co. Ltd formed the first FI-FMC on 31 July 2002. See also Stoyan Tenev and Chunlin Zhang with Loup Brefort, Corporate Governance and Enterprise Reform in China: Building the Institutions of Modern Markets (World Bank Publications, 2002) at 113–114 [hereinafter IFC].

53. China Securities Regulatory Commission, *List of JV Fund Management Companies* (as of December 2005), available at <www.csrc.gov.cn/en/jsp/detail.jsp?infoid=1136943496100& type=CMS.STD> (6 February 2006). See also *23 November 2004 Report*, supra note 46.

Member Regulations and the initial FI-FMC Establishment Rules were more than six months late. Important implementing and explanatory regulations for these commitments were issued even more than six months late. The increase of the permissible level of foreign capital to 49 per cent in a FI-FMC had not been implemented as of 31 December 2004.[54] Other issues have been raised in the transitional review mechanism set up under 18 of China's Protocol of Accession, bilaterally and by relevant industry groups.[55] This section of the chapter briefly reviews a number of concerns related to China's implementation of its securities sector commitments.

The JVSC Rules and FI-FMC Rules contain significant capital requirements, set at a fixed level, that can hinder foreign providers' access to the securities sector.[56] These high-capital requirements are discussed in China's 2002, 2003 and 2004 18 transitional reviews, and have been defended by the Chinese government as prudential in nature.[57] Capital requirements cushion against potential losses by securities intermediaries and reduce systemic risk facing a securities market. Two principal capital requirement approaches are available:

- the Capital Adequacy Directive used by European Union Member States; and
- the net capital approach used by the U.S., Japan and other non-EU jurisdictions.[58]

---

54. Ibid., at p. 44.

55. *World Trade Organization, Accession Protocol of the People's Republic of China*, WT/L/432 (23 November 2001) at 18 [hereinafter *Accession Protocol*]. The Chinese government has expressed its opposition to having bodies subsidiary to the Council on Trade in Services conduct any form of transitional review, stating that any such effort amounts to re-negotiating and re-defining China's protocol of accession. At most, in the Chinese government's view any review by a subsidiary entity might take place during the last meeting, during any given calendar year, of such subsidiary body. Further, the Chinese government has viewed the ¶18 review as an opportunity for China to query other WTO members about their compliance with WTO requirements and commitments. See, for example, Committee on Trade in Financial Services, *Report of the Meeting Held on 4 June 2002*, S/FIN/M/35 (8 July 2002) pp. 26–29.

56. For example, the JVSC Rules state that a JVSC's minimum registered capital must exceed RMB 500 million, the same as for a domestic comprehensive-type securities company. JVSC Rules, supra note 19. Foreign investors to a FI-FMC must have paid-in capital in excess of RMB 300 million, the FI-FMC itself must have registered capital in excess of RMB 10 million, and each fund must raise more than RMB 200 million to be established. FI-FMC Rules, supra note 19.

57. Committee on Trade in Financial Services, *Report of the Meeting Held on 21 October 2002* (24 October 2002) p. 34; Committee on Trade in Financial Services, *Report of the Meeting Held on 1 December 2003*, S/FIN/M/43, (4 December 2003) pp. 39–40; 23 November 2004 Report, supra note 46, at pp. 37 and 46, 54; see also, U.S. China Business Council, *China's WTO Implementation: An Assessment of China's Second Year of WTO Membership Written Testimony by the US-China Business Council*, (10 September 2003), p. 3.

58. *Joint Forum of Basel Committee on Banking Supervision, International Organization of Securities Commissions, and International Association of Insurance Supervisors*, Risk Management Practices and Regulatory Capital: Cross-Sectoral Comparison (Basel Committee

China's fixed-level approach is inconsistent with either international standard and does not reflect a foreign provider's scope of operations. On the front-end, the high capital requirements could hinder market access. China's approach could cause an entity to satisfy statutory requirements but have insufficient capital to cover potential losses. The Chinese government should evaluate methods to create a more flexible, market-based approach to capital requirements for all JVSCs and FI-FMCs.

In 2(C)1 of its Accession Protocol, the Chinese government committed to providing access to, and the opportunity to comment on, all relevant trade-related laws, regulations, and other measures well before such measures are enforced. Observance of this commitment has been uneven, and has been discussed in China's 2002 and 2004 transitional reviews.[59] Despite recent regulatory changes, Chinese regulators often release draft regulations to selected industry players on an ad hoc basis and no standardized process is available by which the Chinese government releases draft laws to all industry.[60] Though China promulgated its Legislation Law on 15 March 2000, which came into force on 1 July 2000, and according to the law, a draft law or regulation can be presented to the public for comments,[61] relevant provisions have not been effectively implemented. In addition, timing issues often prevent thoughtful analysis and comment. The CSRC, for example, issued an initial draft of the Securities JV Rules on 12 December 2001 and an initial draft of the FI-FMC Establishment Rules appeared on 21 December 2001, and requested final comments

---

on Banking Supervision, 2001), pp. 39–40, available at <www.bis.org/publ/joint04.pdf> (5 February 2006) (referred to in this chapter as the Joint Forum). The net capital approach requires securities firms to maintain minimum levels of liquid assets sufficient to satisfy promptly all of its obligations. Ibid., p. 40. Minimum capital requirements for U.S. broker-dealers are specified at 17 CFR 240.15c3–1 (2004). The Capital Adequacy Directive (93/6/EEC) is derived from the Basel II Accord, and applies both to banks and investment firms in the European Union. Ibid., pp. 94–95.

59. Committee on Trade in Financial Services, *Report on the Meeting Held on 21 October 2002* (24 October 2002) p. 21.2.f and p. 37; November 23, 2004 Report, supra note 46, p. 56; See also Working Party on Domestic Regulation, *Report on the Meeting Held on 3 December 2003*, S/WPDR/M/24 (22 January 2004) pp. 37–38.

60. See American Chamber of Commerce-Beijing, 2003 White Paper, *American Business in China,* available at <www.amcham-china.org.cn/publications/white/2003/en-12.htm> (5 February 2006) (referred to in this chapter as the AmCham White Paper). See also Office of the United States Trade Representative, *2003 Report to Congress on China's WTO Compliance*, pp. 65–66, available at <www.ustr.gov/assets/document_library/reports_publications/2003/asset_upload_file425_4313.pdf> (7 February 2006); American Chamber of Commerce-Beijing, *WTO Implementation Report Fall*, 2002, available at <www.amcham-china.org.cn/publications/position/wto/wto_11.htm> (5 February 2006).

61. See Legislation Law of the People's Republic of China (adopted by the Third Session of the Ninth National People's Congress on 15 March 2000) at §§34, 35 and 58, available at <www.csrc.gov.cn/en/jsp/detail.jsp?infoid=1132730852100& type=CMS.STD> (5 February 2006).

and input on both no later than 31 December 2001.[62] China must continue to upgrade compliance with its notice and comment transparency commitments.

As could be expected, the formation and operation of FI-FMCs and JVSCs requires several levels of application, review, and approval. Despite the commitment in paragraph 308 of the Working Party Report to ensure that licensing procedures are not unnecessarily burdensome, the FI-FMC Establishment Rules and Securities JV Rules each require potential applicants to satisfy a multi-step application, registration, and operational review process. Unless scheduled as an exception to its national treatment obligations, licensing procedures should be administered in a national treatment-compliant manner.[63] The multi-step registration and approval process has been raised in China's 2002 transitional review.[64] Some simplification may be on the horizon because:

- in July 2004, the State Council issued the Reform of the Investment System Decision that altered significantly the examination and approval system required of projects not using government funds; and
- in October 2004, the National Development and Reform Commission (NDRC) issued the Administration of the Verification of Foreign-invested Projects Tentative Procedures, which specified how the NDRC would regulate the new registration system.[65] Under the new registration system, foreign investors only need to file one project application report to the NDRC for approval before commencing any investment project.[66] In practice, at least as of the end of 2005, the NDRC-related 'simplifications' have created some level of uncertainty, in that these simplifications empower a local development and reform commission to supplement MOFCOM's approval process with a locally-based investment approval process.[67] How these new regulations have affected FI-FMCs or JVSCs

62. Letter from Marc E. Lackritz, President of the Securities Industry Association to John Snow, U.S. Secretary of the Treasury, 28 August 2003, available at <www.sia.com/2003_comment_letters/pdf/snowletterchina_scapmkts.pdf> (5 February 2006).
63. General Agreement on Trade in Services, 15 April 1994, Marrakech Agreement Establishing the World Trade Organization, Annex 1B, §VI:4; see also Working Party on Domestic Regulation, *Report of the Meeting Held on 24 September 2004*, S/WPDR/M/27 (15 November 2004) p. 59; Working Party on Domestic Regulation, *Report on the Meeting Held on 24 June 2004*, S/WPDR/M/26 (8 September 2004), p. 51. The European Union has proposed to extend specific disciplines to licensing procedures to ensure, inter alia, that procedures do not constitute a barrier to trade. Ibid.
64. Committee on Trade in Financial Services, *Report of the Meeting Held on 21 October 2002* (24 October 2002) p. 21.2.g and 37. Committee on Trade in Financial Services, *Report of the Meeting Held on 1 December 2003*, S/FIN/M/43 (4 December 2003) p. 63.
65. State Council, Reform of the Investment System Decision, (issued by the State Council on 16 July 2004 and effective as of the same date), reprinted at *China Law & Prac.* 2100/04.07.16.
66. State Administration for Industry and Commerce, *Procedure for Enterprise Registration Provisions* (issued by the State Administration for Industry and Commerce on 10 June 2004 and effective as of the same date), reprinted at *China Law & Prac.* 2330/04.06.10.
67. See A.L. Sommers, 'Foreign Investment Verification: Reform, Status Quo, or Bafflement?' in *China Business Review,* volume 6, p. 38 (November-December 2005).

in practice is unclear, and the Chinese government must continue to reduce the administrative burdens it imposes through the licensing and reporting processes.

Foreign parties to a FI-FMC or a JVSC are restricted in terms of the pool of Chinese parties available for partnering relationships, an issue that has been raised in China's 2002 and 2003 transitional reviews.[68] In section 314 of its *Working Party Report*, the Chinese government indicated that a foreign party would be free to partner with the Chinese entity of its choice. [69] Limiting the pool of potential venture partners is a de facto quota, and both the FI-FMC Establishment Rules and Securities JV Rules impose significant requirements on Chinese parties that limit such pools. In addition, the CSRC has specified requirements on senior managers in JVSC and FI-FMC.[70] Relevant CSRC experience requirements may be satisfied through:

- a practice qualification certificate issued by the Securities Association of China;

---

68. Committee on Trade in Financial Services, *Report of the Meeting Held on 21 October 2002* (24 October 2002) p. 21.2.e, S/FIN/M/37; see also Letter from David Strongin, Vice President and Director, International Finance of Securities Industry Association to Shi Bin of the China Securities Regulatory Commission, Feb. 5, 2002 [referred to in this chapter as the Strongin Letter], available at <www.sia.com/2002_comment_letters/pdf/china_securities.pdf> (5 February 2006).

69. *Working Party Report on the Accession of the People's Republic of China*, WT/ACC/CHN/49 (1 October 2001), at p. 314. The FI-FMC's chairman of the board, general manager and deputy general manager must possess the qualifications required, and issued, by the CSRC. In addition, many have suggested that the number of persons employed by a FI-FMC or JVSC be left to the entity's discretion.

70. Senior managers in a securities company must have at least:
    - three years' experience in the securities business;
    - five years' experience in a financial, legal or accounting business; or
    - ten years' experience in general business.

    A securities company's general manager, deputy general manager, finance officer or compliance supervisor must have at least:
    - three years' experience in a securities company; or
    - five years' experience in finance business. These types of senior managers cannot engage in any business activity outside of the scope of their employment. China Securities Regulatory Commission, *Administration of Senior Management Personnel of Securities Companies Procedures*, (issued by the China Securities Regulatory Commission on 9 October 2004 and effective as of 15 November 2004), reprinted at *China Law & Prac.* 3700/04.10.09.

    Senior managers in the securities fund management industry must have:
    - obtained necessary qualifications;
    - passed the senior management personnel examination; and
    - at least three years' work experience in finance-related fields and relevant management experience.

    An investment fund management company's independent directors must have more than five years' experience in the financial, legal or financing work field. The fund's manager must have more than three years' experience in securities investment management. Ibid.

- passing a relevant qualification examination;
- passing the CSRC's personnel examination; or
- having relevant foreign qualifications.[71]

The Chinese government must review the impact of these requirements, as they limit the value of China's WTO commitments.

In its Schedule of Specific Commitments, China committed to allowing a JVSC to 'engage in … trading of B and H shares as well as governmental and corporate debts'. The Securities JV Rules only permit a JVSC to engage in proprietary trading of government and corporate bonds. Further, a JVSC's permitted business scope is narrower than that of a comprehensive-type domestic Chinese securities firm, raising a national treatment question. A JVSC cannot engage in lines of business common to securities companies in other jurisdictions, such as:

- asset management services on behalf of its institutional or individual clients;
- domestic private placement financing services, whether for public or private companies;
- consulting or investment advising;
- deal in A-Shares for its own account or as a broker; or
- deal in B-Shares for its own account, as can comprehensive-type domestic securities companies.[72]

The Securities JV Rules do not specify when brokerage licenses will be made available to JVSCs to implement the brokering aspects of its WTO commitments. American industry associations have been pushing for JVSCs to be permitted to underwrite securities issues and engage in proprietary trading of such shares.[73] Finally, the Securities JV Rules appear to limit joint ventures to a single location.[74]

The FI-FMC Establishment Rules, when read with other relevant rules and regulations, seem to require the actual entity making the direct investment into China to satisfy all relevant requirements. In some cases, it appears that an investor can 'borrow' relevant qualifications from a corporate affiliate. However, the apparent requirement that the actual applicant satisfy stated

---

71. Ibid.
72. JVSC Rules, supra note 19, at §5. On 18 December 2003, the CSRC issued the Client Asset Management Businesses of Securities Companies Trial Procedures, effective as of 1 February 2004. Pursuant to the procedures, securities companies are required to apply to the CSRC to engage in client asset management business, which is defined as designated asset management for single clients, collective asset management for multiple clients and special asset management for clients with special needs. Only comprehensive-type securities companies can engage in client asset management business. Although these procedures are silent as to a JVSC offering client asset management services, the procedures seem to have been drafted to include all comprehensive-type securities companies, including JVSCs.
73. Strongin Letter, supra note 68.
74. See AmCham White Paper, supra note 60.

requirements may prevent even significant intermediate operating companies within a corporate group from satisfying relevant CSRC requirements, and seems to restrict unreasonably access to this sector of China's economy.[75]

Article 306 of the Working Party Report and 2(c)1 of the Protocol of Accession require China's trade framework to be administered in a transparent manner including, by extension, making trade-related regulations transparent as to meaning. Each of the FI-FMC Establishment Rules, Special Member Regulations, B-Share Seat Rules and Securities JV Rules contain vague requirements that reserve some degree of discretion to administrative entities.[76] For example, potential foreign parties to an FI-FMC must be from a jurisdiction that has 'perfected' securities law and supervision;[77] the Securities JV Rules require the foreign investor to have 'sound internal control' and 'good reputation and operating results'; foreign shareholders in a FI-FMC must not have been subject to any 'material penalty' in the past three years. Other ambiguous provisions include the reference to 'other relevant laws and regulations'. The new Administrative Licensing Law (ALL) limits the scope of regulatory agencies' administrative discretion, however, since the ALL took effect on 1 July 2004, just how the ALL will impact these licensing issues is unclear.[78] In general, opacity in licensing requirements runs counter to China's transparency commitments and imposes an unnecessary transaction cost on market participants.[79]

Both the FI-FMC Establishment Rules and Securities JV Rules initially excluded the Ministry of Foreign Trade and Cooperation from any role in the registration process by not requiring FI-FMCs or JVSCs to apply for approval as a foreign-invested enterprise. Neither rules explicitly required that FI-FMCs or JVSCs register with the State Administration for Industry and Commerce. These initial oversights were corrected with follow-on regulations, but added a degree of uncertainty to the application process inconsistent with China's

---

75. See W. Hutchens, 'Promises Kept: The CSRC Opens the Door to Foreign Investment in Fund Management Companies', *China Law & Prac.* 16(8) (October 2002).
76. Flexibility is a major goal of Chinese legal rules drafting, and drafters typically use language that creates wide leeway for administrative discretion. Standard drafting techniques include the use of general principles, undefined terms, broadly worded discretion, omissions, and general catchall phrases such as the *nita* clause present in most legal rules. Much in Chinese legislation is fleshed out only over time in implementing regulations and opinions that may take years to be issued or become available. J.M. Zimmerman, *China Law Deskbook: A Legal Guide for Foreign-Invested Enterprises*, (2nd Edition, American Bar Association, 2005); S. Lubman, 'Bird in a Cage: Chinese Law Reform After Twenty Years', 20 *Nw. J. Int'l L. & Bus.* 383 (Spring 2001); D.H. Rosen, *Behind the Open Door: Foreign Enterprises in the Chinese Marketplace* (Institute for International Economics, 1999).
77. FI-FMC Rules, supra note 19, at §6. Whether foreign investors could hold their interest in an FI-FMC through a tax-haven holding company is unclear, because the CSRC seems to want these establishment conditions be fulfilled by the entity that directly holds the FI-FMC shares. Ibid.
78. See Administrative Licensing Law of the People's Republic of China, (issued by the National People's Congress on 27 August 2004 and effective as of 1 July 2004).
79. Accession Protocol, supra note 55, p. 2(c).

WTO transparency commitments. The Chinese government must continue to improve on the transparency of its regulations.

V.   EFFECT OF VOLUNTARY LIBERALIZATIONS

The Chinese government continues to liberalize its securities markets, supplementing implementation of the nation's WTO commitments in a process the Chinese government has characterized as voluntary liberalizations under WTO.[80] This section of the chapter reviews these developments. These actions liberalize foreign access to, and encourage the development of, China's securities market, including, *inter alia*:

- Enabling foreign-invested enterprises to convert into a foreign-invested company limited by shares and make a public offering;[81]
- Fostering the development of foreign-invested venture capital companies;[82]
- Allowing the transfer of certain state-owned shares to foreign investors;
- Promulgating the first nation-wide law regulating securities investment funds;[83]

---

80. See, for example, 23 November 2004 Report, supra note 46, at p. 26.
81. China Securities Regulatory Commission, *Contents and Format of Prospectuses of Foreign-funded Companies Limited by Shares Special Provisions*, (issued on 19 March 2002 and effective as of the same date). A listing FIE must have:

     - passed the foreign investment enterprise joint annual examinations for three consecutive years prior to the listing application;
     - a business scope consistent with the New Catalogue and the 2002 Provisions; and
     - a Chinese controlling party – or a mandatory shareholding requirement for a Chinese party – if required by a relevant regulation. These regulations require enhanced disclosure in prospectuses issued by foreign invested companies limited by shares (FICLS), including those established by Hong Kong, Macao or Taiwan investors.

     The FIC Special Provisions impose a higher disclosure standard on foreign invested issuers than on domestic PRC issuers. A FICLS prospectus must disclose:

     - risks arising from possible changes in PRC laws, regulations and policies granting preferential tax treatment to foreign investment enterprises;
     - foreign exchange risk;
     - connected transactions with foreign investors; and
     - personal details of the FICLS's foreign directors and senior management personnel.

     On 30 December 2003, Zhejiang King Refrigeration Industry Company Limited by Shares became the first FIE to list on the domestic A-share market.
82. Ministry of Foreign Trade and Economic Cooperation, State Administration for Industry and Commerce, Ministry of Science and Technology, State Administration of Taxation, and State Administration of Foreign Exchange Regulation, *Administration of Foreign-Invested Venture Capital Enterprises* (issued on 30 January 2003 and effective as of the same date).
83. Securities Investment Fund Law of the People's Republic of China (issued by the National People's Congress on 28 October 2003 and effective as of 1 June 2004). The Investment Fund Law regulates closed-end funds and open-end funds that are publicly offered and sold.

- Enabling approved securities companies to engage in specified asset management business;[84]
- Specifying the requirements for secondary and follow-on offerings by public companies;[85]
- Allowing the listing of convertible corporate bonds;[86]
- Specifying the procedures pursuant to which domestic and foreign enterprises can take over a Chinese listed company through an equity transaction;[87]
- Enabling group enterprise listings;[88]

Only CSRC-approved fund management companies may establish and manage investment funds. Such fund management company must have:

- registered capital in excess of RMB 100 million;
- principal shareholders in the securities management, securities investment consulting, trust asset management or other financial asset management business; and
- each principal shareholder with registered capital exceeding RMB 300 million.

To establish a fund, a fund management company must apply to CSRC for approval. If approved, the fund management company can start to sell fund units to the public. To achieve a valid public offering for a closed-end fund, the fund management company must sell more than 80 per cent of the total amount of the units approved by CSRC. For an open-end fund, the fund management company must sell more than the minimum amount of units (as approved by CSRC) to a minimum number of buyers (as stipulated by CSRC). Funds can invest only in listed stocks, bonds and other securities products designated by CSRC. The Investment Fund Law prohibits the use of fund assets for:

- underwriting securities, extending loans, or buying other funds;
- making equity investments in the fund management company or custodian; or
- buying securities issued or underwritten by the fund manager's or fund custodian's controlling shareholder. Ibid.

84. China Securities Regulatory Commission, Trial Measures Regarding Asset Management Business of Securities Companies, (issued on 18 December 2003 and effective as of 1 February 2004).

85. China Securities Regulatory Commission, Notice Regarding Relevant Conditions for Issuance of New Shares by Listed Companies (issued on 24 July 2002 and effective as of the same date).

86. Shenzhen Stock Exchange, Convertible Bond Listing Rules of the Shenzhen Stock Exchange, (issued on 1 November 2002 and effective as of the same date); Shanghai Stock Exchange, Convertible Bond Listing Rules of the Shanghai Stock Exchange, (issued on 4 November 2002 and effective as of the same date).

87. China Securities Regulatory Commission, Administration of the Takeover of Listed Companies Procedures, (issued on 28 September 2002 and effective as of 1 December 2002); Ministry of Foreign Trade and Economic Cooperation, State Administration for Industry and Commerce, State Administration of Taxation, and State Administration of Foreign Exchange, Interim Provisions on Mergers and Acquisitions of Domestic Enterprises by Foreign Investors (issued on 12 April 2003 and effective as of the same date) (M&A Provisions). The M&A Provisions allow foreign investors to acquire stock and assets of domestic Chinese enterprises. These types of acquisitions can be accomplished through the purchase of the outstanding equity of shareholders in a domestic Chinese enterprise or through a subscription of newly issued shares of such a company. In either case, the domestic company will be converted into a foreign invested enterprise upon the purchase.

88. In early-2002, the State Council issued the Guideline Opinions on Developing Large Internationally Competitive Group Enterprises.

- Specifying the amount of shares in an initial public offering that should be allotted to existing investors.[89]
- Reforming the split share structure of listed companies by selling down part of shares held by the state and legal persons and gradually allowing these shares to be traded freely in the secondary market.[90]
- Revising the Company Law and the Securities Law for purposes of encouraging investment, promoting the establishment of companies and the development of domestic capital markets, and strengthening the regulation of the markets and improving the protection for investors.[91]

Although this list is impressive, the adoption of a QFII framework, not included in the list, is the most significant development, related or unrelated to WTO implementation, in China's securities market since WTO accession.[92] The Administration of Securities Investments in China by Qualified Foreign Institutional Investors Tentative Procedures (QFII Tentative Procedures) can be one

---

89. On 20 May 2002, the CSRC issued the *Supplementary Notice Concerning Allotment of Shares to Existing Investors* upon an IPO, effective as of that date. The amount of funds raised through an initial public offering may not exceed two times the issuer's unaudited net asset value as of a date one year prior to the issuer's application to publicly list, less any amount of undistributed profits rolled over by existing shareholders. Companies intending to distribute dividends prior to listing must complete relevant procedures before listing. A prospectus must include a special notice as to the amount of undistributed profits rolled over and any plans for a dividend distribution. China Securities Regulatory Commission, Standards for Examination and Verification of Share Issues Memorandum No. 17: Examination and Verification Requirements for Fund Raising of Companies Initially Offering Shares to the Public, (issued by the Department of Public Offering Supervision of the China Securities Regulatory Commission on 11 May 2004 and effective as of the same date), reprinted at *China Law & Prac.* 3710/04.05.11.
90. On 4 September 2005, the CSRC promulgated the Administrative Measures on the Split Share Structure Reform of Listed Companies (effective as of the same date), available at <www.csrc.gov.cn/en/jsp/detail.jsp?infoid=1129278662100& type=CMS.STD> (5 February 2006).
91. See, for example, China Securities Regulatory Commission, *Decision of Amending Company Law*, available at <www.csrc.gov.cn/en/jsp/detail.jsp?infoid=1133400972100& type=CMS.STD> (6 February 2006).
92. China Securities Regulatory Commission and People's Bank of China, *Administration of Securities Investments in China by Qualified Foreign Institutional Investors Tentative Procedures* (issued on 5 November 2002 and effective as of 1 December 2002), (referred to in this chapter as QFII Tentative Procedures), available at <www.csrc.gov.cn/en/jsp/detail.jsp?infoid=1061947782100&type=CMS.STD> (5 February 2006).The QFII Tentative Procedures enable specified foreign institutional investors to form and operate a QFII. A QFII must be a fund management institution, an insurance company, a securities company or another type of asset management institution or an as-yet-undefined 'other' institution. Potential QFIIs must be financially stable, enjoy good credit and satisfy the asset size test and other CSRC requirements. In the QFII context, the asset size test depends on the type of institution seeking licensure:
    - for fund management institutions, to have engaged in fund business for not less than five years and to have managed assets of not less than USD 10 billion in the most recent fiscal year;

of the most significant developments since the formation of China's securities markets in the early 1990s. China did not make a WTO-related commitment calling for a QFII structure to liberalize foreign access to capital markets.[93] As of the end of December 2005, 34 foreign institutions had obtained QFII qualifications, and another 11 foreign institutions had been approved to be QFII custodians.[94]

Institutions that want to become a QFII must submit an application form and a specified list of documents to the CSRC.[95] QFIIs may invest in renminbi-denominated financial instruments, which include A-shares, treasury bonds, convertible and corporate bonds, and any other instrument approved by the CSRC. However, Shanghai Stock Exchange QFII Investing in Domestic Securities Market Securities Trading Implementing Regulations and Shenzhen Stock Exchange QFII Investing in Domestic Securities Market Securities Trading Implementing Regulations, promulgated on, and effective from,

---

- for insurance companies, to have engaged in insurance business for not less than 30 years, to have paid-in capital of not less than USD 1 billion and to have managed securities assets of not less than USD 10 billion in the most recent fiscal year;
- for securities companies, to have engaged in securities business for not less than 30 years, to have paid-in capital of not less than USD 1 billion and to have managed securities assets of not less than USD 10 billion in the most recent fiscal year;
- for commercial banks, to have total assets listed within the world's top 100 and to have managed securities assets of not less than USD 10 billion during the most recent fiscal year. Ibid.

93. The QFII structure allows a capital market to absorb foreign portfolio capital while minimizing its destabilizing effects, such as a fast withdrawal of such capital. Green, supra note 1, at 209, 232. Taiwan formally abolished its QFII structure on 2 October 2003. Taiwan's QFII system was introduced in the late eighties in Taiwan, to act as a buffer to prevent rapid flows of currency in and out of Taiwan. Under this body of regulations, investors needed government approval to remit money into Taiwan for investment, and needed to state the purpose of the remittance. p. Denlinger, *Taiwan Abandons QFII System*, China Business Strategy (3 October 2003) available at <www.china-ready.com/news/Oct03/TaiwanAbandonsQFIISystem100303.html> (5 February 2006).

94. China Securities Regulatory Commission, *List of QFII* (as of December 2005), available at <www.csrc.gov.cn/en/jsp/detail.jsp?infoid=1136943198100&type=CMS.STD> (6 February 2006); China Securities Regulatory Commission, *List of QFII Custodians*, available at <www.csrc.gov.cn/en/jsp/detail.jsp?infoid=1136943092100&type=CMS.STD> (6 February 2006)

95. Joint and several liability applies on the board of directors for deliberate misrepresentations on QFII application. The CSRC must approve or reject a QFII application within 15 working days of receipt. Upon approval, the CSRC notifies the applicant and issues a securities business investment permit. Upon receipt of the permit, the applicant has to apply, through its PRC custodian, for SAFE approval for its intended investment level. SAFE has 15 working days to act on this type of application. Upon SAFE approval, the QFII applicant will be issued of a notification its investment limit and a foreign exchange registration certificate. Upon receipt of the foreign exchange certificate, the QFII can open a special purpose RMB account with its custodian. This account will fund purchases and other related costs as well as holding proceeds. QFIIs are to be fully invested, in the amount approved by SAFE, within 90 days of receipt of the CSRC approval certificate. QFII Tentative Procedures, supra note 92.

1 December 2002 indicate that QFIIs are not permitted – for the moment – to participate in treasury bond repurchases and enterprise bond trading due to 'technical reasons'.[96]

Related to the QFII Tentative Procedures, the State Administration of Foreign Exchange issued the Administration of Foreign Exchange for Securities Investments in the PRC by QFIIs Tentative Provisions effective 1 December 2002, which state that:

- the minimum QFII investment must be USD 50 million with a USD 800 million cap;
- a single QFII cannot hold more that 10 per cent of the aggregate A-shares in a single listed company; and
- the aggregate limit of all QFIIs' investment in a single listed company cannot exceed 20 per cent of the total A-shares.

If QFII holdings exceed such limits, the stock exchange is to issue a sell down notice. Pursuant to that notice, QFIIs must sell A-shares in a quantity to comply with the aforementioned limits. QFIIs have five trading days to comply with the sell-down notice, with excess shares sold on a last-in-first-out basis. QFIIs are required to have a custodial account with a commercial bank within China, and that bank is the custodian of QFII assets.[97] A domestic securities company within China is to execute the QFII's securities trading and QFIIs may only remit proceeds offshore pursuant to relevant guidelines.[98]

The QFII structure significantly, and adversely, affects the attractiveness of the JVSC structure. A QFII has a broader permissible business scope than a JVSC and fewer foreign exchange headaches. In addition, the number and investment limits of QFIIs dwarfs similar JVSC volumes. For this reason, the QFII structure will increase in popularity, and exercise a more significant influence on the development of China's securities sector.

Because the majority of a Chinese listed company's issued and outstanding shares are non-publicly tradable state shares and legal person shares, purchases of this category of shares are quite important – to both domestic and foreign investors – for acquiring corporate control of Chinese listed companies.

---

96. Ibid., at §20. These Implementing Regulations did not specify what the technical difficulties are nor do they provide for any timetable within which such technical difficulties are to be solved.
97. People's Bank of China, *Issues Relevant to the Application by Commercial Banks for Engaging in the Custody Business of Domestic Securities Investments by Qualified Foreign Institutional Investors Circular,* (issued on 17 December 2002 and effective as of the same date), reprinted at *China Law & Prac.* 3610/02.12.17, which specifies the procedures for commercial banks to become QFII custodians. The circular divides applicant banks into domestic and foreign-funded categories.
98. QFIIs can only apply to SAFE to purchase foreign exchange one year after their principal is fully paid. Subsequently, each remittance is capped at 20 per cent of the total principal and must be made three-month intervals. The recipient of the offshore remittance of principal or of profits must be the QFII itself. QFII Tentative Procedures, supra note 92.

According to Chinese law, the purchase of state shares and legal person shares is different from the purchase of freely tradable shares. Special rules apply for purchasing these non-publicly tradable shares.

The *Notice on Relevant Issues Concerning the Transfer to Foreign Investors of Listed Company State-owned Shares and Legal Person Shares (Transfer of State-owned Shares and Legal Person Shares Notice)* jointly promulgated by the CSRC, the Ministry of Finance, and the States Economic and Trade Commission in November 2002 explicitly permits state shares and legal person shares of listed companies to be transferred directly to foreign investors, thus removing an order of which had prohibited the transfer of these shares to foreign investors since September 1995.[99] Foreign investors now have the potential to acquire sole or shared control of China's publicly listed SOEs. As a result, the previously discouraged foreign M&A of listed companies has begun in earnest.

The transfer of state shares and legal person shares in listed companies to foreign investors shall comply with the requirements of the Foreign Investment Industrial Guidance Catalogue.[100] Because the selling company's shares are issued on the Chinese securities market, the transfer must also be in compliance with relevant regulations by the CSRC, including the regulations on acquisition of listed companies and the regulations on information disclosure.[101]

Article 3 of the Notice states the requirements for foreign investors to qualify for accepting transferred shares:

- have comprehensively strong operation and management capabilities;
- be financially strong;
- have relatively good financial positions and reputations
- have the abilities to improve the corporate governance of the target and to promote the continued development of the targets.

If the transfer involves industrial policy and enterprise reorganization, the State Economic and Trade Commission shall be responsible for examination and approval; if the transfer involves the management of state-owned shares, the Ministry of Finance shall be responsible for the examination and approval; any major matters shall be submitted to the State Council for approval.[102] The applicable shares are to be sold by public bid.[103] Foreign investors may transfer their purchased shares 12 months after full payment of the entire transfer price.[104] After the transfer of shares, listed companies shall continue to be governed by

---

99. China Securities Regulatory Commission, Ministry of Finance, and the State Economic and Trade Commission, *Notice on Relevant Issues Concerning the Transfer to Foreign Investors of Listed Company State Shares and Legal Person Shares* (issued on __ November 2002) at §2.
100. Ibid.
101. Ibid., art. 4.
102. Ibid.
103. Ibid., at art. 3.
104. Ibid., at art. 7.

the original relevant policies and shall not enjoy treatment as foreign-invested enterprises.[105]

VI.   SEQUENCING OF LIBERALIZATION AND REFORM

Implementation of its WTO commitments will liberalize foreign access to China's securities sector and augment the Chinese economy's ability to withstand macroeconomic shocks, but will increase the number and complexity of the risks that confront China's financial system.[106] Many of the nations hardest hit by the AFC had completed some degree of financial system liberalization just prior to the AFC's outbreak.[107] Ex-post analyses of the AFC demonstrate that an integrated, risk-based sequencing of liberalization and reform is necessary to minimize those liberalization-related risks that could destabilize a nation's economy.[108] In AFC-affected nations, liberalization without required re-regulation or with partial or incomplete re-regulation enabled excessive risk-taking and accelerated the accumulation of short-term foreign-denominated debt.[109]

---

105. Ibid., at art. 9. Apparent conflicts can be seen between this provision and Article 16 of the *Investment within China by Foreign-invested Enterprises Tentative Provisions,* in that each handles the target differently.

106. M. Kono, et al., *Special Studies: Opening Markets in Financial Services and the Role of the GATS* (World Trade Organization, 1997): 'Liberalization of financial services trade itself does not cause financial crises but, in the presence of inadequate macroeconomic and regulatory policies, it can exacerbate problems'; see also C. Karacadag, V. Sundararajan, and J. Elliot, 'Managing Risks in Financial Market Development: The Role of Sequencing', *International Monetary Fund Working Paper* WP/03/116 (June 2003), p. 14 (referred to in this chapter as Karacadag).

107. Emerging Markets Committee, International Organization of Securities Commissions, *Causes, Effects and Regulatory Implications of Financial and Economic Turbulence in Emerging Markets* (November 1999), p. 29 (referred to in this chapter as Turbulence). As used in the IOSCO Report and in this chapter, 'liberalization' refers to reducing barriers to foreign entry and participation in a nation's financial system.

108. Karacadag, supra note 106. See also Eswar Prasad, et al., 'Putting the Cart Before the Horse? Capital Account Liberalization and Exchange Rate Flexibility in China', *IMF Policy Discussion Paper* 05/1 (January 2005) (referred to in this chapter as 'Cart Before the Horse'); Bank for International Settlements, *Capital Account Liberalization*, BIS Papers, no. 15 (April 2003) (referred to in this chapter as 'BIS 15'), which states that capital account liberalization is more likely to succeed if part of a larger, coherent reform process; Turbulence, supra note 107, p. 69; Committee on Trade in Financial Services, *Communication from Malaysia*, S/FIN/W/28 (30 July 2003), pp. 9–10 and 17; Council for Trade in Services, *Report of the Meeting Held on 14 and 15 December 1998* (14 January 199), p. 53(a).

109. Turbulence, supra note 107, p. 29. In addition, the report notes that the lack of a strong culture of enforcement and accountability led to prudential and other regulations being breached on a consistent basis. Crises such as the AFC are more likely to occur in jurisdictions with weak institutional frameworks. Ibid., pp. 29–31.

Because capital account liberalization is a medium-term objective for the Chinese government, risk minimization through sequencing increasingly is important.[110] A financial market may be divided into a quasi-hierarchy:

- money market;
- foreign exchange market;
- government bond market;
- corporate bond and equity market; and
- derivatives market.[111]

Most of these markets are interrelated and serve complimentary functions, so the aforementioned divisions are not a true hierarchy. Nonetheless, any sequencing strategy should consider the hierarchy and complementarity of financial markets, and deploy risk mitigation strategies at each level. These risk mitigation skills build on one another at each level. The pace and scope of this sequencing must be market-specific and take into account a nation's wealth and size constraints.[112] This section of the chapter reviews the sequencing of liberalization and reform in China's financial system, with particular attention paid to those risk minimization strategies that must be deployed in China's securities markets.

VI.A.   MONEY MARKET

A money market is the base of any financial system, because the market is:

- the medium through which a central bank affects monetary policy and liquidity, and steers short-term interest rates; and
- the mechanism through which financial institutions manage their liquidity.[113]

Developing a broad range of repurchase agreements and money market funds is crucial to money market development.[114] Repurchase agreements can smooth securities yield curve, facilitate interbank lending by reducing the credit risk that faces market participants and help financial institutions gain experience in credit and interest rate risk assessment.[115] A money market is critical to price discovery and supports the development of an active foreign exchange market

---

110.   Cart Before the Horse, supra note 108.
111.   Karacadag, supra note 106.
112.   Ibid; Turbulence, supra note 107, at 71. Committee on Trade in Financial Services, *Report of the Meeting Held on 26 February 2003*, S/FIN/M/39 (7 April 2003) pp. 13–14, 16 and 24.
113.   M. Levinson, *Guide to Financial Markets* (3d ed., Bloomberg Press, 2003), pp. 37–59 (referred to as 'Levinson').
114.   Ibid., p. 37.
115.   Karacadag, supra note 106, at 9; see also Bank for International Settlements, *Implications of Repo Markets for Central Banks, CGFS Publications No. 10*, (March 1999) (referred to as 'CGFS 10').

and government bond market.[116] An active corporate bond and equity market can support money market development by providing high-quality collateral for repurchase agreements. An illiquid money market can harm the development of corporate bond and equity markets by limiting investors' ability to invest in longer-term investments.[117] As a money market increases in size, the disintermediation of commercial banks accelerates.[118]

Money market development without appropriate risk mitigations can lead to large capital inflows and cause credit expansion.[119] Money market development introduces new, and more complex, types of credit, settlement and liquidity risk to a nation's financial system.[120] These types of risks are rooted in the soundness of market participants, and the ease with which participants can gather detailed, timely, and accurate information about potential counterparties. The risks injected by money market development can be mitigated through:

- enforcing timely and detailed financial disclosure standards on market participants, reinforced by regular use of audits;
- strengthening participants' liquidity management skills; and
- augmenting the clearance and settlement system.[121]

China's money market is less developed and less liquid than the money markets in nations with a similar gross domestic product to China's, which means the Chinese financial system is not receiving a similar level of risk mitigation

---

116. Karacadag, supra note 106, p. 8.
117. Ibid., pp. 9–10; see also CGFS 10, supra note 113.
118. Levinson, supra note 113, p. 37. While no precise definition is available of precisely a money market is, the phrase usually refers to the purchase and sale of instruments with a maturity of less than one year. While somewhat similar to bond markets – in the sense that the product being transacted is indebtedness – money market actors are more focused on cash management or the financing of their portfolios. Ibid., p. 38. Many types of money market instruments exist, including, inter alia, commercial paper, interbank loans, treasury bills and repurchase agreements. Ibid., pp. 40–42 and 50–52; see also Karacadag, supra note 106, p. 9.
119. Karacadag, supra note 106, p. 20.
120. Ibid., p. 21. Credit risk is the risk that a counter-party will fail to perform fully its financial obligations. Credit risk includes the risk of default on a loan or bond obligation, as well as a guarantor or derivative counterparty failing to meet its obligations. Securities firms expose themselves to credit risk through making margin loans to customers, entering into derivatives contracts, borrowing or lending securities, and entering into repurchase agreements. Securities companies typically mitigate credit risk through undertaking significant credit analysis of counterparties and holding an appropriate level of liquid capital. Joint Forum, supra note 58, pp. 15–16. Settlement risk is that the system of transfer and payment connected to a specific transaction will fail. Karacadag, supra note 106, p. 27. Liquidity risk is the risk that an entity will be unable to unwind a position in a specific financial instrument at or near its market value because of some form of market disruption or lack of depth in such instrument. Market risks are significant for securities companies, as they tend to operate in a mark-to-market context, and because securities companies may have to maintain large positions in a certain security. Joint Forum, supra note 58, p. 17.
121. Karacadag, supra note 106, p. 22.

experience as comparably sized economies. In November 2004, the national interbank renminbi market's average daily turnover was RMB 50.466 billion (approximately USD 6.097 billion). The repurchase market has been declining in activity, with an average daily turnover in November 2004 – the most recent date for which statistics are available – of RMB 34.137 billion (approximately USD 4.125 billion), down 30.03 per cent year-on-year.[122]

The selection of available instruments on China's money market is narrower than on other nations' money markets. For example, commercial paper, banker's acceptances and international agency paper are insignificant – if at all – instruments on China's money market. In addition, the People's Bank of China's interest rate controls harm the growth of China's money market.[123]

The Chinese government has taken several steps to foster the development of China's money market. Pursuant to the Administration of Money Market Funds Tentative Provisions, securities investment funds, including FI-FMCs, can for the first time invest in:

- cash;
- bank term deposits and certificates of deposit with a term of one year or less;
- bonds with a remaining term of 397 days or less;
- bond repurchases with a term of one year or less;
- central bank bills with a term of one year or less; and
- other highly liquid money market instruments approved by the CSRC and the PBC.[124]

---

122. Monthly Report for RMB, *Report on the Interbank Lending and Bond System in November 2004*, available at <chinamoney.com.cn/content/online2002/english/market2.html> (1 March 2005).

123. Y. Kim, et. al, *Developing Institutional Investors in People's Republic of China*, World Bank Country Study Paper (September 2003), available at <www.worldbank.org.cn/english/content/insinvnote.pdf> (5 February 2006) (referred to as 'Kim').

124. China Securities Regulatory Commission and People's Bank of China, *Administration of Money Market Funds Tentative Provisions*, (issued on 16 August 2004 and effective as of the same date), reprinted at China Law & Prac. 3700/04.08.16 §3. Money market funds may not invest in:

    - stocks;
    - convertible bonds;
    - bonds with a remaining term of more than 397 days;
    - corporate bonds with a credit rating of lower than AAA; or
    - other financial instruments the investment in which is prohibited by the China Securities Regulatory Commission and the People's Bank of China. Ibid., at §4.

    The portfolio of a money market fund must comply with the following provisions:

    - the percentage invested in the short term corporate bonds issued by one company cannot exceed 10 per cent of the net asset value of the fund;
    - the amount deposited with one commercial bank that has fund custodianship qualifications cannot exceed 30 per cent of the net asset value of the fund; the amount deposited

In early 2005, particular pilot commercial banks were given permission to launch fund management companies and operate money market funds.[125] In August 2005, the CBRC, for the first time, authorized non-bank financial institutions to engage in money broking services, including the offering of money market products.[126] However, China must continue to liberalize and reform its money market to ensure the health of its financial system.

VI.B.   FOREIGN EXCHANGE MARKET

The foreign exchange market is the gateway for foreign capital entering and exiting an economy and influences foreign investment patterns and domestic interest and inflation rates.[127] The foreign exchange market consists of the wholesale interbank market and a retail market.[128] Foreign exchange market development introduces exchange rate risk and new levels of credit risk and liquidity risk to a nation's financial system.[129] These risks can be mitigated through:

 – monitoring, and developing instruments to hedge against exchange-rate movements;

---

with one commercial bank that does not have fund custodianship qualifications may not exceed five per cent of the net asset value of the fund;
 – the balance of funds in bond repos on the national interbank bond market may not exceed 40 per cent of the net asset value of the Fund; and
 – other percentage limits imposed by the CSRC and PBC. Ibid., at §5. The average remaining term of the portfolio of a money market Fund may not exceed 180 days. Ibid., at §6. See also China Securities Regulatory Commission, *Securities Investment Information Disclosure of Securities Investment Funds Compilation Rules No. 5: (Information Disclosure for Money Market Funds Special Provisions)* reprinted at *China Law & Prac.* (3700/05.03.25), which specifies information disclosure for money market funds' earnings announcement, ad hoc reports and periodic reports; see also China Securities Regulatory Commission, *Circular on Issues Relevant to Investments in Short-term Financing Bills by Money Market Funds* (issued on, and effective as of, 22 September 2005), reprinted at *China Law & Prac.* (3700/05.09.22), which provides guidance on minimum credit ratings for short-term bills that might be purchased by money market funds.

125.   People's Bank of China, China Banking Regulatory Commission, and China Securities Regulatory Commission, *Administration of Pilot Projects for the Establishment of Fund Management Companies by Commercial Banks Procedures: Announcement of the PBOC, CBRC and CSRC* [2005] no. 4 (issued and effective as of 20 February 2005), reprinted at *China Law & Prac.* (3610/05.02.20) (referred to here as 'Pilot Projects').

126.   China Banking Regulatory Commission, *Measures for the Administration of Pilot Money Brokers*, Order of the CBRC [2005] no. 1 (issued on 8 August 2005 and effective as of 1 September 2005), reprinted at *China Law & Prac.* (3610/05.08.08).

127.   Karacadag, supra note 106, pp. 10–11; Levinson, supra note 113, p. 14.

128.   Karacadag, supra note 106, at 10.

129.   Ibid., pp. 11 and 23. Foreign exchange risk is the risk of a significant loss caused by adverse movements in a currency's exchange rate.

– enforcing strict licensing and capital requirements for market participants; and
– requiring comprehensive, timely and accurate disclosure by market players.[130]

Although relatively small, China's foreign exchange market continued to develop in 2004, with an increasing number of banks operating in the forward foreign exchange space and the implementation of a two-way quotation system.[131] In the first nine months of 2004, the interbank foreign exchange transaction market increased to USD 124.3 billion, an increase of USD 28.1 billion, year-on-year. The average daily turnover increased 30 per cent to USD 658 million.[132] As with the money market, the size of China's foreign exchange market causes the Chinese financial system to not get the same level of risk mitigation experience as similarly sized economies.

Before the announcement by the People's Bank of China of a more-flexible mechanism for renminbi exchange rate on 21 July 2005, China's renminbi's exchange rate moves in a narrow band, and is aimed at preventing foreign speculators from triggering a crisis similar to the AFC.[133] The Chinese government has stated that exchange rate flexibility is a medium term objective.[134] However, the Chinese government is pursuing greater exchange rate flexibility due to external pressure. This change will benefit China by making the country's monetary policy stronger and creating incentives for currency risk management.[135] Despite these efforts, China is required to go further and faster on its way of reforming its mechanism for renminbi exchange rate by the international society.

VI.C.   GOVERNMENT BOND MARKET

An active government bond market provides a market-determined structure of interest rates and enhances the conduct of monetary policy and liquidity management.[136] A vibrant government bond market provides liquid collateral for repurchase agreements, enables the creation of new types of financial

---

130. Ibid., p. 23.
131. People's Bank of China, *China Monetary Policy Report Quarter 3, 2004*, *available at* <www.pbc.gov.cn/english/huobizhengce/huobizhengcezhixingbaogao/Report_2004_3rdQtr.pdf> (1 March 2005).
132. Ibid.
133. BIS 15, supra note 108.
134. Cart Before the Horse, supra note 108.
135. Ibid; see also International Monetary Fund, *People's Republic of China: 2004 Article IV Consultation Staff Report* (6 July 2004) (referred to as the 'PRC Article IV Consultation').
136. Karacadag, supra note 106, p. 11.

instruments, and furthers money market development.[137] A healthy government bond market helps to create an active corporate bond market and can provide:

- market expectation information;
- information on investor confidence in a nation's macroeconomic policies;
- a benchmark discount rate and yield curve to better value a company's earning projections; and
- risk premia to calculate interest rates on bank loans.[138]

The interest rate structure provided by a government debt market is a prerequisite for derivatives market development.[139]

A developing government bond market introduces sovereign credit risk and new levels of credit, liquidity and interest-rate risks to a nation's financial system.[140] Governments must manage the government debt market to minimize the risk of a systemic shock and to build investor confidence in the market.[141] The risks introduced and increased by government bond market development can be mitigated through:

- prudential requirements for risk management by investors;
- reducing market fragmentation;
- requiring transparency in trading data and financial condition; and
- automating settlement on a real-time basis.[142]

China's government bond market is extremely underdeveloped, as indicated in Tables 2 and 3, and uneven government issuances often fail to meet the government bond issuance quota. The Chinese government has been forced to rely on mandatory quota allocation and heavy subsidies to create demand for government bonds.[143]

As indicated in these tables, China's government bond market is smaller than the government bond markets in other Asian jurisdictions, and is less liquid. Developed countries commonly have 60 per cent of their gross domestic product (GDP) as outstanding government debt. China's outstanding government debt, on the other hand, as of the end of 2004, amounts to approximately

---

137. An active money market can, in turn, stimulate short-term demand for government bonds and create a framework for developing longer-term government bonds. Ibid., pp. 12–13.
138. Ibid., p. 12.
139. Ibid., p. 11.
140. Ibid., p. 24.
141. Ibid.
142. Ibid., p. 25.
143. S. Green and D. Wall, *This Little Piggy Becomes a Market: The Challenges of Chinese Capital Market Liberalization,* (prepared for the Organization for Economic Cooperation and Development, December 2000), p. 14 (referred to as 'Green and Wall').

Table 2: Value of Government Bonds Listed (in USD millions)[144]

Exchange	2002	2003	2004
China: Shanghai	40,961.6	55,232.4	94,754.7
China: Shenzhen	1,669.5	23,575.5	30,600.4
China: Aggregate	42,631.1	78,807.90	125,355.1
Australian	43,667.0	54,490.7	54,000.9
Bursa Malaysia	0	0	0
Korea	118,062.3	212,012.6	527,560.8
Hong Kong	13,541.9	15,469.6	21,106.6
Osaka	3,607,008.3	4,422,407.1	5,127,494.0
National Stock Exchange India	174,384.6	252,529.4	319,337.3

Table 3: Value of Government Bond Trading (in USD millions)[145]

Exchange	2002	2003	2004
China: Shanghai	77,099.5	66,453.2	35,780.9
China: Shenzhen	29,980.6	6,523.7	3,880.3
China: Aggregate	107,080.1	72,976.9	39,661.20
Australian	N/A	N/A	N/A
Bursa Malaysia	0	0	0
Korea	40,356.9	173,960.6	336,663.0
Hong Kong	2.3	3.3	5.3
Osaka	0	0	0
National Stock Exchange India	218,993.4	286,178.5	203,967.7

six per cent of GDP.[146] Chinese government bond revenues are used primarily for pump-priming, investment in the social welfare program and to

---

144. World Federation of Exchanges, *2003 Annual Statistics Fixed Income- 2.1: Value of Bonds Listed*, available at <www.fibv.com/publications/Bond103.xls> (5 February 2006) (for 2002–2003 figures); World Federation of Exchanges, *2004 Annual Statistics Fixed Income- 2.1: Value of Bonds Listed*, available at <www.fibv.com/publications/Bond104.xls> (5 February 2006) (for 2004 figures).

145. World Federation of Exchanges, *2003 Annual Statistics Fixed Income- 2.5: Total Value of Bond Trading*, available at <www.fibv.com/publications/Bond503.xls> (5 February 2006) (for 2002–2003 figures); World Federation of Exchanges, *2004 Annual Statistics Fixed Income- 2.5: Total Value of Bond Trading*, available at <www.fibv.com/publications/Bond504.xls> (5 February 2006) (for 2004 figures).

146. Green and Wall, supra note 143, at 14; World Federation of Exchanges, *2004 Annual Statistics Fixed Income- 2.1: Value of Bonds Listed*, available at <www.fibv.com/publications/Bond104.xls> (5 February 2006) (for 2004 bond figures); 'China Revises 2004 GDP Figure to 2 Trillion US Dollars', *People's Daily* (20 December 2005), available at <www.english.people.com.cn/200512/20/eng20051220_229455.html> (7 February 2006).

cover budgetary responsibilities. The interest rate on government bonds is set administratively.[147] The Ministry of Finance (MOF) does not have a cash management system that enables it to predict its short-term cash needs, and most Chinese government bonds tend to be long-term instruments.[148] Chinese government bond yields do not offer much potential for investment returns. A recent 30-year Chinese government bond, for example, yielded just 3.7 per cent; well below yields on similar sovereign-issued bonds.[149] A central depository for government bonds exists, which increases the clearance and settlement risk and increases the transactions costs for Chinese government bonds. As a consequence, China's government bond market can't produce a yield curve so that interest rates could be set on a market basis.[150]

The Chinese government has undertaken limited steps to develop its government bond market. In May 2005, the People's Bank of China authorized approved institutional investors to engage in forward transactions involving government bonds.[151] Further, in 2005, insurance companies received permission to invest part of their funds in the government bond market and banks received permission to operate government bond funds.[152] Nonetheless, China must continue to develop its government bond market to mitigate liberalization-related risks and to be able to absorb the large increase in public debt that is likely to occur in the next several years.

VI.D.   DERIVATIVES MARKET

A derivatives market is interdependent with its underlying market, and does not fit neatly into the hierarchy of markets within a financial system.[153] Derivatives rely on the liquidity of the markets in which the underlying item trades. Derivatives offer new risk management tools that can foster overall market liquidity and price discovery. Many of the nations affected by the AFC had no, or only limited, derivatives markets, therefore, limiting market participants'

---

147.   Green and Wall, supra note 143, p. 14. Developed countries commonly have 60 percent of their GDP as outstanding government debt.
148.   Green, supra note 1, p. 37.
149.   Ibid.
150.   Green and Wall, supra note 143, p. 13. At present, all fixed-income products are priced based on the one-year bank deposit rate. This has precluded the development of a true yield curve that would lead to the accurate pricing of risk and the rational allocation of capital. Ibid.
151.   People's Bank of China, *Administration of Bond Forward Transactions in the National Inter-bank Bond Market Provisions* (issued on 11 May 2005 and effective as of 15 June 2005), reprinted at *China Law & Prac.* 3610/05.05.11.
152.   China Insurance Regulatory Commission, *Tentative Measures for the Administration of Bond Investments by Insurance Institutional Investors* (issued on 17 August 2005 and effective as of the same date) (*Bao Jian Fa*) [2005] no. 72 (referred to as 'Bond Investments'); Pilot Projects, supra note 125.
153.   Karacadag, supra note 106, p. 17.

hedging opportunities.[154] Derivatives markets introduce complex counterparty, settlement, liquidity and interest-rate risks to a nation's financial system, and can be mitigated through increasingly diligent use of the mitigation strategies, as discussed previously in Subsections A through C and later in Subsection E.

China's derivatives market is in its infancy and is limited in size and liquidity, and seems focused on currency-related derivatives.[155] Pursuant to regulations issued in March 2004, only banks trust and investment companies, finance companies, lease-financing companies and auto finance companies may trade derivatives, such as bond, equity and foreign exchange derivatives.[156] China should continue to develop its derivatives market so as to provide market intermediaries and others with an increased number of hedging options.

VI.E.   CORPORATE BOND AND EQUITY (SECURITIES) MARKET

Securities markets play a critical part in the mobilization, allocation, and monitoring of capital in every modern economy. In AFC-affected nations, better functioning securities markets could have reduced the AFC's impact by, *inter alia*, improving market discipline over firm financial disclosures.[157] Active securities markets can:

- prevent concentrating financial intermediation in the banking system and mitigate vulnerability to systemic stresses;
- better-intermediate savings;
- spread and diversify risk;
- smooth credit flows during a downward economic cycle; and
- facilitate the financing of higher-risk products.[158]

---

154. Turbulence, supra note 107, p. 74.
155. See PRC Article IV Consultation, supra note 135.
156. China Banking Regulatory Commission, *Administration of Trading of Derivatives by Financial Institutions Tentative Procedures* (Issued on 4 February 2004 and effective as of 1 March 2005) reprinted at *China Law & Prac.* 3600/04.02.04; Article 3 defines derivatives as a type of financial contract, the price of which shall be decided by one or more underlying assets or indices. The basic types of contract shall include forwards, futures, swaps and options. Derivatives shall also include structured financial instruments containing one or more characteristics of forwards, futures, swaps or options. ABN AMRO Holdings, Credit Suisse First Boston and ING Group were among the first overseas banks allowed to offer derivatives products in China. 'Foreign Players to Offer Derivatives', *People's Daily* (3 November 2004), available at <english.people.com.cn/200411/03/eng20041103_162613.html> (1 March 2005).
157. Turbulence, supra note 107, at 73; see also M. Kawai, et al., *Financial Crises: Nine Lessons from East Asia*, (Ministry of Finance Japan Policy Research Institute, May 2003), p. 32 (referred to as 'Kawai').
158. Karacadag, supra note 106, p. 14; PRC Article IV Consultation, supra note 135. Active corporate debt and equity markets also enable financing of longer-term projects and transacting with longer-term products, as banks tend to focus on short-term opportunities. The more comparable the size of the securities market is relative to other intermediated

As securities markets develop, new and more complex counterparty and liquidity risks are introduced to a financial market.[159] These risks can be mitigated through:

- developing a robust corporate bond market;
- accounting and disclosure standards that provide timely, high quality information to the market;
- prudential regulation of market institutions;
- effective supervision by a regulator; and
- market transparency.[160]

The Chinese government has undertaken these types of risk mitigation strategies, with limited impact. This section of the chapter reviews the mitigation strategies China should undertake in relation to its securities markets, which include:

- fostering a more-active corporate bond market;
- increasing the amount of a listed company's shares that may be traded;
- improving accounting, auditing, and disclosure practices;
- building out the CSRC's capacity; and
- creating a more-effective suspension and delisting process for troubled issuers.

VI.E.1.   Building an Active Corporate Bond Market

Liquid corporate bond markets offer the following benefits:

- serve as an alternative to banks for raising debt capital;
- provide lower-cost capital relative to bank financing;
- mitigate maturity and currency mismatch risks;
- offer investors a wider range of assets in which to invest;
- enable efficient pricing of credit risk; and
- spread credit risk to promote financial stability.[161]

---

financing, and the larger the proportion of companies that can access the loan and securities market, the more these types of benefits increase. E.P. Davis, *Multiple Avenues of Intermediation, Corporate Finance and Financial Stability*, IMF Working Paper WP/01/115, (August 2001). Multiple avenues also restrict the impact of undue limits on credit availability that arise solely from supply-side weakness, whether from liquidity problems in the securities market or liquidity/solvency problems among financial intermediaries. Ibid., p. 15.

159.   Ibid., p. 27.
160.   Ibid.
161.   Emerging Markets Committee of the International Organization of Securities Commissions, *The Development of Corporate Bond Markets in Emerging Market Countries* (May 2002) pp. 3–6.

The disclosure required by a corporate bond market increases the amount of issuer's information that enters the market and assists in more-efficient price discovery. Corporate bond market yields can assist in valuing the issuer's equities.[162] Most AFC-affected jurisdictions did not have an active corporate bond market. The lack of a corporate bond market had the following effects:

- deprived the financial system of much-needed issuer-related information;
- exacerbated existing informational asymmetries;
- created an adverse selection problem; and
- increased the financial system's vulnerability to interest rate and currency risks, as companies relied on short-term foreign currency-denominated instruments rather than on corporate bonds.[163]

Ordinarily, a nation's corporate bond market has a capitalization equal to the nation's equity markets. In comparison, in China, the bond market's capitalization is less than five per cent that of its equity market.[164] China's corporate bond market is extremely underdeveloped, as illustrated in Tables 4 through 7.

Table 4: Corporate Bond Market Size, Number of Corporate Issues[165]

Market	2002	2003	2004	End-December 2005
China: Shanghai	11	19	24	65
China: Shenzhen	0	0	0	27
Australian	82	90	100	N/A
Bursa Malaysia	46	73	73	72
Korea	6,177	6,579	2,460	2,440
Singapore	N/A	N/A	N/A	N/A
Tokyo	428	259	176	118
Hong Kong	11	12	22	N/A

---

162. Turbulence, supra note 107, p. 21. Bond markets are information intensive, because these markets rely on timely cash flows rather than collateral as a basis for credit. Ibid.
163. Ibid, pp. 20–22 and 73–44; Kawai, supra note 157, p. 6. Without a functioning bond market, banks had no reason to market their loans to potential corporate borrowers. These borrowers, in turn, had one less reason to increase their efficiency and could develop high debt to equity ratios. Ibid., p. 33.
164. See 'Corporate Bonds Calls for Acceleration', [2003] *China Daily*, WLNR 10636482 (13 October 2003), which calls for a more-robust bond market.
165. World Federation of Exchanges, *2003 Annual Statistics Fixed Income-2.3 Number of Bonds Listed*, available at <www.fibv.com/publications/bond303.xls> (5 February 2006) (2002 and 2003 data); World Federation of Exchanges, *2004 Annual Statistics Fixed Income-2.3 Number of Bonds Listed*, available at <www.fibv.com/publications/bond304.xls> (5 February 2006) (2004 data); World Federation of Exchanges, *2005 Monthly Statistics Fixed Income- 2.1 Number of Bonds Listed*, available at <www.fibv.com/

Table 5: Corporate Bond Market Size, Number of Corporate Issuers[166]

Market	2002	2003	2004
China: Shanghai	11	19	16
China: Shenzhen	0	0	0
Australian	30	35	31
Bursa Malaysia	40	55	60
Korea	682	685	655
Singapore	N/A	N/A	N/A
Tokyo	317	213	147
Hong Kong	5	6	17

Table 6: Corporate Bond Market, Value of Bonds (in millions of U.S. Dollars)[167]

Market	2001	2002	2003	2004
China: Shanghai	0	3,012.6	5,318.8	6,514.8
China: Shenzhen	0	0	0	0
Australian	2,991	7,432.3	9,509.5	N/A
Bursa Malaysia	1,002.2	1,498.1	2,205.3	1,905.7
Korea	107,517.2	353,089	297,676	111,739
Singapore	N/A	N/A	N/A	N/A
Tokyo	N/A	N/A	53,197.3	36,100.3
Hong Kong	2,320	2,445.9	4,096.6	8,623

publications/bond2105.xls> (5 February 2006> (end-December 2005 data). The WFE data uses the term 'domestic private sector' in dividing the total number of bond issuers; such term is an appropriate proxy for 'corporate' in this analysis.

166. World Federation of Exchanges, *2003 Annual Statistics Fixed Income-2.3 Number of Bonds Listed*, available at <www.fibv.com/publications/bond203.xls> (5 February 2006) (2002 and 2003 data); World Federation of Exchanges, *2004 Annual Statistics Fixed Income-2.3 Number of Bonds Listed*, available at <www.fibv.com/publications/bond204.xls> (5 February 2006) (2004 data).

167. World Federation of Exchanges, *2001 Annual Statistics Table II.3.A- Market Value of Bonds Listed at Year-End*, available at <www.fibv.com/publications/ta2301.xls> (5 February 2006) (2001 data); World Federation of Exchanges, *2003 Annual Statistics Fixed Income Table 2.1: Value of Bond Listed*, available at <www.fibv.com/publications/bond103.xls> (5 February 2006) (2002 and 2003 data); World Federation of Exchanges, *2004 Annual Statistics Fixed Income Table 2.1: Value of Bond Listed*, available at <www.fibv.com/publications/bond104.xls> (5 February 2006) (2004 data).

Table 7: Corporate Bond Market, Value of Bond Trading (in millions of U.S. Dollars)[168]

Market	2001	2002	2003	2004
China: Shanghai	601.0	616.7	3,818.3	1,158.4
China: Shenzhen	0	0	0	0
Australian	N/A	861.0	1,035.2	1,207.6
Bursa Malaysia	287.8	287.8	389.4	414.0
Korea	1,554.9	2,976.9	747.8	867.1
Singapore	N/A	N/A	N/A	N/A
Tokyo	19,781.2	15,127.6	9,216.6	7,198.9
Hong Kong	0.4	0	0	0

China's corporate bond market is divided into three segments – the Interbank, Exchange and Voucher markets – and trading rarely flows between segments.[169] The Chinese government seems to have a preference to allow public – or quasi-public – debt offerings rather than private debt offerings, and prefers that private companies issue equity instead of debt.[170] Chinese tax regulations enable equity, but not debt, to be issued tax-free. Only joint stock limited companies and limited liability companies whose net assets exceed RMB 30 million and RMB 60 million, respectively, can issue publicly-traded debt instruments, provided that the cumulative value of such issuer's debt instruments do not exceed 40 per cent of the issuer's net assets.[171] The issuer's average annual distributable profit over the past three years must be enough to pay a single year's interest on such debt instruments.[172] An issuer may not issue additional debt instruments if:

– previous offers have not been fully subscribed; or
– the issuer has defaulted on any previous debt issue.[173]

---

168. World Federation of Exchanges, *2001 Annual Statistics* Table II.4.B- Total Value of Bond Trading, available at www.fibv.com/publications/TA2402.xls (5 February 2006) (2001 data); World Federation of Exchanges, *2003 Annual Statistics Fixed Income Table 2.5: Total Value of Bond Trading Value of Bond Listed, available at* <www.fibv.com/publications/bond503.xls> (5 February 2006) (2002 and 2003 data); World Federation of Exchanges, *2004 Annual Statistics Fixed Income Table 2.5: Total Value of Bond Trading Value of Bond Listed,* available at <www.fibv.com/publications/bond504.xls> (5 February 2006) (2004 data).
169. Asia Society Conference Report, supra note 47.
170. World Bank, *China: Promoting Growth with Equity*, Report no. 24169-CHA (September 2003), p. 33; *Company Law of the People's Republic of China* (adopted by the National People's Congress on 29 December 1993 and amended on 27 October 2005), at §164 (referred to as 'Company Law').
171. Ibid., at §§159–169. See also Shenzhen Stock Exchange, *Rules for the Listing of Enterprise Bonds (Revised)*, (issued and effective as of 1 September 2000), reprinted at *China Law & Prac.* 3700/2000.09.01/SZ.
172. Company Law, supra note 170, §161(iii).
173. Ibid., at §162.

Corporate bond return rates must be within a 40 per cent band of the relevant bank deposit rate. For this reason, a negligible supply of corporate bonds is available in China.[174] However, China's policymakers are relaxing control over the issuing of corporate bonds. The new amendments to the Company Law delete many of the restrictions on the requirements for companies to issue bonds.[175] As the new amendments will come into force since 2006, their influence on the bond market remains to be seen.

The FI-FMC, QFII and, to a lesser extent, the JVSC structures should foster growth in China's corporate bond market. Recent regulatory developments also will help. In the Capital Market Opinions, the State Council called for the development of more bond products.[176] Responsibility for verification procedures related to the issuance of corporate bonds has been shifted from the CSRC to the stock exchange on which such bonds would be issued.[177] In February 2005, the People's Bank of China (PBOC), the China Banking Regulatory Commission (CBRC) and the CSRC jointly issued the Administration of Pilot Projects for the Establishment of Fund Management Companies by Commercial Banks Procedures, to enable a number of pilot commercial banks to launch fund management companies and operate bond funds, which may augment demand for corporate bonds.[178]

Clarification of convertible bond procedures will also help develop China's corporate bond market. In late 2001, the CSRC clarified particular requirements related to listed companies' issuance of convertible bonds.[179] An issuer's net average return on its net assets for the three financial years previous to the year of issue must exceed 10 per cent, or seven per cent if the issuer is in the energy, raw material or infrastructure sector. The aggregate outstanding

---

174. Kim, supra note 123.
175. See Company Law, supra note 170, at §§154–163. Pursuant to the current version of the Company Law, only joint stock limited companies and limited liability companies whose net assets exceed RMB 30 million and RMB 60 million, respectively, can issue publicly-traded debt instruments, provided that the cumulative value of such issuer's debt instruments do not exceed 40 per cent of the issuer's net assets. Ibid., at §§159–169. The issuer's average annual distributable profit over the past three years must be enough to pay a single year's interest on such debt instruments. Ibid., at §161. An issuer cannot issue additional debt instruments if:

   – previous offers have not been fully subscribed; or
   – the issuer has defaulted on any previous debt issue. Ibid., at §162.
176. Capital Markets Opinions, supra note 4.
177. Securities Law, supra note 2.
178. Pilot Projects, supra note 125.
179. China Securities Regulatory Commission, *Improving the Work Associated with the Issue of Convertible Corporate Bonds by Listed Companies Circular*, (issued on December 25, 1991 and effective as of the same date), reprinted at *China Law & Prac.* 3700/01.12.25; China Securities Regulatory Commission, *Contents and Formats for Information Disclosures by Companies That Offer Securities to the Public Guidelines 13: Prospectuses for Offering of Convertible Bonds* (issued on 24 March 2003, effective as of the same date and revised in 2003), reprinted at *China Law & Prac.* 2330/03.03.24(3), which describes the requirements for a convertible bond prospectus.

corporate bonds issued by the issuer shall not exceed 40 per cent of its net asset value prior to issue, and 80 per cent of its net asset value after issue. Proceeds are to be used in the issuer's main business or in an investment closely related to the issuer's main business. To be listed on the SHSE, the issue must exceed RMB 100 million in face value and have a term of at least three years.[180]

In another positive action for the development of China's bond market, insurance companies, as of August 2005, are free to purchase any corporate bonds rated at least AA up to a limit equal to – if calculated at cost – 20 per cent of its total assets in the last month; up from 10 per cent under previous regulation.[181] As to a specific class of debt issue, an insurance company cannot hold more than the lesser of 15 per cent of the value of that class (up from 10 per cent in previous regulation) or an amount in that class equal to two per cent of the insurance company's total assets in the previous month.[182] Companies that offer investment-linked insurance can establish investment accounts that can invest up to 100 per cent of its total assets in corporate bonds. For universal life insurance, the limit is 80 per cent of the total assets in the account. Under prior regulation, insurance companies only could purchase central enterprise bonds in relation to some infrastructure projects; the issuance of which had been approved by the relevant central government ministry and had a credit rating of at least AA+. Importantly, in December 2004, the PBOC clarified that institutions intending to issue bonds in the interbank bond market, and bonds to be issued thereby are to be subject to credit ratings. These types of credit ratings are to be issued by authorized credit rating institutions.[183]

In August 2003, the CSRC issued regulations to enable securities companies to issue corporate bonds to the public or to private qualified investors.[184] To issue these types of bonds to the public, a potential issuer must have net assets in excess of RMB 1 billion, measured as of the end of the most recent

---

180. Shanghai Stock Exchange, *Convertible Bond Listing Rules*, (issued on 4 November 2002 and effective as of the same date), reprinted at *China Law & Prac.* 3700/02.11.04/SH.
181. Bond Investments, supra note 152.
182. Ibid.
183. People's Bank of China Notice [2004] no. 22 (Issued 30 December 2004), reprinted at *China Law & Prac.* 3610/04.12.30.
184. China Securities Regulatory Commission, *Administration of Securities Company Bonds Tentative Procedures*, (issued on 29 August 2003 and effective as of 3 October 2003), reprinted at *China Law & Prac.* 3700/03.08.29. See also China Securities Regulatory Commission, *Issue of Credit Rating Reports by Credit Rating Institutions on Securities Company Bonds Guidelines* (issued on 29 August 2003 and effective as of 8 October 2003), reprinted at *China Law & Prac.* 2330/03.08.29(5), which specifies the requirements on credit reporting agencies in relation to bond issuance. The CSRC enabled securities companies to issue short-term bonds if the company has:

   – been a member of the national interbank loans market for at least one year;
   – made the required informational disclosures;
   – segregated clients' transaction settlement appropriately;
   – maintained sound internal controls; and
   – valued assets and liabilities by means of a market capitalization approach.

accounting period. Potential issuers should have net assets, measured as of the end of the most recent accounting period, in excess of RMB 500 million to issue bonds to private qualified investors. The regulations define a qualified investor as one with independent analytical and risk bearing capacity, registered capital in excess of RMB 10 million or audited net assets in excess of RMB 20 million. Securities company bonds can be listed only if the total par value exceeds RMB 200 million.

Perhaps most significantly, in February 2004, the Ministry of Labour and Social Security, CBRC, CSRC and CIRC, jointly issued trial procedures to address issues related to the management of corporate supplementary old-age pension insurance funds formed by capital raised through corporate pension plans.[185] These types of funds can only invest in repurchase of short-term bonds, financial bonds and enterprise bonds with credit rating at or above investment grade and convertible bonds.

Overall, these developments are positive and should increase the supply of and demand for corporate bonds. China needs a larger, more-efficient corporate bond market to minimize liberalization risk and develop a robust financial system. An active corporate bond market would also assist China's most dynamic small and middle-sized enterprises to be valued accurately and have access to debt financing.[186]

VI.E.2.   Increasing the Float

As of the end of 2003, only 35.38 per cent of a listed company's shares were publicly tradable.[187] On average, the state owns 47 per cent of a listed company's shares and legal person shares accounted for 17 per cent of a listed company's shares.[188] The 35.38 per cent tradable ratio is, in turn, divided among

---

Short-term bonds cannot exceed 60 per cent of the issuer's net capital and must be issued through an auction lasting not longer than three working days. Capital raised from short-term bonds cannot be used to:

– invest in fixed assets;
– invest in the secondary stock market;
– finance a firm client's securities transactions; or
– make long-term equity investments.

Ibid.

185. Ministry of Labour and Social Security, China Banking Regulatory Commission, China Securities Regulatory Commission and China Insurance Regulatory Commission, *Administration of Enterprise Pension Funds Trial Procedures* (issued on 23 February 2004 and effective as of 1 May 2004), reprinted at *China Law & Prac.* 2410/04.02.23.

186. See Organization for Economic Cooperation and Development, *China in the World Economy: The Domestic Policy Challenges: Synthesis Report* (2003); *Asia Society Conference Report*, supra note 47, p. 13.

187. China Securities Regulatory Commission, China's Securities and Futures Markets (China Securities and Regulatory Commission, April 2004), p. 24.

188. Ibid.

A-Shares (76 per cent of tradable shares), B-Shares (8 per cent) and H-Shares (17 per cent).[189] In AFC-affected jurisdictions, the lack of a free float in the stock of publicly-traded companies impeded the development of high-quality public issuers.[190] Insiders in these types of entities wanted to retain control, which depressed stock values and increased short-term foreign currency denominated borrowing.[191] A low float concentrates ownership, both in a specific firm and across a market. Concentrated ownership:

 – adversely affects market liquidity; and
 – minimizes minority, and particularly individual, shareholders' influence on corporate governance and firm profitability.

Table 8 illustrates the market share held by the ten largest listed companies on specific markets, including the SHSE and SZSE. As illustrated in this table, the market share held by the ten largest listed companies on the SHSE and SZSE increases over the data period, as opposed to decreasing as in other Asian exchanges. As indicated previously, this concentration adversely affects market liquidity.

Table 8: Share of Market Capitalization of Ten Largest Listed Companies[192]

Market	2001	2002	2003	2004
China: Shanghai	19.3%	21.9%	29.2%	29%
China: Shenzhen	9.4%	10.5%	13.7%	14.7%
Australian	46.3%	44%	41.5%	39%
Bursa Malaysia	37.8%	35.1%	33.1%	36.0%
Korea	56.4%	56%	50.5%	47.8%
Singapore	60%	58.6%	53.3%	47.8%
Tokyo	21.5%	22%	19.3%	18.1%
Hong Kong	64.1%	58.6%	55.3%	52.2%

As a result of the unique share structure of Chinese listed companies, the three largest shareholders held, on average, approximately 58 per cent of total shares.[193] In a significant number of firms, the three largest shareholders own

189. Ibid.
190. Karacadag, supra note 106, p. 15.
191. S. Claessens, et al., *Corporate Growth, Financing, and Risks in the Decade before East Asia's Financial Crisis*, WPS 2017 (November 1998).
192. World Federation of Exchanges, *2001 Annual Statistics Table I.7.1, Market Concentration*, available at <www.fibv.com/publications/ta1702.xls> (5 February 2006) (2001 data); World Federation of Exchanges, *2003 Annual Statistics Equity 1.9 Market Concentration*, available at <www.fibv.com/publications/equity903.xls> (5 February 2006) (2002 and 2003 data); World Federation of Exchanges, *2004 Annual Statistics Equity 1.9 Market Concentration*, available at <www.fibv.com/publications/equity904.xls> (5 February 2006) (2004 data).

as much as 80 per cent of a listed company's shares.[194] As a result, few, if any, of China's listed companies have contestable control, meaning that China's securities markets do not discipline effectively public companies' governance.

The share structure, in reinforcing state control, has an adverse affect on firms' performance.[195] Firms majority-owned by the Chinese state are more leveraged, have lower innovative capacity and less effective internal management mechanisms than do firms not majority-owned by the Chinese state.[196] In addition, firms majority-owned by the Chinese government receive relatively more cash infusions from the central government.[197] These infusions increase moral hazard by removing managers' incentive to improve corporate performance.[198]

The share structure of Chinese public companies is, however, consistent with the property rights goals of the Chinese government. One of the Chinese government's goals in developing China's securities sector is 'preserving and increasing the value of *state assets*', which is not the same as maximizing the value *of the firm*. Property rights in Chinese companies reflect the government's goals of profitability, control and inter-firm equality.[199] As such, the state often takes actions that are value-decreasing to the listed company.[200] These types of actions can adversely impact the integrity and viability of the securities market, and by extension, the financial system as a whole.

The low float of public company shares creates two other, dependent problems:

- Chinese individual investors do not tend to participate in the share-holder's annual meeting; and
- Chinese individual investors focus on short-term growth, rather than on long-term appreciation.[201] Individual shareholders in China do not effectively monitor management. As a result, neither the market in general, nor individual investors, effectively monitor corporate perfor-mance, which removes two important checks on insiders' behaviour. Volatility on China's stock markets remains a concern, as Chinese indi-vidual investors tend to hold shares for a far shorter time than individ-ual investors on other markets. The CSRC recently required Chinese public companies to provide to their shareholder a safe, economic and

---

193.   IFC, supra note 52, p. 78.
194.   Ibid., pp. 78–79.
195.   X. Xu and Y. Wang, *Does Corporate Governance Affect Ownership Structure and Corporate Performance: The Case of Chinese Stock Companies*, World Bank Policy Research Working Paper 1794 (June 1997), p. 4 (referred to as 'Xu and Wang').
196.   p. Changhong and Q. Weil, 'Internationalization of Securities Market after China's WTO Accession', [2002] *China & World Economy* 4.
197.   Xu and Wang, supra note 195.
198.   Ibid.
199.   Ibid.
200.   Ibid.
201.   Ibid.

convenient voting network system for off-site exercise of voting rights to compliment in-person voting processes at shareholders' meetings.[202] This can make it easier for individual investors to participate in shareholders meetings, but will not greatly encourage shareholders to play a more-active role in the corporate governance of listed companies.

Other regulatory changes are aimed at increasing the float through corporatization of state assets. On 8 November 2002, the government issued the Use of Foreign Investment to Restructure State-owned Enterprises Tentative Procedures (SOE Tentative Procedures), effective as of 1 January 2003. The SOE Tentative Procedures clarify the regulatory framework for the conversion of SOEs into FIEs, and enable this type of restructuring to be performed by way of equity or asset transfers. On 1 February 2004, the State-Owned Assets Supervision and Administration Commission (SASAC) and the MOF released the Administration of the Assignment of Enterprise State-owned Assets and Equity Tentative Procedures (SOA Procedures), which created a compulsory regime by which any transfer to any domestic or foreign entity of state-owned assets in enterprises must be conducted through qualified equity exchanges.[203] Note, however, that the SOA Procedures do not cover transfers of state-owned assets by financial enterprises or listed companies or the transfer of state-owned assets from Chinese enterprises located abroad.

An increased float would incentivize corporate managers to maximize the firm's profitability, enable better monitoring of corporate insiders, remove the moral hazard attendant with government ownership and decrease the volatile shareholding patterns of individual investors. Fortunately, the Chinese government has realized the importance of increasing the float of listed companies and decreasing the government's stake in listed companies. The most significant measure worthy of mention here is the promulgation of the Administrative Measures on the Split Share Structure Reform of Listed Companies on 4 September 2005, pursuant to which holders of two-thirds of the value of a

---

202. China Securities Regulatory Commission, *Network Voting for Shareholders' General Meeting of Listed Companies Working Guide (Trial Implementation)*, (issued on 29 November 2004 and effective as of the same date), reprinted at *China Law & Prac.* 2300/04.11.29.

203. Ministry of Finance, *Administration of the Assignment of Enterprise State-owned Assets and Equity Tentative Procedures*, which deals with transactions that involve state-owned assets must be conducted at an authorized equity exchange to be legal. Subject to the criteria in the SOA procedures, SASAC has the power to select and authorize equity exchanges to engage in state-owned asset transfers. Upon consummation of the transaction, the equity exchange is to issue an assets transfer certificate that both parties to the transfer must submit to the relevant government departments for registration. In addition, the SOA procedures seem to require that the transaction be settled with one payment, although instalment payments are permitted in cases in which the transaction price is 'relatively high'. Instalment plans require a first payment of 30 per cent of the transaction amount, to be paid within five days of transfer contract's effective date; in addition, the purchaser must also provide a guarantee.

company's non-tradeable shares can elect to convert these types of shares to tradable status.[204]

VI.E.3. Accounting, Auditing, and Disclosure Reform

Accounting, auditing and disclosure standards provide necessary information to the market and investors. Working together, accounting, auditing and disclosure assist the securities market in performing its signalling function.[205] In AFC-affected nations, opaque and ineffective accounting, auditing, and disclosure standards failed to mitigate liberalization risk by reducing the availability and reliability of financial information.[206] Timely and accurate information became too expensive to procure.[207] Stunted development prevented securities markets from exercising a signalling function and created an adverse selection problem whereby investors and creditors could not differentiate between sound and distressed entities. As investor confidence eroded, the 'solution' to the adverse selection problem manifested itself in the herding behaviour that spread the AFC.[208]

Adopted standards must be enforced. On paper, many AFC-affected nations had implemented accounting standards consistent with international standards. However, these standards rarely were observed and, in practice, a lack of qualified accountants and restrictions on the activities of foreign accounting firms compounded problematic accounting.[209] Many AFC-affected

---

204. *China Securities Regulatory Commission*, Circular on Issues Relating to the Pilot Reform of Listed Companies Split Share Structure (CSRC Circular no. 32 of 2005), available at <www.csrc.gov.cn/en/jsp/detail.jsp?infoid=1129278553100&type=cms.std> (7 February 2006).
205. Turbulence, supra note 107, p. 75.
206. Ibid. As used here, the term 'accounting' is defined to mean the process by which financial data is recorded, measured, interpreted and communicated; the term 'auditing' is defined to mean the examination of accounting records by an independent, qualified party; and 'disclosure' is defined to mean the qualitative and quantitative explanation of a company's financial position and operating results and how these types of explanation reaches interested parties. See Kawai, supra note 157, p. 31.
207. Turbulence, supra note 107, p. 21. Disclosure requirements for related-party transactions were not well developed, which put minority shareholders at a disadvantage. Ibid., p. 22. There is also some concern that the use of over-the-counter instruments may have contributed to difficulties in ascertaining the financial exposure of companies and banks during the AFC. Ibid., p. 24. The most significant disclosure problems in the run-up to the AFC were hidden exposures to foreign exchange, interest rate and equity risks among financial institutions, market intermediaries, the corporate sector and even the central bank within several emerging-market jurisdictions. Their eventual discovery or confirmation significantly added to the financial turmoil through sharp revisions in market expectations and, in some cases, required a sharp change in policy direction. Ibid., p. 74.
208. Ibid., p. 22.
209. Ibid., p. 23. Interestingly, one of the five worst affected economies had officially adopted the International Accounting Standards (IAS) and prepared its national accounting standards in line with the international standards and the other four countries' national accounting standards followed the generally accepted accounting principles (GAAP).

nations had also put in place systems to require external audits to verify, and reinforce the credibility of, accounting information prior to public disclosure.[210] In practice, auditors were not independent and were largely ineffective, permitting inaccurate information to reach the markets. Most AFC-affected jurisdictions implemented standards that required the release of material information on periodic and ongoing bases. In practice, the outbreak and severity of the AFC was due in part to poor disclosure in three areas:

- corporate shareholding structures;
- guarantees for bank loans; and
- use of OTC instruments. [211]

Poor accounting, auditing, and disclosure plague China's securities markets in many of the same ways that poor standards plagued affected jurisdictions prior to the AFC's outbreak. For some, the relative failure of the B-Share market is evidence of poor quality of accounting and disclosure standards. In addition, China's securities markets lack mature users of financial information and, as a result, the market is not yet ready to exercise a supervisory function in relation to auditing and accounting professionals and listed enterprises' disclosure practices. This section reviews accounting, auditing and disclosure issues in China, and recommends particular actions that the Chinese government could take to mitigate liberalization risk.

---

210. Technical Committee of the International Organization of Securities Commissions, *Principles of Auditor Independence and the Role of Corporate Governance in Monitoring an Auditor's Independence*, (October 2002) at 2–3 [hereinafter *Auditor Independence*].

211. Turbulence, supra note 107, pp. 23–25. Poor disclosure hid a system of interrelated ownership, enabled some majority shareholders to pursue questionable financial practices, such as favourable transfer-pricing between company subsidiaries to cross-subsidize money-losing units in the group. A lack of transparency is also thought to have made it possible for companies to undertake implicit and explicit cross-guarantees for bank loans. There is also some concern that the use of over-the-counter (OTC) instruments may have contributed to difficulties in ascertaining the financial exposure of companies and banks. Some have argued, for example, that the opacity of OTC exposures given on-balance-sheet accounting techniques – through particular features such as complex pay-off structures and cross-border components – made it easier for market participants in some jurisdictions to circumvent – or at least only partially comply with – domestic capital controls, reporting requirements and prudential regulations; thus effectively hiding the financial system's true exposure to market and liquidity risk from authorities. Many companies met the minimum requirements of the international standards, but differed widely with regard to their conformity to the underlying principle of timely and accurate disclosure of good corporate governance and disclosure. The lack of timely and accurate disclosure by the corporate sector led to an adverse selection problem, whereby many banks to base credit decisions on the availability of collateral rather than on an analysis of cash flows. This adverse selection problem distorted financial institutions' lending decisions and increased the vulnerability of their respective portfolios. Similarly, institutional disclosure was found to be clearly lacking in some of the worst affected jurisdictions. Turbulence, supra note 107, p. 25.

Accounting standards must be of a high, internationally accepted quality and gather and analyze all financial information that could potentially be relevant to investors.[212] Article 63 of the Securities Law, Article 164 of the Company Law, Chapter 7 of the Code of Corporate Governance for Listed Companies in China and other rules, regulations and interpretations require Chinese public companies to maintain an effective accounting system.[213] All Chinese public companies and non-financial services foreign invested enterprises must follow the Accounting System for Business Enterprises (ASBE), as promulgated by the MOF pursuant to a grant of authority under the Accounting Law.[214] Early in 2002, the MOF issued a new, separate Accounting System for Financial Institutions that all listed and foreign investment banks, insurance companies, brokerages, leasing companies and finance companies were required to use, retroactive to 1 January 2002. The Accounting Law delegates responsibility to the MOF to develop Chinese Accounting Standards (CAS) to be consistent with International Accounting Standards issued by the International

---

212. International Organization of Securities Regulators, *Objectives and Principles of Securities Regulation* (October 2003) at §§14 and 16 (referred to here as 'Principles of Securities Regulation').

213. Ministry of Finance, *Provisional Rules Concerning Accounting for Sale of Assets between Affiliate Parties* (issued on 21 December 2001 and effective as of the same date). In addition, if no material evidence can establish the price of a transaction between affiliates as fair, profits from this type of transaction must be deposited into a capital accumulation fund as an affiliate transaction. The Rules require Chinese companies to establish and operate an accounting system consistent with relevant regulation, and specify that annual financial reports must include, inter alia:

      – balance sheet;
      – income statement;
      – statement of cash flow;
      – explanation of financial conditions; and
      – statement of profit distribution.

      PRC, Accounting Law (issued by the National People's Congress on 21 January 1985 and subsequently amended), §7 (referred to as 'Accounting Law'). A limited liability company must deliver its financial and accounting reports to each shareholder within the time limit prescribed by the articles of association. The financial and accounting reports of a joint stock limited company shall be available at the company's premises for shareholders' inspection as from the 20th day prior to the annual meeting of shareholders' general committee. A joint stock limited company established through public share offer shall make public its financial and accounting reports. A Chinese company may not establish any separate accounting book besides the accounting books prescribed by law. Company Law, supra note 170, at §166.

214. In 2000, the State Council issued the Financial Accounting and Reporting Rules for Enterprises (FARR). In January 2001, the MOF adopted a comprehensive Accounting System for Business Enterprises (ASBE), and starting 1 January 2001 all joint stock limited enterprises (JSLEs) were required to follow the ASBE, with enterprises other than JSLEs encouraged to follow the ASBE as well. On 1 January 2002, the MOF extended the applicability of the ASBE to all foreign investment enterprises other than banks, insurance companies and other financial enterprises.

Accounting Standards Board.[215] Since the first-issued CAS in 1997, the MOF has issued sixteen standards, with others under active development.[216]

In practice, Chinese companies follow multiple accounting standards, including IAS, U.S. generally accepted accounting principles ASBE, and other domestic standards, which confuses the end result.[217] Even to the extent that Chinese accounting standards are consistent with international practice, because many IAS standards have no ASBE equivalent, a Chinese enterprise's financial statement could vary significantly from a report generated pursuant to international standards.[218] Chinese accounting rules are geared towards ensuring the entity is levied an appropriate level of income tax.[219] In addition, Chinese accounting standards are less complex and less detailed than international standards, and cause the omission of many complex liability issues from financial statements.

The quality of Chinese accounting standards is low, and China has an insufficient number of accountants. Chinese accountants do not receive sufficient training.[220] Implementation of China's WTO commitments on accounting

---

215. Accounting Law, supra note 213. The Accounting Law is the highest accounting authority and sets out general principles of accounting for all enterprises. Pursuant to the Accounting Law, the MOF administers accounting affairs and establishes uniform accounting regulations and systems that have the force of law.
216. IFC, supra note 52, pp 119–120.
217. Ibid.
218. In recent years, regulators' investigative powers and expertise have been strengthened, as has the investigators' authority to enforce penalties. Important examples are the requirement for supplying the CSRC with an internal control assessment report at the time of new share issues and the requirement for stricter and more-detailed disclosures in relation to restructuring, related-party transactions and mergers and acquisitions. See, for example, Ministry of Finance, *Provisional Measures on Accounting Treatment of Losses of Enterprise Assets* (issued on 3 September 2003 and effective as of 5 October 2003). These Provisional Measures provide that enterprises' asset losses should be classified as:
    – bad debt;
    – inventory loss;
    – loss of fixed assets or construction project loss;
    – guarantee loss;
    – equity investment loss;
    – debt investment loss; and
    – loss from other securities transactions, futures trading and foreign exchange transactions.

    Each type of asset loss is subject to its own accounting treatment. See also Ministry of Finance, *Notice on Issuance of Procedures for Drafting Accounting Principles*, (issued on 10 July 2003 and effective as of the same date). This Notice provides that the Accounting Division of the Ministry of Finance will oversee the drafting of accounting principles. The drafting process will involve the following stages: topic collection, drafting, public comment and final promulgation; and the following documents will be produced during the process: draft for discussion, draft for public comment, preliminary draft and draft for final approval.
219. Green, supra note 1, p. 140; IFC, supra note 52, pp. 13 and 120.
220. IFC, supra note 52, p. 120. More-experienced accountants usually train new staff in on-the-job training.

services, at §II.A.(b) of its Schedule of Specific Commitments, must improve the capacity of the Chinese accounting system. In the meantime, the Chinese government must build the capacity of its accounting sector.

Audits verify the timeliness and accuracy of financial statements, and must be conducted pursuant to well-defined and internationally acceptable standards.[221] Auditors of listed entities must be independent – both in fact and in appearance – of the entity being audited.[222] Listed companies should have an independent audit committee to oversee the selection and appointment of the external auditor and the conduct of the audit. In addition, auditors should be rotated at specified times.[223] Auditors in AFC-affected nations were not sufficiently independent of the entities they audited, and overall audit quality was poor. Audits in AFC-affected nations did not effectively ensure the veracity and accuracy of information reaching the market.

In practice, the Chinese auditing system fails to ensure the completeness and accuracy of financial information disseminated to the market. In a 2001 random review of 32 audit reports, Chinese investigators found that 23 were 'gravely inaccurate'.[224] Compared with international accounting firms, the overall audit quality of local firms, Particularly smaller firms, is questionable.[225]

---

221. Principles of Securities Regulation, supra note 212, at §10.6; Auditor Independence, supra note 210, pp. 45–46; International Organization of Securities Commissions, *Resolution No. 12: Resolution on Harmonization of Accounting and Auditing Standards,* (Nov. 1988); International Organization of Securities Commissions, *Resolution No. 44, Resolution on IASC Standards*, (May 2000).

222. An appropriate national regulator must establish standards that:

   – establish a framework of principles to mitigate threats to auditor independence; and
   – identify appropriate safeguards that the auditor must implement to mitigate threats to independence. The term 'independent' is defined as an environment in which the auditor is free of any influence, interest or relationship that might impair professional judgment or objectivity, or, in the view of a reasonable investor, might impair professional judgment or objectivity. Auditor Independence, supra note 210, p. 3.

223. The audit committee must oversee establishment of the entity's policies to govern the circumstances in which contracts for the provision of permitted non-audit services can be entered into with the company's external auditors and the procedures that must be followed before doing so. The audit committee must also monitor compliance by management with those policies and procedures. The audit committee must establish policies in regard to hiring from an entity's audit firm of senior officers for the entity, including the Chief Executive Officer and the Chief Financial Officer. The audit committee should report to the shareholders on the actions it has taken to safeguard the independence of the auditor, including satisfying itself that the auditor is independent in accordance with applicable standards. Auditor Independence, supra note 210, pp. 45–46; see also Organization for Economic Cooperation and Development, *Principles of Corporate Governance: 2004*, available at <www.oecd.org/document/49/0,2340,en_2649_37439_31530865_1_1_1_37439,00.html> (1 March 2005>.

224. IFC, supra note 52, pp. 120–121.

225. Ibid., Any accounting firm that conducts finance-related auditing must apply to the relevant People's Bank of China (PBOC) branch and the relevant provincial Certified Public Accountants Association (CPPA) for confirmation of its qualification to conduct auditing business. If an accounting firm meets the requirements for large firms, the PBOC branch

Multiple accounting standards implemented by listed entities affect the quality of information available to audit, and audits tend to review compliance with laws rather than review business performance.[226]

China's audit market is overpopulated and fragmented, which causes audit firms to compete on price, which in turn contributes to poor audit quality.[227] As in the accounting sector, too few well-educated auditors are available, and many perform their duties without sufficient training.[228] In addition, as in the accounting sector, many Chinese audit companies compete on price, which contributes to a cycle of poor audit quality.[229]

Relevant Chinese regulation requires auditors to remain independent of the entity they audit. However, because the state owns most listed enterprises and domestic auditing entities, auditor's independence may be illusory.[230] In addition, Chinese regulation does not limit the non-audit services that an audit firm may provide to the client it audits, nor does relevant regulation limit the percentage of an auditor's total income that can be derived from a single client.[231]

In Chinese companies, independent audit committees are permitted, but are not required.[232] Internal quality control policies that ensure that all audit

---

and the provincial CPPA will issue verification letters to the accounting firm, and then submit the verification letters with original application documents to the Bank Regulatory Department of the PBOC and China Certified Public Accountants Association before 30 July 2002. If an accounting firm can only meet the requirements for smaller firms, after examining the application documents, the PBOC branch and the provincial association must specify the relevant information of the accounting firm in a specific form and submit the form to the Bank Regulatory Department of the PBOC and China Certified Public Accountants Association before 20 August 2002. Ibid.

226. IFC, supra note 52, pp. 13 and 119–120; Green, supra note 1, p. 140.
227. IFC, supra note 52, p 121.
228. Ibid., p. 120.
229. Ibid., p. 121.
230. China Certified Public Accountants Association, *Chinese General Standard on Professional Ethics*, (issued in December 2003). In China, in addition to independence in relation to clients, the issue of independence takes the dimension of independence from the government. An important positive step in this regard was the 1998 delinking procedure, as a result of which external auditors have severed their links with their sponsors or government authorities in the areas of personnel, finance and business strategies. However, genuine independence will also require a change in ownership, and is not likely to be achieved without the development of a truly independent, self-regulating accounting body. Currently, the Chinese Institute of Certified Public Accountants is still in its infancy, and its basic role is likely to be monitoring and supervising rather than providing services to CPA firms. To enhance their legal binding power, all standards developed by the institute are promulgated by the Ministry of Finance. However, because Chinese independent auditing and professional standards are only considered accounting profession standards, and the Chinese Institute of Certified Public Accountants is not a government entity, other government entities have not accepted these standards. IFC, supra note 52, pp. 13 and 122; Green, supra note 1, p. 140.
231. IFC, supra note 52, p. 121.
232. China Securities Regulatory Commission and State Economic and Trade Commission, *Code of Corporate Governance for Listed Companies in China*, (Zhengjianfa, no. 1, 2002)

work meets independent auditing standards often do not exist.[233] Communications between external and internal auditors at the time of audit are minimal in China.[234] For these reasons, an International Finance Corporation survey concluded that the overall audit quality affecting listed Chinese firms is questionable.[235]

Relevant Chinese regulation requires periodic auditor rotation, although whether the regulation requires the entire accounting firm to be rotated or only the individual audit accountants who provide auditing services to the relevant organizations is unclear.[236] In addition, auditors can no longer issue explanatory notes in lieu of a qualified opinion, or a qualified opinion in lieu of an adverse opinion.[237] In addition, the CSRC requires companies that issue 300 million or more shares to be audited by an international accounting firm in accordance with international accounting standards.[238] Since the end of 2001,

---

(issued on 7 January 2001 and effective as of the same date) §§52–54 (referred to here as the 'PRC Code of Corporate Governance').

233.   IFC, supra note 52, p. 121.

234.   Ibid., p. 159.

235.   Ibid., p. 121.

236.   Chinese regulation requires audit accountants to be rotated, pursuant to the China Securities Regulatory Commission and Ministry of Finance, *Regulation on Periodic Rotation of Certified Public Accountants Performing Securities and Futures Auditing Services* (issued on 8 October 2003 and effective as of 1 January 2004). The term 'relevant organization' includes listed companies, underwriters, operators of securities and futures markets, stock and futures exchanges, securities investment funds and their management companies and settlement institutions. Audit accountants that have provided auditing services for the 'relevant organization' for five years must be rotated and replaced by new audit accountants. This regulation specifies a two-year ban on hiring a previously retained audit accountant. In addition, auditors of newly listed companies are limited to two-year engagements. Such audit accountant rotation information is to be disclosed in the periodic financial reports for listed companies and the accounting firm must report the rotation status of the auditors to CSRC and the MOF before 15 May of each year.

237.   China Securities Regulatory Commission, *Compilation Rules for Information Disclosures by Companies That Offer Securities to the Public No.14: Audit Opinions That Are Not Standard and Unqualified and the Handling of Relevant Matters*, (issued on 22 December 2001 and effective as of the same date), reprinted at *China Law & Prac.* 2330/01.12.22. If a registered accountant issues an audit opinion on the financial report of a listed company that is not standard and unqualified, the audit report shall clearly state the reasons and bases of such an opinion and the estimated impact of the related matters on the financial report Ibid., at §5. If the company refuses to do so, or if the adjustment is inadequate and the accountant consequently issues an audit opinion that is not standard and unqualified, the stock exchange shall suspend trading of the shares of the company. Ibid., at §7. During the suspension, the China Securities Regulatory Commission will investigate and deal with the relevant matters. Ibid., at §8. If the matters that gave rise to the qualified opinion or adverse opinion threaten to affect the profit of the company and the accountant has estimated the amount affected, the company shall deduct such amount from its distributable profit. If the accountant issues a disclaimer of opinion, the company shall not distribute its current year's profit. Ibid., p. 10.

238.   'Enronitis Delights Local Auditors', *The Economist* (23 March 2002).

the CSRC has begun to investigate disagreements between listed companies and auditors.[239]

The Chinese government must make efforts to improve the quality and independence of public company auditors to ensure that the best quality information reaches the market.

Investors should be provided with full disclosure of material information on an ongoing basis in a clear, reasonably specific and timely manner by means of efficient, effective and timely means of dissemination.[240] Disclosure should be released to all interested parties at the same time, and penalties should be in place for violations of relevant disclosure standards. Effective disclosure would have provided more information – particularly leverage – on companies in AFC-affected nations and could have prevented or minimized the AFC.[241] Poor disclosure contributed to herd behaviour in investors in AFC-affected jurisdictions, which enabled the crisis to jump borders.[242]

Articles 60 through 65 of the Securities Law, Chapter VII of the Code of Corporate Governance for Listed Companies in China and other regulations require public Chinese companies to make periodic disclosure, and impose an ongoing disclosure requirement as to 'material incidents'.[243] Disclosure must include financial statements, specified corporate governance information and details about the holdings of large shareholders.[244] Required disclosures must be

---

239. Green, supra note 1, p. 141.
240. *Principles of Securities Regulation*, supra note 212, at §14. Relevant international best practices provide that disclosure should include audited financial statements showing financial and operating results of a company, company objectives, major share ownership and voting rights, board members and key executives and their remuneration and material risk factors, and governance structure. The term 'ongoing' is generally defined to include all current, continuous and periodic disclosures, other than disclosures at the IPO stage. The term 'periodic' refers to information required to be disclosed at specified dates or intervals. Technical Committee of the International Organization of Securities Commissions, *Principles for Ongoing Disclosure and Material Development Reporting by Listed Entities*, (October 2002).
241. Kawai, supra note 157, p. 25.
242. Ibid.
243. *PRC Code of Corporate Governance*, supra note 232, at Chapter VII. See also Securities Law, supra note 2, at §§63–64.
244. *PRC Code of Corporate Governance*, supra note 232, at §§87–89. Section 89 of the PRC Code of Corporate Governance calls for Internet dissemination. In addition to disclosing material information, a listed company is to disclose corporate governance information including, inter alia,:

   – the members and structure of the board of directors and the supervisory board; and
   – the performance and evaluation of the board of directors and the supervisory board.

   Ibid., at §91. Required disclosures also must include:

   – the performance and evaluation of the independent directors, including their attendance at board of directors' meetings, their issuance of independent opinions and their opinions in regard to related party transactions, and appointment and removal of directors and senior management personnel;
   – the composition and work of the specialized committees of the board of directors;

published in print media or online, as designated by the CSRC.[245] The Board's secretary is responsible for information disclosure, and the Securities Law and other relevant regulations specify liability for underwriters, issuers and others in the event of non-compliance with disclosure requirements.[246]

In practice, Chinese disclosure standards are not fully effective, and non-disclosure seems to occur most frequently in connection with related party transactions, line segment information, accounting policies, impact of extraordinary items, effects of changes in government policies and reporting of important investments, capital commitments, consolidated statements, fair value and contingencies.[247] Selective disclosure, which is disclosure to different investors at different times, is another significant problem for China's securities markets.[248] In part, these disclosure difficulties arise due to the fact that periodic disclosures are governed by detailed requirements that:

- focus on short-term rather than long-term objectives;
- do not emphasize business opportunities and risks; and
- discourage the use of projections.[249]

- the actual state of corporate governance of the company, the gap between the company's corporate governance and the Code, and the reasons for the gap; and
- specific plans and measures to improve corporate governance. A listed company must also disclose detailed information about each shareholder who owns a large percentage of the company's shares.

Ibid., at §92. A company must timely disclose detailed information about each shareholder who owns a comparatively large percentage of shares of the company, the shareholders who actually control the company when acting in concert and the company's actual controllers in accordance with relevant regulations. Ibid., at §93. A listed company also must disclose in a timely manner, changes in the shareholding of the company and other important matters that may cause changes in the shareholding of the company. Ibid., at §94.

245. China Securities Regulatory Commission, *Guideline No. 13 on Information Disclosure Reports of Listed Companies-Special Rules on Contents and Format for Quarterly Reports (amended, 2002)*, (issued on 12 December 2002 and effective as of the same date). These interim financial statements must include a balance sheet, statement of profits, statement of cash flow and notes to accounting statements.

246. *Securities Law*, supra note 2, at §§69, 192 and 193. *PRC Code of Corporate Governance*, supra note 232, at §90.

247. IFC, supra note 52, p. 119. Other problem areas include:

- disclosure related to the use of IPO proceeds show they used funds raised from the public; and
- the quality of audits by certified public accountants varied, which affected both the reliability of audited accounts and the ease with which the accounts could be compared.

In addition, inadequate disclosure was made of line segment information, accounting policies, impact of extraordinary items, effects of changes in government policies and fake receivables (Green, supra note 1, pp. 137–138). 88 per cent of investors surveyed stated their belief that firms provide inaccurate disclosure. The interdependence between listed and a parent company creates strong incentives to distort information, particularly information about related-party transactions, which are frequently used to adjust operating results and financial positions. IFC, supra note 52, pp. 118–119 and 136.

248. Ibid., p. 120.

249. Ibid., p. 125.

As stated previously, the multiple bases for preparing and auditing financial statements contribute to poor disclosure.

China's securities markets do not yet reward better and more-transparent companies with lower-cost funds, because, until recently, criteria for market access were relatively independent of the quality of companies.[250] Problematic disclosure also adversely affects financial analysts and rating agencies that rely on information disclosed by the covered entities and on other publicly available quantitative and qualitative information.[251]

Related to financial disclosures, covered persons, including share controllers – such as proxy holders – and shareholders in listed Chinese companies must submit a Report of Shareholding Changes among the Shareholders of Listed Companies to the CSRC and the stock exchange if:

- their holdings cross (either up or down) the five per cent threshold (holder-initiated transactions of such shares may be restricted); or
- when the holdings for an existing five per cent holder varies by five per cent of the company's total shares (with resale prohibitions provided in the Disclosure Procedures).[252]

A covered person must also notify the issuer and make a public announcement within two days of the transaction's consummation. A covered person is prohibited from transacting in the company's issued shares for three working days following the required public announcement.

The CSRC's recent amendments to the sponsorship system require a listing company's sponsor to supervise their client's conduct for the rest of the year of listing and the subsequent two full fiscal years in the case of an IPO, or the rest of the year of listing and the subsequent one full fiscal year in case of a new issue or issue of convertible bonds. Sponsors are required to independently investigate and verify the information stated in their client's prospectus and:

- must have 'sufficient reasons' to believe their clients have fulfilled all the statutory requirements for stock issue or listing;
- believe their clients' application documents and prospectus contain no false records, misleading representations or material omissions; and
- believe the opinions in the prospectus are based on sufficient and reasonable grounds.

---

250. Ibid., p. 118.
251. Equity analysts are primarily interested in estimating valuation from a discounted earnings model, while the rating agencies are more interested in estimating the risk to the firm's debt issues and use earnings and forecasts on future earnings as an indicator of a firm's ability to repay its debts. Joint Forum, supra note 58, p. 27.
252. China Securities Regulatory Commission, *Administration of the Takeover of Listed Companies Procedures* (issued and effective as of 28 September 2002); China Securities Regulatory Commission, *Administration of Disclosure of Information on the Change of Shareholdings in Listed Companies Procedures* (issued and effective as of 28 September 2002).

After the submission of initial reference documents to the CSRC, sponsors must ensure that their clients respond to the CSRC's comments; proceed with due diligence investigations or verifications on particular relevant matters, as requested by the CSRC; and designate sponsorship representatives to communicate with the CSRC. Sponsors cannot recommend companies that involve special relations or these companies' main affiliates. In addition, a sponsor cannot recommend any company in which any of the sponsor's representative, director, supervisor or any other senior official has an affiliation with the potential issuer. Just how these amendments will improve, in practice, the quality of disclosures made by listed companies is unclear.

Securities investment funds must publicly disclose particular information, including, inter alia, the fund's:

– prospectus;
– custodianship agreement;
– sale of fund shares;
– listing of fund shares;
– net asset value and the net value of the fund shares;
– the prices for purchase and redemption of the fund shares;
– periodic and interim reports; and
– significant personnel changes of the fund manager.

The parties required to make such disclosure include the fund's:

– manager;
– custodian;
– shareholders that convene the fund shareholders' general meeting; and
– related persons specified by relevant regulation.

Disclosure must be made through those publications designated by the CSRC and on the fund's and custodian's Internet sites.[253] In addition, a securities investment fund must make periodic disclosures, and is subject to an ongoing disclosure requirement.[254]

---

253. China Securities Regulatory Commission, *Administration of Information Disclosure of Securities Investment Funds Procedures*, (issued on 8 June 2004 and effective as of 1 July 2004), reprinted at *China Law & Prac.* 3700/04.06.08; China Securities Regulatory Commission, *Contents and Formats for Information Disclosure of Securities Investment Funds Guidelines, (No. 1) – Contents and Format of Listing Announcements*, (issued on 15 June 2004 and effective as of 1 July 2004), reprinted at *China Law & Prac.* 3700/04.06.15(1).
254. China Securities Regulatory Commission, *Contents and Formats for Information Disclosure of Securities Investment Funds Guidelines (No. 2) – Contents and Format of Annual Reports*, (issued on 15 June 2004 and effective as of 1 July 2004), reprinted at *China Law & Prac.* 3700/04.06.15(2); China Securities Regulatory Commission, *Contents and Formats for Information Disclosure of Securities Investment Funds Guidelines (No .3) – Contents and Format of Interim Reports*, (issued on 15 June 2004 and effective as of 1 July 2004), reprinted at *China Law & Prac.* 3700/04.06.15(3); China Securities Regulatory Commission, *Contents and Formats for Information Disclosure of Securities Investment Funds Guidelines (No. 4) – Contents and Format of Quarterly Reports*, (issued on 15 June

These developments are positive, however, the Chinese government must do more to improve the quality and timeliness of public company disclosures.

VI.E.4.   Regulatory Capacity

A securities regulator must, inter alia:

- be operationally independent and accountable in the exercise of its functions and powers;
- have adequate powers, proper resources and the capacity to perform its functions and exercise its powers;
- have comprehensive inspection, investigation and surveillance powers; and
- have comprehensive enforcement powers.[255]

Effective securities market regulation requires a mix of government, exchange, and self-regulatory oversight. Weak regulatory enforcement coupled with the absence of a strong culture of enforcement and accountability exposed AFC-affected jurisdictions to the risks that caused, and worsened, the AFC.[256]

2004 and effective as of 1 July 2004), reprinted at *China Law & Prac.* 3700/04.06.15(4). The fund's listing announcement, to be disclosed by the fund's managers three days prior to listing, is to include information such as verification information, trading code, and number of shares floated. In addition, the fund's listing announcement must include the number of fund shareholders, average holdings, the ratio of shares held by institutional investors and individual investors, and the names, shareholdings and proportions in the total number of fund shares of the top ten shareholders as of two days before the listing announcement. The fund must also release information on the fund's holdings as of two days before the listing announcement is released. The fund's annual and interim reports are to include information on the fund's accounting results for longer of the previous three years or from the fund's inception date. Other information to be disclosed includes the fund's:

- net earnings;
- net earnings per share;
- distributable earnings;
- distributable earnings per share;
- net asset value;
- net value per share;
- weighted average return on net value;
- growth rate of the net value per share;
- growth rate of the cumulative net value per share; and
- distributable earnings over the previous three years.

An interim report shall be signed by at least two-thirds of the find manager's independent directors. A fund's quarterly report must include the same data and must be released within 15 working days of the end of each quarter.

255. *Principles of Securities Regulation*, supra note 212, §§1–5, 8–10.
256. Ralph C. Bryant, *Standards and Prudential Oversight for an Integrating World Financial System, Brookings Discussion Papers in International Economics No. 152*, (Nov. 1999).

In addition, few AFC-affected jurisdictions had any form of non-governmental regulation of financial markets.[257]

Chapter IX and Chapter X of the Securities Law confer on a self-regulatory body and the CSRC, respectively, significant regulatory powers and responsibilities. Chapter XI of the Securities Law and other relevant regulations impose liabilities on market participants for specified acts and omissions. The CSRC has made great strides in implementing an effective regulatory scheme for China's securities markets, using overseas returnees to build capacity, and has an array of administrative powers with which to identify and punish offenders.[258] For example, the CSRC has complete access to trading records, bank and securities accounts and significant funding.[259]

While several problems persist with the regulatory framework as such, and despite the CSRC's best efforts, China's securities market regulation still contains gaps.[260] China's securities markets are notorious for corruption, with up to 30 per cent of stocks alleged to be manipulated at any one time.[261] Some, but in decreasing numbers, view the CSRC as weak because of the long process, concluded with the implementation of the Securities Law in 1998, conferring on the CSRC full oversight over China's securities markets.[262] The CSRC suffers from a twin mandate of being the market regulator and the market developer.[263] In addition, the CSRC has not dealt effectively with fraud or market manipulation, and financial reporting and disclosure are not up to international standards.[264] Punishment for violations of the Securities Law and subsidiary regulation seems rare, and when meted out comes in the form of private administrative warnings. Just how many notices are issued internally is unclear, however, according to insiders, these notices are of little use, because most companies receive the notices periodically. Fines, which rarely exceed a few thousand renminbi, are not a threat to market manipulators.[265]

Chinese courts have only recently begun to deal effectively with securities-related suits, which reinforces the need for a strong front-line regulator. On 4 November 2003, the Supreme People's Court published the Provisions Regarding Several Issues on the Adjudication of Cases Involving Company Disputes, which provided detailed rules on the protection of minority shareholders and the fiduciary duties of directors and senior management personnel.

---

257. *Turbulence*, supra note 107, at 83.
258. Green, supra note 1, at 172–3.
259. Green and Wall, supra note 143, at 29.
260. Ibid.
261. Ibid.
262. Ibid., p. 26. Upon implementation of the Securities Law, the CSRC was upgraded to the rank of 'an organ operating directly under the State Council', and Zhou Zhenqing, a senior ally of ex-Premier Zhu Rongji was appointed CSRC chairman. Ibid., pp. 26–27.
263. Ibid.
264. *Asia Society Conference Report*, supra note 47, at 13; *see also* Paul Gruenwald and Jahangir Aziz, *China and the Asian Crisis*, in China: Competing in the Global Economy (Wanda Tseng and Markus Rodlauer, eds., International Monetary Fund, 2003), p. 101.
265. Ibid.

In 2004, the Supreme People's Court released draft regulations to address corporate disputes and introduce the possibility of shareholder derivative suits. A shareholder can initiate an action against a company's controlling shareholders, directors, managers or officers who breach their duty of loyalty – but not a duty of care – to the company. A potential plaintiff shareholder must have been a shareholder at the time of the alleged breach, and continued to hold such shares. If the company in question is a limited liability company, potential plaintiffs must hold at least 10 per cent of the company's equity; potential plaintiffs against a company limited by shares must hold more than one per cent of the entity's shares. Notice of the alleged breach must be furnished to the company at least two months prior to the initiation of the action and potential plaintiffs must show that the company has not taken any corrective action. The Chinese government must continue to build up the capacity of its courts to hear securities-related cases to better reinforce the CSRC's regulatory authority.

Effective self-regulation by market institutions, such as exchanges and industry groups, can play a valuable complementary role to the efforts of supervisory regulators. Self-regulation, combining private interests with government oversight, is an effective and efficient form of regulation.[266] As indicated previously, Chapter V of the Securities Law covers the regulatory responsibilities of securities exchanges, and Chapter IX of the Securities Law covers the regulatory powers of a stock brokers' association (Securities Association). In 2002, the chairman of the CSRC, Zhou Xiaochuan, ordered governmental departments to grant greater responsibility to non-governmental associations of the securities industry to improve internal supervision.[267] The Securities Association of China (SAC) is a quasi-self-regulatory entity empowered to:

- Formulate rules to be observed by members.
- Arrange for vocational training for the employees of its members and promote professional exchanges among members.

---

266. International Association of Securities Commissions, *Model for Effective Self-Regulation, Report of the SRO Consultative Committee* (May 2000). In its most complete form, self-regulation encompasses the authority to create, amend, implement and enforce rules of conduct with respect to the entities subject to the self-regulatory organization's (SRO) jurisdiction and to resolve disputes through arbitration or other means. Typically, this authority is derived from a statutory delegation of power to a non-governmental entity. In self-regulation, the rules are drafted by market participants with an intimate knowledge of the market who know how to maximize the regulatory benefits while minimizing the business costs. Effective self-regulation must be defined within the context of government oversight. Government oversight is an essential element in the self-regulatory structure. Government oversight of SRO activities ensures that, among other things, all interests are given the proper consideration and voice in all regulatory activities. This oversight provides a system of checks and balances. The governing statute must clearly delineate the respective roles of the statutory regulators and the SROs.
267. 'Securities Watchdog to Give Industry More Leeway', *Xinhua Economic News Service* (3 July 2002).

- Supervise and inspect members' conduct.
- Impose disciplinary sanctions – in accordance with rules – on any member that violates laws, administrative regulations or the charter of the Association.[268]

The Shanghai Stock Exchange's Self Discipline Standard obligates SHSE members, which include foreign special members, to conduct their business operations in good faith and in compliance with all rules, regulations and professional ethics.[269] Despite these developments, Chinese exchanges and the SAC do not exercise the scale or scope of self-regulation that is expected of them.[270] Overall, front-line regulation, judicial oversight and self-regulation must be augmented.

VI.E.5.   Suspension and De-Listing of Listed Companies

Securities market integrity requires nonviable public companies to be suspended from trading or, if warranted, delisted. AFC-affected jurisdictions did not effectively delist nonviable corporations.[271] Articles 55 and 56 of the Securities Law empower the CSRC to suspend and delist, respectively, Chinese public companies in specified circumstances, including, inter alia, if the issuer sustains losses in three consecutive years. The CSRC has clarified that, if a listed company is unable to continuously satisfy its listing requirements, the company must pass a board resolution on trading suspension and submit the resolution to a shareholders' general meeting for discussion.[272]

Both the SHSE and the SZSE can suspend a listed company's shares for specified reasons.[273] The two Exchanges can add '*ST' before the name of a company's listed shares if the company:

- has incurred losses for the two consecutive years prior to the notice;
- has been required by the CSRC to correct its financial statements; or

---

268. See Securities Law, supra note 2, at §164.
269. See, for example, Shanghai Stock Exchange, *The Self Discipline Standard,* (issued on 28 February 2003 and effective as of the same date). The standards establish certain requirements for Shanghai Stock Exchange members – including special members – with respect to their business operations, transaction and communication systems, internal control and membership.
270. Y. Zhang, President and CEO of the Shenzhen Stock Exchange, *The PRC Securities Market: An Overview of its Regulatory Capacity and Efficiency* (2001).
271. *Kawai,* supra note 157, p. 41.
272. China Securities Regulatory Commission, *Suspending and Terminating the Listings of Loss-making Listed Companies Implementing Procedures (Revised)* (issued on 30 November 2001 and effective as of the same date); China Securities Regulatory Commission, *Implementing the "Suspending and Terminating the Listings of Loss-making Listed Companies Implementing Procedures (Revised)" Supplementary Provisions,* (issued on 18 March 2003 and effective as of the same date), reprinted at *China Law & Prac.* 3700/03.03.18.
273. See, for example, Shenzhen Stock Exchange, *Rules for Suspending the Listing of Stocks of a Listed Company* (revised version) (issued on 16 June 2000 and effective as of the same date).

   – has not published its annual report or semi-annual report within the
required time frame.

A company whose stock is suspended from listing can either resume its listing
or be permanently delisted. If the company makes a profit in the first fiscal year
of its grace period, the company can apply to the CSRC to resume its listing.
However, if the company fails to show a profit in its first fiscal year during the
grace period, the company will be permanently delisted.

   As can be discerned in the following table, the suspension and delisting
rules have not been well-enforced.

Table 9: Number of Newly Delisted Issuers and Value in millions of US dollars[274]

Market	2002	2002 Market Cap	2003	2003 Market Cap	2004
China: Shanghai	1	119.4	2	94.2	4
China: Shenzhen	6	722.3	2	217.7	6
China: Aggregate	7		4		10
Australian	78	N/A	57	N/A	74
Bursa Malaysia	2	414.6	17	3,391.3	15
Korea	34	2,580.4	19	1,880.8	26
Singapore	24	3,951.4	9	1,179.1	10
Tokyo	82	63,133.1	67	20,693.3	53
Hong Kong	6	N/A	14	N/A	11

Suspension and delisting are difficult issues, given that local governments are
significant owners of listed companies and are likely to resist the delisting of
companies under their jurisdiction. Buyers often buy stocks of failing companies expecting a government bailout, a safety net not found in most other
markets. As a result, ST and particular transfer stocks often outperform the
market, which makes the use of stock market performance as part of managers'
incentive mechanisms impractical. For this reason, the Chinese government
should require the exit of nonviable firms.

VII.   ROLE OF INSTITUTIONAL INVESTORS

A deep, vibrant institutional investor base is the most important factor in securities market development, and helps create structures to mitigate liberalization

---

274. World Federation of Exchanges, 2003 Annual Statistics Equity 1.4, Number of Newly
     Listed and Delisted Companies, available at <www.fibv.com/publications/equity403.xls>
     (5 February 2006) (2002 and 2003 data); World Federation of Exchanges, 2004 *Annual
     Statistics Equity 1.4, Number of Newly Listed and Delisted Companies*, available at
     <www.fibv.com/publications/equity404.xls> (5 February 2006) (2004 data).

risk.[275] An institutional investor base is important for sequencing and overall market development, because it provides a framework for long-term capital accumulation and is a steady source of demand for long-term instruments.[276] In addition, intermediary development, such as increasing the number of institutional investors, exerts a large causal impact on economic growth.[277]

Institutional investors also:

- – Promote financial system efficiency by competing with commercial banks;
- – stimulate financial innovation, modernize securities markets, enhance transparency and information disclosure, and strengthen corporate governance;[278]
- – promote more efficient primary markets and efficient trading, clearance, and settlement processes that reduce both new issue and trading costs;[279]
- – Provide a credible mechanism for transmitting information to the financial markets;[280]
- – Support the growth of venture capital funds and the provision of private equity, both of which help finance new and expanding smaller firms;
- – Increase the depth and liquidity of securities markets; and
- – Create incentives for robust regulatory and supervisory framework to minimize risk.[281]

A lack of a domestic institutional investor base adversely affected monitoring of corporate governance in AFC-affected jurisdictions.[282] An active domestic institutional investor base could have decreased the probability and quantity of sudden capital flow reversals that triggered the AFC.[283]

China's institutional investor base is small, and must be strengthened to mitigate the risks associated with liberalization. Some 133 securities companies, 34 fund management companies, and 27 QFIIs are active in China's securities

275. Karacadag, supra note 106, p. 18.
276. Ibid.
277. R. Levine, N. Loayza and T. Beck, *Financial Intermediation and Growth: Causality and Causes, World Bank Paper 2059* (February 1999) (referred to as 'Levine I').
278. C. Oman, S. Fries and W. Buiter, *Corporate Governance in Developing, Transition and Emerging-Market Economies, Organization for Economic Cooperation and Development Policy Brief 23* (February 2004); D. Vittas, *Institutional Investors and Securities Markets: Which Comes First?*, paper presented at the ABCD LAC Conference (June 1998), p. 6.
279. Ibid., p. 8.
280. S.L. Gillan and L.T. Starks, *Institutional Investors, Corporate Ownership, and Corporate Governance, World Bank Global Perspectives* (November 2001), p. 7.
281. See also Xu and Wang, supra note 195, p. 22.
282. IFC, supra note 52, p. 22. As a result, the markets did not have access to dependable, comprehensive and timely information, or a mechanism to aggregate shareholders' votes to enable effective intervention in the management approach of the firm. Ibid.
283. Turbulence, supra note 107, p. 21; *Asia-Pacific Economic Cooperation, Compendium of Sound Practices: Guidelines to Facilitate the Development of Domestic Bond Markets in APEC Member Countries* (1999).

markets. The Chinese government has made efforts to increase the number of institutional investors, as indicated in the Capital Markets Opinions. The State Council believes that institutional investors can help grow stock market capitalization by channelling private savings into stocks.[284] Financial resources in China are skewed towards deposits, and must redirect savings to help reform SOEs, restructure the banking sector, and reform pensions and social security.[285] The Chinese government wants to alter the style of stock market investment from one of short-term speculation to one of long-term, professionally managed, portfolio-driven investment.[286] The ultimate aim of the CSRC is to have approximately 50 per cent of stock market capitalization held by and through institutional investors.[287]

The CIRC and CSRC have issued regulations to permit insurance companies to invest in the securities market, provided that an 'insurance institutional investor' may not hold more than 30 per cent of a listed company's A-Shares.[288] In addition, the trial procedures that address the management of corporate supplementary old-age pension insurance funds formed by capital raised through corporate pension plans enables these types of funds to invest – in a limited fashion – in China's securities market.[289]

---

284. Green and Wall, supra note 143, p. 21.
285. Kim, supra note 123.
286. Ibid., p. 22.
287. Green and Wall, supra note 143, p. 21.
288. China Insurance Regulatory Commission and China Securities Regulatory Commission, *Administration of Stock Investments by Insurance Institutional Investors Tentative Procedures* (issued on 24 October 2004 and effective as of the same date); China Insurance Regulatory Commission, *Matters Relevant to Investments in Convertible Corporate Bonds by Insurance Companies Circular* (issued on 23 July 2004 and effective as of the same date), reprinted at *China Law & Prac.* 3700/04.07.23, which provides guidelines for insurance companies related to investments in convertible corporate bonds.
289. Ministry of Labour and Social Security, China Banking Regulatory Commission, China Securities Regulatory Commission and China Insurance Regulatory Commission, *Administration of Enterprise Pension Funds Trial Procedures*, (issued 23 February 2004 and effective as of 1 May 2004), reprinted at *China Law & Prac.* 2410/04.02.23. Trustees of these types of funds should have registered capital in excess of RMB 100 million and net assets in excess of RMB 150 million. Account managers for these types of entities should have registered capital in excess of RMB 50 million. Custodians of these types of funds must have net assets in excess of RMB 5 billion. Investment managers for such funds should have registered capital and net assets in excess of RMB 1 billion, if they are a comprehensive-type securities company, or registered capital and net assets in excess of RMB 100 million if they are a fund management company, trust investment company or insurance asset management company. These types of funds can only invest in bank deposits, treasury bonds and other financial products with high liquidity, including repurchase of short-term bonds, financial bonds and enterprise bonds with credit rating at or above investment grade, convertible bonds, insurance products with an investment nature, securities investment funds and specified stocks. Ibid.

In general, quantitative limits on an institution's investments limit portfolio choice and cause a bias toward government debt, particularly where relevant regulation specifies a minimum level of government debt holding, and undermine the price discovery process. Many Chinese regulations limit the form and value of institutions' investment in listed companies. These limits must be relaxed, and the Chinese government must continue to develop its institutional investor base.

VIII. ECONOMIC IMPACTS OF LIBERALIZATION

Liberalization should increase the size and liquidity of China's capital market by increasing the level of intermediation made through the securities market, and decreasing the level of intermediation made by the banking system.[290] Liberalization reduces the cost of both components of equity, the risk-free rate and the equity premium.[291] Securities market development offers additional avenues for savings intermediation and risk spreading, and is strongly and positively correlated to a nation's long-term economic growth.[292] Equity market liberalization on average should yield an additional one per cent increase in the annual growth rate for real GDP over a five year period starting on the

---

290. China's domestic banking sector almost wholly allocates its capital to the state-owned enterprise sector, and the non-state sector finances itself through foreign direct investment, bank credit or retained earnings. Interestingly, non-state credit is a significant factor in the variance among provincial growth. For this reason, a large deposit base exists due to the high national saving rate and lack of alternative financial assets. Assets intermediated through bank lending have been misallocated to the larger state sector larger. J. Aziz and C. Duenwald, *Growth-Financial Intermediation Nexus in China*, IMF Working Paper WP/02/194 (November 2002), pp. 6–7. Stock market volatility rises in near term after liberalization but is reduced over long term. A. Demirgüç-Kunt and R. Levine, *Stock Markets, Corporate Finance, and Economic Growth: an Overview*, 10 World Bank. Econ. Rev. 223, 232 (May 1996) (referred to as 'Demirgüç-Kunt and Levine I'). Initially, debt increases as equity markets develop then equity substituted for debt. A. Demirgüç-Kunt and R. Levine, *Stock Market Development and Financial Intermediaries*, 10 World Bank. Econ. Rev. 291, 292 (May 1996). Size is defined as the ratio of market capitalization to gross domestic product; liquidity is measured by the ratio of total value traded to gross domestic product and turnover (value of total shares traded/gross domestic product); and volatility is measured using a standard deviation estimate based on market returns. Ibid, pp. 295–299.
291. See N. Fuchs-Schundeln and N. Funke, *Stock Market Liberalizations: Financial and Macroeconomic Implications*, IMF Working Paper WP/01/193, (December 2001) (referred to as Fuchs-Schundeln in this chapter).
292. Karacadag, supra note 106, p. 14; R. Levine and S. Zervos, *Stock Markets, Banks, and Economic Growth*, World Bank Working Paper No. 1690 (Dec. 1996) (referred to as 'Levine and Zervos I'); Levine I, supra note 277, p. 20.

liberalization date, but the liberalization benefit on GDP growth ends about three years after the liberalization date.[293]

Table 10: Liberalization Impact[294]

	Average three years Prior to Liberalization	Liberalization Year	Three years After Liberalization
Market Cap/GDP Growth	3.3	25.9	9.0
Growth in number of Listed Companies	3.4	16.7	11.7
Turnover Ratio Growth	−4.6	56.9	12.1

Table 11: Overall Market Capitalization (in millions of US dollars)[295]

Market	End-2002	End-2003	End-2004	End-2005
China: Shanghai	306,443.6	360,106.3	314,315.7	286,190.3
China: Shenzhen	156,647.6	152,872.4	133,404.5	115,661.9
China: Aggregate	463,091.2	512,978.7	447,720.2	401,852.2
Australian	380,087	585,431	776,402.8	804.014.8
Bursa Malaysia	122,892.4	160,970.3	181,623.8	180,517.5
Korea	216,116.6	298,248.1	398,558.9	718,010.7
Singapore	101,553.7	148,502.6	217,495.4	257,339.8
Tokyo	2,069,299.1	2,953,098.3	3,557,674.4	4,572,901
Hong Kong	463,054.9	714,597.4	861,462.9	1,054,999.3

---

293. See Fuchs-Schundeln, supra note 291.
294. See ibid.
295. World Federation of Exchanges, 2005 *Monthly Data, Domestic Market Capitalization*, available at <www.fibv.com/publications/equ1105.xls> (5 February 2006) (2005 data); World Federation of Exchanges, 2004 *Monthly Data, Domestic Market Capitalization*, available at <www.fibv.com/publications/equ1104.xls> (1 March 2005) (2004 data); World Federation of Exchanges, *Time Series Data 1990–2003, Domestic Market Capitalization*, available at <www.fibv.com/publications/ts2_market_cap.xls> (1 March 2005) (2001–2003 data).

Table 12: Number of Listed Companies[296]

Market	End-2001	End-2002	End-2003	End-2004	End-2005
China: Shanghai	646	715	780	837	833
China: Shenzhen	508	508	505	536	544
China: Aggregate	1,154	1,223	1,285	1,373	1,377
Australian	1,410	1,421	1,471	1,582	1,714
Bursa Malaysia	807	861	902	959	1,019
Korea	688	683	684	683	1,619
Singapore	492	501	551	632	686
Tokyo	2,141	2,153	2,206	2,306	2,351
Hong Kong	867	978	1,037	1,096	1,135

Table 13: Turnover Velocity[297]

Market	2002	2003	2004	End of December 2005
China: Shanghai	N/A	118%	87%	82.1%
China: Shenzhen	N/A	125.8%	120.5%	128.9%
Australian	76.2%	79.9%	81.1%	84%
Bursa Malaysia	24.9%	34.3%	33.8%	28.3%
Korea	254.4%	193.1%	147.2%	206.9%
Singapore	53.8%	74.4%	60.8%	48.4%
Tokyo	67.9%	82.6%	97.1%	115.3%
Hong Kong	39.7%	51.7%	57.7%	50.3%

China's capital markets are not consistently growing in size, as measured by market capitalization (Table 11) or number of listed companies (Table 12). China's securities markets also are becoming less liquid (Table 13). The statistics

---

296. World Federation of Exchanges, Time Series Data 1990–2003, Number of Listed Companies, available at <www.fibv.com/publications/ts1%20nber%20of%20cos.pdf> (1 March 2005) (2001–2003 data); World Federation of Exchanges, 2004 Monthly Data, Number of Listed Companies, available at <www.fibv.com/publications/equ1204.pdf> (1 March 2005) (2004 data); World Federation of Exchanges, 2005 Monthly Data, Number of Listed Companies, available at <www.fibv.com/publications/equ1205.pdf> (6 February 2006) (2005 data).

297. World Federation of Exchanges, 2002 Annual Data, Equity 1.6: Turnover Velocity, available at <www.fibv.com/publications/ta1602.xls> (5 February 2006) (2002 data); World Federation of Exchanges, 2004 Annual Data, Equity 1.8: Turnover Velocity, available at <www.fibv.com/publications/equ804.xls> (5 February 2006) (2003–2004 data); World Federation of Exchanges, 2004 Monthly Data, Equity 1.4: Turnover Velocity, available at <www.fibv.com/publications/equ1405.xls> (5 February 2006) (end-December 2005 data).

in Table 10, however, present a starker picture of the growth of China's securities markets; with the 2002 data as a base:

- China's market capitalization must be approximately USD 692,700 million rather than USD 401,852.2 million;
- Chinese public markets must include 1,781 listed companies, and not 1,377; and
- turnover velocity must be 148.2 per cent, and not 82.1 per cent, for the SHSE, and 158.1 per cent, not 128.9 per cent, for the SZSE.

The liberalization benefits for market capitalization growth and growth rate of listed companies tends to end in the fourth year after liberalization. If one dates China's liberalization date to1 July 2002, which was the date on which the Securities JV Rules and FI-FMC Establishment Rules took effect, the Chinese government is running out of time to leverage some of the benefits of liberalization.

To reduce adverse selection problems, securities market development increases the amount of information that flows through the system, reduces the cost of mobilizing savings and improves allocative efficiency by facilitating investment in most productive investments.[298]

Usually, as securities markets increase liquidity, transactions costs fall, which improves the net of transactions costs return on investment, and increases productive efficiency.[299] Reduced transaction costs increase the volume of equity market activity by increasing the attractiveness of transactions-intensive investments.[300] Because China's securities markets have not increased significantly in liquidity in this liberalization period, one might conclude that transaction costs remain high. Because the liberation benefits for turnover ratio growth end in the second year after liberalization, the Chinese securities markets may already have missed out on liberalization benefits for market liquidity.[301]

Increasing liquidity is also positively and significantly correlated with current and future rates of economic growth, capital growth and productivity growth.[302] Liquidity facilitates investment in longer-term projects that boost economic growth by facilitating more-efficient resource allocation.[303] Liquid

---

298. Demirgüç-Kunt and Levine I, supra note 290, p. 228. R. Levine and S. Zervos, *Stock Market Development and Long-Run Growth*, 10 World Bank Econ. Rev 323 (May 1996) (referred to as 'Levine and Zervos II').
299. V. Bencivenga, B. Smith and R. Starr, *Equity Markets, Transactions Costs, and Capital Accumulation*, 10 World Bank. Econ. Rev. 241, 245 (May 1996).
300. Ibid., pp. 246–263.
301. See Fuchs-Schundeln, supra note 291.
302. Levine and Zervos I, supra note 292. Data from 49 countries from 1976–1993. Liquidity is measured as value of stock trading relative to the stock market and the value F-stock trading as compared to the overall economy. Interestingly, stock market size, volatility and integration are not linked robustly with growth. Banking development, measured as bank loans to private enterprises divided by GDP, are linked robustly with growth. See also Levine and Zervos II, supra note 298.
303. Levine and Zervos I, supra note 292.

securities markets can increase incentives to obtain information about firms and improve corporate governance, and makes linking manager compensation to stock market price much easier.[304]

Interestingly, securities market development must facilitate inter-regional capital mobility, which currently is low.[305] Capital mobility should increase financial integration across China's regions and limit the market distorting effect of local resistance to inter-regional capital flows.[306] In addition, this type of capital mobility may limit the adverse impact that the central government's reallocation of money from more-productive regions to less-productive ones.[307]

IX.   CONCLUSION

China's securities markets have grown dramatically over the past few years, and the implementation of China's significant securities sector commitments will serve to further such growth. Despite significant efforts, China's implementation record for its securities sector commitments is mixed. High capital requirements and burdensome licensing procedures are among the problems that prevent effective implementation. This article also reviewed the link between capital market liberalization and the need for reforms to mitigate liberalization risk. The State Council, in the Capital Markets Opinions, recognizes these risks, and has called for an aggressive reform effort. These reforms must be completed within the next five to ten to best minimize liberalization risk.[308] Among other reforms, the Chinese government should:

- further develop the domestic government and corporate bond markets to mitigate increased market and liquidity risks;
- deepen the roster of institutional investors active on the domestic capital market;
- Improve accounting, auditing, and disclosure systems to ensure that the most accurate and timely material on issuers reaches the market;
- increase the CSRC's capacity, and enable self-regulatory organizations to police their members in an effective manner;
- have the CSRC divorce itself from its market building tasks and focus on market regulation;
- enable the CSRC to conduct more high-profile public investigations and punishments;

---

304. Levine and Zervos II, supra note 298.
305. G. Boyreau-Debray and S.-J. Wei, *Can China Grow Faster? A Diagnosis of the Fragmentation of Its Domestic Capital Market*, IMF Working Paper WP/04/76 (May 2004) (referred to as 'Faster'); see also Prasad, supra note 3, p. 10.
306. Faster, supra note 289.
307. Ibid.
308. C. Karacadag, 'Financial System Soundness and Reform', in W. Tseng and M. Rodlauer (eds.), China: *Competing in the Global Economy* (International Monetary Fund, 2003), p. 150.

- increase the float of tradable shares in listed companies by reducing state ownership therein;
- increase the capacity of Chinese courts to review securities related cases, to help create a culture of enforcement; and
- suspend and de-list troubled issuers on a more consistent basis.

China's securities market will continue to develop at a fast pace, due to both the implementation of WTO commitments and liberalizations supplementary to WTO accession. The liberalizing developments will increase the risks that China's financial system faces, and require effective mitigating reforms. This tension between liberalization and reform will be the major challenge before the Chinese government in regard to China's securities market.

Chapter 7

Insurance in China: Liberalization and Restructuring Post-WTO

*Andreas Kellerhals**

I.   INTRODUCTION

More than four years ago, on 11 December 2001, the People's Republic of China became the 143rd member of the World Trade Organisation (WTO). A good deal of expectation was put on China's WTO accession, which was expected to provide momentum for reforming its political and economic system, over-hauling its legal framework, and rationalising its market structure.[1] Although development has not been without shortcomings, the Chinese government has been diligent in adhering to its WTO commitments to further open the Chinese market. On the eve of China's WTO entry, expecting fierce competition from global players, domestic industries had been arming themselves with any pos-sible means. In fact, most of China's industry sectors have been witnessing fundamental reorganization and reorientation since China's WTO entry. The insurance sector followed suit. Market structure, technologies and products are evolving vigorously alongside regulatory measures. A monolithic, domes-tic oriented and governmental steered industry has been prompted to open up

**   The author would like to thank Dr. Wei Wenbin for his very helpful support in research.
1.   In the past, China's reforms were largely internally driven; see S. Shen, 'WTO and China's legal system', in M. Matsushita and D. Ahn (eds.), *WTO and East Asia: New Perspectives* (London, 2004), p. 267.

Barth et al., *Financial Restructuring and Reform in Post-WTO China*, pp. 245–272.
© 2007 Kluwer Law International BV, The Netherlands.

to foreign competition and to be part of an ongoing process of restructuring and liberalization.[2]

Although still at an immature stage, China's insurance market has grown for a decade at a dazzling velocity, with an average annual premium revenue growth rate of 30 per cent.[3] Despite the fast growth, insurance density (premiums per capita) and insurance penetration (premium as percentage of GDP) in China are still low by international standards.[4] The insurance sector still only accounts for 3.8 per cent of China's financial industry in terms of assets, and total premiums were just 3.4 per cent in 2005 of gross domestic product, compared to 9.36 per cent in the United States.[5] International forecasts on the annual growth rate of China's insurance sector as measured by premium are set at 12 per cent for the next 5 to 10 years, which means that the total size of the Chinese market might increase by 310 per cent in 2010.[6] This huge growth potential is supported by China's rapid economic growth, changing demographics, social welfare reforms and a more supportive and flexible regulatory framework as a consequence of China's WTO commitments. The potential size of the market and its current pace and breadth of development make China a key strategic target for any insurer in the world.[7] Many foreign insurers have been attracted by the prospect of acceding and exploring the world's largest potential market, which is still very much underdeveloped.[8]

---

2. According to Wu Dingfu, Chairman of the China Insurance Regulatory Commission (CIRC), the local insurance industry has already benefited from foreign expertise and know-how. See http://eg2.mofcom.gov.cn/aarticle/chinanews/200505/20050500099615.html).
3. Figures released by Wu Dingfu, chairman of the CIRC, in an interview with China Daily published on 10 October 2005, available at <www.chinadaily.com.cn/english/doc/2005-10/28/content_488515.thm>.
4. By the end of 2001, China's non-life and life insurance penetration rates were 0.9 per cent and 1.3 per cent, respectively, as compared to Germany's 3.6 per cent and 3.0 per cent, and the USA's 4.6 per cent and 4.4 per cent. More stridently, China's non-life and life insurance density rates are at a meagre eight per cent and 12 per cent, see S. Kai-Uwe, 'China; The Dragon Stirs', *Reinsurance Magazine* (1 April 2003).
5. Figures released by Wu Dingfu, chairman of the CIRC, in an interview with *China Daily* on 10 October 2005, available at <www.chinadaily.com.cn/english/doc/2005-10/28/content_488515.thm>.
6. S.M. Harner, *Business Opportunities for Foreign Insurance Companies in China's Changing Marketplace; Facts and Figures for Potential Investors.*
7. In 2005, the premium of insurance companies totalled RMB 492.7 billion, up 14 per cent over the previous year. Of this total, life insurance premium earnings amounted to RMB 324.4 billion, health and casualty insurance premium earnings RMB 45.3 billion and property insurance premium earnings amounted to RMB 123 billion. Insurance companies paid an indemnity totalling RMB 113 billion, of which life insurance indemnity was RMB 30.7 billion, health and casualty insurance indemnity RMB 15.1 billion, and property insurance indemnity was RMB 67.2 billion; see *China Economic News*, no. 4, (3 April 2006), p. 4.
8. By the end of October 2005, 44 foreign insurance companies from 15 countries and regions were offering insurance service in China; see *China Economic News*, no. 1 (2 January 2006), p. 6.

Nevertheless, entering China's insurance market has not proved to be as easy as some foreign insurance companies might have anticipated.[9] Although China's progress in implementing its WTO commitments and in opening up its insurance market to foreign competition is remarkable and should be acknowledged, some limitations and caution are still key characteristics of China's regulations and will continue to be so in the foreseeable future. For these reasons, foreign insurers must adapt to the challenges posed by China's cautious regulatory approach, and to follow China's liberalization efforts closely to ensure that relevant international commitments are fully honoured.

II.	BASIC FRAMEWORK OF CHINA'S INSURANCE LEGISLATION

Chinese legislation, which is rendered and adopted by respective lawmaking bodies at hierarchical levels, carries various statuses of effectiveness and applicability. At the top of the legislature system are the 'laws' of the National People's Congress (NPC) or its Standing Committee. Laws are followed by the administrative regulations of the State Council, in the pursuit of implementing laws. At a lower level, diverse ministries, commissions and departments subordinated to the State Council issue *administrative rules* within their mandates of competences.[10] The insurance-related legislation follows the same legislative order.

II.A.	INSURANCE LAW

In 1995, the Standing Committee of the NPC enacted China's first Insurance Law (1995 Insurance Law), which provided the necessary legal and regulatory framework to support the rapid growth of China's insurance sector and to fight malpractice.[11] The 1995 Insurance Law was very much a framework legislation – which over time was supplemented by regulations dealing with specific parts of the insurance industry[12] – and dealt, in general, with the structure and

---

9. Although the number of foreign insurance companies exceeds that of Chinese companies, foreign companies still only have about a seven per cent share of the insurance market in China; see *China Economic News*, no. 9, (6 March 2006), p. 5.
10. The Legislation Law, promulgated by the National People's Congress on 15 March 2000 and effective as of 1 July 2000.
11. These included kickbacks, excessive agent's commissions and dishonesty in product promotion.
12. Accordingly regulations deal, for example, with:

    – Brokers: Administration of Insurance Brokerages Provisions, effective 1 January 2005;
    – Agents: Insurance Agencies Provisions, effective 1 January 2005; and
    – Assessors: Administration of Insurance Assessors Provisions.

regulation of the insurance industry and insurance contracts.[13] One of the most important clauses of the 1995 Insurance Law classifies the insurance business into two categories: property and casualty, including liability and credit insurance, and life insurance, including accident and health insurance.[14] At that time, promulgating insurance regulations fell within the scope of competences of the central bank, namely, the People's Bank of China (PBOC).[15] In 1998, in the course of strengthening the relevant regulatory system, the China Insurance Regulatory Committee (CIRC) was established as a ministerial-level agency subordinated to the State Council, and assumed the powers and responsibilities for supervising the insurance industry previously vested in the PBOC.[16]

In October 2002, the Standing Committee of the NPC partially amended the 1995 Insurance Law (the amended law '2002 Insurance Law'),[17] to make the law consistent with China's WTO commitments.[18] For example, Article 154 of the 2002 Insurance Law replaced Article 148 of the 1995 Insurance Law, adding wholly foreign-funded insurance companies as one of the legally permissible forms of foreign-invested insurance companies.[19] The former requirement for non-life, personal accident and health insurance businesses to reinsure 20 per cent of the primary risk with China Re was revised to meet China's WTO

In addition, the regulations deal with broader issues, such as:

- administration of insurance companies: Regulations for the Administration of Insurance Companies, effective 15 June 2004;
- equity investment in insurance companies: Provisional Regulations on Equity Investment in Insurance Companies; and
- foreign invested insurance companies: Regulations on Administration of Foreign-Invested Insurance Companies, effective 1 February 2002.

13. According to the 1995 Insurance Law, insurance companies could be joint stock companies or fully state owned enterprises (1995 Insurance Law, Article 69), which could deal only in life or non-life insurance (1995 Insurance Law, Article 91). Foreign investors could only operate through joint ventures or branches (1995 Insurance Law, Article 148). Various formalities were specified for the formation and validity of insurance contracts (1995 Insurance Law, Articles 10–30).

14. Because a company is prohibited to engage in both areas simultaneously, those insurance companies which want to run both businesses must set up separate entities.

15. The PBOC, for example, issued the Interim Rules on Administration of Insurance in 1996, which stated that the PBOC was the competent authority for issuing regulations and supervising the insurance industry; see Article 65 of Interim Rules of Administration of Insurance. This Interim Rule was abolished by the Administration of Insurance Companies Provisions, issued by CIRC on 3 January 2000.

16. See the Notification of the State Council on the Establishment of CIRC (*Guofa*) [1998], no. 37.

17. The 2002 Insurance Law to effect as of 1 January 2003.

18. See the statement by Wu Dingfu, Chairman of CIRC, available at <www.circ.gov.cn/news/wudingfu.htm> (22 September 2003).

19. According to China's insurance commitments, within two years of China's accession to the WTO, foreign non-life insurers were permitted to establish as wholly foreign-owned subsidiaries.

commitment to the gradual reduction of this rate.[20] Other adjustments made to the insurance business by the 2002 Insurance Law entail the reversal from a micro-managing style of regulatory activities to the more market-oriented and policy-based regulatory activities[21] favoured by private insurers over excessive administrative interference with their daily business. In addition, in line with international trends, property insurance companies were freed from the previous restriction to provide short-term health insurance and accidental injury insurance coverage.[22]

II.B.   INSURANCE ADMINISTRATIVE REGULATIONS

The State Council formulates administrative regulations in accordance with the Constitution and the laws enacted by the NPC and its Standing Committee. The most fundamental insurance regulation related to China's WTO obligations is the Regulation on Administration of foreign-funded Insurance Companies, which came into force on 1 February 2002.[23] The regulation provides a special set of rules applicable to foreign insurers' activities in China and in principle incorporates China's commitments made upon its WTO entry in

---

20. Article 102 of the 2002 Insurance Law replaces Article 101 of the 1995 Insurance Law by stating that the 'reinsurance of insurance companies shall be carried out according to the relevant regulations of the insurance regulatory body'. Refer to the discussion of the related WTO commitment by China in section III.B.
21. Major changes to the PRC Insurance Law and new regulations included more-stringent reserve and solvency requirements and their disclosure, greater freedom for insurance companies to develop products to meet market needs; broader investment channels for insurance companies, including allowing insurers to invest in securities markets; tightening of market conduct regulation and increased penalties for violations; phasing out of mandatory reinsurance by the beginning of 2006; and reduction of barriers to entry, including allowing property and casualty insurers to enter the accident and short-time health insurance business; see:

    – Administration of Foreign-funded Insurance Companies Regulations (13 May 2004),
    – Issues Relevant to the Stock Investment and Trading of Insurance Investors Circular (17 February 2005);
    – Administrative Licensing Law (July 2004);
      Fulfilment of WTO Accession Commitments Notice (11 December 2004);
    – Matters Relevant to Investments in Convertible Bonds by Insurance Companies Circular (23 July 2004);
    – Representative Offices in China of Foreign Insurance Institutions Procedures from (1 March 2004);
    – Relevant to the Adjustment of the Clauses and Premium Rates etc. of Third-Party Liability Insurance for Motor Vehicles and Its Rider Urgent Circular (29 April 2004).
22. G. Xu, B. Cao and R. Mertl, 'Amending the Insurance Law: Long-term Policy or Expedient Measures?' *China Law & Practice*, Vol. 16 (1 December 2002).On 1 January 2006, the new Measures Governing the Insurance Clauses and Insurance Rates of Property Insurance Companies entered into force (promulgated on 23 November 2005); *China Economic News*, no. 10 (13 March 2006), p. 10.
23. Order of the State Council, no. 336.

regard to the insurance service. Under the regulation, foreign-funded insurance companies may be established in the form of joint venture insurance companies, wholly foreign-owned insurance companies, and branches of foreign insurance companies.[24]

II.C.   INSURANCE ADMINISTRATIVE RULES

The CIRC was given the mandate to implement reforms in the PRC insurance industry. Among other tasks,[25] one of the major mandates that the State Council delegated to CIRC is 'to formulate policies and rules concerning commercial insurance'.[26] This mandate is confirmed by Article 2 of the Rules on Administration of Insurance Companies,[27] which entitles the CIRC to supervise insurance companies by the authorization of the State Council.[28] Therefore, given the general nature of the laws and administrative regulations promulgated at a higher level, CIRC rules constitute the main body of applicable regulations for the insurance industry in China.[29] Due to its dual role as central legislative body and – simultaneously – the main enforcement agency in the insurance sector, the CIRC's dominant position as an administrative and regulatory body does raise some concerns in regard to its legitimacy under the common understanding of the rule of law.[30] Among the important rules enacted by the CIRC are the Administration of foreign-funded Insurance Companies Regulations Implementing Rules of 13 May 2004, and that took effect as of 15 June 2004.[31]

---

24. These Regulations were formulated to suit the requirements for opening up and economic development, to strengthen the supervision and administration of foreign-funded insurance companies, and to promote the healthy development of the insurance industry (art. 1). The Regulations specify two types of insurance companies, namely, equity joint venture and wholly foreign-owned companies; fix a minimum registered capital of RMB 200 million; and specify additional criteria, such as the requirement of being in the insurance business for at least 30 years, having had a representative office within China for at least two years, and so on.
25. The CIRC focuses on the regulation of the formation, division, takeover or dissolution of insurance companies; the examination and approval of policy terms, unfair competition among insurers, solvency and market behaviour of insurance companies; the use of funds by insurance companies; and the qualification of personnel nominated for senior managerial positions in the insurance industry.
26. See Notification on the Establishment of CIRC, (*Guofa*) [1998], no. 37.
27. Promulgated by CIRC on 13 May 2004 and effective as of 15 June 2004.
28. See Organic Law of the State Council (1982), Article 10.
29. The CIRC is responsible for the drafting of laws and regulations that regulate the insurance industry.
30. See the discussion in section IV.B.3.
31. These Regulations specify, for example, that the ratio of foreign capital in an equity joint venture life insurance company shall not exceed 50 per cent of the total share capital of the company and provides for additional specifications. See <www.clrsonline.com/clrsonline/ChinaLaw/showpage.asp?ok=English&id=3910>.

II.D.   Bifurcated Regulatory Regime: Domestic vs. Foreign

China's reform process and open-door policy have created a bifurcated legal system in which foreign-funded business in China is governed by a set of rules separate from those applicable to Chinese businesses. The logic of a bifurcated legal system is that, while foreign direct investments may foster the in-flow of capital, technologies and managerial expertise, the resulting increased competition could also impose threats to the national economy, particularly where those industries are still in a nascent stage. For these reasons, China's open door policy has been implemented with the bottom-line that foreign direct investment must only be allowed into the country to the extent that that investment enhances local competitiveness and fosters the independence of the national economy, but does not expose the infant Chinese domestic industry to excessive competition.

To achieve this balance, rules were promulgated, according to which foreign insurers are subject to restrictions in terms of ownership, business scope, geographic coverage and so on. Up to the point of China's WTO entry, foreign insurers on the waiting list for market entry complained that the CIRC's practices in implementing foreign-related special rules were arbitrary, bureaucratic and opaque. This made the insurance industry a sticking point in the overall negotiation process of China's entry into the WTO. Insurance-related commitments made by China in relation to its accession to the WTO[32] reflect the high value placed by the international community on expediting the opening of the insurance markets in China, including facilitating the licensing process, eliminating rules on product limitation and reduction of geographic restrictions.[33] China's WTO accession commitments, however, must be translated into national rules before the commitments can apply to foreign insurers' entrance and operation in China.[34] In any case, those areas in which WTO law applies regulations that differentiate between domestic and foreign competitors required justification under international law. Without this justification, international law will ultimately invalidate such a bifurcated regulatory order. Notably, many recent rules[35] issued by CIRC are concurrently applicable to both domestic and foreign funded insurers, indicating a process of consolidation in the regulatory

---

32. See the discussion in section III.B.
33. S.P. D'Arcy and H. Xia, 'Insurance and China's Entry into WTO', *Risk Management and Insurance Review*, vol. 6, issue 1, spring 2003, pp. 7–25.
34. On 11 December 2003, for example, the CIRC issued the Fulfilment of Relevant WTO Accession Commitments Notice, which permits foreign-invested property insurance companies to engage in all non-life insurance businesses, other than the statutory insurance businesses. Five cities, Fuzhou, Xiamen, Ningbo, Shenyang and Wuhan, are open to the outside for insurance business; see *China Law & Practice*, December 2003/January 2004, vol. 17, p. 10.
35. For example:

   – The Administration of Insurance Companies Provisions, promulgated on 13 May 2004 and implemented 15 June 2004

field. China's legal regime with respect to foreign insurers' activities will be the main subject of analysis in section IV.

III.   CHINA'S WTO OBLIGATIONS AND INSURANCE

The Final Agreement setting out the detailed terms on which China entered the WTO is found in some 900 pages of text, including the final Report of the Working Party[36] for the Accession of China;[37] the Protocol of Accession of China and the Annexes; and the Schedule of China's specific commitments on market access for goods and services (service schedule). These three legal documents are interrelated and interconnected, whereby the Accession Protocol is the leading document.[38]

Among the WTO multilateral agreements which China accepted during its accession negotiation process to the WTO, the General Agreement of Trade in Services (GATS)[39] is the most relevant one for the insurance industry. This agreement covers all sectors of services[40] and provides no exception for financial services. In addition, as part of GATS,[41] the Annex on Financial Services[42] and

---

- the Administration of Insurance Assets Management Companies Tentative Provisions, promulgated on 25 April 2004 and implemented 1 June 2004;
- the Rules on Establishment of Reinsurance Companies, promulgated on 17 September 2002 and implemented the same date;
- the Administration of Utilization of Insurance Foreign Exchange Funds Outside China Provisions, promulgated on 9 August 2004 and implemented on the same date;
- the Administration Methods on Approval and Filing of Life Insurance Products Provisions, promulgated on 13 June 2004 and implemented 1 July 2004;
- Risk Control Guideline on Utilization of Insurance Funds (In Trial), promulgated on 28 April 2004 and effective as of 1 June 2004;
- the Administrative Rules on Solvency Margin and Regulatory Benchmarks of Insurance Companies, promulgated on 24 March 2003 and effective as of the same date.

36. The China Working Party was originally established under the General Agreement on Tariffs and Trade (GATT) in 1987 and in 1995 converted to a WTO Working Party. Membership in the Working Party was open to all interested WTO members.
37. The Working Party also monitored the bilateral negotiations China entered into with WTO members, to keep track of their progress and to ensure that all aspects of China's trade policies were dealt with.
38. D. Arner et al., *Financial Regulation and the WTO: Liberalization and Restructuring in China Two Years Post-Accession*, EAIEL Policy Paper no. 1 (March 2004).
39. In force since 1 January 1995.
40. GATS Article I: 3(b): ' "services" includes any service in any sector except services supplied in the exercise of governmental authority'.
41. GATS, Article XXIX provides that Annexes to the GATS are an integral part of the GATS. This makes the Annexes as legally binding as the GATS itself.
42. The Annex on Financial Services is one of the eight Annexes to the GATS, which form an integral part thereof. The Annex contains five paragraphs – 'Scope and Definition', 'Domestic Regulation', 'Recognition', 'Dispute Settlement' and 'Definitions' – and refers to the movement of natural persons supplying services.

the Second Annex on Financial Services[43] directly relate to financial services.[44] According to these GATS regulations[45] financial services encompass the following insurance related services:

- direct insurance, including co-insurance, for example, life and non-life;
- reinsurance and retrocession;
- insurance intermediation, such as brokerage and agency; and
- services auxiliary to insurance, such as consultancy, actuarial risk assessment and claim-settlement services.[46]

China's obligations under WTO law can be divided in two categories:

- general obligations in the area of all services; and
- insurance-specific commitments deriving from China's service schedule.

III.A.   GENERAL OBLIGATIONS

Within the framework of the WTO, the GATS provides for some general obligations in the area of all services, the most important of which concern the Most-Favoured-Nation Treatment (MFN), transparency, domestic regulation, judicial review, market access and national treatment.[47]

III.B.   CHINA'S INSURANCE SPECIFIC COMMITMENTS

Pursuant to its service schedule, China has agreed to a wide range of market-opening measures, effective in some cases from the date of accession, or spread over a maximum five-year period. These commitments to modify its relevant regulations in order to open up its insurance market for foreign insurance service providers mostly concern GATS supply mode 3 ('commercial presence'

---

43.   Unlike the Annex on Financial Services, the Second Annex on Financial Services concerns only the procedures for further negotiations on financial services commitments, leading to the 1995 interim agreement. The Annex, therefore, is only of historical interest.
44.   However, because the GATS is only a framework agreement, detailed commitments must be made through negotiations in particular sectors. Negotiations on financial services, however, did not finish with the completion of the Uruguay Round of negotiations in 1994. Only on 12 December 1997, did the negotiators concluded an agreement (what is known as the 'Financial Services Agreement') with specific commitments and the Most Favoured Nation Treatment (MFN).
45.   China has not made any statement in its service schedule in regard to the Understanding on Commitments in Financial Services, which requires higher degrees of financial services liberalization than the GATS itself; therefore, the Understanding is not binding on China.
46.   Annex on financial services, Section 5.
47.   For further discussion, see D. Arner, et al., *Financial Regulation and the WTO: Liberalization and Restructuring in China Two Years Post-Accession*, EAIEL Policy Paper no. 1 (March 2004).

in China), although other important undertakings apply with respect to GATS supply mode 1 ('cross-border supply' of insurance services).

III.B.1.   Form of Establishment

Upon China's WTO accession, foreign non-life insurers were permitted to establish their businesses in China as a branch or as a joint venture with up to 51 per cent foreign ownership, and within two years after China's accession,[48] the establishment of wholly foreign-owned subsidiaries was permitted.[49] The Catalogue for Guidance on foreign Investment in Industries[50] opened up the non-life insurance sector to wholly foreign-owned enterprises.

Upon China's WTO accession, foreign life insurers were permitted 50 per cent foreign ownership in a joint venture with a local partner of their choice.[51] In addition, the joint venture partners became entitled to agree freely on the terms of their contractual arrangement, provided the parties remained within the limits of the commitments contained in the service schedule. Important to note, however, is that no phase-out period is set out for the elimination of the 50 per cent local participation requirement in the life insurance sector.[52]

---

48. In other words, since 11 December 2003.
49. The following applies to brokerage of insurance of large scale commercial risks and broker-age of reinsurance and brokerage of international marine, aviation, and transport insurance and reinsurance: upon China's WTO accession, joint ventures with foreign equity no more than 50 per cent became permitted; within three years after China's accession – in other words, after 11 December 2004 – the maximum foreign equity share can be increased to 51 per cent; within five years after China's accession – in other words, after 11 December 2006 – wholly foreign owned subsidiaries will be permitted.
50. Passed 11 February 2002, and took effect 1 April 2002.
51. The *Catalogue for Guidance on Foreign Investment in Industries* enabled foreign stakes in life insurance companies up to 50 per cent.
52. Note that, under the GATS and its Schedule of Services Commitments, China is not obliged to extend national treatment to foreign insurance or any other service suppliers with respect to forms of business establishment. In this regard, foreign investors in most of China's service sectors can only establish 'foreign-invested enterprises', as defined in China's service schedule, to avail themselves of the many market access benefits that arise from China's WTO accession. Companies limited by shares are not included in this def-inition of 'foreign-invested enterprises' and are, therefore, apparently not eligible for any of the market access benefits. Because foreign insurers are not permitted to establish com-panies limited by shares, these insurers may find themselves operating at a distinct com-petitive disadvantage, particularly in regard to equity financing, organizational structure and business operations. In particular, foreign-funded insurance companies, unlike Chi-nese domestic insurers, will be barred from listing on the Shenzhen and Shanghai stock exchanges. In this regard, interesting to note is that the 2000 Insurance Companies Pro-visions, applicable to both domestic and foreign-funded insurers, specifically permit the establishment of companies limited by shares, including publicly listed companies; see Administration of Insurance Companies Provisions, art. 26. Domestic insurance compa-nies, therefore, are authorized to do what foreign-funded companies cannot do; see D. Lewis, www.clrsonline.com/clrsonline/ChinaLaw/howpage.asp?ok=English&id=3910. ...

On 11 December 2004 the China Insurance Regulatory Commission issued the Fulfilment of WTO Accession Commitments Notice, effective as of date of issue. Among other issues the Notice stipulates that the ratio of foreign investment shares for the establishment of equity joint insurance brokerages may be up to 51 per cent.[53] In addition, in its accession agreement, China agreed that foreign insurers handling large scale commercial risks, marine, aviation and transport insurance, and reinsurance were to be permitted 50 per cent foreign equity share in a joint venture upon accession, while these foreign insurers would be permitted to own 51 per cent three years after accession and establish as a wholly foreign-owned subsidiary five years after accession.

III.B.2.   Geographic Coverage

China has unequivocally committed to rolling back the stringent geographical restrictions previously imposed to foreign insurance providers operating in China. Such restrictions naturally resulted in a meagre market share for foreign providers. Upon China's WTO accession, foreign life and non-life insurers, and insurance brokers became permitted to provide services in five municipalities.[54] Within two years of China's accession,[55] foreign life and non-life insurers and insurance brokers received permission to provide services in an additional 10 municipalities.[56] Within three years of China's accession,[57] all geographic restrictions were reduced to the level applied to Chinese insurers, as well.[58]

III.B.3.   Business Scope

Upon China's WTO accession, foreign non-life insurers were permitted to provide 'master policy'[59] insurance of large scale commercial risks with no geographic restrictions. In accordance with MFN, foreign insurance brokers were

---

53. *China Law & Practice,* vol. 19 (March 2005), p. 9. The number of insurance brokerage firms has risen quickly in China in recent years, but these firms' business volume has, with a few exceptions, been anaemic. The China Insurance Regulatory Commission, therefore, will push consolidation in the insurance brokerages sector in 2006 and extend support to strong firms to foster an industry that incorporates insurance brokerages, surveyors and intermediaries. In sharp contrast to the case in other industries where the invasion of foreign investors is feared, those in the insurance brokerages sector, rather than panicking, actually welcome their arrival; see *China Economic News,* no. 9 (6 March 2006), p. 8.

54. Shanghai, Guangzhou, Dalian, Shenzhen and Foshan.

55. After 11 December 2003.

56. Beijing, Chengdu, Chongqing, Fuzhou, Suzhou, Xiamen, Ningbo, Shenyang, Wuhan and Tianjin.

57. After 11 December 2004.

58. On 11 December 2004 the China Insurance Regulatory Commission issued the *Fulfilment of WTO Accession Commitments Notice,* effective as of date of issue. Among other issues the Notice removed the geographical restrictions on establishment of foreign-invested insurance institutions; see *China Law & Practice,* vol. 19 (March 2005), p. 9.

59. A master policy is the policy that provides blanket coverage for the same legal person's property and liabilities located in separate places. A master policy can only be issued by

permitted to provide master policy coverage no later than Chinese brokers, under conditions no less favourable. In addition, foreign non-life insurers were permitted to provide insurance of enterprises abroad, as well as property insurance, related liability insurance and credit insurance of foreign-invested enterprises in China upon accession. Within two years of China's accession,[60] foreign non-life insurers received permission to provide the full range of non-life insurance services to both foreign and domestic clients.

Upon accession foreign insurers are permitted to provide individual – not group – insurance to foreigners and Chinese citizens. Within three years of accession, foreign insurers are permitted to provide health insurance, group insurance and pension, annuities insurance to foreigners and Chinese citizens. Upon accession, foreign insurers are permitted to provide reinsurance services for life and non-life insurance as a branch, joint venture, or wholly foreign-owned subsidiary, without geographic or quantitative restrictions on the number of licenses issued. In addition, restrictions concerning group insurance[61] and health insurance have been removed.[62]

On 11 December 2003, the China Insurance Regulatory Commission issued a Notice Fulfilment of Relevant WTO Accession Commitments which allows foreign-invested property insurance companies to engage in all non-life insurance businesses other than the statutory insurance businesses.[63]

On 1 December 2004 the CIRC promulgated the Administration of Insurance Agencies Provisions, effective 1 January 2005 which regulates the insurance agencies business within the territory of the PRC.[64]

---

the business department of an insurer's head office or that of its authorized province-level branch office. Other branches are not permitted to issue master policies.

60. After 11 December 2003.
61. At the beginning of 2005 AVIVA-COFCO Life Insurance Co., Ltd signed in Beijing group insurance policies with three Chinese enterprises. This was the first time for a foreign capital insurance company to sign group insurance policies in the Chinese mainland. AVIVA-COFCO Life Insurance is a joint venture life insurance company launched in early 2003 jointly by the China Cereals, Oils and Foodstuffs Corp and AVIVA of Britain. In line with the commitment to the WTO, China has opened its domestic group insurance market to foreign capital as of 11 December 2004. The CIRC approved the first group of foreign capital insurers, which include AVIVA-COFCO, to operate group insurance business; see *China Economic News*, no. 7 (21 February 2005), p. 3.
62. China's first specialized health insurance company – PICC Health Insurance Co., Ltd. – recently opened for business in Beijing. The company was initiated by five shareholders, in which PICC Holding holds 51 per cent state, DKV of Germany holds a 19 per cent stake and the remainder is held by three Chinese partners. PICC Health has announced that it will initially launch three insurance products, covering medical treatment, serious illness and accident; see *China Economic News*, no. 19 (23 May 2005), p. 4.
63. *China Law & Practice*, vol. 17 (December 2003/January 2004), p. 10.
64. Without the approval of the CIRC, no work unit or individual can engage in, or covertly engage in, insurance agency business within the territory of the PRC (art. 2). An insurance agency that takes the form of a partnership enterprise or a limited liability company shall have registered capital of no less than RMB 10 million (art. 9). The registered capital or capital contribution shall be increased by at least RMB 100,000 for every new insurance

III.B.4. License

China's WTO accession required that licenses were to be issued with no quantitative restrictions on foreign licenses or 'economic needs' test. Licenses must be awarded on the basis of prudential criteria only, which can only consider the soundness of the foreign insurance institutions, without reference to political factors, and must be applied in a non-discriminatory manner.[65] As a result, China is precluded from disallowing licensure or other activities of a foreign insurer on the basis of potential competition, even if the insurer might have a negative impact on Chinese domestic companies.

On 12 December 2001, the State Council promulgated the Administration of foreign-funded Insurance Companies Regulations, which took effect 1 February 2002. These Regulations specify two types of insurance companies, equity joint venture and wholly foreign-owned companies; fix a minimum registered capital of RMB 200 million; and additional criteria, such as being in insurance business for at least 30 years, having had a representative office within China for at least two years, and so on.[66]

---

agency branch or sub-branch, unless the registered capital or capital contribution has reached RMB 2 million (art. 16). Insurance agencies shall pay and deposit 20 per cent of the registered capital or capital contribution as guarantee funds or, alternatively, purchase professional liability insurance policies (art. 21). As on 1 January 2005, overseas-funded banks are able to act as agents of insurance products in the mainland in accordance with relevant regulations. The country's regulatory requirements call for a so-called 'one license for one site' regime, meaning an outlet can only act as an agent of insurance products when the local CBRC arm issues a License for Insurance Agent Services. Overseas-funded banks cannot promote and conduct insurance agent services at its outlets without this type of license or at other venues. A substantive breakthrough has occurred in spring 2005 in overseas-funded banks' efforts to serve as insurance banks in the mainland, with Hong Kong and Shanghai Banking Corporation Ltd. (HSBC) winning approval of the Shanghai arm of the CBRC to act as an agent for insurance products at three of its Shanghai branches; see *China Economic News*, no. 14 (18 April 2005), p. 4.

65. Previously, the process of licensing was influenced by various informal factors. Foreign insurers were required to demonstrate a long-term commitment to China, for example, by offering seminars, setting up research centres or investing in education institutions. The licenses granted were distributed evenly among the major nations with developed insurance markets to encourage diversification and benefit from a wide variety of technologies and experience. Consequently, when granting licenses, Chinese authorities aimed to meet China's foreign policy goals; see C. Ji and S. Thomas, *The Role of Foreign Insurance Companies in China's Emerging Insurance Industry: An FDI Case Study*, Conference on Financial Sector Reform in China (11–13 September 2001); Y. Shen, *China's Insurance Market: Opportunity, Competition and Market Trend*, The Geneva Paper on Risk and Insurance, vol. 25, no. 3 (July 2000), pp. 335–355.

66. However, the Regulations go further than China's WTO commitments and impose additional conditions on foreign insurers (art. 8 [4]–[7]). But these additional criteria do not seem to be particularly onerous and may, therefore, be justified under the 'prudential carve-out' exception of Article 2 of the *Annex on Financial Services of GATS*. See D. Lewis, <www.clrsonline.com/clrsonline/ChinaLaw/howpage.asp?ok=English&id=3910 . . .>.

In May 2004, the CIRC issued as the final implementing rules the Detailed Rules on the Regulations for the Administration of foreign-Invested Insurance Companies. These new rules lower capital requirements for national licenses from RMB 500 million to RMB 200 million, and for branch offices from RMB 50 million to RMB 20 million.

Today, the main prerequisites for establishing a foreign insurance institution are as follows:

- – The investor must be a foreign insurance company with more than 30 years of establishment experience in a WTO Member State;
- – The institution must have had a representative office for two consecutive years in China; and
- – The institution must have total assets of more than US$ 5 billion at the end of the year prior to submitting the application, with the exception of insurance brokers.[67]

Apparently, China puts a great deal of emphasis on a foreign insurer's size and history in business, rather than on the insurer's actual performance. The market, therefore, opened up only for international giants, and smaller and younger insurers were essentially shunned.

III.B.5.   National Treatment

The scope of GATS national treatment is limited in to those sectors inscribed in each Member's Schedule.[68] As a result, national treatment is inapplicable to service sectors not covered by a Member's Schedule; therefore, one Member of the WTO may take discriminatory measures against services and service suppliers of any other Member in those reserved sectors, without violation of the national treatment rule embodied in GATS Article XVII.

As horizontal commitments, which apply to all financial services, China made the following commitments: First, China permitted companies to establish foreign-capital enterprises (wholly-foreign-owned enterprises), joint venture enterprises, branches and representative offices. Second, the land in the People's Republic of China is state-owned. Use of land by enterprises and individuals is subject to maximum term limitations, such as 50 years or 70 years. Third, managers, executives and specialists as senior employees of a representative office, branch or subsidiary in China shall be permitted entry for a period of time.

---

67. At the time of China's WTO accession, insurance brokers had to have total assets in excess of USD 500 million. Within one year after accession (in other words, after 11 December 2002), they must have had total assets of more than USD 400 million. Within two years after accession (in other words, after 11 December 2003), they must have total assets of more than USD 300 million. Within four years after accession (namely, after 11 December 2005), they must have total assets of more than USD 200 million.
68. See GATS Article XVII:1.

In regard to specific commitments in the insurance sector – apart from the restrictions concerning foreign ownership – China excluded the engagement of foreign insurance institutions in the statutory insurance business.[69] In addition, full national treatment should apply since 1 January 2005.

IV.   CHINA'S INSURANCE LEGAL REGIME IN THE
        CONTEXT OF ITS WTO OBLIGATIONS

The 15 year-long negotiation process with China resulted in China's unprecedented commitment to open and liberalize its economy and to offer a more-predictable environment for trade and foreign investment in accordance with WTO rules. Among other areas, China committed to a gradual opening of both its life and non-life insurance sector. Membership in the WTO has brought with it the huge burden of transposing China's many commitments into national laws. This process, which China has undergone in a very impressive way, involves a broad-ranging programme of post-WTO accession legislative innovation. Over the past four years, the country has revised more than 2,300 national laws and regulations that ran counter to WTO rules. Although enforcement remains difficult, China has made significant efforts towards bringing its legal regime up to its WTO obligation.[70]

To date, China has successfully implemented many of its WTO commitments, but a significant number of problems arose in the first years of China's membership. Therefore, a review of China's current insurance legal regime in the light of its WTO obligations indicates positive developments but also reveals certain shortcomings regarding how China's WTO obligations and regulatory implementation is shaping the insurance industry.

IV.A.   Legal Developments in the Call for WTO Compliance

Shortly after acceding to the WTO the CIRC issued several new insurance regulations, including ones directed at the regulation of foreign insurance companies. These Regulations on Administration of foreign Funded Insurance

---

69. On 11 December 2003, the China Insurance Regulatory Commission issued a *Notice Fulfilment of Relevant WTO Accession Commitments,* which enables foreign-invested property insurance companies to engage in all non-life insurance businesses other than the statutory insurance businesses; see *China Law & Practice*, vol. 17 (December 2003/January 2004), p. 10.
70. For example, as of September 2002, some 2,300 government regulations were reviewed and either amended or abolished by over 30 governmental agencies under the State Council; see C. Wei and M.G. DeSombre and H. Zhang, 'China's Post/WTO Reforms in Financial Services: Achievements and Challenges', *China Law & Practice* (1 March 2003); S. Shen, 'WTO and China's Legal System', in M. Matsushita and D. Ahn (eds.), *WTO and East Asia: New Perspectives* (London, 2004), p. 267.

Companies (foreign Insurance Regulation)[71] set forth stipulations regarding the forms of establishment, the market entry prerequisites, the foreign equity percentage licensing procedures and the business scopes. These regulations implemented many of China's WTO commitments, but also created problems particularly in three critical areas: capitalization requirements, transparency and branching.[72]

In 2004 the CIRC enacted revised rules – known as the Implementing Rules for the Regulation on foreign-invested Insurance Companies –[73] which streamlined application processes, shortened approval times and lowered capital requirements for branching.[74] These rules complemented the Administration of Insurance Companies Provisions, which were replaced in 2004 by new provisions.[75] These new legislative act, which introduced in some respects stricter guidelines, relating, for example, to capital adequacy ratios, consist of seven parts that cover insurance organizations, insurance business operations, insurance clauses, insurance premium rates, insurance funds and solvency of insurance companies and supervision and inspection. On the other hand, insurance companies were also given more flexibility in regard to internal decisions on the amount of premiums and the wording of insurance clauses, which must still be reported, but no longer must be approved by the CIRC.[76] In addition, administrative regulations on insurance brokerage,[77] agencies,[78]

---

71. On 12 December 2001, the State Council promulgated the *Administration of Foreign-funded Insurance Companies Regulations*, effective as of 1 February 2002). These Regulations were formulated to suit the requirements for opening up and economic-development, to strengthen the supervision and administration of foreign-funded insurance companies, and to promote the healthy development of the insurance industry (art. 1). The Regulations specify two types of insurance companies: equity joint venture and wholly foreign-owned companies; fix a minimum registered capital of RMB 200 million; and additional criteria, such as being in insurance business for at least 30 years, having had a representative office within China for at least two years and so on.

72. See section IV.B, later in this chapter.

73. Promulgated on 13 May 2004 and effective as of 15 June 2004.

74. These Implementing Rules further maintain the minimum registered capital of foreign-invested insurance companies at RMB 200 million. Another substantive requirement reconfirmed is the requirement that the company must have operated a Representative Office in China for at least two years. Novel is the inclusion of detailed requirements for the setting up of branch offices – additional registered capital of RMB 20 million is required for each branch office. In addition, each office must be registered with the provincial-level CIRC in which the office is established, and can operate only in that province; see <www.wjnco.com/webnews/view.asp?id=200408231147495616>.

75. *Administration of Insurance Companies Provisions*, promulgated 13 May 2004 and effective as of 15 June 2004; see <www.clrsonline.com/clrsonline/ChinaLaw/showpage.asp?id=3910/2004.05.13(1 ... >.

76. See <www.wjnco.com/webnews/view.asp?id=200408231147495616>.

77. Provisions on Insurance Brokerages, promulgated by CIRC on 16 November 2001 and implemented 1 January 2002, revised on 1 November 2004 and effective as of 1 January 2005.

78. Provisions on Insurance Agencies, promulgated by CIRC on 16 November 2001 and implemented 1 January 2002, revised on 1 November 2004 and implemented as of 1 January 2005.

assessors[79] and reinsurance companies[80] were released. The Regulations were issued to implement China's WTO obligations. The following is an evaluation of how the system established by the Chinese Government complies with the requirements of a WTO membership.

In terms of geographic coverage, China has fulfilled its commitment to open up enlarged scopes of cities for foreign insurers. The CIRC has even lifted particular geographic restrictions applicable to foreign life insurers ahead of schedule.[81] As of the end of 2004,[82] foreign insurers are permitted to underwrite province-wide business from any branch in a given province and all the geographic restrictions were lifted,[83] so that by the end of October 2005, 44 foreign insurance companies had opened 100 operational units in China.[84]

In terms of business scope, foreign non-life insurers were permitted to carry on large-scaled commercial business and master policy upon accession as being promised in the Service Schedule.[85] foreign non-life insurers have been permitted to underwrite the full range of non-life policies for all clients since the end of 2003. In addition, since the end of 2003, foreign non-life insurers can conduct short-term health and casualty insurance business,[86] and since the end of 2004,

---

79. Provisions on Insurance Assessors, promulgated by CIRC on 16 November 2001 and implemented as of 1 January 2002.

80. *Provisions on the Establishment of Reinsurance Companies*, promulgated by CIRC on 17 September 2002. These provisions make foreign investment in reinsurance companies in China legally for the first time. The new Provisions apply to the establishment of reinsurance companies generally, making no distinction between China domestic and foreign-invested reinsurance companies. Nevertheless, the special regulations governing foreign investment in insurance companies in China apply as special laws, such as the *Foreign Insurance Regulations*. In addition, China's relevant WTO commitments will also apply to foreign-invested reinsurance companies in certain circumstances. Foreign insurance companies may establish joint venture reinsurance companies or wholly foreign-owned reinsurance companies, provided that they meet the requirements set out in China's Schedule of Commitments for WTO accession. Such requirements have already been implemented by the government in the Foreign Insurance Regulations with respect to the establishment experience (30 years), existing representative office presence in China (two years) and a level of capitalization (a minimum of USD 5 billion). Additional prudential requirements are compensation capability, the existence of a good insurance regulatory system in the home country, and so on; see <www.clrsonline.com/clrsonline/ChinaLaw/new/showpage.asp?ok=Editorial&id=391 . . .>.

81. In early 2002, CIRC approved life insurance operations for U.S. insurers in Beijing, Suzhou and Tianjin, two years before China had committed to do so in its Service Schedule. In 2003, CIRC approved life insurance operations for a U.S. insurer in Chongqing; nearly one year ahead of schedule. Other foreign life insurers must now be provided the same access to those cities; see the *2003 Report to Congress on China's WTO Compliance*, United States Trade Representative, p. 58.

82. *Circular of the Question of Operational Regions of Insurance Companies*, promulgated by CIRC on 2 September 2003.

83. *Proclamation on Implementing WTO Commitments*, promulgated by CIRC on 11 December 2004, which took effect as of the same date.

84. *China Economic News*, no. 1 (2 January 2006), p. 6.

85. Regulations on Administration of Foreign Funded Insurance Companies, Article 15.

86. 1995 Insurance Law, Article 92.

foreign life insurers can offer health, group, and pension/annuity insurance to both foreign and Chinese clients.[87] However, the general prohibition on simultaneous cross-engagement in both life and non-life business is still in place,[88] which also applies to the domestic insurers.[89]

With respect to national treatment, the requirement on non-life, personal accident and health insurance business to reinsure 20 per cent of the primary risk with China Re was reduced to 15 per cent on 11 December 2002 and further reduced to 10 per cent on 11 December 2003 and to five per cent on 11 December 2004, which is fully in compliance with China's WTO concession.

Year-end 2004 was a critical point, because all geographic restrictions had to be phased out and group insurance and annuities markets had to be fully opened up. To implement those changes in its insurance regime in accordance with its WTO commitments, China enacted a series of rules and regulations. In connection with the lifting of all geographical restrictions, some interested WTO member states also brought related issues, such as internal branching and business expansion with existing license under focus during the last round of transitional review on China's implementation efforts.[90]

In the framework of this market-opening process, the Chinese authorities approved the establishment by about 40 foreign insurance companies of 100 insurance operational entities in China, including life insurers, property insurers and re-insurers up to the year-end 2005.[91] Given their more advanced managing skills, product quality and service-oriented business mentality, it comes as no surprise that the market share of foreign-funded insurance companies experienced a faster growth than their local counterparts.[92] According to the CIRC:

> '[T]he growth rate of foreign-funded insurers was 100–200 per cent higher than that of domestic insurers. Compared to the same period of 2003, during the first half of 2004 the insurance premium of (foreign-funded) property insurance companies and life insurers increased 47.1 and 51.2 per cent, respectively. In the same period, the insurance revenue of all property and life insurers in China increased by only 23 per cent and 6.5 per cent, respectively'.[93]

---

87. *Proclamation on Implementing WTO Commitments*, promulgated by CIRC on 11 December 2004, which took effect as of the same date.
88. *Regulations on Administration of Foreign Funded Insurance Companies* Article 16.
89. Insurance Law, Article 92.
90. WTO, S/FIN/M/43, pp. 6–7; WTO, S/FIN/M/47, pp. 5–8; see Section IV.B, later in this chapter.
91. Ibid, p. 3.
92. In Shanghai and Guangzhou, market share of foreign insurers increased from approximately two per cent prior to China's accession to the WTO, to approximately 17 per cent and eight per cent as of 22 December 2002, respectively; see C. Wei, M.G. DeSombre and H. Zhang, 'China's Post/WTO Reforms in Financial Services: Achievements and Challenges', *China Law & Practices* (1 March 2003).
93. WTO, S/FIN/M/47, p. 4.

In addition, important to note is that China implemented those WTO commitments, which allow foreign-invested insurance enterprises to provide health, group and pension/annuities insurance to both foreign and Chinese clients, on schedule.[94]

IV.B. LINGERING ISSUES

Although China has made significant progress in implementing its WTO commitments especially in the area of insurance services – it must also be acknowledged that, in some areas, China's implementation efforts have lacked the necessary degree of commitment and coordination. While some of these concerns are specific to China's accession agreement, others seem to arise out of a particular reluctance of China to embrace key underlying tenets of WTO principles.

IV.B.1. Licensing

The conditions under which a country grants licenses to foreign-funded insurance providers are a major part of WTO market access rights. In its WTO Schedule, China has agreed to award licenses solely on the basis of prudential criteria (soundness of the foreign insurance institution), without reference to political factors and in a non-discriminatory manner. For China, the implementation of these commitments meant a significant change in the country's insurance policy.

China's WTO commitments in regard to the issue of licenses to foreign-funded insurance providers were implemented by the Regulations for the Administration of foreign-funded Insurance Companies and the Detailed Rules on the Regulations for the Administration of foreign-funded Insurance Companies. Due to the enactment of these rules and regulations, the licensing procedure became simpler and faster. This represents a significant improvement and a real step forward towards an open insurance market in China. However, it seems that the full benefit of these procedures has yet to be realized,[95] in particular due to the following difficulties:

IV.B.1.a. *High Capital Requirements*

Even after the elapsing of the phase-out period by the end of 2004, the minimum registered capital, which is required for the establishment of a foreign-funded insurance company, remains RMB 200 million,[96] 20 per cent of which is

---

94. See also D. Jian, 'Reform of pension insurance steps into "minefield" ', *China Economic News*, no. 3, 16 January 2006, p. 7.
95. USCC.gov/hearing, p. 103.
96. *Regulations on Administration of Foreign Funded Insurance Company*, Article 7.

required to be placed in a bank designated by CIRC as guaranteed fund that may not be used for any purpose other than to pay off debts during liquidation procedures.[97] In addition, the working capital of foreign insurance companies is subject to the same minimal requirements. Although lower now than previously, China's capitalization requirements remain high and prudentially probably unjustifiable and may continue to restrict market entry for foreign insurance service suppliers.

In addition, a foreign-funded insurance company must increase its capital by RMB 20 million for each new branch that the company intends to establish, until the company's registered capital reaches the amount of RMB 500 million.[98] These capital requirements are extremely burdensome, particularly in light of the fact that foreign-funded insurance companies – such as Chinese companies – may not carry out business across the border of provinces, and therefore must set up new branches to write insurance in other provinces.[99]

Given the size and scope of China's insurance market, such unusually high capitalization requirements[100] are a source of concern in light of national treatment and market-access commitments. Most of the WTO member States have expressed concern that these capital requirements restrict market access in China in a manner that violates relevant GATS provisions.[101]

IV.B.1.b.   *Lengthy and Burdensome Licensing Procedure*

Still, applying for an insurance license in China is a multi-tier process that may invite uncertainty and delay. Application consists of a three-step process, which lasts roughly for a two year period.[102] This multi-tier licensing process applies not only to the initial establishment in China, but also to the establishing of branches in additional provinces, which can last roughly 9 months.[103] Although this licensing procedure applies to domestic insurance companies at equal

---

97. Article 13, Ibid.
98. *Implementation Rules of the Regulation on Administration of Foreign Funded Insurance Company*, Article 28, promulgated by CIRC on 15 March 2004 and implemented 15 June 2004.
99. Ibid, Article 27.
100. China's capital requirements are much higher than those of other populous countries with no less an interest in preserving a healthy insurance market and they limit therefore the ability of foreign insurers to enter China's market significantly; see the *2003 Report to Congress on China's WTO Compliance*, United States Trade Representative, p. 57.
101. WTO, S/FIN/M/37, pp. 7–8; WTO, S/FIN/M/47. pp. 5–8.
102. The three steps are:
    1. preliminary application, in which CIRC has up to six-months to decide whether to approve the application;
    2. set-up of the company, in which the applicant has one year in which to complete the task before submitting the official application to establish the company; and
    3. registration of the company.

    See *Regulation on Administration of Foreign Funded Insurance Company*, Articles 9–12.
103. Ibid, Articles 30–33.

terms, one has to point out that these requirements have much more restrictive effects on foreign insurers than on domestic ones, as the latter generally dispose already over a widespread national network. Consequently, the lengthy application procedure continues to adversely affect full consummation of market expectation of foreign insurers, despite the fact that all geographic restrictions were technically phased out by the end of 2004.

In May 2004, the CIRC issued the Detailed Rules on the Regulations for the Administration of foreign-invested Insurance Companies which streamlined licensing application procedures and shortened approval times, although some procedures remained unclear.[104] In particular, the new rules did not adequately address branching rights where an often opaque and confusing regulatory framework leaves foreign companies vulnerable to discriminatory treatment of their applications for new branches in additional provinces. It seems that authorities are allowing domestic insurance companies to license new branches concurrently, whereas foreign companies' new licenses are approved only consecutively.[105] Only permitting concurrent branching of insurance companies in multiple provinces would ensure a level playing field. Therefore, it is fair to say that the lengthy licensing procedure does create entry barriers for foreign insurer to further expand their business in China.

Bearing these difficulties in mind, many potential strategic investors[106] opt to make strategic investment in domestic insurance companies, instead of obtaining license to set up an initial or second branch in China. This type of strategic investment provides at least two benefits.

First, because the investee domestic insurance company remains a 'Chinese' company, the investee is not subject to the locality and scope of business restrictions currently applicable to joint venture insurance companies or foreign branches.

Second, this type of investment permits foreign insurers to have an interest in both life and non-life business at the same time, while a joint venture or a branch can only write either of the insurance.

Strategic investments, however, in a domestic insurance company are subject to equity limits rules, in other words, the aggregate foreign ownership in the

---

104. A good example of speeding up the approval process is the Representative Offices in China of Foreign Insurance Institutions Procedures, in which the CIRC is required to make a decision of whether to approve or disapprove an application for the establishment of a representative office within 20 days; see *China Law & Practice*, vol. 18 (February 2004), p. 6.
105. US-China Business Council (2005).
106. In reported cases, such as Millea Asia and Tokyo Marine and Fire Insurance in taking stakes in Sino Life Insurance; Zurich Insurance, International Finance Corp., Meiji Life and Nederlandse FMO in taking stakes in New China Life; ACE INA, ACE Tempest and ACE US in taking stakes in Huatai Insurance; Winterthur Life, Bank Leu, GIC, Softbank, International Finance Corp. in taking stakes in Taikang Life; Goldman Sachs, Morgan Stanley, HSBC in taking stakes in Ping An Insurance; see W.S. Chong, 'Insurers Find Strategic Path for China Investment', *International Financial Law Review*, vol. 22, issue 9, (September 2003), pp. 56–57.

target company must be less than 25 per cent,[107] and a single foreign investor –
including the investor's associated companies – must not take more than 20 per
cent of the shares of the target company.[108]

IV.B.2.   Transparency Obligations

Transparency and fair regulatory processes are absolutely vital in order for
cross-border trade and investment in services to flourish, because all countries
traditionally tend to regulate services very highly. Therefore, the commitment
to transparency is among the most important factors of China's WTO obligations.[109] Lack of transparency creates an uncertain regulatory environment
for companies attempting to conduct business in China and can, therefore, act
as a significant non-tariff barrier to trade. While China's transparency commitments in many ways require a profound historical shift, China has made
important strides to improve transparency and predictability to business dealing across a wide range of national and provincial authorities.[110]

Improvements seem to be necessary especially with regards to:

– the obligation of notification of all laws, regulations and other measures
  which affect trade in services;[111]
– the proper functioning of enquiry points, which China has the obligation
  to establish and which shall answer requests for information on all laws
  and regulations within 30 days;[112]

---

107. *Regulation on Insurance Company*, Article 45.
108. Ibid, Article 43.
109. In a survey made by the US-China Business Council among US companies in 2005 trans-
      parency ranked as the third-most-important issue for their business in China, up from
      sixth the previous year; see The US-China Business Council, *China's WTO Implemen-
      tation: An Assessment of China's Fourth Year of WTO Membership* (Federal Register,
      September 2005), pp. 44, 714–44 and 715.
110. China's Ministry of Commerce (MOFCOM) remains most notable for its impressive
      moves toward adopting WTO transparency norms. However, many other ministries and
      agencies continue to resist the changes called for by China's WTO obligations; see The
      US-China Business Council, 'China's WTO Implementation: An Assessment of China's
      Fourth Year of WTO Membership', *Federal Register*, 14 September 2005, pp. 44, 714–44,
      715.
111. Because the transparency obligation runs through every aspect of trade in insurance ser-
      vices, relevant laws, regulations, rules or other measures to be made public should not be
      narrowed down to market access; this issue, therefore, was raised by some WTO Members
      during the transnational review in the WTO, particularly by the EU.
112. Another important transparency commitment requires China to establish enquiry points,
      where any WTO member or foreign company or individual may obtain information. To
      comply with this obligation, China established a WTO Enquiry and Notification Cen-
      tre, now operated by MOFCOM's Department of WTO Affairs, in January 2002. Other
      ministries and agencies have also established formal or informal, subject-specific enquiry
      points. Since the creation of these various enquiry points, foreign companies have generally
      found them to be responsive and helpful, and have generally received timely replies. In addi-
      tion, some ministries and agencies have created websites to provide answers to frequently

- China's obligation to invite – within a 'reasonable period' – comments from the public before implementing a new law or regulation;[113] and
- China's obligation to provide for translation of 'all laws, regulations and other measures' which affect trade in services or others, into one or more of the official languages of the WTO not later than 90 days after they are implemented or enforced[114] and to publish these laws and so on in an official journal.[115]

However, the WTO's requirement of transparency does not end here. Transparency also requires that judicial decisions and judgements having a bearing on trade issues be published so as to allow foreign governments and businessmen prompt knowledge.[116]

IV.B.3. Rule by Law vs. Rule of Law

Embedded in the legal development of China's post-reform era was the idea that laws must be used to strengthen the state's ability to govern a country of a growing complexity that is resulting from its economic reforms. In other words, the Chinese concept of the law is conceived and operates as an instrument that is used to carry out and consolidate institutional, primarily economic, changes according to predetermined policy.[117] This Chinese understanding of rule by law – rather than Western rule of law – has formed the mind-set that presides over the entire exercise of WTO accession and implementation.

---

asked questions, as well as to provide further guidance and information; see The US-China Business Council, 'China's WTO Implementation: As Assessment of China's Fourth Year of WTO Membership', *Federal Register*, 14 September 2005, pp. 44, 714–44, 715.

113. For example, China did not publicly issue its draft revisions to the 1994 auto-policy Guiding Rule and did not provide an opportunity for foreign companies to comment; see <www.uscc.gov/hearing/20.PDF>, p. 85.

114. *China's Working Party Report*, para. 334.

115. In its WTO accession agreement, China committed to establish or designate an official journal dedicated to the publication of all laws, regulations and other measures pertaining to or affecting trade in goods, services, TRIPS or the control of foreign exchange. China also committed to publish this journal on a regular basis and to make copies of all issues of this journal readily available to enterprises and individuals. China has yet to establish or designate an official journal for this purpose. Rather, China currently relies on multiple channels, including ministry websites, newspapers and a variety of journals, to provide information on trade-related measures. The establishment or designation of a single journal would greatly enhance the ability of WTO members to track the drafting, issuance and implementation of trade-related measures; see the US-China Business Council, 'China's WTO Implementation: An Assessment of China's Fourth Year of WTO Membership', *Federal Register* (14 September 2005), pp. 44, 714–44, 715.

116. S. Shen, 'WTO and China's Legal System', in: M. Matsushita and D. Ahn (eds.), *WTO and East Asia: New Perspectives* (London 2004), p. 283.

117. Z. Yongnian, 'From Rule by Law to Rule of Law? A Realistic View of China's Legal Development', *China Perspectives*, no. 25 (September–October 1999), pp. 31–34; D.J. Lewis, 'China Law Guru Rules Out "Level Playing Field" ', *China Law & Practice* (April 1996), pp. 10–12.

In its WTO accession agreement, China committed to apply, implement and administer its laws, regulations and other measures relating to trade in goods and services in a uniform and impartial manner. In support of these commitments, China agreed to establish an internal review mechanism to investigate and address cases of non-uniform application of laws based on information provided by companies and individuals.[118] China also agreed to establish tribunals for the review of all administrative actions relating to the implementation of laws, regulations, rules and judicial decisions relating to the implementation of trade-related matters. Although China has taken steps to improve the quality of its judges[119] and in October 2002 the Supreme People's Court issued *Rules on Certain Issues Related to Hearing in International Trade Administrative Cases.*[120] It would be simplistic to assume that the implementation of China's WTO obligation is merely a matter of making and revising laws, training lawyers and judges and building up China's legal infrastructure. The daunting challenge presented by China's WTO accession is to reposition the government in the checks and balances of state powers.

WTO law requires not only transparency and accessibility of law, but also calls for an independent judiciary review[121] and for 'uniform, impartial and reasonable' administration of the law.[122] As recent policy moves show, China is taking notice of this problem and has started to take corrective measures.[123] Nevertheless, any real impact of the law on the regulatory style of the CIRC,

---

118. In 2002, China established an internal review mechanism, now overseen by MOFCOM's Department of WTO Affairs, to handle such cases. The actual working of this mechanism still remains unclear (The US-China Business Council, China's WTO Implementation: As Assessment of China's Fourth Year of WTO Membership, 14 September 2005, Federal Register, pp. 44, 714–44, 715).

119. For example, in 1999, the Supreme People's Court began requiring judges to be appointed based on merits and educational background and experience.

120. See <www.ustr.gov/ . . . /2004/2004_National_Trade_Estimate/2004_NTE_Report/asset_upload_file218_4743.pdf>.

121. Protocol of Accession, Article 2(D)1:

    'China shall establish or designate and maintain tribunals, contact points and procedures for the prompt review of all disputes relating to the implementation of laws, regulations, judicial decisions and administrative rulings of general application . . . Such tribunals shall be impartial and independent of the agencies entrusted with administrative enforcement. . . .'

122. Protocol of Accession, Article 2(A)3:

    'China shall administer in a uniform, impartial and reasonable manner all its laws, regulations, rules, decrees, directives, administrative guidance, policies and other measures . . . pertaining to or affecting trade in goods, services, trade-related aspects of intellectual property rights or the control of foreign exchange'.

123. A case in point is the adoption of the Law of Administrative Licensing, approved by the National People's Congress's Standing Committee on 27 August 2003 and which took effect 1 July 2004, which aims to restrict the power of government departments and to introduce a just and transparent, clean and efficient administrative system with standardized practice and good coordination. In addition, the CIRC has enacted supplement rule – Implementing Rules for Administrative Licensing by CIRC, promulgated by the CIRC

if any, will come only in the long term; the idea of judicial review is gaining acceptance only slowly.[124] Eventually, the real acid test of China's commitment to rule of law remains with the future position of the Communist Party and its claim to have the final word in ruling the country.[125]

IV.C.   RECENT REGULATORY TRENDS: DEREGULATION AND
             CONSOLIDATION

Despite the frustration of foreign participant in terms of less fluid than expected opening,[126] the market does present some progress in deregulation as a direct consequence of various WTO obligations. According to the 1995 Insurance Law, once an insurer is licensed by the CIRC to do business in China, the CIRC continues to closely monitor that insurer's operation. The CIRC approves every branch office, every change in the name of the company, the amount of capital, business premise, scope of business and every change of those investors who hold more than 10 per cent of the shares.[127] In addition, the CIRC decides the basic insurance clauses and premium rates for major types of commercial insurance.[128]

It seems obvious that this direct involvement of the CIRC in the daily business of insurance companies does not support the cultivation of a market-based insurance industry. It is another positive result of China's accession to the WTO that the country is accelerating the deregulation process required to meet the pressing need for preparing the major local insurance companies for a more competitive marketplace; a reversal, thus, from a formerly micro-managing style of regulatory activities is underway. An overemphasis on bureaucratic monitoring of the internal operations of insurance companies has been shifted to more market-oriented and policy-based regulation.[129] This

on 3 June 2004 and effective as of 1 July 2004 – to put its licensing activities under the surveillance of the Law of Administrative Licensing.

124. S. Shen, 'WTO and China's Legal System', in: M. Matsushita and D. Ahn (eds.), *WTO and East Asia: New Perspectives* (London, 2004), p. 281.

125. It seems obvious that the major obstacle lies in the path of implementation of these commitments. The links between the courts and administrative agencies and the defects in the legal system – low professional level of judges, independence of individual judges, corruption, local protectionism, but above all interference with the work of courts by government and party officials and so on – all seriously dilute the state capacity of China's institutions to meet this rule of law standards.

126. D. Pilla, 'Open for Business: Ever so Slowly, China's Market Takes Shape as Regulatory Rules Solidify', *Best's Review* (1 May 2004).

127. 1995 Insurance Law, Articles 74, 79 and 81.

128. 1995 Insurance Law, Article 106. A recent example is the *Working Guidelines on Standardization of Personal Insurance Policies (Trial Implementation* (3900/05.11.18), promulgated by the CIRC on 18 November 2005.

129. G. Xu, B. Cao and R.L. Mertl, 'Amending the Insurance Law: Long-Term Policy or Expedient Measures' 'China *Law & Practice*', vol. 18 (1 December 2002).

change in approach has been achieved through two legal amendments. Only insurance policy clauses and premium rates for policy-mandated insurance and new types of life insurance products require preapproval from the CIRC, while clauses and rates for other insurance products will only need to be filed for record.[130] As a result, and as can also be seen in other financial service sectors, more emphasis is put on the prudential regulation of institutions on an ongoing basis, rather than on merely placing access control at the market entrance.[131]

Market deregulation is also seen in the existence of broadened investment channels. The starting points for fund operations by Chinese insurers are a handful of instruments such as bank deposits, corporate bonds, state debentures and investment funds. Limitation on investment channels led to decreasing investment yield and inhibited the industry's development, calling for greater market liberalization measures. Also in this area, recent policy moves have demonstrated a more liberal horizon and practical approach, allowing insurance companies to invest in subordinated bank loan and convertible corporate bonds,[132] directly in stock markets,[133] treasury bonds, financial bonds and so on.[134]

Along the line of this deregulation process, rules governing foreign and domestic insurers are exhibiting a trend of consolidation. Numerous

---

130. Article 107, Insurance Law; Administration on Approval and Filing of Life-insurance Products Provisions, promulgated by CIRC on 30 June 2004 and effective as of 1 July 2004. This new policy grants insurance companies greater latitude to compete through innovation and price advantages.

131. Legislation has been put in place, therefore, in regard to the following for the sake of industry safety and policyholder protection, with no efforts spared:

   – solvency margins and regulatory benchmarks: see *Administrative Rules on Solvency Margin and Regulatory Benchmarks of Insurance Companies*, promulgated by the CIRC on 24 March 2003 and effective as of the same date;
   – to bring the risk management of insurance companies under prudential measures: see *Regulations in regard to reserve funds – Interim Measures on Provisions for Non-life Insurance Business of Insurance Company*, promulgated by the CIRC on 15 December 2004 and effective as of 15 January 2005;
   – safeguard funds: *Provisions on Insurance Safeguard Funds*, promulgated by the CIRC on 23 December 2004 and effective as of 1 January 2005;
   – risk control on fund application: see *Interim Risk Control Guidelines on Utilization of Insurance Funds*, promulgated by the CIRC on 28 April 2004 and effective as of 1 June 2004.

132. See *Circular of CIRC Baojianfa* (2004), no. 77, promulgated on 25 June 2004 and effective as of the same date; *Administration of Utilization of Insurance Foreign Exchange Funds Outside China*, promulgated on 9 August 2004 and effective as of the same date; *Issues Relevant to the Stock Investment and Trading of Insurance Institutional Investors Circular*, issued 17 February 2005 and effective as of the date of issue.

133. The *Interim Provisions on Insurance Institutional Investors' Stock Investment*, jointly promulgated by the CIRC and CSRC on 24 October 2004 and effective as of the same date.

134. *Provisional Measures Governing Bonds Investment by Insurance Institutional Investors*, promulgated and put into force on 17 August 2005.

regulations and rules[135] are applicable to both locals and foreigners, with a general reservation that on those issues that are stipulated otherwise in special foreign-related regulations,[136] such special regulations shall prevail. In fact, special regulations on foreign insurers are confined to the areas of equity composition, legal forms, locality restriction and business scope which have been included in China's WTO accession documents. To put it differently: except for those areas where China made explicit reservation when entering into WTO, foreign insurers are now generally subject to the same regulations as those applicable to the Chinese insurance companies. Whether these commitments are fully honoured in practice and the CIRC applies all rules equally to foreign and local insurers is a question for which the answer depends highly on how effectively the lingering issues addressed in Section IV.B are addressed.

V.   CONCLUSION

China's insurance legal regime in the post-WTO era is imbedded in two interrelated streams of forces. On the one hand is a cautious administrative approach to the implementation of WTO obligations, under which WTO rules are cunningly transposed and interpreted to best suit the interest of protecting and nurturing the domestic industry. This issue is the major source for frustration of foreign insurers who seek to enter the underdeveloped market. On the other hand, the imminent competition between Chinese and foreign insurers as a consequence of China's WTO entry creates a pressing need for the Chinese government to vitalize the local insurance industry. These forces lead to market-oriented measures and deregulation processes. Certainly, China's WTO implementation performance will be shaped by the checks and balances between these two forces, with a long-term perspective of a gradually opening-up and liberalized market. However, this process might present a scenario in which the deregulation and market process will progress to such an extent that China will try to implement its WTO obligations, particularly those with general characters – such as transparency, judicial review and so on – out of its own need, rather than being forced to do so by other Members of the WTO. China has recently begun phasing in many new principles and phasing out old ones. This process needs time and China, therefore, still has much work to do to comply fully with the letter and the spirit of the WTO. It will remain to be seen how China's

---

135. Supra note 35.
136. At this stage, the major regulations specially applicable to foreign insurers include:

   – *Regulations on Administration of Foreign-funded Insurance Companies*, promulgated by the State Council on 12 December 2001 and effective as of 1 February 2002;
   – the Implementary Rules of the Regulation on Administration of Foreign-funded Insurance Companies, issued on 15 March 2004 and effective as of 15 June 2004; and
   – *Administration of Representative Offices of Foreign Insurance Institutions on China Procedures*, issued in January 2004 and effective as of 1 March 2004.

partners within the WTO, particularly the USA and the EU, will cope with this development.

Nevertheless, it must be stressed that, in the insurance sector, China has thus far done a 'fair' job in fulfilling its WTO obligations. Four years after China's accession to the WTO, the rapidly-growing insurance sector remains the only financial sector that has opened its doors for foreign competition almost completely. That this move presents a new experience for China's regulatory authorities is obvious. As Wu Dingfu, Chairman of the CIRC said: 'Joining the WTO is like riding on an international train . . . Because you are not the conductor, you cannot stop the train anytime you want, nor can you jump off'.[137]

---

137. W. Dingfu, Chairman of the CIRC, in *China Daily* (28 October 2005), available at <www.chinadaily.com.cn/english/doc/2005-10/28/content_488515.htm>.

Chapter 8

Financial Conglomerates in the People's Republic of China

George Walker, Qun Wan, Changyuan Lin and Yong Yang

I.   INTRODUCTION

The emergence of increasingly complex financial groups and conglomerate structures has become a significant development in many countries in recent years. The successful management of the inter-relationships created between the separate entities involved in each of the main financial sectors of banking, securities and insurance and the effective supervision and regulation of the extended group as a whole is essential to the stable operation and continued success of any modern economy.

While the traditional response adopted under a number of laws has been to try to continue to impose strict separation rules between each of the main sectors, (principally through controls on cross-share holdings and cross-activities), this practice is increasingly perceived as being difficult, if not impossible, to maintain due to the break down of the underlying differences between the sectors and the continued integration of financial markets and financial services more generally. This has also been considered to be inefficient and anti-competitive, as well as ineffective from a financial stability perspective, due to the degree of consequent inter-dependence that has arisen. Even if a strict separation policy can be followed in one country, the stability of these markets

Barth et al., *Financial Restructuring and Reform in Post-WTO China*, pp. 273–323.
© 2007 Kluwer Law International BV, The Netherlands.

will necessarily be affected by the more-general integration policies followed in other jurisdictions.

A number of different levels of connection or inter-relationship can also be permitted between the main financial sectors not involving strict separation or full integration, which must also be taken into account. Whether a full separation or full integration approach is to be followed, a number of difficult issues have to be resolved in designing any regulatory system that allows some form of financial grouping to be constructed. Appropriate rules must, for example, be adopted with regard to ownership and holding or financial holding company structures, extended management suitability and autonomy requirements, solo and group capital adequacy and capital distribution, intra-group exposures and concentrations, cross-sector or tied (linked) sales, intra-group information transfers and inter-agency exchanges, effective individual and group systems and controls and other non-financial (commercial) linkages.

A number of these issues have been considered by the main international financial committees including the Basel Committee on Banking Supervision, the International Organisation of Securities Commission (IOSCO) and the International Association of Insurance Supervisors (IAS) as well as the inter-group Tripartite Group of Banking, Securities and Insurance Supervisors and its successor Joint Forum on Financial Conglomerates. Despite this work, no fixed or definitive rules have been agreed to, both with regard to the degree of linkage that should be permitted between each sector and the manner in which the new cross-sector exposures created should be controlled. This failure to establish rules is due to the various approaches adopted in many countries and, in particular, in the distinct polices followed in the United States and in Europe.

In addition to these more-specific regulatory or operational difficulties, three additional general policy issues must also be considered in connection with whether a particular country should follow a single market, single regulator and single regulation (or single rules) based approach. Each country must determine to what extent it will allow cross-sector activities and cross-sector markets to develop or maintain a traditional separation policy. The degree of possible integration to be permitted must then be confirmed. The issue of whether a single or multiple institutional or agency structure is to be set up should then considered. A single-regulator approach can, of course, still operate on the basis of either separate underlying sector laws or a single-financial law. To what extent a common or parallel set of rules and regulations are to be applied on a cross-sector basis should also be assessed – particularly where some degree of cross-sector activity is to be permitted. Each of these issues must be considered in constructing an appropriate conglomerate policy in any particular country.

The purpose of this chapter is to consider the relevant regulatory issues that arise with regard to the emergence of financial conglomerates in China and the possible supervisory and regulatory response that can be adopted. This chapter first outlines the current policy in China. Next, the chapter notes the relative advantages and disadvantages of financial-conglomerate structures and refers to the current international response developed to date. This chapter also considers the more-specific problems that arise with regard to ownership, regulation and supervision. In particular, this chapter considers the possible use of holding and financial holding company structures with regard to ownership regulation, which will be of particular importance in China. Finally, this chapter refers to the separate issues that arise in connection with management, capital adequacy, internal systems, intra-group exposures, concentrations and cross-sales and notes the need to supervise groups on a consolidated, business unit and conglomerate basis. This chapter also makes reference to the possible options available for developing effective inter-agency contact and cooperation, including through the use of memoranda of understanding (MoUs), administrative laws or regulations, and the possible creation of a single regulator. This chapter ends with several final recommendations in regard to reform in this area in China.

II. CHINESE LAW AND PRACTICE

II.A. CHINESE PRACTICE & REGULATORY FRAMEWORK WITH FINANCIAL GROUP

II.A.1. The History of China's Financial Business: from Mixture to Separation

From 1953 to the late 1970s, the People's Bank of China (PBOC) was the only de facto banking institution in China and assumed both central and commercial banking roles.[1] The four SOCBs at that time, which were restructured from banking institutions that existed prior to the establishment of the PRC, were merely performing their specialized functions.[2] During that period, practically no other type of financial business existed, except banking. Until 1979, when a number of non-banking financial institutions were gradually set up, such as the China People's Insurance Company, China International Trust and Investment Company and so on, China's financial market began to approach diversified structure and multiplied business operations. In 1980, the State Council stated that banking institutions could develop various trust and investment business.[3] In 1987, China's first securities company was set up,[4] while that same year, banking and other financial institutions were approved to act as agents for

---

1. X. L. Dai (ed.), *A Fifty Years History of the People's Bank of China: The Development of Central Banking System* (Beijing, Chinese Financial Press, 1998), pp. 22–23.
2. Ibid., pp. 20–22.
3. *Interim Regulations on Driving Economic Association*, (Beijing, State Council, 1 July 1980) (ineffective as of 16 May 1994).
4. Refers to the Shenzhen Special Economic Zone Securities Company.

enterprises in the issuance of bonds[5] and the transfer business of enterprise bonds.[6] In the context of insufficient securities companies in the market at that time, most banking and insurance institutions began to increase their involvement in securities business through setting up trust and investment companies, and some banks even directly set up securities department in their organizations.[7] The trust and investment companies handled a large amount of the transfer business of key industry bonds and financial bonds, and also ran diverse business operations through heavy involvement in industrial and commercial sectors by investment and lending.[8] Mixture of financial business was very prevalent before the end of 1993 when the State Council issued its Decision on Financial Reform. This Decision established separation doctrine and prohibited cross-sector operations among banking, securities, insurance and trust and investment companies.[9] This was further highlighted in a formal and legal way with enactment of the Commercial Banking Law and the Insurance Law in 1995, as well as the Securities Law in 1998. As a matter of fact, this type of financial business mixture did not completely come to an end until 2002, when the reorganization of China's trust and investment companies was completed.

A direct reason that led to the adoption of separate business doctrine in China's financial market was the tremendous financial losses and disordered financial market caused by mixture of financial business during the period from 1980s to the mid-1990s.[10] In that period, trust and investment companies invested a large amount of funds into long-term projects and immature stock market, which aggravated the heating of the entire economy. However, as the implementation of macro-economy control policies and the burst of economic bubble, trust and investment companies consequently suffered great losses from their blind investment. To pay off their huge debts, these companies began to draw deposits with higher interests and embezzle guarantee deposits of securities customers. Finally, the central bank had to input huge funds to help trust and investment companies out of their financial liquidity problems. In addition to problematic trust and investment companies, insurance companies also suffered huge losses from their investment into high-risk sectors such as real estate, stock market and various fixed-asset projects. Due to the close fund link between banks, real estate companies and trust and investment companies, banking institutions were also exposed to serious risks as a result of huge

---

5. *Interim Regulations on Administration of Enterprise Bonds (guo-fa)*, no. 21 [1987], art. 21 (Beijing, State Council, 27 March 1987) (ineffective as of 2 August 1993).

6. Ibid., art. 22.

7. B. Xia, 'Thinking about the Route from Business Separation to Mixture till Financial Holding Limited', *International Economic Review*, issue. 6, 2000, pp. 39–43.

8. Ibid.

9. *Decision of the State Council on Financial System Reform*, National Distribution (*guo-fa*) no. 91 [1993] (Beijing, State Council, 25 December 1993) (referred to as 'Decision on Financial System Reform').

10. Detailed analysis of why employed separate business doctrine; see Y. Yang, *The Legal Research on Financial Group* (Beijing: Peking University Press, 2004), pp. 226–230.

lending to their subsidiary trust and investment or real estate companies, which were often granted under normal standards or even against the law.

In fact, chaos and losses in the mixture of financial business at the beginning of China's economic transformation demonstrate the country's insufficient market development and incapable regulatory and legal system. During that period, China's financial market just started to approach a modern banking system, without necessary knowledge and experience to identify features and risks that exist in various financial sectors. For this reason, a large amount of hot money flew from banks to high-bubble real estate companies and stock markets, but without adequate risk identification and control measures. In addition, the entire regulatory and legal system was so immature that lawmakers could not offer the necessary measures to supervise and control risky operations of financial sectors. In addition, no regulatory authority was in place to exert penalties on wrongdoers or prevent the intervention of local governments in the banking business. In this context, separation business doctrine was adopted in China's financial supervisory regime with a purpose of controlling market risks and maintaining financial stability.

II.A.2.   China's Current Legal and Regulatory Regime With Respect of the Separation of Financial Business

The current law in China is based on sector separation with regard to the operations of financial business. Relevant legislation includes the Commercial Banking Law, the Securities Law and the Insurance Law.[11] Each of these laws generally prohibits cross-sector operations and ownership structures. According to the 1995 Commercial Banking Law:

> '[N]o commercial banks shall undertake the business of trust and investment and securities dealing business, nor shall they invest in the non-self-use real property or non-bank financial institutions and enterprises within the People's Republic of China. For investments in the kind made before the promulgation of this law, the State Council will work out rules to deal with them.'[12]

In 2003, the amended Commercial Banking Law added an exception to this regulation; namely, that if prescribed by the state, commercial banks could expand their business scope.[13]

---

11.   See the *Law of the People's Republic of China on Commercial Banks* (10 May 1995); *Securities Law of the People's Republic of China* (29 December 1998); and *Insurance Law of the People's Republic of China* (30 June 1995).
12.   Article 43, *Law of the People's Republic of China on Commercial Banks*, 1995 (revised in 2003).
13.   Ibid., art. 43.

The Securities Law of 1998 makes a similar provision, which stipulates the principle of the divided operation and management applicable to the industries of securities, banking, trust and insurance.[14] The Law provides that the securities companies and the business organs of banks, trust and insurance shall be separately established.[15] The brokerage business, securities business (on its own account) and securities underwriting business are clarified as the major business scope that securities companies could cover in China.[16] Similar to the revised Commercial Banking Law, the revised Securities Law of 2005 lays out an exception clause to the divided business principle.[17]

In addition, Article 6 of the Insurance Law limits commercial insurance business to the insurance company.[18] In addition, an insurance company is not permitted to use its funds to set up securities organizations or invest in enterprises.[19]

In 1999, trust and investment companies were prohibited from handling banking deposits, and from the lending business and stock-dealing business.[20] In 2002, the PBOC issued formal measures that required trust and investment companies not to engage in the deposit and bond issuance business.[21]

Although generally implemented, the separate business doctrine in China's financial market, some cross-sector operations can still carry out business if they would not create risks to the financial system. Commercial banks, for example, can engage in issuing financial bonds; issuing, cashing and undertaking the sale of government bonds as agents; buying and selling government bonds or financial bonds; and handling receipts and payments and insurance business as agents.[22] In addition, commercial banks can handle securities business as agents upon approval.[23] Insurance companies could buy and sell government bonds and financial bonds.[24] These companies were even permitted to invest no more than five per cent of total company assets into securities investment funds.[25] The business scope of trust and investment companies is under strict

---

14. Article 6, *Securities Law of the People's Republic of China*, 1998 (revised in 2005).
15. Ibid.
16. Ibid., art. 129.
17. Ibid., art. 6.
18. Article 6, *Insurance Law of the People's Republic of China*, 1995 (revised in 2002).
19. Ibid., art. 104.
20. *Transfer by the General Office of State Council of the Notice by the PBOC on Reorganizing Trust and Investment Companies* (Beijing, State Council, 7 February 1999).
21. PBOC, *Measures on Trust and Investment Companies* 2002 (Beijing, PBOC, 9 May 2002).
22. Article 3, *Law of the People's Republic of China on Commercial Banks*, 1995 (revised in 2003).
23. PBOC, *Interim Rules on Intermediate Services of Commercial Banks* (Beijing, PBOC, 21 June 2001).
24. Article104, *Insurance Law of the People's Republic of China*, 1995 (revised in 2002).
25. *Interim Measures on Insurance Company Investing in Securities Investment Funds* 1999. From 2000 to 2003, some insurance companies were permitted to increase their investment ratio greatly. See *Notice on Revising "Interim Measures on Insurance Company Investing in Securities Investment Funds"* (*baojian-fa*) no. 6, (Beijing, 17 January 2003).

restrictions; however, these companies can also engage in the investment-fund business, according to laws and regulations, acting as trusted underwriter of state or enterprise bonds.[26] In addition, trust and investment companies could take forms of leases, sales, loans, investment and interbank loans to manage and operate trust property in accordance with trust documents.[27] For this reason, you can see that the separate business doctrine implemented in China aims to prohibit one sector to engage directly in the core business of other sectors; in other words, the banking deposit and lending business, the dealing, underwriting and marketing of securities, insurance underwriting and so on, and some intermediate business including agent and settlement is beyond the prohibition due to their lower risks.[28]

In addition to these laws and regulations, China's Company Law of 1993 also prohibits holding limited company in principle. Article 12 provided that, with the exception of investment companies and holding companies as specified by the State Council, where a company invests in other limited liability companies or joint stock companies limited, the aggregate amount of the investment shall not exceed 50 per cent of the net assets of the company. [29] However, this clause is removed from the revised Company Law in 2005.

In accordance with sector-based legislation, a multiple sector-based, as opposed to a single agency and regulatory approach, is then followed – which is generally referred to as 'separate market, separate supervision' – in China, in combination with a traditional strict separation model for financial regulation.[30] This approach is supported by the retention of separate laws in each of the three key sector areas of banking, securities and insurance.

In China, three separate regulatory agencies control financial markets: the China Banking Regulatory Commission (CBRC), the China Securities Regulatory Commission (CSRC) and the China Insurance Regulatory Commission (CIRC). Each of these agencies also maintains a number of provincial and city offices. The People's Bank of China (PBOC) still retains more general responsibility for the monetary policy and stability of the financial system, although the PBOC's specific function, in regard to continued market oversight and supervision, has been transferred to the CBRC after the revision of the People's Bank of China Law (PBOC Law) in 2003.

---

26. Article 20, *Measures on Trust and Investment Companies*, no. 5 (Beijing, PBOC, 9 May 2002).
27. Ibid., Article 22.
28. Y. Yang, *The Legal Research on Financial Group* (Beijing, Peking University Press, 2004), p. 246.
29. Art.12, *Company Law of the People's Republic of China,* 1999 (revised in 1999, 2004 and 2005).
30. For discussion of the various models used in respect to financial regulation and their interaction with conglomerate law and financial structure, see D. Arner and J. Lin, *Financial Regulation: A Guide to Structural Reform* (Hong Kong: Thomson Sweet & Maxwell, 2003).

II.A.3.   China's Current Financial Groups

Despite the adoption of a more traditional separation doctrine, some large complex groups have already begun to emerge in China, either directly or through the use of financial holding companies based in Hong Kong or elsewhere.[31] So far, four main types of financial groups exist in China.

The first type is the financial groups that are formed by financial institutions, with interests in banking, securities and insurance, as well as in trust and investment companies. This type of financial conglomerate model includes China International Trust and Investment (CITIC) group, which is the largest financial group on mainland China,[32] as well as the China Everbright Group[33] and the Pinan Group.[34] The major features of this type of financial groups are:

– the non-banking financial group solely owns or absolutely controls banking, securities, insurance and some non-financial subsidiaries;

---

31. See 'Financial holding companies are vividly portrayed', *China Securities* (29 August 2002). For general discussion, see C. Y. Lin, 'Financial Conglomerates in China' (University of London, unpublished paper under supervision of G. A. Walker', 26 February 2003).
32. CITIC was originally set up on 4 October 1979 by Mr. Rong Yiren, former Vice-President of the PRC. CITIC has since been expanded to include more than 38 subsidiary countries across the world. Total assets were in excess of USD 54 billion (RMB 432.6 billion) by the end of 2001. 78 per cent of total assets are financial in nature, with 18 per cent industrial and one per cent services-based. The financial elements are now held under a 'vertical' holding company structure under CITIC Holding Limited, with all other industrial and service subsidiaries held under CITIC directly. CITIC is China's first financial holding limited company, and was approved by the State Council on December 2001. The main financial subsidiaries include CITIC Industrial Bank; CITIC Securities; Changscheng Fund Management Co; CITIC Fund Management Co; CITIC Prudential Life Insurance Co Ltd; CITIC Asset Management Co Ltd; CITIC Futures Broker Co Ltd; CITIC International Financial Holding Co Ltd (HK); CITIC Ka Wah Bank Ltd (HK); CITIC Capital Markets Holding Co Ltd (HK); and the CITIC International Asset Management Co Ltd (HK). See <www.citic.com>.
33. China Everbright Group developed from a foreign trade and investment group to include increasingly significant financial operations within its group structure, a number of which are based in Hong Kong. The Group had total assets of USD 37.75 billion (RMB 302 billion) by the end of 2001, with 96 per cent of the assets being financial. A financial holding company was set up in 1994 – China Everbright Holdings Co Ltd (CEH) – which manages most of the Group's commercial banking, investment banking and insurance operations. The China Everbright Bank was set up in 1992 with commercial banking also being conducted through the International Bank of Asia Ltd. The China Everbright Group also continues to hold its domestic securities company (Shenyin & Wangguo Securities) and insurance operation (China Everbright Sun Life Insurance) directly through the company's head office in Beijing. See <www.ebchina.com>.
34. The Pinan Group is major in insurance business and developed from Pinan Insurance Company. In 2001, the Pinan Insurance Company was approved to establish Pinan Holding Co Ltd, which holds shares in Pinan Life Insurance, Pinan Property & Casualty Insurance, Pinan Annuity Insurance, Pinan Asset Management Company, Pinan Overseas (Holding), and Pinan Trust and Investment Company. Pinan Trust and Investment Company hold an equity interest in Pinan Securities Company. See <www.pinan.com.cn>.

- the group is responsible for establishing development strategies, risk control, financial auditing and product innovation;
- subsidiaries have independent legal identity and engage in various businesses in accordance with separate business doctrine.[35]

The second type of financial groups is the financial holding limited companies, which is solely or jointly funded by the four state-owned commercial banks; namely the Bank of China (BOC),[36] the China Construction Bank (CCB),[37] the Industrial and Commercial Bank of China (ICBC)[38] and the Agricultural Bank of China (ABC).[39]

In addition, the four asset management companies, which were set up in 1999 to acquire 1.4 trillion non-performing loans (NPLs) from the state commercial banks, have taken equity interests in some large state owned enterprises (SOEs) through debt-equity swap scheme and in some bankrupt securities houses under the instruction of the central bank.

The third category of financial groups in China is the financial holding limited companies that are funded by industrial sectors. Some SOEs and private sector corporations have invested into financial sectors, for example, the China Merchants Group,[40] Shandong Electronic Group, Haier Group, Delong

---

35. J.S. Pan, 'Development of China's Financial Holding Companies', *Almanac of China's Finance and Banking 2003* (Beijing, Editor Board, Almanac of China's Finance and Banking, 2003), pp. 696–697.

36. The BOC was originally set up in 1912 as the central bank of the Republic of China. The BOC was taken over in 1949 and acted as the country's only foreign exchange and foreign trade bank until 1994 when the bank was converted into a state-owned commercial bank. The BOC had previously established a finance company in Hong Kong in 1979 (China Construction Finance (HK) Ltd) and a securities operation in 1983 (Bank of China Securities Ltd). A holding company was set up in July 1996 (the Bank of China International Holdings Ltd) although this company was to be based in the UK rather than in mainland China. Insurance operations began in 1992 (BOC Group Insurance Co Ltd) and subsequently expanded in 1998 (BOC Group Life Insurance Ltd).

37. CCB transferred its earlier fiscal agent and policy lending functions to the Ministry of Finance and the State Development Bank (SDB) in 1994 as part of the reform of the financial system. CCB then entered into a joint venture with Morgan Stanley (US) and other financial firms to form China International Capital Corporation Ltd, of which CCB holds the largest share.

38. ICBC has developed its non-bank financial activities through Hong Kong. This includes the acquisition of the securities operations of the National Westminster Bank, which is now operated through a joint venture with the Bank of East Asia of Hong Kong, the ICBC-East Asia Financial Holdings Co.

39. The ABC set up the Agricultural Bank of China Finance Co Ltd (HK) to develop non-bank financial business mainly in the securities and insurance areas again through Hong Kong and separate from its Mainland banking operation.

40. China Merchants Group established the first shipping insurance company in 1875 and the first Chinese bank in 1879. More recently, the Group has consolidated its banking and insurance operations, including the acquisition of the Union Bank of Hong Kong in 1986 and the establishment of the first joint stock commercial bank, China Merchants Bank in 1987, and the first corporate funded insurance company, Ping An Insurance Company of China Ltd, in 1988. The company bought two UK insurance companies – the Scottish

Group, Hope Group and so on.[41] Under this type of financial group, the holding limited companies are non-financial entities with controlling interests in banking, insurance and securities, as well as trust and investment companies.

In addition, some local governments, for example, Shenzhen and Shanghai, have set up large financial holding companies by reorganizing local financial resources, including banking, securities, insurance and trust and investment companies.[42]

The entry of foreign owned financial groups and conglomerates must also be taken into consideration in addition to the continued expansion of these large domestic operators.

II.A.4.　　　　Problems and Risks in the Operations of China's Financial Groups

From this description, one can see that China's financial groups mainly take the form of financial holding Co. Ltd. or bank parent-subsidiary companies, and some large financial holding limited companies control both financial and commercial sectors. Subsidiary financial institutions operate on the sector-based doctrine. In addition, the operations of China's financial groups are strongly administration-oriented with deep government involvement – for example, their establishment and the appointment of high management must attain approval from the State Council – rather than upon market disciplines.

Without sufficient supervision in place, China's financial groups have confronted certain financial risks in their business operations. Firstly, complex arrangements in shareholding structure among parent companies and their subsidiaries implicit risks in capital adequacy. For example, if a parent company holds shares in a financial subsidiary, and the financial subsidiary then invests in a commercial company that is not regulated by financial supervisors and reversely takes equity interest in the parent company, the capital base of parent company and its subsidiary can be repeatedly computed. Because the companyhas not set up a smooth channel for information exchange among

---

　　　Lion Insurance Co. Ltd. and Houlder Insurance Brokers Group – in 1988 with another Hong Kong insurance company – China Merchants Insurance Co Ltd. The Group subsequently acquired interests in securities activities, including the China Merchants Securities Co. Ltd. in 1997. The company disposed of its interest in the Union Bank in June 2000, but retained and renamed the securities CM-CCS Securities Ltd. The Group has also more recently moved into fund and asset management. The China Merchants Finance Holding Co Ltd (CMFH) was then set up in 1999 as a financial holding company with the Group's other major interests being in transportation infrastructure, logistics and real estate. See <www.cm-finance.com>.

41.　For a detailed discussion, see J.S. Pan, 'Development of China's Financial Holding Companies', in *Almanac of China's Finance and Banking* (Beijing, Editor Board, Almanac of China's Finance and Banking, 2003).

42.　Ibid.

various supervisory bodies and the system of preventing insider trading is still developing, capital adequacy in the financial group faces great challenges.

Second, serious management risk is involved in the financial groups. Generally, the high-level management of parent companies is also in charge of the operations of financial subsidiaries, but their qualification review is beyond supervision. As a result, their unqualified management and even illegal operations led to a great deal of bad assets and financial risks in the company.

Third, a popular practice in China's financial groups is that parent companies and their financial subsidiaries have a large amount of connected or inside trading. Due to complex shareholding structure arrangements and non-transparent information disclosure, identifying the risks related to connected or inside trading among the group members is usually difficult, and as a result, a great deal of banking funds, particularly those that flow illegally to the stock market, have become bad debts and led to a bubble stock market.

Finally, financial groups involve high-leverage financial risks. Generally, the parent company obtains funds through three channels to invest in financial subsidies: the first is to issue bonds to acquire investment funds; the second is to borrow money from the bank by setting mortgages on its own assets; and the third is to offer guarantee to the company's subsidiaries, who are then free to borrow money from the bank to invest in another financial subsidiary. Apparently, these operations easily expose the entire group to huge potential risks.

The adoption of separate business doctrine is against the backdrop of China's economic transformation from a planned and closed system to a market and open system. First, sector-based supervision is relatively choice for China's current financial market. Preventing connected dealings among subsidiaries and parent companies in the financial group is still rather difficult. In addition, the corporate governance of the entire market is still developing, with insufficient risk control system and serious asset quality problems. In a transitional market, China's financial sector has been in confronting deep government involvement and even severe intervention for the sector to support the survival of SOEs and maintain social stability. As a result, interest conflicts exist widely among SOEs, state-owned commercial banks and other types of state-owned investment companies. In addition, a large scale of banking funds flowed into risky and unstable stock market can affect the stability of the banking market. And finally, the underdeveloped regulatory and legal regime in China's financial market could not provide sufficient approaches and techniques to supervise various issues in the operations of financial group. In particular, these issues become more complex when the central bank and the three financial supervisory organs still must make the balance between development and stability. Moreover, the quality and credibility of supervisory authorities is evolving, which could not offer effective supervision to the complex financial conglomerates. It has been stated that stable macroeconomic environment and effective financial supervision are vital to the profits of financial mixture in the developing countries; otherwise, it would create huge room for financial institutions to abuse their diversified business qualifications.[43] The effective supervision of financial conglomerates relies greatly upon a mature market with highly developed self-discipline and well-functioning legal systems with strong enforceability.

The Chinese authorities are, nevertheless, aware of the potential benefits of permitting financial groups to develop on a cross-sector basis. Several large conglomerates in China have been approved by the State Council with more groups having applied for authorization. While the anticipated policy will remain a separate, law-based agency and sector, some relaxation of the demarcation that exists between the main sectors is being considered and the consequent necessary regulatory amendments are being examined.

All of these developments will create significant challenges for the regulation of financial markets and maintenance of financial stability within China. The following sections consider the main issues that arise with regard to the possible benefits (advantages) and exposures (disadvantages) that can arise from a more-open market policy, along with the possible regulatory responses that can be adopted.

Current laws in China are sector-based. Relevant legislation includes the Commercial Banking Law, the Securities Law and the Insurance Law.[44] Each of these laws generally prohibits cross-sector operations and ownership structures. Despite the adoption of a more traditional separation doctrine, some large complex groups have already begun to emerge in China either directly or through the use of financial holding companies based in Hong Kong and elsewhere.[45]

The largest financial group on mainland China is the China International Trust and Investment Corporation (CITIC), which was established on 5 December 2002.[46] Other state-owned conglomerate models include the China

---

43. C.U. Uche, 'The Adoption of Universal Banking in Nigeria' (2001) 10*JIBFL*, p. 35.
44. See the Law of the People's Republic of China on Commercial Banks of 10 May 1995; Securities Law of the People's Republic of China of 29 December 1998; and Insurance Law of the People's Republic of China of 30 June 1995. A number of substantial amendments to China's Securities Law 1998 were approved by the Standing Committee of the National People's Congress on 27 October 2005. The revised Securities Law consists of 12 chapters and 240 articles and came into effect on 1 January 2006. The revisions include changes to the securities administrative supervision procedures, strengthening accuracy and accountability of information disclosure to enhancing legal protection for investors. The revised law is expected to have a significant and positive impact on the protection of investors and the flow of funds into the Chinese stock market. The 1995 Insurance Law 1995 is also under second revision. After its revision, the amended Law is expected to be submitted to the National Congress at the end of 2006 and the beginning of 2007.
45. See 'Financial holding companies are vividly portrayed', *China Securities* (29 August 2002). For general discussion, see C. Lin, 'Financial Conglomerates in China' (University of London, unpublished paper under supervision of G.A. Walker, 26 February 2003).
46. CITIC was originally set up on 4 October 1979 by Mr. Rong Yiren, former Vice-President of the PRC. CITIC has since been expanded to include more than 38 subsidiary countries around the world. Total assets were in excess of USD 54 billion (RMB 432.6 billion) by the

Everbright Group[47] and the China Merchants Group[48] as well as the four state-owned commercial banks that continue to dominate the banking industry in China: the Bank of China (BOC),[49] the China Construction Bank (CCB),[50]

---

end of 2001. 78 per cent of total assets are financial in nature with 18 per cent industrial and one per cent services-based. The financial elements are now held under a vertical holding company structure under CITIC Holding Limited, with all other industrial and service subsidiaries held under CITIC directly. The main financial subsidiaries include the CITIC Industrial Bank; CITIC Securities; Changscheng Fund Management Co; CITIC Fund Management Co; CITIC Prudential Life Insurance Co Ltd; CITIC Asset Management Co Ltd; CITIC Futures Broker Co Ltd; CITIC International Financial Holding Co Ltd (HK); CITIC Ka Wah Bank Ltd (HK); CITIC Capital Markets Holding Co Ltd (HK); and CITIC International Asset Management Co Ltd (HK). See <www.citic.com>.

47. China Everbright Group developed from a foreign trade and investment group to include increasingly significant financial operations within its group structure, a number of which are based in Hong Kong. The Group had total assets of USD 37.75 billion (RMB 302 billion) by the end of 2001 with 96 per cent of this being financial. A financial holding company was set up in 1994 – China Everbright Holdings Co Ltd (CEH) – which manages most of the Group's commercial banking, investment banking and insurance operations. The China Everbright Bank had been set up in 1992, with commercial banking also being conducted through the International Bank of Asia Ltd. The China Everbright Group also continues to hold its domestic securities company (Shenyin & Wangguo Securities) and insurance operation (China Everbright Sun Life Insurance) directly through the company's head office in Beijing.

48. China Merchants Group established the first shipping insurance company in 1875 and the first Chinese bank in 1879. More recently, the Group has consolidated its banking and insurance operations, including the acquisition of the Union Bank of Hong Kong in 1986 and the establishment of the first joint stock commercial bank, the China Merchants Bank, in 1987, and the first corporate funded insurance company – the Ping An Insurance Company of China Ltd – in 1988. Two UK insurance companies – the Scottish Lion Insurance Co. Ltd and the Houlder Insurance Brokers Group – were purchased in 1988 with another Hong Kong insurance company – the China Merchants Insurance Co. Ltd. The Group subsequently acquired interests in securities activities, including the China Merchants Securities Co. Ltd, in 1997. The Group disposed of its interest in the Union Bank in June 2000, but the securities are retained and renamed CM-CCS Securities Ltd. The Group has also more recently moved into fund and asset management. The China Merchants Finance Holding Co Ltd (CMFH) was then set up in 1999 as a financial holding company with the Group's other major interests being in transportation infrastructure, logistics and real estate. See <www.cm-finance.com>.

49. The BOC was originally set up in 1912 as the central bank of the Republic of China. The BOC was taken over in 1949 and then acted as the country's only foreign exchange and foreign trade bank until 1994, when the BOC was converted into a state-owned commercial bank. The BOC had previously established a finance company in Hong Kong in 1979 – the China Construction Finance (HK) Ltd – and a securities operation in 1983 – the Bank of China Securities Ltd. A holding company was set up in July 1996 – the Bank of China International Holdings Ltd – although this company was to be based in the UK rather than in mainland China. Insurance operations began in 1992 – the BOC Group Insurance Co Ltd – and subsequently expanded in 1998 – as the BOC Group Life Insurance Ltd. The BOC has total assets of USD 423.75 billion (RMB 3,390 billion).

50. CCB transferred its previous fiscal agent and policy lending functions to the Ministry of Finance and the State Development Bank (SDB) in 1994 as part of 'the Reform of the Financial System'. CCB then entered into a joint venture with Morgan Stanley (US) and

the Industrial and Commercial Bank of China (ICBC)[51] and the Agricultural Bank of China (ABC)).[52] Other state-owned enterprises (SOEs) and private sector corporations are also anxious to develop their own financial operations, including Haier Group and the Delong Group in Xinjiang Province. The entry of foreign-owned financial groups and conglomerates must also be taken into consideration, along with the continued expansion of these large domestic operators.

In China, financial markets are controlled through three separate regulatory agencies: the China Banking Regulatory Commission (CBRC), the China Securities Regulatory Commission (CSRC) and the China Insurance Regulatory Commission (CIRC). Each of these agencies also maintains a number of provincial and city offices. The People's Bank of China (PBC) also retains more general responsibility for the monetary policy and stability of the financial system, although the PBC's specific function with regard to continued market oversight and supervision is unclear in advance of the revision of the PBC Law, which is currently under consideration.

A multiple sector-based, rather than single-agency, structure has accordingly been adopted in China in combination with a traditional strict separation model for financial regulation.[53] This structure is supported by the retention of separate laws in each of the three key sector areas of banking, securities and insurance. Since then, China has followed a sector-based agency and regulatory approach, which is generally referred to as 'separate market, separate supervision'. The Chinese authorities are nevertheless aware of the potential benefits of allowing financial groups to develop on a cross-sector basis. The first conglomerate in China, CITIC Holdings, has since been approved by the State Council with three additional groups having applied for authorization. While the anticipated policy will remain a separate agency and sector-law based, some relaxation of the demarcation that exists between the main sectors is being considered, and the consequent necessary regulatory amendments are being examined.

All of these developments will present significant challenges for the regulation of financial markets and maintenance of financial stability within China. The following sections describe the main issues that arise with regard to the

---

other financial firms to form the China International Capital Corporation Ltd, of which CCB holds the largest share.

51. ICBC has developed its non-bank financial activities through Hong Kong. These activities include the acquisition of the securities operations of the National Westminister Bank, which is now operated through a joint venture with the Bank of East Asia of Hong Kong: the ICBC-East Asia Financial Holdings Co.

52. The ABC set up the Agricultural Bank of China Finance Co. Ltd (HK) to develop non-bank financial business mainly in the securities and insurance areas again through Hong Kong and separate from the company's mainland banking operation.

53. For a discussion of the various models used in respect to financial regulation and their interaction with conglomerate law and financial structure, see D Arner and J Lin, *Financial Regulation: A Guide to Structural Reform* (Thomson Sweet & Maxwell, 2003).

possible benefits (advantages) and exposures (disadvantages) from a more-open market policy, along with suggestions for the possible regulatory responses that the country can be adopted.

III.   INTERNATIONAL PRACTICE

III.A.   CONGLOMERATE ADVANTAGES AND DISADVANTAGES

A number of relative advantages and disadvantages arise with regard to financial conglomerates. Possible advantages include economies of scope and scale, which can generate lower costs, reduce prices and improve product and service innovation.[54] Sector linkages and synergies can also improve general competitiveness, while overall stability is increased through diversified revenue streams. Product variety and innovation can increase customer loyalty and market penetration and development. New corporate structures also permit maximum commercial advantage to be gained, while complying with relevant statutory permissions and restrictions.[55] While some writers refer to this as a separate advantage, this can also be considered to constitute a form of regulatory avoidance, which may or may not be considered desirable, depending on the purpose and content of the underlying restrictions imposed.[56]

Against these advantages, difficulties can arise with regard to 'double gearing' of capital, risk management capacity, intra-group exposures, conflicts of interest and lack of sufficient management authority and autonomy. Supervisory problems can also arise in terms of transparency and the identification of the proper centre of management and control.[57] The most significant additional risk that arises is the possibility of loss transfer between entities in the group and consequently between the separate financial sectors involved. The close nature of the corporate, legal and financial linkages created in the conglomerate will necessarily increase the risk of intra-group contagion and possible

---

54. See G A Walker, *International Banking Regulation – Law, Policy and Practice* (Kluwer Law, 2001), Chapter 3, Section 2.
55. The inclusion of sector and financial holding companies within a conglomerate structure can be used to avoid some of the commercial or economic restrictions that may otherwise apply. Other advantages can then arise in raising capital, share or stock liquidity and taxation depending upon local conditions. Benefit can also arise in terms of product or service innovation where restrictions that may otherwise apply to individual financial institutions can be bypassed. This can, for example, include geographic restrictions – such as inter-state banking in the US – or controls on the types of financial activities that may be carried out – such as under the Glass-Steagall provisions of the US Banking Act of 1933 that separated commercial and investment banking. See Section III.D, later in this chapter.
56. See K.K Mwenda and A. Flemming, *International developments in the organisational structure of financial services supervision*, available at<www.imf.org>; D. Scott, *Regulation and Supervision of Financial Conglomerates*, available at<www.imf.org>; and K. Koguchi, 'Financial Conglomeration', in *Financial Conglomerates* (1993), OECD. See also Walker, Section 6.VII(c).
57. See Walker, Chapter 3, Section 6.I(a).

cross-sector loss transfer. Significant losses suffered in a more volatile area of group activity such as in a derivatives, currency or securities subsidiary can then be transferred to the insurance and banking parts of the same group. Even in the absence of actual legal or financial liability, this contagion can spread through reputational damage alone. This danger of potential cross-sector loss transfer is possibly the most significant difficulty that arises with regard to conglomerate business structures.[58] The traditional method for dealing with such possible loss transfer is to impose restrictions on the main types of activities that financial institutions may conduct. Separation rules or structural regulation can then be used to distinguish the main financial sectors such as under the original US Glass-Steagall model.[59] Institutions in one sector are then prohibited from conducting activities in another.

The alternative to a system of strict separation is to impose additional regulatory requirements and, in particular, capital controls on institutions that are active in more than one of the main financial areas. This approach is the policy adopted in Continental Europe, where the large universal banks are authorized to conduct banking and securities, as well as other ancillary financial activities, from within the same corporate or legal form. Additional capital requirements are then imposed on each of the distinct financial risks identified, including, in particular, credit risk (in the banking or 'loan book'), market risk (in the securities or 'trading book') as well as interest rate risk, currency risk and other risks (including financial derivatives and commodity related risks) and operational risks. This alternative model then operates through subsequent loss absorption rather than initial loss prevention under a separation option.[60]

While strict sector separation would appear to prevent loss transfer, the increasingly complex and inter-connected nature of modern financial markets will often not permit such strict demarcation to be maintained. Financial crisis within one sector can more easily spread into other sectors with alternative regulatory and financial stability responses being required. Even in cases in which a strict sector separation policy is adopted in a conglomerate (including through the use of holding or financial holding company requirements and supporting 'firewalls'), contagion can still spread through reputational damage and exposure alone with the expectation that a parent or related group company will inevitably support its corporate affiliate.

This risk of cross-sector contagion can be further aggravated where gaps or omissions in the regulatory framework – due to underlying design faults – permit particular group activities to be unsupervised or unregulated.[61] Losses arising in such areas can then undermines the stability of the entire financial

---

58. See Walker, Chapter 3, Section 4.I.
59. This policy was also followed in Japan following the Second World War, but has been substantially relaxed subsequently. See the authorities cited in Walker, Chapter 3, no. 81.
60. See Walker, Chapter 3, Section 5.
61. This arises from financial and regulatory mismatch, which results from the underlying financial structure and regulatory design flaws. A particular country's financial regulatory structure may not correspond closely with the structure of its financial sector with

group, which will, in turn, result in losses from one sector being transferred to another with the consequent contagious damage that that could cause.

The more-general recent trend in developed markets has been to allow financial groups to realize some, if not many, of the benefits of conglomerate business structures rather than maintain traditional full strict separation rules. Various restrictions and controls must nevertheless be imposed through a range of ownership, regulatory and supervisory requirements to ensure that a safe balance is maintained. The degree of residual control affected will then depend upon the size and structure of the economy and its relative stage of development. No fixed rules can be set with the degree and nature of the controls imposed being dependent upon the amount of cross-sector holding and cross-sector activity permitted. It must nevertheless be expected that stricter ownership and other control requirements will generally be imposed in transitional and emerging economies, although requirements may still be further relaxed over time as markets and regulatory familiarity and experience and expertise develop.

III.B.   International Regulatory Response

International authorities became concerned with the emerging problems that arise with conglomerates during the late 1980s and early 1990s. These problems were initially highlighted by the Basel Committee, in a number of the Committee's biannual reports during the late 1980s. The Committee then issued particular principles in regard to the supervision of financial conglomerates in September 1992.[62] The Report identified a number of specific difficulties that arose with conglomerates and attempted to establish certain general principles of supervision for financial conglomerates.

IOSCO issued a separate Report at its 17th Annual Conference in London in October 1992.[63] In its Report, IOSCO also attempted to establish certain general principles for the risk assessment of conglomerates that could be used, as much as possible, to direct the development of regulatory practice and co-operation in the area. Eight general principles are identified in a substantially shorter paper than the September 1992 Basel paper. A separate Tripartite Group of Supervisors was then established at the suggestion of the Basel

---

significant regulatory gaps arising. Larger unsupervised groups may, in particular, develop within a strict separation l system in which firms are regulated on a sector and not a group basis. This can then generate significant risks at the group level that are not otherwise managed or controlled. Partly in response to this fact, various forms of consolidated or group supervision have been developed, although this may still be insufficient where the sector regulator has inadequate powers to deal with the exposures created. See Section III.E.2.e., later in this chapter.

62. See Basel Committee, *Principles for the Supervision of Financial Conglomerates* (September 1992). For comment, see Walker, Chapter 3, Section 6.I.

63. See IOSCO, *Principles for the Supervision of Financial Conglomerates* (November 1992).

Committee consisting of representatives from the Basel Committee, IOSCO and the IAIS. The Tripartite Group was set up in February 1993 and issued a progress report in April 1994, which was followed by a final report in July 1995.[64] The 1994 Progress Report contained several general recommendations with regard to supervisory approaches, cooperation, capital adequacy, structure, ownership and management, contagion, external auditors and supervisory arbitrage.[65]

In its full July 1995 Report, the Tripartite Group provided a much more substantial examination of the structure and operation of financial conglomerates and the supervisory issues that arose. The Tripartite Group defined a conglomerate as any group of companies under common control, whose exclusive or predominant activities consisted of providing services in at least three different financial sectors: banking, securities and insurance. Various supervisory issues are identified, including capital, contagion, intra-group exposures, large exposures, conflicts of interest, suitability, transparency, management autonomy, shareholders, access to information, supervisory arbitrage, moral hazard and mixed conglomerates. The final report includes a number of provisional recommendations.[66]

In light of the perceived continuing importance of the need to supervise conglomerates effectively, the earlier Tripartite Group was replaced by a more-formal Joint Forum on Financial Conglomerates at the beginning of 1996.[67] The new Joint Forum produced a Progress Report in April 1997 (in advance of the Denver G7 Summit), which was followed by a series of consultation documents in February 1998.[68] The February 1998 consultation package consisted of a series of separate papers on capital adequacy, fit and proper principles, information sharing and supervision.[69] Two further papers were released in July 1999 on intra-group transactions and exposures (ITEs) and risk concentrations (RCs).[70] A series of revised final documents were then issued in December 1999.[71]

---

64. See Tripartite Group, *Progress Report on the Supervision of Financial Conglomerates* (April 1994); and Tripartite Group, *Report on the Supervision of Financial Conglomerates* (July 1995).
65. See Walker, Chapter 3, Section 6.III.
66. See Walker, Chapter 3, Section 6.IV.
67. The Joint Forum is made up of 25 persons, representing the banking, securities and insurance sectors.
68. See Joint Forum, *Progress Report* (April 1997); and Joint Forum, *Supervision of Financial Conglomerates* (February 1998). See Walker, Chapter 3, Section 6.V.
69. See Joint Forum, *Capital Adequacy Principles* (February 1998); Joint Forum, *Fit and Proper Principles* (February 1998); Joint Forum, *Framework for Information Sharing* (February 1998) and *Principles for Information Sharing* (February 1998); Joint Forum, *Co-ordinator* (February 1998). See Walker, Chapter 3, Section 6.VII.
70. See Joint Forum, *Intra-group Transactions and Exposures* (July 1999); and Joint Forum, *Risk Concentrations* (July 1999). See Walker, Chapter 3, Section 6.VII.
71. See collectively Joint Forum, *Supervision of Financial Conglomerates* (December 1999).

These documents, and in particular the series of supervisory papers issued by the Joint Forum, contain a number of important recommendations for the supervision of financial conglomerates. These recommendations are generally based on a series of principles in each of the key areas of suitability (fit and proper), information sharing, coordination and intra-group exposures and concentrations. In connection with capital adequacy, three specific techniques are identified for use in assessing group-wide capital, including a building block prudential approach, a risk-based aggregation method and a risk-based deduction method. These techniques are designed to allow for a total group capital figure to be calculated, but are otherwise too concerned with revising the existing separate capital rules that apply to banks, securities firms and insurance companies.[72] The operation of each is also necessarily dependent upon local accounting and reporting requirements.

The papers issued by the Joint Forum are useful, although essentially limited in themselves, and must be understood with the earlier, more-general reports and, in particular, the September 1992 Basel Committee and July 1995 Tripartite Group Reports. The effect is generally to identify a number of specific issues that must be taken into account in terms of regulatory adjustment or revision. This revision can then be given effect to either in a separate 'conglomerate law' or through revision to the separate sector statutes involved – or possibly a conglomerate supplement or amendment to these sector laws. The international papers issued to date do not deal with the more-general problems of sector separation and the use of holding company and financial holding company models, as well as the more-significant problem of loss transfer and extended market (lender of last resort) support. Each of these issues must also be taken into account in designing any effective national response.

III.C.   BANK HOLDING AND FINANCIAL HOLDING COMPANY RULES

In areas in which a non-separation policy is adopted, such as in Continental Europe, universal banks are entitled to carry on a range of activities, which include core deposit taking and securities trading and underwriting.[73] If sector separation is to be maintained, the two main types of controls are business or activity restrictions – through authorization or licensing – and ownership controls. The most common device is to define narrowly the permitted activities

---

72. See Section III.E.1.b, later in this chapter. A number of worked examples are nevertheless provided on each measurement technique in the supplementary paper on capital adequacy. This assists understand how each operates in practice.
73. See, for example, Annex to the Second Banking Directive; as restated in the Banking Consolidated Directive. See Directive 2000/12/EEC of May 2000, relating to the taking up and pursuit of the business of credit institutions.

that a financial institution may undertake. This device is often referred to as the 'general prohibition' in each of the mina financial laws.[74] Institutions may be permitted to carry out particular ancillary activities, although these will not involve any other core service in a separate sector.[75]

Where activity or authorisation restrictions are imposed, these restrictions are usually supported by ownership rules to prevent avoidance through holding and subsidiary company relationships. Bank holding company controls were initially developed in the US, although originally to restrict the geographic expansion of branch networks.[76] Bank holding companies were required to register with the Federal Reserve under the Banking Law of 1933 before they could vote their voting stock in their subsidiary banks.[77] The development of substantial banking groups was then further restricted with the Bank Holding

---

74. See, for example, sect. 19(1) of the Financial Services and Markets Act 2000 in the UK, which prohibits any person from undertaking a regulated activity as defined unless otherwise authorized or exempt. Narrower restrictions were formerly imposed on banking, securities and insurance companies under the relevant legislation, including, in particular, the Banking Act 1987, the Financial Services Act 1986 and the Insurance Companies Acts.

75. US law generally uses terms such as 'closely related to banking as to be a proper incident thereto' 12 USC SS 1843 (C)(8). Financial holding companies may also undertake any other activity that is 'financial in nature or incidental to such financial activity' or 'complementary to a financial activity' (provided that it does not 'pose a substantial risk to the safety or soundness of depository institutions or the financial system generally'). Gramm-Leach-Bliley Act, Pub. L. No. 106-102, ss 103(a) (adding a new 12 U.S.C. SS 1843 (K)(a)), 113 Stat. 1338, 1342–50 (1999).

76. Many states introduced anti-branching laws at the beginning of the 20th century, which forced controlling shareholders to acquire and operate banks in separate locations. The McFadden Amendment Act of 1927 then prohibited national banks from branching across state lines. McFadden Act, Ch. 191 SS 7, 44 Stat. 1224 (1927) (codified at 12 U.S.C. SS 36(c)). Banking holding companies were subsequently prohibited from acquiring banks across state lines unless expressly permitted by the host state under the Douglas Amendment to the Bank Holding Company Act. Act of May 9, 1956, Ch. 240, 70 Stat 134 (originally codified at 12 U.S.C. SS 1842(d)). See generally, P.A. McCoy, *Banking Law Manual* (Lexus Publishing, Loose-leaf), Chapter 1.

77. Companies that acquire banks cannot generally own voting stock in non-bank companies subject to particular exceptions. Banking holding companies cannot directly or indirectly own or control other companies except:

    – companies engaged in banking or in managing or controlling banks and their authorized subsidiaries;
    – companies that furnish services to the holding company's subsidiaries; and
    – companies engaged in exempt non-bank activities.

    Banking Act 193, Ch 89, SS 2(b), 48 Stat. 162. Registration was nevertheless avoided by surrendering Federal Reserve membership or relying on non-voting control with the effect that less than 15 per cent of all bank holding companies were supervised by the Federal Reserve by 1954. See McCoy, para. 4.01.

Company Act in 1956 (BHCA).[78] The objective was accordingly to restrict the
territorial, financial and non-financial expansion of bank groups.[79]

The earlier restrictions impose under the BHCA in the US were subsequently relaxed after an extended period of lobbying which led to the adoption
of the Financial Competitiveness (Gramm-Leach-Bliley) Act in 1999.[80] This
followed some earlier relaxation of the bank holding company restrictions during the 1990s.[81] Gramm-Leach-Blile then provided for the establishment of
'financial holding companies' which may own subsidiary operations in each of
the major financial areas. Financial holding companies may conduct the same
activities as bank holding companies as well as any other activity that is 'financial in nature or incidental to such financial activity' ('financial activities') and
activities that are 'complementary to a financial activity' provided that these
activities do 'not pose a substantial risk to the safety or soundness of depository institutions or the financial system generally'.[82] Financial holding companies must be well capitalised and well managed with their subsidiary banks
and thrifts having a satisfactory or outstanding Community Reinvestment Act
rating.[83]

Although originally established to restrict geographic expansion and consolidation, the use of bank holding companies in increasing financial stability has also been recognised subsequently.[84] Early 'net worth maintenance
agreements' (or 'capital maintenance commitments') were used with regard to

---

78. The BHCA prohibited individuals from becoming bank holding companies and therefore
    from owning banks; bank holding companies were prohibited from abusing a monopoly
    position and unreasonable restraints on trade; non-bank activities were limited to those
    'closely related to banking', which prevented direct industry tie-ups; with the Douglas
    Amendment prohibiting inter-state expansion. Bank Holding Company Act of 1956,
    SS 3(d), 70 Stat. 133, 135 (formerly codified as amended 12 U.S.C. SS 1842(d)). Any com-
    pany that acquires control of a bank or a bank holding company becomes a bank holding
    company under US law. 'Control' is defined to include 25 per cent stock ownership, ability
    to elect a board majority or other effective control of management. Banking holding com-
    panies were also brought within the restrictions imposed under the BHCA in 1970. Bank
    Holding Company Act Amendments of 1970, Pub. L. No. 91/607, SS 101, 84 Stat. p 1,760.
79. Despite these restrictions, bank holding companies controlled 96 per cent of all bank assets
    by 1998 with only one-fifth of US banks operating without a holding company with most
    of these being small state banks. See McCoy, para. 4.01.
80. Gramm-Leach-Bliley Act, Pub. L. No. 106-102, SS 103(c)(1)(B) (adding a new 12 U.S.C.
    SS 1841 [P]), 113 Stat. 1338, 1351 (1999). See Olive and Arner, 'Sectoral Regulation in the
    United States: Financial Services Modernization in the US and the Gramm-Leach-Bliley
    Act of 1999', in Arner and Lin, no. 10 above.
81. The Douglas Amendment was repealed under the Riegle-Neal Interstate Banking and
    Branching Act of 1994. Pub. L. No. 103-328, 1994 U.S.C.C.A.N. (108 Stat.) 2338.
82. SS 103(a).
83. SS 103(b).
84. The US Supreme Court described the objectives of the BHCA as being:

    – to restrict the control of banking and non-banking enterprises by a single business entity;
    – to prevent anti-competitive tendencies in national credit markets through restrictions on
      concentration; and

thrifts during the 1970s to require holding companies to support their under-performing subsidiaries. This was extended in the 1980s under the Federal Reserve's 'source of strength doctrine' which requires bank holding companies to support the solvency of their bank and thrift subsidiaries where necessary, including through capital injections.[85] This is clearly contrary to traditional doctrines of the limited liability of corporate entities, although it does reflect the close nature of the relations that exist between group companies and the need to protect the instability of the banking markets. The source of strength doctrine is further supported by cross-guarantee provisions that make affiliated banks and thrifts responsible for any losses suffered to the Federal Deposit Insurance Corporation (FDIC) from the failure of a related bank.[86]

One of the other major difficulties that arose in negotiating the US Gramm-Leach-Bliley Act was in connection with the exchange of non-public customer information and cross-marketing. This situation caused significant difficulty, because the major banking groups wanted to retain the right to make full use of this sort of valuable information. The compromise agreed upon was to allow information exchange in the holding company, subject to customers opting out of sales of their personal information to unaffiliated third parties. This compromise is also subject to exceptions, including where considered necessary to carry out the institution's functions.[87] Financial institutions have also been required to adopt appropriate privacy policies to protect non-public personal information with relevant standards being developed by the Federal authorities and the Federal Trade Commission. Enforcement of these provisions has been conferred on the federal regulators. The provisions also made it illegal to obtain non-public customer information under false pretences, except where necessary for law enforcement purposes or other specified investigations.

    – to ensure the safety and soundness of banks and the safety and soundness of their bank holding companies

    See *First Lincolnwood*, 439 U.S. pp. 243 and 248.

85. Policy Statement, 52 Fed. Reg. 15, 707, (1987). Regulation Y was also interpreted in 1994 to require holding companies to serve as a source of financial and managerial strength to their subsidiary banks and prevent them from conducting their operations in an unsafe or unsound manner. 12 C.S.R. SS 225.4(a)(1).

86. See Financial Institutions Reform, Recovery and Enforcement Act of 1989 (FRREA), 12 U.S.C. SS 1821(i)(2); and 12 U.S.C. SS 1815(e) (on cross-guarantees). This provided for the horizontal consolidation of holding companies and ensured affiliate although it did not extend to non-bank affiliates or their holding companies. Vertical consolidation was subsequently also provided for under the Federal Deposit Insurance Corporation Improvement Act 1991 (FDICIA). This introduced 'prompt corrective action' provisions that required bank or thrift subsidiaries that became under capitalized either to submit a capital restoration plan with financial guarantees produced by the parent holding company or incur operating restrictions, including interest rate caps, restrictions on asset growth and activities, management amendments and inter-bank deposit balance. 12 U.S.C. SS 1831(d)(2)(A)-(C). For comment, see McCoy, para. 4.05.

87. Gramm-Leach-Bliley Act, Pub. L. No. 106-102, SS 502-503, 113 Stat. 1338, pp. 1,347–1,349 (1999).

III.D.   REGULATORY AND SUPERVISORY REVISION

Where some level of cross-sector conglomerate activity is to be permitted, the main regulatory and supervisory requirements that apply with regard to each of the financial institutions involved must be reviewed. This review is required to ensure that they continue to operate in an effective manner. The main regulatory issues that arise include matters such as intra-group exposures, capital allocation, management autonomy, internal systems and controls and crisis management. Ensuring that financial groups are supervised on a consolidated basis is also essential.[88] While consolidated supervision has become an essential element of almost all modern regulatory systems, many have also extended this to include significant business or management unit supervision[89] and financial conglomerates more generally.[90] The objective of each of these initiatives is to ensure that conglomerates are subject to effective regulation and supervision as they are allowed to develop.

III.D.1.   Regulatory Revision

Certain adjustments must be made to sector-based legislative frameworks to ensure that they continue to be relevant in a conglomerate situation. The main areas involved have already been referred to.[91] The following particular issues can be referred to:

III.D.1.a.   Intra-Group Exposures

A range of exposures can arise between subsidiary and parent companies in a conglomerate structure. These exposures include direct draw-down facilities, loans and cross-guarantees. Other indirect exposures can also arise, for example, with regard to negative pledges and cross default clauses in general loan documentation, which can be triggered by an affiliate's default. The Basel Committee referred to the contagion difficulties that were significantly exacerbated by complex intra-group exposures created as a result of direct and indirect claims, including credit lines, equity investments, trading exposures, liquidity management, guarantees and commodities.

---

88. See Walker, 'Consolidated Supervision', BIJBFL [1998].
89. See Walker, 'Bank Supervision', Ch. 4 in W Blair, Walker and others, *Banking and Financial Services Regulation* (2nd ed., Butterworths, 1998,), Ch 4; and Walker, 'Banking Supervision' in Blair, Walker and others, *Banking and Financial Services Regulation* (3rd ed., Butterworths, 2002), Chapter 6.
90. See Walker, 'Conglomerate Law and International Financial Market Supervision' *Boston University Annual Review of Banking Law*, vol. 17: 287, 1998), p. 287; and Walker, *International Banking Regulation – Law, Policy and Practice*, Chapter 4).
91. See Basel Committee, IOSCO, Tripartite Group and Joint Forum papers.

III.D.1.b.   *Capital Calculation and Distribution*

Separate difficulties arise with regard to the calculation of total group capital within a conglomerate and with ensuring that this capital is properly distributed across the companies concerned. One of the major problems that arise with group structures is with the double-gearing of capital. This occurs whenever intra-group investments are included in available group capital.[92] As the same capital is effectively transferred from the asset to the liability side of the balance sheet each time, the original capital invested does not increase, although the total groups figure will be considerably higher. Best practice, accordingly, is to deduct intra-group holdings and investments in unregulated non-financial entities.[93]

Various techniques have been developed to attempt to calculate total capital within heterogeneous groups. Four systems in particular have been identified, although only three have been approved at this stage.[94]

– the building-block prudential approach: involves using the consolidated accounts at the parent company level;
– the risk-based aggregation approach: totals the solo capital requirements of the regulated group and compares the result with group capital; and
– the risk-based deduction method: examines each company in turn, beginning at the lowest group level, with subsidiary investments being subject to a risk deduction calculated on the basis of the own funds of the subsidiary assessed on a solo-plus basis less the capital requirement of the subsidiary multiplied by the proportion of shares held in the subsidiary.[95]

Rather than impose any specific model, the Joint Forum confirmed that groups should adopt any of these three methodologies. The selection will depend on the type and structure of the conglomerate involved. Capital would also still have to beproperly distributed within the group to ensure that each operating

---

92. Long chains of vertical investment may arise which produce a large total capital figure.
93. See Joint Forum, *Capital Adequacy Principles Paper* (February 1999). Where unregulated entities conduct activities similar to regulated firms, a comparable or notional capital proxy may be estimated by applying the capital requirements of the most analogous regulated industry. Otherwise, holdings in unregulated non-financial entities should be excluded from group capital.
94. The fourth technique is referred to as block capital adequacy, which involves the classification and aggregation of assets and liabilities according to risk types. This can achieve an accounting based consolidation within heterogeneous groups although this will require the development of harmonized standards, which can be impracticable for some time. See Tripartite Group, July 1995 Report, para. 109–110. See also Joint Forum, *Capital Adequacy* (February 1999).
95. See Tripartite Group, para. 111–129. See also Joint Forum, *Capital Adequacy* (February 1999).

entity was adequately capitalized in accordance with the relevant regulatory provisions.[96]

III.D.1.c.   *Management Authority and Autonomy*

It is essential that management within each regulated entity be suitable and have sufficient authority to carry out their functions. Conglomerate management will necessarily involve some degree of centralisation, although it is also essential that proper and effective oversight be maintained at the regulated entity level. Supervisors and regulators must ensure that regulated and non-regulated holding companies have adequate strength of management to ensure that total group risk is prudently managed. A series of fit and proper principles designed to ensure proper management suitability were developed by the Joint Forum in its February 1988 paper.[97] These are generally based on suitability, review and consultation. Sufficient management autonomy must also be conferred on each regulated entity to ensure that it complies with relevant regulatory obligations. This is, in particular, necessary to avoid any conflicts of interest arising at the regulated entity level. Supervisors should know who is responsible for compliance with legal and supervisory requirements and be informed of any significant changes in shareholders, as well as significant management changes within the group.[98]

III.D.1.d.   *Systems and Controls and Conflict of Interest*

Adequate systems and controls must be maintained at the regulated entity and group level. Unfortunately, little guidance has been provided in this regard at the international level. The adequacy of any specific financial firm's systems and controls will have to be assessed at the national level both on initial authorization and on a continuing basis subsequently. Serious conflicts of interest can arise where various parts of the group act for the same customers or investors. This can be partly dealt with through 'Chinese walls' although their operation would have to be subject to strict conditions at the national level and subject to effective continued oversight.

Difficulties can also arise in situations in which banking or insurance entities in the conglomerate make loans or invest assets in the group outside the usual approval processes or where investors with substantial holdings have separate contractual relationships in the group, creating both shareholder and credit conflicts.[99] No detailed recommendations have been issued in this regard, although these will generally be dealt with through management and

---

96. See Basel Committee, *Principles for the Supervision of Financial Conglomerates* (September 1992).
97. See Joint Forum, *Fit and Proper Principles* (February 1998).
98. See Tripartite Group, July 1995 Report, para. 80.
99. Ibid., para. 73–74.

shareholder suitability, management authority and autonomy and effective internal control systems. This remains a significant problem which must be considered within any particular national regulatory systems.[100]

III.D.1.e.   Crisis Management

Effective crisis management systems must be maintained within regulated firms to ensure that any difficulties that arise are properly identified and corrected. This process will generally be carried out as part of the ongoing risk management functions of the entity, although additional exposures can arise through direct and indirect intra-group relations.

III.D.2.   Supervisory Adjustment

It is essential to ensure that all complex groups are subject to effective supervision. This, in particular, requires that adequate information is obtained with regard to regulated entity and group activities and that this information is capable of necessary exchange and proper distribution. These issues were considered by the Joint Forum in its framework and information-sharing papers.[101] The Joint Forum produced a number of principles for information sharing, based generally on sufficiency, cooperation, full communication, distribution and necessary contact and trust.

While these types of general principles are of value, individual entities and groups must be effectively supervised on a continuing basis in practice. For this purpose, most countries have developed relatively complex consolidated supervision systems to ensure that regulated firms are properly supervised on a solo and group basis. Certain countries have since extended this supervision to include significant management or business units, with additional information also being obtained in connection with more complex conglomerate structures.

---

100.   In the UK, conflicts of interest are highlighted within the General Principles that the FSA expects firms to comply with at all times. In the PRIN section in Block, 11 general principles are set out in the *FSA Handbook of Rules and Guidance*. The FSA has confirmed since the FSMA came into effect on 1 December 2001 that it will enforce breaches of these general principles strictly. Equivalent provisions may have to be considered in other systems. See, generally, Walker, *Financial Services Authority and Financial Services and Markets Act* in Blair, Walker and others, (3rd edn, Butterworths, 2002), Chapter 2.
101.   See Joint Forum, *Framework for Information Sharing* (February 1999); and Joint Forum, *Principles for Supervisory Information Sharing* (February 1999).

III.D.2.a.   *Consolidated Supervision*

Consolidated supervision was originally adopted at the international level by the Basel Committee in 1979.[102] Consolidated supervision was then included within the Committee's Revised Concordat in 1983 which established particular general principles governing the supervision of internationally active banks.[103]

Consolidated supervision was adopted in the EU under the first Consolidated Supervision Directive in 1983 and subsequently extended to include securities subsidiaries and holding companies in 1992.[104] These requirements have since been restated in the 2000 Banking Supervision Directive,[105] which is based on the definition of a credit institution (bank) and financial institution (non-bank financial entity),[106] as well as a financial holding company.[107] Within the scope of consolidation, the EU provisions also include ancillary banking services undertakings,[108] with information requirements also being imposed on mixed-activity holding companies and insurance companies.[109] Mixed-activity holding companies are required to provide information on group activities, which information can be verified under the inspection procedures provided for.[110]

---

102. See Basel Committee, *Consolidated Supervision of Bank's International Activities* (March 1979). This followed an earlier 1978 paper by the Committee, *Consolidation of banks' balance sheets: aggregation of risk-bearing assets as a method of supervisory bank solvency* (October 1978). See Basel Committee, *Compendium of Documents* (April 1997), vol. 1, pp. 83–84. For comment, see Walker, Chapter 1, pp. 139–141.
103. See Basel Committee, *Principles for the supervision of banks' foreign establishments* (May 1983). This followed the Committee's earlier First Concordat, *Report on the supervision of banks' foreign establishments* (September 1975). See generally, Walker, Chapter 1.
104. See Council Directive 83/350/EEC of 13 June 1983 on the supervision of credit institutions on a consolidated basis; and Council Directive 92/30/EEC on the supervision of credit institutions on a consolidated basis.
105. Council Directive 2000/12/EEC of the European Parliament and of the Council of 20 March 2000, relating to the taking-up and pursuit of the business of credit institutions, Title V, Chapter 1, Articles 52–56. See Annex 4.
106. See Banking Consolidation Directive, Annex 1, para. 2–12.
107. A financial holding company is a financial institution, the subsidiary undertakings of which are either exclusively or mainly credit institutions or financial institutions one, at least, of which subsidiaries is a credit institution. See BCD, Article 1.21. The terms 'subsidiary' and 'parent undertaking' are borrowed from corresponding company law requirement. See Directive 83/349/EEC.
108. An undertaking the principal activity of which consists in owning or managing property, managing data-processing services or any other similar activity that is ancillary to the principle activity of one or more credit institutions. BCD, Article 1.23.
109. A 'mixed-activity holding company' is a parent undertaking, other than a financial holding company or a credit institution, the subsidiaries of which included, at least, one credit institution. See BCD, Article 1.22.
110. Articles 55 and 56.

III.D.2.b.   *Business Unit Supervision*

Certain countries, such as the UK, have since extended supervision to include other significant business, as well as legal subsidiaries within the scope of consolidation. The limitation of consolidated supervision is that it only applies to separate legally incorporated entities. More-complex financial groups are rarely organized on a legal entity basis in practice, but rather on geographical or product lines. The effect of consolidation is then to bring these separate corporate entities within the scope of supervision, although not the underlying business and management units involved. Under the UK rules, a 'significant management unit' is one that carries on any separately identifiable revenue generating activity with a group.[111]

This management unit requirement was developed as part of a larger revision of the nature of modern bank supervision in the UK. Following the collapse of Barings in 1995, the Bank of England had commissioned a report by the Board of Banking Supervision in July 1995 into the circumstances surrounding the collapse.[112] A number of immediate supervisory changes were made and a separate report commission by Arthur Andersen which was produced in July 1996.[113] A number of consultation documents were subsequently issued on the revision of bank supervisory practice, which included a proposed paper on the adoption of a risk-based approach, which is referred to as the RATE framework.[114] The objective was to develop a new 'supervision by risk' approach based on the identification of a bank's specific risks (CAMEL B) as against its control capability COM (Internal Controls, Organisation and Management). CAMEL consists of a bank's capital, assets, market risk and earnings as well as a generalbusiness factor (B), which constituted a revised form of the

---

111. The original Quantitative Consolidated Supervision Guideline produced by the Bank of England, before the assumption of the responsibility for the supervision of banks by the FSA, defined a significant management unit as one that satisfied one of four quantitative criteria or was otherwise considered by the authorities or by the management of the reporting institution to give rise to any significant business or control risk. The quantitative criteria were that the unit generated five per cent or more of revenue, five per cent or more of pre-tax profit or loss of the consolidated pre-tax profits, five per cent or more of the consolidated capital requirement or if the group's investment in the unit is deducted and the investment represents five per cent or more of the consolidated capital base before deduction. See Bank of England, *RATE Framework* (1997), Annex I.

112. See Board of Banking Supervision, 'Inquiry into the circumstances of the Collapse of Barings' HC (1994–1995) p. 673.

113. See Arthur Andersen, *Findings and Recommendations of the Review of Supervision and Surveillance*(July 1996). See also Bank of England, *The Bank's Review of Supervision* (July 1996).

114. See Bank of England, *A Risk Based Approach to Bank Supervision (The RATE Framework)* (June 1997). A separate risk-based approach was also developed for overseas banks, although this approach was subsequently integrated within the RATE framework. See Bank of England, *A Risk Based Approach to the Supervision of Non-EEA banks (the SCALE framework)* (July 1997).

US CAMEL (Capital, Asset, Management, Earnings and Liquidity).[115] This RATE framework has since been revised and developed in the FSA's larger new regulatory approach and operating framework adopted since the enactment of the Financial Services and Markets Act in December 2001.

It is not necessary that China consider adopting this type of approach, at least initially, and with regard to all financial institutions. This should, nevertheless, be considered with some management unit requirements possibly being applied with regard to more-complex groups over time.

III. D.2. c.   Conglomerate Supervision

Few countries have any sophisticated, direct form of conglomerate supervision. The EU Banking Consolidation Directive extends consolidated supervision generally to include banks and securities firms with additional information requirements being imposed on insurance related and other mixed-activity groups. No specific guidance, however, is provided as to how the supervision is to be conducted. Only general information collection principles have been developed at the international level with no specific direction being provided in connection with conglomerate supervision. A general obligation of 'supplementary supervision' is imposed on 'financial conglomerates' – as defined in the EU proposed Directive on Financial Conglomerates – although this only applies to the matters listed, including financial position, coordinated appointment and cooperation and exchange of information.

The UK has attempted to develop a new regulatory approach that applies to all financial institutions on a common and integrated basis. This approach was considered necessary following the enactment of the Financial Services and Markets Act and the creation of a single regulatory framework under the authority of the FSA. In connection with this, the FSA has been developing a new regulatory approach and operating system,[116] based on the identification of a number of probability and impact factors designed to enable the FSA to assess the extent to which it has complied with its regulatory objectives, as set out in the Financial Services and Markets Act, Section 2(2). The FSA has also produced a single Handbook of Rules and Guidance, issued under Sections 138 and 157 of the Act. This handbook includes a number of interim prudential sourcebooks that have generally adopted the previous sector based financial and systems and controls requirements imposed on financial firms.

In designing the new rulebook, it had to be accepted that the FSA would not have time to develop a fully integrated set of financial and control requirements for all firms by the time the Act came into effect and that these earlier, sector-based rules would have to be continued on an interim basis. The FSA

---

115. See Walker, 'Banking Supervision' in Blair, Walker and others, *Banking and Financial Services Regulation* (2nd ed., Butterworths), para. 4.4 and 4.40–84.

116. Ibid., Chapter 6.

has since issued a draft integrated prudential sourcebook – referred to as the 'PRU' – which will replace the earlier interim measures. This also adopts a supervision-by-risk system, although this system is revised to refer to risk-by-risk, because the system extends the previous bank-based RATE to include all major market risks. The PRU will then apply to credit risk, market risk, insurance risk, group risk and liquidity risk. The PRU includes separate chapters on each of these risks with a financial institution being subject to one or more of these, depending upon the type and scope of the financial activities conducted. The effect of this new risk-by-risk system is to develop a new model approach that could apply to all financial risk on an integrated basis. This can then be suitable for use in connection with financial conglomerates in particular. The PRU is not expected to come into effect until 2004 with sections having been postponed until 2006 to parallel the proposed capital amendments under Basel Committee's proposed New Capital Accord (Basel II).[117] The adoption of a risk-by-risk approach would be considered inappropriate in China at this stage, particularly because China has not adopted a single legislative framework but rather continues supervision and regulation on a sector basis. The construction of this type of cross-risk approach may, nevertheless, be examined further over time as markets and financial groups develop.

III.E.   CONGLOMERATE LAW MODELS

To date, few distinct or full conglomerate laws have been adopted. Many countries have created a single regulator, although these systems have often only continued to apply the separate sector laws that previously applied.[118] A smaller number of countries have adopted a further single-regulatory approach that attempts to create a single legislative framework for all services and markets. The most developed example of this is the UK.

Where a single legislative framework has not been established, most conglomerate measures operate through regulatory or supervisory adjustment within the existing sector laws.[119] The effect of this is to incorporate revisions or adjustments into existing regulatory and supervisory provisions to ensure that they are capable of proper and effective application in a conglomerate situation. One of the most important attempts to construct a single set of coherent

---

117. See Walker, 'Capital Consultation' *Financial Regulation International* (July 2003), p. 1.
118. Countries with single supervisors for all financial intermediaries include: Denmark, Estonia, Germany, Hungary, Ireland, Japan, South Korea, Latvia, Malta, Norway, Singapore, Sweden and the United Kingdom. Countries that have single supervisors for banks and insurers or banks and securities firms include: Australia, Austria, Canada, Columbia, El Salvador, Finland, Iceland, Jamaica, Luxembourg, Malaysia, Mauritius, Mexico, Pakistan, Paraguay, Peru and Venezuela. Other countries that are considering adopting an integrated supervisory framework include Bulgaria, Kazakstan, Poland, Slovakia, Slovenia, South Africa, the Ukraine and Indonesia. See de Luna-Martinez and Rose, in D Arner and Lin, supra note 30.
119. See Section E(1) and (2).

provisions that draws all of these amendments and revisions together in an integrated approach is that set out in the proposed EU draft Directive on Financial Conglomerates.[120] The objective of the proposed EU law is to lay down rules for the supplementary supervision of regulated entities within a financial conglomerate.

The proposed EU Directive includes a series of new and revised definitions including financial conglomerate[121] and mixed financial holding company (Article 2).[122] Separate threshold conditions are imposed on the definition of a financial conglomerate (Article 3) and an identification obligation (Article 4). The Directive contains further provision with regard to supplementary supervision (Chapter II), including financial position, appointment of a coordinator, cooperation and exchange of information, third country reciprocity, creation of a Financial Conglomerate Committee (Chapter III) and a series of amendment provisions (Chapter IV). A separate provision is included with regard to asset management companies (Chapter V) and particular transitional and final provisions (Chapter VI).

---

120. See draft directive 2002/87/EEC of the European Parliament and of the Council of 16 December 2002 on the supplementary supervision of credit institutions, insurance undertakings and investment firms in a financial conglomerate and amending Council Directives 73/239/EEC, 79/267/EEC, 92/49/EEC, 92/96/EEC, 93/6/EEC and 93/22/EEC and Directives 98/78/EC and 2000/12/EC of the European Parliament and of the Council (OJ L 035, 11/02/2003, P 0001–0027.

121. A 'financial conglomerate' means a group that meets the following conditions (subject to Article 3 of the FCD):

    – a regulated entity within the meaning of Article 1 is at the head of the group or, at least, one of the subsidiaries in the group is a regulated entity within the meaning of Article 1;
    – where a regulated entity exists in the meaning of Article 1 at the head of the group, it is either a parent undertaking of an entity in the financial sector, an entity which holds a participation in an entity in the financial sector or an entity linked with an entity in the financial sector by a relationship within the meaning of article 12(1) of Directive 83/349/EEC;
    – where no regulated entity in the meaning of Article 1 is at the head of the group, the group's activities mainly occur in the financial sector within the meaning of article 3(1);
    – at least one of the entities in the group is within the insurance sector and at least one is within the banking or investment services sector; and
    – the consolidated and or aggregated activities of the entities in the group within the insurance sector and the consolidated and/or aggregated activities of the entities within the banking and investment services sector are both significant within the meaning of article 3(2) or (3). Any sub-group of a group that falls within this definition shall also be considered as a financial conglomerate. See FCD, Article 2.14.

122. A parent undertaking, other than a regulated entity, that together with its subsidiaries, at least one of which is a regulated entity which has its head office in the EU and other entities, constitutes a financial conglomerate. FCD, Article 1.15.

The EU draft Directive on Financial Conglomerates is an important initiative in developing a necessary framework for the supplementary supervision of financial conglomerates. This initiative is particularly relevant where existing sectoral supervisory and regulatory systems are to be maintained. Supplementary supervision is then developed as an adjunct, complementary or supporting mechanism to existing sector based supervision. This also has the advantage of giving effect to all of the main elements of the Joint Forum recommendations including, in particular, capital, intra-group exposures, concentrations, suitability and information exchange. The draft EU Directive contains some provisions that would be of value in China. Little assistance, however, is provided with regard to detailed regulatory content as the Directive is concerned with establishing the more general principles that should apply. A number of other matters are also dealt with in other existing Directives such as consolidated supervision and information exchange. The Directive is accordingly of value but it must be considered with other supporting European measures that would apply.

III.F.   INSTITUTIONAL RELATIONS AND STRUCTURE

Appropriate inter-agency relations must be established, in which more than one authority is responsible for the supervision and regulation of financial markets in any particular country. This need for general inter-agency cooperation then increases in importance where financial groups include companies active in more than one other financial sector. Appropriate arrangements governing these relations can either be set out in an administrative law or regulation of some form or under a memorandum of understanding entered into between the relevant agencies.

   Agreed inter-agency relations are necessary wherever a financial institution may undertake some cross-sector activity or cross-sector holdings or ownership are otherwise permitted. This would only be unnecessary where no cross-sector interest or exposure of any form were involved. The residual issue in such cases would then only be market support (lender of last resort) although even this would be restricted to the banking markets and managed through the central bank. If some cross-sector activity or holdings are to be permitted in China, appropriate inter-agency relations would have to be established either in the form of a memorandum of understanding or administrative law or regulation. The longer-term option that may be considered would be to merge the existing sector agencies and establishing a single financial regulator.

III.F.1.   Memorandum of Understanding

Various mechanisms can be developed to facilitate cooperation between supervisory authorities. These include establishing a college mechanism such as that used in the case of BCCI[123] or the appointment of a lead regulator or coordinator.[124] This can be supported by further separate committee arrangements at the regional or international level, such as through the Contract Group (*Groupe de Contact*) in the EU, which considers issues of common interest with regard to the supervision of particular banks or banking groups. These mechanisms are generally designed to support the collective supervision of individual financial institutions or groups. Specific problems will be discussed and general policy or coordinated action will be agreed upon.

In addition to these collective mechanisms, day-to-day cooperation between individual authorities – either on a bilateral or multilateral basis – is generally effected through the conclusion of an appropriate memorandum of understanding (MoU) or more specifically a Financial Information Sharing memorandum (FISMoU).[125] An MoU is an agreement between two or more agencies that set out the terms under which the agencies will cooperate on a continuing basis. This will include provisions with regard to the exchange of information and document access, supporting investigations or verifications and enforcement or corrective action. A FISMoU is a more-limited type of MoU originally developed by the UK authorities for the exchange of specified information on a regular basis such as with regard to risk assessment determinations and financial compliance by individual institutions or groups. An MoU can also include some affirmative action, such as with regard to the mandatory reporting of firms that experience financial difficulties. Here, affirmative action generally requires that something is monitored and acted on positively rather than only in response to a passive request for assistance.

An increasingly complex network of MoUs has been entered into between sector authorities, both nationally and globally. Although initially adopted in the securities area principally, this practice has since spread into the banking and insurance markets. Previously, banking cooperation tended to be restricted to more-general policy discussion and the production of best practice supervisory and regulatory guidelines, such as through the Basel Committee on Banking Supervision. Most financial authorities are now connected with a large number of others, both nationally and globally, and within the same sector or across sectors through an extended number of individual MoUs.[126] These

123. See Lord Justice Bingham, 'Inquiry to the Supervision of the Bank of Credit and Commerce International' (22 October 1992).

124. See Walker, 'Conglomerate Law and International Financial Market Supervision', *Boston Annual Review of Banking Law* (Vol. 17, 1998). See also Walker, *International Banking Regulation – Law, Policy and Practice*, Chapter 4.

125. See Walker, 'International Supervisory Co-operation' in Blair, Walker and others, *Banking and Financial Services Regulation* (Third Edition), paras 17.7–17.16. See also IMF, *International Capital Markets: Developments, Prospects and Policy Issues* (August 1995), Annex III, 'Mechanics for International Co-operation in Regulation', p. 161.

126. For a list of the MoUs concluded between 1992 and 1994, see IMF, *International Capital Markets: Developments, Prospects and Key Issues* (September 1996), Annex IV, 'International Co-operation of Supervision and Regulation of Financial Institutions', Box. A

authorities can also be entered into on a bilateral or multilateral basis, such as the May 1995 Windsor Declaration.[127]

To facilitate the further use and common development of MoUs, IOSCO has produced a set of common standards governing the content and operation of MoUs in the securities area.[128] These standards contain a number of specific provisions with regard to the scope of relevant subject matter, confidentiality obligations, implementation procedures, the rights of persons subject to MoU requests, regular consultation, public policy exceptions, types of assistance, participation by requesting authorities and cost sharing. These are intended to apply to MoUs entered into between securities authorities and between securities and other authorities.

The IOSCO Principles and the use of MoUs and FISMoUs generally should be fully supported. However, important to bear in mind is that these are not formal international documents and lack the formal authority of treaties and conventions. It is this informality, however, that facilitates the conclusion of MoUs, which would otherwise be obstructed by protracted negotiations in such sensitive and difficult areas.

Although an advantage in terms of negotiation, this informality creates consequent problems in terms of enforcement with the validity and effect of such arrangements generally being dependent upon sufficient goodwill and commitment between the authorities concerned. No formal enforcement mechanisms can be included although authorities can cooperate and coordinate their unilateral corrective responses. The other main difficulty that arises is that MoUs will generally include a 'public policy' exception that permits authorities to refuse to provide assistance or co-operation where this may otherwise violate domestic policy considerations.[129] This can be triggered in any case where sovereign, national security or other essential interests can be effected.

---

list of the main MoUs currently in place is also generally kept on the IOSCO website at <www.iosco.org>.

127. This followed a meeting of the regulatory authorities from 16 countries responsible for the supervision of the world's leading futures and derivatives exchanges. See also the Future Industry Association Global Task Force on Financial Integrity, *Financial Integrity Recommendations for Futures and Options Markets and Market Participants* (June 1995). See Walker, 'Financial Derivatives – Global Regulatory Developments' [1996] *JBL*, January 66, 70.

128. See Working Party No 4 of the Technical Committee of IOSCO, *Principles for Memorandum of Understanding*, Documents of the XVI Annual Conference of IOSCO, No 5, September 1991 (the IOSCO Principles). IOSCO produced a separate multilateral Memorandum of Understanding (MOU) concerning co-operation and exchange of information between regulatory authorities in 2002. IOSCO, *Multilateral Memorandum concerning Consultation and Co-operation and the Exchange of Information* (May 2002). This replaces the earlier guidance document on the use of MOUs in the securities area. The purpose is to establish a series of common standards for consultation and cooperation between authorities to operate on a global basis.

129. See IOSCO Principles, Principle 6.

MoUs are accordingly of considerable value in facilitating inter-agency and cross-sector and cross-border cooperation, although their limitations especially in terms of enforcement and public policy exception must be taken into consideration. These MoUs are of particular use in providing for the necessary exchange of relevant information although appropriate confidentiality obligations should be imposed both on the providing and recipient authorities with clear and express channels (or 'gateways') through which this type of information can be exchanged. Care will also have to be taken generally in drafting the terms of an appropriate MoU. Reference must also be made to the IOSCO principles and existing model MoUs available.

III.F.2. Administrative law or Regulation

Rather than attempt to deal with inter-agency relations through an informal MoU, an administrative law or regulation can be considered, at least, for use at the national rather than international level. The obvious advantages are transparency and predictability as well as authority and enforceability. This may be of particular use where countries have less developed administrative laws more generally. The opportunity can then be taken to formalise particular general principles and rights of action through such a law or regulation. The additional advantage created would then be in terms of confirming and clarifying the rights of action available by regulated entities and private parties against administrative agents.

The most simple administrative law or regulation could provide for the identification of the agencies covered and appropriate definitions – such as regulatory authority, financial institution, relevant law, board or governing body. The law or regulation could then provide for the institution and board structure of the regulatory agencies, which include appointment rules, composition, duration, prohibitions and procedures; management, which include appointment, duration and duties; personnel; other divisions and committees or subcommittees; and funding and budget. These provisions may not be considered necessary where they are already dealt with in each of the separate sector Laws and the decision has been taken to continue these in place.

Additional equivalent provisions to those that would otherwise be set out an appropriate inter-agency MoU could also be incorporated as this would include identification of relevant information, confidentiality obligations and exchange of information requests and procedures. Appropriate 'gateways' must be provided for.[130]

Immunity clauses can also be included to avoid regulatory agencies and their, staff as well as appointed external parties from beingheld liable for loss

---

130. See, for example, the Banking Act 1987 in the UK. These provisions have since been replaced by equivalent measures adopted under the Financial Services and Markets Act 2000.

caused otherwise than by action taken in bad faith.[131] Immunity is necessary to limit unnecessary and potentially penal liability on the part of regulatory authorities as well as to protect staff from intimidating or abusive threats of unmerited litigation. Staff protection is, in particular, necessary to ensure that appropriately qualified and experienced people are attracted and retained within the supervisory service.

Additional rights of action should also be provided to ensure the proper judicial review of administrative action. This would be based generally on accountability through an express right of administrative or judicial review. This can then be supported by liability in appropriate cases although again generally limited to bad faith or clear negligence. This issue has become of particular importance in a number of countries where the supervisory authorities have been sued, in particular, by depositors or other creditors that have suffered loss as a result of the failure of a bank or other financial institution.[132] It is accordingly essential to clarify the nature of the rights of action available and limits of potential review and liability. The adoption of an appropriately drafted administrative law and regulation may accordingly be considered more appropriate in China rather than a more informal MoU. This would more clearly and formally clarify the relations between the authorities as well as create supporting rights of action against the statutory agencies at the same time as limit their potential liability within expected and reasonable grounds. If such an administrative or regulatory law or regulation is not to be adopted, an appropriate MoU should be entered into between the POBC and the relevant sector agencies.

III.F.3.   Single Regulator

The alternative to maintaining separate sector regulators and attempting to manage their relations would be to create a single authority for all financial market supervision and regulation. This would represent a considerably more fundamental form of revision but one that could be considered as an interim if not longer-term option. Since 1986, over 29 countries have merged their supervisory functions either in whole or in part.[133] Institutional and regulatory

---

131. See, for example, Section 3 of the Banking Act 1987 in the UK; and the succeeding Paragraph 19, sch. 1 of the Financial Services and Markets Act 2000.
132. The Bank of England in the UK is currently being sued by a number of the former depositors of BCCI that have suffered loss as a result of the bank's closure in July 1991. The Bank is being sued for £10 billion in compensation. Preliminary hearings have determined that the action should proceed on the basis of the tort of misfeasance in public office. The trial date has been set to begin in January 2004. For comment, see Walker, 'Three Rivers', *International Regulator Report* (2002), p. 1.
133. Countries with single supervisors for all financial intermediaries include: Denmark, Estonia, Germany, Hungary, Ireland, Japan, South Korea, Latvia, Malta, Norway, Singapore, Sweden and the United Kingdom. Countries that have single supervisors for banks and insurers or banks and securities firms include: Australia, Austria, Canada,

integration have become significant trends in recent years. The arguments for and against must accordingly be considered in China and the relative potential advantages and disadvantages assessed.

A number of studies and papers have been published on institutional or regulatory revision. Earlier papers considered whether monetary policy and supervisory or regulatory policy should be conducted by the same institution.[134] Subsequent papers have then considered whether financial supervision should be conducted on a unitary or separate sector basis. Early studies in this area tended to focus on the distinction between 'institutional' regulation (the type of financial firm or intermediary) and 'functional' regulation (type of activity conducted) regulation.[135] Later papers have focused on the distinction between systemic stability and consumer protection functions[136]or on possible

---

Columbia, El Salvador, Finland, Iceland, Jamaica, Luxembourg, Malaysia, Mauritius, Mexico, Pakistan, Paraguay, Peru, Venezuela.

Other countries that are considering adopting an integrated supervisory framework include: Bulgaria, Kazakstan, Poland, Slovakia, Slovenia, South Africa, the Ukraine, and Indonesia. See, Freshfields, *How Countries Supervise their Banks, Insurers and Securities Markets* (2001). For discussion, see, Martinez and Rose, 'International Survey of Integrated Supervision' in Arner and Lin, no. 10, Chapter 1.

134. Arguments against an integrated policy function include potential conflicts of interest or policy objectives, consequent credibility problems and the maintenance of price stability as the key objective of the central bank and functional diversity in product or service development. The arguments against separation include the need to maintain the essential link between the lender of last resort and the conduct of supervisory policy, necessary payment system support or dependence with the central bank generally being responsible for payment system stability and the need for basic policy consistency. See, for example, C. Goodheart and D. Schoenmaker, *Institutional Separation Between Supervisory and Monetary Agencies*, Financial Markets Group (FMG, April 1993). For discussion, see Walker, 'United Kingdom Regulatory Reform: A New Beginning in Policy and Programme Construction' in Arner and Lin, no.10, Chapter 1.

135. On the use by the US of the distinction between institutional and functional regulation in the reform of the Glass-Steagall Act, see R.S. Karmel, 'Functional Regulation', *Practising Law Institute, Corporate Law and Practise Course Handbook* (18 November 1985), PLI No. B4–6733 (501 PLI/CORP), p. 9; and M.L. Fein, 'Functional Regulation: A Concept for Glass-Steagall Reform?' 2 *Stanford Journal of Law, Business & Finance* (1995), p. 89. On more general usage in connection with financial reform and demarcation of regulatory responsibility, see J.J. Norton, *Financial Sector Reform in Emerging Economies* (London, BIICL, 2000), Chapter 1, sect. 3. An equivalent distinction between 'structural' and 'conduct' regulation can also be drawn. See, for example, Kay and Vicers, 'Regulatory Reform in Britain', *Economic Policy* [1988] pp. 285 and 312–325. See Olive and Arner, supra note 80 for an alternative formulation.

136. Michael Taylor draws a clear distinction between the systemic stability and consumer protection functions within a financial system and recommends that these are discharged by separate agencies. See, Taylor, 'Twin Peaks: A regulatory structure for the new century' (CSFI, December 1995); Taylor, 'Peak Practice: How to reform the UK's regulatory system' (CSFI, October 1996); and Taylor, 'Regulatory Leviathan: Will Super-SIB Work?' (October 1997). See also, Richard K. Abrams and Michael Taylor, 'Assessing the Case for Unified Financial Sector Supervision' Chapter 1 in Arner and Lin, supra note 30.

regulatory objectives more specifically.[137] Other writers have supported the creation of a single regulator[138] while the use of a holding company or financial holding company system remains a useful intermediate or transitional model.

A number of advantages and disadvantages can be developed for and against the creation of a single regulator.[139] Various general principles can also be developed against which effective regulation can be measured. These include proper objectives, full scope, necessary resources, cost effectiveness, effective enforcement, political independence and proper accountability.[140] A number of separate policy, institutional and operational factors can then be compared in assessing whether a single or multiple sector based regulatory solution should be adopted. While a number of advantages and benefits can be identified in each case, a number of corresponding difficulties and costs can also be noted. In terms of relevant policy, the main advantages are policy integration, consistency, simplicity, ease of review and flexible development. Against this have to be considered possible lender of last resort and moral hazard confusion and extension, consequent lack of reputational incentives, loss of specialist service providers and the need for additional protection for focused or specialist interest groups.

In institutional terms, improved administrative control, increased contact and communication, better allocation and use of resources, improved training and enhanced internal and external accountability have to be balanced with possible excessive size and administrative complexity, potential conflicts of interest and regulatory culture friction, abuse of power, additional and specialist training demands and confused or reduced accountability.

---

137. Other regulatory objectives can also be identified. Goodhart and others, for example, identify six consisting of: systemic regulator, non-bank potential regulator, conduct of business regulator, wholesale business regulator, markets and exchanges regulator and competition regulator. See C.A.E. Goodheart, P. Hartmann, D.T. Llewellyn, L. Rojas-Suarez and S.R. Weisbrod, *Financial Regulation: Why, How and Where Now?* (6 June 1997), Monograph for the Central Bank Governors' Meeting, Bank of England. For a discussion of how this can be applied in relation to regulatory structure and, in particular, in the context of Australia, see J Carmichael, 'Options for Financial Regulatory Structure', Chapter 1 in Arner and Lin, supra note 30.

138. On the UK system, see Clive Briault, *The Rationale for a Single National Financial Services Regulator* (May 1999), FSA Occasional Paper 5; and Briault, *Revisiting the Rationale for a Single National Financial Services Regulator* (February 2002), FSA Occasional Paper 16. See also, Walker, 'United Kingdom Regulatory Reform: A New Beginning in Policy and Programme Construction', Ch. 7 in Arner and Lin, supra note 30.

139. Arguments in favour include: the need to follow market developments; competitive neutrality; regulatory flexibility; regulatory efficiency; staffing; and accountability. Arguments against include: unclear objectives; diseconomies of scale; limited synergies; and moral hazard. See, Abrams and Taylor, n. 107. Other relevant factors in support include: relative simplicity; coherence; unified regulation; reduced compliance; scale and scope; co-operation and communications; prestige and reputation; and transparency. Arguments against also include: concentration; internal division difficulties; conflicting policy and interests; and accountability. See authorities referred in notes 105–110.

140. See Abrams and Taylor, supra note 136.

With regard to operational and implementation issues, operational efficiency (including economies of scope and scale, simplified management and administrative structure and improved expertise and experience), increased responsiveness, flexibility, reduced costs and the elimination of cross-sector competition have to be considered against any inherent operational inefficiency, supporting slow decision taking and response time, the danger of over-standardised responses, increased costs (in certain areas) and more general loss of regulatory competition and consequent incentive and internal accountability as well as high levels of concentration.[141]

A number of corresponding arguments for and against the construction of a single regulatory regime can accordingly be developed. The degree of relative advantage and disadvantage is dependent upon the relationships or effects of the particular regulatory decision taken having regard to all of the supporting financial, legal and administrative factors that characterize any particular legal system and economy. Whichever option is adopted (single agency or multiple agencies), certain adjustments will always have to be made to ensure that the consequent difficulties that arise are eliminated or, at least, reduced and managed. Provided that these limitations are properly identified and controlled, a single or multiple model may be workable in any particular country. The fundamental issue is possibly not then one of initial theoretical design or absolute model selection but of subsequent corrective adjustment.[142]

Different single or hybrid models have been tried in various countries. Australia has adopted a three part system with the core functions of consumer protection, prudential regulation and systemic stability as well as payments system oversight being conferred on separate agencies.[143]These also exchange

---

141. Walker, 'United Kingdom Regulatory Form: A new beginning in policy programme construction', in Arner and Lin, supra note 30.
142. See Walker, in Arner and Lin, supra note 30.
143. A Financial System Inquiry was announced by the government in June 1996 which would be conducted by a five member committee chaired by Stan Wallis, President of the Business Council of Australia. The inquiry report was subsequently produced in March 1997, 'Financial System Inquiry Final Report' (March 1997) (referred to as the Wallis Report). This contained 115 recommendations to overhaul the regulatory framework in the financial services area. The committee, in particular, recommended the establishment of three objective based agencies responsible for consumer protection and market integrity, prudential regulation and systemic stability and payment systems oversight. The Government subsequently set up the Australian Prudential Regulatory Authority (APRA) under the Australian Prudential Regulation Authority Act 1998. This specified the functions and powers of APRA, ensures its independence, details its internal organisational arrangements with additional provisions concerning financing and confidentiality. The Australian Securities and Investments Commission (ASIC) was also set up in 1988 under the Financial Sector Reform (Amendments and Transitional Provisions) Act 1998, Sch 1, 'Amendment to the Australian Securities Commission Act 1989'. This represents an extension of the earlier Australian Securities Commission although its functions are now extended to include consumer protection and market integrity. ASIC is also required to co-operate with the Australian Competition and Consumer Commission.

information and co-operate through an umbrella agency.[144] A more experimental tripartite objective rather than institutional or functional approach has accordingly been attempted in Australia.

Japan has, in contrast, established a single regulator with its Financial Services Agency.[145] The Financial System Reform Law was enacted on 5 June 1998 which amended 21 earlier statutes.[146] Although important, the Japanese reforms were more an internal political reaction rather than a considered policy response to chances in financial markets. The concern was to remove responsibility for financial supervision from the discredited MoF but at the same time continue to separate legislative and operational authority in this area. Japan has also continued to operate on the basis of separate sector laws rather than attempt to integrate those at this stage. A similar approach has been followed in Germany where a single regulator has been created but legislative separation maintained.[147] Korea is presently in the process of integrating

---

144. The Council of Financial Regulators set up under recommendation 112 of the Wallis Committee Report. The Financial Sector Advisory Council was subsequently set up as a high-level non-statutory agency by the Treasurer in March 1998. Its function is to report directly to the Treasurer on regulatory and other changes required to make Australia a leading financial centre in the Asia Pacific region.

145. The Japanese FSA was originally established as the 'Financial Supervisory Agency' by the Diet on 16 June 1997 following transfer of supervisory responsibility for the financial sector from the Ministry of Finance (MoF). The FSA was to act as a separate public authority under the Prime Minister's Office. See Government Release 'Reforms to the Financial Regulatory System' (February 1998). The Financial Supervisory Agency was subsequently replaced by the 'Financial Services Agency' on 1 July 2000 following the integration of the Financial Supervisory Agency with the MoF's Financial System Planning Bureau. On Japanese financial reform, see also Yoshihisa Hayakawa, 'Crisis and Regulation: The Japanese Case' in Arner and Lin, Ch 8; and Mamiko Yokoi-Arai, 'A Single Regulator with a Difference: The Japanese Case' in Arner and Lin, n. 10, Ch 8.

146. Law Amending Related Laws for Financial System Reform of 5 June 1998. This amended a number of earlier statutes including the Banking Law, the Securities and Exchange Law, the Securities Investment Trust Law and the Insurance Business Law to promote liberalisation and innovation within financial markets. This included the abolishment of the earlier Glass-Steagall style restrictions (firewalls) between banking and securities activity and permitted the creation of financial holding companies and bancassurance groups. This followed an earlier package of 'Six Reforms' of the Japanese administration, fiscal structure, social security structure, economic structure, financial system and education adopted by the new Prime Minister Ryutaro Hashimoto on 11 November 1996. The outline proposals for the Japanese Big Bang was subsequently produced in June 1997. Ministry of Finance, 'Financial System Reform: Toward the Early Achievement of Reform' (13 June 1997). This was based on the revised financial system being free, fair and global.

147. The *Bundesanstalt fur Finanzdienstleistungsaufsicht* was established by the German Federal Parliament, the Bundestag, on 1 March 2002. See *Bundesgesetzblatt (Federal Law Gazette)*, 2002-I, 1310. The new Federal Regulatory Authority is responsible for banking, securities and insurance supervision replacing the earlier Federal Banking Supervisory Office (the BundesaufsichtsaImnt *fur das Kreditwesen*) under the Banking Act (the *Kreditwesengesetz*) of 1961 and the Securities Supervisory Office (the *Bundesaufsichtsamnt fur den Wertpapierhandel*) under the Securities Trading Act (the *Wertpapierhandelsgesetz*) of 1998 and the Federal Insurance Supervisory Office under the Insurance Supervision Act

its separate laws, which are currently operating under a single regulator structure.[148]

The most fundamental regulatory reform that has taken place in recent years in any financial system has been in the UK. The incoming Labour Government announced in May 1997 that the structure and content of financial services regulation would be subject to fundamental revision.[149] The earlier Securities and Investments Board was subsequently reconstituted as the Financial Services Authority on 28 October 1998 with responsibility for bank supervision being transferred from the Bank of England under the Bank of England Act 1988.[150] The Financial Services and Markets Act was subsequently adopted on 14 June 2000 which provided for the assumption of responsibility for the supervision and regulation of all other financial areas by the FSA and for the creation of a new integrated regulatory regime under the 'rules' and 'guidance' to be issued by the FSA.[151] The FSA has since produced a full Handbook of Rules and Guidance under the powers conferred. This includes a number of separate blocks and sections that make provision for the regulation and supervision of all financial services and markets in the UK.[152] This includes a

---

(the *Versicherungsaufsichtsgesetz*) of 1901. The new authority is based in both Frankfurt and Bonn and is headed by a President, Vice President and three Deputies for banking, insurance and securities trading. An Administrative Council has also been established to monitor and support the administration. Inter-agency co-operation continues under a Forum for Financial Market Supervision (*Forum fur Finanzmarktaufisicht*) which was set up between the three Federal Supervisory Offices, the Bundesbank and the Federal Ministry of Finance on 3 November 2000. The Forum has been given formal status under the new laws and assigned further advisory functions with regard to the general stability of financial markets. The *Bundesbank* also continues to collect information on market operations and oversee supervision in the regions. Market support (lender of last resort) is managed through the separately incorporated Liquiditats-Konsortialbank which was set up following the collapse of Bankhaus Herstatt in 1974. Day-to-day liquidity is managed in Germany through the Bundesbank with emergency support being provided by the Konsortialbank. On the recent German financial reforms, see generally Jens-Hinrich Binder, 'Financial Market Regulation in Germany: A New Institutional Framework' in Arner and Lin, supra note 30, Ch 9.

148. See Y Shim, 'Korean Financial Regulatory and Supervisory Structure' Ch 10, in Arner and Lin, supra note 30.

149. See Walker, 'United Kingdom Regulatory Reform: a New Beginning in Policy and Programme Construction' in Arner and Lin, supra note 30.

150. See Michael Blair, Walker and others, *Guide to the Financial Services and Markets Act 2000* (London: Blackstones, 2001). See also, Blair, Walker and others, *Banking and Financial Services Regulation* (Butterworths, 2nd ed, 1998), Ch 2; and (Butterworths, 3rd edn, 2001), Ch 2; and M Blair and G Walker, *Financial Services Law* (Oxford: OUP, 2006), Ch 1.

151. Nine earlier regulatory authorities were abolished and the regulatory statutes under which they operated repealed. The date on which the FSA assumed responsibility for banking supervision was referred to as 'N1' with the date of assumption to other markets as 'N2' (1 December 2001). It was subsequently announced that the FSA would also be responsible for mortgage advice and insurance brokerage with effect from 2004 (referred to as 'N3').

152. See Walker, 'The Financial Services Authority and Financial Services and Markets Act' in Blair, Walker and others, (3rd edn), Ch 2. See also, Walker, 'United Kingdom Regulatory

number of general 'high level' standards, specific market sourcebooks and common 'process' manuals (including authorisation, supervision and enforcement). Integrated redress is also provided under the internal and FSA complaints sourcebooks as well as the creation of a single appeal system and compensatory fund.

The UK regime accordingly provides for both institutional (agency) and substantive (regulatory) integration with the FSA's new 'handbook'. This is, in turn, based on a 'rules' approach which has the advantage of relative flexibility, ease of amendment (without the need for full statutory revision) and clarity as well as ease of access (with rules being set out in supporting sourcebooks or manuals rather than full laws). Although not classified as laws as such, these 'statutory rules' have the effect of law. Statutory provision is then restricted to constitutional matters and framework powers and duties. The rules are also supported by 'statutory guidance' which facilitates their interpretation and understanding and consequent ease of application.

While other countries have established single regulators and have attempted to develop common sets of rules, nothing has been attempted on the size and scale of the UK approach under the Financial Services and Markets Act. This accordingly represents the most developed and sophisticated example of a 'single market', 'single regulator' and 'single regulation (rules)' approach. This anticipates future market integration and development at both the national and international levels and attempts to realise the full regulatory benefits of available especially in terms of cost-effectiveness, operational efficiency and consequent market stability. The associated disadvantages and difficulties have also been fully recognised and appropriate mechanisms adopted to ensure, in particular, sufficient transparency (consumer education) and accountability.

IV.   CHINESE CONGLOMERATE POLICY REVISION
           AND REFORM

The following recommendations can be made with regard to the reform of the laws governing financial groups and financial conglomerates in China. These recommendations are generally concerned with the extent to which China has followed a single-market, single-regulator and single-regulation approach to financial policy revision. More specific recommendations with regard to future legal and regulatory reform in this area are made in the following section.

IV.A.   GENERAL POLICY

An appropriate policy must be constructed, with regard to financial groups that properly balances regulatory (prudential) safety and stability with financial

---

Reform: A New Beginning in Policy and Programme Construction', in Arner and Lin, supra note 30.

flexibility and innovation. The general approach adopted in China is currently based on sector separation, with distinct financial regulators and laws, under a 'separate market, separate supervision' policy). This approach has the advantages of specialization and separate sector expertise, although these benefits must be set against the lack of central oversight and possible regulatory inconsistency and unnecessary regulatory restraint. The existing sector-based response can be maintained, although this response must be supported by the creation of an appropriate coordination mechanism between the separate sector regulators – the CBRC, the CSRC and the CIRC – and between these agencies and the PBC. This support is essential to enable a consistent and coherent approach to be developed and applied over time. China could consider establishing a new single authority for financial groups or conglomerate supervision, however, this authority would be both expensive and administratively inconvenient. This authority would also be contrary to the more-recent agency simplification programme followed elsewhere. It would accordingly be preferable to proceed by way of revision of the existing institutional structure rather than the creation of any new agency at this time.

China must, therefore, continue its existing sector and separate agency-based system at this time. This system will, in particular, reinforce individual sector supervision and help avoid any significant risk of cross-sector loss transfer at this stage in its transition from a managed to a market economy. To enable this policy to work effectively, a number of reforms must be considered. China must, in particular, adopt a clear and consistent policy on financial groups; set up an appropriate set of cross-sector supervisory mechanisms; develop extended group supervisory reporting and information requirements; and impose appropriate regulatory obligations on all financial group companies. Effective institutional and inter-agency relations must also be set up between all of the authorities involved, including necessary internal departments or divisions. The system must also be reviewed over time and any further regulatory reforms adopted as necessary. This can include the eventual establishment of a single regulatory agency with a China Financial Regulatory Commission. China can also consider moving to a single financial law and common set of regulatory rules for all financial sectors at some point. Whether these reforms will be possible will depend upon the way in which financial markets and financial regulation develop over time.

IV.B.   FINANCIAL GROUPS

A clear policy must be adopted both with regard to the establishment of large groups within particular financial sectors – banking, securities and insurance – as well as more complex groups made up of firms from more than one sector – financial groups or financial conglomerates. The existing financial laws must be revised to ensure that the laws permit single-sector groups to be set up and supervised in a consistent manner.

A separate Law on Financial Groups (or Law on Financial Conglomerates) should then be adopted for cross-sector groups. This law could also be effected through regulation, although preferable would be if a separate law were passed in light of the importance of the issue in terms of financial market stability and the future development of the Chinese economy. Because China presently only permits financial groups to set up financial groups rather than conduct cross-sector activity directly, it may be clearer to refer to the 'Law on Financial Groups', rather than the 'Law on Financial Conglomerates' at this stage. This can still be reconsidered, depending upon what amendments are adopted in future, including under the proposed revisions to the Commercial Bank Law and the Securities Law.

China must either adopt a financial group policy based on direct control, through holding companies, or through indirect control, through the regulated financial entities within a group. The alternative would be to set up an inter-mediate form of group supervision combining the most important advantages of both. Direct control, based on an American model, requires that holding companies be separately authorized and regulated in the same way as if the companies were conducting financial business. The advantage is that more-substantial control can be imposed on the holding company, including business restrictions, capital adequacy and support obligations for subsidiary compa-nies. These requirements are then enforced directly against the holding com-pany, which becomes a 'regulated entity', rather than through the financial firms within the group. The disadvantages are the additional financial, administrative and regulatory costs imposed on firms – and the regulatory authorities – and the restrictions created on group expansion, group activities and financial inno-vation. Under an indirect system, such as that used in Europe, requirements are imposed on financial firms rather than the holding company. Persons who acquire – or dispose of – any significant interest must notify the authorities, who will either provide or refuse consent, as appropriate. Group information is also collected through the completion of capital and other returns on a group or consolidated basis by regulated firms with the authorities being able to impose additional capital, liquidity and other regulatory requirements on the financial companies – but not the holding companies – if necessary.

Under an intermediate or partial financial holding company model, hold-ing companies would require notification and consent and possibly be sub-ject to some direct reporting but additional regulatory requirements would not be imposed, such as on capital adequacy or affiliate support obligations. This requirement would permit effective oversight and control, but without the added requirement for severe compliance and regulatory costs for firms and the authorities, such as under a full holding-company model. This approach would be the most appropriate option for China, at least initially. The approach could then be reviewed, over time, in light of market and financial group develop-ments and be revised accordingly. China must decide whether to adopt a pure 'financial holding company' or an 'operating holding company' system. Under a pure system, the parent company will only be permitted to hold shares in financial companies and possibly some other financial related business but not regulated activities, including banking, securities and insurance. A regulated institution, such as a bank, a securities firm or an insurance company will not be permitted to act as a financial holding company. Under an operating company model, the holding company can also be a financial firm. If China wishes to continue its strict separation policy at this stage in the development of its financial market system, it should initially follow a pure holding company approach although this can again be relaxed subsequently.

Whether a strict non-commercial policy is to be continued must also be confirmed. The existing financial laws generally prohibit commercial companies from owning financial firms and financial firms from engaging in non-financial business. The objective is to try to prevent contagious risks spreading from the commercial sector into the financial markets. If these prohibitions are to be continued, this should be restated under the new law to be adopted.

Some concessions can be considered by permitting financial firms to hold investments in non-financial firms up to particular limits. Financial firms can, for example, hold up to 15 per cent of own funds (capital) in commercial undertakings in Europe, with a total limit of 60 per cent of own funds. This approach could be considered in China over time, to the extent that this would not create any significant threat to financial instability. This would, however, not be appropriate until other existing difficulties are fully resolved, including, in particular, the NPL problem.

One exception that may have to be provided for under the new law would be for group parent companies that hold shares in a financial holding company. The financial holding company can operate under a group parent, which either owns a separate industrial holding company or other commercial interests directly, with the commercial interests than being held in a separate group 'arm' distinct from the financial entities under the financial holding company. Practice again differs across countries, although this approach has been used in China.

While a pure system would prohibit any commercial interests in a group that contained financial firms, this system might be unnecessarily restrictive, because this would require a number of groups to divest their financial group companies. The most appropriate policy might then be to permit mixed groups to develop but to require that financial firms be held in a separate arm under a financial holding company. This would then have to be taken into account in determining the relevant definitions to be used and holding company rules to be adopted. This policy would be reviewed over time and further relaxed or tightened, as appropriate.

The most appropriate system for China can then be an intermediate financial holding company model that combines the benefits of direct approval and oversight but without all of the additional costs involved with a full supporting regulatory regime. This would also be easier and cheaper to set up initially and can be reviewed and adjusted over time. Financial firms must also be prohibited from engaging in commercial activities or from holding interests in commercial firms, at least until the NPL problems is resolved after which some non-financial investment can be permitted, subject to certain limits. Mixed holding companies would, however, have to be permitted to hold shares in the financial holding company with all financial and commercial interests than being separated and held within distinct arms within the larger group.

IV.C.   FINANCIAL GROUPS

Cross-sector supervision can either be dealt with through the appointment of a single authority to be responsible for financial groups, such as the CBRC or the PBC, or through the appointment of a coordinator – a 'lead regulator' – on an individual group basis.

The general approach adopted with regard to the cross-border supervision of complex groups at the international level is to use a lead regulator mechanism, with the primary authority being the supervisor of the largest financial entity within the group whether it is a bank, a securities firm or an insurance company. This can also be used within a particular country – between local domestic authorities – although the appointment of a single permanent entity is often preferable on a cost and personnel – expertise and experience – basis. The related problem that arises with the use of a variable lead regulator is that the largest financial entity may change from time to time, depending upon which definition of comparable size or value is used.

The most suitable body to be appointed to supervise complex financial groups would be the PBC, based on the cross-sector nature of the oversight required, as well as the link between this and general financial stability and financial assistance (lender of last resort support). The existing agencies – the CBRC, the CSRC and the COIRC – would continue to supervise single sector groups.

With the previous removal of supervisory responsibility from the PBC, this change would require amendment to the proposed new PBC Law to confer the necessary power on the PBC to carry out this function. Arguably, this responsibility will fall within the scope of 'financial stability' responsibility more generally, which will be conferred on the PBC under the proposed revisions; although it would be preferable if this responsibility were to be clarified to avoid confusion and possible challenge.

The alternative to appointing the PBC on its own as a new financial group supervisor would be to set up a combined approach by means of the PBC and a new Joint Committee (or Joint Financial Stability Committee) with the existing supervisory agencies. The creation of a joint committee is legally and operationally necessary whenever financial groups include firms from more than one financial sector. The CBRC, CSRC and the CIRC would then have to be represented. In the absence of creating a new single regulatory authority, this cross-sector activity could be most easily achieved through the establishment of a joint regulatory committee at this stage. The Joint Committee would oversee the development of more-complex financial groups in China, including taking all major decisions with regard to approval, reporting and enforcement or closure. The joint nature of the membership would also promote contact and cooperation between the sector authorities and enable the coordination of inter-agency relations, including exchange of information and co-decision where relevant.

IV.D.   CONSOLIDATED AND CONGLOMERATE SUPERVISION

Consolidated supervision must be introduced in each of the main sectors, including, in particular, in the banking and securities areas, and with additional information being collected on insurance companies. Other financial firms must also be brought within the scope of this consolidation to the extent possible. These additional reporting requirements are necessary to ensure that the authorities are provided with all the relevant information in regard to group structures, control systems and financial condition.

This basic consolidated supervision – on a legal-entity basis – could also be extended to include other 'significant business units' or 'significant management units' within a group. The objective would be to ensure that all active management units, as well as earnings units, in a financial entity or financial group are identified and monitored. Firms and groups would, in particular, be required to provide separate diagrams (organograms) for their legal and internal management structures. The limitation of consolidated supervision is that it only applies to subsidiaries and separate legal entities in the group and does not include other more complex management units based on product, geographic or regional lines. This type of business unit supervision has been introduced in the UK and other countries.

Some form of further 'conglomerate supervision' could also be created over time, based on the collection of all relevant information with regard to regulated firms and closely connected financial (or non-financial) entities in an extended group. While full accounting consolidation may not be required for all elements, such as insurance and particular financial operations, sufficient information must be collected and made available as appropriate on an initial and continuing basis.

Necessary information can either be collected through the regulated firms or the holding company. In practice, regular 'prudential' information must generally be collected through the sector agencies: the CBRC, the CSRC and CIRC. Relevant returns must be completed by firms on both an individual (solo) and group (consolidated) basis. This information must then be examined at the sector level, within the particular department responsible for group supervision within the CBRC, the CSRC and CIRC. More general financial group information would then be passed on to the relevant division in the PBC.

Investigations and inspections must generally be conducted through the separate sector authorities under the powers conferred under the existing financial laws. These powers should be reviewed and extended and revised to the extent necessary to ensure that all appropriate information can be collected in practice. Some residual power to conduct investigations and inspections can be conferred on the PBC – in the event that the other agencies fail or refuse to do – or, at least, a power given to direct that the other agencies carry this out where necessary. The availability of such a power of direction would assist avoid disagreement in practice.

IV.E.   REGULATORY REVISION

To the extent that the existing financial laws – and separate sector regime – are to be continued for the foreseeable future, appropriate regulatory adjustments, such as revisions or amendments, must be made to the main laws. Some further revision might also be necessary in dealing with SOEs, as opposed to market-managed firms, although these must generally be treated in identical terms, insofar as possible, to promote transparency, certainty and competitive equality. This would also generate investor confidence and consequent internal and external investment within China.

Proper suitability standards must initially be applied within each financial sector to ensure that regulated entities are properly managed on both an individual (solo) and group (consolidated) basis. Appropriate policies must be developed to ensure that all persons who either manage regulated entities and holding companies or control them are suitable. Such standards will then be applied to managers (internally) and to controllers (externally). Relevant considerations include necessary expertise and training and with the persons concerned not otherwise being disqualified to act, such as following a criminal conviction or bankruptcy.

Additional systems and controls obligations must also be imposed to ensure the effectiveness of group and conglomerate management. Sufficient authority and autonomy must be conferred at the regulated entity level at the same time that the efficiency and effectiveness of internal systems are reviewed and revised, as necessary.

Appropriate measures to limit or control conflicts of interest must be introduced, and supported by necessary management authority and autonomy requirements, as well as effective internal control systems obligations. Proper controls will also have to be put in place on the use and exchange of client information within large financial groups. These controls must be extended to include the collection, protection and transfer of confidential client information. This would apply to any non-public information or information concerning an individual client not otherwise available through publicly accessible information systems.

In regard to client confidentiality, firms must also be required to develop appropriate privacy policies that should be notified to clients at the time that the business relationship begins with any necessary consents with regard to the subsequent use of confidential information being obtained from the client at that stage. If the necessary consent is not obtained, financial firms and groups should be prohibited from using any non-public information collected with regard to individual clients. Whether confidential information can be exchanged between group members without express client consent should be made clear. This is permitted in some countries, such as in the US, but more strictly controlled in others.

Effective crisis management procedures must be introduced at the regulated entity and financial group level. The establishment and proper operation of such systems should be confirmed as part of any extended or supplementary group or conglomerate supervision conducted.

IV.F.   AGENCY RELATIONS AND JOINT COMMITTEE

Appropriate internal arrangements must be set up in all the agencies involved with financial group supervision. Cross-sector group supervision must preferably be conducted through either a permanent department or division within the PBC. The limited number of significantly large conglomerates in China and the need for the development of necessary expertise would require a fixed rather than flexible response. The coordination of responsibilities and activities between the sector agencies and the PBC could then be most easily dealt with through the establishment of the Joint Financial Stability Committee. This would enable all necessary exchange of information and co-decision between the relevant agencies.

The Joint Committee could be set up by regulation issued by the State Council, although it would be preferable if the committee were established by law to confirm its authority and status. This could be achieved under either the new Law of Financial Groups, or alternatively in the revised PBC Law. The most appropriate and easy to access would be the Law on Financial Group Law. The power of the PBC to participate in this type of committee must still be clarified in the PBC Law.

The Joint Committee should be chaired by a State Commissioner or Deputy Prime Minister to ensure sufficient political and operational authority. As a reporting committee to the Sate Council, the Joint Committee would have authority over each of the PBC, as well as over the CBRC, CSRC and CIRC in connection with all matters that fall within the scope of its authority. The Committee would be served for administrative purposes by the Financial Groups Division which would form part of the Financial Stability Department the PBC. The PBC would be given necessary legal authority to act in the areas referred to, including financial stability (under the revised PBC Law) and complex group supervision (under the proposed new Law on Financial Groups). These functions could also be extended to include financial restructuring and insolvency, under the PBC Law and proposed new insolvency or restructuring and liquidation law.

Because the Financial Stability Department within the PBC would carry out a series of essential support functions for the Joint Committee, the Governor – or Deputy Governor – of the PBC must also be appointed co-Chair of the Joint Committee to clarify lines of responsibility and authority. The lack of clear lines of authority would undermine the effectiveness of the new integrated regime to be set up. This should not be left unspecified as this will only otherwise lead to disagreement and ineffective systems and operations. (Alternative co-chairs may nevertheless be appointed in certain circumstances where, for example, the largest entity with a large financial group was a securities firm or an insurance company in which case the head of the CSRC or the CIRC could act as co-chair.)

Confirming the chairman is also necessary to ensure that the Joint Committee – and the Financial Stability Department in the PBC – have sufficient authority over the large number of branches of the CBRC, the CSRC and CIRC throughout China, as well as the provincial state councils and local government authorities that will still have the power – as major shareholder – over publicly owned banking and financial institutions. It is essential to ensure that a consistent policy is followed in all cases. While the activities of the PBC, CBRC, CSRC and CIRC could be coordinated through a memorandum of understanding (MoU) entered into between them, this would not be required to the extent that all necessary obligations, including cooperation, exchange of information and secrecy, are set out under the new law supporting rules or regulations. Most of this could be dealt with in the proposed 'Law on Financial Groups'.

V.   CONCLUSION

The current law in China is based on sector separation. This follows the underlying policy of 'separate market, separate supervision'. It must be accepted that this is a safe and prudent approach to follow, certainly at this stage in the transition of the Chinese economy from a managed to a market system. The disadvantage of this law is that some of the economic benefits that may otherwise arise with a more open market policy may be lost. Of particular importance in this regard may be the ability of the larger financial groups in China to restructure further and expand to allow them to compete with other large global conglomerates and financial groups especially after financial liberalisation pursuant to its WTO commitment by end-2006.

Of more-immediate concern from China's perspective, however, may be the fact that a number of increasingly complex groups have already been constructed or are proposed on the Chinese mainland at the same time as certain larger groups have already used Hong Kong and other overseas centres to avoid the domestic regulatory constraints with regard to group structures. The current policy will then limit innovation, as well as promote regulatory avoidance. The Chinese authorities may also find that they are not able to collect sufficient information about these non-mainland or other foreign based groups, nor exercise any form of control on their activities if any concerns arise. China may wish to continue on a separate sector agency and law based approach for a period. This would be supportable in terms of risk separation and consequent market stability as the economy moves from a managed to a market basis. As market practice and supervisory and regulatory experience develops, however, China may wish to consider creating a single regulatory authority on the model adopted in a number of other countries. The particular advantage in the case of China would be that this would focus personnel and funding resources to allow the agency to develop its capability, reputation and authority as quickly as possible (such as on the model of the UK FSA). China might then also wish to continue its existing sector laws for a period under the direction and management of the new single agency (on the German model). China may, over time, want to consider the adoption of a fully integrated substantive regulatory model with a single set of rules and regulations (on the UK model). Whether this transition was effected in stages or in a single 'big bang' would have to be considered. The most appropriate time period within which such a transition could be effected would also have to be carefully assessed.

Chapter 9

Financial Institution Insolvency in the PRC*

George A. Walker and Douglas Arner

I.   INTRODUCTION

The purpose of this chapter is to examine the main issues that arise with regard to the design and structure of a possible bank and financial insolvency law in China. The key procedural or operational options available are examined, including the relative advantages and disadvantages of each of the main resolution mechanisms generally used in other countries. These mechanisms are reviewed in regard to the current financial and economic conditions in China.

    The fundamental difficulty that must be taken into consideration is the need to balance the requirements of both a planned and market-based economic system, as well as provide effective transitional and continuing mechanisms that can operate on a short and medium-to-long term basis. As China moves towards the adoption of a number of the main attributes of a market economy, but within a planned market system, a series of adjustments may have to be considered to the main operational options otherwise available. These must then also apply on an interim or transitional basis while certain existing economic difficulties are resolved including, in particular, the large volume of non-performing loans

*   The authors would like to thank Yu Yueting, Research Fellow, Asian Institute of International Financial Law, for research assistance and comments.

(NPLs) within the banking and financial system at the same time. The new law must also then contribute to the construction of a larger effective legal framework that will support the longer-term continued development of the Chinese economy.

In carrying out these reforms, the growth and stability of financial markets must be protected at the same time as the rights of the State and individuals properly respected. The new adjusted market place must also operate internally as well as continue to attract substantial external investment to allow China to participate fully in the new international trading system operating under the auspices of the World Trade Organisation (WTO). The new law to be adopted must then have proper regard to the special characteristics and attributes of the current Chinese financial system but also allow the economy to develop in an optimum manner that properly balances the advantages of a planned and market economic system. A series of recommendations are made in this regard.

The structure of this chapter is as follows. The nature and purpose of insolvency law more generally is considered and the specific characteristics of bank insolvency noted. The general principles that underlie the establishment of an effective insolvency regime are then outlined with the possible establishment of either a court or administrative agency based system. The main resolution mechanisms or devices available are then considered in further detail in turn. These include

- pre-closure conservation (or asset protection);
- court or agency appointed administration (or managed rehabilitation);
- other officially managed rehabilitation or restructuring operations;
- voluntary and compulsory (official) liquidation; and
- the possible need for a separate creditor driven mandatory bankruptcy mechanism.

While these resolution mechanisms reflect the main options currently available under the laws in other countries or proposed revisions, these can be simplified to consist solely of three main options of administration (official or creditor), rehabilitation and final closure (or liquidation). This chapter reviews the advantages and disadvantages of each of these options.

The various resolution options that can be available as part of rehabilitation or restructuring (rescue) programme are also noted separately in light of their importance. The main rules governing the possible provision of individual bank support by the central bank through some form of more traditional 'lender of last resort' or alternative financial support mechanism are considered. This chapter also provides comments with regard to the potential relevance and value of each of these main resolution options in China. The additional, more-procedural provisions that would also have to be included within any new law on bank rehabilitation and liquidation are also referred to. Final recommendations are made on possible future policy development within this area in China.

II.   FINANCIAL INSTITUTION INSOLVENCY

II.A.   Insolvency and Bank Insolvency Procedures

Corporate insolvency law is generally concerned with the distribution of available assets of an institution to its creditors following dissolution. The dissolution is often determined by more general corporate or company laws with asset realization and distribution being effected in accordance with relevant insolvency law rules. This can generally be considered to constitute a form of asset and liability resolution. The assets of the institution are realised and distributed to discharge outstanding claims either on a full, an agreed priority or proportionate basis or combination of these. Bank insolvency can then be dealt with either under a general liquidation or bankruptcy law, or through some more-specialist dedicated laws or procedure. In developed economies in which established appointment and recovery procedures are in place with suitably qualified staff available to manage the relevant procedures, bank insolvency can be conducted under the general law. In the event that an effective general insolvency culture is unavailable, a dedicated or specialist regime can be considered more appropriate in light of the special characteristics and importance of bank insolvency. Bank insolvency is of importance in light of the essential role that banks carry out in any economy. Banks perform a range of savings, credit and payment functions without which any market based economy could not operate.[1] Banks are also an important source of available employment and

---

1. See generally World Bank and International Monetary Fund [IMF], *Legal, Institutional and Regulatory Framework to Deal with Insolvent Banks,* Joint Report on Bank Insolvency (Draft, August 2003). The paper was prepared as part of the Global Bank Insolvency Initiative (GBII) originally launched in January 2002 in coordination with the Bank for International Settlements (BIS), the Financial Stability Institute (FSI), the Basel Committee on Banking Supervision and the Financial Stability Forum (FSF). The report sets out the principal elements of the legal and institutional framework required to deal with insolvent banks and follows an extended consultative exercise conducted by the World Bank and IMF between January 2003 and July 2003.
The original principles of the GBII were:

- to identify the appropriate legal, institutional and regulatory framework for addressing cases of bank insolvency,
- to build an international consensus towards the acceptance of this framework and
- to provide a basis for a policy dialogue between international financial institutions and countries on these issues and to facilitate provision of technical assistance to countries that want to improve their national legislative and regulatory systems.

See also Basel Committee on Banking Supervision, *Supervisory Guidance on Dealing with Weak Banks* (March 2002); and IMF, *Orderly & Effective Insolvency Procedures* (1999). The Basel Committee paper was prepared by a Task Force on Dealing with Weak Banks and was concerned with the definition and identification of weak banks and the development of possible resolution options. The IMF paper was prepared by the Legal Department (LEG) of the IMF. In addition to considering the various stages and procedures available, including rehabilitation and liquidation). The paper examined the general objectives and features of

generate significant wealth as independent commercial sectors within most economic systems.

Apart from the importance of the underlying economic functions discharged, the difficulty that arises with regard to banking markets is that these markets are inherently unstable and susceptible to collapse. Banks essentially borrow sight or short-term funds, which are pooled and then on-lent on a medium to long-term basis. The effect is to create an inherently non-disposable or non-transferable asset pool in the form of bank loans, supported by sight or on-demand borrowing or credits. A fundamental term or maturity mismatch (or transformation) then arises between the short term nature of the funding and long term nature of its application.

Banks generally retain a reserve – historically one-third of their deposit base – in the form of cash or other easily liquefiable assets to cover anticipated ongoing withdrawal demands. A typical bank balance sheet can then be made up of 70–75 per cent loans and 30–35 per cent cash or easily disposable securities, usually in the form of Government bonds, bills or gilts. This reserve may nevertheless be exhausted in the event of an unexpectedly large amount of withdrawal demands being made within a short period of time. In such an event, the bank will either try to obtain further funds from other institutions on the interbank markets, or directly from the central bank either through the bank's general operations in the primary money market or on an individual, lender-of-last-resort basis.[2]

Under the general lender of last resort rules initially developed by Henry Thornton and Walter Bagehot during the 19th century,[3] the central bank will

---

insolvency procedures and includes a number of 'principal conclusions' through the text. The UNCITRAL Moral Law on Cross-Border Insolvency is also attached as an Appendix to the IMF paper.

2. The difficulty that arises is that the commercial and financial standing of a bank will be affected by the bank's perceived stability in the market place. Once a 'run' has started on the credit of a bank, managing or stopping the run is highly difficult. Runs can often be irrational in cause and nature, with the original trigger possibly only being based on rumour or uninformed speculation. Irrational panic can, nevertheless, destroy the credit standing of an otherwise respectable – and solvent – bank. In the event that a run commences, the reserve assets of the bank can be quickly exhausted and, if the bank's credit position has been sufficiently undermined, the bank will be unable to borrow any further funds in the inter-bank markets or from other financial institutions on a wholesale basis. In the event that no other funds are available, the bank will be forced to approach the central bank, which can either advance or refuse to advance funds, depending upon its solvency and ability to advance collateral or size and consequent potential threat to the stability of the financial system. On the risks in financial market and lender of central bank support, see G.A. Walker, *International Banking Regulation – Law, Policy and Practice* (Kluwer Law, 2001), Chapter 3, Section 4(I), no. 61.

3. See generally, H. Thornton, *An Enquiry into the Nature and Effects of the Paper Credit System of Great Britain* (1802); and W. Bagehot, *Lombard Street* (1873). See also T.M. Humphrey, 'Lender of Last Resort: the Concept in History', 75:2 *Fed. Res. B. Richmond Econ. Rev.* 8 (March/April 1989). For a discussion, see Walker, no. 11. See also *Joint Report on Bank Insolvency*, para 2.5.

advance secured lending to illiquid but solvent banks. Funds will only be advanced to insolvent banks where their collapse may otherwise create a systemic threat to the financial system. This arises from the contagious (or domino effect) of individual bank closure spreading to other banks and then to the financial system as a whole. The ultimate responsibility of the central bank is to ensure that all necessary liquidity is made available to protect the financial system from such collapse both on a general daily and individual emergency basis.[4]

The other particular characteristic that has to be taken into account in considering bank rather than general insolvency is that the primary assets held in the balance sheet of a bank are financial claims: mainly loans, but also some securities. These do not have the same characteristics as physical goods or otherwise easily disposable assets. Under the laws of many countries, intangible claims are difficult to transfer with onerous obligations generally applying. Under the Law of Property Act 1926 in the United Kingdom, these types of transfers can only be affected by legal assignment, which requires that the sum involved be unconditional, the transfer be effected in writing and all debtors be properly notified. Satisfying all of these conditions is often difficult, including, in particular, non-conditionality in a modern market system. The requirement for individual debtor notice also causes significant administrative inconvenience in the event of the collapse of a large bank.

In considering bank insolvency, the importance of the underlying functions carried out by banks are relevant, although the key issues are the need to prevent systemic collapse in a financial system and, where appropriate, to facilitate a speedy rescue or support operation before the credit and consequent asset position of the bank is unduly threatened. The decision as to whether a restructuring or support operation of some form is to be effected must be taken quickly. In practice, this should be decided within the first two to five days of any significant threat arising with regard to the stability of the bank. If some form of support or rescue operation is to be effected and it has not been put in place within that time period, the asset position and credit standing of the bank may be significantly if not irremediable damaged.

Every effort must also be made more generally to protect the value of the assets of the bank if any difficulties arise. Residual reserve assets should be protected from unnecessary dissipation while the credit standing of the bank more generally is supported to prevent or limit the damage caused by a bank run. In designing a bank insolvency law, the need for possible support, early resolution and asset protection must all be taken into consideration.

---

4. Acting as 'lender of last resort' can either be used to both or only the second of these functions.

II.B.   COURT AND ADMINISTRATIVE BASED SYSTEMS

One of the main policy issues that must be determined in setting up any general
or special bank, or bank and financial insolvency regime, is whether the bank
must operate on an agency (administrative) or court (judicial) basis. An administrative procedure generally operates on an extra-judicial basis with commencement and appointment decisions being taken by the supervisory agency
directly without any formal court approval or involvement. This can be conducted by, or in cooperation with, a deposit protection or insurance agency,
although this is unusual where the deposit support system only consists of a
'pay box' form that makes payment to entitled depositors with little active oversight or involvement in the resolution process.[5] A judicial based system requires
that the decision on the commencement of the proceedings and the appointment of the conservator, administrator or liquidator is taken by a court with
the proceedings than generally continuing under court oversight. The court will
accordingly be involved at the initial, continuing and termination stages.

    The advantages of an administrative process are that this type of pro-
cess is considered to be more flexible and immediate, protective, accurate,
and informed – relying on specialist insolvency practitioners rather than
non-trained judges – and consequently more efficient and effective. The disadvantages are that the system is more costly and potentially bureaucratic, non-
transparent and lacks proper due process with the rights of private parties being
cancelled or adjusted without formal legal approval or authority. The main difficulty that generally arises in practice is with non-judicial claims adjustment
with decisions being taken by an administrative agency rather than a court.
Conferring this type of authority on a non-court based agency is considered to
be unacceptable in a number of countries, because this authority undermines
the legitimate rights of private parties. This objection can be partially corrected
through the adoption of appropriate appeals or review procedures within an
administrative system. The availability of these types of procedures, in and of
themselves, however, can then create further significant delays and obstruct the
supposed advantages of immediacy and flexibility otherwise available under an
administrative option.

    The only major developed country that has retained an effective extra-
judicial resolution system is the United States, which is effected through its
Federal Deposit Insurance Corporation (FDIC). The FDIC is a well-funded,
well-staffed administrative institution that has been able to develop significant
experience since the early 1930s in the management of financial crisis and bank
resolution situations. The operations of the FDIC are also supported by an

---

5. On the nature of the structure and operation of deposit protection schemes, see Financial
    Stability Forum [FSF], *Report on Guidance on Deposit Insurance* (2001). See also FSF, 'Terms
    of Reference: FSF Study Group on Deposit Insurance,' Press Release (19 November 1999);
    and *FSF Working Group on Deposit Insurance*, Background Paper (June 2000). For comment,
    see Walker, no. 11, Chapter 5, Section 5(V).

extended system of administrative laws, rules and regulations in the United States, with relevant core procedures further revised and adjusted over time. Few other countries have an as effective administrative agency with as clear and developed a supporting body of laws, rules and regulations.

Switzerland has also considered transferring bank insolvency from a court to an extra-judicial regime, although this regime is supported by an effective administrative law and appeals procedures that will protect the interests of shareholders and creditors. Other extra-judicial regimes operate in countries such as Italy and Norway although most other European and developed Western economies operate on a judicial rather than administrative basis. Difficulties have arisen in other smaller or emerging economies such as the Philippines and Moldova, where sufficiently strong supporting legal and administrative procedures are not in place. The general tendency in many countries has then been to adopt some form of court based system or, at least, court supported regime.

The principal advantages of a court based system are that the system has immediate authority and validity, which is particularly important with regard to interim measures and property or claims adjustment. Any decisions taken are supported by necessary enforcement and sanction mechanisms with full due process applying at all times including proper notice and hearing. A court-based system also generally provides for finality and completion possibly not otherwise available under an administrative regime, depending upon the terms of operation agreed. The potential disadvantages are possibly delay, cost and lack of commercial or specialist technical expertise. These issues can be dealt through of special short summary procedures and the setting up of specialist courts, if necessary.

Apart from an express administrative or court based option, some from of hybrid system may also be adopted. This would involve assigning as much administrative discretion as possible to the relevant insolvency agency but with all significant decisions being subject to court approval or confirmation. This would then combine immediacy and flexibility with authority and validity. This would apply with regard to such stages as commencement, interim measures, disposal, enforcement and completion. Other more-administrative matters could then be dealt with on a delegated basis including procedural conditions, management operations, meetings and negotiations, compromises, collections, interim and final payments.

The two key issues that arise from an operational perspective are possibly then authority and finality which require court involvement. Any underlying property or claims adjustment must be subject to core approval or confirmation. Full due process must be respected in all cases. This can nevertheless be affected without any unnecessary cost or delay by only requiring minimal decisions to be referred to a judicial authority and with the court's discretion being limited under the relevant laws and regulations.

An appropriate combined or hybrid model can accordingly be constructed that attempts to achieve the main benefits from both policy options. This model is perhaps the most desirable compromise option in practice that benefits from the advantages of both of the pure model regimes.

Whether a separate court should be established for insolvency purposes and, in particular, bank insolvency depends upon the state of development, credibility and effectiveness of the existing court system. If the courts are considered to operate sufficiently quickly and credibly with judges having a necessary degree of relevant general experience this may not be considered necessary. If any concerns arise in this regard, specialist insolvency courts should be set up. While these would operate within the general court system, judges would be given specialist training with separate procedures being set up to govern their operation. Whether any separate bank insolvency rather than general insolvency courts would be required would also depend upon expected usage. Separate specialist courts may not be required where a sufficiently large amount of relevant business was involved, although separately trained judges may be of use in such cases. A substantial amount of experience, however, might not be required, because the discretion of the judges would be restricted under the relevant laws and regulations to avoid delay or interference. Local conditions and opinions would have to be further considered to determine whether a special insolvency court system must be set up in China, although this is unlikely at this stage.

II.C.   Policy Options

A range of policy options can be identified in developing a new insolvency law in the banking area. These options include conservation (or asset protection) managed under a conservator, administration under an appointed administrator, restructuring or rehabilitation, voluntary and compulsory liquidation and bankruptcy. Which resolution option or mechanism would apply in any particular case would depend upon whether the relevant triggers set were satisfied or not. These triggers generally include not being able to pay debts as they fall due (a liquidity test), assets exceeding liabilities (an insolvency or balance sheet test) or a capital falling below prescribed levels (a regulatory test).[6] Other factors can include license revocation or the business otherwise being conducted in a manner considered prejudicial to the interests of shareholders or credits. The tests or triggers set with regard to each resolution option would be adjusted to ensure that they operate in a consistent and coherent manner.

The resolution mechanisms available can be classified in various ways and with various combinations being adopted. The most basic functions discharged are asset protection (conservation) and interim administration (for a limited period under protection against creditor actions), which can include restructuring and closure (voluntary or compulsory liquidation). Conservation and

---

6.   See no. 21.

administration can also be combined with the insolvency agency with the power to appoint an administrator to carry both an asset protection and interim management or rehabilitation function. A separate full bankruptcy procedure could also be included which would allow third parties to petition the court for bank closure. Mandatory liquidation and bankruptcy can nevertheless be combined depending upon whether the supervisory or insolvency agency are to be given power to appoint a liquidator directly or whether an appointment would require court approval in all cases. If the appointment requires court consent, these two mechanisms could be combined with both the supervisory or insolvency agency and third party creditors being able to apply to the court for the commencement of the relevant procedure. A separate agency appointed liquidator and court commenced bankruptcy procedure would then be unnecessary.

The nature of possible support operations including central bank lender-of-last-resort funding and other rescue options must also be considered. Additional restructuring or rehabilitation options can include shareholder, third party or central bank capital injections, as well as other asset transfers (to an existing or special purpose bank) or share transfers (mergers or acquisitions). The main resolution procedures are considered next. Possible support or rescue options are examined in the following section.

II.C.1.   Conservation

The purpose of conservation (or conservatorship) is to permit the central bank or supervisory agency to assume control of a bank through the appointment of a conservator. The conservator will be given control over the assets, books and records of the bank, which will enable the assets and the value of the bank to be protected as a going concern. This will either operate on an interim basis until the financial difficulties involved are resolved or another more informal insolvency proceeding is commenced.

Appropriate triggers would have to be imposed, which would generally include being unable to pay debts as they come due, capital falling below 25 per cent or liabilities exceeding assets. One or more of these triggers could be used, depending upon the regulatory obligations imposed under the Banking Law. Additional automatic grounds would also include where the bank's authorization or license has been revoked or a petition made for the voluntary or mandatory liquidation of the bank. The objective in each case would be to have a conservator appointed immediately to protect the assets and value of the bank on a going concern. A further test could also be included where otherwise justified by the interests of depositors or creditors.

While the first three triggers could operate on a discretionary basis, the following three must be mandatory. It would also be preferable if the first three were automatic as this would remove any discretion on the part of the regulatory or supervisory agency. The retention of unnecessary discretion creates the danger of forbearance and consequent delay with the supervisory or insolvency agency being reluctant or hesitating to proceed. The use of mandatory triggers in certain cases creates certainty and predictability for regulated institutions and officials.

Some additional discretionary triggers can also be included, such as when the bank fails to carry out a regulatory or administrative order, direction or instruction or this can otherwise be considered appropriate in the interests of shareholders or creditors. This would operate on a discretionary basis. As well as permitting additional asset protection, this would also support the other sanctions exercised and authority of the supervisory or regulatory agency more generally.

An appropriate appointment procedure would have to be provided for. The immediate appointment would generally be effected by the supervisory or regulatory agency to ensure a quick and effective response. The effect would be to suspend the powers of the management and shareholders of the bank subject to the direction or instruction of the conservator. The powers of the conservator to enter the premises of the bank and take control of all assets, books and records would be provided for. The conservator would be subject to an obligation to examine the condition of the bank and prepare a report within a specified period, for example, 30 days. This obligation would include producing recommendations for the rehabilitation or possible closure of the bank.

To ensure proper due process and validity of the action taken, some form of court consent would be required. Preconsent would not be desirable unless this could be provided immediately on application by the supervisory or regulatory authority. Otherwise court consent should be obtained within a period of one to five days following the appointment of the conservator.

Court approval would also be required in connection with any action taken by the conservator that would affect the rights of third parties. Court consent would be required in all cases in which third party rights were affected. Such persons should have the right to make representations and apply for any decisions to be reviewed within a specified period, for example, 10 days from any decision being taken, including the initial appointment of a conservator. Appropriate court procedures and facilities would have to be set up.

The intervention powers of the conservator should also be specified. These can, for example, include suspending access to, and payment on, accounts for particular periods such up to three months. This would, in particular, prevent the effects of a bank run or assets being immediately withdrawn. This would require court consent.

Appropriate termination provisions would have to be included. Termination would generally take place on the expiry of the initial period designated or such shorter period as the supervisory or insolvency agency or the court may specify. Appointment terms would be subject to extension on proper cause. On termination of the appointment, the conservator should be required to return control of all assets, books and records obtained and general management responsibility for the running of the bank. The conservator should also be required to produce a final report and accounting on the conduct of the conservatorship.

II.C.2.   Administration

A separate administration procedure may also be provided for. This administration would be equivalent to Chapter 11 in the US[7] or the administration procedure under the Insolvency Act in the United Kingdom.[8] The objective would be to permit the court to appoint an administrator to assume control over the affairs, business and property of the bank for a period to attempt to deal with any immediate financial difficulties and restore the profitability and stability of the institution.[9]

Appropriate triggers would again have to be specified. These may, for example, include where the company is, or is likely to become, unable to pay its debts (UK Insolvency Act 1986, ss 8(1)(a) and 123) or the appointment would assist ensure the survival of the company either in whole or part as a going concern, a more advantageous realization of the company's assets would be effected rather than through a winding-up or any other formal insolvency petition has already been made (Insolvency Act, s 8(3)). Petitions for an application may be made by the company or any of its directors or by one or more of the bank's creditors (Insolvency Act s 9(1)).

The effect of the application is to prevent any other petitions being made such as for the winding-up of the institution (Insolvency Act s 19[1]). This will then allow the bank to trade for an interim period under court protection against any separate filings for winding-up or bankruptcy. Equivalent protection is provided for under the Chapter 11 procedure in the US. On the making of an administration order, any existing petitions for winding-up or the appointment of another receiver are cancelled (s11[1]).

The administrator is given power to do all such things as may be necessary for the management of the affairs, business and property of the company and without prejudice to the generality of these will be given a number of express powers – s 14(1)(a) and (b) and Schedule 1. These include the power to take possession of, collect and get in the property of the company and take such proceedings as may be expedient, power to sell or otherwise dispose of the property of the company by public auction or private contract, raise or borrow money and grant security, appoint solicitors, accountants or other professional parties, bring and defend actions or commence or terminate arbitration, take out

---

7. See K.R. Macey, G.P. Miller and R.S. Carnel, *Banking Law and Regulation* (3rd edn, Aspen Law & Business).
8. See generally, G. Lightman, G. Moss and R. Snowden, *The Law of Receivers and Administrators of Companies* (Sweet & Maxwell, 2000); and A. Campbell and P. Cartwright, *Banks in Crisis* (Ashgate, 2002). See also A. Keay, *McPherson's Law of Company Liquidation* (Sweet & Maxwell, 2001).
9. See *Joint Report on Bank Insolvency*, Chapter 4.

insurance and use the company's seal as well as to any other acts and execute in the name and on behalf of the company any other deed, receipt or document.

Administration is similar to the conservation although the purpose is to enable the bank to continue in business for a period under legal protection from its creditors to attempt to restore its business profitability and sustainability. This overlaps with conservatorship, although its specific objective is to protect the assets of the bank against damage or dissipation in the event that a financial difficulty has or is expected to materialise in early course. Conservatorship then focuses on asset protection while administration on business and financial restructuring although this will include a protective element. Conservatorship is also commenced by the supervisory or insolvency agency alone while administration may be petitioned by the company, its management or creditors as well as by the supervisory or insolvency agency.

The protective effects of conservatorship and the restructuring effects of administration are both highly desirable. The inclusion of both functions must be considered with any new insolvency model. The alternative to providing for these functions through separate procedures would be to combine them. In such a case, the relevant triggers and appointment rules would be adjusted accordingly although this would not create any difficulties. The distinction would then not be between conservatorship and administration as such but whether the administration was being used principally for protective or restructuring purposes. Both of these objectives could nevertheless be carried within the use of the same procedure. All of the points made above with regard to commencement, powers and duties, reporting and accounts and termination would be equally applicable.

II.C.3. Restructuring or Rehabilitation

A separate formal restructuring or rehabilitation procedure can also be provided for in any new or revised law. The objective would be to allow for a rehabilitation plan to be implemented. This plan would operate either as part of, or in parallel with, a financial (lender of last resort) support facility. The effect of providing for an express restructuring procedure would be to formalize the availability of such support and include express provision with regard to the provision's availability and operation in the insolvency law.

One option would be for the supervisory or insolvency agency – such as the China Banking Regulatory Commission (CBRC) – to be able to make recommendations for the restructuring of a bank to the People's Bank of China (PBOC) or the State Council. The relevant restructuring programme would then be subject to political or legislative support or confirmation. The advantage of this programme is that it would avoid reputational damage on the part of the PBOC or the CBRC, where either or both considered that a rescue was inappropriate for economic as opposed to political reasons. The availability of necessary funding would then be determined in accordance with the relevant provisions set out in the Law of the PBOC.

A further restructuring option would be for the assets of the bank to be transferred to a newly established bank set up for the purpose of assuming and managing those loans and other claims, which are referred to as 'bridge' banks in the US.[10] The transfer made by order of the court on the application of the supervisory or insolvency agency with power being conferred on the court under the insolvency law to allow this to be effected without requiring the consent of the shareholders or creditors of the bank. The transfer would be published by notice in the official gazette and take effect on the following day or a date otherwise specified in the notice. The transfer can also exceptionally be made by an administrative agency provided that appropriate safeguards are provided and supporting judicial review possible.

Other rehabilitation options would include a simple asset (or liability) transfer subject to an appropriate discount or share transfer, including a merger or acquisition (including a US 'purchase and assumption').

Each of these options could either be set out in the powers conferred on the supervisory or insolvency agency with regard to possible resolution options. The agency could then be given separate power to develop relevant supporting procedures internally. The alternative would be to include formal options within an express rehabilitation procedure set out in the insolvency law or regulation. Provided that the availability and possible use of each option is publicised, whatever conferment policy is followed (delegated power or express rehabilitation procedure), the practical effects should be the same.

II.C.4. Liquidation

Most insolvency laws provide for both a voluntary and mandatory liquidation procedure.[11]

II.C.4.a. *Voluntary Liquidation*

Voluntary liquidation enables the owners of a bank to apply for its dissolution. This may be affected once the trading position of the bank has otherwise become undesirable or otherwise threatened. Compulsory rather than voluntary liquidation will usually apply where the authorisation or license of the bank has been revoked, for whatever reason.

The availability of a voluntary liquidation procedure must not be permitted to prejudice the interests of creditors of the bank, including existing depositors. Most laws, accordingly, will only allow a voluntary liquidation if the bank is solvent and capable of paying off all existing claims and liabilities.

---

10. See *Joint Report on Bank Insolvency*, Chapter 5; and Basel Committee on Banking Supervision, *Supervisory Guidance on Dealing with Weak Banks* (March 2002), Part II; and IMF, *Orderly & Effective Insolvency Procedures* (1999), Chapter 2. See also Section II.C.4.e., later in this chapter.
11. See generally, *Joint Report on Bank Insolvency*, Chapter 6.

The application or petition for the liquidation must then be accompanied by appropriate documentation and accounts and other supporting evidence to the extent necessary.

Subject to the relevant conditions being satisfied, a court should be given power to dissolve a bank on a voluntary basis. The supervisory or regulatory authority may nevertheless be given power to object on cause shown. In the event that any conditions are not satisfied or the interests of depositors or creditors or the public more generally may otherwise be threatened, the supervisory or insolvency agency should be given power to apply for an administrator to be appointed or for the mandatory liquidation of the bank under its direction as appropriate.

II.C.4.b.   Compulsory Liquidation

A mandatory or automatic liquidation procedure should also be provided for. This procedure would generally enable the supervisory or regulatory agency to apply for a bank to be dissolved through the appointment of a liquidator. The liquidator could either be a member of the staff of the supervisory or insolvency agency or an independent third party – usually a qualified accountant or solicitor specializing in insolvency matters. Relevant conditions of appointment would have to be specified. A compulsory liquidation could either be effected where the authorisation or license of a bank has been revoked or on any of the more general grounds referred to above. These would include liquidity, balance sheet and regulatory insolvency.[12]

Specific triggers could be adjusted to reflect the conditions used under either an administration or liquidation. The capital test could, for example, be set at 25 per cent for an administrator being appointed, or 50 per cent for a liquidator. A more-general discretionary public interest test can also be used, for example, such as threat to safety and soundness of the bank or otherwise 'just and equitable' (UK).[13] This test would be subject to a separate petition for rehabilitation being made to support or rescue an individual bank, such as in cases in which systemic concerns arise or the interests of depositors or the public may otherwise be affected.

---

12. See no. 21.
13. The Financial Services Authority (FSA) in the UK can apply for the compulsory winding up of a bank that is unable to pay its debts, or where the court is of the opinion that it is just and equitable for the bank to be wound up. *Financial Services and Markets Act 2000*, sect. 367(3). Relevant factors to be considered in determining whether a bank must apply for an order are set out in Chapter 10 of the *FSA's Enforcement Manual*, which forms part of the FSA's *Handbook of Rules and Guidance*. See M. Blair, G.A. Walker et al., *Guide to the Financial Services and Markets Act* (Blackstones, 2000); W. Blair, G.A. Walker et al., *Banking and Financial Services Regulation* (3rd edn, Butterworths, 2002); W. Blair, G.A. Walker et al., *Financial Services Regulation* (Butterworths, Five Volumes, Looseleaf); and M. Blair, G.A. Walker et al., *Encyclopaedia of Banking Law* (Butterworths, 5 Volumes, Looseleaf).

Appropriate provision should be included in the relevant law or regulation in connection with entitlement to petition or apply for a relevant order, court consent, appointment of a liquidator, representations and appeal, effect of the order, powers and duties of the liquidator, reports, records, payments and termination and accounting. Some of these provisions would overlap with the supporting provisions adopted in connection with administrators, although further provision would also have to be included for asset realisation, determination of qualifying claims, priority of claims, payments and any further rights of appeal.

The general objective would be to give the liquidator sufficient powers to realise the residual assets of the bank and make all appropriate payments in accordance with the relevant priority rules set under the relevant law or regulation. The court would again have to be involved at key appointment, property adjustment, and termination stages. The objective would be to ensure full due process and legal certainty with ultimate finality of relevant proceedings. Appropriate immunities would also have to be conferred on the liquidator to ensure that there was no personal liability other than where action was taken in bad faith.

Relevant priority rules could include: inland revenue or inland revenue service debts; customs and excise duty debts; social security contributions; occupational and other contribution schemes contribution; employee remunerations; other preferential creditors; depositors; other general creditors.[14] More-developed rules can also be included with regard to payments to central or regional authorities and possibly for court awards including, for example, personal injury claims. After all of these entitlements are satisfied, subordinated debt holders would be paid with any residual amounts being paid to shareholders. Payments would again be made according to any relevant sub-priority rules set out in the relevant company law or articles or memorandum of the bank concerned. Separate provision may also be included for the court to give effect to creditor agreements or compromises including power to compel the operation of these on a minority in which an appropriate distribution had been agreed upon by the others generally or within any particular category of creditor claims.

Further provision must also be included for possible pre-insolvency offences by managers and third parties and for cross border insolvency issues.

II.C.5.   Bankruptcy

Some laws include provision for a separate bankruptcy procedure. The objective is to disapply the general law of bankruptcy and provide for specific third party creditor rights against banks. Petitions may be made by any creditor of the

---

14. See, for example, Schedule 6 to the UK Insolvency Act 1986.

bank and are determined on the basis of one of the general tests including liquidity, balance sheet and regulatory insolvency. The main difference between a compulsory liquidation and bankruptcy procedure where both are used is that liquidation will only be commenced by the supervisory or regulatory agency and for a regulatory failure including, in particular, authorization or license revocation. Bankruptcy is then a more-general closure remedy available to all creditors of the bank.

Because the supervisory or regulatory agency can also be given power to apply for bankruptcy under the general test provided for, and as many of the supporting procedures for the appointment of a liquidator and conduct of the closure are identical, the two procedures may be combined. It would only be necessary to include separate rights of application or petition for the supervisory or insolvency agency and general creditors. These rights could be included in a new insolvency law for China.

II.D.	SUPPORT OR RESCUE OPTIONS

In addition to determining whether the insolvency regime must operate on a court or extra-judicial basis, and which specific resolution procedures must be made available, such as asset protection, administration or closure, possible support or rescue mechanisms must also be considered within the restructuring or rehabilitation options available.[15] These mechanisms will operate as an alternative to the possible provision of central bank funding on a general or emergency, lender-of-last-resort basis. The provision of such support will always be discretionary, although this may either operate on a formal or informal basis.

In the absence of established experience in the management and discharge of these types of functions, the creation of a more formal procedure would be advisable in that would clarify the number and functions of each of the parties involved. This could, for example, be effected under some form of early resolution procedure, including a 'stability review' to determine whether any such support should be provided. A separate 'regulatory hearing' or 'regulatory (or protective) receivership' can also be considered, which would link the market support process with possible conservation and asset protection.

These support procedures would apply at an early stage following confirmation that a bank was experiencing financial difficulty. In addition to these early procedures, other support or rescue operations should also be considered either immediately or at a stage in the resolution process. These may include further secured lending, capital injections or asset or share transfers.

The following sections describe each of these procedures in more detail.

---

15. See generally, the *Joint Report on Bank Insolvency*, Chapter 5.

II.D.1.   Market Support (Lender of Last Resort)

The central bank must initially device whether or not it will make any financial assistance support available. While the provision and operation of such funding might not be specified in many older central bank laws, express provision in this regard is commonly provide for in newer laws. The advantage of this is that it clarifies the relevant procedures and responsibilities.

One way in which an initial decision could be taken with regard to the possible provision of financial support would be set up some type of stability review procedure. The objective of the review would be to place the central bank under an express statutory obligation to review the potential consequences and impact of the closure of a particular institution and then to determine whether some form of support should be provided.[16] This may have to be cross-referred to statutory functions of the central bank as set out in relevant legislation. This type of support would, of course, only be made available in the event of a systemic threat to the financial system and then only in accordance with the traditional rules developed (only support illiquid but solvent banks except in case of a larger systemic threat).[17]

II.D.2.   Restructuring or Rehabilitation (Regulatory Hearing or Regulatory Receivership)

As well as determining whether any financial support should be provided, it is necessary to confirm whether any other restructuring or rehabilitation options might be available. Supervisory staff would then be required to meet with bank management to discuss possible proposals. One way in which this could be affected would be to set up a sort of 'regulatory hearing' procedure with the 'line management' in the CBRC meeting with senior bank management and the major shareholders – but only if they constituted a sufficiently accessible group – to discuss a possible restructuring, which may include capital or liquidity injection or change of management or a takeover or merger, including either or both of an asset and share purchase.

In the event that the owners are a large or diverse group or otherwise oppose the restructuring or asset or share sale proposed which is otherwise considered desirable, the authorities should be able to apply to the court for an order to approve the 'rescue' arrangements proposed. A court order would be necessary to the extent that company law, property and other rights were otherwise being interfered with without consent. The order would be approved where the relevant authorities were able to establish that the proposed arrangements were in the best interests of the bank or public interest more generally.

Any person or persons who objected must be given a right to be heard, although care would have to be taken to ensure that no abuse or undue delay

---

16.   See supra notes 3 and 4.
17.   See supra note 4.

resulted. One option would be the restructuring or rescue to be given effect to immediately on a provisional or interim basis subject to this being confirmed by the court at a later stage after all interested parties had been heard.

In the event that it was considered necessary for the assets of the bank to be protected in some way, the authorities should have the right to apply to the court for the immediate appointment of some form of 'regulatory receiver'. This would be necessary, for example, to safeguard the assets of the bank from dissipation. This regulatory receiver would obviously overlap with a conservator or administrator. It would only then be necessary to confirm tat the powers of the administrator extended to assisting or giving effect to an agreed restructuring or rehabilitation programme.

II.D.3.   Secured Lending and Capital Injections

The financial position of the bank may also be supported by third party liquidity or capital injections. This can be provided either by existing shareholders or outside third parties, or in exceptional cases by the central bank. The objective would be to strengthen the stability and credibility of the bank in the market place. It would generally not be possible to require existing shareholders or prospective new owners to inject capital, except possibly where these were already state owned enterprises (SOEs). Commercial freedom would otherwise apply. To the extent that the PBOC or the CBRC provided capital, they would effectively be partially nationalising the bank. Additional funding could also be made available to a bank at any time. This would generally be on commercial terms with the advance being fully secured and an appropriate interest rate imposed.

II.D.4.   Asset and Liability Transfers

Asset transfers may either be affected by having the loan book of the bank assigned to another existing bank or to a newly established ('bridge') bank. A combined asset and liability transfer is generally referred to as 'purchase & assumption' in the United States.[18] The purchase of the loan book by an existing bank would be made at a discount, taking into account the quality of the underlying loans and the inability of the assignee to undertake the same original credit assessments. In the event that a significant reduction was required, this may amount to a 'fire sale'. After the assets are transferred, the assignor would be wound up with the discount price being distributed to the outstanding creditors including depositors and then shareholders.

A newly established bank might also be set up to manage the loan book. The advantage would be that this would be able to operate without the credit or reputational damage suffered by the original bank. The financial standing

---

18.   See *Joint Report on Bank Insolvency*, para. 5.4–5.5. See also K.R. Macey, G.P. Miller and R.S. Carnel, *Banking Law and Regulation* (3rd edn, Aspen Law & Business).

of the new bank could also be further strengthened through additional capital injections. The new bank can either be set up to operate on an interim basis pending the further transfer or closure of the loan book or with a view to continuing on a general basis.

II.D.5.   Share Transfers

Rather than transfer assets, the shares of the bank can be transferred through a merger or acquisition, either by a third-party enterprise or an SOE. Whether this is another financial institution would depend upon the holding company or other qualifying holding rules adopted.[19]

II.E.   SUPPORTING STATUTORY PROVISIONS

The draft laws or regulations to be adopted will have to include a number of additional substantive and procedural provisions. A number of points have already been made in this regard under each of the resolution option that may be set up. These would include the triggers for each insolvency mechanism to be adopted as well as appointment rules. The effects of the appointment should also have to be specified with the duties and powers of the appointees, such as a conservator, administrator and liquidator. Report, record and review requirements will also have to be specified with the appropriate court consent stages being determined. Termination provisions will also be included for each resolution mechanism. In addition to these specific mechanism related provisions, additional measures should also be included with regard to distribution priorities, appeals, hearings, party immunities and final procedural closure or resolution. Appropriate provisions will have to be included within the draft law or regulations in respect of each.

III.   OVERVIEW OF CHINESE BANKRUPTCY LAW

III.A.   INTRODUCTION OF CHINESE CORPORATE INSOLVENCY LAW FRAMEWORK

Currently, the insolvency of financial institutions in China is governed by a number of separate laws. No single or special insolvency law applied for banks and other financial institutions, nor a single bankruptcy system for enterprises generally.[20] SOEs are dealt with under the Law of the People's Republic of

---

19. See *Joint Report on Bank Insolvency*, para. 5.4.
20. A new draft enterprise bankruptcy law (Draft Law) has recently been submitted to the Standing Committee of the National People's Congress (SCNPC) for deliberations and approval. The proposed Draft Law consists of 11 Chapters and 164 Articles and includes

China on Enterprise Bankruptcy of 2 December 1986. This law provides for a 'declaration of bankruptcy', in which enterprises demonstrate 'poor operations and management' resulting in serious losses with the entity being 'unable to repay debts' (Article 3).[21]

Other enterprises were subject to the liquidation and bankruptcy proceedings set out in the Civil Procedure Law of China of 9 April 1991 (Chapter XIX). This law enabled creditors of an enterprise to apply to a People's Court to declare the debtor bankrupt, in cases in which the enterprise has suffered serious losses and is unable to replay its debts (Article 199). A 'liquidation team' can then be established to value and dispose of property and distribute the assets (Article 201). The law contained separate provision for enforcing compromise agreements (Article 202).

The Supreme People's Court subsequently issued a series of interpretations on enterprise bankruptcy, including the Provisions on Some Issues concerning the Trial of Enterprise Bankruptcy Cases of 18 July 2002, which came into effect 1 September 2002. The objective was to establish a consistent understanding of the Law on Enterprise Bankruptcy and the relevant provisions in the Civil Procedure Law. A number of directions were, in particular, issued with regard to:

- jurisdiction: Articles 1–3);
- application and acceptance of proceedings (Articles 4–20);
- reporting of claims (Articles 21–24);
- conciliation and rectification (Articles 25–30);
- issuance of the bankruptcy declaration (Articles 31–38);
- creditors meetings (Articles 39–45);
- appointment and functions of the liquidation team (Articles 47–54);
- bankruptcy claims (Articles 55–63);
- relevant property (Articles 64–72);
- repayment, collection and distribution (Articles 73–87);

---

a number of new bankruptcy rules new to China. The first deliberation by the SCNPC took place in June 2004, and the second took place in October 2004. Following the third deliberation, the draft law was expected to be passed sometime in 2006. The draft law is intended to create a unified bankruptcy law for all enterprises whether state or privately owned. While state-owned commercial banks and insurance companies are technically covered by the Draft Law, difficulties arose in the deliberations as to whether financial institutions should fall within the scope of the amended bankruptcy law. Although it was agreed, after extensive discussion during the second deliberation, that the provisions of the Draft Law should be applicable to the bankruptcy of financial institutions including commercial banks and insurance companies, it is still unclear whether such entities can be dealt with separately in regard to the special nature of their activities and the risks to the financial and economy as a whole. See Section I, previously in this chapter.

21. For the purposes of this Report, this situation is referred to as 'liquidity insolvency'. The other key tests (or triggers) are 'balance sheet' insolvency, in which liabilities exceed assets, and 'capital insolvency' or 'regulatory insolvency', in which required capital levels are breached. Equivalent definitions are used in the *Joint Report on Bank Insolvency*.

- expenses (Articles 88–91);
- distribution (Articles 92–95);
- termination (Articles 96–99);
- other miscellaneous provisions (Articles 100–106).

In practice, the majority of cases of corporate insolvency are policy-related bankruptcy. For policy related bankruptcy, the People's courts essentially apply to regulations of the State Council in priority instead of the laws. In 1996, the Supreme People's Court issued an Urgent Notice Regarding Problems in Enterprises Bankruptcy Cases.[22] This notice stressed that policy-related SOE bankruptcy must apply to the 1994 Regulation No. 59 of the State Council.[23]

China began to draft a new bankruptcy law in 1994. Thus far, no version can pass the National People's Congress. The latest available version is the October 2004 Draft. The law is still restricted to 'legal person enterprises bankruptcy'; financial institution insolvency is excluded in this draft.[24]

III.B.   INTRODUCTION OF CHINESE FINANCIAL INSTITUTION INSOLVENCY
              LAW FRAMEWORK

Separate provisions were contained within other specific laws and regulations for financial institution insolvency, including the Commercial Bank Law,[25] the Securities Law,[26] the Insurance Law,[27] the Trust and Investment Law,[28] the Company Law,[29] Banking Supervision Law[30] and the Administrative Measures on Trust Investment Company.[31] Additional measures were also provided for in connection with foreign-funded financial institutions, financial leasing companies, enterprise group finance companies and rural credit cooperatives.[32] While particular general provisions were included, such as with regard to the use of a debts test (unable to pay debts), consistent and coherent procedures are not provided for financial institutions.

---

22. The Supreme People's Court, *Urgent Notice Regarding Problems in Enterprises Bankruptcy Cases*, no. 431 (*Fa Min Chuan*) (1996).
23. The State Council, *Notice Regarding Problems Pertaining to the Trial Implementation of State Owned Enterprises Bankruptcy in Certain Cities*, no. 59 (*Guo Fa*) 1994.
24. The Draft PRC Bankruptcy Law (October 2004), Article 149.
25. The Commercial Bank Law, Articles 71–72.
26. The Securities Law, Article 19.
27. The Insurance Law, Articles 87–89.
28. The Trust and Investment Law, Article 18.
29. The Company Law, Articles 189 and 196.
30. The Banking Supervision Law (2004), Articles 38–39.
31. The Administrative Measures on Trust Investment Company (2002), Articles 16–19.
32. See Regulation on Administration of Foreign-Funded Financial Institutions; Measures of Administration on Financial Leasing Companies; Measures of Administration on Enterprise Group Finance Companies; and Rules of Administration on Rural Credit Cooperatives.

So far, only one case of financial institution bankruptcy has been reported: the Guangdong International Trust and Investment Company (GITIC) bankruptcy case (1999).[33] Several cases of assume control or close have been reported.[34]

III.C.   PROBLEMS OF CHINESE FINANCIAL INSTITUTION INSOLVENCY
                      FRAMEWORK

A series of additional operational difficulties also arise in practice in the insolvency area. These difficulties are generally concerned with the lack of market discipline and awareness of the proper function and value of insolvency proceedings within a market economy. Specific problems identified include the failure of borrowers to repay loans without sanction or enforcement, the failure of banks to make full provision for value impaired assets (loss provisions), the ability of enterprise debtors to carry unpaid deposits at full value on their books, the full official repayment of individual deposits held with insolvent banks (in the absence of any separate deposit protection scheme) and the lack of effective sanction or incentives for managers an shareholders of insolvent institutions.[35]

The first difficulty is generally concerned with possible lack of proper credit determinations being made by banks on the initial advancement of credit. This issue is clearly a significant problem in regard to state-owned banks, which has resulted in significant levels of NPLs arising. This problem can then be aggravated by the lack of effective enforcement policy in financial institutions.

Apart from these asset-side problems, more-significant difficulties can arise on the liability side of the balance sheet, in particular, with the lack of effective market discipline and sanction being applied to poorly run institutions. The last three operational difficulties referred to are all concerned with market discipline failures by individual and corporate depositors as well as managers are shareholders. Managers should be rewarded for good practice and success, at the same time as disciplined for poor performance. Shareholders must monitor and discipline management while depositors should oversee the safety of their

---

33. HCA 15651/1999 (HKSAR) or The People's High Court of Guangdong, Yue Fa Jing – Po Zi, no. 1–9 (1999).
34. Bank of China Trust and Investment Company, China Rural Development Trust and Investment Company, Hai Nan Development Bank and China New Technology Creation and Investment Company.
35. This issue of 'moral hazard' is particularly severe as it applies with regard to both depositors – those who have no incentive to monitor and sanction banks through the withdrawal of funds through the availability of de facto full deposit protection – and mangers and shareholders, who have no threat of loss. It is essential that relevant and effective 'incentives' be created to enable proper market principles to apply and operate. Basel Committee on Banking Supervision, *Supervisory Guidance on Dealing with Weak Banks* (March 2002); and IMF, *Orderly & Effective Insolvency Procedures* (1999), no. 1.

funds and, if necessary, transfer them to another bank or depository institution. Financial institutions should be judged in terms of their performance and punished for bad practice. Financial regulation will ensure that institutions are established and operate in a safe and prudent manner. Regulatory sanctions must nevertheless be supported by market discipline which includes the risk of insolvency and closure.

The general purpose of bank and financial regulation (as opposed to insolvency) is to establish a series of market entry conditions to ensure that financial entities are properly structured, capitalised and managed. Such institutions must then be operated in a safe and prudent manner on a continuing basis. This is the basic function of authorization (or licensing) and continuing supervision. These regulatory controls on market entry must then be supported by necessary exit rules, including effective bank insolvency procedures. Inefficient and poorly run institutions must be restructured or closed, with their liabilities and assets either being assumed by other institutions or distributed to depositors and creditors.

The two main procedures applicable to banks previously were the assumption of control and bankruptcy provisions set out in the Law of Commercial Banks. The POBC could assume control over a bank where it 'may suffer a credit crisis' seriously affecting the interests of depositors (Article 64). The objective was to protect the interests of depositors and enable the bank to resume normal business. Although orders may be continued, the maximum period for this statutory intervention is two years. Control terminates when the bank is either able to resume normal business or merged or declared bankrupt (Article 71). A People's Court could then issue an order declaring the bank bankrupt in cases in which the bank is unable to pay its debts (Article 71). The assets of the bank will be realized and depositors and other creditors paid in priority of wages, employee benefits, liquidation expenses and individual deposits. Little guidance, however, was provided in regard to the detailed application and operation of these procedures in practice.

Further confusion could arise if one or more of the other solvency or bankruptcy procedures available are also triggered, such as under the Company Law or the Law of Civil Procedure. Inconsistency could again arise, depending upon the nature of the financial institution and whether any of the other financial laws apply.

A series of deficiencies accordingly arose with regard to the structure, content and operation of the insolvency laws in China in the financial area. The initial tests or triggers were inadequately defined and articulated, the rights of parties to petition unspecified and relevant procedures undeveloped. A single series of alternative but coherent and consistent mechanisms or procedures should be available depending upon the severity of the financial difficulty being experienced by the bank or financial institution concerned. These procedures may then be either protective or rehabilitatory in nature or both, but also supported by full closure rules where necessary. The relationship between statutory insolvency procedures and other market support mechanisms, such as central bank liquidity or emergency provision (lender of last resort) and deposit protection schemes should also be considered. A consistent, or at least parallel, framework must be set up across the financial area.

IV.   FINANCIAL INSTITUTION INSOLVENCY LAW
             REFORM IN CHINA

The special issues and difficulties that arise in designing and setting up an appropriate insolvency law for banks and other financial institutions have been outlined in this chapter. The principal options available for reform of the Chinese laws in this area have also been examined and reviewed. A new more general Enterprise Bankruptcy has since been proposed in China,[36] although it is unlikely that this will provide all of the necessary safeguards and protections required to govern the conduct of bank and other financial institution insolvencies.

The residual core issues that arise in designing an effective insolvency law for particular application in the financial area are considered in the following sections. The purpose is not to be prescriptive nor recommend the adoption of any specific procedure within China. The objective is rather to review possible alternatives for consideration and assessment having regard to the specific needs of the Chinese economy and the underlying political and market system in place. More-detailed recommendations and conclusions are made in the final section.

IV.A.   GENERAL POLICY

In light of the importance of the banking area and the absence of any clear or unified set of relevant provisions within China, the adoption of a special insolvency law for banks should be considered as a matter of urgency. This could also be extended to other financial institutions although particular provisions would only apply with regard to banks such as in connection with rehabilitation and market support. These provisions could be included within the revised Commercial Bank Law (currently being considered), although these provisions should preferably be set out in a separate law, in light of the further delay that negotiating these provisions would cause and due to the length and complexity of the provisions required, as described later in this chapter.

Because the general objective is to promote effective market operations and market discipline, a dedicated insolvency law would also clarify respective rights, duties, obligations, procedures and recoveries. This might also be preferable in light of the difficulties that have arisen in agreeing to any additional general enterprise-insolvency requirements and the particular sensitivity and special characteristics of banking and financial markets.

---

36. No. 21 supra.

The existing law on Enterprise Bankruptcy can be used as a basic model, although a number of the provisions would have to be revised to provide for a series of new, clear and consistent procedures, as described later. The interpretations issued by the Supreme People's Court are also of value, including, in particular, the 2002 Provisions on Some Issues concerning the Trial of Enterprise Bankruptcy Cases. These Provisions provide useful procedural and operational details, and can either be included within the revised insolvency law or incorporated as supporting regulations, although subject to necessary revisions to reflect the new procedures adopted. In cases in which existing laws must not be used, these laws must be expressly disapplied to avoid confusion, and possibly overlapping and contradictory proceedings.

While this can be referred to as a new 'Law on Bank Insolvency' or 'Law on Bank Bankruptcy', it would be preferable to use 'Law on Bank Restructuring and Liquidation'. This description would more-accurately reflect its purpose and content and avoid confusion in regard to terms such as 'bankruptcy' or 'insolvency'. The new law can be applied both to privately owned and managed firms, as well as SOEs. The only difference that would arise in practice is that the relative tests or standards (triggers) for the commencement of proceedings may be applied in a different manner. While this can create particular differences in practice, the same provisions must preferably be applied in all cases insofar as possible.

The system adopted must operate on the basis of an appropriate underlying legal framework that provides proper respect and protection for property rights including intangible financial claims, for reasons of transparency, validity (authority) and finality. A significant amount of administrative power and discretion can nevertheless be conferred, provided that appropriate judicial procedures are included at all necessary stages, including commencement, approval of property rights adjustments and distributions and termination. A separate court system for insolvency procedures would generally not be necessary unless any specific concerns arose with regard to delay or relevant judicial expertise.

The new law should preferably include a series of general principles concerning the operation, purpose and function of insolvency law. These types of general principles have already been used in other laws, including the Commercial Bank Law. These principles should, in particular, confirm the general purpose and operation of a market-based economy, including the need to promote market discipline (and avoid moral hazard) to remove inefficient institutions. These principles could also attempt to correct misunderstandings in regard to some of the residual problems in the current system, including failure to repay debts, absence of adequate loss provisions, holding blocked assets at inflated values, the need for meaningful depositor and shareholder oversight and proper management incentives and efficiencies.

These general statements of objective could be based on some of the principles issued by various international bodies in the insolvency and bank insolvency area.[37] Although this practice of including general principles within a law is not common in other countries, these principles are of value in clarifying the objectives and underlying rules and procedures that must apply. This appears to be of particular benefit where China has adopted new laws that promote more general market rather than managed economy based ideas and approaches.

IV.B.   AGENCY RESPONSIBILITY

The day-to-day supervision of banks must continue to be managed though the CBRC, with the PBC being responsible for monitoring the stability of the financial system stability more generally. It is understood that this stability is to be provided for under the proposed revisions to the PBC Law and that the PBC will, in future, have an express legal basis for action in this area. The system would then operate generally with the PBC monitoring and overseeing the stability of the financial system and banks and other financial institutions. The conduct of this type of oversight could most easily be achieved through the setup of a new 'Financial Stability Department' in the PBC through which all market stability-related matters would be dealt with.

Bank restructuring and liquidation would then be conducted through a specialist department or division in the CBRC. In addition, equivalent sections must be set up in the CSRC and the CIRC to deal with difficulties experienced by other types of financial institutions. The bank insolvency department or division could have been located within the PBC, although it would be preferable for department or division to be in the CBRC for reasons of familiarity of CBRC supervisory staff (line management) with individual institutions, necessary information access, immediacy of action, possible operational consistency as well as administrative convenience and low cost. Bank restructuring and liquidation could alternatively be transferred to an independent insolvency agency although this would require separate funding, staff and training with the other advantages of contact and proximity or immediacy being lost.

The other alternative would be for this function to be discharged by the deposit protection agency – once established – although the same relative disadvantages would again necessarily apply. This can be considered further at such time as China establishes a formal deposit protection scheme, and its scope and nature of operation are confirmed. While the main bank restructuring and liquidation division or section would be established within the CBRC, a separate parallel division should be set up within 'Financial Stability Department' in the PBC. This division could, for example, be referred to as the 'Financial Restructuring Division' or 'Financial Resolution Division'. The objective would be to

---

37. See, for example, World Bank General Insolvency 'Principles and Guidelines' in Annex III. See also World Bank and IMF, *Joint Report on Bank Insolvency*; and Basel Committee, supra note 1.

monitor the financial soundness of the banking and financial sector, specifically in regard to the stability of major banks and financial groups.

In the event that concerns arise over the soundness of an individual institution, these concerns would be referred by supervisory staff to the restructuring department or division in the CBRC, which would advise the corresponding section in the PBC. If the matter could be dealt with by the CBRC itself, the PBC would not be involved further, and would only advised of the manner in which the issue was resolved. If further action was required, including the possible provision of emergency (lender of last resort) financing, appropriate action would be coordinated by the Financial Restructuring Division and the other divisions within the Financial Stability Department.

IV.C.   JOINT REVIEW COMMITTEE

To promote cooperation and coordinated action between the CBRC and the PBC, a joint review committee must be established, consisting of representatives of the PBC and the CBRC, as well as any separate deposit protection agency once established. This joint review committee could also include representatives of the MOF, or at least report to the MOF in the event that any specific concerns arise. This function could be carried out by the same joint committee set up for complex groups and financial stability. The main function of the joint committee would be to consider whether the financial condition of any individual institution was a cause of concern and the appropriate action to be taken. The joint committee would, in particular, consider whether the collapse of an individual institution could create a systemic threat to the financial system. The effect of the closure of a bank on other institutions would be examined and the possibility of any contagion assessed. While the general administrative management of a restructuring would be dealt with through the CBRC, any more general policy or strategic decisions, including financial support, would be taken through the Joint Committee. The restructuring or closure of a larger financial group would also have to be dealt with on a joint basis, with representatives from the CSRC and the CIRC attending depending upon the structure of the particular group. This type of continuing joint representation could be most easily achieved through the use of the separate Joint Committee. Complex group supervision and financial stability, including larger restructuring or insolvency work, would then be combined by extending the functions of the Joint Financial Stability Committee to include all market stability related issues of major concern.

The Joint Financial Stability Committee would be chaired by a State Commissioner and co-chaired by the Governor of the PBC. The Committee would report directly to the State Council. Administrative support would be provided through the Financial Stability Department of the PBC, which would include separate divisions on Financial Stability, Financial Groups, Financial Support, Financial Restructuring and Financial Insolvency or Liquidation. Using the

Joint Financial Stability Committee in this way would, as a result, accordingly enable the creation of a fully integrated framework for the oversight of the financial system in general, including complex financial group supervision and financial restructuring, support and, where necessary, closure. While specific tasks would continue to be carried out by dedicated divisions (or sections) within the existing agencies, all major decisions could be taken on a joint basis where necessary, and by a committee that would have sufficient political authority to ensure that these were given full effect in practice.

IV.D.   INSOLVENCY MECHANISMS

The main procedural mechanisms to be provided under the new Law on Bank Restructuring and Liquidation should include, at a minimum, some form of administration, rehabilitation and liquidation. Administration and liquidation would require court consent although restructuring would only require court involvement in cases in which any property rights or claims were adjusted without consent. Administration would enable a bank to be managed for a defined period – which could be extended – under the control of either the CBRC or an externally appointed third party. The assets of the bank would be under the control of the administrator and the bank legally protected from other third-party enforcement proceedings during the course of the administration. As part of the rehabilitation procedure, a range of disposal or rehabilitation options would be made available including asset and liability transfers, mergers and acquisitions or new bank transfers. This would enable a more flexible and cost-effective set of resolution options to be made available to deal with institutions that experience financial difficulties on a more flexible, cost effective, and ultimately more successful basis.

Rehabilitation plans would be developed in parallel with possible financial support decisions (lender of last resort). This might be of use in cases in which direct financial support would be quicker and more efficient, or if some form of rehabilitation might not otherwise be possible in the particular case. Rehabilitation and financial support (lender of last resort) would then be closely coordinated in practice. A simplified liquidation procedure must also be introduced in the event that a bank is incapable of rehabilitation or where its assets and liabilities have already been transferred to another institution.

Other procedures could be considered, including possible 'conservation' or 'regulatory receivership', which operate on a protective basis to safeguard the assets of the bank against dissipation. The same results can nevertheless be achieved through the use of a single administration procedure that would permit the CBRC – or possibly the PBC in the event that the CBRC refused to act in a particular case – to appoint an administrator as soon as a bank or other financial institution experienced difficulties. Allowing administration to be used for such protective purposes would simplify the structure and operation of the new insolvency system as a whole, but without undermining the system's effectiveness. The administration could also be extended in practice to support possible restructuring or rehabilitation options, where necessary. Restructuring could either be conducted by the bank directly, through the CBRC or with the assistance of an administrator. Court involvement would only be required where property rights or claims were adjusted without consent. Administration would then become a flexible protective and corrective device in practice.

Other forms of creditor 'receivership' might also be considered. These generally provide secured creditors with certain rights of intervention and recovery against corporate borrowers – including banks – although their availability depends upon the nature of the underlying corporate security law in place. While this may not be a problem where the availability of such rights is limited, if third parties are to be allowed to exercise significant powers against banks, the authorities (the CBRC and the PBC) must be given the right to oppose the appointment of a receiver (or other agent of the creditor) in cases where this may otherwise undermine the stability of a bank or the it is considered that the claim can be repaid in some other less obtrusive or damaging manner or the appointment would otherwise not in the public interest.

Sufficient legal safeguards must be provided for including court consent for each of the major procedural steps (commencement, asset realisation and distribution and closure) and ongoing rights of review or appeal. These rights of appeal should not, however, be allowed to delay or interfere with the general operation of the resolution process. Appropriate time limits must be incorporated in to the law and the authorities permitted to act in emergency situations subject to subsequent court consent or sanction.

The system must also allow for maximum administrative (agency) management autonomy and discretion, although these powers would be exercised in a more-general, court-based system to provide necessary validation and finality. In this way, speed and flexibility would, accordingly, be balanced with legal certainty and validity.

IV.E.   INSOLVENCY PROCEDURES

The three principal insolvency mechanisms to be set up would consist of some form of administration, restructuring (rehabilitation) and formal closure (on either on a voluntary or compulsory basis). Whichever procedure applied would depend upon the particular circumstances and relevant tests (triggers) to be set out in the new law or regulation. In the event that a crisis arises within a particular bank, the possibility of some refinancing or reconstruction should be initially considered. This may include secured or unsecured borrowing or some form of capital injection. Asset or share transfers either to an existing or special purpose (new or bridge) bank basis can also be considered. This would avoid the need for any separate financial assistance (lender of last resort) support.

In situations in which a systemic issue arises, the nature and amount of any financial support to be provided would also have to be confirmed as a matter of urgency. This type of decision could initially be considered within the Financial Support Division in the PBC, although any final decision must be referred to the Joint Financial Stability Committee for determination to the extent necessary. This type of support should generally only be made available where an institution is illiquid but solvent. Assistance should only be provided to an insolvent institution where the institution's closure would otherwise create a systemic threat. Support should generally be secured, although unsecured funding can be made available in exceptional circumstances.

In the event that the financial condition of a particular bank has become unsustainable but no systemic threat arises through its closure, some form of liquidation or closure procedure should be commenced. While the existing court based systems in China may be continued, a simplified liquidation procedure should be considered.

Three parallel sets of tests (or triggers) should generally be used for the commencement of formal proceedings, including 'liquidity insolvency' (unable to pay debts as they fall due), 'balance sheet' insolvency (where liabilities exceed assets) and 'capital insolvency' or 'regulatory insolvency' (where set capital levels are breached). The use of all three tests would enable creditors to protect their legitimate interests (using the first two tests) as well as official intervention in appropriate cases (using the third test). Other tests could license revocation (to apply automatically) or a more general discretionary public interest standard (either 'threat to the safety and soundness of the bank' or on 'just and equitable' basis).

The authorities must have the right, in appropriate cases, to oppose any closure procedure commenced by a third party. This right would generally apply where the claim could otherwise be satisfied, or the closure of the institution would be considered to pose a systemic threat. Petitions by creditors in liquidation proceedings must be limited to two-party applications to prevent a single creditor commencing vexatious or otherwise unjustified action.

IV.F.   ADMINISTRATION

A new administration procedure must be created to enable the insolvency agency – generally the CBRC – to assume control over the operation and assets of a bank and protect them from removal or dissipation. This agency could operate on either an automatic or discretionary basis in the event that relevant tests were met with the administrator then continuing in office until the administration (conservation) was formally terminated or a separate formal process commenced (either rehabilitation or liquidation).

In the event that it was considered that a bank could 'work out' its financial difficulties, the administrator would manage its affairs for an interim period to be determined by the agency or a court, for example, three moths subject to extension. This would allow the bank to continue in operation on a commercial basis with only the rights of the managers and shareholders being suspended to the extent considered necessary by the administrator. The administration would continue in operation until formal termination or being superseded by another formal procedure.

The right to apply for such an administrative procedure should be extended to include the official insolvency agency – generally the CBRC, but possibly also the PBC – as well as the directors and creditors of the bank. This is common in a number of countries. Where a third party applied, however, the insolvency agency would be able to oppose the appointment in appropriate cases. The availability of such a private right of action would ensure that pressure was placed on the insolvency agency to take appropriate action in all cases or be pre-empted by an individual petition. A court would then rule on whether the administrator should or should not be appointed. Court hearings to consider appointments and any objections should be taken within limited time periods (such as five business days) to avoid delay and unnecessary uncertainty and damage to the financial condition of the bank.

The effects of the appointment of the administrator should be set out in the law. These effects would include preventing any other enforcement action being commenced (a moratorium) or continuing against the institution during the course of the administration unless otherwise approved by the court. The appointment would also transfer all power and authority to manage the assets of the bank to the administrator with the rights of existing managers and shareholders being suspended unless otherwise agreed to by the administrator. The administrator would be given general power to dispose of or liquidate assets and commence or defend legal proceedings in the name of the bank. The new law should also include power to apply to the court to reopen or nullify particular transactions entered into for fraudulent purposes or otherwise not at fair market a value. Certain time limits may have to be provided (such as two years) to avoid protracted litigation and delay in such cases.

IV.G.   RESTRUCTURING

In cases in which more-formal action was required to enable the bank to continue in business beyond simple managed administration, various rehabilitation devices must be made available. The CBRC – or, failing which, the PBC – must be given express power to propose and give effect to such arrangements either with the consent of the shareholders (if possible) or under a court order. Appropriate devices would include asset or liability transfers (to another bank or an asset management company), mergers and acquisitions or new (bridge) bank transfers. The objective would be to attempt to preserve the business of the bank as a going concern, or to dispose of assets separately. The objective would be to produce a rehabilitation plan or programme to enable the institution to deal with any financial difficulties and avoid closure. The restructuring plan can be prepared by any party, including bank management, shareholders, creditors or the administrator, if appointed, or the CBRC.

While some restructuring may be possible, either through the bank's existing management or shareholders directly or with the involvement of the CBRC, other more-complex arrangements can be implemented following the appointment of an administrator. Whether an administrator must be appointed would be decided on by the CBRC on a case-by-case basis. The powers of the administrator would have to include the ability to participate in such restructuring arrangements.

The new law must confer on the CBRC the power to propose or accept any restructuring proposal considered to be in the best interests of the bank, although this restructuring could take a number of different forms. Other refinancing or restructuring can be given effect to by the bank directly, which would not require CBRC or court involvement.

Under more-complex arrangements, various technical matters may have to be dealt with, including valuations, share transfers and the treatment of losses and accrued rights, minority rights and delisting of listed securities. The implications and effects of these are dependent on underlying company, accounting and securities or stock exchange laws and regulations in place as well as more general property laws. The treatment of this type of matter would be set out in the restructuring plan or programme produced. The objective of the restructuring procedures is to ensure the implementation of a transparent, complete and certain (irreversible) transfer. While necessary powers might be given to an administrative agency to carry out the transfer, court consent is desirable to ensure that the other objectives – those of transparency, completeness and certainty – are secured. A significant number of other separate provisions or amendments to other laws might otherwise be required.

Court involvement can either be provided on an *ex ante* (initial consent) or *ex post* (subsequent approval) basis. While certain, more-limited actions may be permitted to be taken by the administrator under the powers conferred, more-substantial action, such as giving effect to a restructuring programme, should preferably require prior court consent. Private parties should be given rights to make representations although the court will be given power to take the final decision on whether a restructuring should proceed or not. Court involvement is desirable in the interests of due process, validity and finality whenever private rights are effected. The use of these types of restructuring or rehabilitation devices should be coordinated with the possible provision of direct financial support from the PBC. The most appropriate option will depend upon the particular circumstances.

IV.H.   LIQUIDATION

In appropriate cases, formal closure or liquidation must be available. This can again operate on either a voluntary basis, following an appropriate resolution being passed by the owners or shareholders of the bank, or on a compulsory basis, in the event that a certain test is satisfied. Voluntary liquidation must only be available in situations in which the assets of the bank will cover all liabilities. Compulsory liquidation should occur where defined conditions are met. This situation would generally include liquidity, balance sheet and regulatory insolvency, such as a 50 per cent below required capital requirement. The lower capital figure of 25 per cent can also be considered, although this would force a bank into liquidation quicker without possible corrective action (para. 24, previously). If the tests are satisfied, the court must be required to commence the proceedings. The availability and decision whether to apply to the court would be discretionary. Other compulsory tests can still be provided to include revocation of the banking license. The CBRC could then be required to petition for closure if the license was revoked for any reason. The CBRC or PBC must be entitled to oppose a petition in cases in which this might create a systemic threat or some other, more-effective resolution option is available, such as under a proposed restructuring or rehabilitation package.

A separate 'bankruptcy' procedure might be considered to permit other creditors or third parties to apply for the winding-up of an individual bank. The alternative is for this to be combined with the liquidation procedure by allowing creditors to apply for the court to issue commencement order. This would then allow for the possible appointment of either an internal agency appointed liquidator – under a compulsory liquidation by the CBRC – or an external independent liquidator. This would simplify the available options and procedures. The parties that might be appointed to act as liquidator must be confirmed. This can include experienced personnel in the CBRC or PBC – possibly transferred to a new Financial Restructuring or and Recovery Division – or external experts, including lawyers and accountants with the necessary relevant experience. Relevant qualification requirements must be included within the proposed new law.

The conduct of the liquidation and closure of a financial institution could be carried out in accordance with the provisions set out in the existing Enterprise Law, although restating all the relevant provisions in a single source for banks and financial institutions would be of value. Relevant sections could either be copied into the new law or incorporated by reference with any necessary amendments. The provisions set out in the Supreme Court's *Provisions on Some Issues concerning the Trial of Enterprise Bankruptcy Cases* can also be included or incorporated by reference to the extent necessary.

The alternative to using the existing procedures would be to provide for a simplified mechanism that provided for the appointment of a single liquidator who would be responsible for the realisation of the banks' assets and their distribution in accordance with the priority rules set out in the new law. This would enable a quicker and possibly more-efficient realization of the residual assets of the institution. There would be no need for the use of any more-complicated or protracted procedure, because a bank closure can be simpler than an industrial or commercial entity or the assets and liabilities of the bank may already have been dealt with under one of the restructuring or rehabilitation mechanisms provided for.

IV.I.   Powers and Duties

All appropriate powers and duties must be conferred on administrators and liquidators as appropriate. These powers and duties must be laid out in the new law to ensure certainty and transparency. The powers of the administrators and liquidators should be supported by corresponding duties, which should include relevant provisions with regard to matters such as reports, records, notice, review or appeal, immunity from prosecution. Private parties must be given necessary rights of review and appeal. These rights are essential to protect legitimate private and State interests. Rights of review or appeal must nevertheless be subject to strict time limits and provide for final resolution or determination by the court to avoid delay and abuse. Appropriate immunity protections from actions for damages by creditors or shareholders must be conferred on administrators and liquidators. These protections would apply to all actions taken within the proper discharge of their functions and not involving bad faith. This is essential to protect them from unnecessary or vexatious litigation. All relevant parties must be required to cooperate in cross-border or other international insolvency procedures as appropriate. This would include the CBRC and PBC to the extent relevant, administrators and liquidators as well as the People's Court. China must comply with all relevant international treaties, conventions or arrangements to which it is a party.

IV.J.   Policy Coordination

The availability and use of the main resolution options provided for must be properly coordinated in practice. This will be achieved through a dedicated department or division set up within the CBRC which would liaise with the corresponding division in the PBC. Which administration, rehabilitation and closure procedures would then be used in any individual case would depend upon the particular circumstances involved. The operation of the insolvency procedures must also be coordinated with other support or redress mechanisms, including lender of last resort and possible deposit protection. This coordination would be facilitated in practice with the transfer of responsibility for major decision to the Joint Financial Stability Committee and supported by the establishment of separate divisions for restructuring and recovery – or insolvency – set up within the PBC. This transfer would enable close contact and cooperation between the CBRC and the PBC, with any consequent action been taken in a consistent and fully coordinated manner.

China must reconsider the establishment of some form off deposit protection or insurance scheme. It is understood that this type of scheme is currently thought to be inappropriate in light of the extent of the outstanding NPL problem. The advantage of a bank-funded deposit cover scheme is that it would place considerably less pressure on State funds, as under the present *de facto* full refinancing of most banks in financial difficulty. The adoption of partial rather than full cover scheme, such as with percentage limits or maximum payment amounts, would also promote market discipline with depositors having an incentive to monitor bank performance and punish poor results through the withdrawal and transfer of funds elsewhere. This would also promote competition between banks which should lead to better customer services. The availability of deposit protection payment would also still act as a disincentive for bank runs which would limit claims under against the PBC (as lender of last resort). The creation of such a scheme should accordingly be considered as early as conditions will permit.

The general operation and success of the new restructuring and recovery processes should be monitored and reviewed over time. Developments within the structure and operation of financial markets and elsewhere should be considered and supporting best supervisory and regulatory practice on a national and global basis taken into account. This review function could be undertaken by the existing Research Bureau within the PBC although its responsibility in this regard should be clarified and strengthened with the Bureau being required to cooperate closely with the divisions within the new Financial Stability Department and the Joint Financial Stability Committee. Any necessary revisions or amendments should be made as appropriate.

Further reforms must only be considered to the extent that financial market developments and improvements in supervisory and regulatory experience and practice permit. The overall objective must be to ensure that China is able to promote the continued safe and stable expansion of its financial markets and financial system at the same time as prevent any avoidable crisis or collapse.

V.   CONCLUDING OBSERVATIONS AND
          RECOMMENDATIONS

An effective exit (insolvency) policy must be adopted to deal with inefficient banks and other financial institutions based on a new of Law on Bank Restructuring and Liquidation. This law must outline the main procedures available, but also include a series of general principles in regard to the operation, purpose and function of the law. Supporting regulations should be considered that would contain further procedural and operational details. Significant administrative power and discretion should be conferred to allow the system to operate in as quick and efficient a manner as possible although the main stages in any formal process should require court consent. This is necessary for transparency, validity (authority) and finality reasons. Court involvement should nevertheless be limited to apply only at key stages in the each process (including commencement, approval of property rights adjustments and distributions and termination). The system should also operate within strict time limits to avoid unnecessary delay and cost with judicial discretion being restricted through strict drafting to provide legal predictability and limit abuse. A separate insolvency court is not necessary at this stage unless any major concerns arise with regard to expertise, delay or abuse in practice.

Bank restructuring and liquidation should be conducted through a specialist department (or division) within the CBRC. Transferring this function to an independent insolvency agency would not be desirable at this stage due to the separate funding, staff and training required and loss of contact and familiarity of CBRC staff with relevant institutions. A separate oversight division should also be set up within the PBC (to be referred to as the 'Financial Restructuring Division' (or 'Financial Resolution Division') which would operate within a new 'Financial Stability Department'). The function of the Department generally would be to monitor the financial soundness of the banking and financial sector which would also include the oversight of the restructuring of any major bank or financial group within the specialist Financial Restructuring Division. In the event that difficulties arose with regard to the soundness of an individual bank, this would initially be managed within the restructuring department (or division) within the CBRC.

Coordinated action between the CBRC and the PBC would be supported by a joint review committee (the 'Joint Financial Stability Committee') made up of representatives of the PBC and the CBRC as well as the MOF. The restructuring of more complex financial groups would also be coordinated through the Joint Committee with representatives of the CSRC and the CIRC also attending. The Committee would be chaired by a State Commissioner and co-chaired by the Governor of the PBC. It would report directly to the State Council. Administrative support would be provided through the Financial Stability Department within the PBC.

Use of the Joint Financial Stability Committee would allow the creation of an integrated framework to be constructed for the oversight of the financial system including financial stability oversight, complex groups supervision, financial restructuring, financial support and (where necessary) financial closure. While particular tasks would continue to be carried out by relevant divisions (or sections) within the sector agencies, these functions would be monitored by the Financial Stability Department within the PBC with any common decisions being taken through the Joint Financial Stability Committee.

The new Law on Bank Restructuring and Liquidation must provide for three main insolvency procedures, consisting of administration, restructuring (rehabilitation) and liquidation. Administration and liquidation would require court consent; however, restructuring would only require court involvement where any property rights or claims were adjusted without consent.

Three parallel tests would be used for administration and liquidation proceedings consisting of 'liquidity insolvency' (unable to pay debts as they fall due), 'balance sheet' insolvency (where liabilities exceed assets) and 'capital insolvency' or 'regulatory insolvency' (where set capital levels are breached). Other tests can also be used. These could include license revocation or more general public interest (either 'threat to the safety and soundness of the bank' or on 'just and equitable' basis). The first three (and license revocation) would apply on an automatic and compulsory basis while the other (public interest ground) would be discretionary which would limit uncertainty and delay.

The right to apply for an administrator or liquidator to be appointed would be available to the bank, its directors, a creditor and the CBRC (and the PBC in the event that the CBRC refused to act without proper cause). An application by creditors for a liquidator to be appointed should require, at least, two parties (that than only one). The CBRC (and the PBC) would be able to oppose any petition wherever they considered inappropriate to close an individual bank (such as where the claim could otherwise be satisfied or the closure of the institution would create a systemic threat).

Administration would allow a bank to be managed for a set period (subject to extension) under the control of the CBRC or an externally appointed third party. The assets of the bank would be held by the administrator and the bank legally protected from other third party enforcement proceedings during the course of the administration. The administrator would be responsible for the management of the business of the bank until the financial difficulties experience had been resolved. The administrator would prepare a report on the conduct of the administration, which can include recommendations for some more-formal restructuring or for the closure (liquidation) of the institution. Restructuring or rehabilitation would be managed through the restructuring department (or division) within the CBRC. The objective would be to produce a rehabilitation plan or programme to enable the institution to deal with any financial difficulties and avoid closure. The restructuring plan may be prepared by any party, including bank management, shareholders, creditors, the administrator (if appointed) or the CBRC. The restructuring plan might include any one or more of a number of mechanisms including secured or unsecured borrowing, liquidity or capital injections, asset or liability transfers and share transfers, such as mergers and acquisitions or new bank transfers.

The function of the CBRC in relation to rehabilitation would be to assess the validity of any plan produced and determine whether it would be in the interests of the bank or the general public interest to proceed. In the event that a plan or programme required individual property or financial rights (claims) to be altered in some way (with the relevant consents being unavailable), court approval would be required. Approval would again be considered, in regard to the interests of the bank and the general public.

Direct financial assistance might also be provided by the PBC (under a general or emergency lender of last resort procedure). This practice is distinct from restructuring, to the extent that this is dependent on existing bank or third party rather than official support. Financial assistance would generally only be considered in the event that no separate restructuring or rehabilitation was possible or had already failed. The provision of such assistance could be coordinated through a separate Financial Support Division within the Financial Stability Department in the PBC although this would liaise with the Financial Restructuring Division and the CBRC. Any joint decisions would again be taken through the Financial Stability Committee.

In the event that the institution could not be rehabilitated and the provision of direct financial assistance was considered unnecessary or inappropriate, formal closure proceedings would begin. Again this would generally require court consent although the grounds would be set out in the Law with the court to avoid unjustifiable refusal where the conditions were satisfied. Closure would be carried out through a simplified liquidation procedure with the appointment of a single liquidator (rather than a liquidation team) to enable a quick and effective realization of the assets of the bank and payment of outstanding liabilities in accordance with the priority rules set out under the Law.

All appropriate powers and duties would have to be conferred on administrators and liquidators as appropriate. These duties must be set out in the new law to ensure certainty and transparency. Additional provisions must also be included in regard to matters such as reports, records, notice, review or appeal, immunity from prosecution, as well as enforcement of cross-borer orders or proceedings under any relevant international treaties, conventions or other arrangements.

The operation of the new restructuring and recovery processes should be monitored and reviewed over time with any necessary revisions or amendments being made as appropriate. Further reforms should only be considered to the extent that financial market developments and improvements in supervisory and regulatory experience and practice permit. The overall objective must be to ensure that China is able to promote the continued safe and stable expansion of its financial markets and financial system at the same time as prevent any avoidable crisis or collapse.

Chapter 10

China's Banking Law and Free Trade Agreements: The Case of CEPA

Wei Wang

I. INTRODUCTION

On 11 December 2001, China became a Member of the WTO.[1] Therefore, undoubtedly, China is under the obligation to bring its laws, regulations and administrative procedures into compliance with WTO agreements. On 29 June 2003, the Closer Economic Partnership Arrangement (CEPA) between Mainland China and Hong Kong was signed and took effect.[2] On 27 August 2004, the two sides reached a Summary of Minutes to provide further liberalization measures on trade in goods and services for the second stage of the CEPA.[3] Two months later, based on the Summary of Minutes (*Huiyi Jiyao*), the two sides signed a formal supplement to further liberalize trade in goods and trade

---

1. In this article, 'China' generally refers to People's Republic of China (PRC), not including separate customs territories (Hong Kong, Macao and Taiwan) unless otherwise stated. This expression is also used in the *Protocol on the Accession of the People's Republic of China*; see the Preamble of the protocol.
2. For the official text (in Chinese) of the CEPA, see www.tid.gov.hk/sc_chi/cepa/fulltext.html, last updated 22 March 2004. For the official English translation of the CEPA, see <www.tid. gov.hk/english/cepa/fulltext.html> or the WTO official document, WT/ REG162/1.
3. See <search.mofcom.gov.cn/china/getDetail.jsp?site_id=www&articleid=20040800270018 & p_ keyword=CEPA&old_key=CEPA>.

Barth et al., *Financial Restructuring and Reform in Post-WTO China*, pp. 363–385.
© 2007 Kluwer Law International BV, The Netherlands.

in services (CEPA II).[4] China shall, without question, implement the CEPA in the territory of China, which will have a significant impact on China's existing laws, regulations and rules.

The CEPA is a Free Trade Agreement (FTA) between two separate customs territories under a single country, under the background of the WTO.[5] From the perspective of China, this concerns at least two relations. One is the external relation, in other words, the relation between the CEPA and the World Trade Organization (WTO). Mainland China and Hong Kong are both WTO Members,[6] therefore, the FTA between them shall be constrained by relevant WTO rules. The other relation is the internal relation, in other words, the relation between the CEPA and China's domestic laws. This chapter touches upon the two relations, with the emphasis on how to adjust China's banking laws under two different regimes. Section II discusses the relations between the CEPA and the WTO. Section III analyzes China's special commitments in banking services under the CEPA, and compares these commitments with those under the WTO. Section IV focuses on the relations between China's banking laws and the CEPA, discusses their conflicts and the implementation issue. Section V provides tentative ways to coordinate China's banking laws with two separate, but connected, trade regimes.

II.   RELATIONS BETWEEN THE CEPA AND THE WTO

The CEPA, like other Free Trade Agreements, lays down more-liberal conditions for trade of goods and services between China and Hong Kong than China's WTO commitments. The CEPA appears to be a departure from the WTO, in that CEPA accords more-favoured treatment only to the two parties. Is this a breach of WTO obligations, for example, and most significantly, MFN treatment? In essence, the relation between the CEPA and the WTO is the relation between two trade regimes, in other words, the multilateral trade regime and the regional trade regime, both of which China and Hong Kong participate in positively.

II.A.   WTO MECHANISM OF EXAMINING REGIONAL TRADE
                           AGREEMENTS

The WTO tries to restrain regional trade agreements by Article XXIV of the General Agreement on Tariffs and Trade (GATT), the Enabling Clause

---

4. *Supplement to the Mainland and Hong Kong Closer Economic Partnership Arrangement* (27 October 2004), available at <www.tid.gov.hk/english/cepa/files/sa_main_e.doc>.
5. WT/REG162/N/1, S/C/N/264, which indicates that the purpose of the CEPA is to establish a Free Trade Area within the meaning of GATT Article XXIV and GATS Article V.
6. China accessed to the WTO in December 2001. Hong Kong became a WTO Member in January 1995. See <www.wto.org/english/thewto_e/whatis_e/tif_e/org6_e.htm>. In this article, for the sake of convenience, the term 'China' refers to Mainland China, and 'Hong Kong' refers to the Hong Kong Special Administrative Region (HKSAR).

(Differential and More Favourable Treatment Reciprocity and Fuller Participation of Developing Countries) and Article V of the General Agreement on Trade in Services (GATS) to prevent regional trade integration from raising barriers to trade of non-regional countries. Paragraphs 4, 5, 6, 7 and 8 of GATT Article XXIV constitute legal requirements for regional economic integration regarding trade in goods among WTO Members.[7]

The Enabling Clause reached by the Contracting Parties of the GATT at the end of the Tokyo Round[8] provides more-favoured treatment for regional trade agreements between developing countries.[9] In the case of European Communities – Conditions for the Granting of Tariff Preferences to Developing Countries, the Appellate Body and the Panel held that the Enabling Clause is an exception to GATT Article I (MFN Article).[10] Important to note is that the Enabling Clause only covers trade in goods, and could be viewed as *lex specialis,* which prevails over GATT Article XXIV, as an exception to GATT Article I, with respect to regional trade agreements between developing countries.[11] The Enabling Clause is still valid under the framework of the WTO, as an instrument forming part of the GATT 1994.[12]

---

7. For the discussion of GATT Article XXIV, see J.H. Mathis, *Regional Trade Agreements in the GATT/WTO: Article XXIV and the Internal Trade Requirement* (T.M.C. Asser Press, 2002).

8. L/4903, Decision of 28 November 1979.

9. Paragraphs 1 and 2(c) of the Enabling Clause provide that:

   'Notwithstanding the provisions of Article I of the General Agreement, contracting parties may accord differential and more favourable treatment to developing countries, without according such treatment to other contracting parties.
   The provisions of paragraph 1 apply, *inter alia,* to: [. . .]
   (c) Regional and global arrangements amongst less-developed countries for mutual reduction or elimination of tariffs, and according to conditions set down by CONTRACTING PARTIES, for the mutual reduction or elimination of non-tariff measures, on products imported from each other.'

10. Appellate Body Report, *European Communities – Conditions for the Granting of Tariff Preferences to Developing Countries*, WT/DS246/AB/R, pp. 90 and 99, which states that the Enabling Clause is an exception to GATT Article I:1, based on the ordinary meaning of the term 'notwithstanding' of paragraph 1 of the Enabling Clause.

11. See *Legal Note on Regional Trade Arrangements under the Enabling Clause*, Note by the Secretariat, WT/COMTD/W/114, pp. 4–5.

12. GATT 1994, art. 1(b)(iv); see also L. Bartels, *The WTO Enabling Clause and Positive Conditionality in the European Community's GSP Program*, 6(2) Journal of International Economic Law 507 (2003), pp. 515–516; see also the Appellate Body Report, *European Communities – Conditions for the Granting of Tariff Preferences to Developing Countries*, WT/DS246/AB/R, p. 90, which states that the Enabling Clause has become an integral part of GATT 1994; Footnote 192, which indicates that the participants and third participants all agreed that the Enabling Clause is one of the 'other decisions of the contracting parties' within the meaning of Paragraph 1(b)(iv) of the language of Annex 1A, incorporating the GATT 1994 into the WTO Agreement.

GATS Article V specifies the requirements for regional economic integration in regard to trade in services.[13]

The Understanding on the Interpretation of Article XXIV of the GATT 1994, reached during the Uruguay Round, partly clarifies some procedural and substantial ambiguities in the GATT Article XXIV, for example, the concept of 'reasonable length of time', referred to in Paragraph 5(c) of Article XXIV.[14] An outstanding improvement of the Understanding on Interpretation of Article XXIV of the GATT 1994 is that the Article introduces the WTO dispute settlement mechanism into the disputes concerning Article XXIV.[15]

In addition to these legal requirements for regional trade agreements, for the purpose of examining regional trade agreements, the WTO established the Committee on Regional Trade Agreements (CRTA) as a permanent institution in 1996,[16] in lieu of the temporary Working Party established on a case-by-case basis in the practice of the GATT.

In spite of legal requirements set up by GATT Article XXIV and GATS Article V, important to note is that the actual effect of those legal requirements on regional trade agreements is highly limited. As Jackson pointed out:

> '[T]the GATT and its Article XXIV, as well as the more ambiguous legal framework of the 1979 enabling clause, are woefully inadequate for the tasks required of a multilateral system to provide some sort of adequate supervision and discipline on certain of the more dangerous tendencies of trading blocs'.[17]

The WTO has noted the issues and in the Doha agenda, regional trade is one of the negotiated topics.[18]

II.B.   APPLICATION OF THE ENABLING CLAUSE

Some have argued that the CEPA between Mainland China and Hong Kong, or between Mainland China and Macao, may take advantage of the Enabling

---

13. The regional trade agreements related to trade in services between developing countries are covered by GATS, Article V, and not by the Enabling Clause.
14. For details of the changes, see the *Understanding on the Interpretation of Article XXIV of the GATT* (1994), paras. 2–11.
15. See the *Understanding on the Interpretation of Article XXIV of the GATT* (1994), para. 12.
16. WT/L/127. The terms of reference of the CRTA include examination of regional trade agreements, developing procedures for the examination, considering the systemic implications of regional trade agreements for the multilateral trading system and other additional functions assigned by the General Council.
17. J.H. Jackson, 'Regional Trade Blocs and the GATT', in *The Jurisprudence of GATT and the WTO: Insights on Treaty Law and Economic Relations* (Cambridge University Press, 2,000), pp. 99–109 (originally published in 16 *World Economy* 2, [1993] pp. 121–130).
18. For the main issues related to the WTO regional trade rules, see *Compendium of Issues Related to Regional Trade Agreements*, Background Note by the Secretariat, TN/RL/W/8/Rev.1 (1 August 2002).

Clause, because Mainland China is a developing country.[19] In fact, the CEPA is not subject to the Enabling Clause, but to GATT Article XXIV and GATS Article V, because only if *both* sides of a regional trade agreement are developing countries can they invoke the Enabling Clause.[20] Because Hong Kong is not a developing country,[21] the CEPA is not an FTA between developing countries. The CEPA Notification from China and Hong Kong to the WTO clearly indicates that the CEPA must be notified pursuant to GATT Article XXIV and GATS Article V, not to the Enabling Clause, and 'the CEPA establishes a free trade area *within the meaning of Article XXIV of the GATT 1994* and ... *Article V of the GATS*' (emphasis added).[22]

II.C.   WTO-CONSISTENCY ISSUE

Obviously, the drafters of the CEPA recognized the importance of consistence with the WTO rules from the beginning of the CEPA negotiations. For example, during the WTO Trade Policy Review of Hong Kong in 2002, some WTO Members, such as Canada[23] and Japan,[24] raised the question of whether the CEPA under negotiations would be consistent with GATT Article XXIV and GATS Article V, or would constitute barriers to the trade of other WTO Members.[25] Hong Kong replied that both sides – China and Hong Kong – agreed that 'the CEPA should be fully consistent with WTO rules',[26] and 'will be fully consistent with relevant WTO rules, including those pertaining to sectoral coverage of FTAs',[27] and 'would not raise barriers to trade with third parties'.[28] During the period of 2003 Transitional Review for China, Japan once again raised the issue that the CEPA must be consistent with the WTO.[29] The EC also wanted

---

19.   M. Yaping and S. Hong, *Discussing the Necessities and Legal Basis of Establishing a Pan-China Free Trade Agreement* (*Jianli Fanzhongguo Ziyou Maoyiqu de Biyaoxing jiqi Falv Yiju Tantao*), available at <www.cel.net.cn/print.asp?a_id=972>.

20.   *Legal Note on Regional Trade Agreements under the Enabling Clause*, Note by the Secretariat, WT/COMTD/W/114, para. 3, which states that the Enabling Clause contains a provision for the establishment of regional trade agreements 'among developing countries'.

21.   Under the WTO, 'country' does not mean 'state'. Rather, the term 'country' refers to any separate customs territory Member of the WTO. See the Explanatory Notes of the WTO Agreement.

22.   Supra note 5.

23.   *Trade Policy Review Body, Minutes of Meetings (16 and 18 December 2002) for the Trade Policy Review of Hong Kong*, WT/TPR/M/109, Part IV, para. 42 (17 February 2003).

24.   Ibid., para. 90.

25.   See the *Addendum of the Minutes of Meeting for Trade Policy Review of Hong Kong, China*, WT/TPR/M/109/Add.1, 'Question 4', para. 24 (17 February 2003).

26.   See Ibid., Answer, para. 24.

27.   See Ibid., para. 46.

28.   Supra note 26, Part V, para. 21.

29.   Communication from Japan, *Transitional Review Mechanism in Connection with paragraph 18 of the Protocol on the Accession of the People's Republic of China*, S/C/W/228, paras. 21 and 22 (12 September 2003).

to know whether the CEPA would be compatible with the GATS.[30] In deed, the implications of the WTO on the CEPA took place even before the conclusion of the CEPA.

One day prior to the implementation of the CEPA, Hong Kong stated that China and Hong Kong committed the consistency of the CEPA with the WTO.[31] On 27 December 2003, the CEPA was notified to the WTO,[32] and WTO Members may review the CEPA in accordance with the rules of the WTO. On 26 January 2004, the Terms of Reference of the examination of the CEPA were adopted by the CRTA, which read as follows:

> To examine, in light of the relevant provisions of the GATT 1994, the Closer Economic Partnership Arrangement between China and Hong Kong, China and to submit a report to the Council for Trade in Goods. It is understood that the understanding read out by the Chairman of the Council for Trade in Goods under Item 7 of the agenda of the meeting of the Council for Trade in Goods on 20 February 1995, as contained in document WT/REG3/1, will apply *mutatis mutandis* to the examination of the agreement. It is also understood that, during the examination, due account will be taken of the intrinsic differences between customs unions and free-trade areas.[33]

Several points in the CEPA relate to the WTO-consistency issue. First, one principle of the CEPA is that the CEPA must be consistent with WTO rules.[34] The fact that the WTO-consistency is deemed to be a principle shows that relevant WTO rules (GATT Article XXIV or GATS Article V) are to be strictly observed by China and Hong Kong, and should penetrate all aspects of the CEPA. Second, CEPA Article 6 provides that 'neither side shall apply non-tariff measures inconsistent with WTO rules to goods imported and originated from other sides'. Third, CEPA Article 8 states: 'The two sides reiterate their observance of the WTO "Agreement on Subsidies and Countervailing Measures", and Article XVI of "the General Agreement on Tariffs and Trade 1994"'. Fourth, CEPA Article 18 states: 'The "CEPA" and provisions in its Annexes shall not affect the ability of the Mainland or Hong Kong to maintain or adopt exception measures consistent with the rules of the WTO'. Fifth, CEPA Article 20(1) further provides: 'Except as otherwise provided in the "CEPA", any action taken

---

30. *Communication from the European Communities, China's Transitional Review Mechanism*, S/C/M/229 (10 November 2003), para. 30.
31. See the Press Release of the Trade and Industry Department of the Hong Kong Special Administrative Region [HKSAR], issued on 30 December 2003, 'Hong Kong Reading to Fully Implement CEPA on 1 January 2004', available at: <www.tid.gov.hk/textonly/english/aboutus/pressspeech/2003/cepa2004.html> (30 December 2003).
32. Notification from the Parties (27 December 2003), WT/REG162/N/1, S/C/N/264 (20 January 2004).
33. Terms of Reference of the Examination adopted on 26 January 2004, WT/REG162/2 (9 March 2004).
34. See the CEPA, art. 2(2).

under it shall not affect or nullify the rights and obligations of either side under other existing agreements to which it is a contracting party'. Here, 'other existing agreements' definitely include the WTO agreements of which Hong Kong and China are members. From these five points, it becomes clear that the WTO has a strong impact on the CEPA, because the CEPA must be consistent with the WTO rules and does not affect or nullify China or Hong Kong's rights and obligations under the WTO unless otherwise provided in the CEPA.

II.D.   Impact of the CEPA on China's WTO Commitments: Non-Application of Some Rules

While the WTO has a significant impact on the CEPA, the CEPA also impacts the WTO. According to CEPA Article 4, some provisions of China's WTO accession legal documents are not applicable between Hong Kong and China, including Articles 15 and 16 of the China Accession Protocol and Paragraph 242 of the Working Party Report.

II.D.1.   Anti-dumping and Countervailing

Article 15 of the China Accession Protocol stipulates 'price comparability in determining subsidies and dumping', which gives other WTO Members more-favoured treatment than the existing WTO rules do when addressing anti-dumping and countervailing issues with China.[35] The CEPA Article 4 excludes the application of the disadvantageous article in the China's WTO accession document, which partly reduces the sacrifices that China has made for the WTO-entry. In addition, CEPA Article 7 and Article 8 exclude the application of anti-dumping measures and countervailing measures to goods imported and originated from each other.

II.D.2.   Special Safeguard Measures

Article 16 of the China Accession Protocol provides 'transitional product-specific safeguard mechanism', which gives other WTO Members the right for 12 years to take advantage of the special safeguard measures against China. Paragraph 242 of the Working Party Report confers other WTO Members a special safeguard power with respect to textiles and apparel products, which may seriously limit China's export of textiles and apparel products to foreign countries.[36] Article 16 of the China Accession Protocol, for example, replaced

---

35.   For the disadvantages of the Article.
36.   Z. Weitian, *On the Jurisprudence Nature of the 'Special Safeguard Clause'* (*Lun Teshu Baozhang de Fali Benzhi*), available at <www.cel.net.cn> (11 June 2004), which argues that the 'special Safeguard Clause' separates GATT requirements of invoking the safeguard measures by adopting lower standards); see also S. Yanlu and G. Zhuangzhi, 'Shortcoming

the 'serious injury' standard in GATT Article XIX[37] with the 'material injury' standard,[38] which relaxes the standard of taking safeguard measures by other WTO Members against China. However, this disadvantageous safeguard measure clause was repealed by the CEPA. Hong Kong will use the traditional 'serious injury' standard in determining whether to take safeguard measures against China in case of a sharp increase in imports of a product from Mainland China. Therefore, the distortion of the WTO safeguard measure provisions by the China Accession Protocol is corrected by the CEPA for the benefit of China, in other words, the WTO safeguard measures standards are 'resumed' within the scope of China and Hong Kong.

Article 15 and 16 of the China Accession Protocol and paragraph 242 of the Working Party Report, as binding obligations to China under the WTO, are deemed to be part of the dues that China must pay for accession to the WTO,[39] and the deviation from GATT Article XIX. The non-application of the CEPA provisions disadvantageous to China is beneficial primarily to the Mainland. To some extent, the non-application reduces the obligations that China must undertake under the WTO. Important to note is that CEPA Article 4 does not conflict with CEPA Article 20(1), because the former constitutes an 'exception' of the latter; therefore, although CEPA Article 4 may affect or nullify the rights of Hong Kong under the WTO, the CEPA is still viable under the CEPA.

III.   CHINA'S SPECIFIC COMMITMENTS IN BANKING
            SERVICES UNDER THE CEPA

III.A.   Two Important Concepts in the CEPA

Service trade is covered in the CEPA.[40] The core of CEPA service trade is Mainland China's Schedule of Specific Commitments on Opening Service Trade to Hong Kong (hereinafter China's CEPA Schedule), as Annex 4 to the CEPA, which lists the financial service sector. To analyze China's banking commitments in the CEPA, one must look to two important concepts: banking service and banking service suppliers.

---

        of China's WTO-entry Commitments in Safeguard Measures' (*Woguo Rushi dui Baozhang Cuoshi Falv Chengnuo de Quexian*), *China Lawyers* (*Zhongguo Lvshi*), no. 4 (2003).

37. GATT, art. XIX:1.
38. The China Accession Protocol, art. 16(4).
39. Some have even gone so far as to argue that China's full WTO membership will only become complete at the end of the 12-year time span of the special safeguard article. See F. Spadi, 'Discriminatory Safeguards in the Light of the Admission of the People's Republic of China to the World Trade Organization', 5(2) *Journal of International Economic Law* (2002), pp. 421 and 442–43 (2002).
40. See the CEPA, Chapter 4.

III.A.1.   Banking Service

China's CEPA Schedule includes following banking services:

- acceptance of deposits and other repayable funds from the public;
- lending of all types, including consumer credit, mortgage credit, factoring and financing of commercial transaction;
- financial leasing;
- all payment and money transmission services, including credit, charge and debit cards, travellers cheques and bankers drafts, including import and export settlement;
- Guarantees and commitments;
- Trading for own account or for account of customers: foreign exchange.

In comparison to China's WTO banking service commitments,[41] the scope of banking services in China's CEPA Schedule is equal to that in China's WTO Schedule. The fact that China's CEPA Schedule does not include more categories of banking services indirectly shows that the scope of banking services in China's WTO commitments is sufficiently broad. However, in the CEPA II, the scope of banking services is broadened to include insurance agency business, which will be discussed in following sections.

III.A.2.   Banking Service Suppliers

According to GATS Article XXVIII (g), the term 'service supplier' refers to any person who supplies a service. 'Person' means either a natural person or a juridical person.[42] Because the concept of 'natural person' is meaningless in supplying banking services, 'juridical person' is the focus of analysis. GATS Article XXVIII (m)(i) stipulates that a 'juridical person' of another Member refers to a juridical person who is constituted or otherwise organized under the law of that other Member, and is engaged in substantive business operations in the territory of that Member or any other Member.[43] Under the WTO, no minimum operation time is required for being a 'service supplier'. However, according to CEPA Annex 5, 'Definition of "Service Supplier" and Related Rules', the standards of a Hong Kong service supplier (HKSS) providing service by way of a juridical person include the following:

- establishment or registration based on HKSAR Corporation Regulations or other regulations, with a valid business registration certificate or license;

---

41. WT/ACC/CHN/49/Add.2.
42. See GATS, art. XXVIII(j).
43. In the case of the supply of a service through commercial presence, owned or controlled by either natural persons of that Member; or juridical persons of that other Member. See GATS, art. XXVIII (m)(ii).

– being engaged in substantive business operations in Hong Kong for at
least three years. Thus, the tests to determine engagement in substantive
business operation in Hong Kong include, *inter alia*, a minimum number
of three years of registration and operation in Hong Kong.[44]

The conditions for becoming a Hong Kong banking service supplier are stricter
than those for becoming an ordinary HKSS. To be a Hong Kong banking
service supplier, a Hong Kong bank or a Hong Kong finance company should
have engaged in substantive business operations for five years or more after it
has been granted a licence by the Hong Kong Monetary Authority (HKMA)
pursuant to the Hong Kong Banking Ordinance.[45] An applicant for the status
of a Hong Kong banking service supplier should submit its applications for
a Certificate of HKSS to the Trade and Industry Department (TID) of the
HKSAR through the Banking Supervision Department of the HKMA.[46] After
obtaining a Certificate of HKSS from the TID, the Hong Kong banking service
supplier must apply to the China Banking Regulatory Commission (CBRC) to
obtain the CEPA treatment.[47]

Important to note is that foreign banks and finance companies can receive
the benefits of the CEPA by way of investment in Hong Kong banks or finance
companies. In accordance with Annex 5 of the CEPA, if more than 50 per
cent of the equity of a Hong Kong service supplier has been owned for at least
one year after a merger or acquisition by a foreign-service supplier, the service
supplier which has been merged or acquired will be regarded as a Hong Kong
service supplier.[48] foreign banks and finance companies, therefore, can indirectly obtain the status of 'Hong Kong banking service suppliers' in order to
obtain the more-favourable treatment from China. To some extent, the CEPA
will stimulate foreign direct investment (FDI) in Hong Kong, which is a good
example of China's support to Hong Kong's economy. Meanwhile, the drafters
of the CEPA noted the possibility of foreign 'shell companies' to benefit from
CEPA's favourable treatment by only registering a company in Hong Kong,
therefore, the drafters designed the five-year substantive business operation
standard, more than 50 per cent equity requirement and one year requirement
after merger or acquirement, all of which aim to prevent foreign 'shell companies' from taking advantage of the CEPA benefits.

---

44. See CEPA, Annex 5, 'Definition of "Service Supplier" and related Rules', 3.1.1, 3.1.2(2). In
addition to the operation year requirement, other requirements apply for being a HKSS, for
example profit tax, business premises, employment of staff. See CEPA Annex 5 'Definition
of "Service Supplier" and related Rules', 3.1.2(3), (4) and (5).
45. Ibid., 3.1.2(2).
46. Notice to Service Suppliers No. 2 (2003), Application Procedures for Certificate of Hong
Kong Service Supplier, issued by the TID of the HKSAR Government, WT 324/9/5/7
(14 November 2003), para. 9.
47. See Annex 5 of the CEPA, art. 7, and the *Notice to Service Suppliers,* no. 2 (2003), Application Procedures for Certificate of Hong Kong Service Supplier, issued by the TID of the
HKSAR Government, WT 324/9/5/7 (14 November 2003), para. 14.
48. Annex 4 of the CEPA, Footnote 2.

After the implementation of the CEPA, for the purpose of gaining the benefits of the CEPA, a number of foreign banks branches in Hong Kong have changed their status to Hong Kong banks. For example, in 2004, the Citibank Hong Kong branch became the Citibank (Hong Kong) Ltd.,[49] and the Standard Chartered Hong Kong Branch became a Hong Kong bank; namely, the Standard Chartered (Hong Kong) Ltd.,[50] which is wholly-owned by the Standard Chartered Bank.

III.B.   MARKET ACCESS COMMITMENTS IN BANKING SERVICES
                 UNDER THE CEPA

As to specific market access commitments, China provides more favourable treatment to Hong Kong banking service suppliers under the CEPA.[51] First, the minimum total assets requirement for a Hong Kong bank to establish a branch or juridical person in China is USD 6 billion. This requirement reduces the threshold of market access by allowing medium size Hong Kong banks to enter the Chinese market.[52] For example, a medium-size Hong Kong local bank, Wing Lung Bank, set up a branch in Shenzhen on 29 March 2004,[53] which became the first beneficiary of CEPA's reduction of the minimum total assets requirement. In June 2004, two other medium size banks from Hong Kong – DahSing Bank and Shanghai Commercial Bank – opened branches in Shenzhen.[54] From 1 January 2004 to 30 December 2004, the CBRC, China's banking supervisor, granted approval for five Hong Kong banks to establish branches in China.[55] By the end of 2004, 90 per cent of Hong Kong banks whose total assets reached the CEPA requirement were approved to enter China.[56] Second, no precondition applies for a Hong Kong bank to set up a representative office before establishing a joint-equity bank or joint-equity finance company. Third,

---

49. <www.info.gov.hk/hkma/chi/press/2004/20041029c4.htm> (29 October 2004).
50. <www.standardchartered.com.hk/chi/news/2004/c_press_20040511.pdf> (11 May 2004).
51. See Specific Commitments on Opening Service Trade Area, Table 1 of Annex 4 of the CEPA. The existing schedule of specific commitments under current CEPA is unilateral. There are only service commitments made by the Mainland China to the HKSAR. According to the arrangement, Mainland China and the HKSAR will negotiate service commitments to be made by the HKSAR to Mainland China, which will be contained in Table 2 of Annex 4 of the CEPA. See Specific Commitments on Opening Service Trade Area, Annex 4 of the CEPA.
52. Prior to the CEPA, only four large banks in Hong Kong had set up branches in China, namely, the HSBC, Hang Seng Bank, Bank of East Asia and Bank of China Hong Kong Limited. See <www.southcn.com/news/hktwma/jingji/200307040705.htm> (4 June 2003).
53. <www.china.org.cn/chinese/zhuanti/qkjc/688897.htm> (26 October 2004).
54. <finance.sina.com.cn/b/20040604/1658797123.shtml> (4 June 2004), and <www.gd.xinhuanet.com/newscenter/2004-06/22/content_2358044.htm> (22 June 2004).
55. See the CBRC news release on 30 December 2004, at <www.cbrc.gov.cn/chinese/module/infomore.jsp>.
56. Ibid.

the conditions for a branch of a Hong Kong bank located in China to apply for Renminbi (RMB) business include: two years business operation in China; and comprehensive consideration of whole branches operation to determine whether the bank satisfies the profitable qualification, unlike individual consideration of a single branch operation applicable to non-HK foreign bank branches. As of 30 December 2004, China gave approval to 26 Hong Kong bank branches to open RMB business.[57] Fourth, by the CEPA II, China will allow Chinese branches of Hong Kong banks to conduct insurance agency business upon obtaining approval.[58]

In comparison, China's WTO commitments in banking services are stricter. First, the minimum total assets requirement to establish a foreign bank subsidiary is USD 10 billion at the end of the year prior to filing the application, while the minimum total assets requirement to establish a foreign bank branch is USD 20 billion at the end of the year prior to filing the application, and the minimum total assets requirement to establish a joint-equity bank is USD 10 billion, while for Hong Kong banks, the total assets requirement is reduced to USD 6 billion. Second, under the WTO, the conditions for foreign-funded banks to engage local currency business are three-years' business operation in China and being profitable for two consecutive years prior to the application, rather than the CEPA's requirement of two years operation. Third, according to China's WTO financial commitments, China is not obliged to allow branches of foreign banks to conduct insurance agency business. China's special commitment to Hong Kong banks to conduct insurance agency business provides more favourable treatment to Hong Kong banks than to the banks of other WTO Members.

III.C.   FINANCIAL COOPERATION COMMITMENTS UNDER THE CEPA

To strengthen banking cooperation and embody the support from China to Hong Kong, the drafters of the CEPA devised a special article, Article 13, which provides financial cooperation between the two sides. According to CEPA Article 13, China adopts four supporting measures. First, China supports wholly state-owned commercial banks (*guoyou shangye yinhang*)[59] and certain joint-stock commercial banks (*gufenzhi shangye yinhang*)[60] in relocating their

---

57. Ibid.
58. Annex 3 of the CEPA II, 'Supplements and Amendments to the Mainland's Specific Commitments on Liberalization of Trade in Services for Hong Kong', Sector 7, available at <www.tid.gov.hk/english/cepa/files/sa_annex3_e.doc>.
59. Four state-owned commercial banks do business in China: the Industrial and Commercial Banking of China (*zhongguo gongshang yinhang*); the Agricultural Bank of China (*zhongguo nongye yinhang*); the Bank of China (*zhongguo yinhang*); and the China Construction Bank (*zhongguo jianshe yinhang*).
60. Currently, 11 joint-stock commercial banks conduct business in China: the Bank of Communications (*jiaotong yinhang*): the CITIC Industrial Bank (*zhongxin shiye yinhang*); China Everbright Bank (*zhongguo guangda yinhang*); Huaxia Bank (*huaxia yinhang*); Guangdong

international treasury and foreign exchange trading centres to Hong Kong.[61] Second, China supports its banks in developing network and business activities in Hong Kong through acquisition.[62] Third, China supports the full utilization of financial intermediaries in Hong Kong during the process of reform, restructuring and development of the financial sector in China.[63] Fourth, China supports eligible companies, including private enterprises in listing in Hong Kong.[64] In addition to these four supporting measures, the financial regulators of China and Hong Kong shall strengthen regulatory cooperation and information sharing.[65] These supportive measures aim to strengthen Hong Kong's position as an international financial centre in Asia.

III.D.   RELATIONS OF CHINA'S BANKING COMMITMENTS UNDER THE WTO AND THE CEPA

As opposed to China's WTO Schedule, which contains three columns of specific commitments – market access commitments, national treatment commitments and additional commitments – [66]China's CEPA Schedule contains only one column of specific commitments: market access column. Does that mean China's CEPA Schedule is irrelevant to national treatment? Or has China not made national treatment commitments in the CEPA? This issue is a highly confusing one. Paragraph 3 of the Annex 4 of the CEPA states:

> 'In respect of the service sectors, sub-sectors or relevant measures not covered by this Annex, the Mainland [China] will apply Annex 9 of the "Schedule of Specific Commitments on Services List of Article II MFN Exemptions" of the "Protocol on the Accession of the People's Republic of China [to the WTO]"'.

This Paragraph appears to connect China's CEPA Schedule with China's WTO Schedule so as to complicate the seemingly simple commitments in the CEPA. Because national treatment limitation measures are covered in China's WTO Schedule, are these measures, as 'relevant measures', also covered in China's CEPA Schedule according to Paragraph 3 of Annex 4 of the CEPA? And if so, China's specific commitments concerning national treatment – as well as market access commitments and additional commitments – in the WTO Schedule must

Development Bank (*Guangdong fazhan yinhang*;, Shenzhen Development Bank (*shenzhen fazhan yinhang*); China Merchants Bank (*zhaoshang yinhang*); Shanghai Pudong Development Bank (*shanghai pudong fazhan yinhang*): Industrial Bank Co. Ltd. (*xingye yinhang*); China Minsheng Banking Corp. Ltd. (*zhongguo minsheng yinhang*); and Evergrowing Bank (*hengfeng yinhang*). See <www.pbc.gov.cn> (20 June 2004).

61.   CEPA, art. 13(1).
62.   CEPA, art. 13(2).
63.   CEPA, art. 13(3).
64.   CEPA, art. 13(5).
65.   CEPA, art. 13(4).
66.   See WT/ACC/CHN/49/Add.2.

be incorporated into the CEPA as part of China's commitments to Hong Kong under the CEPA framework.

It is highly possible that this was the intention of the draftsmen of the CEPA; otherwise, why is China's WTO Schedule mentioned in the CEPA? It is China's WTO obligation to abide by its WTO specific commitments; a fact which therefore makes the CEPA's confirming of China's WTO obligations unnecessary. Such confirmation, if any, is redundant, unless there are special considerations. According to the principle of effectiveness, *ut res magis valeat quam pereat*, which is used in WTO cases on many occasions,[67] Paragraph 3 of Annex 4 of the CEPA must be interpreted so as to make this paragraph meaningful and effective. In the first WTO Appellate Body Report, the Appellate Body held that an interpretation could not result in reducing whole clauses or paragraphs of a treaty to 'redundancy or inutility'.[68] According to the principle

---

67. Panel Report on *Canada – Term of Patent Protection*, WT/DS170/R, para. 6.49, Footnote 30, which states that 'the principle of effective interpretation reflects the general rule of interpretation, which requires that a treaty be interpreted to give meaning and effect to all the terms of the treaty'; Appellate Body Report, in *Japan – Taxes on Alcoholic Beverages*, WT/DS8/AB/R, WT/DS10/AB/R, WT/DS11/AB/R, adopted 1 November 1996, sect. D, which states that 'the principle of effectiveness' is a fundamental interpretation principle; Appellate Body Report, *United States – Import Prohibition of Certain Shrimp and Shrimp Products*, WT/DS58/AB/R, adopted 21 November 2001, para. 131, and Footnote 116, which interprets the concept of 'exhaustible natural resources' in line with the principle of effectiveness; Appellate Body Report, *United States – Restrictions on Imports of Cotton and Man-Made Fibre Underwear*, WT/DS24/AB/R, adopted on 25 February 1997, sect. IV:1, DSR 1997:I, para. 24, which invokes the principle of effectiveness in treaty interpretation; Panel Report, *Korea – Definitive Safeguard Measure on Imports of Certain Dairy Products*, WT/DS98/R, adopted 12 January 2000, paras. 4.609, 7.37, which states that all terms must be given full meaning and must be interpreted to avoid inconsistencies and inutility; Appellate Body Report, *Korea – Definitive Safeguard Measure on Imports of Certain Dairy Products*, WT/DS98/AB/R, adopted 12 January 2000, para. 81, which states that it is the duty of any treaty interpreter to give meaning to all provisions of a treaty; Appellate Body Report, *Canada – Measures Affecting the Importation of Milk and the Exportation of Dairy Products*, WT/DS103/AB/R, WT/DS113/AB/R, adopted 27 October 1999, para. 133, which applies 'the fundamental principle of *effet utile*' and states that the treaty interpreter must give effect to a 'legal operative meaning for the terms of the treaty'; Appellate Body Report, *Argentina – Safeguard Measures on Imports of Footwear*, WT/DS121/AB/R, adopted 12 January 2000, para. 88, which holds that 'the Panel failed to give meaning and legal effect to *all* the relevant terms of the WTO Agreement'; Appellate Body Report, *United States – Section 211 Omnibus Appropriations Act*, WT/DS176/AB/R, adopted 1 February 2002, para. 161, 338; Panel Report on *EC – Trade Description on Sardines*, WT/DS231/R, adopted 23 October 2002, para. 7.76, which states that the principle of effectiveness is 'a corollary of the general rule of interpretation in the Vienna Convention'; Appellate Body Report, *United States – Continued Dumping and Subsidy Offset Act of 2000*, WT/DS217/AB/R, WT/DS234/AB/R, adopted 27 January 2003, para. 271, which states that the interpretative principle of effectiveness must guide the interpretation of the WTO Agreement.

68. Appellate Body Report, in *United States – Standards for Reformulated and Conventional Gasoline*, WT/DS2/AB/R, adopted on 20 May 1996, section IV. The Appellate Body also cited some famous international cases and teachings of some highly qualified publicists,

of interpretation of effectiveness, it is highly probable[69] that Paragraph 3 of Annex 4 of the CEPA has incorporated China's WTO Schedule into the CEPA to supplement China's CEPA Schedule. If this interpretation is correct, the two service schedules under two different trade regimes are closely related, particularly in respect to national treatment commitments.

If China's specific national treatment commitments in China's WTO Schedule are incorporated into the CEPA based on Paragraph 3 of Annex 4 of the CEPA, China's national treatment commitments in banking services under the framework of the WTO are also regarded as China's banking commitments under the framework of the CEPA.

IV. IMPLEMENTATION OF THE CEPA IN CHINA

How to implement the CEPA in China is a very interesting issue. Can the CEPA be applied by the People's Courts of China? Because the CEPA is not a treaty or an international agreement at all, there is not a problem of 'direct effect' or 'indirect effect', or a problem of 'domestic application of international agreements'.[70] However, even so, the CEPA inevitably must be implemented in China; otherwise the CEPA would be a mere scrap of paper. The implementation of the CEPA may lead to many questions. For example, if conflicts arise between the CEPA and China's existing laws, which will prevail? Is it China's obligation to revise or amend its existing laws to be consistent with the CEPA?[71] These problems are not merely based on assumption.

IV.A. THE STATE COUNCIL NOTICE

In fact, the CEPA is being performed by relevant Chinese governmental departments as an agreement with *de facto* legal effect, and more surprisingly, the legal basis of the implementation is not from laws made by the National People's Congress (NPC) or its Standing Committee, but from a low-level notice issued by the General Office of the State Council (*Guowuyuan Bangongting*); that is, the Notice on Relevant Works for Implementing the CEPA (*Guanyu Zhuohao*

---

for example, Corfu Channel Case (1949) I.C.J. Reports, see Footnote 45 of this Appellate Body Report.

69. Although the principle of effectiveness is a fundamental principle of interpretation, it should be treated with some caution. See M. Lennard, 'Navigating by the Stars: Interpreting the WTO Agreements', 5(1) *Journal of International Economic Law* 17, pp. 59–60 (2002).

70. As to the question of domestic application of international agreements, see J.H. Jackson, 'United States', in F.G. Jacobs and S. Roberts (eds.), *The Effect of Treaties in Domestic Law* (Sweet & Maxwell 1987), pp. 141–169.

71. China's legal system is still undergoing a large-scale reform to comply with the WTO rules, and many laws, regulations, rules and measures have been repealed, amended based on China's WTO-entry commitments and the requirements of the WTO rules.

Shishi Neidi yu Xianggang Aomen Gengjinmi Jingmao Guanxi Anpai youguan Gongzuo de Tongzhi) (also known as the State Council Notice).[72] The first sentence of the Notice shows that the State Council had authorized the Ministry of Commerce (MOFCOM) to sign the CEPA and the leaders of the State Council had approved the implementation items in the State Council Notice. The main content of the State Council Notice is that all government agencies and local areas should make corresponding revisions or formulate relevant policies and rules based on the CEPA.[73] But a prerequisite for the effect of the State Council Notice is its nature and legality. In other words, does the State Council Notice have binding force on its receivers?

According to the PRC Legislation Law (2000),[74] the State Council has power to formulate administrative regulations (*xingzheng fagui*) based on China's Constitution and laws made by the NPC and its Standing Committee.[75] However, the State Council Notice, which was not issued by the State Council, but by the General Office of the State Council, is not an administrative regulation in strict sense. There is no place for such a 'notice' in the PRC Legislation framework. Strictly speaking, the State Council Notice is neither a law nor a regulation, but an administrative 'measure' with *de facto* legal force. Although the measure is not a law made by the NPC or a regulation made by the State Council, it could still be regarded as a rule in the broadest sense, and could be subject to the review of the WTO if it is taken by a government or an authority and affects trade in services.[76] So far, a number of Chinese governmental departments have changed relevant administrative rules based on the State Council Notice. For example, to be consistent with the CEPA, based on the State Council Notice, the Judicial Department revised the Administrative Rules on Representative Offices Established in the Mainland by Law Firms from the HKSAR and Macao SAR.[77] Some government departments even issued special rules to implement the CEPA.[78]

---

72. *Guobanfa* [2003] No.95, 2 December 2003.
73. The State Council Notice, 2(2).
74. The PRC Legislation Law was adopted at the Third Session of the Ninth National People's Congress on 15 March 2000 and took effect on 1 July 2000.
75. The PRC Legislation Law, art. 56.
76. See GATS, art. 1, paras. 1 and 3(a).
77. See the Decision on Revising the Administrative Rules on Representative Offices Established in the Mainland by Law Firms from the HKSAR and Macao SAR, issued by the Ministry of Justice of the PRC on 30 November 2003 and entered into force on 1 January 2004, *Sifabu* Order No. 84.
78. For example, the Ministry of Information Industry issued the Proclamation on Relevant Issues of Implementation of the CEPA (30 September 2003); The Customs General Administration issued the Rules on Implementation of the Rules of Origin for Trade in Goods under the CEPA with Hong Kong (30 December 2003), Haiguanzongshu Order [2003] No. 106, available at <www.customs.gov.cn/flfg/flfg.asp>; The State Administration for Industry and Commerce issued the Relevant Opinions on Implementation of the CEPA with Hong Kong and the CEPA with Macao and to Facilitate Mutual Economic

However, even if the State Council Notice has binding force on administrative departments and institutions under the State Council, is it necessarily binding on the CBRC? This question is not as simple as it appears. According to the State Council Notice, its receivers are the governments of all provinces (*sheng*),[79] autonomous regions (*zizhiqu*)[80] and municipalities directly under the Central Government (*zhixiashi*),[81] all departments of the State Council (*guowuyuan buwei*),[82] and institutions directly under the State Council (*guowuyuan zhishu jigou*).[83] Is the CBRC one of them?

The State Council is composed of six categories:

- the General Office of the State Council;[84]
- departments;[85]
- special institutions directly under the State Council (*guowuyuan zhishu teshe jigou*);[86]
- institutions directly under the State Council;[87]
- working Institutions under the State Council (*guowuyuan banshi jigou*)[88]
- institutional units directly under the State Council (*guowuyuan zhishu shiye danwei*)[89]

The CBRC, together with China's insurance regulator (CIRC) and securities regulator (CSRC), belongs to the sixth category, which is not one of the receivers of the State Council Notice. As a result, the State Council Notice on the implementation of the CEPA in China, if legal, has no binding force on the CBRC. It is unclear why the State Council Notice did not address to the CBRC or some other institutional units under the State Council. This ignorance, no matter whether it is intentional or unintentional, adds more legal difficulties to the implementation of the CEPA in China's financial areas.

Development between the Mainland, Hong Kong and Macao, *Gongshangwaiqizi* [2003] No.149 (30 December 2003).

79. In addition to two special administrative regions (Hong Kong and Macao) and the disputed Taiwan, China is divided into 22 provinces: Heilongjiang, Jilin, Liaoning, Hebei, Shanxi (Taiyuan), Gansu, Qinghai, Shanxi (Xi'an), Henan, Shandong, Anhui, Jiangsu, Hubei, Hunan, Sichuan, Yunnan, Guizhou, Jiangxi, Zhejiang, Fujian, Guangdong and Hainan.

80. China includes five autonomous regions: Tibet, Xinjiang, Neimenggu, Ningxia and Guangxi.

81. There are four municipalities directly under the Central Government, including Beijing, Shanghai, Tianjin and Chongqing.

82. There are 28 departments under the State Council. See Notice on Institutional Establishment issued by the State Council, *Guofa* [2003] No. 8, Section 2, 21 March 2003.

83. There are 18 institutions directly under the State Council. See ibid., *Guofa* [2003] No. 8, Section 4.

84. See ibid., Section 1.

85. For 28 departments under the State Council, see ibid., Section 2.

86. There is only one special institution directly under the State Council, namely, the Regulatory and Administrative Committee of State-Owned Assets. See ibid., Section 3.

87. For 18 institutions directly under the State Council. See ibid., Section 4.

88. There are four working institutions under the State Council, see ibid., Section 5.

89. There are 14 Institutional Units directly under the State Council, see ibid., Section 6.

IV.B.   THE CBRC NOTICE

Although the CBRC is not bound by the State Council Notice, it has been implementing the CEPA and devoting much attention to the implementation work since the CEPA took effect on 1 January 2004.[90] On 28 August 2003, the CBRC sent out the Notice on Implementation of the CEPA (*Guanyu Luoshi Neidi yu Xianggang Guanyu Jianli Gengjinmi Jingmao Guanxi de Anpai de Tongzhi*) (referred to as the CBRC Notice).[91] Unlike other implementation notices issued by the administrative departments and institutions directly under the State Council, which usually quote the State Council Notice as their legal foundation, the CBRC Notice neither mentions the State Council Notice or other legal sources. The CBRC Notice directly makes the following arrangements to implement the CEPA:

- Introducing China's supportive measures in the CEPA to Hong Kong banking industry;[92]
- Instructing local banking regulatory bureaus to study the CEPA and implement those measures in the CEPA;[93]
- Instructing local banking regulatory bureaus to accept applications from Hong Kong banks for setting up branches and operating RMB business.[94]

Undoubtedly, the CBRC Notice reflects the determination of the CBRC to implement the CEPA in China's banking areas and has binding force on local supervisory bureaus. However, the CBRC Notice lacks a legal base to make itself legally valid.

Because the PRC Constitution neither provides how to implement international agreements in China, nor stipulates how to implement internal agreements between the Mainland and its Special Administrative Regions in China, no authoritative legal model exists for the CEPA's implementation. In my view, the implementation of the CEPA in China could follow the method of the implementation of the WTO agreements in China. In other words, the CEPA can be applied by transforming into Chinese domestic laws, regulations or rules. From the perspective of agreement effect, the CEPA is not as high as treaties like the WTO Agreement. If treaties must be transformed into Chinese domestic laws before the treaties are applicable to China, the CEPA, as an interregional agreement or a semi-treaty must also be transformed into Chinese domestic laws in order to be implemented unless the CEPA is viewed as part of Chinese

---

90. The CBRC News release on 30 December 2004, available at <www.cbrc.gov.cn/chinese/module/infomore.jsp>.
91. *Yinjiantong* [2003] No. 22.
92. Ibid., Paragraph 1.
93. Ibid., Paragraph 2.
94. Ibid., Paragraph 3.

domestic laws, which seems impossible. In addition, the transformation application corresponds to the requirement of the consistency of the CEPA with the WTO.[95] Interesting to note is that one of China's administrative departments, the MOFCOM, which is in charge of both China's WTO negotiations and CEPA negotiations, takes the view that the implementation of the CEPA is parallel with the implementation of the WTO, by incorporating China's CEPA commitments into China's regulations and rules.[96] Based on this analysis, in the case of China's banking laws, I suggest the adjustment process of China's banking laws to the CEPA synchronize and coordinate with the reconstructive process of China's banking laws to the WTO.

V.   HOW TO ADJUST CHINA'S BANKING LAW UNDER
         THE CEPA AND WTO

V.A.   CONFLICTS BETWEEN CHINA'S BANKING LAWS AND THE CEPA

Hong Kong banks are accorded more favoured treatment than ordinary foreign banks in establishing branches or subsidiaries in China, based on the CEPA. However, some provisions in China's current banking laws and regulations are in conflict with China's banking commitments under the CEPA.

First, according to the Regulation on Administration of foreign-Funded Financial Institutions of the People's Republic of China (*Zhonghua Renmin Gongheguo Waizi Jinrong Jigou Guanli Tiaoli*), which is referred to as the *FFFI* Regulation, effective on 1 February 2002,[97] which is also applicable to HK-funded banks in China,[98] one of the conditions to establish a subsidiary or a branch in China is to have a representative office in China for at least two years.[99] As to the establishment of a joint venture bank, the requirement is to have a representative office (no two-year term requirement).[100] As described previously, however, under the CEPA, no precondition applies for a Hong Kong bank to set up a representative office before establishing a joint equity bank or a joint equity finance company.

Second, the current scope of business of foreign banks does not cover insurance agency business. According to the FFFI Regulation, the scope of

---

95. One of the principles of the CEPA is to be consistent with the WTO rules. See CEPA, art. 2.
96. *See* MOFCOM Notice on Law-Based Administration to Do foreign-Funded Enterprise Examination Work (*Shangwubu guanyu Yifa Xingzheng Zhuohao Waishang Touzi Qiye Shenpi gongzuo de Tongzhi*), Paragraph 6, issued by the MOFCOM on 21 January 2005, *Shangzihan* [2005] no. 3, available at <search.mofcom.gov.cn/china/getDetail.jsp?site_id=www&articleid=20050300022107&p_keyword=CEPA&old_key=CEPA>.
97. PRC State Council Decree, no. 340 (20 December 2001).
98. See the FFFI Regulation, art. 50.
99. See the FFFI Regulation, art. 6(2), art. 7(1).
100. See the FFFI Regulation, art. 8(2).

foreign-banks business includes the following items: public deposit, loans, draft acceptance and discount, government bond, financial bond, foreign currency, letter of credit and guarantee service, settlement, foreign exchange, foreign currency exchange, inter-loan, banking card, safe box service, credit investigation and counselling service, and other business approved by the banking regulator.[101] Insurance agency business is also outside the business scope of Chinese domestic banks.[102] So far, there has been no legal basis for allowing branches of Hong Kong banks the treatment to do insurance agency business in China unless the current banking laws, regulations, or rules are amended.

V.B.   TWO APPROACHES

The PRC Commercial Banking Law (2003 amended) and PRC Banking Regulation and Supervision Law (2003) are both silent on whether they are applicable to Hong Kong banks. Under the framework of the 'One Country, Two Systems',[103] most Chinese laws do not apply to Hong Kong.[104] Therefore, the two banking laws do not apply to Hong Kong banks located in Hong Kong. Theoretically, Hong Kong banks are not *'foreign banks'*, but 'Chinese banks' in the broadest sense of the words. Accordingly, Hong Kong-funded banks in China are not 'foreign-funded financial institutions', but 'Chinese financial institutions'. The Chinese nature comes from the concept of 'One Country'. However, in practice, Hong Kong-funded banks in the Mainland enjoy the same treatment with foreign banks, which indicates the impact of another concept, 'Two Systems'.

Article 50 of the Regulation provides that the regulation applies, *mutatis mutandis*, to Hong Kong (Macao and Taiwan) banks that establish and do business in China. Therefore, the Regulation is the main target of adjustment under the influence of the CEPA. As discussed in the previous section, under the CEPA, no precondition exists for a Hong Kong (or Macao) bank to set up a representative office before establishing a joint equity bank or joint equity finance company, therefore, the different provisions in the existing Regulation should be adjusted into two parts. In the first part, the existing two-year term requirement of a representative offices remains which applies to non-CEPA states. In the second part, no two-year term requirement applies for Hong Kong

---

101. The FFFI Regulation, art. 17.
102. See PRC Commercial Banking Law (2003), art. 3.
103. See the preamble of the HKSAR Basic Law. Basic Law of the Hong Kong Special Administrative Region of the People's Republic of China, 4 April 1990 (entered into force 1 July 1997), available at <www.info.gov.hk/basic_law/fulltext/>.
104. According to Paragraph 2 of Article 18 of the HKSAR Basic Law, China's national laws (*quanguoxing falv*) shall not be applied to the HKSAR except for those listed in Annex III of the HKSAR Basic Law. Six laws are listed in Annex III, including the Resolution on the Capital, Calendar, National Anthem and National Flag, Resolution on the National Day of the PRC, Nationality Law of the PRC and so on.

(or Macao) banks. The 2004 Rules must have made corresponding revisions in accordance with the CEPA. Unfortunately, the 2004 Rules issued by the CBRC have not made special arrangements for Hong Kong-funded banks.

In addition to these points, because the CEPA has incorporated China's specific national treatment commitments – and most market access commitments – under the WTO, China's banking laws should make adjustments to national treatment requirements based on both the WTO and the CEPA. Therefore, in regard to national treatment obligations and market access obligations, the adjustment of China's banking laws to the WTO can be coordinated with their adjustment to the CEPA.

For the purpose of adjusting China's banking laws under CEPA and WTO, two different approaches could be considered. The first approach is to make a parallel legislation to particularly regulate Hong Kong-funded banks in China. This idea originates from the *de facto* dual legal systems of China's foreign investment law. In addition to the Corporation Law, China has a series of foreign-funded enterprises laws which are at the same level with the Corporation Law. This parallel mode of legislation is also introduced to the area of foreign banking laws. Although China, *de jure*, has the Commercial Banking Law and the Banking Regulation and Supervision Law which are applicable to both domestic-funded banks and foreign-funded banks, however, foreign-funded banks are *de facto* regulated by one Regulation, one Rule, and a large number of relevant measures that only regulate foreign-funded banks. According to this legislation ideology, the easiest way in which to regulate Hong Kong-funded banks is to enact special laws, regulations, rules or measures only applicable to Hong Kong; in other words, to enact a parallel legislation. However, this approach is time-consuming, and seems, under current Chinese legal system, impossible to put into practice. The CEPA is only an agreement between two different regions under one country, and not a treaty or international agreement.[105] Under this situation, it is impossible for the NPC to include any CEPA-related topic in its legislation plan. In this respect, the CEPA differs from the WTO. China signed a treaty with the WTO to achieve accession,[106] and that treaty was ratified, although before signing by the NPC.[107] For this reason, China's

---

105. The CEPA took effect immediately after signature without ratification or review of the NPC.
106. The Protocol on Accession of the People's Republic of China. See *Accession of the People's Republic of China, Decision on 10 November 2001*, WT/L/432 (23 November 2001).
107. Unlike normal ratification which takes place after agreement has been reached, China's 'ratification' of the WTO Accession Protocol was prior to the reach of the document. On 25 August 2000, more than a year before the signature of the China Accession Protocol, the Standing Committee of the National People's Congress passed a special decision authorizing the highest administrative institution of the PRC, i.e. the State Council, to negotiate and accept the WTO accession protocol, and the PRC President to ratify it. Although Part III:1 of the China Accession Protocol provides that the protocol shall be open for acceptance by China until 1 January 2002, one day after the signature of the China Accession Protocol (11 November 2001), China's President of the time, Jiang Zemin, accepted the

duty under international law is to implement the WTO. However, implementing the CEPA lacks international law duty. Whether the CEPA, as a free trade agreement under one country, has an international element is doubtful. Therefore, without NPC's legislation support, or its authorization, the State Council cannot make a special regulation on the CEPA, let alone a special regulation to implement CEPA's financial services liberalization requirements.

The second approach is to add a number of special articles, rather than a separate regulation, applicable only to Hong Kong into the current foreign banking regulations, rules and measures. In this way, the current foreign banking legal framework needs not to be separated into several parts by regional trade agreements. A practical method is to have a special chapter in the Regulation and 2004 Rules, entitled 'Banks Related to Hong Kong, Macao'. However, this approach has a potential political problem. Under the Chinese legal system, the issues related to Hong Kong, Macao and Taiwan are usually dealt with together. For example, Article 50 of the Regulation put the banks from the three areas at the same footing. When the Regulation was formulated in 2001, the CEPA was not under negotiation. Nowadays, there are two free trade agreements with Hong Kong and Macao. Taiwan has not been included in the CEPA negotiations, and, for political reasons, concluding a Free Trade Agreement between Mainland China and Taiwan is highly complicated. If China's banking regulations and rules contained chapters only applicable to Hong Kong and Macao, this would lead to a potential result, that is, Taiwan banks would be treated more and more like 'foreign' banks, which is something the Mainland China is unwilling to see. Therefore, how to deal with Article 50 of the Regulation – in other words, how to equalize Hong Kong, Macao and Taiwan, politically more than economically, symbolically more than practically – becomes a difficult issue for China's banking regulators, and for the CBRC in particular. However, the CBRC can only resolve banking regulatory issues, not political issues. Therefore, the final resolution depends, at least in part, on the political decision.

It seems the CBRC tends to adopt the second approach. In January 2006, the CBRC issued the Measures for Implementing Administrative Licensing Matters of foreign-Funded Financial Institutions.[108] Article 8 of the Measures takes into account of the implementation of the CEPA. Firstly, the last sentence of the Article 8(3) stipulates that there is no need to have a representative office before establishing a joint venture bank or a wholly-foreign-owned bank if the sole foreign shareholder or the largest foreign shareholder is a Hong Kong bank or a Macao bank. Secondly, the last sentence of Article 8(4) stipulates that the

China Accession Protocol without seeking approval from the Standing Committee of the National People's Congress.

108. Measures of the CBRC for Implementing Administrative Licensing Matters of foreign-Funded Financial Institutions (*Zhongguo Yinhangye Jiandu Guanli Weiyuanhui Waizi Jinrong Jigou Xingzheng Xuke Shixiang Shishi Banfa*), issued on 12 January 2006, effective as of 1 February 2006, CBRC Decree [2006] no. 4, available at <www.cbrc.gov.cn/mod_cn00/jsp/cn004002.jsp?infoID=2234&type=1.

minimum total assets requirement for establishing a joint venture bank or a wholly-foreign-owned bank is reduced from USD 10 billion to USD 6 billion if the sole foreign shareholder or the largest foreign shareholder is a Hong Kong bank or a Macao bank. The two new provisions directly come from China's CEPA commitments, and they are incorporated in the special foreign banking rule, not in a separate CEPA banking rule.

However, important to note is that the State Council has not revised the FFFI Regulation. Strictly speaking, Article 8(3) and Article 8(4) conflict with the FFFI Regulation. According to the order of legal effect, the legal effect of the FFFI Regulation is higher than that of CBRC's banking rules. Therefore, the legality of relevant sentences in Article 8(3) and Article 8(4) is uncertain unless the State Council revises the FFFI Regulation.

VI.   CONCLUSION

It is predictable that China will conclude more and more regional trade agreements, mainly FTAs, with some countries that are also WTO Members. In each FTA, some special commitments will grant more favoured treatment to the other party of the agreement, and those special commitments may directly impact China's existing laws, which are still under the process of adjustment to the WTO. Therefore, China's current law adjustment is facing double challenges: one from the WTO, the other from regional trade agreements, all of which demand different obligations of China. With respect to China's banking law, it seems the current banking law system has not been well-prepared for the double challenges, particularly the potential impact from regional trade agreements. From the practice of the CEPA's implementation in China, the CBRC, China's banking regulator, has taken a stopgap measure which cannot cope with the complex situations caused by a series of regional trade agreements. However, the blame should not be put only on the CBRC. It is impossible to completely resolve the issue without the participation of the State Council, and particularly the legislation of the NPC. The NPC did not make a necessary measure to streamline the implementation of the WTO in China. With the arrival of regional trade agreements in China, it remains to be seen whether the NPC will lose the second chance or mend fences by making the necessary legislation to coordinate the implementation of the WTO and regional trade agreements.

INTERNATIONAL BANKING AND FINANCE LAW SERIES

1. Jan Job de Vries Robbé, *Innovations in Securitisation. Yearbook 2006*. (2006) ISBN 90-411-2533-7

2. Jim Bartos, *United States Securities Law: A Practical Guide*, Third edition. (2006) ISBN 90-411-2362-8

3. Hui Huang, *International Securities Markets: Insider Trading Law in China*. (2006) ISBN 90-411-2557-4

4. Barth et al., *Financial Restructuring and Reform in Post-WTO China*. (2007) ISBN 90-411-2573-6